Guide to Reference Books

Guide to Reference Books

Ninth Edition

SUPPLEMENT

Edited by

EUGENE P. SHEEHY

With the assistance of
RITA G. KECKEISSEN
EILEEN Mc ILVAINE
DIANE K. GOON
Columbia University Libraries

Pure and Applied Sciences compiled by
RICHARD J. DIONNE
ELIZABETH E. FERGUSON
ROBERT C. MICHAELSON
Kline Science Library, Yale University

Major Data Bases compiled by
MARTHA E. WILLIAMS
University of Illinois

AMERICAN LIBRARY ASSOCIATION

Chicago 1980

Library of Congress Cataloging in Publication Data

Sheehy, Eugene Paul, 1922–
Guide to reference books, 9th edition.

Includes index.
1. Reference books—Bibliography.
I. Title.
Z1035.S43 1976 suppl. 011'.02 79-20541
ISBN 0-8389-0294-4

Printed in the United States of America

Contents

Preface

❖This *Supplement* to the ninth edition of the *Guide to Reference Books* focuses on works published between Fall 1974 and Fall 1978. Much as one would like to establish strict chronological coverage, that is not really practical in a work of this nature: just as some volumes bearing 1973 imprints and worthy of inclusion in the ninth edition were not available for examination at the time work on that volume was completed, so numerous others bearing 1978 imprints were received too late for inclusion in this *Supplement.* Items were added in some sections as late as December 1978, but October of last year represents a more realistic cutoff date for the work as a whole. In addition, the compilers of this *Supplement* have taken the opportunity to include a number of works which were unfortunately omitted from the ninth edition of the *Guide.*

No attempt was made to set strict numerical limits for the individual sections of the *Supplement,* and a few categories may appear disproportionately long in relation to corresponding sections of the parent work. However, the great number of recently published volumes relating to women, ethnic groups, blacks, energy, and cinema studies, and the many publications inspired by our nation's bicentennial celebration have made inevitable a certain weighting of relevant sections. As a general policy, I have tried not to "second guess" my collaborators in either increasing or decreasing the number of entries in individual categories.

Because computer searches utilizing machine-readable data bases have become an integral part of reference work at many libraries, a special survey of some of the major data bases has been contributed by Martha E. Williams and added at the end of the *Supplement.* Reference to on-line access to material in printed sources is made in the main text as applicable.

Following a precedent established in supplements to earlier editions of the *Guide,* newly published parts of works noted as "in progress" in the ninth edition have been entered in this *Supplement.* Titles of continuing series, however, have not been carried forward unless a change of content or character seemed to warrant special attention in the *Supplement.* Whenever available, prices have been supplied: this was done on the assumption that some librarians will use the *Supplement* as a selection tool for expanding or updating their reference collections. Prices were derived from a wide variety of sources; they are meant to indicate the price range of the items, but they may no longer be exact. As in the ninth edition, the Library of Congress class mark is usually given, but if a class mark appeared for an item in the ninth edition it has not been carried forward for a "continuation" entry or for a new edition in the *Supplement.* Form of entry again conforms to Library of Congress practice in almost all cases. CIP information was widely utilized, but if a Library of Congress printed card was found to use a different form of entry, the latter was accepted.

In general, arrangement of the entries follows the pattern of the ninth edition of the *Guide.* In the interest of saving space, however, there has been some simplification of the overall outline, with subheadings often omitted when there were only a few entries for a given topic. On the other hand, it has occasionally been necessary to introduce a new heading for a topic or type of work not previously included.

Subject headings used in the index follow Library of Congress practice, with occasional simplification. When a subject heading would merely duplicate a title entry, we have elected not to enter the subject term in the index.

Not long after publication of the ninth edition of the *Guide* I indicated that, in view of the greatly accelerated growth and expansion of the field of reference publications, I would no longer continue as editor of the *Guide to Reference Books.* It is with some misgivings, then, that I appear as general editor of this *Supplement.* It was only because the several colleagues whose names appear on the title page were willing to play a greater role than heretofore or to undertake compilation of various sections outside my fields of interest or competence that I agreed to continue as editor. Had not Donald E. Stewart, the American Library Association's Associate Executive Director for Publishing, recruited Richard Dionne and his Yale colleagues to assemble the Pure and Applied Sciences sections, this *Supplement* quite possibly would not have appeared.

Veterans of both the ninth edition of the *Guide* and supplements to its predecessor, Rita Keckeissen and Eileen McIlvaine have shared with me the work on all phases of this *Supplement,* from selection of reference works and writing annotations through proofreading and indexing. Miss Keckeissen again took major responsibility for the sections on language dictionaries, genealogy, and religion. In addition to continued responsibility for the History and Area Studies sections, Miss McIlvaine also did most of the work for the music and fine arts categories. Although Diane Goon was a late addition to our team of compilers, I cannot over-emphasize her very important contribution: she prepared the lion's share of the Social Sciences entries and organized those entries within the appropriate sections.

The names of the many individuals who, in one way or another, contributed to the completion of this work would make a very long list. Rather than offend by omission of a name or names, let me express on behalf of my Columbia colleagues and myself an all-embracing "thank you": to the departmental librarians and their staffs, the bibliographers and catalogers at the Columbia University Libraries whose collecting and processing efforts have made compiling this *Supplement* possible; to the many helpful librarians in the New York metropolitan area, particularly those at the Research Libraries of the New York Public Library, the Mid-manhattan Library, Teachers College, Fordham University, and Union Theological Seminary; and to those who took the time to write to me concerning omissions from the ninth edition of the *Guide.*

I cannot, however, leave unnamed the members of the Columbia University Libraries reference staff who have been obliged, willy-nilly, to become associated with this compilation—whether through selecting or reviewing reference books, or simply by "being there" to allow work on the *Supplement* to proceed. They are Laura Binkowski, Paul Cohen, Anita Lowry, Mary Ann Miller, and former staff members Barbara Noda and Doris Ann Sweet. To all of them, my warmest thanks. Our Yale colleagues offer a special word of appreciation to Anthony M. Angiletta and Joseph A. Miller.

EUGENE P. SHEEHY

Columbia University Libraries
January 1979

Abbreviations

❖*Abbreviations used in the citations and annotations of this* Supplement *conform to those established for the ninth edition of the* Guide to Reference Books, *pages xvii–xviii. Following is a list of foreign currencies which do not appear in the* Guide.

BFr. (Belg.): Belgian Franc
Cr (Brazil): Cruzeiro
F (France): Franc
fl (Neth.): florin
Fmk (Finland): Finnish mark
gldr. (Neth.): guilder
I£ (Israel): Israeli pound
k (Russ.): kopek
K (Swed.): Krona
Kcs (Czech.): Koruna
L (Italy): Lira
n (Zambia): ngwee
n.kr. (Norway): Norwegian krone
pta. (Spain): peseta
£ (Eng.): pound
r (Russ.): ruble
R (India): Rupee
R (So.Afr.): Rand
S (Ecuador): Sucre
S$ (Singapore): Singapore dollar
sch. (Austria): schilling
Sw.Fr. (Switz.): Swiss Franc
Y (China): Yuan
zł (Poland): złoty

The dollar sign ($) used with "Austral.," "Fiji," and "N.Z." denotes the dollar currency of Australia, Fiji, and New Zealand, respectively.

pa. has been used following a price when the volume is paperbound rather than hardback.

A

General Reference Works

A A

Bibliography

GENERAL WORKS

Guides

Malclès, Louise-Noëlle. Manuel de bibliographie. 3. éd. rev. et mise à jour par Andrée Lhéritier. Paris, Presses Universitaires de France, [1976]. 398p. 130F. **AA1**

2d ed. 1969 (*Guide* AA5).

A revised edition with some new illustrative examples, etc.

Z1002.M28

Bibliography of bibliography

Arnim, Max. Internationale Personalbibliographie. Begründet von Max Arnim fortgeführt von Franz Hodes. Band III/IV, 1944–1975, 2. überarbeitete und bis zum Berichtsjahr 1975 fortgeführte Aufl. von Band III (1944–1959). Mit Nachträgen zur Zweiten Aufl. von Band I/II (1800–1943). Stuttgart, Hiersemann, 1978– . Lfg.1– . (In progress) **AA2**

Contents: Lfg.1, Aafjes-Baudin.

For Bd.1–2 and previous ed. of Bd.3 *see Guide* AA13.

This new edition of Bd.3 extends the period of coverage through 1975 and also incorporates new references for persons included in Bd.1–2 of the set (the latter names being marked with an asterisk). Bd.4 is to provide indexes to the full set.

Bibliographical services throughout the world, 1970/74. [Ed. by] Marcelle Beaudiquez. [Paris], UNESCO, 1977. 419p. (Documentation, libraries and archives: bibliographies and reference works, 3) **AA3**

Also published in French.

For earlier volumes *see Guide* AA16.

Covers 120 countries, surveying publications and developments in bibliographical services for the 1970–74 period.

Synoptic tables concerning the current national bibliographies. Comp. by Gerhard Pomassl and a working group of the Deutsche Bücherei. Berlin & Leipzig, 1975. unpaged (25 folded leaves) 36cm. DM25. **AA4**

At head of title: Bibliotheksverband der Deutschen Demokratischen Republik; Deutsche Bücherei, Leipzig.

An earlier, mimeographed version was distributed at the IFLA meeting in Grenoble in 1973.

Presents in tabular form information on current national bibliographies published throughout the world. Arranged by continent, then alphabetically by country. As far as available, tables indicate for each country: statistics on book production (1967/68 data), year of legal deposit regulation, editor/compiler (i.e., government agency, national library, institution, or commercial firm) of the national bibliography, title of the bibliography, together with its frequency, scope, contents, arrangement, indexes, titles listed per year, indication of delays in publication, and comments on special features.

Toomey, Alice F. A world bibliography of bibliographies, 1964–1974; a list of works represented by Library of Congress printed catalog cards. A decennial supplement to Theodore Besterman, A world bibliography of bibliographies. Totowa, N.J., Rowman and Littlefield, [1977]. 2v. $85. **AA5**

Compiled as a supplement to the 4th ed. of Besterman (*Guide* AA14). Limited to separately published bibliographies represented by Library of Congress printed cards, "including, however, some offprints of bibliographies which originally appeared as part of a larger work."—*Note.* Z1002.T67

Africa

Besterman, Theodore. A world bibliography of African bibliographies. Rev. and brought up to date by J. D. Pearson. Totowa, N.J., Rowman and Littlefield, [1975]. 241col. $25. **AA6**

Includes the entries for the various African subjects as found in the 4th ed. of Besterman's *World bibliography of bibliographies* (*Guide* AA14), plus additional works published through 1972. Arranged by geographical division, with subdivisions by region and subject as pertinent. Indexed. Z3501.A1B47

Australia

Borchardt, Dietrich Hans. Australian bibliography: a guide to printed sources of information. [3d ed. Rushcutters Bay, N.S.W.], Pergamon, [1976]. 270p. $14.40 Austral. **AA7**

2d ed. 1966 (*Guide* AA35).

A bibliographic survey of printed sources intended for the serious student, much enlarged in this edition. Includes chapters on libraries and library catalogs, encyclopedias and general reference works, general bibliographies, subject bibliographies, sources of biographical information, and government publications. Indexed. Z4011.B65

Brazil

Basseches, Bruno. A bibliography of Brazilian bibliographies. Una bibliografia das bibliografias brasileiras. Detroit, Blaine Ethridge, [1978]. 185p. $14. **AA8**

Introductory matter in English and Portuguese.

An author (or other main entry) listing of nearly 2,500 Brazilian bibliographies published as separates, in periodicals, or as parts of books. Includes works published outside Brazil on Brazilian topics. Index of authors and subjects. Z1671.B37

Bulgaria

Bibliografiia na bulgarskata bibliografiia. 1973– . Sofiia, Narodna Biblioteka "Kiril i Metodii," 1974– . Annual. (Natsionalna bibliografiia na NR Bulgariia, ser.8) **AA9**

For full information *see Suppl.* AA106.

China

Tsien, Tsuen-Hsuin. China; an annotated bibliography of bibliographies. Comp. . . . in collaboration with James K. M. Cheng. Boston, G. K. Hall, [1978]. 604p. $45. **AA10**

Lists "a selection of over 2500 bibliographies concerning China, mainly in English, Chinese, and Japanese, with some in French, German, Russian, and other European languages."—*Introd.* Includes separate publications, bibliographies in periodicals and monographs, surveys of the literature of specific fields, etc. In two sections, each with numerous subdivisions: (1) General and special bibliographies; (2) Subject bibliographies (e.g., classics and philosophy, religion, history, geography, literature, etc.). Author, title, and subject indexes. Z3106.T87

Cuba

Robaina Fernández, Tomás. Bibliografía de bibliografías cubanas [1859–1972]. [La Habana, Biblioteca Nacional José Martí, 1973] 340p. **AA11**

A classed bibliography of nearly 1,400 items. Includes bibliographies of individuals, periodical indexes, specialized bibliographies, etc. Indexed. Z1511.A1R6

Finland

Grönroos, Henrik. Finlands bibliografiska litteratur: kommenterad förteckning. Ekenäs, Ekenäs Tryckeri, 1975. 388p. Fmk.125. **AA12**

An annotated bibliography of Finnish bibliographies, both those published in Finland and works published abroad which include sections on Finland. In four main sections: (1) general bibliographies; (2) Finland in foreign literature and foreign countries in Finnish literature; (3) subject bibliographies; (4) author bibliographies. Indexed.

India

Kalia, D. R. and **Jain, M. K.** A bibliography of bibliographies on India. Delhi, Concept Pub. Co., [1975]. 204p. Rs.60. **AA13**

A bibliography of bibliographies arranged alphabetically by subject. 1,243 entries; index of authors and subjects. Numerous brief annotations. Z3201.A1K34

Indonesia

Tairas, J. N. B. Indonesia: a bibliography of bibliographies. Daftar karya bibliografi Indonesia. [N.Y., Oleander Pr., 1975] 123p. $13.50. **AA14**

A revised edition of *Daftar karya bibliografi Indonesia* published in Jakarta, 1973.

Foreword and subject headings in English and Indonesian.

A classified listing of 661 items. Includes: (1) all types of bibliographical works published in Indonesia; (2) bibliographies dealing wholly or partly with Indonesia, published outside Indonesia; (3) important bibliographical listings published as parts of books. Brief descriptive notes in English. Author-title-subject index.

Latin America

Gropp, Arthur Eric. A bibliography of Latin American bibliographies published in periodicals. Metuchen, N.J., Scarecrow, 1976. 2v. (1031p.) $37.50. **AA15**

A companion to the same author's *Bibliography of Latin American bibliographies* (*Guide* AA60).

A classed listing of more than 9,700 items, mainly from the period 1929–65, but including some earlier publications. Lists not only articles which are bibliographic in nature, but also articles which have substantial bibliographies appended. Fully indexed. Z1601.A2G76

Philippines

Hart, Donn Vorhis. An annotated bibliography of Philippine bibliographies, 1965–1974. [De Kalb], Center for Southeast Asian Studies, Northern Illinois Univ., 1974. 160p. (Northern Ill. Univ. Ctr. for Southeast Asian Studies. Occasional papers, 4) $7.50 pa. **AA16**

Intended to supplement Charles O. Houston's *Philippine bibliography* (Manila, 1960) and Shiro Saito's *The Philippines* (1966; *Guide* DG28). An author listing of 280 items, with index of titles and subjects. Z3291.A1H37

Poland

Czachowska, Jadwiga and **Loth, Roman.** Przewodnik polonisty: bibliografie, słowniki, biblioteki, muzea literackie. Wrocław, Zakład Narodowy Imienia Ossolińskich Wydawnictwo, 1974. 620p. 120 zł. **AA17**

An extensive guide to Polish dictionaries, general bibliographies, and bibliographies of Polish literature and related fields, plus sections on libraries and museums. Classed arrangement with author and subject indexes. Z2528.P5C95

South Africa

Musiker, Reuben. South African bibliography; a survey of bibliographies and bibliographical work. Supplement 1970–1976. Johannesburg, The Library, Univ. of the Witwatersrand, 1977. 34p. R.1.50. **AA18**

For the main volume *see Guide* AA72.

Supersedes an earlier supplement published 1975. Follows the plan of the main volume. Adds about 150 items.

Thailand

Hart, Donn Vorhis. Thailand: an annotated bibliography of bibliographies. [De Kalb], Center for Southeast Asian Studies, Northern Illinois Univ., distr. by Cellar Book Shop, Detroit, 1977. 96p. (Occasional paper, no.5) $6 pa. **AA19**

Cites 205 bibliographies relating specifically to Thailand and more than ten pages in length. Arranged alphabetically by author or issuing body, with subject index. Annotations indicate number of entries, arrangement, kinds of indexes, languages of works cited, special features. DS563.5

Yugoslavia

Bibliografija jugoslovenskih bibliografija, 1956–1960. Beograd, [Jugoslovenski Bibliografski Institut], 1975. 295p. **AA20**

Slobodan M. Komadinić, ed.

More than 1,400 items in classed arrangement with author and subject indexes. Z1002.B5688

UNIVERSAL

Bibliography

U.S. Library of Congress. Monographic series. Jan./Mar. 1974– . Wash., Lib. of Congress, 1974– . 3 qtrly. issues per yr. plus annual cumulation. (1977: $160) **AA21**

At head of title: Library of Congress catalogs.

"Compiled and edited by the Catalog Publication Division of the Processing Department, Library of Congress."—*verso of t.p.*

Includes reproductions of Library of Congress printed cards on which a series statement appears in parentheses following the collation. Arrangement is according to series entry which is shown in capital letters preceding the reproduction of the cards for that series. Includes unnumbered as well as numbered series. Z881.U49U54a

Library catalogs

National libraries

National union catalog, pre-1956 imprints.... [London], Mansell, 1976–78. v.425–594. (In progress) **AA22**

For previously published volumes and annotation *see Guide* AA96.

Contents: v.425–594, Nurnberga–Tiny times.

v.53–56 (The Bible) are not yet published.

British Museum. Dept. of Printed Books. Subject index of modern books acquired, 1951–1955. London, pub. for the British Library Board by British Museum Publs., Ltd., 1974. 6v. **AA23**

Fills the gap between the 1946/50 and 1956/60 volumes of the library's *Subject index* . . . (*Guide* AA101). About 175,000 entries; uses the more specific forms of subject headings adopted for the 1956/60 compilation.

A single index for the 1961–70 period is in preparation.

Paris. Bibliothèque Nationale. Catalogue général des livres imprimés. Auteurs. Paris, Impr. Nationale, 1974–77. v.221–27. (In progress) **AA24**

For previously published volumes and annotation *see Guide* AA105.

Contents: v.221–27, Wellspacher–Wuzel.

Rome. Centro Nazionale per il Catalogo Unico delle Biblioteche Italiane e per le Informazioni Bibliografiche. Primo catalogo collettivo delle biblioteche italiane. Roma, 1975. v.8. (In progress) **AA25**

For previously published volumes and annotation *see Guide* AA107.

Contents: v.8, B–Balmus.

Nonnational libraries

Harvard University. Library. Widener Library shelflist. Cambridge, Harvard Univ. Library; distr. by the Harvard Univ. Pr., 1974–75. no. 49–55. **AA26**

For previously published volumes and annotation *see Guide* AA111.

Contents: no. 49–50, German literature (*Suppl.* BD124); no.51–52, Italian history and literature (*Suppl.* DC70); no. 53–54, British history (*Suppl.* DC39); no.55, Ancient history (*Suppl.* DA28).

Festschriften

Leistner, Otto. Internationale Bibliographie der Festschriften mit Sachregister. International bibliography of Festschriften with subject-index. Osnabrück, Biblio Verlag, 1976. 893p. DM320. **AA27**

The "List of Festschriften arranged by name of the personality or institution honoured" (which provides the citations to the homage volumes) is followed by a subject index to the general content of the works cited. There is no list of the individual essays and their contributors, and therefore no specific subject indexing of the contents. A "List of frequently employed terms in foreign languages with German and English translations," and a section of "General abbreviations" completes the volume. Z1033.F4L43

New York. Public Library. Research Libraries. Guide to *Festschriften.* Boston, G. K. Hall, 1977. 2v. $120. **AA28**

Contents: v.1, The retrospective *Festschriften* collection of the New York Public Library: materials cataloged through 1971; v.2, A dictionary catalog of *Festschriften* in the New York Public Library (1972–1976) and the Library of Congress (1968–1976).

The first volume is a reproduction of the catalog cards for "over 6,000 *Festschriften* collected by NYPL over a fifty-year period, ending in December 1971" *(Introd.)*, and therefore includes some imprints prior to the 1920s. Unfortunately this is a main-entry arrangement only, with no cross references from names of honorees, editors, etc., and no subject approach.

v.2, an infinitely more satisfactory compilation, is a computer-produced dictionary catalog of *Festschriften* added to the NYPL collections 1972–76, plus entries for *Festschriften* available in the Library of Congress MARC data base 1968–76. It offers multiple access: main entry, secondary entries (for editors, persons honored, etc.), and subjects. Z1033.F4N48

Reproductions

Dodson, Suzanne Cates. Microform research collections: a guide. Westport, Conn., Microform Review, [1978]. 410p. (Microform Review series in library micrographics, 8) $35. **AA29**

A title listing of some 200 microform research collections. As far as possible, information given for each includes publisher, date, format, price, reference to published reviews, notes on arrangement and bibliographic control, bibliographies or indexes which serve as keys to the collection, and notes on scope and content of the collection. Index of authors, editors, compilers, and titles of the microform collections and of the bibliographies, indexes, etc., upon which they are based. A valuable work for the reference librarian, the acquisitions librarian, and the cataloger. Z1033.M5D64

Guide to microforms in print, incorporating International microforms in print. 1977– . Westport, Conn., Microform Review Inc., 1977– . Annual. **AA30**

John J. Walsh, ed.

A continuation of *Guide to microforms in print* (*Guide* AA120) with expanded coverage; *International microforms in print* (*Guide* AA121) ceased publication after the 1974/75 issue. With the 1978 volume, the companion publication *Subject guide to microforms in print* (*Guide* AA120a) is also published by Microform Review Inc. and incorporates the international listings.

Microlist; an international record of new micropublications. v.1, no.1– , Jan. 1977– . Westport, Conn., Microform Review, 1977– . 10 nos. per yr. **AA31**

An author/title and subject listing of new micropublications from publishers throughout the world. Includes books, periodicals, newspapers, government documents, and microform collections.

National register of microform masters, 1965–1975. Wash., Lib. of Congress, 1976. 6v. $190. **AA32**

For annual volumes *see Guide* AA123.

A cumulation, with all reports for the period in a single alphabetical sequence (i.e., the 1965–69 listings originally arranged by catalog card number are here integrated into the main-entry listing).

Anonyms and pseudonyms

United States and Great Britain

Clarke, Joseph F. Pseudonyms. London, Book Club Associates, [1977]. 252p. **AA33**

Not limited to pen-names, but extends to "anyone well known who changed his or her name. Of the 3400 pseudonyms listed, pen-names account for roughly half the collection, stage names a third; the remainder of the entries cover personalities in the various spheres of politics, sport, crime, painting and sculpture, and music."—*Introd.* Many entries include brief remarks on background and choice of pseudonym. Z1041.C57

Australia

Nesbitt, Bruce and **Hadfield, Susan.** Australian literary pseudonyms; an index, with selected New Zealand references. Adelaide, Libraries Board of South Australia, 1972. 134p. $3.30 Austral., pa. **AA34**

Covers a literature that abounds in pseudonyms. Pseudonyms and real names are listed in a single alphabet, the pseudonym being entered as a *see* reference to the original name. Z1107.N47

Canada

Amtmann, Bernard. Contributions to a dictionary of Canadian pseudonyms and anonymous works relating to Canada. Contributions à un dictionnaire des pseudonymes canadiens et des ouvrages anonymes relatifs au Canada. Montreal, Author, 1973. 144p. **AA35**

Text in English or French.

A listing by pseudonym or anonymous title, without indication of source of the attribution. Addenda, pp.137–44. Z1047.A47

Vinet, Bernard. Pseudonymes québécois. Québec, Éditions Garneau, [1974]. 361p. $10.95. **AA36**

"Édition basée sur l'oeuvre de Audet et Malchelosse intitulée: Pseudonymes canadiens."—*t.p.*

Adds numerous pseudonyms not found in the Audet and Malchelosse work (*Guide* AA143) and cites additional sources. Z1047.V55

India

Chatterjee, Amitabha. Dictionary of Indian pseudonyms. Calcutta, Mukherji Book House, [1977]. 170p. Rs.75; $18. **AA37**

A dictionary of about 3,500 pseudonyms used by Indian writers in all Indian languages and in English. Gives real name, an identifying phrase, and (when possible) date of birth. Index of real names giving reference to page number only—not to pseudonym. Sources not indicated.

Virendra Kumar. Dictionary of pseudonmys [sic] in Indian literature. [Delhi], Delhi Library Assoc., 1973. 163p. (Delhi Lib. Assoc. English ser., no.7) Rs. 40. **AA38**

An initial attempt to provide a guide to the real names of pseudonymous Indian authors. Includes writers in various Indian languages. Under the pseudonym is indicated the real name, language, and year of birth of the writer. A second section provides a guide from original name to pseudonym. Z1087.I5V57

Romania

Straje, Mihail. Dicţionar de pseudonime, alonime [sic], anagrame, asteronime, criptonime ale scriitorilor şi publiciştilor români. Bucureşti, Editura Minerva, 1973. 810p. Lei 32. **AA39**

A dictionary of Romanian pseudonyms, etc., with references to sources of identification. Z1080.R6S8

Russia

Leningrad. Publichnaia Biblioteka. Russkie anonimnye i podpisannye psevdonimami proizvedenniia pechati: 1801–1926: bibliograficheskii ukazatel'. [Sost. G. Z. Guseva i dr.] Leningrad, Gos. Publichnaia Biblioteka, 1977– . v.1– . (In progress) **AA40**

Contents: v.1– , A–M.

A title listing of works published anonymously or pseudonymously, with indication of authorship and source of attribution. Does not include material covered in I. F. Masanov's *Slovar' psevdonimov* . . . (*Guide* AA164).

Slovak authors

Kormúth, Dezider. Slovník slovenských pseudonymov 1919–1944. Martin, Matica Slovenská, 1974. 594p. (Slovenská národná retrospektívna bibliografia) Kčs. 29.50. **AA41**

The first section gives the pseudonym and the corresponding true name. A second section arranged by the Slovak authors' real names gives references to publications in which the pseudonyms were used. PG5402.K6

ANCIENT, MEDIEVAL, AND RENAISSANCE MANUSCRIPTS

Bibliography

Ker, Neil Ripley. Medieval manuscripts in British libraries. Oxford, Clarendon Pr., 1977. v.2. (In progress) **AA42**

For v.1 and annotation *see Guide* AA184.
Contents: v.2, Abbotsford–Keele.

Illumination

Oxford. University. Bodleian Library. Illuminated manuscripts in the Bodleian Library, Oxford. Comp. by Otto Pächt and J. J. G. Alexander. Oxford, Clarendon Pr., 1973. v.3. **AA43**

For v.1–2 and annotation *see Guide* AA203.
Contents: v.3, British, Irish, and Icelandic schools, with addenda to v.1 and 2.

EARLY AND RARE BOOKS

Union lists

Gesamtkatalog der Wiegendrucke. Hrsg. von der Kommission für den Gesamtkatalog der Wiegendrucke. 2. Aufl., durchgeschener Neudruck der 1. Aufl. Stuttgart, A. Hiersemann; N.Y., Kraus, 1976. Bd.8, Lfg.4. (In progress) **AA44**

For previously published parts and annotation *see Guide* AA220.
Contents: Bd.8, Lfg.4, Faber Stapulensis–Festus.

Book collecting

Heard, Joseph Norman, Hoover, Jimmie H. and **Hamsa, Charles F.** Bookman's guide to Americana. 7th ed. Metuchen, N.J., Scarecrow, 1977. 403p. $16. **AA45**

6th ed. 1971 (*Guide* AA239).
"The seventh edition, like its predecessors, is an alphabetically arranged compilation of quotations gleaned from recent out-of-print booksellers' catalogs. It is intended to provide the bookseller or book buyer with a record of prices asked for out-of-print titles in the broad field of Americana, including factual or fictional works relating to America or written by Americans."—*Pref.* Z1000.5.H4

Historical children's books

U.S. Library of Congress. Rare Book Division. Children's books in the Rare Book Division of the Library of Congress. Totowa, N.J., Rowman and Littlefield, 1975. 2v. $100. **AA46**

Contents: v.1, Author; v.2, Chronological.
"As a result of the federal copyright regulations, the Library of Congress has assembled an immense collection of American children's books. For its period—the 19th and 20th centuries—and its country of origin—the United States—this collection outranks any other in the world. From these holdings the Rare Book Division has brought together on its shelves approximately 15,000 volumes of particular interest, maintaining them separately as a special collection, which this publication describes."—*Introd.* Also includes other children's books in the Rare Book Division which are not part of the separate children's book collection. Reproduces the catalog cards describing the books; includes numerous temporary entries for works not found in the *National union catalog.* Z1038.U5U54

Printers' marks, etc.

Reilly, Elizabeth Carroll. A dictionary of colonial American printers' ornaments and illustrations. Worcester, Amer. Antiquarian Soc., 1975. 515p. il. $45. **AA47**

"The purpose of the dictionary is to aid both bibliographers and historians in their studies of the colonial period. Used judiciously, the listings may facilitate the bibliographer's identification of many books, pamphlets, and broadsides which lack imprints or colophons. The index of printers records the ornaments and illustrations used by each printer and thus provides the means for a study of the changes in his printing stock."—*Introd.* Z208.R43

PRINTING AND PUBLISHING

General works

Directories

Book publishers directory. no.1– , June 1977– . Detroit, Gale, 1977– . Quarterly with annual cumulated indexes. $75 per yr. **AA48**

Subtitle: An information service covering new and established, private and special interest, avant-garde and alternative, organization and association, government and institution presses.
Elizabeth Geiser and Annie Brewer, eds.
Each issue aims to provide directory information (address, principal officers, brief description, subjects, discount and returns policies, selected recent titles published) on 500 to 600 publishers not usually found in standard lists. Arranged alphabetically by name of publisher, with "Publishers and personnel," subject, and geographic indexes in each issue; the indexes cumulate in the fourth issue for the year.

Bowker Editores Argentina. La empresa del libro en América Latina; guía seleccionada de editoriales, distribuidores y librerías de América Latina. [2. ed.] [Buenos Aires], Bowker Editores, [1974]. 307p. $16.95 pa. **AA49**

1st ed. 1968 (*Guide* AA272).
A revised and expanded edition. Z490.5.B67

Clarke, Tim. International academic and specialist publishers directory. N.Y., Bowker, [1975]. 555p. $26.50. **AA50**

A country-by-country listing of publishers, giving address and indication of special subjects published. Index of subjects, and index of publishers and imprints. Z282.C616

Directory of Indian publishers. Ed.1– . New Delhi, Federation of Publishers & Booksellers Associations in India, [1973]– . **AA51**

Ed.1 is in four sections: (1) Publishers—private sector (arranged by language in which their works are published); (2) Corporate bodies; (3) Book industry adjuncts (e.g., exporters, importers, book review media, book trade journals); (4) Geographical index of publishers.

Directory of publishing opportunities. 3d ed. Chicago, Marquis Academic Media, [1975]. 850p. $44.50. **AA52**

1st ed. 1971 had title *Directory of scholarly and research publishing opportunities.* 2d ed. 1973 by Mary Butcher Ross.
This edition "includes more than 2,600 specialized and professional journals, about 800 of which appear for the first time in this edition."—*Introd.* Entries are arranged alphabetically within 69 subject fields. Gives address, beginning date, changes of title, subscription data, editorial description, and information for submitting manuscripts. Indexes of: (1) periodicals; (2) subjects; (3) publishers and sponsoring organizations; (4) editorial staff. Z6944.S3D57

Gli editori italiani: indirizzi e punti di vendita. [Milano], Bibliografica, 1976. 398p. **AA53**

A directory of publishers' addresses, together with lists of their affiliates and bookstores.

Internationales Verlagsadressbuch. Publishers' international directory. Ausgabe 1– . München, Verlag Dokumentation, 1964– . (Handbuch der internationalen Dokumentation und Information, Bd.7) Irregular. (7th ed.: $62.50) **AA54**

Explanatory matter in German and English.

About 38,000 publishers (including a greatly increased number of small firms) in the 7th ed. (publ. 1977). An "International ISBN publishers' index" (which identifies publisher by number and *vice versa*) appeared as a companion volume to the 6th ed., but is included as a separately paged supplement in the 1977 volume. Z282.I65

Répertoire international des éditeurs et diffuseurs de langue française. Publié sous l'égide de l'Union des Éditeurs de Langue Française. Paris, Cercle de la Librairie, 1975. 467p. 159 F. **AA55**

Represents a new edition of the *Répertoire international des éditeurs de langue française* (1971; *Guide* AA281) with greater emphasis on booksellers and distributors of French-language publications. Z282.R45

Dictionaries

Collins, Frederick Howard. Authors and printers' dictionary. 11th ed., rev. by Stanley Beale. London, Oxford Univ. Pr., 1973. 474p. £2.50. **AA56**

10th ed. 1956 (*Guide* AA290).

An updating of this standard work, deleting obsolescent and little used terms, and adding new ones. PE1628.C53

Móra, Imre. Wörterbuch des Verlagswesens in 20 Sprachen. The publisher's practical dictionary in 20 languages. Pullach/München, Verlag Dokumentation, 1974. 389p. DM98. **AA57**

Arranged on a German base, with indexes from the other languages. Equivalent terms only, not definitions. Z1006.M6

Orne, Jerrold. The language of the foreign book trade: abbreviations, terms, phrases. 3d ed. Chicago, Amer. Lib. Assoc., 1976. 333p. $6.50. **AA58**

2d ed. 1962 (*Guide* AA297).

This edition expanded to include 15 languages—Finnish, Hungarian, and Romanian having been added. Z1006.O7

Schuwer, Philippe. Dictionnaire de l'édition; art, techniques, industrie et commerce du livre. Dictionary of book publishing; creative, technical and commercial terms of the book industry. Paris, Cercle de la Librairie, [1977]. 309p. 120F. **AA59**

French-English and English-French.

Each section lists the words with their equivalents in the other language. Z118.S53

Stiehl, Ulrich. Satzwörterbuch des Buch- und Verlagswesens, Deutsch-Englisch. Dictionary of book publishing; with 12000 sample sentences and phrases, German-English. München, Verlag Dokumentation, 1977. 538p. DM88. **AA60**

Introduction in German and English.

Gives the English equivalent of the German terms, usually followed by one or more examples of English usage. In addition to publishing in general, includes terms relating to editing and copyright, marketing, library science, etc.

History and biography

Maxted, Ian. The London book trades, 1775–1800; a preliminary checklist of members. [Folkestone, Kent], Dawson, [1977]. 257p. **AA61**

"The aim of the work is to provide, by approaching a limited selection of wide-ranging sources, a checklist of members of the book and allied trades in the London area which would be sufficiently comprehensive to serve as a basis for further study and as a much needed stop-gap for the poorly documented period of the late eighteenth century."—*Pref.* Entries for about 4,000 individuals and firms with brief biographical information and notes on publishing and book trade activity (including printing, engraving, binding, music and book selling, etc.). "Key to sources," pp.xiv–xvii.

Robinson, Francis John Gibson and **Wallis, P. J.** Book subscription lists; a revised guide. Newcastle upon Tyne, H. Hill for The Book Subscriptions List Project, 1975. 120p. £2.50 pa. **AA62**

Earlier, preliminary lists were issued in duplicated form.

An introductory section provides background and description of subscription lists and points out their potential uses. The "Catalogue of book subscription lists" is chronologically arranged within two main sections: "Lists to 1761" and "Lists 1761–1974." Author index; book trade index; provincial imprint index.

Rouzet, Anne. Dictionnaire des imprimeurs, libraires et éditeurs des XVe et XVIe siècles dans les limites géographiques de la Belgique actuelle. Nieuwkoop, B. de Graaf, 1975. 287p. (Collection du Centre National de l'Archéologie et de l'Histoire du Livre. Publ. 3) 210 fl. **AA63**

Biographical sketches in alphabetical sequence, with tables according to place of activity and addresses by city. Z350.R68

Copyright

Crawford, Tad. The writer's legal guide. N.Y., Hawthorn Books, [1977]. 271p. $10.95. **AA64**

Chapters include: Copyright; Rights of the writer; Contents of written works; Contracts; Marketing literary property; Self-publication and vanity presses; Income taxation; The writer's estate; Public support for writers. Indexed.

Johnston, Donald F. Copyright handbook. N.Y., Bowker, 1978. 309p. $14.95. **AA65**

A guide to the new (1976) copyright law. An introductory chapter on the subject of copyright and the principal features of the new law is followed by chapters which "examine the components of the new copyright law and include such areas as copyrightable subject matter, copyright notices, registration, exclusive rights, fair use, and library reproduction rights."—*Pref.* Appendixes include text of the Copyright Act of 1976; fair use guidelines; library reproduction guidelines, etc. Detailed table of contents and index. Intended for publishers, librarians, educators, and authors. KF2994.J63

Copy preparation

Butcher, Judith. Copy-editing: the Cambridge handbook. [London], Cambridge Univ. Pr., [1975]. 326p. £6.50. **AA66**

Based on the author's experience at Penguin Books and the Cambridge University Press, but intended as a guide for copy-editors in general. Covers much specialized material as well as general aspects of the work. Detailed index. Appendixes include a glossary and a good "checklist of copy-editing." PN162.B86

SELECTION OF BOOKS

Guides

Hackett, Alice Payne and **Burke, James Henry.** 80 years of best sellers, 1895–1975. N.Y., Bowker, 1977. 265p. $15. **AA67**

Previous ed., 1967, had title: *60 years of best sellers, 1895–1955* (*Guide* AA338). This volume follows the plan of its predecessors. Z1033.B3H342

The reader's adviser; a layman's guide to literature. 12th ed. N.Y., Bowker, 1974–77. 3v. $25 per v. **AA68**

Contents: v.1, The best in American and British fiction, poetry, essays, literary biography, bibliography, and reference, ed. by Sarah

L. Prakken. 808p.; v.2, The best in American and British drama and world literature in English translation, ed. by F. J. Sypher. 774p.; v.3, The best in the reference literature of the world, ed. by Jack A. Clarke. 1034p.

For earlier editions *see Guide* AA339.

"For the first time the work of revising each chapter of the first [two] volume[s] of this edition has been entrusted to a single editor who has special expertise in the area of his chapter."—*Pref.* Those sections are signed with the initials of the contributing editors. v.3 is the work of the general editor of that volume. In addition to expanded coverage, there has been some rearrangement of material within sections and new introductory notes. v.1 has separate indexes for authors and for titles and subjects; v.2 and 3 have indexes of authors and of titles.

Books for college students

Books for college libraries; a core collection of 40,000 titles. A project of the Association of College and Research Libraries. 2d ed. Chicago, Amer. Lib. Assoc., 1975. 6v. $65. **AA69**

1st ed. 1967 (*Guide* AA349).

Contents: v.1, Humanities; v.2, Language and literature; v.3, History; v.4, Social sciences; v.5, Psychology, science, technology; v.6, Index.

"New aspects include the sharp reduction in number of titles to a minimal 'core collection'; the expansion of individual entries to provide more complete cataloging and classification information; and the use of automated techniques for the production of the list itself."—*Introd.* Z1035.B72

Opening day collection. Prep. under the supervision of Richard K. Gardner, ed. 3d ed. Middletown, Conn., Choice, 1974. 59p. il. **AA70**

Previous ed. 1968 (*Guide* AA354).

This edition originally appeared in the Dec.1973–Mar.1974 issues of *Choice,* with some updating and addition of an author-title index for the separate publication. Z1035.O683

Books for children and young people

Children's literature abstracts. no.1– , May 1973– . [Birmingham, Eng.], Sub-section on Library Work with Children, International Federation of Library Associations, 1973– . Quarterly. £2.75 per yr. **AA71**

Includes brief abstracts of books about children's literature and reading as well as notes on books for children. No cumulative indexing to date. Z1037.C5446

Good reading; a guide for serious readers. 21st ed. J. Sherwood Weber, ed. N.Y., Bowker, [1978]. 313p. $12.95. **AA72**

For earlier editions *see Guide* AA364.

A thorough revision. "More than half of its chapters have been prepared by new editors, and many have new or substantially revised introductions; all its annotated book lists have been updated, and several have been expanded; data about authors, books, editions, and translations are current as of January 1978."—*p.ix.* Z1035.G63

Wilson, H. W., *firm, publishers.* Junior high school library catalog. 3d ed. 1975. Ed. by Ilene R. Schlechter and Gary L. Bogart. N.Y., Wilson, 1975. 991p. $42. **AA73**

2d ed. 1970 (*Guide* AA376).

"The Third Edition includes 3,791 titles and 10,673 analytical entries that have been considered appropriate for grades seven through nine."—*Pref.* Z1037.W675

Withrow, Dorothy, Carey, Helen B. and **Hirzel, Bertha M.** Gateways to readable books: an annotated graded list of books in many fields for adolescents who find reading difficult. 5th ed. N.Y., Wilson, 1975. 299p. $12. **AA74**

1st–4th eds., 1944–66, by R. M. Strang and others (*Guide* AA374).

About 1,000 titles, 85% of them new in this edition. Z1039.S5W58

Reference books

Beaudiquez, Marcelle and **Zundel-Benkhemis, Anne.** Ouvrages de référence pour les bibliothèques publiques; répertoire bibliographique. Paris, Cercle de la Librairie, [1974]. 195p. 49.60F. pa. (Cercle de la Librairie. Répertoire bibliographique, 1) **AA75**

A selective guide to representative reference works in the broad range of subject fields likely to be of interest in public libraries. Arranged according to the simplified Universal Decimal Classification used in the "Livres du mois" section of *Bibliographie de la France—Biblio,* with an expanded section for "Généralités" (encompassing encyclopedias, dictionaries, annuals, bibliographies, periodicals, etc.) and an added section for "Domaines étrangers." 723 items, most of them briefly annotated. In general, foreign-language publications are included only if there is no French-language equivalent. Index of authors, anonymous titles, and subjects. Z1035.B13

A guide to reference materials on India. Comp. and ed. by N. N. Gidwani and K. Navalani. Jaipur, Saraswati Publs., 1974. 2v. (1536p.) Rs. 300. **AA76**

A classified guide to the whole range of reference works relating to India. In addition to monographs and multi-volume works, a special effort was made to list reference sources published in series or as parts of books. Aims to be comprehensive rather than selective. Includes numerous brief annotations, detailed contents of various multi-volume sets, occasional references to reviews, etc. Cutoff date is early 1972; supplements are planned. Index of authors, titles and subjects. Z3206.G84

Musiker, Reuben. Guide to South African reference books. 4th cumulative supplement, 1970–1976 to 5th rev. ed. Johannesburg, The Library, Univ. of the Witwatersrand, 1977. 112p. **AA77**

For the 5th ed. *see Guide* AA392.

About 100 titles added in this supplement, bringing the total number of supplementary entries to 283.

Peterson, Carolyn Sue. Reference books for elementary and junior high school libraries. 2d ed. Metuchen, N.J., Scarecrow Pr., 1975. 314p. $10. **AA78**

1st ed. 1970.

Intended as a buying guide. Arranged by subject and type of reference work. Annotated; indexed. Z1037.1.P4

Ryder, Dorothy E., ed. Canadian reference sources. Supplement. Ottawa, Canadian Lib. Assoc., 1975. 121p. $7 pa. **AA79**

For the main volume *see Guide* AA395.

Lists new works and editions up to Dec. 1973. Z1365.R8

U.S. Library of Congress. The Library of Congress Main Reading Room reference collection subject catalog. Comp. by Katherine Ann Gardner. Wash., Lib. of Congress, 1975. 638p. $13. **AA80**

Offers an alphabetical subject approach to the approximately 14,000 titles (about 11,000 monographs and 3,000 serials) in the Library's Main Reading Room collection. All subject headings appearing on Library of Congress printed cards for volumes in the collection have been used, and some additional headings have been added by the General Reference and Bibliography Division staff. The Library intends to issue a companion catalog in classified arrangement by call number. Z1035.1.U526

Walford, Albert John. Guide to reference material. 3d ed. London, Lib. Assoc., 1975–77. v.2–3. **AA81**

Contents: v.2, Social & historical sciences, philosophy & religion. 647p. $30; v.3, Generalities, languages, the arts & literature. 710p. $35.

For v.1 and previous ed. *see Guide* AA404, EA9.

The total number of entries in each of these volumes represents an increase of about 15% over the corresponding volumes of the 2d edition (v.1 publ. 1968; v.2, 1970). Cutoff date for v.2 was Apr. 1974, wth a few later additions; for v.3, mid-Aug. 1976.

For a fuller note on v.2 *see Suppl.* CA2.

Among the subjects "highlighted" in v.3 are: documentation, librarianship, government publications, linguistics, antiques, the film, sport, non-European literatures. "An appreciable amount of valuable older reference materials, now available as reprints, is included. As in previous volumes, announcements of forthcoming works or volumes are mentioned. 'Hidden' bibliographies, appearing in periodicals or forming parts of books, continue to find a place."—*Introd., v.3.*

v.3 includes a cumulated subject index to the three volumes of the 3d edition (pp.627–49) and also a cumulated author-title index (pp.651–710).

Book review indexes

Book review digest. Author/title index 1905–1974. Ed. by Leslie Dunmore-Leiber. N.Y., Wilson, 1976. 4v. $245. **AA82**

For the series which these volumes index *see Guide* AA411.

Covers nearly 300,000 books. Variant forms of author entries have been reconciled and cross references provided.

Children's book review index. v.1, no.1– , Jan./Apr. 1975– . Detroit, Gale, 1975– . 3 issues per yr. $18 per yr. **AA83**

Citations are derived from the listings in the *Book review index* (*Guide* AA412)—i.e., citations to reviews of works identified as children's books are repeated in this publication.

Current book review citations. v.1, no.1– , Jan. 1976– . N.Y., H. W. Wilson, 1976– . Monthly (except Aug.), with annual cumulation. $75 per yr. **AA84**

Brings together the book review citations from all the various Wilson periodical indexes. An author (or other main entry) listing gives the full review citation, including the reviewer's name when known; this is followed by a title index. The full list of periodicals (with addresses and subscription rates) appears in the January issue and the cumulation only. Z1035.A1C86

Guía a las reseñas de libros de y sobre Hispanoamérica. 1972– . Detroit, Blaine Ethridge-Books, [1976–]. Annual (1975 pub. 1977). $45 per v. **AA85**

Added title page in English: A guide to reviews of books from and about Hispanic America.

Antonio Matos, comp. and ed.

Introductory matter in Spanish and English; annotations in English or Spanish.

Continues a publication of the same title published in Río Piedras, Puerto Rico, in 1965 covering the years 1960–64, and a second volume (published in Río Piedras in 1973) covering 1965. The intervening years have not yet been covered.

Provides summaries of the reviews as well as citations to reviews. "Hispanic America" as here defined "includes, in addition to Spanish-speaking countries, Brazil, French, Dutch, and English-speaking areas of the Caribbean."—*Pref.* Arranged alphabetically by author, with title index.

SELECTION OF PERIODICALS

Katz, William A. and **Richards, Berry Gargal.** Magazines for libraries: for the general reader and school, junior college, college, university, and public libraries. 3d ed. N.Y., Bowker, 1978. 937p. $37.50. **AA86**

1st ed. 1969 (*Guide* AA419a); 2d ed. and suppl., 1972–74.

About 6,500 periodicals are annotated and evaluated in this edition. As before, "titles have been selected to include: (1) some general, nonspecialist periodicals of interest to the layperson; (2) the main English-language research journals sponsored by distinguished societies in the United States, Canada, and Great Britain; (3) some high-quality commercial publications commonly found in academic/special libraries. No attempt has been made to represent the full scope of research publications available for specialized collections. There has been an attempt, however, to provide a balance, by discipline, between specialist vs. layperson interests, student vs. faculty use, and general science vs. research concerns."—*Pref.* About 95% of the annotations from previous editions were edited and revised for this edition.

AUDIO-VISUAL MATERIALS

Brown, Lucy Gregor. Core media collection for secondary schools. N.Y., Bowker, 1975. 221p. $16.95. **AA87**

Aims "to provide a qualitative selection guide to approximately 2,000 titles of nonprint media—filmstrips, film loops, transparencies, 16mm motion pictures, phonodiscs, audiotapes, art prints, study prints, kits, specimens, slides, and models—covering a wide variety of subjects and ability levels."—*Pref.* Alphabetical subject arrangement, with each title annotated under its appropriate subject heading; numerous cross references. Title index; producer/distributor directory. LB1043.Z9B76

Index to instructional media catalogs; a multi-indexed directory of materials and equipment for use in instructional programs. N.Y., Bowker, 1974. 272p. $19.50. **AA88**

For the curriculum planner. Aims to provide "a simple guide to the catalogs of the suppliers of specific instructional materials."—*p.vii.* The bulk of the volume is a "Subject/media index" arranged by broad subjects (e.g., language arts, mathematics, science, social studies) appropriately subdivided by more specific topics, then by type of instructional aid. There is also a "Product and services index" and a directory of companies. LB1043.Z9I52

International index to multi-media information. v.4, no. 1– , Spr. 1973– . Pasadena, Calif., Audio-Visual Associates, 1973– . Quarterly. $60 per yr. **AA89**

Continues *Film review index* (*Guide* AA429) and continues its numbering. Z5784.M9F5

National Audiovisual Center. A reference list of audiovisual materials produced by the United States government, 1978. Wash., D.C., The Center, 1978. 354p., xlvip. **AA90**

1974 ed. had title: *A catalog of United States government produced audiovisual materials.*

"This is a list of over 6,000 audiovisual materials selected from over 10,000 programs produced by 175 Federal agencies covering a wide range of subjects. Major subject concentrations in the Center's collection include medicine, dentistry, and allied health; education; science; social studies; industrial/technical training; safety; and the environmental sciences."—*Introd.* A title section provides the full information on a given item, including availability through rental or sale; a subject section serves as an index to the titles. Price list included.

Rufsvold, Margaret Irene. Guides to educational media: films, filmstrips, multimedia kits, programmed instruction materials, recordings on discs and tapes, slides, transparencies, videotapes. 4th ed. Chicago, Amer. Lib. Assoc., 1977. 159p. $5 pa. **AA91**

3d ed. 1971 (*Guide* AA428).

Enlarged and rewritten. "This edition identifies and describes 245 educational media catalogs, indexes, and reviewing services; in addition, 35 related publications are mentioned in the annotations."—*Pref.* Z5814.V8R8

NATIONAL AND TRADE

Bibliography

Commonwealth national bibliographies: an annotated directory. London, Commonwealth Secretariat, [1977]. 97p. £.50 pa. **AA92**

A country-by-country listing, with full descriptions, of national bibliographies (plus some nationally produced serials lists and periodical indexes), published in Commonwealth countries. "Most of the bibliographies appearing in the directory have been produced nationally, but some regional publications have also been included so as to cover those Commonwealth states and dependencies that are too small to warrant their own national bibliographies. In addition, the Accessions Lists produced by Library of Congress Offices for the use of librarians in the U.S.A. have been included so as to supplement inadequate bibliographic coverage in some regions."—*Introd.*

Reprints

Books on demand: author guide; 84,000 selected books available as on-demand reprints. Ann Arbor, Mich., University Microfilms, 1977. 803p. $24.50 (free on microfiche). **AA93**

Books on demand: subject guide . . . . Ann Arbor, Mich., University Microfilms, 1977. 786p. $24.50.

Books on demand: title guide . . . . Ann Arbor, Mich., University Microfilms, 1977. 831p. $24.50.

The above three volumes, offering variant approaches to the same 84,000 works, are available separately or as a set ($73.50). The "on-demand" reprint program makes the works listed in the catalogs available by xerography as full-size bound books or in microfilm. The lists include many early and rare books, but also include "books published in the past ten years but no longer in stock that publishers wish to continue to make available to librarians, bookstores, and individuals."—*Introd.* Prices of the reprints are indicated.

A review in *Library journal* 103:1384 (July 1978) concludes that the set is "essential for any acquisitions department," but warns that "some of the books listed here are still in *Books in Print* at more reasonable prices."

A supplement for each volume is promised for 1978.

Internationale Bibliographie der Reprints. International bibliography of reprints. Ed. by Christa Gnirss. München, Verlag Dokumentation, 1976– . Bd.1– . (In progress) **AA94**

Contents: Bd.1, Teil 1–2, Bücher und Reihen; Teil 3, Register. $130 the 3-pt. set.

Introductory matter in German and English.

"The term 'reprint' is here used to describe all reprinted works produced by photomechanical means in so far as the publisher is not identical with the publisher of the original work."—*Foreword.* Information was initially derived from publishers' catalogs, lists and prospectuses, but additional searching in national bibliographies was done in order to supply full information, including original publication date where possible. Aims "to present a comprehensive bibliography of available reprints published up to the end of 1973." Bd.2 is to list reprints of periodicals and yearbooks.

The quarterly *Bulletin of reprints* (*Guide* AA437) provides coverage since 1973. Z1033.R41572

United States

Early

Bowe, Forrest. French literature in early American translation; a bibliographical survey of books and pamphlets printed in the United States from 1668 through 1820. Ed. by Mary Daniels. N.Y., Garland Pr., 1977. 528p. $60. **AA95**

For full information *see Suppl.* BD142.

Molnar, John Edgar, comp. Author-title index to Joseph Sabin's Dictionary of books relating to America. Metuchen, N.J., Scarecrow, 1974. 3v. (3196p.) $115. **AA96**

For a note on the Sabin compilation *see Guide* AA451.

Authors and titles in a single sequence; some identification of pseudonyms. Z1201.S222

Current

Bowker (R.R.) Company, New York. Dept. of Bibliography. Books in series in the United States, 1966–1975: original, reprinted, in-print, and out-of-print books, published or distributed in the U.S. in popular, scholarly, and professional series. N.Y., Bowker, [1977]. 2486p. $52.50. **AA97**

"In compiling *Books in Series* . . . these sources of series information were reviewed: the Library of Congress MARC (MAchine Readable Cataloging) files from 1969 through May 1976; the *Books in Print* Active and Out-of-Print files from 1968 to August 1976; series listings included in the *Publishers' Trade List Annual* for the years 1966 to 1976; the *American Book Publishing Record* for the years 1966 to 1969 (to provide cataloging information on pre-MARC records); and *Irregular Serials and Annuals* . . . . 86,500 books issued by 1000 publishers in 9370 series are represented in this volume. Included are titles in series which were in print, or came into print, whether in original or reprinted editions, during the ten-year span of 1966–1975."—*Pref.* The "Series index" is followed by an author index, a title index, and a subject index to series. Z1036.B7

——— Books in series supplement. N.Y., Bowker, [1978]. 1000p. $34.50.

Adds some 10,700 titles, both pre-1976 publications and those bearing 1976–77 publication dates.

Bowker (R.R.) Company, New York. Dept. of Bibliography. Large type books in print, 1976: subject index, title index, author index. [2d ed.] N.Y., [1976]. 455p. **AA98**

1st ed. by R. A. Landau and J. S. Nyren (1970; *Guide* AA470).

Lists 2,552 large type books available from 44 publishers, with no attempt at selectivity. The subject part is in two main sections: (1) General reading and (2) Textbooks, each appropriately subdivided. Z5348.B69

Africa

The African book publishing record, v.1, no. 1– , Jan. 1975– . [Oxford, Eng., Hans Zell Ltd.], 1975– . v.1– . Quarterly. £18 ($40) per yr. **AA99**

Offers subject, author, and title lists of English, French, or African vernacular language books recently published or in press on the African continent. Each issue includes articles on and news of the book trade in Africa, reviews of new magazines or special issues of journals. Beginning with the Apr. 1977 issue, reviews of major publications are included. A directory of publishers is a useful feature. Annual table of contents for the volume, but no index. Z465.7.A35

The African book world & press; a directory. Répertoire du livre et de la presse en Afrique. Comp. by the African Book Publishing Record, Hans M. Zell, ed. Oxford, Zell; Detroit, Gale, [1977]. 296p. $40. **AA100**

Introduction and section headings in English and French; directory information in English or French. A country-by-country listing covering 48 African nations. For each country is given information under as many of the following headings as applicable: (1) University, college, and public libraries; (2) Special libraries; (3) Booksellers; (4) Publishers; (5) Institutional publishers; (6) Periodicals and magazines; (7) Major newspapers; (8) Book industry associations and literary societies. Appendixes include directories of printers, dealers in African books in Europe and the United States, and book clubs; subject index of special libraries; subject index of periodicals; bibliography of publishing in Africa.

Bangladesh

Bangladesh national bibliography, 1972– . Dacca, Directorate of Archives and Libraries, Ministry of Education, 1974– . Annual. **AA101**

"A subject catalogue of new books published in Bangladesh and received under the provision of Copyright Ordinance, 1962; classified with modification according to the Dewey Decimal Classification (16th edition), provided with a full author, title and subject index and a list of Bangladesh publishers whose books have been included in the Bibliography."—*1972 ed., p. 109.*

Title also in Bengali.

In two parts: (1) Bengali; (2) English.

Barbados

The national bibliography of Barbados. Jan./Mar. 1975– . Bridgetown, Barbados, Public Library, 1975– . Quarterly, the 4th issue being an annual cumulation. **AA102**

Intends "to list all new works published in Barbados; as well as those works of Barbadians authorship published abroad."—*Pref.* Classed arrangement according to Dewey Decimal Classification, with author/title/series index.

Belgium

Bibliotheca belgica. Bibliographie générale des Pays-Bas. Bruxelles, Culture et Civilisation, 1975. v.7. **AA103**

Contents: v.7, Index général. 500p.

For v.1–6 and annotation *see Guide* AA500.

This volume provides much more detailed indexing than the indexes of authors and of printers found in v.6.

Cockx-Indestege, Elly and Glorieux, Geneviève. Belgica typographica, 1541–1600 .... Nieuwkoop, B. de Graaf, 1977–78. v.2[1-2]. (In progress) **AA104**

For full citation, v.1, and annotation *see Guide* AA501.

Contents: v.2, fasc.1–2, Items 4983–6612 (A–Rantzovius).

The second volume lists, describes bibliographically, and locates items in Belgian libraries other than the Bibliothèque Royale.

Bolivia

Costa de la Torre, Arturo. Catálogo de la bibliografía boliviana. La Paz, Universidad Mayor de San Andres, 1973. v.2. (In progress) **AA105**

Contents: v.2, Adiciones al "Segundo suplemento de la Bibliografía boliviana" de Gabriel René Moreno—1900–1908; Folletos anónimos en general—1908–1963. 1069p.

For v.1 and annotation *see Guide* AA509.

A third volume is to provide a bibliography of foreign authors, 1909–63.

Bulgaria

Natsionalna bibliografiia na NR Bulgariia. Sofiia, Narodna Biblioteka "Kiril i Metodii," 1974– . **AA106**

Beginning 1974, the various bibliographic services for Bulgaria are brought together under this general title and issued by the National Library. The following series are included:

Ser.1, *Bulgarski knigopis; knigi, notni, graficheski i kartigrafski izdaniia.* v.78– , 1974– . Bi-weekly with annual cumulation. Subtitle also in English: Books, music, prints, maps. Supersedes, in part, *Bulgarski knigopis* (*Guide* AA520) and continues its numbering.

Ser.2, *Bulgarski knigopis; sluzhebni izdaniia i disertatsii.* v.78– , 1974– . Monthly with annual index. Subtitle also in English: Official publications and dissertations. Supersedes, in part, *Bulgarski knigopis* (*Guide* AA520) and continues its volume numbering. The entries for dissertations are also included in:

Bulgarski disertatsii. 1973– (publ. 1974–). Annual.

Ser.3, *Bulgarski gramofonni plochi.* 1972– (publ. 1974–). Annual.

Ser.4, *Bulgarski periodichen pechat.* 1972– (publ. 1974–). Annual. Title also in English: Bulgarian periodicals, newspapers, journals, bulletins and periodical collections. Supersedes a publication of the same title covering 1965–71. Includes all periodical publications listed in the bi-weekly issues of Ser.2 (above) as well as non-official serial publications.

Ser.5, *Letopis na statiite ot bulgarskite spisaniia i sbornitsi.* v.23– . 1974– . Bi-weekly. Title also in English: Articles from Bulgarian journals and collections. Supersedes and continues the volume numbering of a publication of the same title covering 1972–73, which in turn partially superseded *Letopis na periodichnaia pechat* (*Guide* AE197).

Ser.6, *Letopis na statiite ot bulgarskite vestnitsi.* v.23– , 1974– . Monthly. Title also in English: Articles from Bulgarian newspapers. Supersedes and continues the volume numbering of a publication of the same title covering 1972–73, which in turn partially superseded *Letopis na periodichnaia pechat* (*Guide* AE197).

Ser.7, *Bulgariia v chuzhdata literatura (Bulgarika).* 1972– (publ. 1974–). Annual. Title also in English: Bulgaria in foreign literature. Continues a publication of the same title covering 1964–71.

Ser.8, *Bibliografiia na bulgarskata bibliografiia.* 1973– (publ. 1974–). Annual. Title also in English: Bibliography of Bulgarian bibliographies. Continues a publication of the same title covering 1963–72.

Canada

Amtmann, Bernard. Contributions to a short-title catalogue of Canadiana. Montreal, 1973. v.4. **AA107**

For v.1–3 and annotation *see Guide* AA521.

Contents: v.4, Pratt–Zubek. Completes the set.

Canadian books in print: author and title index. 1975– . Toronto, Univ. of Toronto Pr., 1976– . Annual. **AA108**

Continues *Canadian books in print* (*Guide* AA531). With the 1973 edition of the earlier series the French title was dropped, and only those French-language titles issued by predominantly English-language Canadian publishers are now included (the French-language publications being adequately covered by the annual *Répertoire de l'édition au Québec,* 1972–75, which has been superseded by the annual *Edi-Québec,* 1976–). Beginning with the 1975 volume (published 1976), the subtitle, "Author and title index" appears on the title page; a companion volume is published as:

Canadian books in print: subject index. 1975– . Toronto, Univ. of Toronto Pr., 1976– . Annual. **AA109**

Continues *Subject guide to Canadian books in print,* 1973–74. Martha Pluscauskas, ed.

A companion publication to the author/title section of *Canadian books in print* (above), listing all the books included therein under some 674 subject headings. Includes an alphabetical list of subject headings and a list of publishers with addresses. Z1365.S9

Canadiana, 1950– . Ottawa, Nat. Lib. of Canada, 1951– . Monthly, with annual cumulations. **AA110**

For earlier information on the series *see Guide* AA532.

Automation of the production of *Canadiana* proceeded in stages from 1973 and was completed at the end of 1977, with various changes during the transition period. Beginning 1974, the bibliography appeared in eight parts: (1) Monographs (fully catalogued and classified) [now includes sheet music and scores]; (2) Theses in microform; (3) Serials (fully catalogued and classified) [now includes monographic series]; (4) Pamphlet file material; (5) Sound recordings (fully catalogued and classified); (6) Films, filmstrips and videotapes [not included after the Dec. 1976 issue; thereafter these materials are listed in an annual publication, *Film Canadiana,* prepared by the Canadian Film Institute in cooperation with the National Library]; (7) Publications of the government of Canada; (8) Publications of the provincial governments of Canada. Separate cumulated annual indexes were published for Section 1 (comprising pts.1–2) and for Section 2 (comprising pts.3–8); from 1978 there will presumably be a single annual index for all seven parts as announced in the Jan. 1978 issue.

——— 1968–1976 index. Ottawa, Nat. Lib. of Canada, 1978. 10v. $50 the set in Canada; $60 elsewhere. pa.

"This index is the cumulation of Index A information for all of the manually-prepared text of CANADIANA for the years 1968 to 1976; for 1968 to 1973 this included all parts, for 1974 parts III–VIII, and for 1975 and 1976 parts V and VI only. It attempts to provide every type of specific entry under which a publication may be sought. It includes authors (personal and corporate), titles, added entries (i.e. associated names such as editors, joint authors, etc.) and series. It also includes cross-references from headings not used, and where relevant, histories of corporate bodies occurring as authors."—*v.1, [p.1].* Users are

cautioned that changes in cataloging rules and filing procedures sometimes mean that separate alphabetical sequences must be searched for publications of a given organization.

Caribbean area

The CARICOM bibliography, v.1– . Georgetown, Guyana, Caribbean Community Secretariat Library, 1977– . Annual. $6 per yr. **AA111**

Subtitle: A cumulated subject list of current national imprints of the Caribbean Community member countries, arranged according to the Dewey Decimal Classification, 18th ed., and catalogued according to the British text of the Anglo-American rules (1967) and the International Standard Bibliographic Description for Monographs and Serials.

Aims "to list all material currently published" (*Pref.*) in Antigua, Bahamas, Barbados, Belize, Dominica, Grenada, Guyana, Jamaica, Montserrat, St. Kitts/Nevis/Anguilla, St. Lucia, St. Vincent, Trinidad and Tobago. Full information appears in the classified section; index of authors, titles, series. Excludes periodicals (except first issue, changes of title, and annual reports) and certain types of government publications. v.1 covers mainly 1976 publications, with some of earlier date.

Chile

Williams, Lee H. The Allende years, a union list of Chilean imprints, 1970–1973, in selected North American libraries .... Boston, G. K. Hall, 1977. 339p. $24. **AA112**

For full information *see Suppl.* DB64.

China

Chinese cooperative catalog. Jan. 1975– . Wash., Lib. of Congress, 1975– . Monthly, with annual cumulation. (1976: $350) **AA113**

Intended as an aid for libraries acquiring Chinese-language materials, this catalog presents "Library of Congress printed cards, preliminary cards prepared in the Library of Congress at the initial stage of cataloging, and catalog cards submitted by 12 of the larger Chinese collections in the United States. Although most of the entries are monographs, serials are also included."—*Foreword.* Arranged alphabetically by romanized title. Not to be considered a union catalog, since only a single location is usually indicated. Z881.U49C49

Ecuador

Anuario bibliografico ecuatoriano, 1975– . Quito, Universidad Central del Ecuador, 1976– . Annual. **AA114**

At head of title: Universidad Central del Ecuador, Biblioteca General.

The annual volume represents a cumulation of the bimonthly issues of the *Bibliografía ecuatoriana* and includes the sixth number of that series.

A classed listing in two sections: (1) Bibliografía monográfica, and (2) Bibliografía analítica, the latter providing analytics for collective works and selected periodicals. Indexes of names, titles, and subjects.

Ethiopia

Höjer, Christianne. Ethiopian publications. Books, pamphlets, annuals and periodical articles published in Ethiopia in foreign languages from 1942 till 1962. Addis Ababa, Haile Sellassie I Univ., Inst. of Ethiopian Studies, 1974. 146p. **AA115**

Intends to fill the gap between Stephen G. Wright's *Ethiopian incunabula* (Addis Ababa, 1967) and the annual *Ethiopian publications* (*Guide* AA590). A classified list with annual index.

France

Répertoire bibliographique des livres imprimés en France au seizième siècle .... Baden-Baden, Heitz, 1973–76. Fasc.13–25 (fasc.15 omitted in numbering). (Bibliotheca bibliographica Aureliana, 48–49, 51, 53–54, 57–59, 62–65) (In progress) **AA116**

For previously published parts and annotation *see Guide* AA608.

Current

Bibliographie de la France—Biblio. Paris, Cercle de la Librairie, 1972– . Année 161– . Weekly. **AA117**

For history of the publication *see Guide* AA613.

Certain changes have been effected in the make-up and frequency of portions of Pt.1, *Bibliographie officielle.* The weekly classed lists in the *Livres* section continue to cumulate monthly in a classed arrangement designated as *Les livres du mois.* However, the quarterly cumulation, *Les livres du trimestre* has been superseded (1977) by the quarterly *Tables trimestrielles des nouveautés* which cumulates entries from the previous three months in an author listing with an alphabetical title list which indicates author's name and subject class for each title. An "Index cumulatif annuel" for the 1977 *Livres* section was published as a supplement to no.52 of Dec. 28, 1977; this will presumably be an annual feature.

There are now four numbered supplements which appear regularly as part of the *Bibliographie officielle:* I, Publications en série (monthly); II, Publications officielles (bimonthly); III, Musique (quarterly); IV, Atlas, cartes et plans (three times a year [varies]). Additional, special supplements also appear from time to time.

Les livres disponibles, 1977– . [Paris], Cercle de la Librairie, 1977– . Annual. **AA118**

Also called *French books in print.*

Subtitle: La liste exhaustive des ouvrages disponibles publiés en langue française dans le monde. La liste des éditeurs et la liste des collections de langue française.

Issued in two parts: (1) Auteurs; (2) Titres. (A subject volume arranged by Universal Decimal Classification was added with the 1978 edition.)

Supersedes *Le catalogue de l'édition française* (*Guide* AA614), last published 1976 (éd. 5). Includes books published in French regardless of place of publication. Excludes theses, pamphlets, periodicals, musical scores, and annuals of associations. The lists of publishers and distributors and of publishers' series appear in both volumes.

Germany

Gesamtverzeichnis des deutschsprachigen Schrifttums (GV); 1911–1965. Hrsg. von Reinhard Oberschelp; bearb. unter der Leitung von Willi Gorzny, mit einem Geleitwort von Wilhelm Totok. München, Verlag Dokumentation, 1976–78. v.1–76. (In progress) **AA119**

To be in 150v.; DM16500 the set.

Contents: v.1–76, A–Land.

Represents a cumulation and integration of the main entries from some fifteen series of German-language national bibliographies and dissertation lists. (Entries from the original publications have been interfiled and photographed, not re-set). Citations are drawn from the *Deutsches Bücherverzeichnis* (*Guide* AA631), *Deutsche Bibliographie* (*Guide* AA634), *Deutsche Nationalbibliographie* (*Guide* AA627), and from the various German, Austrian, and Swiss dissertation lists. These publications are not, however, fully superseded since the subject indexes are not similarly cumulated and integrated, and all portions of some series are not represented in the new work. Z2221.G47

Current

Leipzig

Deutsche Nationalbibliographie. Reihe C. Leipzig, VEB Verlag für Buch- und Bibliothekswesen, 1968– . Monthly. **AA120**

For Reihe A and Reihe B *see Guide* AA627.

Beginning 1968, "Dissertationen und Habilitationsschriften" are listed in Reihe C; for full information *see Suppl.* AH10.

Frankfurt am Main

Deutsche Bibliographie. Wöchentliches Verzeichnis. Frankfurt a. M., Buchhändler-Vereinigung GMBH, 1975– . Weekly. **AA121**

For history of the publication *see Guide* AA632.

A new weekly section, *Neuerscheinungen-Sofortdienst (CIP),* began publication July, 1975, cumulating monthly and quarterly; weekly issues follow a classed arrangement, the cumulations are main entry listings with *see* references from titles, editors, etc., as appropriate. Entries are based on information supplied for "cataloging-in-publication," thus providing advance listings for persons involved in book selection. Full bibliographic information derived from examination of the book itself is provided in Reihe A of the *Bibliographie* following publication.

For the "Hochschulschriften-Verzeichnis" section of the *Bibliographie see Suppl.* AH9.

Great Britain

Allison, Antony Francis and **Goldsmith, V. F.** Titles of English books (and of foreign books printed in England); an alphabetical finding-list by title of books published under the author's name, pseudonym or initials. [Folkestone, Eng.], Dawson; Hamden, Conn., Archon Books, [1976–77]. 2v. $45. **AA122**

Contents: v.1, 1475–1640; v.2, 1641–1700.

v.1 offers a title approach to Pollard and Redgrave's *Short-title catalogue . . . 1475–1640* (*Guide* AA647), including some references to the new edition now in progress. v.2 provides a similar approach to Wing's *Short-title catalogue* (*Guide* AA660).

A review of v.1 by Paul Morgan (*TLS* 9-24-76, p.1221) expresses reservations about the completeness of the work and the form of entry chosen for many titles. Z2001.A44

Pollard, Alfred William and **Redgrave, Gilbert Richard.** A short-title catalogue of books printed in England, Scotland, & Ireland and of English books printed abroad, 1475–1640. 2d ed., rev. & enl., begun by W. A. Jackson & F. S. Ferguson, completed by Katharine F. Pantzer. London, Bibliographical Society, 1976– . v.2– . (In progress) **AA123**

Contents: v.2, I–Z. £40.

The first published part of the new edition of this important catalog. "The earlier completion of volume 2 is the result of Miss Pantzer's taking over the work of final revision on the death of William A. Jackson in 1964 at the letter R. The later letters of the alphabet represented a later stage in Jackson's own revision, and Miss Pantzer has felt that this, and the fact that she has personally overseen all these parts of the work, enable her and the Society to lay this volume before the public as having reached as definitive a stage as is possible in a work of this nature."—*Pref.*

v.1, A–H, is projected for publication in 1980, with a third volume containing an index of printers and booksellers, as well as additions and corrections, to follow in another two years.

1st ed. 1926 (*Guide* AA647). Z2002.P77

Shaaber, Matthias Adam. Check-list of works of British authors printed abroad, in languages other than English, to 1641. N.Y., Bibliographical Soc. of America, 1975. 168p. $15. **AA124**

"British authors" are here defined as "(1) all writers born in the British Isles, including those who spent most of their lives abroad, (2) all writers born elsewhere who spent considerable parts of their mature lives in the British Isles."—*Pref.* Anonymous works are included if there is "direct evidence" or a consensus of opinion that they are of British origin." Locates copies. Z1012.S49

Current

British national bibliography, 1950– . London, 1950– . **AA125**

For full information *see Guide* AA667.

Beginning in 1977 the *BNB* carries advance cataloging information in the form of CIP (cataloging in publication) records in the weekly lists, thus increasing the bibliography's usefulness as a current selection tool since the entries appear as much as two months in advance of publication of the books themselves. Such entries are identified in the annotations as "CIP entry." As titles are published and deposited in the Copyright Receipt Office the corresponding entries are expanded to include full cataloging information and the full form appears in subsequent interim cumulations and in the annual volume identified as "CIP rev."

Greece

Ntelopoulos, Kyriakos. Hellēnika vivlia. Greek books. 1975– . Athēnai, "Manoutios," 1976– . Annual. **AA126**

Added title page in English. Preface in Greek and English.

"A contribution to the Greek bibliography."—*t.p.*

Lists books published in Greece in the Greek language during the year of coverage and available in the book trade. Arranged according to a modified Dewey Decimal Classification. Indexes of names and of series (Greek names and foreign names in separate alphabets). Does not include Greek publications in foreign languages, nor publications in Greek published abroad. Entries are derived mainly from the quarterly issues of *Nea vivlia—New books,* the bibliographic bulletin of the Hestia bookstore, with some augmentation from other sources. Volumes for 1976– include a supplement for the preceding year.

Guyana

Guyanese national bibliography. 1973– . Georgetown, Guyana, National Library, [1974–]. Quarterly with annual cumulation [i.e., the 4th issue of the year is the annual cumulation]. $10 per yr. **AA127**

"A subject list of new books printed in the Republic of Guyana, based on the books deposited at the National Library, classified according to the Dewey Decimal Classification 16th edition, catalogued according to the British Text of the Anglo-American Cataloguing Rules, 1967 and provided with a full author, title and subject index and a List of Guyanese Publishers."—*t.p., 1973.*

Beginning 1975, includes nonbook materials; classification follows the 18th edition of Dewey; subject entries are omitted from the index; and a "List of single bills, acts, subsidiary legislation and parliamentary debates" forms an appendix to each issue. Z1791.G88

Hungary

Magyar nemzeti bibliográfia könyvek bibliográfiája. évf.32[16]– , Aug. 31, 1977– . Budapest, Országos Sepchényi Könyvtár, 1977– . Semimonthly. **AA128**

Represents a change of title for *Magyar nemzeti bibliográfia. Bibliographica Hungarica* (*Guide* AA705), which closed with évf.32, füzet 15 (Aug. 15, 1977), and continues its volume numbering. Classed arrangement (with index) remains the same, and the issues will continue to be cumulated in *Magyar könyvészet* (*Guide* AA703).

Iceland

Íslenzk bókaskrá. The Icelandic national bibliography. 1974– . Reykjavík, Landsbókasafn Íslands, 1975– . Annual. **AA129**

Prefatory matter in Icelandic and English.

"The Icelandic National Bibliography is a continuation of two older bibliographies, the 'Íslenzk rit' which appeared in 'Arbok Landsbókasafns Íslands' (Year Book of the National Library) 1945–75, and 'Bókaskrá Bóksalafélags Íslands' (Bookseller's Association List) 1937–73. These two works had different functions, the first being a bibliographic source for Icelandic publications and the second a practical aid for booksellers; the new bibliography is intended to combine the two functions."—*Pref. 1974.*

An alphabetical author/main entry listing, with a classified section; a separate section for maps and charts; and a statistical summary of the year's publishing output. Entries in the alphabetical section appear under an author's given name, not the surname. 5-year cumulations are promised.

"A preliminary edition appears in *Íslenzk bókatidindi,* published by the Society of Icelandic Publishers."—*Pref.*

India

National bibliography of Indian literature, 1901–1953. Gen. eds.: B. S. Kesavan and V. Y. Kulkarni. New Delhi, Sahitya Akademi, [1974]. v.4. **AA130**

For v.1–3 and annotation *see Guide* AA712.

Contents: v.4, Sindhi, Tamil, Telugu, Urdu. Completes the set.

Italy

Michel, Suzanne P. and **Michel, Paul-Henri.** Répertoire des ouvrages imprimés en langue italienne au XVIIe siècle conservés dans les bibliothèques de France. Paris, Éditions du Centre National de la Recherche Scientifique, 1975–76. v.5–6. (In progress) **AA131**

For v.1–4 and annotation *see Guide* AA738.

Contents: v.5–6, L–P.

Jamaica

Jamaican national bibliography, 1964–1970 cumulation. Comp. by Rosalie I. Williams. Kingston, West India Reference Library, Institute of Jamaica, 1973. 322p. **AA132**

For annual volumes of the bibliography and its predecessor *see Guide* AA747.

Although called "1964–1970," the introduction states that this cumulation covers "accessions for the ten year period 1960–1970." No annual volumes were published for 1971–74, but a cumulative volume for that period is in preparation. Beginning 1975, the current bibliography became a quarterly [irregular], with the last issue for the year being the annual cumulation.

Latin America

Libros en venta en Hispanoamérica y España; por autor, por título, por materia. Servicio informativo preparado por el equipo de Bowker Editores baja la dirección de Mary C. Turner. 2. ed. Buenos Aires, Bowker, 1974. 2v. (2185p.) $57.50. **AA133**

1st ed. 1964; suppls. 1–4 covered 1964/66–71 (*Guide* AA760).

This edition includes listings for some 120,000 books. About 1,300 publishers and distributors are represented. Separate author, title, and subject listings.

Suplemento 1975 (304p.) was published 1977; *Suplemento 1976/1977* (539p.) appeared 1978. Z1601.L593

United Nations Educational, Scientific and Cultural Organization. Centro Regional para el Fomento del Libro en América Latina. Boletín bibliográfico CERLAL. Año 1, no.1– , Julio 1974– . Bogotá, UNESCO, Centro Regional para el Fomento del Libro en América Latina, 1974– . Quarterly. **AA134**

A regional current bibliography covering Spanish and Portuguese publications of Bolivia, Colombia, Chile, Ecuador, Peru and Venezuela. Classed listing with author and title indexes. No cumulations to date. Z1601.U5a

Latvia

Jēgers, Benjamiņš. Latviešu trimdas izdevumu bibliografija, 1940–1960. [Stockholm], Daugava, [1972]. v.2. **AA135**

For v.1 *see Guide* AA762.

Contents: v.2, Serials, music, maps, programmes & catalogues. v.2 includes indexes.

——— ———, 1961–1970. [Stockholm], Daugava, [1977]. 460p. **AA136**

Added title page in English: Bibliography of Latvian publications published outside Latvia, 1961–1970.

Continues the listings from the earlier compilation covering 1940–60 (*Guide* AA762), with items numbered consecutive to the entries in the first two volumes. This volume covers books and pamphlets, serials, music, maps, etc., in separate listings. Indexes of subjects, places of publication, publishers, persons, and titles.

Malaysia

Bibliografi negara Malaysia. Malaysian national bibliography. 1967– . Kuala Lumpur, Perkhidmatan Perpustakaan Negara, Arkib Negara Malaysia, 1969– . Quarterly. $40 ($55 overseas). **AA137**

Issued annually 1967–74; 1975– , quarterly, the fourth issue being an annual cumulation.

Lists "materials published in Malaysia which are deposited in the National Library of Malaysia under the provisions of the *Preservation of Books Act, 1966,* and includes books, pamphlets, Government publications, new serial titles, maps and posters. However, it excludes popular magazines, comics, commemorative and travel brochures, souvenir programmes and trade catalogues."—*Pref., 1975 annual.*

In two sections: (1) a classified section according to Dewey Decimal Classification in which the full bibliographic information is given; and (2) an alphabetical author/title/series index. An alphabetical subject index to the Dewey class numbers is added in the annual cumulation. Z3261.B5

New Zealand

Bagnall, Austin Graham, ed. New Zealand national bibliography to the year 1960. Wellington, Govt. Printer, 1975. v.4. (In progress) **AA138**

For previously published volumes and annotation *see Guide* AA799.

Contents: v.4, 1890–1960, P–Z.

v.4 completes the 1890–1960 sequence; v.1 (pre-1890 imprints), index and supplement are still to appear.

Nigeria

The national bibliography of Nigeria, 1973– . Lagos, National Library of Nigeria, 1974– . Annual. **AA139**

1st–21st annual cumulations (1950/52–1972) had title *Nigerian publications* (*Guide* AA807).

Covers "books and pamphlets published in Nigeria and received under the legal deposit provisions . . . as well as those about Nigeria or by Nigerians published abroad. In addition, it includes a section on Nigerian periodicals and newspapers."—*Pref. 1974.* Originally arranged by author or other main entry within five sections: (1) works in English; (2) government publications; (3) works in vernacular (i.e., Nigerian languages); (4) Nigeriana published outside the country; (5) Nigerian periodicals and newspapers. Beginning with the issue covering 1976 a single classified sequence (with index) is used for types 1–4, and there is a separate listing of new Nigerian periodicals and newspapers. Z3597.N37

Pakistan

The Pakistan national bibliography, 1947–1961. [Karachi], National Book Centre of Pakistan, [1975]. Fasc.2. (In progress) **AA140**

For Fasc.1 and annotation *see Guide* AA816.

Contents: Fasc.2, Social sciences to languages, 300 to 492.

Paraguay

Fernández-Caballero, Carlos F. S. Paraguái tai hũme tove Paraguái arandu taisarambi ko yvy apére. The Paraguayan bibliography, volume two. Amherst, Mass., Seminar on the Acquisition of Latin American Library Materials, Univ. of Mass. Library, 1975. 221p. (Seminar on the Acquisition of Latin American Library Materials. Bibliog., no.3) $5 pa. **AA141**

For the earlier volume (1970) *see Guide* AA820.

This volume includes additions to the bibliographies of Paraguayan authors as found in [v.1], and lists "works published from the eighteenth century to 1974, by: (1) Paraguayans and non-Paraguayans on the specific subject of Paraguay; and by (2) Paraguayans on any topic."—*Prologue.* 2,363 entries listed by author or other main entry; subject index. Separate subject index for [v.1], pp.217–21. Z1821.F45

Philippines

Bernardo, Gabriel Adriano. Philippine retrospective national bibliography: 1523–1699. [Manila], Nat. Lib. of the Philippines, [1974]. 160p. il. (Occasional papers of the Dept. of History, Ateneo de Manila bibliographical ser., no.3) **AA142**

Includes three categories of foreign and Philippine imprints: "(1) those which deal in whole or in part with the Philippines and were printed abroad, (2) all those printed in the Philippines of any nature, and (3) those written by Filipinos."—*Introd.* Chronological listing in two main sections, (1) Foreign imprints; (2) Philippine imprints. Author/subject index. 760 items. Z3298.A35B47

Philippine union catalog. Jan./Mar. 1974– . Quezon City, Univ. of the Philippines Library, 1974– . 3 quarterly issues per yr. plus annual cumulation. **AA143**

Supersedes *Philippine bibliography* 1963–1972 (*Guide* AA832) and the *Filipiniana union catalog* 1968–1973 (in preparation).

"An author list of Filipiniana materials currently acquired by the University of the Philippines Library and other libraries."—*t.p.*

Gives full catalog entries for "Filipiniana materials including books, theses, music scores, phonodiscs, tapes, microfilms, new serial titles and other materials, or reproductions of any of these forms. It also includes government documents and publications except individual acts, bills and ordinances. Pamphlets of less than five pages, unless of research value, are excluded."—*Introd.* Includes both current materials and older works recently acquired by participating libraries. Author listing with title and subject indexes.

Poland

Estreicher, Karol J. T. Bibliografia polska XIX. stulecia. Wyd.2. Kraków, [Państwowe Wydawn. Naukowe, Oddział w Krakowie], 1975–76. v.8–11. (In progress) **AA144**

For v.1–7 and annotation *see Guide* AA834a.

Contents: v.8–11, G–I.

Rhodesia

Hartridge, Anne, comp. Rhodesia national bibliography, 1890 to 1930. Salisbury, National Archives, 1977. 50p. (National Archives of Rhodesia. Bibliographical ser., no.2) **AA145**

A first step toward providing coverage from 1890 (the date of "commencement of administration and modern commerce within Rhodesia"—*Foreword*) to 1961, the beginning date for annual bibliographic records for the area (*see Guide* AA850).

Classed arrangement according to the Dewey Decimal Classification, with index of authors, editors, etc. and titles. Lists books, pamphlets, maps, serials (including newspapers), and government publications published in Rhodesia.

Russia

Leningrad. Publichnaia Biblioteka. Opisanie izdanii . . . . Dopolneniia i prilozheniia. Sost. T. A. Bykova, M. M. Gurevich, P. I. Kozintseva. Leningrad, 1972. 272p. 91k. **AA146**

At head of title: Biblioteka Akademii Nauk SSSR. Gosudarstvennaia Publichnaia Biblioteka imeni M. E. Saltykova-Shchedrina. Leningradskoe Otdelenie Instituta Istorii SSSR. Akademii Nauk SSSR.

For earlier volumes *see Guide* AA860.

Scope has been extended to cover through December 1727, and information from sources not searched for compilation of the basic volumes is included here.

Svodnyi katalog russkoi knigi grazhdanskoi pechati XVIII veka, 1725–1800. Dopolneniia, razyskivaemye izdanniia utochneniia. [Redaktsionnaia kollegiia: N. M. Sikorskii] Moskva, Kniga, 1975. 189p. 85k. **AA147**

For main set and annotation *see Guide* AA862.

Lists acquisitions of participating libraries from 1967; corrections to v.1–4; citations to reviews and indexes. Includes a list of unlocated books.

Slovakia

Matica Slovenska, Turčiansky sv. Martín. Knižnica. Katalóg slovacikálnych kníh vydaných do roku 1918 v knižnici Matice slovenskej, zost. Anna Podmanická. Martin, Matica Slovenská, 1974. 2v. (1205p.) (Slovenské knižnice, zv. 10–11) Kčs. 27 per v. **AA148**

Added title page in Latin: Catalogus librorum slovacicorum usque ad annum 1918 impressorum qui in Bibliotheca 'Matica slovenská' asservantur.

A listing by author or other main entry. Index by place of publication, subdivided by publisher. Z2137.S6M38

Spain

Goldsmith, Valentine Fernande. A short title catalogue of Spanish and Portuguese books, 1601–1700, in the Library of the British Museum (The British Library—Reference Division). Folkestone, Dawsons of Pall Mall, 1974. 250p. £30. **AA149**

Includes "1. Books written wholly or partly in Spanish or Portuguese, no matter where published; 2. Books, in no matter what language, published or printed at any place which today forms part of Spain or Portugal."—*Definitions.* Books lost or destroyed during World War II are listed whether or not the library has replaced them. Continues chronologically the Museum's *Short-title catalogue of books printed in Spain and of Spanish books printed elsewhere in Europe before 1601* (*Guide* AA892).

Errors and shortcomings of the work are pointed out in D. W. Cruickshank's review in *The library,* ser. 5, 29:463–67 (Dec. 1974). Z2686.G64

Llordén, Andrés. La imprenta en Málaga; ensayo para una tipobibliografía malagueña. Málaga, Caja de Ahorros Provincial, [1973]. 2v. **AA150**

Arranged by printer or press; an historical note is followed by a bibliography of the works published by each. Z174.M22L55

Palau y Dulcet, Antonio. Manual del librero hispano-americano; bibliografía general española e hispano-americana .... 2.ed., corr. y aum. por el autor. Barcelona, Librería Palau, 1975–77. v.26–28. (In progress) **AA151**

For previously published volumes and annotation *see Guide* AA885.

Contents: v.26–28, Vega–Z.

The main alphabetical sequence is now complete; a title index and supplement are planned.

Sri Lanka

Sri Lanka national bibliography. Colombo, Dept. of Nat. Archives, 1977– . v.10, no.5/12– , May/Dec.1972– . **AA152**

Continues the *Ceylon national bibliography* (*Guide* AA906), which ceased with v.10, no.4, Apr. 1972, and assumes its numbering. Arrangement remains the same as in the earlier series.

Swaziland

Swaziland national bibliography ... with current information. 1973/76– . Kwaluseni, Univ. of Botswana and Swaziland, Univ. College of Swaziland, 1977– **AA153**

The first volume covers 1973–76; subsequent issues are to appear annually. Lists "all known publications issued in Swaziland ... with the exception of certain ephemeral items and those items which are regarded as confidential or restricted. In addition, all publications in Siswati, including those published outside Swaziland, are included in the bibliography."—*Pref.* Arranged by Dewey Decimal Classification with author/title index. Appendixes include a list of foreign publications on Swaziland, Swaziland legislation and law reports, and forthcoming books and works in progress.

Serves in part to supplement *Swaziland official publications, 1880–1972* (*see Suppl.* AG26).

Sweden

Swedish imprints, 1731–1833; a retrospective national bibliography, prep. at the Center for Bibliographical Studies, Uppsala (CBSU). Uppsala, Dahlia Books, 1977– . Introd. & pt.1– . (In progress) **AA154**

Rolf E. DuRietz, gen. ed.

An effort toward a comprehensive retrospective bibliography of works printed and/or published in the area constituting the sovereign territory of Sweden during the 1731–1833 period. The bibliography is being published in parts, each part having its own index; cumulated indexes are to be published at regular intervals. Within each part arrangement is chronological-alphabetical. Supplementary entries in later parts will correct and augment information appearing in the first entry for a given work.

Switzerland

Das schweizer Buch .... Bern, 1901– **AA155**

For full information *see Guide* AA924.

Beginning 1976, the bibliography is no longer issued in two parts (i.e., titles formerly listed in pt.B, "outside the booktrade," are no longer separately treated); instead, a single combined list is published semimonthly and covers all types of publications. The classified arrangement with author/subject index is retained. The semi-annual cumulated index discontinued in 1976 was reinstated in 1977.

Tunisia

Bibliographie nationale de la Tunisie. Publications non officielles. 1956/68– . Tunis, Service Documentaire, 1974– . **AA156**

At head of title: République Tunisienne. Ministère des Affaires Culturelles. Bibliothèque Nationale.

Added title page in Arabic.

The issue noted as "Série II, Année 1, 1969" in *Guide* AA926 has been superseded by retrospective compilations covering 1956/68 (publ. 1974) and 1969/73 (publ. 1975); an annual volume for 1974 was published 1976. Each volume is a classed listing according to the Universal Decimal Classification system, with separate sections for French and Arabic publications.

al-Maktabah al-Qawmiyah. Bibliographie nationale: publications non-officielles, 1956–1968. Tunis, Service Documentaire, 1974. 167p., 165p. **AA157**

At head of title: République Tunisienne. Ministère des Affaires Culturelles. Bibliothèque Nationale.

Added title page in Arabic.

Offers retrospective coverage for the period prior to the beginning of the current *Bibliographie nationale de la Tunisie* (*Guide* AA926). In two parts: (1) Western languages; (2) Arabic. Each part employs a classed arrangement according to the Universal Decimal Classification with author and title indexes.

Venezuela

Anuario bibliográfico venezolano, 1967/1968– . Caracas, Congreso de la República, 1977– . Irregular. **AA158**

At head of title: República de Venezuela. Biblioteca Nacional. Centro Bibliográfico Venezolano.

A continuation of the earlier bibliography of the same title (*Guide* AA936), with plans calling for filling the gap from 1954 (i.e., volumes covering 1955–66 and 1969–74 have been announced as in preparation). An annual volume covering 1975 appeared in 1977.

Zambia

The national bibliography of Zambia. 1970/71– . Lusaka, National Archives of Zambia, [1972]– . Annual (beginning with the issue covering 1972). (1972: 45n.) **AA159**

Attempts to list "all work published in Zambia and received by National Archives of Zambia under the Printed Publication Act" during the period covered. Includes "books, pamphlets, first issues of new serials, publications of statutory bodies and Government publications, excluding Acts, Bills, parliamentary debates and gazettes." —*Introd.* Arranged by Dewey Decimal Classification, with author and title index. Z3573.Z3N37

A B

Librarianship and Library Resources

GENERAL WORKS

Bibliography

Harris, Michael H. A guide to research in American library history. 2d ed. Metuchen, N.J., Scarecrow Pr., 1974. 275p. $9. **AB1**

1st ed. 1968.

Sections on "state of the art," philosophy and methodology for research in American library history, and basic sources are followed by "An annotated bibliography of graduate research in American library history," pp.41–253. Indexed. Z731.H3

Knoop-Busch, Hedda. Beiträge aus deutschen Festschriften auf dem Gebiet des Buch- und Bibliothekswesens 1947–1965. Göttingen, Evan. Bibliothekar-Lehrinst., 1970. 67*l.* (Arbeiten aus dem Evangelischen Bibliothekar-Lehrinstitut Göttingen, 3) **AB2**

Some 58 commemorative volumes are listed and their contents analyzed in a classified arrangement. Author index. Contributions are mainly in German. Z666.K58

Dissertations

Library and information studies in the United Kingdom and Ireland, 1950–1974: an index to theses. Ed. by Peter J. Taylor. [London], Aslib, [1976]. 69p. £4.50. **AB3**

A bibliography of theses in librarianship and information work which "seeks to bring together in one list all of those theses accepted in full or partial requirement for [higher] degrees, either in library schools or other departments of the universities."—*Introd.* Chronological listing with author and detailed subject indexes. Theses accepted after 1974 are listed in the Library Association's *RADIALS bulletin.* Z666.L374

Magnotti, Shirley. Master's theses in library science, 1960–1969. Troy, N.Y., Whitston, 1975. 366p. $18. **AB4**

——— ———, 1970–1974. Troy, N.Y., Whitston, 1976. 198p. $10.50.

The basic volume lists about 2,500 master's theses from 31 accredited library schools; the supplement adds some 700 titles from 24 schools (plus a few titles from the earlier period). The 1960–69 volume is an author listing with subject index; the 1970–74 supplement repeats the full citation in the subject section. Z666.M27

Schlachter, Gail A. and **Thomison, Dennis.** Library science dissertations, 1925–1972; an annotated bibliography. Littleton, Colo., Libraries Unlimited, 1974. 293p. (Research studies in library science, no. 12) $12.50. **AB5**

A chronological listing, with author and subject indexes. Drawing their citations from the standard American dissertation lists, the compilers have listed "those doctoral studies which were either accepted by library schools or concerned with areas bearing a close relationship to the field of librarianship (e.g., communications, information services, education, etc.)."—*Introd.* As far as possible, each entry is annotated as to purpose, procedure, and findings. Z674.R4 no.12

Handbooks of usage

Cook, Margaret Gerry. The new library key. 3d ed. N.Y., Wilson, 1975. 264p. il. $5 pa. **AB6**

2d ed. 1963 (*Guide* AB21).

"This edition includes the latest editions or revisions of standard reference works, as well as new reference books, some of major importance, published since the 1963 edition. . . ."—*Pref.* Z711.2.C75

Downs, Robert Bingham and **Keller, Clara D.** How to do library research. 2d ed. Urbana, Univ. of Illinois Pr., [1975]. 298p. $7.95. **AB7**

1st ed. 1966.

Sections on "America's libraries," library catalogs, and "Practical use of reference books" are followed by what are essentially annotated bibliographies of various types of reference works, plus a section on non-book materials. Z1035.1.D68

Encyclopedias

Encyclopedia of library and information science. Allen Kent and Harold Lancour, eds. N.Y., Dekker, [1976–78]. v.17–25. (In progress) **AB8**

For earlier volumes and annotation *see Guide* AB23.

Contents: v.17–25, Malawi–Rochester.

Directories

International

Fang, Josephine Riss and **Songe, Alice H.** International guide to library, archival, and information science associations. N.Y., Bowker, 1976. 354p. $15.95. **AB9**

A preliminary ed. (1973) had title: *Handbook of national and international library associations* (*Guide* AB34).

"The general criteria for selection are nonprofit associations related to librarianship, documentation, and information science, archives, including institutions, staff (both professional and nonprofessional), and professional education."—*Introd.* In two sections: (1) International associations; (2) National associations. Includes a list of official journals of the associations, an alphabetical list of chief officers, a general bibliography, and an index of official names. Z673.A1F33

United States

North American film and video directory: a guide to media collections and services. Comp. by Olga S. Weber. N.Y., Bowker, 1976. 284p. $25. **AB10**

Represents "both a revision and extension of the pioneer *Directory of film libraries in North America,* published by the Film Library Information Council in 1971, in that in addition to updating data on film and other media services, information has been expanded to include institutions offering video services and/or maintaining video tape collections."—*Pref.* PN1998.A1W36

Subject directory of special libraries and information centers. Ed. 1– . Detroit, Gale, 1975– . Irregular. **AB11**

Ed. by Margaret L. Young [and others].

1977 issue in 5v. called "4th ed." ($125; individual vols., $30).

"A subject classified edition of material taken from *Directory of special libraries and information centers* covering special libraries." —*t.p.*

Contents: v.1, Business and law libraries; v.2, Education and information science libraries; v.3, Health sciences libraries; v.4, Social sciences and humanities libraries; v.5, Science and technology libraries.

A re-arrangement of the entries from the *Directory of special libraries. . . .* (*Guide* AB44).

Canada

Directory of library associations in Canada. Ed.1– . Ottawa, Library Documentation Centre, Nat. Lib. of Canada, 1974– . Biennial? (Ed.2, 1976) **AB12**

Provides information regarding founding date, objectives, meetings, publications, officers, etc. Z673.A1D57

Biography

Dictionary of American library biography. Editorial board: George S. Bobinski, Jesse Hauk Shera, Bohdan S. Wynar. Littleton, Colo., Libraries Unlimited, 1978. 596p. $65. **AB13**

A collection of biographical sketches (about 1,000 to 6,000 words each) of 302 outstanding men and women of the library field. Emphasis is on "figures of national importance, based on the following criteria: contributions of national significance to library development; writings that influenced library trends and activities; positions of national importance . . . ; major achievements in special fields of librarianship; significant scholarly, philanthropic, legislative, or governmental support or activity that affected American libraries. To ensure proper historical perspective, only those people deceased as of June 30, 1976, were considered for inclusion."—*p.xxxi.* Articles are signed and include bibliographies. Supplementary sketches are to appear in the *Journal of library history.* Z720.A4D5

Yearbooks

American Library Association. ALA yearbook. 1976– . Chicago, Amer. Lib. Assoc., 1976– . il. Annual. (1977: $30) **AB14**

Subtitle: A review of library events 1975– .

An annual record of the events, activities, topics of current interest, etc., which reflect the varied concerns of the Association and its members. Includes obituary notices, state reports, etc. Indexed. Z673.A5Y14

LIBRARY RESOURCES

United States

Ash, Lee, comp. Subject collections; a guide to special book collections and subject emphases as reported by university, college, public, and special libraries and museums in the United States and Canada. 4th ed., rev. & enl. N.Y., Bowker, 1974. 908p. $39.95. **AB15**

3d ed. 1967 (*Guide* AB98).

Now computer-produced for easier expansion and updating of future editions. Some listings from the previous edition are omitted at the request of the holding library or because a library failed to respond to the compiler's questionnaires. Z731.A78

Directory of Jewish archival institutions. Ed. by Philip P. Mason. Detroit, pub. for the National Foundation for Jewish Culture by Wayne State Univ. Pr., 1975. 76p. il. $3.75 pa. **AB16**

A brief guide to the major archival collections in the American Jewish Archives, American Jewish Historical Society, Leo Baeck Institute, Bund Archives of the Jewish Labor Movement, Dropsie University, Hebrew Union College–Jewish Institute of Religion Manuscript Library, Library of the Jewish Theological Seminary of America, and YIVO Institute for Jewish Research. Z6366.D57

East Central and Southeast Europe: a handbook of library and archival resources in North America. Paul Horecky, chief ed., David H. Kraus, assoc. ed. Santa Barbara, Calif., Clio Pr., [1976]. 467p. (Joint Committee on Eastern Europe. Publ. ser., 3) $35.75. **AB17**

Intends "to provide scholars, librarians, students, and researchers with a basic reference tool for the study of the essential collections available in major libraries, archives, and research institutions in the United States and Canada, by outlining the profiles of these collections and offering broad guidance to their subject and area contents. The focus is on the humanities and the socioeconomic and political sciences."—*Foreword.* Covers material on Albania, Bulgaria, Czechoslovakia, East Germany, Greece, Hungary, Poland, Romania, and Yugoslavia. Collections of some forty libraries, archives, and research institutions are described, with major surveys of up to 5,000 words in length. Descriptions are signed by contributors and include bibliographic citations. Institutions are arranged alphabetically. An "Area and subject guide" serves as an index. Z2483.E2

Meckler, Alan M. and **McMullin, Ruth.** Oral history collections. N.Y., Bowker, 1975. 344p. $22.50 **AB18**

For full information *see Suppl.* DB14.

U.S. National Archives and Records Service. Guide to the National Archives of the United States. Wash., for sale by Supt. of Docs., 1974. 884p. $12.30. **AB19**

For full information *see Suppl.* DB15.

Williams, Sam P., comp. Guide to the research collections of the New York Public Library. Chicago, Amer. Lib. Assoc., 1975. 336p. $35. **AB20**

Supersedes Karl Brown's *Guide to the reference collections of the New York Public Library* (1941; *Guide* AB105).

A guide to the principal resources and special collections in this vast library system. In four main sections, each with numerous subdivisions: (1) General materials; (2) The humanities; (3) The social sciences; (4) The pure and applied sciences. Index of subjects and collections. Z733.N6W54

Canada

Association of Canadian Archivists. Directory of Canadian records and manuscript repositories. Ottawa, Bonanza Pr., 1977. 115p. **AB21**

Aims "to list archival repositories in Canada and to provide enough pertinent information about their nature and operations to enable users to contact them for additional details."—*Introd.* Entries give name of institution, address, name of curator, telephone number, hours, and a brief note on holdings.

Ottawa. National Library. Research collections in Canadian libraries. [Ottawa, Information Canada, 1972–76] [pt.] I$^{1-6}$; [pt.] II$^{4-5}$. (In progress) **AB22**

Contents: [pt.] I, Universities: 1, Prairie provinces; 2, Atlantic provinces; 3, British Columbia; 4, Ontario; 5, Quebec; 6, Canada; [pt.] II, Special studies: 4, Slavic and East European resources in Canadian academic and research libraries; 5, Collections of official publications.

Comprises results of a survey undertaken by the National Library of Canada. Reports take different forms, offering descriptive and/or statistical information by subject. Z735.A1O88

Germany

Archive. Archive im deutschsprachigen Raum. 2. Aufl. Berlin, W. de Gruyter, 1974. 2v. (1418p.) DM480. **AB23**

At head of title: Minerva-Handbücher.

Aufl. 1, 1932, published as *Minerva-Handbücher:* 2. Abt. Die Archive, Bd.1 (*Guide* AB38).

Offers information on about 8,000 archives in Germany (both East and West Germany), Austria, Switzerland, Luxembourg and Lichtenstein, together with a few archives in Czechoslovakia and Poland. Indexes by type of archive, by country, and by city. Includes private as well as public archives. CD1000.A72

Gebhardt, Walther. Spezialbestände in deutschen Bibliotheken: Bundesrepublik Deutschland einschl. Berlin (West). Im Auftrag der Deutschen Forschungsgemeinschaft. Berlin, W. de Gruyter, 1977. 739p. **AB24**

Added title page: Special collections in German libraries: Federal Republic of Germany incl. Berlin (West.).

Preface in English and German.

"The special collections in this catalogue are to be understood as products of the printing press (including printed graphics) as well as phototechnical or other methods of reproduction, collected because of their subject matter or because of their external form or by reason of their . . . origin, e.g., scholars' personal libraries, monastic libraries, church and school libraries. They must also be of a certain size and be useful as source material for the researcher."—*Pref.* Arranged by city, with a subject index. Z801.A1G4

Welsch, Erwin K. Libraries and archives in Germany. Pittsburgh, Council for European Studies, [1975]. 275p. **AB25**

Intended as "a practical and portable guide primarily for those scholars planning a first research trip abroad."—*Introd.* In addition to information on the collections, facilities, etc. of individual libraries and archives, there is a section on regional catalogs and union lists, and separate sections on "Library bibliography" and "Archive bibliography." Z675.R45W45

Great Britain

Downs, Robert Bingham and **Downs, Elizabeth C.** British library resources; a bibliographical guide. Chicago, Amer. Lib. Assoc.; London, Mansell, 1973. 332p. $25. **AB26**

Intends to "record all published library catalogs—general and special; all checklists of specialized collections in libraries; calendars of manuscripts and archives; exhibition catalogs; articles descriptive of library collections; guides to individual libraries and their holdings; directories of libraries—both general and in specialized fields; union lists of periodicals, newspapers, and other serials; and any other records, descriptive, analytical, or critical, that may guide the scholar, research worker, or advanced student in finding significant materials to meet his needs."—*Introd.* Includes libraries of the United Kingdom and Eire. Classed arrangement with index. Z1002.D63

Latin America

Naylor, Bernard, Hallewell, Laurence and **Steele, Colin.** Directory of libraries and special collections on Latin America and the West Indies. [London], Athlone Pr., 1975. 161p. (London. Univ. Inst. of Latin American Studies. Monographs, no.5) £3.50. **AB27**

For full information *see Suppl.* DB55.

Poland

Lewanski, Richard Casimir, comp. Guide to Polish libraries and archives. Boulder, Colo., East European Quarterly (distr. by Columbia Univ. Pr.), 1974. 209p. (East European monographs, no.6) $11. **AB28**

Aims "to provide American and other English-reading scholars and researchers a comprehensive guide to materials in Polish repositories of manuscript and printed records."—*Introd.* Emphasis is on resources for study of Polish history, civilization, and society. Listing is by city, then by repository. A "subject profile" for each library is usually supplemented by a listing of special collections or unique features. Published catalogs and descriptions of the libraries or special collections are noted. Subject index. Z817.A1L48

Union of Soviet Socialist Republics

Grimsted, Patricia Kennedy. Archives and manuscript repositories in the USSR: Moscow and Leningrad. Supplement 1: Bibliographical addenda. Zug, Switzerland, Inter-Documentation Co., [1976]. 203p. (Bibliotheca Slavica, 9) Sw.Fr.37.50. **AB29**

For main volume *see Guide* AB117.

A bibliographical supplement listing publications appearing through the end of 1973 (and including numerous pre-1970 publications which were omitted from the original volume) plus a few 1974 imprints. Items in the supplement which are available in the publisher's (i.e., IDC) microfiche series are so noted, and a "microfiche correlation table" for items in the main volume is provided.

Yugoslavia

Jovanović, Slobodan and **Rojnić, Matko.** A guide to Yugoslav libraries and archives. Paul L. Horecky, chief ed.; Elizabeth Beyerly, tr. and assoc. ed. [Columbus, Ohio, Am. Assoc. for the Advancement of Slavic Studies, 1975] 113 p. (Joint Committee on Eastern Europe publ. ser., 2) **AB30**

Offers historical notes on the libraries, descriptions of book and manuscript collections, and references to published writings on the libraries. Z841.A1J68

LIBRARY SCIENCE

Handbooks

Art library manual; a guide to resources and practice. Philip Pacey, ed. London & N.Y., Bowker in assoc. with the Art Libraries Assoc., [1977]. 423p. $22.50. **AB31**

A manual for art librarians; chapters by specialists are concerned with "problems of acquisition, organization, accomodation, exploitation and conservation."—*Introd.* Materials discussed include general art bibliographies, quick reference sources, art books, photographs and reproductions, slides and filmstrips, loan collections of original works of art, etc. Z675.A85A79

Handbook of special librarianship and information work. 4th ed. W. E. Batten, ed. London, Aslib, 1975. 430p. £11. **AB32**

3d ed. 1967 by Wilfred Ashworth (*Guide* AB121).

"Despite the rapid development of new techniques and aids for the special librarian—particularly in the area of mechanization . . . , this fourth edition retains all of the essential philosophy associated historically with the manual era."—*Pref.* Z675.A2A75

Harleston, Rebekah M. and **Stoffle, Carla J.** Administration of government documents collections. Littleton, Colo., Libraries Unlimited, 1974. 178p. $9.50. **AB33**

". . . a manual of the procedures involved in processing government documents, in libraries with either separate or integrated collections of federal documents."—*Introd.* Concerned with United States government documents. Bibliography; index. Z7164.G7H37

Larsgaard, Mary. Map librarianship; an introduction. Littleton, Colo., Libraries Unlimited, 1978. 330p. $15. **AB33a**

"The focus . . . is on the actual techniques of map librarianship, from the selection and acquisition of individual maps . . . to the administration of an entire map library."—*Introd.* Chapters cover: (1) Selection and acquisition of maps; (2) Map classification; (3) Map cataloging and computer applications; (4) Care, storage, and repair of maps; (5) Public relations and reference services; (6) Administration; (7) Map librarianship: a brief overview. Numerous appendixes list publishers, reference works, review sources, suppliers of maps and map library equipment, etc. Bibliography and supplemental readings. Indexed.

Harold Nichols' *Map librarianship* (London, Bingley; Hamden, Conn., Linnet Books, 1976. 298p. $12.50) covers subject areas similar to those in the Larsgaard book, but with a British emphasis; it is intended for the practicing map librarian or curator and has less of a textbook approach. Z692.M3L37

Manual of business library practice. Malcolm J. Campbell, ed. London, Clive Bingley; Hamden, Conn., Linnet Books, [1975]. 186p. $10. **AB34**

A text concentrating on British experience in business and commercial libraries. Chapters by librarians and information specialists on the structure of business information, organization and administration of libraries, and information sources. Z675.B8M35

Manual of law librarianship: the use and organization of legal literature. Ed. by Elizabeth M. Moys. Boulder, Colo., publ. for the British and Irish Assoc. of Law Librarians [by] Westview Pr.; London, André Deutsch, 1976. 733p. $32.50 **AB35**

A thorough manual of law librarianship in the British Isles, with chapters contributed by specialists. Bibliographies at the end of each chapter; "Index of works cited," pp.663–715. Z675.L2M27

Mount, Ellis. University science and engineering libraries, their operation, collections, and facilities. Westport, Conn., Greenwood Pr., [1975]. 214p. (Contributions in librarianship and information science, no. 15) $15. **AB36**

Discusses the major aspects of science-engineering library service. "The plan of the book is to proceed from broad topics, such as the general nature of the libraries involved and their organization, to more specific points, e.g., staffing, collection development, reference services, uses of computers, and the planning of library facilities."—*Pref.* Bibliographic notes; index. Z675.U5M68

Acquisitions work and technical services

Nickel, Mildred L. Steps to service: a handbook of procedures for the school library media center. Chicago, Amer. Lib. Assoc., 1975. 124p. $4.50 pa. **AB37**

". . . designed to give practical help and guidance to inexperienced and beginning professionals and to serve as a review for those who may want to reevaluate their own programs."—*Pref.* Includes sections on (1) functions of the school library media center; (2) standards; (3) administration; (4) activities; (5) facilities. Glossary; directory of publishers, producers, and suppliers; index. Z675.S3N63

Carter, Mary Duncan, Bonk, Wallace John and **Magrill, Rose Mary.** Building library collections. 4th ed. Metuchen, N.J., Scarecrow Pr., 1974. 415p. $9. **AB38**

1st ed. 1959.

Essentially a textbook for library school students, with extensive bibliographies and lists of selection aids for the practicing librarian. In three sections: (1) Selection (giving attention to principles of selection and variations by type of library; selection aids; surveying and weeding collections, etc.); (2) Acquisitions; (3) Appendices (giving text of the Library Bill of Rights and related documents; sample selection policies, etc.). Indexed. Z689.C29

How to start an audiovisual collection. Myra Nadler, ed. Metuchen, N.J., Scarecrow Pr., 1978. 157p. $7. **AB39**

A manual for the inexperienced librarian or administrator who needs to start an audiovisual collection or services. Chapters were contributed by librarians and consultants with practical experience in the field. "Definitions and glossary," pp.106–51. Z717.H68

Katz, Bill and **Gellatly, Peter.** Guide to magazine and serial agents. N.Y., Bowker, 1975. 239p. $14.95. **AB40**

Not simply a directory of serials agents as such, but a work designed to give "enough background information concerning serials and their management to provide an understanding of the agent-library relationship" (*Pref.*) together with "facts, details, and descriptions of the major and selected smaller domestic and foreign serials subscription agents." Directory of subscription agents, pp.199–239. Z689.K33

Kim, Ung Chon. Policies of publishers: a handbook for order librarians. Metuchen, N.J., Scarecrow Pr., 1976. 132p. $8.50 pa. **AB41**

An alphabetical listing of publishers, giving information for each of the following points: address for orders, prepayment, discount policy, return policy, shipping and billing policy, back order policy, standing order plan. Z475.K55

Magrill, Rose Mary and **Rinehart, Constance.** Library technical services: a selected, annotated bibliography. Westport, Conn., Greenwood Pr., 1977. 238p. $14.95. **AB42**

In seven main sections: (1) Organization of technical services; (2) Acquisition of materials; (3) Organization of materials; (4) Maintenance of materials; (5) Circulation of materials; (6) Serials; (7) Special materials (e.g., non-book materials, government publications, maps, microforms). Brief annotations; name and subject indexes. More than 1,200 items, with emphasis on recent publications. Z688.5.M25

Archives

Evans, Frank Bernard. Modern archives and manuscripts: a select bibliography. [Wash., D.C.] Soc. of Amer. Archivists, 1975. 209p. **AB43**

"This publication is confined almost exclusively to writings in the English language and its emphasis is upon archival theory and practice in the United States. It is intended only as an introduction to the subject, and does not eliminate the need for more comprehensive or annotated bibliographies on selected subjects."—*Introd.* Classed arrangement within four main sections: (1) Introduction to archives administration; (2) Survey of archival functions; (3) American archival agencies and archives: an overview; (4) International archival developments. Subject and author indexes. Z5140.E87

Cataloging

Daily, Jay Elwood. Cataloging phonorecordings: problems and possibilities. N.Y., M. Dekker, [1975]. 172p. $13.75. **AB44**

The volume "is not meant to advocate a method of cataloging . . . [but] is offered as a means of understanding what the possibilities are."—*Pref.* ML111.5.D34

Subject headings

Sainsbury, Ian M. Legal subject headings for libraries. London, Butterworths, 1974. 108p. £3.80. **AB45**

A work of British origin based on subject headings used in the Inns of Court libraries. Z695.1.L3S24

U.S. Library of Congress. Subject Cataloging Div. Library of Congress subject headings. 8th ed. Wash., Lib. of Congress, 1975. 2v. (2026p.) $35. **AB46**

Previous eds. had title: *Subject headings used in the dictionary catalogs of the Library of Congress* (*Guide* AB180).

"Incorporates material through 1973; kept up to date by quarterly cumulative supplements."—*verso of t.p.*

A greatly expanded list, though unfortunately out of date at time of publication thus making constant reference to the supplements essential. Users of the list will need to be aware of the new filing rules explained in the introduction: "Although not yet applied to the Library of Congress card catalogs, the rules are being used in the computer-generated bibliographic products of the LC Processing Department."

A useful feature for both the cataloger and the reference worker is the section of "Most commonly used subdivisions" (pp.xviii–lxxii) wherein "each subdivision which could offer difficulties in application is provided with a scope note explaining . . . the points to observe in assigning the subdivision, the nature of the publication to which it should be assigned, how it may overlap in meaning with other subdivisions, and what other related or similar subdivisions should be considered at the same time."—*Introd.* Z695.U4749

Documentation, information storage and retrieval

Hayes, Robert Mayo and **Becker, Joseph.** Handbook of data processing for libraries. 2d ed. Los Angeles, Melville Pub. Co., [1974]. 688p. $22.50. **AB47**

1st ed. 1970.

Aims "to ensure that practicing librarians and that students in library schools approach the world of automation with knowledge of its capabilities and limitations and with the techniques of systems analysis by which to analyze and evaluate alternative answers to the library's processing problems."—*Pref.*

In four main sections: (1) Introduction to library data processing; (2) Management of library data processing; (3) Data processing technology; (4) Library subsystems [e.g., ordering, cataloging, serials records, circulation systems]. Z678.9.H36

Williams, Martha E. and **Rouse, Sandra H.** Computer-readable bibliographic data bases: a directory and sourcebook. Wash., American Society for Information Science, 1976. 1v., looseleaf. $68. **AB47a**

For annotation *see Suppl.* EJ49.

Interlibrary loan

International Federation of Library Associations. Committee on Union Catalogues and International Loans. International loan services and union catalogues; a manual . . . under the editorship of Valentin Wehefritz. Frankfurt am Main, V. Klostermann, [1974]. 258p. (Zeitschrift für Bibliothekswesen und Bibliographie. Sonderheft, 17) DM68.50. **AB48**

An earlier ed. (1961) had title: *Guide to union catalogues and international loan services* (*Guide* AB95).

This edition arranged by country, giving for each (as far as possible): (1) principal national bibliographies; (2) printed union catalogs; (3) unpublished union catalogs; (4) information on international loan policies, national lending centers, principal libraries with legal deposit, and principal special collections. Z695.83.I58

International Federation of Library Associations. Office for International Lending. A brief guide to centres of international lending and photocopying. Ed. by Anne M. Digby and Barry P. Thompson. Boston Spa, Eng., IFLA Office for Intl. Lending, 1975. unpaged. **AB49**

A country-by-country directory, indicating whether there is a national union catalogue, a central national lending service, and procedures to be followed in placing requests for loan or photocopy. Z713.I67

Thomson, Sarah Katharine. Interlibrary loan policies directory. Chicago, Amer. Lib. Assoc., 1975. 486p. $7.95 pa. **AB50**

". . . displays the general, nation-wide interlibrary lending policies of 276 of the major lending libraries in the United States: academic, medical, special, federal, public libraries, plus all state public library agencies and the national libraries."—*p. 1.* Includes information on photocopying services as well as general loan policies or restrictions on specific types of materials (e.g., dissertations, technical reports). Based on responses to a questionnaire distributed in the summer of 1974. Z713.5.U6T5

Photoreproduction

Gaddy, Dale. A microform handbook. Silver Spring, Md., Nat. Microfilm Assoc., 1974. 66p., 52p. il. $5 pa. **AB51**

Developed for use in junior and community colleges "as a primer for persons who are unfamiliar with the educational uses of microforms" (*Pref.*), but with wider application. Includes a glossary of terms, a review of the micrographics field, information on types of microforms and microform hardware, and a summary of factors to be considered in designing an educational microform system. A "Buyer's guide to micrographics equipment, products and services" forms Appendix A. Z681.G33

Microfilm Association of Great Britain. A directory of British photoreproduction services for libraries, 1974. Guilford, Eng., Microfilm Assoc. of Gt. Brit., 1974. 81p. £2.50 **AB52**

Indicates type of photoreproduction services available and price per exposure. Information was gathered late 1972 and early 1973. Geographical listing. Z681.M54

National Microfilm Association. Guide to micrographic equipment. Ed.6– . Silver Spring, Md., 1975– . il. **AB53**

Hubbard W. Ballou, ed.

Supersedes the Association's *Guide to microreproduction equipment* (*Guide* AB208) and continues its numbering.

Ed.6– issued in three parts: (1) Production equipment; (2) User equipment; (3) COM recorders.

Reference work

Katz, William A. Introduction to reference work. 3d ed. N.Y., McGraw-Hill, [1978]. 2v. **AB54**

1st ed. 1969 (*Guide* AB212); 2d ed. 1974.

Contents: v.1, Basic information sources (367p.; $13.95); v.2, Reference services and reference processes (288p.; $12.95).

A revised and updated edition of this now standard work. Z711.K32

Murfin, Marjorie E. and **Wynar, Lubomyr R.** Reference service: an annotated bibliographic guide. Littleton, Colo., Libraries Unlimited, 1977. 294p. $15. **AB55**

A bibliographic guide to the literature of reference service, covering publications on all aspects of library reference work appearing during the period 1876–1975. Topically arranged in 14 chapters, with author and title indexes. Z711.M86

A C

Encyclopedias

ENGLISH AND AMERICAN

The Harper dictionary of modern thought. Ed. by Alan Bullock and Oliver Stallybrass. N.Y., Harper & Row, [1977]. 684p. $20. **AC1**

Also published in England under title: *The Fontana dictionary of modern thought* (London, Fontana, 1977).

Aims to steer "a middle course between an ordinary dictionary and an encyclopaedia. It takes some 4,000 key terms from across the whole range of modern thought, sets them within their context, and offers short explanatory accounts (anything from ten to a thousand words) written by experts, but in language as simple as can be used without *over*simplification or distortion."—*Pref.* Generally speaking, "modern" is here equated with "twentieth-century," although numerous older terms are included because of continuing importance or new ramifications. Articles are signed with initials; select bibliographic references are often provided; cross references. Some British orientation.

The new Columbia encyclopedia. Ed. by William H. Harris and Judith S. Levey. 4th ed. N.Y., Columbia Univ. Pr., 1975. 3052p. il. $65. **AC2**

Eds.1–3 had title: *The Columbia encyclopedia* (*Guide* AC6).

A brief mention of this work was appended to the annotation for the 3d ed. (*Guide* AC6). As noted there, this is a fully revised and updated edition of some 50,000 articles; maps and line drawings are now interspersed with the text; and the work was computer set, allowing presentation of more information per page. It follows the tradition of earlier editions as a work of ready reference, offering articles "on the arts and literature, geography, the life and physical sciences, and the social sciences."—*Pref.* As far as possible, information was current as of the end of 1974; population figures were the most recent available at time of writing; and "coverage of Africa, Asia, and South America has been greatly expanded. In keeping with the increased knowledge and sophistication of readers, the science entries in this edition include more advanced and detailed technical information than those in previous editions." All articles in the 3d ed. were reviewed and revised or replaced as necessary. Cross references are generously provided; pronunciation is indicated for unfamiliar or difficult names and terms; brief, selected bibliographies appear at the end of many articles. The volume remains an excellent reference source for home or office as well as for quick reference in libraries of all sizes. AG5.C725

The Random House encyclopedia. James Michell, ed. in chief. N.Y., Random House, [1977]. 2856p. il., maps. $70. **AC3**

A new work, planned as a family encyclopedia and with no one particular level of readership in mind. In two main sections: (1) Colorpedia and (2) Alphapedia. "The function of the *Colorpedia* section is to provide general knowledge [i.e., through lengthy articles with color illustrations on topics arranged in sections on the universe, the earth, life on earth, man, history and culture, man and science, man and machines]; the function of the *Alphapedia* section is to provide brief answers to factual questions [i.e., through concise entries on very specific topics, alphabetically arranged]."—*p.12.* Cross references are provided from the "Alphapedia" to the longer articles in the other section, and "every important person, place, or thing mentioned on a *Colorpedia* page has an *Alphapedia* entry." Articles are unsigned, but each "Colorpedia" section has an introduction by an outstanding scholar, and there is a list of major contributors and consultants. Bibliography pp.2698–2706; atlas section pp.2726–2856. AG5.R25

Guides

Encyclopedia buying guide, 1975/76– . N.Y., Bowker, 1976– . Triennial. (2d ed.: $17.50) **AC4**

Kenneth Kister, ed.

Serves as a continuation of Walsh's *General encyclopedias in print* (1963–74; *Guide* AC8).

The 2d ed. (publ. 1978) contains profiles of 36 English-language, non-specialized encyclopedias published or distributed in the United States. Coverage ranges from single- to multi-volume works, and from children's to adult level encyclopedias. Z1035.W267

FOREIGN LANGUAGE

Dutch

Grote Winkler Prins. Encyclopedia in twintig delen. [7. geheel nieuw druk] Amsterdam, Elsevier, 1974–75. v.19–20. **AC5**

For previously published volumes and annotation *see Guide* AC30.

Contents: v. 19–20, Urey–Zype. Completes the set.

——— ——— Supplement, 1976. Amsterdam, 1976. 720p.

Offers articles on economic, political, social, scientific developments throughout the world. Necrology covers 1966–75.

Estonian

Eesti noukogude entsüklopeedia. Tallinn, [Valgus], 1973–76. v.5–8. il. **AC6**

For previously published volumes and annotation *see Guide* AC31.

Contents: v.5–8, Maap–Yver. Completes the set.

French

La grande encyclopédie. Paris, Larousse, [1974–78]. v.9–21. il. **AC7**

For previously published volumes and annotation *see Guide* AC38.

Contents: v.9–20, France–Zwingli; v.21, Index. Completes the set.

Universalia, 1974– . Les événements, les hommes, les problèmes en 1973– . Paris, Encylopaedia Universalis, 1974– . Annual. (1975: 196F.) **AC8**

At head of title: Encyclopaedia universalis.

A series of yearbooks supplementing the *Encyclopaedia universalis* (*Guide* AC34). Each volume in five sections: (1) La marche du temps (a brief summary of the year's events chronologically presented); (2) Points d'histoire (essays on contemporary events and problems); (3) Thèmes et problèmes (alphabetically arranged articles on events, countries, personalities, and special topics); (4) Vies et portraits (obituary notes on figures who died during the year covered); (5) Statistiques pour l'année (graphs, tables, and explanatory texts).

German

Brockhaus Enzyklopädie in zwanzig Bänden. 17. völlig neubearb. Aufl. des Grossen Brockhaus. Wiesbaden, Brockhaus, 1976. v.23–24. il. **AC9**

For previously published volumes and annotation *see Guide* AC43.

Contents: v.23, Ergänzungen J–Z; v.24, Bildwörterbuch der deutschen Sprache. Completes the set.

Meyers enzyklopädisches Lexikon. In 25 Bänden. 9., völlig neubearb. Aufl. Mannheim, Bibliographisches Institut, 1975–78. v.15–22. il. (In progress) **AC10**

For previously published volumes and annotation *see Guide* AC47.

Contents: v.15–22, Let–Sud.

Hebrew

Encyclopaedia hebraica. [Jerusalem, 1973–75] v.23, 25–27. (In progress) **AC11**

For previously published volumes and annotation *see Guide* AC52.

Russian

Bol'shaia sovetskaia entsiklopediia. 3. izd. Glav. red. A. M. Prokhorov. Moskva, Izd. Sovetskaia Entsiklopediia, 1975–77. v.20–26. il. (In progress) **AC12**

For previously published volumes and annotation *see Guide* AC72.

Contents: v.20–26, Plata–Ul'ianovo.

Great Soviet encyclopedia; a translation of the third edition. N.Y., Macmillan; London, Collier Macmillan, [1973–78]. v.2–18; Index to v.1–15. (In progress) **AC13**

For annotation *see Guide* AC73.

As previously indicated, a new cumulative index is issued after the appearance of each five volumes; thus, the index to v.1–15 supersedes the one which covered v.1–10.

Spanish

Gran enciclopedia Rialp, G E R. Madrid, Ediciones Rialp, 1971–76. 24v. il. **AC14**

Contents: v.1–23, A–Z; v.24, Index.

A new work featuring signed articles with bibliographies. Most articles are of considerable length; few run to less than half a column. Bibliographies emphasize Spanish-language materials. List of contributors and advisory editors (with indication of qualifications) in v.1. Elaborately illustrated with black-and-white and color photos; charts, maps, diagrams. AE61.G75

Turkish

Türk ansiklopedisi. Ankara, Millî Egitim Basimevi, 1972–74. v.20–21. (In progress) **AC15**

For previously published volumes and annotation *see Guide* AC87.

Contents: v.20–21, Îbrahim Paşa, Makbul–Kethüda.

A D

Language Dictionaries

ENGLISH LANGUAGE

Bibliography

See also Suppl. AD31.

Kister, Kenneth F. Dictionary buying guide: a consumer guide to general English-language wordbooks in print. N.Y., Bowker, 1977. 358p. $15.95. **AD1**

A successor to S. P. Walsh's *English language dictionaries in print* first published by Bowker in 1965 and issued as part of *Home reference books in print* in 1969 (*Guide* AA405).

Intended for the consumer who is contemplating purchase of a dictionary, and "especially designed to assist individuals—parents, students, educators, word buffs, gift givers, secretaries, professional people of all kinds—who want authoritative information about the numerous and sometimes indistinguishable dictionaries currently available from American publishers and distributors."—*Pref.* Reviews at some length (giving full bibliographic citation plus information on purpose and scope, authority, vocabulary treatment, encyclopedic features, graphics, a summary of strong and weak points, and references to other critical opinions) 58 general adult English-language dictionaries; evaluates more briefly some sixty school and children's dictionaries; and offers concise coverage of about 225 "special-purpose dictionaries and wordbooks" (dictionaries of etymology, slang, synonyms, idioms and usage; style manuals; secretary's handbooks, etc.). Author-title-subject index. Z2015.D6K57

American

Desk dictionaries

The Doubleday dictionary for home, school, and office. Sidney I. Landau, ed. in chief. Garden City, N.Y., Doubleday, [1975]. 906p. il. $5.95. **AD2**

A new desk dictionary of some 85,000 entries. Letter-by-letter alphabetization. Indicates syllabication, pronunciation, parts of speech, and brief etymology. "In entries for words having several senses, the order in which the definitions appear is, wherever possible, that of frequency of use, rather than semantic evolution."—*Guide to use.* PE1625.D6

The Random House college dictionary. Rev. ed. [N.Y., Random House, 1975] 1568p. il. $8.95. **AD3**

"Based on The Random House dictionary of the English language, the unabridged edition. Jess Stein, editor in chief."—*t.p.*

1st ed., 1968, had title *The Random House dictionary of the English language, College edition* (*Guide* AD14).

A number of new terms and new meanings have been added, and some definitions have been modernized or improved. PE1625.R34

The Scribner-Bantam English dictionary. Edwin B. Williams, gen. ed. N.Y., Scribner's, [1977]. 1093p. $8.95. **AD4**

Indicates syllabication, pronunciation, etymology, part of speech, irregular inflections, definitions, synonyms and antonyms. Includes lists or charts of colleges and universities of the United States, languages of the world, Indo-European languages, foreign alphabets, signs and symbols, proofreader's marks, weights and measures, periodic table of elements, forms of address. PE1625.S3

English

Murray, *Sir* James Augustus Henry. Oxford English dictionary, . . . A supplement to the Oxford English dictionary. Ed. by R. W. Burchfield. Oxford, Clarendon Pr., 1976. v. 2. (In progress) **AD5**

For v.1 and annotation *see Guide* AD27.

Contents: v.2, H–N.

Desk dictionaries

The concise Oxford dictionary of current English. Based on the Oxford English dictionary and its supplements. First ed. by H. W. Fowler and F. G. Fowler. 6th ed., ed. by J. B. Sykes. Oxford, Clarendon Pr., [1976]. 1368p. $11.95. **AD6**

5th ed. 1964 (*Guide* AD30).

In this edition "the changes made include revisions and additions resulting from a detailed scrutiny of the whole work, as well as modifications of typography and format to allow greater ease of use. . . . The opportunity has been taken to eliminate some matter that can no longer be regarded as pertaining to current English, to add many new words, phrases, and meanings that have entered the language in recent years (including technical expressions found in general literature), to increase the contribution from the English-speaking world outside the British Isles, to incorporate the appendix of abbreviations into the main list, to systematize the definitions of interrelated terms, to eliminate some duplication of definitions, to expand some unduly concise wordings, and to add an enlarged Introduction . . . explaining the use of the dictionary."—*Pref.* Appendixes: Weights and measures; The Greek and Russian alphabets; Principal monetary units of the world.

Abbreviations

De Sola, Ralph. Abbreviations dictionary. New international 5th ed. N.Y., Elsevier, [1978]. 654p. $27.50. **AD7**

4th ed. 1974 (*Guide* AD34).

The subtitle now reads: Abbreviations, acronyms, anonyms and eponyms, appellations, contractions, geographical equivalents, historical and mythological characters, initials and nicknames, short forms and slang shortcuts, signs and symbols. PE1693.D4

Gale Research Company. Acronyms, initialisms, & abbreviations dictionary: a guide to alphabetic designations, contractions, initialisms, abbreviations, and similar condensed appellations. v.1. Ed. by Ellen T. Crowley [and others]. 5th ed. Detroit, Gale, [1976]. 757p. $38.50. **AD8**

4th ed. 1973 (*Guide* AD36).

A revised and expanded edition. A supplement, now entitled *New acronyms, initialisms, & abbreviations* (1977 ed.: 172p. $35) and designated as v.2 of the set, continues to be published between editions and cumulates annually (e.g., the 1977 edition of *New acronyms* includes the entries from the 1976 supplement). A third volume is entitled *Reverse acronyms, initialisms, & abbreviations dictionary* (1976 ed.: 754p. $45). P365.G3

Pugh, Eric. Second dictionary of acronyms & abbreviations. More abbreviations in management, technology and information science. [Hamden, Conn.], Archon Books; [London], Clive Bingley, [1974]. 410p. $16.50. **AD9**

"This book is a supplement to Eric Pugh's *A dictionary of acronyms and abbreviations,* second edition 1970 [*Guide* AD39]; it does not cumulate any of the material therein, but does update it in many cases."—*Publisher's Note.*

About 10,000 entries. T8.P82

——— Third dictionary of acronyms & abbreviations; more abbreviations in management, technology and information science. London, Bingley; Hamden, Conn., Archon Books, [1977]. 208p. $12. **AD10**

2d ed. 1970 (*Guide* AD39).

A supplementary volume rather than a new edition. About 5,000 entries—most of them new, the others updating earlier entries.

Etymology

See also Suppl. AD5.

Eponyms dictionaries index. Ed. by James A. Ruffner. Detroit, Gale, [1977]. 730p. $45. **AD11**

"A reference guide to persons, both real and imaginary, and the terms derived from their names, providing basic biographical identification and citing dictionaries, encyclopedias, word books, journal articles, and other sources for additional information: includes acts, analyses, awards, axioms, bills, cases, circles, codes, coefficients, collections, commissions, complexes, costumes, diseases, dynasties, effects, equations, expeditions, experiments, forces, formulas, functions, laws, maneuvers, medals, methods, mixtures, organs, paradoxes, phenomena, presses, prizes, processes, ratios, reactions, rebellions, rules, schemes, societies, solutions, styles, syndromes, systems, techniques, tests, theories, trophies, unity, and wars."—*t.p.* PE1596.E6

Morris, William and **Morris, Mary.** Morris dictionary of word and phrase origins. N.Y., Harper & Row, [1977]. 654p. $15. **AD12**

Incorporates new material with that previously published in the three volumes of the same authors' *Dictionary of word and phrase origins* (N.Y., 1962–71). There has been some revision and shortening of the earlier material, and an index has been provided in lieu of the *see* references previously employed in the body of the work. Popular treatment, with very little scholarly apparatus. A review by Anthony Burgess appears in *TLS* Mar. 24, 1978, p.347. PE1580.M6

Idioms and usage

Mager, Nathan H. and **Mager, Sylvia K.** Encyclopedic dictionary of English usage. Englewood Cliffs, N.J., Prentice-Hall, [1974]. 342p. $10.95. **AD13**

In addition to matters of usage, the work lists frequently misspelled words, indicates pronunciation for difficult words and names, shows plural forms, capitalization, etc. PE1628.M23

Morris, William and **Morris, Mary.** Harper dictionary of contemporary usage. N.Y., Harper & Row, [1975]. 650p. $15. **AD14**

"With the assistance of a panel of 136 distinguished consultants on usage."—*t.p.*

". . . treats of virtually every aspect of today's language—idioms, slang, vogue words, and regionalisms, as well as all the vast range of words used in formal speech and writing."—*Introd.* Opinions of the "usage panel" are reported in the form of percentages of approval and disapproval and in quotations from opinions of individual panel members. PE1680.M59

Oxford dictionary of current idiomatic English. Comp. by A.P. Cowie and R. Mackin. London, Oxford Univ. Pr., 1975. v.1. (In progress; to be in 2v.) **AD15**

Contents: v.1, Verbs with prepositions & particles. $13.50.

Intends to provide a specialized dictionary of idiomatic usage "which is sufficiently broad in scope to answer the various practical requirements of the learner."—*Gen. Introd.* Idiomatic phrases are defined in "concise and readily intelligible statements . . . which do not assume an understanding of . . . expressions given elsewhere in the dictionary." Examples of usage from contemporary speech and writing are given; caveats against wrong usage or wrong constructions are frequently included. A valuable work for the foreign-language speaker learning English. PE1689.O94

New words

6,000 words; a supplement to Webster's third new international dictionary. Springfield, Mass., G. & C. Merriam Co., [1976]. 220p. $8.50. **AD16**

"To try to keep abreast of the living language, Merriam editors added an eight-page Addenda section to Webster's Third in 1966 and increased it to sixteen pages in 1971."—*Pref.* This volume is "essentially the most recent Addenda section of Webster's Third New International Dictionary."—*Pref.* PE1630.S5

Pronunciation

Lass, Abraham Harold and **Lass, Betty.** Dictionary of pronunciation. N.Y., Quadrangle, [1976]. 334p. $12.50. **AD17**

A guide to pronunciation of 8,000 English-language words which are frequently mispronounced or have one or more acceptable variant pronunciations. Pronunciations are given phonetically (and a "pronunciation key" appears on every right-hand page of the book) for each variant accepted by four standard desk dictionaries; a small numeral beside each pronunciation serves to indicate consensus of preference. PE1137.L38

Slang

Wentworth, Harold and **Flexner, Stuart Berg.** Dictionary of American slang. 2d supplemented ed. N.Y., Thomas Y. Crowell, [1975]. 766p. $12.95. **AD18**

Previous ed. 1967 (*Guide* AD93).

The original (1960) edition was reprinted in 1967 and a 48-page supplement was added. In this latest edition the main section again remains unchanged, but the new supplement includes "all of the material that appeared in the first supplement of 1967 plus about 1,500 new slang terms and definitions that have become current since then."—*Pref. to the Suppl.* PE2846.W4

Synonyms and antonyms

Bernstein, Theodore Menline. Bernstein's Reverse dictionary. With the collaboration of Jane Wagner. [N.Y.], Quadrangle, [1975]. 277p. $10. **AD19**

Not a "reverse dictionary" in the usual sense of the term. The intent here is to enable the user to work from a definition to the term; functions also as a dictionary of synonyms. PE1591.B45

The Doubleday Roget's Thesaurus in dictionary form. Sidney I. Landau, ed. in chief. Garden City, N.Y., Doubleday, 1977. 804p. $4.95. **AD20**

A dictionary of synonyms rather than a thesaurus in the sense of Roget's classified arrangement. A list of antonyms is given for many of the words. PE1591.D6

Webster's Collegiate thesaurus. Springfield, Mass., G. & C. Merriam, [1976]. 944p. $8.95. **AD21**

". . . a wholly new book resulting from long study and planning and differing from existent thesauruses in a number of significant respects."—*Pref.* Employs a conventional dictionary arrangement, and gives synonyms, related terms, idiomatic equivalents, antonyms, and contrasted words as applicable. Cross references are indicated by placing relevant words in small capitals. PE1591.W38

Regional and dialect

British

Commonwealth

Beeton, Douglas Ridley and **Dorner, Helen.** A dictionary of English usage in Southern Africa. Capetown & N.Y., Oxford Univ. Pr., 1975. 196p. $9.50. **AD22**

Preliminary work for the *Dictionary* was carried out through the journal *English usage in Southern Africa.* Aims to provide a glossary of local vocabulary and idiom; to indicate mistakes and problems which are characteristically South African, as well as those common to speakers of English in general; and to list departures from standard English encountered in South African speech. PE3451.B36D5

Branford, Jean. A dictionary of South African English. Cape Town, Oxford Univ. Pr., 1978. 308p. **AD23**

"South African English—the English of South Africans of whatever race, colour or national group—is in every sense, culturally, lexically, grammatically and phonologically, a 'mixed bag'.... It teems therefore with words, ideas, structures and concepts from many cultures...."—*p.xi.*

Offers a wide-ranging, but carefully selected vocabulary intended for the South African with an interest in dialect, its background and usage, for the tourist or immigrant, and for the overseas student of South African literature. In general, an entry gives pronunciation (for non-English terms), grammatical designation, definition, etymology, and illustrative quotations (usually drawn from fairly recent sources).

Johnston, Grahame. The Australian pocket Oxford dictionary. Melbourne, Oxford Univ. Pr., [1976]. 975p. $14.25. **AD24**

"Based on *The pocket Oxford dictionary of current English,* first edited by F. G. and H. W. Fowler [1924]."—*t.p.*

"The distinctive feature of this book is its attempt to cover as informatively and comprehensively as possible within limited space the vocabulary, idioms, and pronunciation of Australian English."—*p.xx.* PE3601.Z5J6

Scottish

Craigie, *Sir* William Alexander. Dictionary of the older Scottish tongue.... Ed. by A. J. Aitken [and others]. Chicago & London, Univ. of Chicago Pr., 1975–77. Pts.27–29. (In progress) **AD25**

For previously published parts, full citation and annotation *see Guide* AD118.

Contents: pts.27–29, O–Pavil(l)ion.

Scottish national dictionary, ... Edinburgh, Scottish Nat. Dictionary Assoc., 1975–76. v.10,pts.1–4. **AD26**

For previously published parts and annotation *see Guide* AD122.

Contents: v.10^{1-3}, W–Z, Miscellanea, Suppl. A–Dad; 10^4, Suppl. Dadgil–Zetlandicus. Completes the work.

The "Miscellanea" section includes lists of personal names, place-names, fairs and markets, Scottish currency, weights and measures. The "List of works quoted in the Dictionary" follows the Supplement; "A list of scientific terms with Scottish connections" concludes the work.

Anglo-Norman

Anglo-Norman dictionary. Under the general editorship of Louise W. Stone and William Rothwell. London, Modern Humanities Research Assoc., 1977– . Fasc.1– . (In progress) **AD27**

At head of title: The Modern Humanities Research Association in conjunction with the Anglo-Norman Text Society.

Contents: Fasc.1, A–Cyvere.

"The purpose of this Dictionary is to facilitate the reading and understanding of a wide variety of texts written in the French used in the British Isles between the time of the Norman Conquest and the late fifteenth century. To this end, each separate sense of each word listed is illustrated by a quotation, chosen on semantic rather than on historical grounds."—*Introd.*

Anglo-Saxon

Jember, Gregory K. English-Old English, Old English-English dictionary. Boulder, Colo., Westview Pr., [1975]. 178p. $15. **AD28**

In two parts: (1) English-Old English; (2) Old English-English. Each section provides equivalents for about 5,000 of the most common words. Intended as an aid to the student in writing Old English. PE279.J4

Middle English

Middle English dictionary. Hans Kurath, ed.; Sherman M. Kuhn, assoc. ed. Ann Arbor, Univ. of Michigan Pr., 1975–77. Pts.M^{1-6}. (In progress) **AD29**

For previously published parts and annotation *see Guide* AD126.

Contents: pts.M^{1-6}, M–much(e).

Foreign words and phrases

Pei, Mario Andrew and **Ramondino, Salvatore.** Dictionary of foreign terms. N.Y., Delacorte Pr., [1974]. 366p. $8.95. **AD30**

Indicates the language from which the word or phrase derives, pronunciation, and meaning of "useful, interesting and timely" foreign terms frequently encountered in the English-speaking world. PE1670.P44

FOREIGN LANGUAGES

Bibliography

Brewer, Annie M., ed. Dictionaries, encyclopedias, and other word-related books, 1966–1974. Detroit, Gale, [1975]. 591p. $48. **AD31**

Subtitle: A classed guide to dictionaries, encyclopedias, and similar works, based on Library of Congress catalog cards, and arranged according to the Library of Congress classification system. Including compilations of acronyms, Americanisms, colloquialisms, etymologies, glossaries, idioms, and expressions, orthography, provincialisms, slang, terms and phrases, and vocabularies in all languages.

Reproduces the catalog cards for the works concerned. Table of contents (outlining the classification system) and a keyword index to the classification system, but no index of authors and titles. Z7004.D5B65

Bibliographie der Wörterbücher, erschienenen in der Deutschen Demokratischen Republik, Rumänischen Volksrepublik, Tschechoslowakischen Sozialistischen Republik, Ungarischen Volksrepublik, Union der Sozialistischen Sowjetrepubliken, Volksrepublik Bulgarien, Volksrepublik Polen.... Warszawa, Wydawnictwa Naukowo-Techniczne, 1974–76. [v.6–7] **AD32**

For previously published volumes and annotation *see Guide* AD130.

Contents: [v.6], 1971–72; [v.7], 1973–74.

Walford, Albert John and **Screen, John Ernest Oliver.** A guide to foreign language courses and dictionaries. 3d ed., rev. and enl. London, Library Assoc., 1977. 343p. £10. **AD33**

2d ed. (1967) by A. J. Walford had title: *A guide to foreign language grammars and dictionaries* (*Guide* AD135).

A complete revision, considerably expanded as to the number of languages covered. The work now "provides a running commentary on selected courses, audio-visual aids and dictionaries in most of the main European languages, plus Arabic, Chinese and Japanese. It is intended for teachers, students, graduates taking up a particular language for the first time, scientists (for acquiring a reading knowledge of a language on a minimum of grammar), tourists, business men and librarians (for book-selection and stock revision)."—*Introd.* Information is presented in sections according to type and level of user. Z5818.L35

Afrikaans

Kritzinger, Matthys Stefanus Benjamin. Handige woordeboek: Afrikaans-Engels. Pretoria, J. L. van Schaik, [1976]. 750p. R. 8.50. **AD34**

Afrikaans-English and English-Afrikaans.

Includes "most of the words which the intelligent reader uses and needs."—*Foreword.*

Woordeboek van die Afrikaanse taal. Pretoria, Die Staatsdrukker, 1976. v.6. (In progress) **AD35**

For earlier volumes and annotation *see Guide* AD140.

Contents: v.6, Kla–Kolyk.

Amharic

Leslau, Wolf. Concise Amharic dictionary: Amharic-English, English-Amharic. Wiesbaden, Harrassowitz, 1976. 538p. DM98 pa. **AD36**

Intends to provide an up-to-date reference work for the student of Amharic. PJ9237.E7L424

Arabic

Deutsche Morgenländische Gesellschaft. Wörterbuch der klassischen arabischen Sprache.... Wiesbaden, Harrassowitz, 1974–78. v.2^{3-5}. (In progress) **AD37**

For previously published parts and annotation *see Guide* AD150.

Blachère, Régis, Chouémi, Moustafa and **Denizeau, Claude.** Dictionnaire arabe-français-anglais. (Langue classique et moderne) . . . Paris, Maisonneuve et Larose, 1974–78. v.$3^{8/9}$–4^{1} (fasc.32/33–37). (In progress) **AD38**

For full citation, previously published parts, and annotation *see Guide* AD149.

Fasc.36 completes v.3. Beginning with fasc.37, editorship was assumed by Moustafa Chouémi and Charles Pellat.

Assyro-Babylonian

Chicago. University. Oriental Institute. The Assyrian dictionary.... Chicago, Oriental Inst., 1977. v.10^{1-2}. (In progress) **AD39**

For full citation, previously published parts, and annotation *see Guide* AD170.

Contents: v.10^{1-2}, M.

Editors vary.

Soden, Wolfram von. Akkadisches Handwörterbuch unter Benutzung des lexikalischen Nachlasses von Bruno Meissner.... Wiesbaden, Harrassowitz, 1974–77. v.3^{1-3} (Lfg.12–14). (In progress) **AD40**

For previously published parts and annotation *see Guide* AD173.

Contents: v.3^{1-3} (Lfg.12–14), S–Tēšû(m).

Chinese

Chi, Wen-shun. Chinese-English dictionary of contemporary usage. Berkeley, Univ. of California Pr., [1977]. 484p. $20. **AD41**

A dictionary of some 1,200 entries for new words and words with new definitions resulting from the institutional and ideological changes of the last forty years. PL1455.C59.

Bibliography

Hixson, Sandra and **Mathias, Jim.** A compilation of Chinese dictionaries. New Haven, Conn., Far Eastern Publs., Yale Univ., 1975. 87p., 37p. $5. **AD42**

Compiled by the Secretariat Staff of CETA (Chinese-English Translation Assistance) Group.

Lists more than 1,000 Chinese dictionaries located in the Library of Congress and in private libraries. A subject listing is followed by a section of general dictionaries. Both monolingual and bilingual dictionaries are included. Z3108.L5H58

U.S. Library of Congress. Chinese-English and English-Chinese dictionaries in the Library of Congress: an annotated bibliography. Comp. by Robert Dunn. Wash., Lib. of Congress, 1977. 140p. $6. **AD43**

In two main sections: (1) special subject dictionaries listed alphabetically by subject field; (2) general language dictionaries. Indexes of authors and titles, plus a Chinese-character author and title list. 569 items with annotations. Z3109.U53

Coptic

Černý, Jaroslav. Coptic etymological dictionary. Cambridge & N.Y., Cambridge Univ. Pr., [1976]. 384p. $75. **AD44**

"My guiding principle in compiling this dictionary has been to adopt only etymologies which I considered certain, probable or at least possible."—*Pref.* Serves as a complement to W. E. Crum's *Coptic dictionary* (*Guide* AD205) which omits etymologies, and offers references to Crum's work. Gives bibliographic references to sources for the etymologies.

For a review of this "great work of scholarship" see the appraisal by H. S. Smith in the *Bulletin* of the School of Oriental and African Studies 41:358–62 (1978). PJ2163.C4

Dutch

Woordenboek der Nederlandsche taal. 'sGravenhage, Nijhoff, 1973–77. v.$12^{4(3-4)}$, $17^{2(11-13)}$, $17^{3(1-4)}$, 22^{3-4}, 23^{1-4}. (In progress) **AD45**

For previously published parts and annotation *see Guide* AD237.

Editors vary.

Finnish

Hurme, Raija and **Pesonen, Maritta.** Englantilais-suomalainen suursanakirja. English-Finnish general dictionary. [Porvoo], Söderström, 1973. 1182p. Fmk. 82. **AD46**

"The editors have primarily had in mind a general dictionary to meet the needs of Finnish readers.... Throughout the work, however, we have taken pains not to forget foreign users with their special problems."—*Foreword.* Gives pronunciation and examples of usage. PH279.H8

French

Grand Larousse de la langue française.... Paris, Larousse, [1976–77]. v.5–6. (In progress) **AD47**

For earlier volumes, full citation and annotation *see Guide* AD265.

Contents: v.5–6, O–sur.

Originally planned for completion in six volumes, the title now carries the phrase "en sept volumes."

Imbs, Paul. Trésor de la langue française; dictionnaire de la langue du XIXe et du XXe siècle (1789–1960). Paris, Éditions du Centre National de la Recherche Scientifique, 1974–78. v.3–6. (In progress) **AD48**

For v.1–2 and annotation *see Guide* AD267.

Contents: v.3–6, Ange–Désobliger.

Robert, Paul. Dictionnaire alphabétique & analogique de la langue française. [Nouvelle éd.] [Paris], Société du Nouveau Littré, 1977. 2171p. 158F. **AD49**

On cover: Petit Robert.

1st ed. 1967 (*Guide* AD272).

A revised and expanded (i.e., about 200 additional pages) edition of this excellent dictionary.

Etymology

Dauzat, Albert, Dubois, Jean and **Mitterand, Henri.** Nouveau dictionnaire étymologique et historique. 3e éd. rev. et corr. Paris, Larousse, [1974]. 804p. 18.60F. **AD50**

1st ed., 1938, by Albert Dauzat. Earlier eds. entitled *Dictionnaire étymologique de la langue française.*

A work for the general reader and the student, giving brief etymological information, date of earliest usage, definition, derivatives, etc. PC2580.D35

Wartburg, Walther von. Französisches etymologisches Wörterbuch; . . . Basel, Zbinden Druck and Verlag AG, 1975–76. Lfg.139–140. (In progress) **AD51**

For previously published parts, full citation and annotation *see Guide* AD286.

Contents: Lfg.139 (v.24$^{1(3)}$), advenire–alacer; Lfg.140 (v.22^{1}), Materialen unbekannten oder unsicheren Ursprungs, Teil 1.

Idioms and usage

Brueckner, John H. Brueckner's French contextuary. Englewood Cliffs, N.J., Prentice-Hall, [1975]. 613p. $30. **AD52**

Aims "to provide full contextual illustrations of over 11,500 basic English words used in combination and translated into idiomatic French. . . . It also provides the native French speaker with a clear analysis of English meanings and many of the common uses of the same basic words."—*Gen.Introd.* In four main sections: (1) adjectives, (2) nouns, (3) verbs, (4) adverbs and other parts of speech. English and French in parallel columns. PC2460.B78

Dournon, Jean-Yves. Dictionnaire d'orthographe et des difficultés du français. Paris, Hachette, [1974]. 648p. 40F. **AD53**

About 38,000 entries, with indication of part of speech, gender, etc., as applicable. Some 8,000 terms are marked with a dot and an explanation of the point of difficulty is provided. PC2460.D65

Gerber, Barbara L. and **Storzer, Gerald H.** Dictionary of modern French idioms. N.Y., Garland, 1976. 2v. (1228p.) $80. **AD54**

Intended "to serve both as a dictionary of expressions and as a handbook for colloquial usage."—*Pref.* In pt.1 the idioms are presented topically (e.g., travel and transportation, dining, stores, apartments, schools), with sentences to illustrate meaning in context, and review exercises at the end of each section. Pt.2 is the dictionary proper, taking the form of French and English indexes to the idioms. PC2460.G46

Marks, Georgette A. and **Johnson, Charles B.** The new English-French dictionary of slang and colloquialisms. [N.Y.], Dutton, 1975. 299p. $12.95. **AD55**

Published in Great Britain as *Harrap's English-French dictionary of slang and colloquialisms* (1974).

A companion to Joseph Marks's *French-English dictionary of slang and colloquialisms* (*Guide* AD289).

For the non-specialist. Intends to enable French-speaking people "to cope with the English slang and colloquialisms they are likely to come across [in travel or in reading], and also to help English speakers to find the French equivalents of current words and expressions in non-standard English."—*Foreword.* PE3721.M28

Bibliography

Baldinger, Kurt. Introduction aux dictionnaires les plus importants pour l'histoire du français; recueil d'études. [Paris], Klincksieck, 1974. 184p. 50F. (Bibliothèque française et romane. Série D: Initiation, textes et documents, 8) **AD56**

A collection of essays (one by Baldinger, the remainder by his seminar students) on the purpose, scope, strengths and weaknesses of the important etymological and historical French dictionaries from Wartburg (*Guide* AD286) to DEAF (*Guide* AD282). PC2571.B3

Klaar, R. M. French dictionaries. [London, Centre for Information on Language Teaching and Research], 1976. 71p. £2. **AD57**

At head of title: Specialised bibliography.

An annotated list of French monolingual, French-English and English-French dictionaries available in Dec. 1975. Includes dictionaries of etymology, phonetics, place names, proper names, and slang.

German

Grimm, Jakob Ludwig Karl and **Grimm, Wilhelm.** Deutsches Wörterbuch. Hrsg. von der Deutschen Akademie der Wissenschaften zu Berlin in Zusammenarbeit mit der Akademie der Wissenschaften zu Göttingen. Neubearbeitungen. Leipzig, Hirzel, 1974–77. Bd.1^{6}, 6$^{5-7}$. (In progress) **AD58**

For previously published parts and annotation *see Guide* AD319.

Contents: Bd.1, Lfg.6, abschieszen–absolut; Bd.6, Lfg.5–7, demütigen–Direktor.

Wahrig, Gerhard. Deutsches Wörterbuch; mit einem "Lexikon der deutschen Sprachlehre" . . . Sonderausgabe, ungekürzt völlig überarbeitete Neuauflage. Gütersloh, Bertelsmann, [1975]. 4320col. DM39. **AD59**

A revised and updated edition of Wahrig's *Das grosse Wörterbuch* (1966; *Guide* AD326); an earlier edition with the new title appeared in 1974.

Wörterbuch der deutschen Gegenwartssprache. Hrsg. von Ruth Klappenbach und Wolfgang Steinitz. . . . Berlin, Akademie Verlag, 1974–76. v.5^{3}–6^{6} (Lfg.43–56/57). **AD60**

For previously published parts and annotation *see Guide* AD327.

Contents: v.5^{3}–6^{6} (Lfg.43–56/57), Seidel–Zytologie. Completes the work.

The final volume contains an "Alphabetisches Verzeichnis der Quellen."

Bilingual

Harrap's Standard German and English dictionary. Ed. by Trevor Jones. London, Harrap, [1974]. pt.1 [v.3]. (In progress) **AD61**

For previously published parts and annotation *see Guide* AD330.

Contents: pt.1 [v.3], German-English, L–R.

Spalding, Keith. An historical dictionary of German figurative usage. Oxford, Blackwell, 1974. fasc.28–29. (In progress) **AD62**

For previously published parts and annotation *see Guide* AD336.

Contents: fasc.28–29, Hemisphere–Hutzel.

New words

Heberth, Alfred. Neue Wörter: Neologismen in der deutschen Sprache seit 1945. Wien, Verband der Wissenschaftlichen Gesellschaften Österreichs, 1977. 240p. **AD63**

A dictionary of new words which have achieved currency in German speech since World War II. Indicates derivation of terms, country of origin for loan-words, etc.

Greek

Snell, Bruno and **Fleischer, Ulrich.** Lexikon des frühgriechischen Epos. . . . Göttingen, Vandenhoeck & Ruprecht, 1976. Lfg.8. (In progress) **AD64**

For full citation, previously published parts and annotation *see Guide* AD352.

Contents: Lfg. 8, 'Αρισταῖος – 'Ατρεΐδης.

Hebrew

See also Suppl. BB38–BB39.

Koehler, Ludwig and **Baumgartner, Walter.** Hebräisches und aramäisches Lexikon zum Alten Testament. 3. Aufl. neu bearb. von Walter Baumgartner. . . . Leiden, Brill, 1974. Lfg.2. (In progress) **AD65**

For Lfg.1 and annotation *see Guide* AD391.

Editors vary.

Sivan, Reuben and **Levenston, Edward A.** The new Bantam-Megiddo Hebrew & English dictionary. N.Y., Schocken Books, [1977]. 399p., 294p. $18.95. **AD66**

First published N.Y., Bantam Books, 1975.

Added title page in Hebrew.

Hebrew-English and English-Hebrew. Based on *The Megiddo modern dictionary* (Hebrew-English by R. Sivan; English-Hebrew by E. A. Levenston and R. Sivan. Tel-Aviv, Megiddo, 1965–66. 2v.).

"The Hebrew column in both parts of the dictionary is given in the *plene* spelling, in accordance with the latest rules of the Hebrew Language Academy."—*Pref.* PJ4833.S56

Hungarian

A magyar nyelv történeti-etimológiai szótára. Budapest, Akadémiai Kiadó, 1976. v.3. **AD67**

For v.1–2 and annotation *see Guide* AD414.

Contents: v.3, P–Zs. Completes the work.

Indonesian

Echols, John M. and **Shadily, Hassan.** An English-Indonesian dictionary. Ithaca, N.Y., Cornell Univ. Pr., [1975]. 660p. $29.50. **AD68**

Includes "the most common words and phrases in American English . . . with the Indonesian equivalent."—*Pref.* Intended primarily for the use of Indonesians. PL5076.E23

Irish

Vendryes, Joseph. Lexique étymologique de l'irlandais ancien. Dublin, Dublin Inst. for Advanced Studies; Paris, Centre National de la Recherche Scientifique, 1974. [fasc.3] (In progress) **AD69**

For previously published parts and annotation *see Guide* AD434.

Contents: [fasc.3], R–S.

Italian

Battaglia, Salvatore. Grande dizionario della lingua italiana. Torino, Unione Tipografico-Editrice Torinese, 1975. v.9. (In progress) **AD70**

For earlier volumes and annotation *see Guide* AD437.

Contents: v.9, Libecciale–Medusòide.

Bilingual

Dizionario delle lingue italiana e inglese. Vladimiro Macchi, ed. Firenze, Sansoni, 1975. v.2². **AD71**

For previously published parts and annotation *see Guide* AD443.

Contents: v.2², Inglese–Italiano, M–Z. Completes the set.

Reynolds, Barbara, comp. The concise Cambridge Italian dictionary. [London], Cambridge Univ. Pr., [1975]. 792p. $19.95. **AD72**

"The Italian-English section is based on *The Cambridge Italian Dictionary* [*Guide* AD450], which it follows closely in style and conventions. The English-Italian section represents a selection of material compiled in preparation for the English-Italian volume of that publication."—*Introd.* PC1640.R44

Khmer

Cambodian-English dictionary. [Ed. by] Robert K. Headley, Jr. [et al.]. Wash., Catholic Univ. of Amer. Pr., 1977. 2v. (1495p.) il. (Publications in the languages of Asia, 3) $49. **AD73**

Intended as a "reasonably comprehensive, accurate, and, above all, usable" (*Pref.*) compilation including "not only current literary and standard spoken forms of Khmer, but also archaic, obsolete, obsolescent, dialectal, and argot forms." Gives etymologies "for almost all known or suspected Indo-European loan words as well as for most of the Chinese, Thai, and Vietnamese borrowings." PL4326.C3

Jacob, Judith M. A concise Cambodian-English dictionary. London & N.Y., Oxford Univ. Pr., 1974. 242p. £15. **AD74**

Aims "to provide a handy reference book of basic modern Khmer vocabulary for the English-speaking reader. Every effort has been made to cover the recurrent vocabulary of 20th-century prose publications—newspapers, novels, articles, etc.—as well as that of the spoken language."—*Introd.* PL4326.J3

Latin

Oxford Latin dictionary. Oxford, Clarendon Pr., 1976–77. fasc.5–6. (In progress) **AD75**

For previously published parts and annotation *see Guide* AD492.

Contents: fasc.5–6, Libero–Qualitercumque.

Thesaurus linguae latinae, ... Lipsiae, Teubner, 1974–77. v.$7^{2(8-11)}$, $9^{2(4-5)}$. (In progress) **AD76**

For full citation, previously published parts and annotation *see Guide* AD480.

Contents: v.$7^{2(8-11)}$, lego–ludibundus; v.$9^{2(4-5)}$, oenanthe–oppugnatio.

Medieval

Arnaldi, Francesco. Latinitas italicae medii aevi . . . lexicon imperfectum. . . . Bruxelles, 1977. Addenda, fasc.4 (*In* Bulletin Du Cange, v.40, 1977) (In progress) **AD77**

For full citation and previously published parts *see Guide* AD495.

Contents: Addenda, fasc.4, Craricula–Dyspnoea.

Latham, Ronald Edward. Dictionary of medieval Latin from British sources. Prep. . . . under the direction of a committee appointed by the British Academy. London, Publ. for the

British Academy by Oxford Univ. Pr., 1975– . fasc.1– . (In progress) **AD78**

Contents: fasc.1, A–B. $53 pa.

"This dictionary is designed to present a comprehensive picture of the Latin language current in Britain from the sixth century to the sixteenth. . . . Sources later than 1550 are normally excluded, though some use has been made of Latin records in the Medieval tradition as late as the seventeenth century."—*Pref.* Three categories of material are distinguished, with varying fullness of treatment: "(a) The use by British authors of CL words in approximately their basic classical meanings" is afforded fairly brief treatment; "(b) Words and usages that belong to the post-classical development of Latin as a whole are dealt with more fully"; and (c) "The fullest treatment is reserved for what is distinctively British, either because of its links with Anglo-Saxon, Anglo-Norman, or some other vernacular . . . , or because it reflects the growth of institutions with specifically British features." Etymology is indicated where not self-evident. Quotations are dated in boldface type. Bibliography of sources cited in fasc.1, pp.xvi–xlv. PA2891.L28

Mittellateinisches Wörterbuch bis zum Ausgehenden 13. Jahrhundert. . . . München, C. H. Beck, 1974–76. Bd.2$^{6-7}$. (In progress) **AD79**

For previously published parts and annotation *see Guide* AD499.
Contents: Bd.2$^{6-7}$, cognoscitivus–comprovincialis.

Niermeyer, Jan Frederik. Mediae latinitatis lexicon minus. Leiden, Brill, 1976. fasc.12, Abbreviationes. **AD80**

For previously published parts and annotation *see Guide* AD500.
Contents: fasc.12, vaccarius-zucarum; Abbreviationes et index fontium, composuit C. van de Kieft. Completes the work.

Novum glossarium mediae latinitatis ab anno DCCC usque ad annum MCC. . . . [Hafniae], Ejnar Munksgaard, 1975. (In progress) **AD81**

For full citation and previously published parts *see Guide* AD501.
Contents: O–Ocyter, ed. by Franz Blatt.

Pali

Trenckner, Vilhelm. A critical Pali dictionary. . . . Copenhagen, Commissioner: Munksgaard, 1973–75. v.2$^{8-9}$. (In progress) **AD82**

For full citation, previously published parts and annotation *see Guide* AD528.
Contents: v.2$^{8-9}$, Ugghāṭiyati–Upakkama, ed. by L. Alsdorf.

Polish

Polska Akademia Nauk. Słownik staropolski. Warszawa, 1973–76. v.7$^{1-6}$. (In progress) **AD83**

For previously published parts and annotation *see Guide* AD537.
Contents: v.7$^{1-6}$, Póć–Rodzić.

Skorupka, Stanisław. Słownik frazeologiczny jezyka polskiego. Wyd. 2. Warszawa, Wiedza Powszechna, 1974. 2v. 360zł. **AD84**

1st ed. 1967–68 (*Guide* AD538). PG6689.S5

Bilingual

Stanisławski, Jan. Wielki słownik polsko-angielski. [Wyd. 3] Warszawa, Wiedza Powszechna, 1975–77. 2v. and suppl. 400zł. **AD85**

Added title-page in English: *The great Polish-English dictionary.* Prefatory matter in Polish and English.
1st ed. 1969 (*Guide* AD546) in 1v.
A companion to the *Great English-Polish dictionary* (1964; *Guide* AD545). "It comprises about 180,000 words, phrases and expressions commonly used in the Polish language. A considerable number of terms have also been included which belong to special branches of learning such as technology, medicine, science, etc."—*Pref.* The supplement adds about 10,000 entries, both new terms and meanings supplementary to entries in the basic set. PG6640.S84

Etymology

Sławski, Franciszek. Słownik etymologiczny jezyka polskiego. Kraków, Nakł. Tow. Miłośników. Jezyka Polskiego, 1974–76. v.4^{5}–5^{2}. (In progress) **AD86**

For previously published parts *see Guide* AD549.
Contents: v.4^{5}–5^{2}, Łabet–Łom.

Romanian

Dicţionarul limbii române (DLR). Serie nouâ. Bucureşti, Editura Academiei Republicii Populare Române, 1974–75. T.VIII^{A2-A}–IX. (In progress) **AD87**

For previously published parts and annotation *see Guide* AD577.
Contents: t.VIII^{A2-A}, Pe–Pînar; t.IX, R.

Romansh

Società Reto-romantscha. Dicziunari rumantsch grischun, . . . Cuoira, Bischofberger, 1974–77. v.6$^{4-12}$. (In progress) **AD88**

For full citation, previously published parts and annotation *see Guide* AD574.
Contents: v.6$^{4-12}$, Femna–Furiar, ed. by Alexi Decurtins and Hans Stricker.

Russian

Akademiia Nauk SSSR. Institut Russkogo IAzyka. Slovarnyi Sektor. Slovar' russkikh narodnykh govorov. Sostavil F. P. Filin. Leningrad, Nauka, 1974–76. v.10–11. (In progress) **AD89**

For previously published parts and annotation *see Guide* AD586.
Contents: v.10–11, Zaglazki–Zubrënka.

Daum, Edmund and **Schenk, Werner.** A dictionary of Russian verbs: bases of inflection; aspects; regimen; stressing; meanings. Leipzig, VEB Verlag, [1974]. 750p. DM30. **AD90**

"With an essay on the syntax and semantics of the verb in present-day Russian by Professor Rudolf Ruzicka.—*t.p.*
A translation of *Die russischen Verben* (München, 1963).
About 20,000 verbs in alphabetical order, with inflected forms, etc. PG2271.D313

Etymology

Vasmer, Max. Etimologicheskii slovar' russkogo iazyka. Perevod s nemetskogo i dopolneniia O. N. Trubacheva. Pod red. i s predisl. B. A. Larina. Moskva, Progress, 1964–73. 4v. 12r.,51k. **AD91**

Added title page: *Russisches etymologisches Wörterbuch.*
A Russian translation of the Heidelberg edition (*Guide* AD603) with additions and corrections (by the Russian editors) indicated. PG2580.V316

Synonyms

Slovar' sinonimov; spravochnoe posobie. Leningrad, Izdatel'stvo "Nauka," 1975. 648p. 3.11r. **AD92**

At head of title: Akademiia Nauk SSSR. Institut Russkogo IAzyka.
Editor, A. P. Evgen'eva.
Evgen'eva is also the editor of the more comprehensive *Slovar' sinonimov russkogo iazyka* (*Guide* AD605). PG2591.S58

Bibliography

Zalewski, Wojciech. Russian-English dictionaries with aids for translators; a selected bibliography. Stanford, Stanford Univ. Libs., 1976. 51p. **AD93**

Attempts to include "all significant Russian-English dictionaries published after World War II. A rigorous selection has been applied to general bilingual dictionaries, while subject bilingual dictionaries have been emphasized."—*Introd.* Brief descriptive annotations for most items.

Sanskrit

Mayrhofer, Manfred. Kurzgefasstes etymologisches Wörterbuch des Altindischen. A concise etymological Sanskrit dictionary. Heidelberg, C. Winter, 1975–76. Lfg.25–26 (v.3^{8-9}). (In progress) **AD94**

For previously published parts and annotation *see Guide* AD613.

Contents: Lfg.25–26 (v.3^{8-9}). Completes v.3 and includes a section of "Nachträge und Berichtungen."

While the main work is now complete, a small v.4 containing a "Wörtregister" is to be published.

Serbo-Croatian

Jugoslovenska Akademija Znanosti i Umjetnosti. Rjecnik hrvatskoga ili srpskoga jezika. Obraduje D. Danicic. U Zagrebu, U Knizarnici L. Hartmana, 1972–76. v.20^{3}-23^{2}. **AD95**

For previously published parts and annotation *see Guide* AD616.

Contents: v.20^{3}–23^{2}, užimavati-žvuknuti. Completes the set.

Includes a "Popis kńiga i rukopisa upotrijeblenih za rječnik" (list of books and manuscripts cited in the dictionary).

Shona

Hannan, M. Standard Shona dictionary. 2d ed. [Salisbury, Rhodesia Literature Bureau, 1974] 996p. **AD96**

1st ed. 1959.

"Comp. for the Rhodesia Literature Bureau."—*t.p.*

A Shona-English dictionary with an English index of words that appear in the definitions. PL8681.4.H3

Slovak

Slovenska Akademija Znanosti in Umetnosti, Ljubljana. Institut za Slovenski Jezik. Slovar slovenskega knjižnega jezika. Ljubljana, Slovenska Akademija . . . , 1975. v.2. (In progress) **AD97**

For full citation, previously published volume and annotation *see Guide* AD630.

Contents: v.2, I–Na.

Spanish

Academia Española, Madrid. Diccionario histórico de la lengua española. Seminario de Lexicografía: Director, Rafael Lapesa Melgar. Madrid, 1972–76. fasc. 10–12. (In progress) **AD98**

For previously published parts and annotation *see Guide* AD637.

Contents: fasc.10, ajarafe–alá [completes v.1]; fasc.11–12 (v.2^{1-2}), álaba–alexifármaco.

Simon and Schuster's Concise international dictionary: English/Spanish, Spanish/English. Tana de Gámez, ed. in chief. N.Y., Simon and Schuster, [1975]. 1379p. $12.95. **AD99**

Added title page in Spanish: *Diccionario conciso internacional Simon and Schuster.*

Introductory matter in English and Spanish.

An abridgment of the 1973 *Simon and Schuster's International dictionary* (*Guide* AD648), with the addition of some new material. PC4640.S48

Swedish

Svenska Akademien. Ordbok öfver svenska språket. Lund, Lindstedt, 1975–77. v.27^{1-2}, Suppl. **AD100**

For previously published parts and annotation *see Guide* AD669.

Contents: v.27^{1-2} (häfte 284–293), Skräpp–Sluv; Supplement, Källförteckning.

Turkish

İngilizce-Türkçe Redhouse sözlüğü. Redhouse English-Turkish dictionary. İstanbul, Redhouse Yayinevi, [1977]. 1152p. 140.00TL. **AD101**

Based on the *Revised Redhouse dictionary, English-Turkish* (1950; *Guide* AD703).

"The dictionary reflects the American point of view of its editors; however British usages in vocabulary, meanings, spelling and pronunciation have usually been noted."—*Pref.* PL191.I49

Ukrainian

Podvez'ko, M. L. and **Balla, M. I.** Anhlo-ukraïns'ky slovnyk; bliz'ko 65000 sliv. Kiiv, "Radyans'ka shkola," 1974. 663p. 3.90 r. **AD102**

Added title page in English: English-Ukrainian dictionary; about 65,000 words. PG3891.P6

Slovnyk ukraïns'koi movy. [Red. kolehiia: I. K. Bilodid (holova), ta inshi] Kyiv, Nauk. Dumka, 1974–76. v.5–7. (In progress) **AD103**

For previously published parts and annotation *see Guide* AD712.

Contents: v.5–7, N–Pryrobliaty.

Welsh

Geiriadur prifysgol cymru; a dictionary of the Welsh language. . . . Caerdydd, Gwasg Prifysgol Cymru, 1975–76. Pts.27–28. (In progress) **AD104**

For full citation, previously published parts and annotation *see Guide* AD717.

Contents: pts.27–28, Gwlyddaidd–Haint.

A E

Periodicals

BIBLIOGRAPHY

Bakunina, Tatiana A. L'émigration russe en Europe; catalogue collectif des périodiques en langue russe, 1855–1940, établi par Tatiana Ossorguine-Bakounine. Paris, Institut d'Études Slaves, 1976. 340p. (Institut d'Études Slaves. Bibliothèque russe, t.40[1]) 180F. pa. **AE1**

Lists and locates files of Russian émigré publications published in the Russian language in European countries other than Russia. In two parts: 1855–Feb. 1917, and Mar. 1917–1939, each being an alphabetical title listing. Entries are given in Cyrillic characters, with notes on holdings, etc., in French. Indexes of transliterated titles and of names cited. About 1,400 entries. Z6956.R9B25

International directory of little magazines & small presses. Ed. 9– . Paradise, Calif., Dustbooks, 1973– . Annual. (12th ed., 1976/77: $9.95) **AE2**

Supersedes *Directory of little magazines* (*Guide* AE5) and continues its numbering.

Len Fulton, ed.

Entries for little magazines and for small presses appear in a single alphabetical listing. In addition to the expected directory information, listings usually include comments by the editors regarding policies and types of material published, and lists of recent contributors. Z6944.L5D5

Sources of serials. Ed. 1– . N.Y., Bowker, [1977–]. (A Bowker serials bibliography) (Ed.1: $52.50) **AE3**

"An international publisher and corporate author directory."—*t.p.*

Based on a name authority file developed by Bowker in connection with publication of *Ulrich's International periodicals directory, Irregular serials and annuals,* and *Ulrich's Quarterly.* The first edition "includes 63,000 publishers and corporate authors arranged under 181 countries, listing 90,000 current serial titles they publish or sponsor."—*Pref.* Entry is by name of publisher or sponsoring body and includes address, co-publisher information if any, distributor information, and lists of titles of serials with indication of frequency and ISSN designation. Publisher imprints and subsidiaries of publishing houses are interfiled as entries for publishers. Cross references; index of publishers and corporate authors.

Ulrich's Quarterly; a supplement to Ulrich's International periodicals directory and Irregular serials and annuals. v.1, no.1– , Spr. 1977– . N.Y., Bowker, 1977– . Quarterly. $24 per yr. **AE4**

Supersedes *Bowker serials bibliography supplement* (1972–76).

Provides a record of new serial titles, title changes, and cessations between issues of the biennial publications (*Guide* AE10; AE8) mentioned in the subtitle. Indexes of titles, title changes and cessations cumulate in each issue of a given volume.

Abbreviations

Alkire, Leland G. Periodical title abbreviations. 2d ed. Detroit, Gale, [1977]. 436p. $32. **AE5**

"Covering periodical title abbreviations in science, the social sciences, the humanities, law, medicine, religion, library science, engineering, education, business, art, and many other fields."—*t.p.*

1st ed. 1969, by C. E. Wall (*Guide* AE15).

Nearly 20,000 entries in this edition. Z6945.A2W34

Guides for authors

Birkos, Alexander S. and **Tambs, Lewis A.** Academic writer's guide to periodicals. Littleton, Colo., Libraries Unlimited, 1975. v.3. (In progress?) **AE6**

For v.1–2 and a note on the series *see Guide* AE18.

Publisher varies.

Contents: v.3, African and black American studies (205p.; $11.50).

This volume focuses "on serial publications with either a primary or an occasional interest in any of the areas of Africa . . . , the African nations of the Middle East, or the nations or colonies on the African continent. Included also are publications that deal with Black American interests in Canada, Latin America, and the United States."—*Introd.*

United States

Devers, Charlotte M., Katz, Doris B. and **Regan, Mary Margaret,** eds. Guide to special issues and indexes of periodicals. 2d ed. N.Y., Special Libraries Assoc., 1976. 289p. $14.50. **AE7**

1st ed. 1962 (*Guide* AE28).

Provides information on, "in alphabetical sequence, 1,256 periodicals which publish one or more of the following: *Specials* (features, supplementary issues and/or sections appearing on a continuing annual/semi-annual/quarterly basis); an *Editorial Index* (other than a table of contents); and an *Advertiser Index* (a page locator of the advertisers appearing in the issue)."—*Introd.* Subject index. Z6951.S755

Edgar, Neal L. A history and bibliography of American magazines, 1810–1820. Metuchen, N.J., Scarecrow, 1975. 379p. $15. **AE8**

The major portion of the work is an annotated bibliography of American magazines (pp.85–257), giving very full information about more than 200 periodicals of the period. Appendixes include a list of exclusions, a chronological list, a register of printers, and a selected bibliography. Indexed. PN4877.E3

Guide to alternative periodicals. [2d ed.] St. Petersburg Beach, Fla., Sunspark Pr., [1977]. 69p. plus index. **AE9**

Periodicals are grouped under the following headings: Environmental conservation; Homesteading and natural living; Spirituality and consciousness; Arts and crafts; Outdoor recreation and survival; Health and nutrition, natural healing; Alternative energy/appropriate technology; Community cooperation; Children and education; Social, political and economic change. For each title gives address, frequency, subscription price, and a brief note on content. Title index.

Murphy, Dennis D. Directory of conservative and libertarian serials, publishers, and freelance markets. [Tucson, Ariz., Author], 1977. 64p. $3.50 pa. **AE10**

". . . includes organizations which publish or distribute, and some bookstores and book clubs which specialize in, libertarian or conservative works."—*Introd.* Entries for serials are briefly annotated, and indicate book reviews, availability of free sample copies, and editorial policy on freelance material. Subject index. Z475.M87

Africa

Advertising & press annual of Southern Africa. 1977– . Cape Town, National Pub. Co., 1977– . Annual. $45 per yr. **AE11**

Supersedes *Advertising & press annual of Africa* (*Guide* AE31).

Now concerned only with Southern Africa. 1977 ed. in three main sections: (1) Press guide (to newspapers and periodicals of Southern Africa); (2) Radio, TV, cinema and outdoor advertising; (3) Mail advertising and postal information. Brief "who's who in advertising and publishing."

Argentina

Ferreira Sobral, Eduardo F. Publicaciones periódicas argentinas, 1781–1969. Buenos Aires, Ministerio de Agricultura y Ganadería de la Nación, 1971– . v.1– . (In progress) **AE12**

v.1 is an alphabetical list of Argentinian periodicals for the long period indicated. v.2 is to provide chronological and geographical lists and statistical summaries.

Bulgaria

Bulgarski periodichen pechat 1844–1944; anotiran bibliografski ukazatel. Sofiia, Nauka i Izkustvo, 1962–69. 3v. 16.43 leva. **AE13**

Added title page in German: Bulgarische periodika 1844–1944; annotiertes bibliographisches Verzeichnis.

Comp. by Dimitur P. Ivanchev.

v.1–2 are an exhaustive alphabetical listing of Bulgarian periodicals, with notes on the history, editors, etc., of each. v.3 lists foreign-language periodicals published in Bulgaria, includes a section of additions and corrections, and provides full indexing for the set. Z6956.B9B88

Bulgarski periodichen pechat. 1972– . Sofiia, Narodna Biblioteka "Kiril i Metodii," 1974– . Annual. (Natsionalna bibliografiia na NR Bulgariia, ser.4) **AE14**

For full information *see Suppl.* AA106.

Letopis na statiite ot bulgarskite spisaniia i sbornitsi. Sofiia, Narodna Biblioteka "Kiril i Metodii," 1974– . v.23– . Biweekly. (Natsionalna bibliografiia na NR Bulgariia, ser.5) **AE15**

For full information *see Suppl.* AA106.

Spasova, Mariia Vladimirova. Bulgarski periodichen pechat, 1944–1969: bibliografski ukazatel. Sofiia, Narodna Biblioteka "Kiril i Metodii," 1975. 3v. **AE16**

At head of title: Narodna Biblioteka "Kiril i Metodii."

Added title page in German: Bulgarische Periodika.

Continues the bibliographic record of Bulgarian periodicals begun with the three-volume *Bulgarski periodichen pechat, 1844–1944* (*Suppl.* AE13).

v.3 comprises indexes and tables. Z6956.B9S76

Canada

Canadian serials directory. Répertoire des publications sériées canadiennes. 1976– . Toronto, Univ. of Toronto Pr., [1977]– . (1976 ed.: $75) **AE17**

Martha Pluscauskas, ed.

Text in English and French.

An alphabetical listing of serials (magazines, annuals, yearbooks, proceedings and transactions of societies, special-interest newspapers) published in Canada. Subject index and index of publishers and sponsoring bodies. Indicates type of publication, frequency, format, price, circulation, etc.

France

Place, Jean Michel and **Vasseur, André.** Bibliographie des revues et journaux littéraires des XIXe et XXe siècles. Paris, Éditions de la Chronique des Lettres Françaises, 1974–77. v. 2–3. (In progress) **AE18**

For full information *see Suppl.* BD141.

Germany

Deutsche Bibliographie: Zeitschriften-Verzeichnis, 1971–1976. Neuerscheinungen, Änderungen und Abschlüsse. Frankfurt am Main, GMBH, 1977. 3v. **AE19**

For earlier volumes and a note on the series *see Guide* AE56.

Contents: Bd.1–2, Titelnachweise im Anschluss an das Zeitschriften-Verzeichnis 1958–1970; Bd.3, Verfasser, Titel- und Stichwortregister. (Issued in three bound volumes.)

The 1958–70 segment of the series is still incomplete, Lfg.1–4 having appeared 1971–76.

Kirchner, Joachim. Bibliographie der Zeitschriften des deutschen Sprachgebietes bis 1900. Stuttgart, Hiersemann, 1971–77. Bd.2, Lfg.1–5; Bd.3, Lfg.1–8/9. **AE20**

For Bd.1 and annotation *see Guide* AE58.

With the publication of Bd.2, Lfg.5 and Bd.3, Lfg.8/9, the set is complete.

Great Britain

British directory of little magazines and small presses. Ed. 1– , 1974/75– . New Malden, [Eng.], Dustbooks, 1974– . (Ed.1: £1) **AE21**

An alphabetical listing by name of magazine or press. Gives name of editor, address, type of material published, brief comment by editors, list of recent contributors, frequency, price, founding year, size, format, etc. Information appears to be drawn from the *International directory* . . . (*Suppl.* AE2). Z6944.L5B73

Madden, Lionel and **Dixon, Diana.** The nineteenth-century periodical press in Britain; a bibliography of modern studies, 1901–1971. N.Y., Garland, 1976. 280p. (Garland reference library of the humanities, v.53) $25. **AE22**

A relatively brief section on "Bibliographies, finding lists and reports on bibliographical projects" is followed by a fairly long one on "General history of periodicals and newspapers"; both are arranged chronologically by date of publication. The bulk of the volume is devoted to section C, "Studies of individual periodicals and newspapers," and section D, "Studies and memoirs of proprietors, editors, journalists and contributors," each arranged alphabetically by title/name, then chronologically by date of the study. Author index only; some brief annotations. About 2,600 items. Z6956.G6M3

Spiers, John. The underground and alternative press in Britain; a bibliographical guide with historical notes. [Brighton, Eng.], Harvester Pr., 1974. 77p. £6.50. **AE23**

"Published with a title and chronological index as a companion to the Underground/Alternative Press collection prepared for microfilm publication by Ann Sexsmith and Alastair Everitt."—*t.p.*

Offers bibliographic and historical notes on sixty-odd British underground and alternative press periodicals. Z6944.U5S64

The Waterloo directory of Victorian periodicals, 1824–1900. Phase I. [Montreal], publ. for the Univ. of Waterloo by Wilfrid Laurier Univ. Pr., [1976]. 1187p. $135. **AE24**

"Sponsored by the Research Society for Victorian Periodicals and Waterloo Computing in the Humanities."—*t.p.*

Editors: Michael Wolff, John S. North, Dorothy Deering.

An attempt to make "conveniently available in one alphabetical listing the newspaper and periodical titles published in England, Ireland, Scotland, and Wales at any time between 1824 and 1900."—*Pref.* Includes some 29,000 entries (about 4,400 of them cross references), covering all fields of publication: government, church, trade, the professions, the sciences and humanities. Titles were gleaned chiefly from the *British union catalogue of periodicals* (*Guide* AE146), the *Union list of serials* (*Guide* AE133), the British Museum's catalog of newspapers for 1801–1900 (*Guide* AF40), and the Times's *Tercentenary handlist of English and Welsh newspapers, magazines and reviews* (*Guide* AF42). Information available on many titles is admittedly sketchy, but the following points are covered as far as possible: subtitle, numbering, publication dates, editor, place of publication, publisher, printer, price, size, frequency, illustrations, circulation, sponsoring body, indexing, mergers, alternate titles, and descriptive or explanatory notes. Discrepancies between earlier listings are also noted.

"Phase II" of the project is planned to result in "a comprehensive directory . . . based on the alphabetical listing of Phase I, augmented and corrected by actual shelf-checks" (*Pref.*) and supplying additional categories of information. A subject guide to the present volume is in preparation.

Hungary

Magyar nemzeti bibliográfia időszaki kiadványok repertóriuma. Évf. 32[15]– , Aug. 15, 1977– . Budapest, Országos Széchényi Könyvtár, 1977– . Semimonthly. **AE25**

Represents a change of title for the *Magyar folyóiratok repertóriuma* (*Guide* AE207), which closed with évf. 32, füzet 14 (July 13, 1977), and continues its volume numbering. Coverage and arrangement remain the same. Forms a companion publication to *Magyar nemzeti bibliográfia könyvek bibliográfiája* (*Suppl.* AA128).

Indonesia

Nagelkerke, G. A. Bibliografisch overzicht uit periodieken over Indonesie. Bibliographical survey based on periodicals on Indonesia, 1930–1945. Leiden, Bibliotheek, Koninklijk Instituut voor Taal– , Land– en Volkenkunde, 1974. 232p. 15.60 fl. **AE26**

A bibliography of articles from thirty-odd periodicals dealing with Indonesia. Arranged by geographic area, with subject index. Z3276.N33

Reid, Anthony, Jubb, Annemarie and **Jahmin, J.** Indonesian serials, 1942–1950, in Yogyakarta libraries, with a list of government publications in the Perpustakaan Negara, Yogyakarta. Canberra, Australian Univ. Pr. in assoc. with the Faculty of Asian Studies, Australian Nat. Univ., 1974. 133p. $5.95. (Oriental monograph ser., 15) **AE27**

Includes newspapers as well as periodicals. Listing is by place of publication. Indexed. Z3275.R44

Iran

A directory of Iranian periodicals. 1969– . Tehran, Tehran Book Processing Centre, 1969– . Irregular. **AE28**

Poori Soltani, comp.

Publisher varies. Also published in Persian.

Issue covering "21st March 1976 - 20th March 1977" publ. June 1977.

Each issue is a listing of periodicals (i.e., magazines appearing at least twice a year) currently published during the period covered. Alphabetical title listing, with subject and name indexes.

Latin America

Maison des Sciences de l'Homme. Service d'Échange d'Informations Scientifiques. Liste mondiale des périodiques spécialisés: Amérique Latine. World list of specialized periodicals: Latin America. Paris, Mouton, [1974]. 186p. (*Its* Publications, série C. Catalogues et inventaires, 5) 59F. **AE29**

Provides directory and brief descriptive information on 381 periodicals devoted to Latin America (regardless of where published) and limited to the "social and human sciences" (i.e., social and cultural anthropology, sociology, political science, economics, demography, linguistics, social psychology). Arranged by country of publication. Subject and title indexes. Z1605.M33

Philippines

Golay, Frank H. and **Hauswedell, Marianne H.** An annotated guide to Philippine serials. Ithaca, N.Y., Southeast Asia Program, Dept. of Asian Studies, Cornell Univ., 1976. 131p. (Data paper, 101) $5 pa. **AE30**

Based on the holdings of the Cornell University Library. Arranged as two lists, each with its own index: (1) non-governmental serials; (2) government serials. Z6958.P5G64

Union of Soviet Socialist Republics

Letopis' periodicheskikh i prodolzhaiushchikhsia izdaniia. 1971– . Moskva, Kniga, 1972– . Annual with quinquennial cumulation. **AE31**

Continues *Letopis' periodicheskikh izdanii SSSR* (*Guide* AE114) which ceased with the 1966/70 cumulation (published 1972–75 in 2v.). The 1966/70 cumulation of the earlier title supersedes only the *Novye* section, not the annual *Trudy* parts for those years.

Annual issues now bear the subtitle *Novye, pereimenovannye i prekrashchennye izdaniem zhurnaly i gazety,* and no annual volume is issued in the last year of each quinquennial cumulation.

Yugoslavia

Bibliografija Jugoslavije: serijske publikacije. 1975– . Beograd, Jugoslovenski Bibliografski Institut, 1975– . Quarterly with annual index. **AE32**

Title page in Croat, Serbian, and Macedonian.

Continues *Bibliografija jugoslovenske periodike* (*Guide* AE130) which ceased with the volume covering 1974.

UNION LISTS

United States

Danky, James Philip. Undergrounds: a union list of alternative periodicals in libraries of the United States and Canada. Madison, State Historical Soc. of Wis., 1974. 206p. $12.95 pa. **AE33**

"The purpose of this list is to bring a heterogeneous group of often little-known periodicals to the attention of North American researchers and librarians."—*Introd.*

An alphabetical listing, with geographic index. Gives title, place of publication, and library location, but no indication of holdings or dates of publication. Indicates availability on microfilm, indexing in *Alternative press index* (*Guide* AE177), and citations in other lists or directories. Z6944.U5D3

New serial titles, 1950–1970, subject guide. N.Y., Bowker, 1975. 2v. (3692p.) $138.50. **AE34**

"Based on the *New Serial Titles 1950–1970* published by Library of Congress and R. R. Bowker Company."—*t.p.*

Offers a subject approach, according to the Dewey Decimal Classification, of the titles appearing in the 1950–70 cumulation of *New serial titles* (*Guide* AE134). Information from the cumulation was edited and refined to provide greater consistency and utility. A list of subject headings in alphabetical sequence (with Dewey class number indicated) and an index to the subject headings serve as guides for the user. There is also a list of the subject headings in numerical sequence, and a correlation table indicating the range of Dewey numbers included in the subject heading numbers employed in the guide. Z6945.N42

France

Paris. Bibliothèque Nationale. Département des Périodiques. Catalogue collectif des périodiques du début du XVIIe siècle à 1939. . . . Paris, 1977. v.1. (In progress) **AE35**

For previously published volumes and annotation *see Guide* AE142.

Contents: v.1, A–B.

Published in reverse order, the 4-volume alphabetical title sequence of the catalog is now complete. A fifth volume providing access to titles through the names of societies and other issuing bodies will be published (projected date, 1980) as the final volume of the set and will include addenda and corrigenda.

Germany

Bruhn, Peter. Gesamtverzeichnis russischer und sowjetischer Periodika und Serienwerke. Wiesbaden, Harrassowitz, [1973–76]. Lfg.19–20. **AE36**

For previously published parts, full citation and annotation *see Guide* AE144.

Contents: Lfg.19, Nachtrag (completes Bd.3); Lfg.20, Register. Completes the set.

Great Britain

Travis, Carole and **Alman, Miriam.** Periodicals from Africa: a bibliography and union list of periodicals published in Africa. Boston, G. K. Hall, [1977]. 619p. $55. **AE37**

At head of title: Standing Conference on Library Materials on Africa.

Aims to present "as comprehensive a list as possible of periodicals published in Africa, and at the same time, to give locations for those titles held in libraries in the United Kingdom."—*Introd.* (Egypt is excluded, and only those South African periodicals held in U.K. libraries are listed.) Arrangement is alphabetical by country of publication, then by title; comprehensive title index. Holdings of "some 60 university, national, government and private libraries, representing the major African collections in the United Kingdom" are recorded, but bibliographic information on many titles not located in those libraries is also given. Z3503.T73

Italy

Catalogo dei periodici esistenti in biblioteche di Roma. Roma, 1975. 986p. **AE38**

At head of title: Unione Internazionale degli Istituti de Archeologia, Storia e Storia dell'Arte in Roma.

A union list of periodical holdings of some 35 libraries in Rome. Z6945.C343

Southeast Asia

Nunn, Godfrey Raymond. Southeast Asian periodicals: an international union list. [London], Mansell, [1977]. 456p. $50. **AE39**

A union list of "some 26,000 periodicals published since the beginning of the nineteenth century."—*Introd.* Arrangement is by country (Burma; Cambodia; Indonesia; Laos; Malaysia, Singapore and Brunei; Philippines; Thailand; Timor; Vietnam), then by title or other main entry. In addition to locations in libraries of the countries covered, selected libraries in Australia, Canada, France, India, Great Britain, Netherlands, Portugal, Spain, and the United States are represented.

Spain

Spain. Dirección General de Archivos y Bibliotecas. Catálogo colectivo de publicaciones periódicas en bibliotecas españolas. [Madrid, 1973–76] v.3–5[1]. (In progress) **AE40**

For previously published parts and annotation *see Guide* AE157.

Contents: v.3, Agricultura y veterinaria; v.4, Ciencias de la educación; v.5, Humanidades, tomo I: Ciencias historicas.

INDEXES AND ABSTRACT JOURNALS

International

Arts & humanities citation index. Jan./Apr. 1978– . Philadelphia, Inst. for Scientific Information, 1978– . $1500 per yr. **AE41**

Publ. in two softbound issues (Jan./Apr. and May/Aug.) and a hardbound cumulative issue (covering Jan./Dec.) each year. Each issue in two physical parts: (1) Guide and journal lists; Citation index; "Permuterm" subject index; (2) Source index; Corporate index.

Patterned on the *Science citation index* and *Social sciences citation index,* and using the same general format and approach to indexing. This is "a multidisciplinary index to the journal literature of the arts and humanities. It covers every substantive item in each journal issue indexed: articles, letters, editorials, notes, meeting abstracts, discussions, corrections, errata; poems, short stories, excerpts from books, plays, music scores; chronologies, bibliographies, discographies, filmographies, etc.; and reviews of books, films, records, art exhibits, TV and radio programs, and dance, music, and theatrical performances."—*Introd.* About 900 journals are covered in the first year. To overcome the problem of articles with non-descriptive titles an "enrichment policy" has been inaugurated, and such articles are indexed as though the titles contained the name of an artist, work of art or literary work which the article concerns; illustrations of works of art, musical scores, etc., are also indicated.

United States and Great Britain

❖A comparison of the coverage and content of eight new periodical indexes with the *Readers' guide* (*Guide* AE169) may be found in the article "Indexing of popular periodicals: the state of the art," by Brian Aveney and Rod Slade, *Library journal* 103:1915–23 (Oct. 1, 1978).

Abstracts of popular culture. v.1– . Bowling Green, Ohio, Bowling Green Univ. Popular Pr., 1976– . Quarterly. $75 per yr. **AE42**

Subtitle: A quarterly publication of international popular phenomena.

"By 'Popular Culture' we mean all aspects of life which are not academic or creative in the narrowest and most esoteric sense of the words. . . . Important topics such as film, television, radio, popular literature, fairs, parades, theater, amusements, music, circuses, carnivals, urban and rural life, the counter culture, ethnic and women's studies, folklore, the family sports, leisure and work, humor, and all other aspects of the 'New Humanities' " (*Introd., v.1A*) are included.

With the third issue of v.1 abstracts of articles from slightly less than 300 journals were being published, with much of the abstracting being done by volunteers. The aim is to expand the list of periodicals to some 600 titles. Full citations appear in an author listing, and there is a subject index. Also aims to provide information on unpublished papers on popular culture and to serve as a clearinghouse for copies of such papers. Z7164.S66A27

Access; the supplementary index to periodicals. Jan./Apr. 1975– . Syracuse, N.Y., Gaylord Professional Pubs., 1975– . 3 times a yr., the 3d issue being an annual cumulation. $75 per yr. **AE43**

John Gordon Burke and Ned Kehde, eds.

Intends to complement rather than duplicate the efforts of other general periodical indexes. (As a general principle, titles picked up by *Readers' guide* will be dropped from *Access.*) The first issue indexes 130 titles representing "regional and city magazines as well as a balanced subject-oriented list of general and special interest periodicals."—*Introd.* Author and subject entries in separate sections.

The American humanities index. v.1, no.1/2– , Spr./Sum. 1975– . Troy, N.Y., Whitston, 1975– . Quarterly with annual cumulation. (1976 annual cumulation in 3v.: $89.50) **AE44**

Stephen Goode, ed.

An author and subject index to scholarly and critical magazines, plus a number of little magazines. Designed to complement rather than duplicate other indexing services. 96 periodicals indexed in the first issue, with list expanded to about 300 titles by v.3. AI3.A278

Bloomfield, Barry Cambray. An author index to selected British 'little magazines,' 1930–1939. [London], Mansell, 1976. 153p. £12.50. **AE45**

Indexes 73 periodicals of the period, less than a dozen of which are included in the *Comprehensive index to English-language little magazines* (*Suppl.* AE51). With the exception of *Caravel* (published in Majorca, but containing "a considerable amount of poetry by young

British writers"—*Pref.*) all were published in the United Kingdom. With a few exceptions noted in the preface, all magazines are fully indexed. This is an author index only, although the form heading "Films reviewed" provides cross references to film reviews, and cross references to book reviews are provided under the name of the author of the book reviewed. AI3.B56

Index to American little magazines, 1900–1919. Comp. by Stephen H. Goode. Troy, N.Y., Whitston, 1974. 3v. $82.50. **AE46**

"To which is added a selected list of British and continental titles for the years, 1900–1950, together with addenda and corrigenda to previous indexes."—*t.p.*

Indexes about 100 titles for the period. Together with other retrospective volumes of this title and the *Index to little magazines* (*Guide* AE184), provides indexing from 1900 through 1967.

Index to periodical articles by and about blacks. 1974– . Boston, G. K. Hall, 1977– . Annual. (1975: $56) **AE47**

Represents a change of title for *Index to periodical articles by and about Negroes* (*Guide* AE187) which ceased with the volume covering 1972.

Work on the index was disrupted in 1974 when a tornado struck the Hallie Q. Brown Memorial Library, Wilberforce, Ohio, where the index is prepared. As a result, the 1973 volume has not yet appeared, but it will presumably bear the new title when eventually published.

Index to U.S. government periodicals 1972– . Chicago, Infordata Intl. Inc., 1974– . Quarterly, the 4th issue being an annual cumulation. $175 per yr. **AE48**

". . . published quarterly in May, August, November and March. Indexing for the fourth quarter is included in the annual cumulative issue published in March."—*verso of t.p.*

Began publication with the quarterly issues for 1974; retrospective annual volumes for 1972 and 1973 were subsequently published.

"A computer-generated guide to 156 selected titles by author and subject."—*t.p., 1976.* The number of periodicals indexed varies from year to year. Includes various periodicals not sent to Depository Libraries, and many which are distributed directly by department or issuing agency rather than through the Government Printing Office. Z1223.Z9I5

The new periodicals index. v.1, no.1– , Jan./June 1977– . Boulder, Colo., Mediaworks Ltd., 1977– . Semiannual. $25 per yr. **AE49**

". . . indexes all articles from a list of alternative and new age magazines, journals, newspapers and newsletters. The purpose of the index is to provide access to the wealth of important new information these periodicals offer on the New Culture, the still-evolving manifestation of the recent wave of change in technology, spiritual life, lifestyles, energy, ecology, health, diet, feminism, community, art, music, politics and the media."—*Introd., v.1, no.1.* Initially indexed 62 titles. A subject-author index (author entries being provided for "major" articles). No cumulations.

Popular periodical index. no 1– , Jan./June 1973– . Camden, N.J., 1973– . Semiannual. $9.70 per yr. **AE50**

A subject index (with some author entries) indexing (by 1977) some 29 popular periodicals not covered in the standard periodical indexes. Book reviews are grouped under "Book reviews." No cumulations. AI3.P76

Sader, Marion, ed. Comprehensive index to English-language little magazines, 1890–1970. Series one. Millwood, N.Y., Kraus-Thomson, 1976. 8v. $590. **AE51**

An index to 100 English-language little magazines of the period indicated, 59 of which are "partly or totally American."—*Pref.* It aims to index complete files of defunct publications; magazines which are still current are completely indexed through 1970, with some 1971 issues included. Selection of titles for this first series—it is indicated that work has begun on a second series—was made by Felix Pollak, formerly of the University of Wisconsin Libraries, with the advice of Charles Allen, well-known authority on the American little magazine. Indexing is by personal name only, with designation of "Works by" and/or "Works about" under each name. Book reviews are entered under both the author of the book and the name of the reviewer, with an additional subject entry if the book is a biography or a critical work devoted to an individual writer or artist, etc. In addition to the expected details of pagination, date, etc., each contribution has been categorized as to type (article, poem, excerpt, illus., etc.). Z6944.L5S23

Guide to indexes

Marconi, Joseph V. Indexed periodicals; a guide to 170 years of coverage in 33 indexing services. Ann Arbor, Mich., Pierian Pr., 1976. 416p. $65. **AE52**

". . . an alphabetically arranged listing of those periodical and serial titles identified as being indexed in some 33 (counting title changes) American, British and Canadian periodical indexes, showing the indexes in which they were covered and the dates indexed. . . . The overall scope of this volume ranges from 1802 into mid-1973, consisting of approximately 11,000 periodical and serial titles, title changes, and cross references."—*Introd.*

East Europe

Terry, Garth Michael. A subject and name index to articles on the Slavonic and East European languages and literatures, music and theatre, libraries and the press, contained in English-language journals, 1920–1975. Nottingham, Nottingham Univ. Lib., 1976. 198p. £3.25 pa. **AE53**

Indexes about 4,800 articles from some 37 journals (including changes of title). Alphabetical subject arrangement with a name index. Locates files of the journals in British libraries.

France

French periodical index, 1973/74– . Westwood, Mass., Faxon, 1976– . Annual. (1973/74: $28) **AE54**

Comp. by Jean-Pierre Ponchie.

Preface and table of contents in English and French.

Intended as a guide to "up-to-date information concerning contemporary France."—*Pref.* The 1973/74 volume indexes seven periodicals; in the 1976 volume this number had been increased to ten. Indexing is under broad subject headings (arranged alphabetically according to the French form of the heading) roughly corresponding to the categories used in weekly news magazines (e.g., business and economy, food, art, entertainment, environment, armed forces, medicine and health, religion, sports). Within categories the listing is chronological (except that the "people" section is alphabetical by name); titles are usually given as they appear in the original publication. Articles of at least a column or more are indexed. Further refinement of subject categories would greatly increase facility of use. AI7.F7

Latin America

Hispanic American periodicals index, 1975– . Los Angeles, UCLA Latin American Center Publs., Univ. of California, [1977–]. Annual. **AE55**

At head of title: HAPI.

Barbara G. Cox, ed.

A subject and author index to articles of interest to Latin Americanists appearing in some 200 journals published in South and Central America, the United States, Europe, and the Caribbean. "The journals were selected with the assistance of the SALALM Committee on Bibliography and an international panel of indexers for their scholarly value and representative coverage of editorial viewpoint, subject matter, and geographical area. Included are leading journals in all major disciplines of the social sciences and the humanities: archaeology and anthropology; art; economics, development, and finance; folklore; film; geography; history; language and linguistics; literature; music; philosophy; political science; sociology; and others."—*Introd.* Journals published in Latin America are indexed in full; those published elsewhere are selectively indexed for items relevant to Latin America. Author and subject listings in separate sections; full bibliographic citations are furnished in both sections. Book reviews are listed in the subject section under author of the book.

Switzerland

Bern. Schweizerische Landesbibliothek. Bibliographische Auskunftsstelle. Analytische Bibliographie der Gesamtregister schweizerischer Zeitschriften; Bibliographie analytique des tables générales des périodiques suisses. Bern, 1974. 125p. **AE56**

"Zusammengestellt von Maja Studer."—*t.p.*

A classed listing of Swiss periodicals having one or more cumulative indexes, with indication of type of index and period covered. Alphabetical title index.

Union of Soviet Socialist Republics

Letopis zhurnal'nykh statei. T.1– , 1926– . Moskva, 1926– . Weekly. **AE57**

Frequency varies.

Title varies: 1926–37, *Zhurnal'naia letopis'.*

A weekly index of wide scope covering more than 1,700 journals, series, and continuing publications of academies, universities and research institutes in humanities, science, and the social sciences. Excluded are popular magazines, children's literature, and government publications. Entries, averaging some 3,500 an issue, are arranged in the 31 sections of the Soviet classification scheme. Each issue identifies the specific journal numbers indexed; the annual *Spisok zhurnalov* . . . cumulates this information. Indexes of names and localities were published quarterly 1956–77; starting 1978, indexes are issued bi-monthly. AI15.L4

Masanov, IUrii Ivanovich, Nitkina, N. V. and Titova, Z. D. Ukazateli soderzhaniia russkikh zhurnalov i prodolzhaiushchikhsia izdanii 1755–1970 gg. Moskva, "Kniga." 1975. 437p. 1r.,84k. **AE58**

At head of title: Gosudarstvennaia publichnaia biblioteka im. M. E. Saltykova-Shchedrina.

A bibliography of indexes to individual Russian journals. Arranged alphabetically by title of the journal. Indexed. Z6956.R9M37

Yugoslavia

Bibliografija rasprava i članaka. Zagreb, Leksikografski Zavod, 1965–77. v.8–12. (In progress) **AE59**

Contents: v.8–10, Pt.4, sect. 1, Historija [with index]; v.11, Pt.4, sect. 2, Historija jugoslavenskih naroda; v.12, Pt.5, Likovne umjetnosti.

Represents a change of title for *Bibliografija rasprava, članaka i književnih radova* (*Guide* AE232).

AF

Newspapers

BIBLIOGRAPHIES AND UNION LISTS

International

Newspaper and gazette report. 1976– . Wash., Lib. of Congress, 1976– . 3 nos. per yr. Free. **AF1**

Supersedes *Foreign newspaper and gazette report* (originally *Foreign newspaper report*), 1973–75 (*Guide* AF5). 1977 issues called "v.5."

"The title change . . . marks the expansion of the current program and enables us to include information on both foreign and domestic newspapers."—*no.1, 1976.* Beginning 1977, the December issue contains an annual index; a cumulative index covering 1973–76 was published 1978.

U.S. Library of Congress. Catalog Publication Division. Newspapers in microform. 1973– . Wash., Lib. of Congress, 1975– . Annual. (1975 publ. 1976: $11.25 pa.) **AF2**

Serves as a supplement to both *Newspapers in microform: foreign countries, 1948–1972* (*Guide* AF10) and *Newspapers in microform: United States, 1948–1972* (*Guide* AF26), listing reports for foreign and domestic newspapers in separate sections, with a combined title index.

——— **Serial Division.** Newspapers received currently in the Library of Congress. Ed. 4– . Wash., Lib. of Congress, 1974– . (Ed. 4: $.95) **AF3**

Supersedes *Newspapers currently received & permanently retained* . . . (3d ed., 1972; *Guide* AF12).

The 4th ed. "lists 302 United States and 1,016 foreign newspapers which are received and retained on a permanent basis and an additional 324 United States and 76 foreign newspapers retained on a current basis only."—*Pref.* Z6945.U5N42

Webber, Rosemary. World list of national newspapers: a union list of national newspapers in libraries in the British Isles. London, Butterworths, [1976]. 95p. £9.50. **AF4**

Comp. under the auspices of the Standing Conference of National and University Libraries in contract with the Social Science Research Council.

A title listing with index by country. For British and Irish newspapers, "all newspapers having national circulation have been listed" (*Introd.*), as have regional newspapers which regularly carry a significant amount of national news; all foreign newspaper holdings are reported. Holdings of the British Library's Newspaper Library at Colindale have *not* been included. Z6945.W385

United States

Directory of newspaper libraries in the U.S. and Canada. Grace D. Parch, ed. N.Y., Special Libraries Assoc., 1976. 319p. $9.75 pa. **AF5**

"Project of the Newpaper Division, Special Libraries Association."—*t.p.*

A directory of libraries maintained by newspaper publishers. Aims "to provide convenient, complete, accurate and up-to-date information on newspaper libraries including their collections, services and personnel."—*Pref.* Geographical arrangement, with personnel and place-name indexes. Notes on library resources include availability of

indexes (published and unpublished) and of microfilm files of the newspaper, and indication of services available to outsiders.
Z675.N4D57

Wynar, Lubomyr Roman and **Wynar, Anna T.** Encyclopedic directory of ethnic newspapers and periodicals in the United States. 2d ed. Littleton, Colo., Libraries Unlimited, 1976. 248p. $15. **AF6**

1st ed. 1972 (*Guide* AF27).

A revised and updated edition adding new titles (and a new section on the "multi-ethnic" press) and deleting defunct publications. 977 entries in this edition. Z6953.5.A1W94

Australia

Newspapers in Australian libraries; a union list. 3d ed. Canberra, Nat. Lib. of Australia, 1973–75. 2v. **AF7**

2d ed. 1967 (*Guide* AF30).

Contents: pt.1, Overseas newspapers; pt.2, Australian newspapers.

This edition lists and locates about 2,300 overseas newspapers and some 4,000 Australian papers.

Belgium

Bertelson, Lionel. La presse d'information: tableau chronologique des journaux belges. [Bruxelles, 1974] 287p. **AF8**

At head of title: Institut pour Journalistes de Belge.

In two main sections: (1) Les journaux disparus (subdivided by period); (2) Les journaux actuels (subdivided as "quotidiens" and "hebdomadaires"). Within subsections, the newspapers are listed by beginning date of publication. Index of titles. Z6956.B4B43

Bulgaria

Letopis na statiite ot bulgarskite vestnitsi. Sofiia, Narodna Biblioteka "Kiril i Metodii," 1974– . v.23– . Monthly. (Natsionalna bibliografiia na NR Bulgariia, ser.6) **AF9**

For full information *see Suppl.* AA106.

Germany

Hagelweide, Gert. Deutsche Zeitungsbestände in Bibliotheken und Archiven. Düsseldorf, Droste Verlag, [1974]. 372p. (Bibliographien zur Geschichte des Parlamentarismus und der politischen Parteien. Heft 6) **AF10**

Added title page in English: German newspapers in libraries and archives; a survey.

Introductory matter in German and English.

"Hrsg. von der Kommission für Geschichte des Parlamentarismus und der politischen Parteien und dem Verein Deutscher Bibliothekare e. V."—*t.p.*

An effort to provide reasonably up-to-date information on files of German newspapers. "For the period from 1700 to 1969 (with several supplements up to 1972), it covers a total of 2,018 German newspapers with an overall number of 4,411 titles arranged according to 222 German places of publication, within the German frontiers of 1939, which have been and are of special historic interest as far as the press is concerned."—*Publishers' pref.* Title index.
Z6956.G3H33

Great Britain

British Library. Newspaper Library, Colindale. Catalogue of the Newspaper Library, Colindale. London, Publ. for the British Library Board by British Museum Publs. Ltd., 1975. 8v. £150. **AF11**

Contents: v.1, London; v.2, England and Wales, Scotland, Ireland; v.3–4, Overseas countries; v.5–8, Alphabetical title catalogue.

"The Newspaper Library at Colindale (formerly the British Museum Newspaper Library) contains about half a million volumes and parcels of daily and weekly newspapers and periodicals, including London newspapers and journals from 1801 onward, English provincial, Scottish and Irish newspapers from about 1700 onward, and large collections of Commonwealth and foreign newspapers. It contains no London newspapers published before 1801 (which are in the Burney Collection at Bloomsbury), no newspapers in oriental languages (which are in the Department of Oriental Manuscripts and Printed Books at Bloomsbury), and very few periodicals which appear monthly or less frequently."—*Introd.*

Union of Soviet Socialist Republics

Kuznetsov, Ivan Vasil'evich and **Fingerit, Efim Markovich.** Gazetnyi mir Sovetskogo Soiuza. 1917–1970 gg. Moskva, Izd-vo Mosk. Un-ta, 1972–76. 2v. il. (v.1, 1r.,48k.; v.2, 1r.,71k.) **AF12**

Contents: v.1, Tsentral'nye gazety; v.2, Respublikanskie, kraevye, oblastnye i okruzhnye gazety.

A listing of Russian newspapers of the period, with extensive notes on the publishing history of each. In v.1 newspapers are arranged in chronological sections; v.2 is arranged by individual Soviet republics, then by title. Volumes are separately indexed. PN5274.K8

INDEXES

United States

New York Times index. v.1– ,1913– . N.Y., Times, 1913– . **AF13**

For full information *see Guide* AF67.

Beginning 1978, three quarterly cumulative issues are published in addition to the semimonthly issues and the annual cumulation for each year.

Users of the *Index* should be aware that in the weekday editions of the newspaper with special feature sections ("Sports Monday," "Living," etc.) the parts are designated by the letters A, B, C and D, but these are represented in the *Index* by the Roman numerals I, II, III and IV, respectively.

Beginning 1978, quarterly cumulations of the *Index* are issued for the first three quarters of the year, with the annual volume "serving, in effect, as the fourth quarterly cumulation covering the entire year."

——— Prior series. N.Y., New York Times Co., [1973–76]. v.10–15. **AF14**

For earlier volumes and annotation *see Guide* AF68.

Contents: v.10, 1907 (publ. 1976); v.11, 1908 (publ. 1976); v.12, 1909 (publ. 1975); v.13, 1910 (publ. 1976); v.14, 1911 (publ. 1973); v.15, 1912 (publ. 1974). Completes the series.

Newspaper index: Chicago tribune. 1972– . Wooster, Ohio, Bell & Howell, 1972– . Monthly with annual cumulation. **AF15**

Newspaper index: Los Angeles times. 1972– . Wooster, Ohio, Bell & Howell, 1972– . Monthly with annual cumulation. **AF16**

Newspaper index: the New Orleans times-picayune. 1972– . Wooster, Ohio, Bell & Howell, 1972– . Monthly with annual cumulation. **AF17**

Newspaper index: the Washington post. 1972– . Wooster, Ohio, Bell & Howell, 1972– . Monthly with annual cumulation. **AF18**

For the period 1972–74 the above four indexes were available in a monthly "4-in-1" index (*see Guide* AF69) covering all four newspapers, with a separate annual cumulation for each. Beginning 1975, each index has been issued separately, both the monthly issues and the annual cumulation, and the "4-in-1" combination abandoned.

Bibliography

See also Suppl. AF5.

Milner, Anita Cheek. Newspaper indexes: a location and subject guide for researchers. Metuchen, N.J., Scarecrow, 1977. 198p. $8.50. **AF19**

Information relates mainly to card files and unpublished indexes, and was gathered by questionnaires sent to libraries, newspapers, historical and genealogical societies. The first part of the volume is a listing by state and county of the various newspapers indexed, with indication of dates and special topics covered, together with location of the index; the second part is a listing of indexes by repository, with notes on type of indexes maintained. Z6951.M635

France

France-actualité; index de la presse écrite française. v.1, no.1– , jan. 1978– . Québec, Microfor Inc., 1978– . Monthly with annual cumulation. $450 per yr. **AF20**

A computer-generated indexing/abstracting service for French newspapers. The first volume provides selective indexing of the dailies *Le monde, Le figaro* and *L'humanité,* and full indexing of the weeklies *Le nouvel observateur* and *Le point* as well as the monthly *Le monde diplomatique.* Emphasis in selection is on trends in French public opinion.

Each issue is in two parts: (1) Section analytique and (2) Section chronologique. The former is arranged alphabetically by subject "descriptors"; the chronological listing includes abstracts of the articles. An English-French glossary of descriptors is issued every three months.

Le temps. Tables du journal Le temps. Paris, Éditions du Centre National de la Recherche Scientifique, 1974–75. v.6–7. (In progress) **AF21**

For previously published volumes and annotation *see Guide* AF74.
Contents: v.6, 1886–1888; v.7, 1889–1891.

Germany

Zeitungs-Index. Jahrg. 1, nr.1– , Jan./März 1974– . Pullach bei München, Verlag Dokumentation, 1974– . Quarterly. DM248 per yr. **AF22**

"Verzeichnis wichtiger Aufsätze aus deutschsprachigen Zeitungen."—*t.p.*

Willi Gorzny, ed.

A subject index to 19 German-language newspapers (mainly weeklies), including two Zürich publications and one from Vienna. Listing is chronological under topical heading. Entry includes author's name (for the high percentage of signed articles), title of article, newspaper abbreviation, volume number, date, and page. The index itself does not cumulate, but an annual "Register" issue includes a "Verfasser-register," a "Systematisches Register," and a "Geographisches Register." AI9.Z44

Great Britain

The Times index. Jan./Mar. 1973– . Reading, Eng., Newspaper Archive Developments, 1973– . Monthly, with annual cumulation beginning 1977. **AF23**

Published quarterly 1973–76. Also called *London Times index.*
Supersedes *Index to the Times* (*Guide* AF76).

Now indexes *The Times, The Sunday Times, The Times literary supplement, The Times educational supplement, The Times educational supplement Scotland,* and *The Times higher education supplement.* Indexing practices of the preceding series are continued (e.g., book reviews are listed under the name of the author of the book as well as under "Books reviewed and noticed"; obituaries under name of the deceased; theater reviews under "Theatrical productions," and motion picture reviews under "Films").

A G

Government Publications

INTERNATIONAL

Newspaper and gazette report. 1976– . Wash., Lib. of Congress, 1976– . Wash., Lib. of Congress, 1976– . 3 nos. per yr. Free. **AG1**

For full information *see Suppl.* AF1.

Palic, Vladimir M. Government publications; a guide to bibliographic tools. 4th ed. Wash., Lib. of Congress, 1975. 441p. $6.70. **AG2**

3d ed., 1942, by James B. Childs, had title: *Government document bibliography in the United States and elsewhere* (*Guide* AG2).

"This guide outlines bibliographic aids in the field of official publications issued by the United States, foreign countries, and international government organizations. It is intended to be a practical guide directing the researcher, the student, and, last but not least, the reference librarian to bibliographic tools which may help him to identify or locate the materials needed."—*Pref.* In three main sections: (1) United States of America; (2) International governmental organizations; (3) Foreign countries. Indexed. Z7164.G7C5

UNITED STATES

Guides

Downey, James A. U.S. federal official publications: the international dimension. Oxford, Pergamon, [1977]. 352p. (Guides to official publications, v.2) $12.50. **AG3**

1975 ed. had title: *U.S. federal government publications.*

"This account of United States Federal Government publications is written with the foreign user in mind. . . . it is concerned with . . . what is being published and how, especially for the foreigner, to acquire it."—*Pref.* Pt.I discusses bibliographic control and acquisitions through agencies, commercial firms, NTIS, etc. Pt.II lists the major government agencies, some of their publications of particular international interest, and acquisitions methods. Indexed. Z1223.Z7D68

Leidy, William Philip. A popular guide to government publications. 4th ed. N.Y., Columbia Univ. Pr., 1976. 440p. $25. **AG4**

3d ed. 1968 (*Guide* AG11).

About 3,000 items, mainly from the period 1967–75. Various new subject headings are introduced in this edition. Z1223.Z7L4

Morehead, Joe. Introduction to United States public documents. Littleton, Colo., Libraries Unlimited, 1975. 289p. $10. **AG5**

A guide for the librarian and the student which intends "to set forth an introductory account of public documents, their locus, diffusion, habitation, and use."—*Pref.* Sections on the Government Printing Office, the Superintendent of Documents, the Depository Library system, Administering documents collections, General guides to federal publications, Legislative branch materials, Publications of the presidency, Department and agency publications, Documents of independent and regulatory agencies, Reports of advisory committees and commissions, and Publications of the Judiciary. Indexed.

A 2d ed. appeared in late 1978. Z1223.Z7M67

Bibliography

Guide to U.S. government publications. [New ed.] McLean, Va., Documents Index, [1976–78]. 4v. **AG6**

Ed. by John L. Andriot.

Contents: v.1, Class A; v.2, Classes C–H; v.3, Classes I–W; v.4, Classes X–Z, and index.

For 1973- looseleaf ed. *see Guide* AG18.

"With the publication of this new edition, the looseleaf service has been superseded by a set of four bound volumes. . . . The arrangement is again by SuDocs classification numbers. The contents of Volumes 1 and 2 of the 1973 looseleaf edition have been combined into a single sequence."—*Foreword, v.1.*

Volume-by-volume revision and updating is to be effected at 6-month intervals.

Catalogs and indexes

See also Suppl. AE48.

Congressional Information Service. CIS U.S. serial set index. Wash., Congressional Information Service, [1975–78]. Pt.1–3, 9–12. (In progress) $4,320 the set (prepaid); $400 per pt. **AG7**

Contents: Pt.1, American state papers and the 15th–34th Congresses, 1789–1857 (3v., publ. 1977); Pt. 2, 35th–45th Congresses, 1857–1879 (3v., publ. 1977); Pt.3, 46th–50th Congresses, 1879–1889 (3v., publ. 1978); Pt. 9, 69th–73d Congresses, 1925–1934 (3v., publ. 1975); Pt. 10, 74th–79th Congresses, 1935–1946 (3v., publ. 1976); Pt. 11, 80th–85th Congresses, 1947–1958 (3v., publ. 1976); Pt.12, 86th–91st Congress, 1st session, 1959–1969 (3v., publ. 1976). Pts.4–8, scheduled for publication late 1978 and 1979, will cover the intervening Congresses. Each part consists of a 2v. "Index of subjects and keywords" and a volume of "Finding lists" (i.e., "Private relief and related actions—Index of names of individuals and organizations"; "Numerical list of reports and documents"; "Schedule of serial volumes").

Aims to provide an index to the complete "U.S. Serial set" for the period 1789–1969. (It also serves as point of access to the CIS full text collection of the "Serial set" on microfiche.) Titles and reference numbers of "Serial set" documents were converted to machine-readable form, "making extensive use of existing secondary sources of this information such as the Government Printing Office's *Numerical Lists and Schedule of Volumes* and its predecessor, the *Document Index.*"—*User guide.* Accuracy was verified through cross-checking with the "Serial set" volumes themselves, and a subject and keyword index was computer-generated. Editorial effort was focused "on careful review and revision of the subject-keyword index, to increase its ease of use, to structure extensive listings into meaningful breakdown, to reduce distracting redundancy, to eliminate meaningless terms, and to improve the thoroughness of the coverage."

The "Private relief and related actions" section of each part is "a separate index for documents concerned with . . . actions of Congress affecting specified individuals in specific circumstances. Such separate coverage provides access to reports on specific legislation, and at the same time allows exclusion of voluminous listings from the Index of Subjects and Keywords."—*User guide.* It is an alphabetical index to names of persons and organizations cited as recipients of proposed relief or related action. It is important to remember that the distinction between public actions (which are covered in the "Subject and keywords index") and private actions cannot always be clearly made, and both indexes should be consulted for thorough research.

Although the enriched keyword and subject indexing of this compilation should obviate the use of Poore (*Guide* AG20), Ames (*Guide* AG21), the *Document catalog* (*Guide* AG24), and the *Monthly catalog* (*Guide* AG25) for locating "Serial set" documents of the relevant periods, those earlier indexes are not superseded for listings of the many other publications not included in the "Serial set." Moreover, because of variations in indexing practice between the earlier publications and the CIS set, the former may sometimes provide a more satisfactory approach to a given topic (i.e., despite the "enrichment," subject indexing appears to be mainly keyword-in-title). Z1223.Z9C65

Rich, Margaret. Index to U.S. government serials (1956–1960), as published by Readex Microprint Corp. N.Y., Readex, 1975. 282p. **AG8**

Aims to facilitate the use of government serials appearing in the Readex Microprint editions (both the depository and non-depository collections) of U.S. government publications, eliminating the need to search the *Monthly catalog* listings for these items. Z1223.Z9R53

U.S. Library of Congress. Serial Division. Popular names of U.S. government reports. 3d ed. comp. by Bernard A. Bernier, Jr., Katherine F. Gould, Porter Humphrey. Wash., Lib. of Congress, 1976. 263p. $6.50. **AG9**

For previous ed. *see Guide* AG29.

"Entries in this edition have been greatly expanded to include extensive annotations and other added information useful to both reference librarians and researchers."—*Foreword.* A subject index has also been added. Z1223.A199U54

U.S. Superintendent of Documents. Monthly catalog of United States government publications, 1895- . Wash., Govt. Prt. Off., 1895- . Monthly. **AG10**

For full information *see Guide* AG25.

Beginning with the issue for July 1976, the catalog is converted to MARC format, with full cataloging according to Anglo-American cataloging rules shown for each item. "The *Monthly Catalog* utilizes AACR and Library of Congress main entries. Subjects are derived from *Library of Congress Subject Headings* 8th edition and its supplements. The catalog consists of text and four indexes—author, title, subject, and series/report number."—*Pref., July 1976.*

Beginning 1977, the "Directory of United States government periodicals and subscription publications" formerly appearing as an appendix to the February issue is replaced by a separate "Serials supplement" with its own indexes. (In 1977 entries in the supplement are assigned item numbers between those of the April and May issues of the catalog.)

Congressional committee prints and hearings

A bibliography and indexes of United States congressional committee prints from the sixty-first Congress, 1911, through the ninety-first Congress, first session, 1969, in the United States Senate Library. Ed. by Rochelle Field. Westport, Conn., Greenwood Pr., [1976]. 2v. $395. **AG11**

Contents: v.1, Bibliography; v.2, Indexes.

The bibliography is organized by type of committee (House standing committees, House select and special committees, Joint committees, Senate standing committees, Senate select and special committees), then by keyword of committee and subcommittee names. Indexes by title and by Congress/session/year. "This Bibliography . . . has been prepared to accompany the Greenwood Press microfiche collection of committee prints."—*p.xi.* Z7165.U5B52

U.S. Congress. Senate. Library. Cumulative index of Congressional committee hearings. Fourth quadrennial supplement from ninety-second Congress (Jan. 21, 1971) through ninety-third Congress (Dec. 20, 1974) in the United States Senate Library. Wash., Govt. Prt. Off., 1976. 823p. $15. **AG12**

For earlier volumes *see Guide* AG36.

"The index to committee prints, issued as an appendix in prior editions, is omitted from this volume and a separate publication of this index is planned."—*Pref.*

Executive branch

U.S. Congress. Senate. Library. Presidential vetoes, 1789–1976. Wash., Govt. Prt. Off., 1978. 533p. $5.25 pa. **AG13**

Previous ed. 1969 (*Guide* AG43).

Extends the record through the 94th Congress, 1976.

State publications

Parish, David W. State government reference publications: an annotated bibliography. Littleton, Colo., Libraries Unlimited, 1974. 237p. $11.50. **AG14**

A state-by-state listing which intends "to include not only the most important state documents but also those considered representative of the works issued by each state."—*Introd.* Z1223.5.A1P37

Municipal publications

Municipal government reference sources: publications and collections. Ed. for the American Library Association Government Documents Round Table by Peter Hernon [and others]. N.Y., Bowker, 1978. 341p. $15.95. **AG15**

"This source guide is a cooperative, pioneering effort to identify municipal reference sources on a large scale. Under the auspices of the Task Force on Local Documents of the American Library Association's Government Documents Round Table, information was gathered by over one hundred volunteer workers under the direction of the project's editors. Concentration is on large urban areas. The arrangement is by state and, within state, by municipality. When pertinent, an overview of a given city is provided, describing special characteristics of that municipality's publishing program or distinctive features of its government—its history or structure."—*Pref.* Subject index.

BRAZIL

Lombardi, Mary. Brazilian serial documents: a selective and annotated guide. Bloomington, Indiana Univ. Pr., 1974. 445p. $15. **AG16**

Listing is by issuing agency, with index of titles and agencies. A detailed table of contents serves as an outline of government structure. About 1,400 entries with full bibliographical details and notes on the agencies. Z1679.L65

EAST AFRICA

Howell, John Bruce. East African community: subject guide to official publications. Wash., Lib. of Congress, 1976. 272p. $6.65. **AG17**

"This is a subject guide to official publications of the East African Community and its predecessors for the period 1926 to 1974, and of the East African region (including Kenya, Tanzania, and Uganda) for the period 1859 to 1974 issued by Great Britain or one of the three partner states."—*Pref.* Subject arrangement similar to that used in *Africa South of the Sahara* (*Guide* DD55). Indexed. Z3582.H69

FRANCE

Commission de Coordination de la Documentation Administrative. Répertoire des publications périodiques et de série de l'administration française. [Paris, Documentation Française, 1973] 368p. 40F. **AG18**

Lists and describes about 850 serial publications (periodicals, annuals, series of various kinds) issued by French official agencies. Listing is by ministry or other sponsoring body, with title and subject indexes. Information was current as of 1972. Z2169.C64

GREAT BRITAIN

British Library. Official Publications Library. Check list of British official serial publications. Ed. 7– . [London], The British Lib., [1975–]. Irregular. (8th ed., 1976: £3.50 pa.) **AG19**

1st–6th eds. (1967–72) issued by the British Museum State Paper Room.

A listing of serial publications of the British government. Listing is by title, except in cases where the issuing body is considered an essential part of the title—e.g., annual reports, bulletins, etc.—and is entered first. Indicates issuing body, availability, frequency, latest part received in the British Library. Z2009.B87

Gt.Brit. Parliament. House of Commons. House of Commons sessional papers of the eighteenth century. Ed. by Sheila Lambert. Wilmington, Del., Scholarly Resources, Inc., [1975]. 2v. **AG20**

A session-by-session list; within each session entries are grouped as bills, reports, or accounts and papers. An index in v.2 (pp. 425–83) provides a subject approach. The papers have been reproduced on microfilm by Scholarly Resources, Inc. J301.K625

Gt.Brit. Stationery Office. Cumulative index to the annual catalogues of Her Majesty's Stationery Office publications, 1922–1972. Comp. by Ruth Matteson Blackmore. Wash., D.C., Carrollton Pr., 1976. 2v. $195. **AG21**

Represents "a merger of twenty-three separate annual and quinquennial indexes" *(User's guide)* into a single alphabet, giving references to entries in the original catalogs (*Guide* AG87, AG88). Variant forms of subject headings used at different periods have not been reconciled and cross references from such forms are not always provided. Basic purpose of the cumulation was to provide an index to the microfilm edition of documents for the period published by United States Historical Documents Institute. Z2009.G85

Richard, Stephen. British government publications; an index to chairmen and authors, 1900–1940. London, Lib. Assoc., Reference, Special and Information Section, 1974. 174p. £5.50. **AG22**

A chronological predecessor to A. M. Morgan's index for the 1941–66 period (*Guide* AG96). Listing is by name of chairman or author, with full citation to the report (including Command number as relevant). An "Alphabetical list of Royal Commissions and distinctive titles of Committees, 1900–1940" is included as an appendix; the name of the chairman follows the title of the commission or committee. Z2009.R535

IRELAND, NORTHERN

Maltby, Arthur. The government of Northern Ireland, 1922–72; a catalogue and breviate of Parliamentary papers. Dublin, Irish Univ. Pr.; N.Y., Barnes & Noble, [1974]. 235p. $25. **AG23**

Patterned after the Ford breviates for British Parliamentary papers (*Guide* AG91–AG95). Aims "to catalogue and summarize the principal Northern Ireland papers for the fifty-year span from March 1922, the date of the first command paper, to the time of the prorogation of Stormont in March 1972."—*Introd.* Entries are grouped in categories such as: Machinery of government, National finance, Agriculture and food supply, Transport, Labour, Social security, Housing, Social problems. Indexed. Z2035.M34

LATIN AMERICA

Latin American serial documents. Comp. by Rosa Quintero Mesa. Ann Arbor, Mich., University Microfilms International, 1977. v.12. **AG24**

For earlier volumes and a note on the series *see Guide* AG103. Contents: v.12, Venezuela. 313p.

NIGERIA

Stanley, Janet. Nigerian government publications, 1966–1973; a bibliography. Ile-Ife, Nigeria, Univ. of Ife Pr., [1975]. 193p. $19. **AG25**

Aims "to include all publications of the federal government of Nigeria, the four regional governments (January 1966 to May 1967) and the twelve state governments (June 1967 to December 1973)."—*Introd.* Serves as a continuation of S. B. Lockwood's *Nigeria: a guide to official publications* (*Guide* AG107). Z3597.S73

SWAZILAND

Pretoria. State Library. Swaziland official publications, 1880–1972; a bibliography of the original and microfiche edition. Pretoria, State Lib., 1975. 190p. (*Its* Bibliographies, no.18) R.15. **AG26**

A classed bibliography, with the first four sections "arranged in a sort of logical development-of-the-Territory order: historical background, concessions, constitutional development and parliament."—*Notes.* Includes both official and semi-official publications. Indexed.

UGANDA

Gray, Beverly Ann. Uganda: subject guide to official publications. Wash., Lib. of Congress, 1977. 271p. $7.25. **AG27**

Comp. in the African Section, General Reference and Bibliography Division, Library of Congress.

A topical listing of "official publications of Uganda for the period 1893 to 1974. Every attempt was made to include documents issued by Uganda, Great Britain, and the East African Common Services Organization and its predecessors before October 1962, and by Uganda, the East African Common Services Organization, and the East African Community after independence. Included also are publications prepared by organizations and individuals on behalf of the Uganda government."—*Pref.* Indexed. Z3586.G7

A H

Dissertations

GUIDES AND MANUALS

Chauveinc, Marc. Guide on the availability of theses. Groningen, [Univ. Library], 1978. 331p. 20 fl. pa. **AH1**

Presents information (regarding publication requirements, interlibrary loan, consultation within library, photocopying, etc.) in tabular form concerning the availability of academic theses at individual institutions in some sixty countries. Information was gathered by questionnaire, with resulting unevenness in reporting. Existence of a national thesis bibliography for the country is indicated, but the title thereof, unfortunately, is not given.

Modern Language Association of America. MLA handbook for writers of research papers, theses, and dissertations. N.Y., Modern Language Assoc., 1977. 163p. **AH2**

Based on the *MLA style sheet* (2d ed. 1970), with the recommendations therein amplified and certain sections extended so as to serve as a "supplementary text in a writing course or as a reference book for undergraduate or graduate students to use independently."—*Pref.* Many illustrative examples; index. Information on submitting manuscripts for publication and on proofreading of printed copy as found in the *MLA style sheet* is not included.

Turabian, Kate L. A manual for writers of term papers, theses, and dissertations. 4th ed. Chicago, Univ. of Chicago Pr., [1973]. 216p. $8.50; $3.45 pa. **AH3**

3d ed. 1967 (*Guide* AH5).

A thorough revision, with some re-arrangement of contents, additional sample footnote references, etc. LB2369.T8

BIBLIOGRAPHY

Bibliography of bibliography

Reynolds, Michael M. A guide to theses and dissertations; an annotated, international bibliography of bibliographies. Detroit, Gale, [1975]. 599p. $35. **AH4**

"This bibliography is a retrospective international listing of bibliographies of theses and dissertations produced through 1973, which appear as separate listings."—*Introd.* Includes both serial and one-time publications. Subject arrangement, with indexes of institutions, of names and titles, and of specific subjects. Z5053.R49

International

See also Suppl. AH7.

Dissertation abstracts international [Section] C: European abstracts. v.37, no.1– , Autumn 1976– . [Ann Arbor, Mich.], University Microfilms International, 1976– . 4 issues per yr. $295. **AH5**

Forms a third section of *Dissertation abstracts international* (*Guide* AH14) and carries its numbering.

Subtitle: Abstracts of dissertations submitted for doctoral and post-doctoral degrees at European institutions.

Each issue follows the subject arrangement of sections A and B of *DAI*, with author and subject indexes. (Only the author index cumulates annually.) A full bibliographic citation to the dissertation is followed by an indication of the language of the work (if other than English), and a brief abstract; University Microfilms order number is given when the full text is available on demand from U.M.I. Western European universities contribute the bulk of the listings (and the representation from some countries is disappointingly small in the early issues), with relatively little Eastern European coverage at the outset. Efforts are being made both to expand coverage and to increase the availability of the dissertations in microform.

Bulgaria

Bulgarski disertatsii. 1973– . Sofiia, Narodna Biblioteka "Kiril i Metodii," 1974– . Annual. **AH6**

For full information *see* contents note for *Natsionalna bibliografiia na NR Bulgariia* (*Suppl.* AA106).

Lazarov, Mikhail and **Dancheva, Iota.** Disertatsii zashtiteni v chuzhbina ot bulgari 1878–1968; bibliografski ukazatel. Sofia, 1975. 333p. **AH7**

At head of title: Narodna Biblioteka "Kiril i Metodii."

An international list of dissertations submitted by Bulgarians at universities throughout the world. Classed arrangement with indexes by author, language, and university. Z5053.L39

France

Bibliographie analytique des thèses de doctorat des universités de France (1966–1974). Avec la collaboration de Françoise Grivot [et al.]. Paris, AIDLUPA; Sherbrooke, Québec, Éditions Naaman, [1977]. 98p. $10 pa. **AH8**

At head of title: Association Internationale des Docteurs (Lettres et Sciences Humaines) de l'Université de Paris et des Autres Universités de France.

An earlier *Bibliographie analytique* ... covering 1899–1965 was published by the Association in 1967.

Listing is by year, then by university, with an author index. There are also cumulative indexes by personal name as subject, by topical subject, and by geographic terms figuring in the titles for the two volumes (i.e., 1899–1965 and 1966–74) of the bibliography.

Germany

Deutsche Bibliographie. Hochschulschriften-Verzeichnis. Frankfurt a. M., Buchhändler-Vereinigung, 1972– . Monthly with annual cumulative index. **AH9**

Forms part of the *Deutsche Bibliographie* (*Guide* AA632).

Lists German academic theses from 1971 on. Classed arrangement with author, title, subject index in each issue, the index cumulating annually.

Deutsche Nationalbibliographie ... Reihe C, Dissertationen und Habilitationsschriften. Leipzig, VEB Verlag für Buch- und Bibliothekswesen, 1968– . Monthly. **AH10**

A classed listing of academic theses from German universities, together with some dissertations written in German but submitted in other countries (mainly Switzerland). Includes published and unpublished works. Index of authors and subjects in each issue, but no cumulative index.

Jahresverzeichnis der Hochschulschriften. Jahrg. 88– , 1972– . Leipzig, VEB Verlag für Buch- und Bibliothekswesen, 1975– . **AH11**

Continues the *Jahresverzeichnis der Hochschulschriften der DDR, der BRD und Westberlins* (Jahrg. 86–87, covering 1970–71) which in turn superseded the *Jahresverzeichnis der deutschen Hochschulschriften* (*Guide* AH43) which ceased with Jahrg. 85 covering 1969; *Jahrgang* numbering has been continuous throughout the periods of title variation, and arrangement and coverage remain the same.

Great Britain

Retrospective index to theses of Great Britain and Ireland, 1716–1950. Roger R. Bilboul, ed. Santa Barbara, Calif., American Bibliographical Center–Clio Pr., [1975–77]. 5v. **AH12**

Contents: v.1, Social sciences and humanities ($125); v.2, Applied sciences and technology ($70); v.3, Life sciences ($85); v.4, Physical sciences ($50); v.5, Chemical sciences ($75).

"The aim of this publication is to provide information for scholars on the existence of theses completed for higher degrees in Great Britain and Ireland up to 1950 when Aslib began the annual publication of its lists [*Guide* AH44]."—*Foreword.* Concentrates on theses in manuscript or typescript and "does not attempt to list the earlier printed theses whether they are full texts of theses by individuals or the broadsheets announcing the propositions to be disputed and the names of the candidates." Intended as a checklist only, and does not pretend to strict bibliographical accuracy.

Each volume is in two parts: (1) an alphabetical subject arrangement under index headings based on those used in the *British humanities index;* and (2) an author index; both parts give the full citation. Subject indexing was done manually, mainly on the basis of titles (although this is not a keyword-in-title index as such).

Hungary

Budapest. Müszaki Egyetem. Központi Könyvtar. A Magyar müszaki egyetemeken elfogadott doktori disszertációk jegyzéke. 1958/63– . Budapest, 1964– . **AH13**

Title also in German, Russian, and English (*Guide to theses accepted by Hungarian technical universities for doctors' degrees*). Titles of dissertations given in Hungarian, English, German, and Russian; abstracts in Hungarian.

1958–63 publ. in 1v.; biennial 1964/65–1970/71; annual 1972– . Arranged by faculty, with author and subject indexes.

India

Inter-university Board of India and Ceylon. A bibliography of doctoral dissertations accepted by Indian universities, 1857–1970. New Delhi, 1974–75. [v.7–24] **AH14**

For previously published volumes and annotation *see Guide* AH49.

Contents: [v.7] English, Chinese, French, German; [v.8] Geography; [v.9] Physics; [v.10] Hindi; [v.11] Kannada, Malayalam, Tamil, Telugu; [v.12] Assamese, Bengali, Gujarati, Marathi, Oriya, Punjabi; [v.13] Earth sciences; [v.14] History, fine arts; [v.15] Engineering, technology; [v.16] Pali, Prakrit, Sanskrit; [v.17] Botany; [v.18] Chemistry; [v.19] Philosophy, religion; [v.20] Urdu, Persian, Arabic; [v.21] Agriculture, animal husbandry; [v.22] Zoology; [v.23] Palaeontology, anthropology, biology; [v.24] Medical sciences.

Romania

Teze de doctorat, 1948–1970: lucrări susţinute în ţară de autori români şi străini şi lucrări susţinute in străinătate de autori români. Bucureşti, 1973. 627p. **AH15**

At head of title: Biblioteca Centrală Universitara Bucureşti.

A classed listing with indexes of authors, names mentioned in titles of the theses, and directors of the theses. Z5055.R64B878

A J

Biography

GENERAL WORKS

Bibliography

Slocum, Robert B. Biographical dictionaries and related works. 2d supplement. Detroit, Gale, [1978]. 922p. $35. **AJ1**

For basic volume and first supplement *see Guide* AJ1.

This supplement lists about 3,800 additional works.

Indexes

Biographical dictionaries master index. Ed.1– , 1975/76– . Detroit, Gale, [1975–]. Biennial? (Ed.1 in 3v.: $65) **AJ2**

Dennis La Beau, Gary C. Tarbert, eds.

Ed.1 has subtitle: A guide to more than 725,000 listings in over fifty current who's whos and other works of collective biography.

Birth dates are given in most instances, but there is no other identifying information in the entry, merely a reference to the work in which a biographical sketch is to be found. Z5305.U5B56

Lobies, Jean-Pierre. Index bio-bibliographicus notorum hominum. Osnabrück, Biblio Verlag, 1972–77. (In progress) **AJ3**

For earlier parts and annotation *see Guide* AJ11.

"Pars B," the list of biobibliographical works, is complete in ten fasc. (884p.) publ. 1972–73.

"Pars C," *Corpus alphabeticum,* has been published through v.9 (issued 1977) and covers the letter A and supplementary entries through "Agazzari." Following the appearance of fasc.30 (which completed v.3 of "Pars C") the work has been issued in bound volumes rather than in fascicules.

Marquis Who's Who Publications: Index to all books. 1974– . Chicago, Marquis, [1975–]. Biennial. **AJ4**

An index to the names of all persons whose biographical sketches appear in current editions of eleven Marquis biographical directories, with reference to the work in which the biography appears.

INTERNATIONAL

Biographisches Lexikon zur Geschichte Südosteuropas. München, Oldenbourg, 1973–76. Bd.1, Lfg.2/3–Bd.2. (In progress) **AJ5**

For Lfg.1 and annotation *see Guide* AJ18.

Contents: Bd.1, Lfg.2/3–Bd.2 (Auersperg, Karl–Kyrillos).

Beginning with Bd.2, no longer published in *Lieferungen.*

Chiappe, Jean-François. Le monde au féminin: encyclopédie des femmes célèbres. [Paris], Somogy, [1976]. 296p. il. 78F. **AJ6**

Brief biographical sketches of famous women of all countries and periods. Bibliographical references at the end of many articles. HQ1123.C48

Contemporary authors: permanent series. A bio-bibliographical guide to current authors and their works. Detroit, Gale, [1975]– . v.1– . Irregular. $38 per v. **AJ7**

Clare D. Kinsman, ed.

"The *Permanent Series* will consist of biographical sketches which formerly appeared in regular volumes of *Contemporary Authors* [*Guide* AJ33]. Sketches . . . have been removed from regular volumes at the time of revision for one of two reasons: (1) The subject of the sketch is now deceased; (2) The subject of the sketch is approaching or has passed normal retirement age and has not reported a recently published book or a new book in progress."—*Pref.* Some revision and updating is done prior to publication of a sketch in this series. The cumulative index to the current series of *Contemporary authors* includes references to sketches in the "permanent series." Z1010.C65

Lewytzkyj, Borys and **Stroynowski, Juliusz.** Who's who in the Socialist countries: a biographical encyclopedia of 10,000 leading personalities in 16 communist countries. N.Y., K.G. Saur; München, Verlag Dokumentation, 1978. 736p. $99. **AJ8**

Offers biographical sketches of contemporary figures (a few recently deceased persons are included) in socialist countries, compiled mainly from information in the editors' personal archives. In addition to political leaders, figures from the fields of economics, the arts and sciences, the military, and religion are included. The prefatory matter does not specify countries covered, but the list includes Albania, Bulgaria, China, Cuba, Czechoslovakia, East Germany, Estonia, Hungary, Laos, Latvia, Lithuania, Poland, Romania, U.S.S.R., Vietnam, and Yugoslavia; country representation and depth of coverage varies widely. CT120.L44

The New York Times biographical service; a compilation of current biographical information of general interest. v.6, no.1– , Jan. 1975– . N.Y., Times, 1975– . Looseleaf. Monthly. $85 per yr. **AJ9**

Represents a change of title for the *New York Times biographical edition* (*Guide* AJ37), continuing its volume numbering, format, and coverage.

Obituaries from the Times 1961-1970; including an index to all obituaries and tributes appearing in the Times during the years 1961–1970. Reading, Eng., Newspaper Archive Developments Ltd., [1975]. 952p. **AJ10**

Frank C. Roberts, comp.

In two parts: "The second contains an index of all entries appearing in the obituary columns of *The Times* between January 1, 1961 and December 31, 1970. The first part reprints in full an alphabetically-arranged selection of about 1,500 obituary notices of the period. The selection has been made with regard to the public importance of the subject of the obituary, the intrinsic interest of what was written about him, and the need to reflect the wide range of nationalities and walks of life which *The Times* obituary columns encompass."—*Pref.* CT120.O15

———1971–1975; including an index to all obituaries and tributes appearing in the Times during the years 1971–1975. [Reading, Eng.], Newspaper Archive Developments Ltd.; [Westport, Conn.], Meckler Books, [1978]. 647p. $60. **AJ11**

The first of a promised series of 5-year supplements to the volume covering 1961–70 (above). Reprints a selection of about 1,000 obituaries from the 1971–75 period, and provides an index to all obituaries and tributes appearing in the *Times* during those years.

Robert, Paul. Dictionnaire universel des noms propres, alphabétique et analogique. Rédaction générale: Alain Rey et Josette Rey-Debove. Paris, Société du Nouveau Littérature, 1974. 4v. il. 749F. **AJ12**

A dictionary of personal and place names, fictional and mythological characters, titles (using the French form) of literary works, motion pictures, etc. Information is often surprisingly full (e.g., country articles are sometimes several pages in length); illustrations are excellent and copious. AG25.R6

Who's who in world Jewry. [Ed. 4] Tel Aviv, Olive Books of Israel, 1978. 974p. **AJ13**

For earlier editions *see Guide* AJ39.

[Ed. 4] has subtitle: A biographical dictionary of outstanding Jews.

About 12,000 biographies in this edition, including for the first time Jews living in Soviet Russia.

UNITED STATES

Abajian, James. Blacks in selected newspapers, censuses and other sources: an index to names and subjects. Boston, G. K. Hall, 1977. 3v. $320. **AJ14**

Reproduction of a card file maintained by the compiler and published "without refinements, corrections, or investigations for accuracy."—*Pref.* All entries "refer to black people or their activities unless otherwise stated." The newspapers covered are mainly West Coast publications. Z1361.N39A28

Biographical directory of the governors of the United States, 1789–1978. Ed. by Robert Sobel and John Raimo. Westport, Conn., Meckler Books, [1978]. 4v. $195. **AJ15**

Offers short biographies, a page or less in length, incorporating such basic information as dates of birth and death, ancestry, family, religion, political affiliation, electoral results, and political and private careers. Arranged alphabetically by state, then in chronological order of the governorship. Short bibliographies included. Contributors are identified, but biographical sketches are not signed. An index of names of biographees in the full set appears in each volume.

A review by Sally Linden in *Library journal* 103:1968 (Oct.1, 1978) points out certain factual errors. E176.B573

Dictionary of American biography. Supplement 5, 1951-1955, with an index to the supplements. John A. Garraty, ed. N.Y., Scribner's, 1977. 799p. $45. **AJ16**

For the basic set and earlier supplements *see Guide* AJ41.

The preface states that "certain 'standard' facts not necessarily important for the individual . . . [which were included in earlier supplements] for the benefit of sociologists and other scholars interested in collective biography" are generally omitted from this supplement. Such information, however, was gathered on data sheets which will be on file with the *DAB* papers in the Library of Congress. An "Index guide to the supplements" provides a cumulative list of biographees treated in all five supplementary volumes.

Concise dictionary of American biography. 2d ed. N.Y., Scribner's, [1977]. 1229p. $50. **AJ17**

Joseph G. E. Hopkins, ed.

1st ed. 1964, *Guide* AJ42.

Presents the essential facts of every article in the *Dictionary of American biography* (*Guide* AJ41) and its first four supplements in summary form. As in the parent work, no subject who died later than 1950 is included, but in a few cases where recent scholarship has revealed new information, some revisions have been made. Outstanding titles by authors are listed, but bibliographical sources are omitted. About 16,000 entries in this edition. E176.D564

Dockstader, Frederick J. Great North American Indians: profiles in life and leadership. N.Y., Van Nostrand Reinhold, [1977]. 386p. il. $16.95. **AJ18**

Offers biographical sketches of about 300 notable native Americans. List of books for further reading, pp.355-69. Tribal listing, chronology, and an "Index of names" which includes names of all people mentioned in the text, together with variants of the Indian names. Many portraits. E89.D55

Garraty, John Arthur and **Sternstein, Jerome L.** Encyclopedià of American biography. N.Y., Harper & Row, [1974]. 1241p. $22.50. **AJ19**

For each biographee there is a factual account of the subject's life, followed by an interpretive essay which evaluates the person's total career. The factual summaries were provided by graduate students (mainly history students at Columbia University); the interpretive essays are signed by the contributor (frequently the author of a full-length study of the biographee). About 1,000 entries; living persons are included. Suggestions for further reading are most often limited to a single reference at the end of the article. CT213.G37

National cyclopaedia of American biography. Index [to] permanent series (numbered volumes); current series (lettered volumes). Clifton, N.J., J. T. White & Co., 1975. 546p. **AJ20**

Supersedes the 1971 index (*Guide* AJ44). Covers through v.54 of the numbered series; v."L" of the lettered series.

Van Doren, Charles Lincoln and **McHenry, Robert.** Webster's American biographies. Springfield, Mass., G. & C. Merriam, [1975]. 1233p. $14.95. **AJ21**

More than 3,000 biographical sketches averaging 350 words in length. Besides presenting basic facts about each person, the work seeks "wherever possible to describe the shape of a life, to place it in juxtaposition to other, similar lives, and to set it in the context of surrounding events."—*Introd.* CT213.V36

Wakelyn, Jon L. Biographical dictionary of the Confederacy. Westport, Conn., Greenwood Pr., 1977. 601p. $29.95. **AJ22**

Provides biographical information on "the political, business, and intellectual figures of Rebel society" *(Pref.)* as well as the military leaders. Five appendixes offer lists and tables showing: (1) Geographical mobility before and after the Civil War; (2) Principal occupations; (3) Religious affiliation; (4) Education; (5) Prewar and postwar political party affiliation. Bibliography; index. E467.W2

Who was who in America; a companion biographical reference work to Who's who in America. Chicago, Marquis, 1976. v.6. (In progress) **AJ23**

For earlier volumes and annotation *see Guide* AJ52.

Contents: v.6, 1974–76. Includes a cumulated index to all *Who was who* volumes.

College graduates

Sibley, John Langdon. Biographical sketches of those who attended Harvard College with bibliographical and other notes. Boston, Mass. Historical Soc., 1975. v.17. (In progress) **AJ24**

For earlier volumes *see Guide* AJ56.

Contents: v.17, 1768–1771.

Contemporary

Directory of American scholars; a biographical directory. 6th ed. N.Y., Bowker, 1974. 4v. $148.50. **AJ25**

For earlier editions and annotation *see Guide* AJ63.

Some 38,000 biographies in this edition. Arrangement of contents follows that of the 5th ed., again with complete alphabetical index of names in v.4. A geographical index appears at the end of each subject volume.

A new edition was scheduled for publication in late 1978.

Ukrainians in North America; a biographical directory of noteworthy men and women of Ukrainian origin in the United States and Canada. Ed., Dmytro M. Shtohryn. Champaign, Ill., Assoc. for the Advancement of Ukrainian Studies, 1975. 424p. $20. **AJ26**

Approximately 1,800 entries. The principal selection criteria were: "(1) positions of responsibility held (2) scientific-scholarly and/or professional work (3) cultural, social and/or political activities and (4) past positions and services."—*p.xi.* E184.U5U486

Who's who among black Americans. Ed.1– , 1975/76– . Northbrook, Ill., Who's Who Among Black Americans, Inc., 1976– . (Ed.1: $35) **AJ27**

"Reference value" is cited as the prime basis of selection. "Individuals became eligible for listing by virtue of positions achieved through election or appointment to office and by distinguished achievement in meritorious careers."—*Pref.* As far as possible, information was collected by questionnaires to the biographees. About 10,000 entries in the first edition; this was increased to about 13,500 in the second (1978: $49.95).

AFGHANISTAN

Adamec, Ludwig W. Historical and political who's who of Afghanistan. Graz, Akademische Druck- u. Verlagsanstalt, 1975. 385p. 560 sch. **AJ28**

Offers concise biographical information on about 1,500 persons. In four parts: Who is who, 1945–1974; Who was who, 1747–1945; Afghan government positions, 1901–1974; Genealogies of important Afghan families in 92 tables. DS355.A3

AFRICA

Dictionary of African biography. N.Y., Reference Publs. Inc., [1977–]. v.1– . il. (In progress) **AJ29**

At head of title: The encyclopaedia Africana.

Contents: v.1, Ethiopia, Ghana. 367p. $57.95.

To be in 20v. The idea for the dictionary originated with W. E. B. DuBois and has been carried forward as a cooperative effort of the African states. Articles deal with "the personalities of the past who . . . influenced the history and development of their various countries."—*Introd.* Living persons are excluded. Each country section is preceded by a historical introduction. Articles are signed by the contributors (including some European and American, as well as African, scholars) and carry bibliographies. DT18.D55

Les élites africaines. Ed. 1– , 1970/71– . Paris, Ediafric, 1971– . (Ed.3, 1974: 252F.) **AJ30**

Issued as "Numéro spécial du Bulletin de l'Afrique noire."

On cover, éd.3: Cameroun, RCA, Congo, Côte d'Ivoire, Dahomey, Gabon, Haute-Volta, Mali, Mauritanie, Niger, Sénégal, Tchad, Togo.

A who's who of government officials for the countries named above. DT533.A2E4

ARGENTINA

Cutolo, Vicente Osvaldo. Nuevo diccionario biográfico argentino (1750–1930). Buenos Aires, Editorial Elche, 1975. v.4. (In progress) **AJ31**

For earlier volumes and annotation *see Guide* AJ73.

Contents: v.4, L–M.

Sosa de Newton, Lily. Diccionario biográfico de mujeres argentinas. Buenos Aires, [Author], 1972. 414p. **AJ32**

Brief biographical sketches of outstanding Argentinian women, including living persons. CT3290.S67

AUSTRALIA

Australian dictionary of biography. [Melbourne], Melbourne Univ. Pr., 1976. v.6. (In progress) **AJ33**

For earlier volumes and annotation *see Guide* AJ79.

Contents: v.6, 1851–1890, R–Z. Includes corrigenda list.

AUSTRIA

Österreichisches biographisches Lexikon, 1815–1950. Graz-Köln, Böhlaus, [1973–77]. Lfg. 26–34. (In progress) **AJ34**

For full citation, earlier volumes, and annotation *see Guide* AJ85.

Contents: Bd.6–7[4] (Lfg.26–34), Maier, Stefan–Pechmann von Massen.

BELGIUM

Académie Royale des Sciences, des Lettres, et des Beaux-arts de Belgique. Biographie nationale. Bruxelles, Bruylant, 1973–74. v.38. (In progress) **AJ35**

For earlier volumes and annotation *see Guide* AJ89.

Contents: v.38, Supplément v.10.

Suppl.9 was complete in 1 fasc.; Suppl. 10 was issued in 3 fasc.

Nationaal biografisch woordenboek. Brussel, Paleis der Academiën, 1972–74. v.5–6. (In progress?) **AJ36**

For earlier volumes and annotation *see Guide* AJ91.

CANADA

Dictionary of Canadian biography. Toronto, Univ. of Toronto Pr., [1976]. v.9. (In progress) **AJ37**

For previously published volumes and annotation *see Guide* AJ101.

Contents: v.9, 1861–1870.

CHINA

Association for Asian Studies. Ming Biographical History Project Committee. Dictionary of Ming biography, 1368–1644. L. Carrington Goodrich, ed. N.Y., Columbia Univ. Pr., 1976. 2v. (1751p.) $85. **AJ38**

Signed biographies (with bibliographies) of important persons from the 300 years of the Ming dynasty. Indexes of names, titles of books, and detailed subjects. DS753.5.A84

CZECHOSLOVAKIA

Biographisches Lexikon zur Geschichte der böhmischen Länder. Hrsg. im Auftrag des Collegium Carolinum von Heribert Sturm. Wien, Oldenbourg, 1974–76. Bd.1, Lfg.1–4. (In progress) **AJ39**

Contents: Bd.1, Lfg.1–4, A–Et.

The completed work (to be in 2v. of 8 or 9 Lfg. each) is expected to include about 10,000 brief biographical sketches. References to other biographical sources are given at the end of the articles. CT933.B56

ETHIOPIA

See also Suppl. AJ29.

The dictionary of Ethiopian biography. [Addis Ababa, Institute of Ethiopian Studies, 1975–] v.1– . (In progress) **AJ40**

Editors: Belaynesh Michael, S. Chojnacki, Richard Pankhurst.

Contents: v.1, From early times to the end of the Zagwe dynasty c.1270 A.D.

"Because of the limited historical sources available for the early period covered [in v.1] . . . the majority of entries are devoted to kings, religious leaders, warriors and other personalities who appear on coins, inscriptions and in manuscripts."—*Pref.* Includes persons "irrespective of nationality who, for good or ill, played a significant rôle in the area." Signed articles; bibliographies. CT2153.D53

FRANCE

Dictionnaire de biographie française. Paris, Letouzey, 1973–78. v.13[4]–14[3]. (In progress) **AJ41**

For earlier volumes and annotation *see Guide* AJ146.

Contents: v.13[4]–14[3] (fasc.76–81), Faure–Fouret.

Hommes et destins (Dictionnaire biographique d'outre-mer). Paris, Académie des Sciences d'Outre-Mer, [1975]–77. 2v. in 3. (Académie des Sciences d'Outre-Mer. Publications. Travaux et mémoires, n.s., no.2, 5) (v.1: 60F) **AJ42**

A new biographical series concerned with outstanding figures in French colonial territories, including citizens of the new nations, explorers, administrators, missionaries, doctors, anthropologists, engineers, etc., who made significant contributions in those areas. Includes about 500 signed biographies, mainly of 20th century figures. Bibliographies include writings by and about the individual. Index in v.2. CT1014.H65

GERMANY

Neue deutsche Biographie. Hrsg. von der Historischen Kommission bei der Bayerischen Akademie der Wissenschaften . . . Berlin, Duncker und Humblot, 1974–77. Bd.10–11. (In progress) **AJ43**

For earlier volumes and annotation *see Guide* AJ158.
Contents: Bd.10–11, Hufeland–Kleinfercher.

Rössler, Hellmuth and **Franz, Günther.** Biographisches Wörterbuch zur deutschen Geschichte. 2., völlig neubearb. und stark erw. Aufl. bearb. von Karl Bosl, Günther Franz, Hanns Hubert Hofmann. München, Francke Verlag, [1973–75]. 3v. (Bd.1: DM158) **AJ44**

Contents: Bd.1–3, A–Z.
1st ed. 1952 in 1v. (*Guide* AJ159).
A new and enlarged edition, with numerous articles added and bibliographies updated. The work now covers down to the present, and about four-fifths of the material is either new or rewritten.
Reviews in *Erasmus* 27:426–30 (1975) and 30:630 (1978), while recognizing the importance of the work, point to "weaknesses in conception and execution" as well as certain factual errors in the text. DD85.R572

Who's who in Germany. 6th ed. Ottobrunn nr. Munich, Who's Who-Book & Pub., 1976. 2v. **AJ45**

For earlier editions *see Guide* AJ162.
6th ed. has subtitle: A biographical encylopedia containing some 23,000 biographies of prominent personalities in Germany and a listing of 2,400 organizations.

Who's who in the arts. Ed.1– . Ottobrunn nr. Munich, Who's Who-Book & Pub., 1975– . (Ed.1 in 2v.: DM 200) **AJ46**

Ed. by Otto J. Groeg.
Subtitle, ed. 1: A biographical encyclopedia containing some 13,000 biographies and addresses of prominent personalities, organizations, associations and institutions connected with the arts in the Federal Republic of Germany.
Includes persons in all the arts except literature, a separate publication being planned for that field. Includes an index by field or specialty; appendix lists galleries, museums, awards, festivals, orchestras, opera houses and theaters, publishers, etc.

GREAT BRITAIN

Bellamy, Joyce M. and **Saville, John.** Dictionary of labour biography. [London], Macmillan; [Clifton, N.J.], A. M. Kelley, [1974–77]. v.2–4. (In progress) **AJ47**

For v.1 and annotation *see Guide* AJ167a.
Cumulated index of names in v.1–4 in v.4.

Reel, Jerome V. Index to biographies of Englishmen, 1000–1485, found in dissertations and theses. Westport, Conn., Greenwood Pr., [1975]. 688p. $30. **AJ48**

Provides an analytical index to biographical information appearing in about 175 dissertations and theses completed at universities in the United States, Great Britain, and Canada. Some brief information is provided on the biographee, but the user is referred to the relevant dissertation for details of a career. Z5305.G7R43

INDIA

Sen, Siba Pada, ed. Dictionary of national biography. Calcutta, Inst. of Historical Studies, 1973–74. v.2–4. (In progress?) **AJ49**

For v.1 and annotation *see Guide* AJ196.
Contents: v.2–4, E–Z. Completes the main set.
Promised supplements for the 1947–72 period have not yet been received. CT1502.S46

ITALY

Dizionario biografico degli italiani. Roma, Istit. della Enciclopedia Italiana, 1975–77. v.18–20. (In progress) **AJ50**

For earlier volumes and annotation *see Guide* AJ208.
Contents: v.18–20, Canella–Carusi.

Il movimento operaio italiano: dizionario biografico, 1853–1943. [A cura di] Franco Andreucci, Tommaso Detti. [Roma], Editori Riuniti, [1975–78]. v.1–4. il. (In progress) **AJ51**

Contents: v.1-4, Abbo–Suzzara. L8000 per v.
Offers signed articles of substantial length, with bibliographies, on persons active in the Italian workers' movement. HD8483.A1M68

LUXEMBOURG

Biographie nationale du pays de Luxembourg depuis ses origines jusqu'à nos jours; collection présentée par Jules Mersch. Luxembourg, Impr. de la Cour Victor Buck, 1975. v.11 (fasc.21–22). **AJ52**

For earlier volumes and annotation *see Guide* AJ226.
Contents: v.11 (fasc.21-22). Completes the set.
The final fascicule is a "Table des principaux personnages traités dans les volumes 1 à 11" which indicates birth and death dates and an identifying note as well as giving reference to volume and page for the biographical sketch.

MEXICO

Camp, Roderic Ai. Mexican political biographies, 1935–1975. Tucson, Univ. of Arizona Pr., [1976]. 468p. $27.50. **AJ53**

For full information *see Suppl.* CJ127.

NEPAL

Who is who—Nepal. 1972/74– . Kathmandu, Kathmandu School of Journalism, [1974–]. (Ed.1: Rs.100) **AJ54**

Subtitle: A biographical dictionary of the distinguished Nepali personalities.
The first work of its kind for this country. CT1529.W48

NIGERIA

Orimoloye, S. A. Biographia Nigeriana: a biographical dictionary of eminent Nigerians. Boston, G. K. Hall, [1977]. 368p. $40. **AJ55**

An attempt to provide a who's who of contemporary Nigerians and other prominent figures living and working in Nigeria. Information was gathered from questionnaires; there is some emphasis on academic figures. CT2526.O74

NORWAY

Norsk biografisk leksikon. Redaktion: Edv. Bull, Anders Krogvig, Gerhard Gran. Oslo, Aschehoug, 1973–77. v.17^4–19^1 (hft. 84–91). (In progress) **AJ56**

For earlier volumes and annotation *see Guide* AJ246.
Contents: v.17^4–19^1 (hft.84–91), Ullmann–Wexelsen.

POLAND

Akademja Umiejetności, Kraków. Polski słownik biograficzny. Kraków, Nakł. Polskiej Akademja Umiejetności, 1974–77. v.19³–22³ (zeszyt 82–94). (In progress) **AJ57**

For earlier volumes and annotation *see Guide* AJ258.
Contents: v.19³–22³ (zeszyt 82–94), Malicki–Nawój.

RHODESIA

Prominent African personalities of Rhodesia. [Salisbury, Rhodesia], Cover Publicity Services, [1976?]– . Ed.1– . il. Annual? **AJ58**

A who's who type of directory. Principles of selection are not indicated in the first edition.

SAUDI ARABIA

Who's who in Saudi Arabia, 1976/77– . Jeddah, Saudi Arabia, Tihama; London, Europa Publs., [1977]– . [Ed.1]– . **AJ59**

An English-language who's who for Saudi Arabia.

SCOTLAND

Watt, Donald Elmslie Robertson. A biographical dictionary of Scottish graduates to A.D. 1410. Oxford, Clarendon Pr., 1977. 607p. $66. **AJ60**

"The intention has been to be as thorough as possible in collecting information on all Scots who had university training" *(Introd.)* from about 1150 to 1410 when St. Andrew's University was founded. As far as possible, biographies are uniformly presented, with references to sources of information provided.

SWEDEN

Svenskt biografiskt lexikon. Redaktionskommitté: J. A. Almquist [o.a.]. Redaktör: Bertil Boëthius. Stockholm, Bonnier, 1974–77. v.20³–22² (Hft.98–107). (In progress) **AJ61**

For earlier volumes and annotation *see Guide* AJ278.
Contents: v.20³–22² (Hft.98–107), Johansson–Larsson.

TURKEY

Türkiye' de kim kimdir. Istanbul, Tanitim Yayinlari, 1977. 324p. il. **AJ62**

An earlier work of the same title (Istanbul, 1961-62) was published in English translation as *Who's who in Turkey* (Wash., 1963; *Guide* AJ292).

VIETNAM

Who's who in Vietnam. [Ed.1–] Saigon, Vietnam Pr., 1967– . Irregular. **AJ63**

3d ed. 1974.

Persons selected for inclusion are "those who are holding elected positions, high-ranking government posts, and those who have scored outstanding achievements in social, cultural and economic domains."—*3d ed.* DS557.A5A555

AK

Genealogy

UNITED STATES

Guides

Beard, Timothy Field and **Demong, Denise.** How to find your family roots. N.Y., McGraw-Hill, [1977]. 1007p. $7.95. **AK1**

In four sections: (1) How to find your ancestors; (2) Books to help you search; (3) Tracing your family's history in America; (4) Tracing your family's history abroad. The first section offers essays on methods and sources; the remainder is principally long lists of published sources and directory information on archives and societies relevant to genealogical research. CS16.B35

Blockson, Charles L. and **Fry, Ron.** Black genealogy. Englewood Cliffs, N.J., Prentice-Hall, [1977]. 232p. $8.95. **AK2**

Includes chapters on the use of family and public documents, slave records, and other sources useful in tracing Afro-American genealogy. Two appendixes: A "directory of research resources" listing names and addresses of record and information centers in the United States and abroad; a list of newspapers important in black genealogical searching. Index; bibliography. CS21.B55

Filby, P. William. American & British genealogy & heraldry: a selected list of books. 2d ed. Chicago, Amer. Lib. Assoc., 1975. 467p. $25. **AK3**

1st ed. 1970 (*Guide* AK3).

"In six years some 3,000 new or newly noted titles, including over 300 periodical articles, have been added, and the total of almost 2,000 titles in 1968 has grown to over 5,000 titles in the present volume." —*Pref.* Cutoff date for the new edition is 1974. Z5311.F55

Rottenberg, Dan. Finding our fathers; a guidebook to Jewish genealogy. N.Y., Random House, [1977]. 401p. $12.95. **AK4**

An introductory guide to research in Jewish genealogy, with emphasis on "American Jews of European ancestry, and especially East European ancestry."—*Pref.* Chapters on methods, archives and general sources are followed by "A source guide to Jewish family genealogies" (pp.141–375), an alphabetical listing of family names (including cross references from variant and related forms) with references to sources of information. Bibliography, pp.376–401. CS21.R58

Smith, Clifford Neal and **Smith, Anna Piszczan-Czaja.** American genealogical resources in German archives (AGRIGA): a handbook. München, Verlag Dokumentation; N.Y., Bowker, 1977. 336p. $35. **AK5**

An English-language handbook "devoted to the primary source materials of German-American genealogical interest to be found in the archives of [West] Germany" and West Berlin, focusing on the "direct documentary links between the old and new worlds."—*Pref.* Drawn from the as yet unpublished *Americana in deutscher Sammlungen,* the new inventory of German archival materials which bear on America, compiled by the Deutsche Gesellschaft für Amerikastudien at the University of Cologne. Geographic, subject, and name indexes.

Wellauer, Maralyn A. A guide to foreign genealogical research: a selected bibliography of printed material with addresses. Rev. and enl. ed. Milwaukee, Wellauer, [1976]. 228p. $10.50. **AK6**

1st ed. 1973.

Offers bibliographies of books and periodicals for most countries or areas of the world, with addresses of archives, libraries, genealogical societies, consulates, and tourist offices. A guide for the American researcher who has identified an immigrant ancestor and wishes to find overseas sources of information. Z5311.W44

Bibliographies and indexes

American genealogical-biographical index to American genealogical, biographical and local history materials. . . . Middletown, Conn., 1974–78. v.86–102. (In progress) **AK7**

For earlier volumes and annotation *see Guide* AK9.

Contents: v.86–102, Hubbard, Ernest–Lent, Jacobus.

New York. Public Library. Local History and Genealogy Division. Dictionary catalog of the Local History and Genealogy Division. Boston, G. K. Hall, 1974. 20v. $1540. **AK8**

Contents: v.1–18, Dictionary catalog of the Local History and Genealogy Division; Supplement, v.1–2, United States local history catalog.

Reproduction of the catalog cards for this extensive collection covering local history, genealogy, nomenclature (forenames and surnames), heraldry, and vexillology. Represents some 100,000 volumes. "Contains entries for materials cataloged for the collection through December 1971. Beginning in January 1972, all additions to the collection of the Local History and Genealogy Division have been included in the Dictionary catalog of the Research Libraries [*Guide* AA112]." —*Foreword.*

The two-volume supplement (which may be purchased separately; $155) is subtitled "A modified shelf list arranged alphabetically by state, and alphabetically by locality within each state"; it represents the Libraries collection of county, city, town, and village histories of all areas of the United States. The publisher's *Bibliographic guide to North American history,* 1977– , serves as an ongoing supplement to this section. Z881.N59

U.S. Library of Congress. Genealogies in the Library of Congress; a bibliography. Ed. by Marion J. Kaminkow. Supplement 1972–1976. Baltimore, Magna Carta, 1977. 285p. $23.50. **AK9**

For main volume *see Guide* AK21.

Includes some older works as well as publications of the 1972–76 period.

Yantis, Netti Schreiner. Genealogical books in print. [Springfield, Va., Author, 1975] 311p. $4 pa. **AK10**

Subtitle: A catalogue of in-print titles, useful and interesting to those doing genealogical research; including prices and complete ordering information for over 5000 items. Z5313.U5Y35

Dictionaries and compendiums

Burke's Presidential families of the United States of America. 1st ed. London, Burke's Peerage, 1975, 676p. il. £16.95. **AK11**

Hugh Montgomery-Massingberd, ed.

A chapter is devoted to each of the 37 presidents, Washington through Ford, each chapter divided into sections for: (1) biography; (2) portraits; (3) chronology; (4) writings; (5) lineage; (6) descendants; (7) brothers and sisters; and (8) notes. Indexed. CS69.B82

Smith, Clifford Neal and **Smith, Anna Piszczan-Czaja.** Encyclopedia of German-American genealogical research. N.Y., Bowker, 1976. 273p. $35. **AK12**

Attempts to "survey the material available to the genealogist seeking to link American lineages with their origins in German-speaking Europe" (*Pref.*) through bibliographical essays. Includes some background material on German customs, sociological stratification and governmental organization useful to the genealogist. Indexed. E184.G3S66

FRANCE

Dictionnaire des dynasties bourgeoises et du monde des affaires, publié sous la direction de Henry Coston. Paris, Éditions Alain Moreau, [1975]. 599p. 120F. **AK13**

Aims to provide historical and background information on the leading families of France not of the nobility. Gives information on their origin; financial, industrial, and commercial enterprises which they direct; political affiliations, etc. HC272.5.A2D5

Sereville, Etienne de and **Saint Simon, François de.** Dictionnaire de la noblesse française. Paris. Soc. Française au XXe Siècle, [1975]. 1214p. plates. 240F. **AK14**

The main portion of the work is an alphabetical listing of "Notices sur les familles nobles," giving place of origin, description of arms, and a historical note on the family, documenting its elevation to noble status. Includes statistics on the French nobility in 1975; a bibliography, pp.65–89; a glossary; and an "Index des noms de terre." CS587.S47

GERMANY

Genealogisches Handbuch des Adels. . . . Limburg a.d. Lahn, C. A. Starke, 1974–78. v.57–67. il. (In progress) **AK15**

For previously published volumes and annotation *see Guide* AK31.

Contents: Adelslexikon, v.2–4, 1974–78; Adelige Häuser: A, v.13–14, 1975–77; B, v.11–12, 1974–77; Freiherrliche Häuser, A, v.9–10, 1975–77; B, v.6, 1976; Gräfliche Häuser, A, v.8, 1976.

GREAT BRITAIN

See also Suppl. AK3.

Barrow, Geoffrey Battiscombe. The genealogist's guide: an index to printed British pedigrees and family histories, 1950–1975. London, Research Pub. Co.; Chicago, Amer. Lib. Assoc., 1977. 205p. £9; $12.50. **AK16**

Supplements G. W. Marshall's *Genealogist's guide* (1903; *Guide* AK47) and J. B. Whitmore's *Genealogical guide* (1953; *Guide* AK48) both by updating and by including books and articles omitted in those earlier volumes. Cites surname and abbreviated title of source of information. Z5313.G69B36

Debrett's Peerage and baronetage, with Her Majesty's royal warrant holders. 1976– . Kingston upon Thames, Kelly's Directories, Ltd., 1976– . Irregular. **AK17**

Supersedes in part *Debrett's Peerage, baronetage, knightage, and companionage* (*Guide* AK55) which ceased with the volume for 1973/74.

"Comprises information concerning the royal family, the peerage, privy counsellors, Scottish Lords of Session, baronets, and chiefs of names and clans in Scotland."—*t.p., 1976.*

"In future, Debrett will be published at longer intervals than previously."—*p.14, 1976.* Users are referred to *Kelly's handbook* (*Guide* AJ177) for information on the knightage and companionage.

Thomson, Theodore Radford. A catalogue of British family histories. [3d ed.] London, Research Pub. Co., [1976]. 184p. £4. **AK18**

1st ed. 1928.

"This book purports to be a complete list of British Family Histories, that is, books written as histories of families generally acknowledged to be English, Scots, Welsh or Irish."—*Pref.* Does not include reprints from periodicals, collections of pedigrees, biographies, histories of businesses, books dealing with more than one family, or books published in America. Z5315.G69T4

FORMS OF ADDRESS

Montague-Smith, Patrick W. Debrett's Correct form; an inclusive guide to everything from drafting wedding invitations to addressing an archbishop. [Rev. ed.] [Kingston upon Thames], Debrett's Peerage Ltd., [1976]. 423p. £5.95. **AK19**

1st ed. 1970 (*Guide* AK74).

Besides revision of existing text, new sections have been added for "American Usage" and "Usage in other foreign countries."

Titles and forms of address; a guide to their correct use. 15th ed. London, A. & C. Black, [1976]. 188p. £1.75. **AK20**

13th ed. 1966 (*Guide* AK75); 14th ed. 1971.

Minor changes reflect current practice and less strict formalities.

HERALDRY

Roll of Scottish arms. Ed. by Lt. Col. Gayre of Gayre and Nigg, and Reinold Gayre of Gayre and Nigg the Younger. Edinburgh, the Armorial, 1969. pt. I, v.2. (In progress) **AK21**

For v.1 and annotation *see Guide* AK91.

Contents: pt. I, v.2, H–Z.

ORDERS AND DECORATIONS

Werlich, Robert. Orders and decorations of all nations: ancient and modern, civil and military. 2d ed. [Wash., D.C., Quaker Pr., 1974] 476p. il. $29.95. **AK22**

1st ed. 1965.

Illustrates and describes the major awards of all countries. Arranged by country; general index. CR4509.W4

FLAGS

Smith, Whitney. Flags through the ages and across the world. N.Y., McGraw-Hill, [1975]. 357p. col. il. $39.95. **AK23**

In three main sections: (1) Flags through the ages (History of flags; Flags that made history: Customs and etiquette; National flag histories); (2) Flags across the world (Flags of the world's 157 nations and their subdivisions; International flags; Ethnic minority flags); (3) Symbols. A good deal of background information and explanatory text accompanies the illustrations. Glossary of terms; index. JC345.S57

NAMES

American and British

Puckett, Newbell Niles. Black names in America: origins and usage. Ed. by Murray Heller. Boston, G. K. Hall, [1975]. 561p. $29.50. **AK24**

At head of title: Newbell Niles Puckett Memorial gift, John G. White Department, Cleveland Public Library.

Chapters 1–4 offer background material, chronological and regional lists of names, and various types of statistics. Chapter 5 is a "Dictionary of African origins." There is also an "Index of unusual names" and a bibliography of principal sources. E185.89.N3P82

Withycombe, Elizabeth Gidley. The Oxford dictionary of English Christian names. 3d ed. Oxford & N.Y., Clarendon Pr., [1977]. 310p. £4.50. **AK25**

2d ed. 1950 (*Guide* AK116).

"The present edition contains about forty names not included in the previous editions, as well as a number of new cross-references. The main work of revision, as before, consists of many small corrections, emendations, and additions to existing articles, many of which reflect the changes in usage, frequency, and status of names. . . ."—*Pref.* CS2375.G7W5

African

Madubuike, Ihechukwu. A handbook of African names. Wash., D.C., Three Continents Pr., [1976]. 233p. $9. **AK26**

The author acknowledges that "the work in its present form and content is tentative."—*Pref.* Sections are devoted to specific ethnic groups, and a brief discussion of naming conventions and practices for each is followed by a selected list of typical names and their meanings. There is an "Alphabetical list of some African names," pp.181–227. CS375.A33M3

Jewish

See also Suppl. AK4.

Kaganoff, Benzion C. A dictionary of Jewish names and their history. N.Y., Schocken Books, [1977]. 250p. $10.95. **AK27**

The "history," pp.1–115, is concerned with both first names and family names; the "Dictionary of selected Jewish names," pp. 117–211, gives brief information on the origin and meaning of family names. Indexes of names and of subjects. CS3010.K28

Portuguese

Guérios, Rosário Farâni Mansur. Dicionário etimológico de nomes e sobrenomes. 2. ed., rev. e ampl. São Paulo, Editora Ave Maria, 1973. 231p. **AK28**

1st ed. 1949.

An introductory essay on names (pp.13–43) precedes the dictionary section. Includes both given names and surnames. CS2761.G8

Russian

Unbegaun, Boris Ottokar. Russian surnames. Oxford, Clarendon Pr., 1972. 529p. £8. **AK29**

Aims "to discuss the modern system of Russian surnames in both its morphological and its semantic aspects."—*Pref.* Historical data are included "whenever they throw useful light on the modern system," but the work is not a history of Russian surnames. More than 10,000 surnames are cited. Bibliography; indexes of all quoted surnames and of surname-terminations. PG2576.U5

B

The Humanities

B A

Philosophy

GUIDES

Bertman, Martin A. Research guide in philosophy. Morristown, N.J., General Learning Pr., [1974]. 252p. $5.95 pa. **BA1**

A research guide for the undergraduate, with information on research methods, use of the library, selective bibliography, glossary of terms, etc. B52.B43

BIBLIOGRAPHY

Bibliography of bibliography

Guerry, Herbert. A bibliography of philosophical bibliographies. Westport, Conn., Greenwood Pr., [1977]. 332p. $25. **BA2**

In two parts: (1) Bibliographies of individual philosophers (alphabetical by philosopher); (2) Subject bibliographies (alphabetical by subject). 2,353 items, with selective, brief annotations. In general, includes "only bibliographies that have been published separately or appeared as contributions to journals," but lists "a few significant

bibliographies which were published as appendixes to monographs or as parts of larger bibliographies."—*Introd.* Author index.
Z7125.A1G83

International

The philosopher's index; a retrospective index to U.S. publications from 1940. Bowling Green, Ohio, Philosophy Documentation Ctr., Bowling Green State Univ., [1978]. 3v. $195. **BA3**

Contents: v.1–2, Subject index; v.3, Author index.

An index to "approximately 15,000 articles from U.S. journals published during the 27 year period, 1940–1966, and approximately 6,000 books published during the 37 year period, 1940–1976."—*p. vii.* It thus offers retrospective indexing for journal articles published prior to the beginning of the quarterly *Philosopher's index* (*Guide* BA24), and complementary coverage for book publications from the longer period. A second retrospective edition is planned for books and journal articles published in English outside the United States.

Tobey, Jeremy L. The history of ideas: a bibliographical introduction. Santa Barbara, Calif., Clio Books, [1975–76]. v.1–2. v.1, $17.25; v.2, $19.75. (In progress?) **BA4**

Contents: v.1, Classical antiquity; v.2, Medieval and early modern Europe.

v.1 offers a series of bibliographic essays on "the important research and reference tools and scholarly works on the history of ideas and its related fields of philosophy, science, aesthetics, and religion in antiquity."—*Postscript.* A similar plan is followed in v.2.
Z7125.T58

Dissertations

Bechtle, Thomas C. and **Riley, Mary F.** Dissertations in philosophy accepted at American universities, 1861–1975. N.Y., Garland, 1978. 537p. (Garland reference library of the humanities, v.112) $32. **BA5**

An author listing of more than 7,500 doctoral dissertations accepted at 120 United States and Canadian universities. "As a rule, only those authors have been included whose dissertations are primarily concerned with philosophy and whose degrees have been earned in a department of philosophy."—*Pref.* There were, however, numerous variant situations wherein content of the dissertation (i.e., whether or not it was "essentially concerned with philosophical concepts") determined its inclusion or exclusion. Detailed subject index.
Z7125.B38

Colombia

Herrera Restrepo, Daniel. La filosofía en Colombia: bibliografía 1627–1973. Cali, Universidad del Valle, División de Humanidades, [1974?]. 247p. **BA6**

In two parts: (1) Parte historica; (2) Parte sistematica. Lists writings of Colombian scholars on all aspects of philosophy and all periods.
Z7129.C6H47

India

Dr. C. P. Ramaswami Aiyar Research Endowment Committee. A bibliography of Indian philosophy. Madras, 1963–68. Pt.1–2. (In progress?) **BA7**

Intended as a bibliography for research in Sanskrit and philosophical studies. Pt.1 is a bibliography "of source-books in Sanskrit and, where available, of their translations in English, relating to the Upanishads, the Bhagavad Gita, the Nyaya, the Vaiseshika, the Sankhya, the Yoga, the Mimamsa and the Vedanta systems comprising Advaita, Visishtadvaita and Dvaita."—*Pref.* Pt. 2 lists works relating to Navya Nyaya, Jainism, Buddhism, Saiva, Siddhanta, the Vedas, the Dharma Sutras, Sakta Tantra and works on Bhakti.
Z7129.I5D63

DICTIONARIES AND ENCYCLOPEDIAS

Dictionary of the history of ideas.... N.Y., Scribner's, [1974]. [v.5] **BA8**

For v.1–4, full citation and annotation *see Guide* BA50.

Contents: [v.5], Index. 479p.

A detailed index with reference to volume, page, and column.

The encyclopedia of Indian philosophies [by] Sibajiban Bhattacharya [and others]. Delhi, Publ. for Amer. Inst. of Indian Studies by Motilal Banarsidass, 1977. [v.2] **BA9**

For v.1 *see Guide* BA35.

Contents: [v.2], Indian metaphysics and epistemology: the tradition of Nyaya-Vaisesika up to Gangesa. Ed. by Karl H. Potter.

Lacey, Alan Robert. A dictionary of philosophy. London, Routledge & Kegan Paul, [1976]. 239p. £4.75. **BA10**

A work for "the layman or intending student" which aims "to take some of the commonest terms and notions in current English-speaking philosophy and to give the reader some idea of what they mean to the philosopher and what sort of problems he finds associated with them."—*Pref.* Cross references; some bibliographies. B41.L32

Urmson, James Opie, ed. The concise encyclopedia of Western philosophy and philosophers. [2d ed. rev. in new format] London, Hutchinson, [1975]. 319p. £5.50. **BA11**

1st ed. 1960 (*Guide* BA63).

A work for the non-specialist, with signed articles of a "minimum length compatible with accuracy and intelligibility."—*Introd.* Principles of selection included "a fairly narrow interpretation of what constitutes philosophy"; emphasis on the needs of the non-specialist, with a minimum of attention to "very technical problems and the philosophers who specialized in them"; and English-language orientation (i.e., "philosophers whose works are not available in translation into English have been omitted or given treatment shorter perhaps than their merits"). B41.U7

INDIVIDUAL PHILOSOPHERS

Bergson

Gunter, Pete Addison Y. Henri Bergson: a bibliography. Bowling Green, Ohio, Philosophy Documentation Ctr., Bowling Green Univ., [1974]. 457p. $17.50. **BA12**

A chronological listing of Bergson's works is followed by an alphabetical author listing of works concerning Bergson. Z8089.9.G85

Erasmus

Margolin, Jean-Claude. Neuf années de bibliographie Érasmienne (1962–1970). Paris, Vrin; Toronto, Univ. of Toronto Pr., 1977. 850p. (De Pétrarque à Descartes, 33) 250F. pa. **BA13**

Continues the listings in the same compiler's Erasmus bibliographies covering 1936–49 and 1950–61 (*Guide* BA82–BA83).

Plato and Socrates

McKirahan, Richard D. Plato and Socrates: a comprehensive bibliography, 1958–1973. N.Y., Garland, 1978. 592p. (Garland reference library of the humanities, v.78) **BA14**

Supplements the bibliography "Plato (1950–1957)" by H. F. Cherniss which appeared in *Lustrum,* v.4–5 (1959–60). Separate sections for Plato and Socrates, each topically subdivided. Author index. About 4,600 items. Z8696.M34

B B

Religion

GENERAL WORKS

Guides

Adams, Charles Joseph, ed. A reader's guide to the great religions. 2d ed. N.Y., Free Pr., [1977]. 521p. $17.95. **BB1**

1st ed. 1965 (*Guide* BB1).

Revised and updated. Lacunae have been filled, and new chapters added for fuller and more comprehensive treatment. New sections are: the ancient world; Sikhs; Jainas; early and classical Judaism; medieval and modern Judaism. Appendix: "The history of the history of religions," by Charles H. Long. Author and subject indexes. Z7833.A35

Kennedy, James R. Library research guide to religion and theology: illustrated search strategy and sources. Ann Arbor, Mich., Pierian Pr., 1974. 53p. il. $8.50; $3.50 pa. (Library research guides ser., no.1) **BB2**

A manual, principally for the undergraduate, on methods of searching topics in religion and theology and on writing term papers. Includes information on use of the card catalog, basic reference tools, choosing a research topic, evaluating sources. BL41.K45

Bibliography

Capps, Donald, Rambo, Lewis and **Ransohoff, Paul.** Psychology of religion: a guide to information sources. Detroit, Gale, [1976]. 352p. (Philosophy and religion information guide ser., v.1) $18. **BB3**

A section of general works in psychology of religion is followed by sections for each of the six "dimensions" of religion: the mythological, ritual, experiential, dispositional, social, and directional. Each section has four to eight subsections, and there are author, title, and subject indexes. Materials are largely limited to publications from the period 1950–74, with fuller coverage for 1960–74 inasmuch as W. W. Meissner's *Annotated bibliography in religion and psychology* (N.Y., 1961. 235p.) is very comprehensive for the earlier years. Books and articles of special merit are annotated. Z7204.R4C36

Ofori, Patrick E. Black African traditional religions and philosophy; a selected bibliographic survey of the sources from the earliest times to 1974. Nendeln, Liechtenstein, KTO Pr., 1975. 421p. $87. **BB4**

"This bibliography covers all the major ethnic groups of black Africa. Black Africa, as used in the context of this bibliography, means Africa south of the Sahara, and it includes all the major ethnic groups drawn roughly from Senegal in the West, along the southern boundary of the Sahara desert, through Central Ethiopia to Somalia in the East, through west, central, eastern and Southern Africa, including Madagascar."—*Introd.* Arranged by geographic area (Africa in general, West Africa, Central Africa, East Africa, Southern Africa), then by country and by ethnic groups within country sections. Some of the larger ethnic sections are subdivided according to such categories as "Religious beliefs and conceptions," "Birth, initiation and funeral rites," "Festivals," "Myths, superstitions, taboos," etc. Author and ethnic indexes. Z834.A3O34

Thompson, Laurence G. Studies of Chinese religion: a comprehensive and classified bibliography of publications in English, French, and German through 1970. Encino, Calif., Dickenson Pub. Co., [1976]. 190p. $12.95. **BB5**

"... deals solely with Chinese *religion,* and includes items pertaining to the so-called Classics and philosophy only when these address themselves to religious matters."—*Pref.* In three main sections: (1) Bibliography and general studies; (2) Chinese religion exclusive of Buddhism; and (3) Chinese Buddhism; pts.2 and 3 are topically subdivided. Index of authors, editors, compilers, etc. Includes books and periodical articles. Z7757.C6T56

Turner, Harold W. Bibliography of new religious movements in primal societies. Boston, G. K. Hall, [1977]– . v.1– . (In progress) **BB6**

Contents: v.1, Black Africa. $25.

To be in 4v. "The religious movements with which this bibliographic series is concerned are defined as those which arise in the interaction of a primal society with another society where there is great disparity of power or sophistication."—*Introd.* Later volumes are to deal with North America, Latin America and the Caribbean, and Asia and Oceania.

v.1 is designed to "correct, cumulate and update" Turner and Mitchell's *Comprehensive bibliography of modern African religious movements* (*Guide* BB7) and its two supplements which appeared in the *Journal of religion in Africa* (1968 and 1970). While the new work adds material through mid-1976, it is more selective and omits some material from the earlier lists. Some Islamic movements are now included. Geographical arrangement with "Index of authors and sources." About 1,900 items. Brief annotations (mainly descriptive) for most items. Z7833.T87

Ward, Arthur Marcus [and others]. A theological book list, 1971. [London, Theological Education Fund, 1971] 5pts. in 1v. **BB7**

Contents: Works in English, comp. by A. M. Ward; French, comp. by J.-J. von Allmen; German, comp. by H. C. Deppe; Portuguese, comp. by A. Sapsezian; Spanish, comp. by E. Castro.

Forms a third supplement to the work of R. P. Morris (*Guide* BB8). Covers mainly the period 1966–70.

Williams, Ethel L. and **Brown, Clifton F.** The Howard University bibliography of African and Afro-American religious studies; with locations in American libraries. Wilmington, Del., Scholarly Resources, [1977]. 525p. $24.95. **BB8**

Some 13,000 entries (books, periodical articles, parts of books) in five main sections: (1) African heritage; (2) Christianity and slavery in the New World; (3) The black man and his religious life in the Americas; (4) Civil rights movement; (5) The contemporary religious scene. Appendix I is a selected listing of manuscripts; Appendix II is an "Autobiographical and biographical index" which includes references to biographical material in periodical articles and parts of books. Indexed. No standards for inclusion are mentioned, and works listed range from scholarly works to popular accounts appearing in national weeklies.

Indexes and abstract journals

Religion index one: periodicals. July/Dec. 1977– . Chicago, American Theological Lib. Assoc., 1978– . Semiannual, with biennial cumulation. **BB9**

Subtitle: A subject index to periodical literature, including an author index with abstracts and a book review index.

Represents a change of title for the *Index to religious periodical literature* (*Guide* BB15). Follows the policies of the earlier title and employs the three-part arrangement introduced with the 1975 *Index:* (1) Subject index; (2) Author index with abstracts; and (3) Book review index. The final issue published under the old title (Jan./June 1977) will be cumulated with the July/Dec. 1977 and Jan./June 1978 semiannuals, plus new materials for July/Dec. 1978, to form v.13 (1977–78) of the new title.

Religion index two: multi-author works (*Suppl.* BB10) is a companion publication.

Religion index two: multi-author works, 1976– . [Chicago], American Theological Lib. Assoc., 1978– . [v.1–] Annual. $60 per yr. **BB10**

A companion to *Religion index one: periodicals* (*Suppl.* BB9), this new series indexes, by subject and author, composite works by various authors published during the year covered. "Each volume will appear about a year after the end of the imprint year of the majority of books indexed."—*Pref., 1976.* Includes Western-language publications which are collections by more than one author, which are intended to be scholarly, and which have a religious or theological subject focus. 241 books are indexed in the 1976 volume. Subjects and authors in separate sections.

Bibliography

Regazzi, John J. and **Hines, Theodore C.** A guide to indexed periodicals in religion. Metuchen, N.J., Scarecrow, 1975. 314p. $10. **BB11**

An alphabetical listing of some 2,700 periodicals with indication of which of 17 abstracting and indexing services includes each title. An "inverted title listing" which lists the journals under each important word in the title is intended as an aid for locating garbled or partially remembered titles. Z7753.R34

Dictionaries and encyclopedias

Dictionnaire de spiritualité, ascétique et mystique, doctrine et histoire, fondé par Marcel Viller, F. Cavallera et J. de Guibert, S.J., continué par A. Rayez, A. Derville et A. Solignac, S.J. . . . Paris, Beauchesne, 1974–77. fasc. 57/58–64/65. (In progress) **BB12**

For earlier volumes and annotation *see Guide* BB46.

Contents: v.8^4–$10^{1/2}$ (fasc. 57/58–64/65), Joseph-Marie de Jésus d'Agreda.

Ferguson, John. An illustrated encyclopaedia of mysticism and the mystery religions. London, Thames and Hudson; N.Y., Seabury, [1977]. 228p. il. $14.95. **BB13**

Brief articles on names, terms, and movements relating to various forms of mysticism. Demonology, magic, and witchcraft are excluded. "Bibliography of secondary sources," pp.217–27.
BL625.F44

Reallexikon für Antike und Christentum; Sachwörterbuch zur Auseinandersetzung des Christentums mit der antiken Welt. In Verbindung mit Carsten Colpe, Ernst Dassmann, Albrecht Dihle. . . . Stuttgart, Hiersemann, 1974–78. v.9^3–10^5. (In progress) **BB14**

For earlier volumes and annotation *see Guide* BB56.

Contents: Bd.9^3–10^5 (Lfg. 67–78), Gefangenschaft–Gewand.

Rice, Edward. Eastern definitions. Garden City, N.Y., Doubleday, 1978. 433p. il. $10. **BB15**

Subtitle: A short encyclopedia of religions of the Orient; a guide to common, ordinary, and rare philosophical, mystical, religious, and psychological terms from Hinduism, Buddhism, Sufism, Islam, Zen, Taoism, the Sikhs, Zoroastrianism, and other major and minor Eastern religions.

"The terms encountered in this work are in most cases those most likely to be met by the average curious reader of both popular and scholarly works written in or translated into English."—*Foreword.* Articles range in length from a few lines to several pages. Cross references; no bibliography.

Theologische Realenzyklopädie. In Gemeinschaft mit Horst Robert Balz [et al.], hrsg. von Gerhard Krause und Gerhard Müller. Berlin & N.Y., W. de Gruyter, 1976– . Bd.1, Lfg.1– . (In progress) DM28 per Lfg. **BB16**

Contents: Bd.1–Bd.2, Lfg.5, A–Anselm von Canterbury; indexes.

To be in 25 volumes of about 800 pages (five *Lieferungen*) each; publishing schedule calls for publication of six *Lieferungen* per year.

In some respects a successor to the *Realencyklopädie für protestantische Theologie und Kirche* (*Guide* BB21), but a new work employing a broader interpretation of "theology" and less concerned with the strictly Protestant point of view. Long, scholarly articles (most of them many pages in length) signed by the contributors, and including extensive bibliographies. Each volume has its own index, and a general index is promised as the final volume of the set.

Directories

Wright, Robert, comp. A directory of religious studies programs; departments of religion in North America. [Waterloo, Ont., Canada], Council on the Study of Religion, [1973]. 237p. **BB17**

United States entries are arranged by state, then by academic institution. Indicates department, type of institution, enrollment, faculty areas of specialization, and courses offered.

CHRISTIANITY

General works

Dictionaries and encyclopedias

Baudrillart, Alfred. Dictionnaire d'histoire et de géographie ecclésiastiques. . . . Paris, Letouzey, 1974–76. v.18^{2-4}. (In progress) **BB18**

For earlier volumes and annotation *see Guide* BB43.

Contents: v.18^{2-4}, France–Frauenthal.

Since v.16 "sous la direction de R. Aubert."

The concise Oxford dictionary of the Christian church. Ed. by Elizabeth A. Livingstone. 2d ed. abr. Oxford and N.Y., Oxford Univ. Pr., 1977. 570p. £7.50; $14.95. **BB19**

An abridgment of the 2d ed. of *The Oxford dictionary of the Christian church* (1974; *Guide* BB50). Answers "the questions who and what" and refers the reader "to the corresponding article in the parent volume" (*Pref.*) for fuller information and bibliography.
BR95.O82

Encyclopedia of theology: the concise *Sacramentum mundi.* Ed. by Karl Rahner. N.Y., Seabury Pr., [1975]. 1841p. $37.50. **BB20**

"This volume contains revised versions of the major articles on theology, biblical science and related topics from *Sacramentum Mundi* [*Guide* BB266], together with a large number of articles from the major German works *Lexikon für Theologie und Kirche* [*Guide* BB22] and *Theologisches Taschenlexikon,* and entirely new articles on topics of major importance written for the occasion by Professor Rahner and others."—*Pref. Note.* BR95.E48

Douglas, James Dixon, ed. The new international dictionary of the Christian church. Grand Rapids, Mich., Zondervan, [1974]. 1074p. $24.95. **BB21**

An international group of about 180 scholars has contributed signed articles on a wide range of topics relating to the history, development, and practices relating to the Christian church. Many biographical sketches. Some articles include bibliographical references. Cross referencing is effected both through conventional *see* references and use of an asterisk following a name or term in the text of an article. Strong in American church history and evangelical movements. BR95.D68

Biography

Bowden, Henry Warner. Dictionary of American religious biography. Edwin S. Gaustad, advisory ed. Westport, Conn., Greenwood Pr., [1977]. 572p. $29.95. **BB22**

With a view to correlating "historical materials related to American religious figures" (*Pref.*), the volume presents biographical sketches of 425 persons from "all denominations that played a significant role in our nation's past." For each biographee, available details of vital statistics, education, and career are briefly noted preceding a discussion of the life work and influence of the figure. Bibliographies at the end of the articles cite works both by and about a person.
BL72.B68

Who's who in religion. Ed.1– , 1975/76– . Chicago, Marquis, [1975]– . Biennial? **BB23**

The 1st ed. contained about 16,000 biographies; this figure was increased to about 18,000 in the 2d ed. (publ. 1977). Names of persons included were drawn from the following general categories: (1) church officials (both lay and clergy); (2) clergy, selected for outstanding contributions to activities of their respective faiths; (3) religious educators in the field of higher education; (4) lay leaders. Information was supplied by the biographees; a few sketches compiled by Marquis editors are marked with an asterisk.

Williams, Ethel L. Biographical directory of Negro ministers. 3d ed. Boston, G. K. Hall, 1975. 584p. $28. **BB24**

2d ed. 1970 (*Guide* BB65).

This edition includes 1,442 biographical sketches of the "who's who" type. BR563.N4W5

Church history and expansion

Statistics

Johnson, Douglas W., Picard, Paul R. and **Quinn, Bernard.** Churches & church membership in the United States: an enumeration by region, state and county; 1971. Wash., D.C., Glenmary Research Ctr., [1974]. 237p. maps. $15 pa. **BB25**

"This report contains statistics by region, state and county on Christian churches and church membership for 1971. Fifty-three denominations are included, representing an estimated 80.8 percent of church membership in the United States."—*Pref.*

Offers tables for (1) churches and church membership by denomination; (2) churches and church membership by region, state and denomination; and (3) churches and church membership by state, county and denomination. BR526.J64

Atlases

Gaustad, Edwin Scott. Historical atlas of religion in America. Rev. ed. N.Y., Harper & Row, [1976]. 189p. $20. **BB26**

1st ed. 1962 (*Guide* BB97).

"Briefly, the changes introduced into this edition are as follows. The generally unrevealing state maps of the earlier edition have now been replaced with county maps for the mid-twentieth century.... New maps have been added ... along with several new charts and updated line graphs. A new fold-out color map reflects denominational distribution in 1970, while an additional map indicates the Protestant-Catholic dominance county-by-county."—*Pref.*
G1201.E4G3

The Bible

Texts

Anchor Bible. Garden City, N.Y., Doubleday, 1974–78. v.6A, 7, 7C, 23, 32, 34–34A, 38, 41, 42, 44. (In progress) **BB27**

For previously published volumes and annotation *see Guide* BB167.

Contents: v.6A, Judges; v.7, Ruth; v.7C, Song of songs; v.23, Book of Daniel; v.32, Corinthians I; v.34, Ephesians, Chapters 1–3; v.34A, Ephesians, Chapters 4–6; v.38, Revelation; v.41, I Maccabees; v.42, Esdras I and II; v.44, Daniel, Esther and Jeremiah—the additions.

Bible. English. New English. The New English Bible, with the Apocrypha. Samuel Sandmel, gen. ed., M. Jack Suggs, New Testament ed., Arnold J. Tkacik, Apocrypha ed. Oxford study ed. N.Y., Oxford Univ. Pr., 1976. 1036p., 257p., 333p., [100p.] maps. $15.95; $9.95 pa. **BB28**

Prep. under the authority of the Joint Committee on the New Testament of the Bible.

Includes introductions to individual books and groups of books as well as general background articles on Scripture; there are also annotations throughout "dealing with literary, historical, theological, geographical, and archaeological aspects of the text, and ... cross-references" (*Pref.*) to related passages. Index of people, places and themes in the Bible; maps with index. BS192.A1 1976 .N48

Bible. Latin. Vulgate. Biblia sacra: iuxta Vulgatam versionem adiuvantibus Bonifatio Fischer ... [et al.] rec. et brevi apparatu instruxit Robertus Weber. Ed. altera emendata. Stuttgart, Württembergische Bibelanstalt, [1975]. 2v. DM68. **BB29**

1st ed. 1969.

Contents: v.1, Genesis–Psalmi; v.2, Proverbia–Apocalypsis, Appendix.

A new Vulgate text based on the important manuscripts and two modern critical editions. BS75

Bibliography

Coldham, Geraldine Elizabeth. A bibliography of Scriptures in African languages. Supplement, 1964–1974. London, British and Foreign Bible Soc., 1975. 198p. £3 pa. **BB30**

Intended for use with the 1966 volume (*Guide* BB109), which it supplements, and not as a separate work. Includes Scriptures published 1964–74 and editions of earlier years omitted from the basic work. Long lists of "Language name corrections" and "Geographical name corrections" help to update a rapidly changing nomenclature.

Concordances

The computer Bible. Editors: J. Arthur Baird [and] David Noel Freedman. [Wooster, Ohio], Biblical Research Associates, 1973–77. v.4–5, 7–13. (In progress) **BB31**

For v.1–3 and annotation *see Guide* BB128.

Contents: v.4, An analytical linguistic key-word-in-context concordance to the Books of Haggai, Zechariah and Malachi, by Yehuda T. Radday; v.5, A critical concordance to the Gospel of John, ed. by A. Q. Morton and S. Michaelson; v.7, A critical concordance to the Acts of the Apostles, ed. by A. Q. Morton and S. Michaelson; v.8, A critical word book of Leviticus, Numbers, Deuteronomy, by Peter M. K. Morris and Edward James; v.9, A linguistic concordance of Ruth and Jonah. Hebrew vocabulary and idiom, by Francis I. Andersen and A. Dean Forbes; v. 10, Eight minor prophets: a linguistic concordance, by Francis I. Andersen and A. Dean Forbes; v.[11], An analytical linguistic key-word-in-context concordance to the Book of Judges, by Yehuda T. Radday; v.12, Syntactical and critical concordance to the Greek text of Baruch and the Epistle of Jeremiah, by R. A. Martin; v.13, A critical concordance to the Letter of Paul to the Romans, by A. Q. Morton, S. Michaelson, J. David Thompson.

Computer Konkordanz zum Novum Testamentum Graece von Nestle-Aland, 26. Auflage, und zum Greek New Testament, 3d edition, hrsg. vom Institut für Neutestamentliche Textforschung und vom Rechenzentrum der Universität Münster, unter besonderer Mitwirkung von H. Bachmann und W. A. Slaby. Berlin, De Gruyter, 1977. col.709–1820; 1–66. **BB32**

Contents: col. 709–1820, (Ζαβουλών–ὠφέλιμος); col.1–66, Anhang.

A computer-produced concordance to the two texts of the *Vollständige Konkordanz* (*Suppl.* BB36), without citation to variants as provided in that work. Overlaps alphabetically with part of Bd.1, Lfg.5 of the larger work and is meant for interim use until the *Vollständige Konkordanz* is complete. BS2302.C65

Hartdegen, Stephen J., gen. ed. Nelson's Complete concordance of the New American Bible. Nashville, Thomas Nelson, [1977]. 1274p. $29.95. **BB33**

A computer-generated verbal concordance to the text of the *New American Bible* (*Guide* p.261). Employs small, but very legible type on a three-column page, with keywords set in boldface capitals to make for ease of use. BS425.H27

Modern concordance to the New Testament. Ed. and rev. following all current English translations of the New Testament by Michael Darton. Garden City, N.Y., Doubleday; London, Darton Longman & Todd, [1976]. 786p. $27.50 **BB34**

"Based on the French *Concordance de la Bible, Nouveau Testament* produced under the aegis of the Association de la Concordance française de la Bible."—*t.p.*

A thematic and verbal concordance in English and Greek designed to serve as a guide to the themes, subjects, and ideas of the New Testament as well as to specific words occurring therein. Its underlying purpose is to lead the student to the Greek text on which modern English translations are founded. "The presentation is by subject matter: 341 themes subdivided under their Greek roots according to sense. In these themes, all the 5,600-odd Greek words (apart from definite and indefinite articles and the most common prepositions) of the New Testament, and the many more words in the vocabulary of English New Testaments, are conveniently grouped so that the Concordance succeeds on the one hand in avoiding the scattering of the texts into as many separate articles or headings as there are distinguishable words, and on the other hand in marking the close connection between words which, though slightly different in form, are similar in derivation or meaning."—*p.xii.* Headings are in English, with the Greek words given at the beginning of each subsection and with English and Greek indexes. BS2305.M6

Novae concordantiae Bibliorum sacrorum iuxta Vulgatam versionem critice editam quas digessit Bonifatius Fischer OSB. [Stuttgart-Bad Cannstatt], Frommann-Holzboog [1977]. 5v. DM2000. **BB35**

A computer-produced concordance based on the two-volume *Biblia sacra iuxta Vulgatam versionem adiuvantibus Bonifatio Fischer* (Stuttgart, Württembergische Bibelanstalt, 1975; *Suppl.* BB29).

Vollständige Konkordanz zum griechischen Neuen Testament; unter Zugrundelegung aller modernen kritischen Textausgaben und des Textus receptus in Verbindung mit H. Riesenfeld, H.-U. Rosenbaum, Chr. Hannick, neu zusammengestellt unter der Leitung von K. Aland. Berlin & N.Y., De Gruyter, 1975–77. Lfg.1–5. (In progress) (Lfg.5: DM118) **BB36**

Contents: Bd.1, Lfg.1–5, A – Ζηλωτής.

A new concordance which takes into account modern New Testament scholarship and includes variants from all important sources. BS2302.V64

Dictionaries and handbooks

Blair, Edward P. Abingdon Bible handbook. Nashville, Abingdon Pr., [1975]. 511p. il. $15.95. **BB37**

For the intelligent layman. Intended as a companion to serious Bible study, not as a commentary on each book of the Bible. In three sections: "The Bible today"; "The Bible in history" (with sections on the Old Testament, the Apocrypha, the New Testament, and the background of the Bible); and "The Bible and faith and life." Indexed. BS475.2.B5

Botterweck, G. Johannes and **Ringgren, Helmer.** Theologisches Wörterbuch zum Alten Testament. Stuttgart, Kohlhammer, 1973–78. Bd.1–3²/³. (In progress) DM198 per v. **BB38**

Issued in *Lieferungen* beginning 1970; title page of Bd.1 is dated 1973. To be in about 8v.

Contents: Bd.1–3²/³, 'āb–j'l.

An English translation is appearing as: BS440.B57

——— Theological dictionary of the Old Testament. John T. Willis, translator. Grand Rapids, Mich., Wm. B. Eerdmans, [1974–75]. v.1–2. (In progress) $18.50 per v. **BB39**

A translation of the *Theologisches Wörterbuch zum Alten Testament* (above).

Contents: v.1–2, 'ābh–gālāh.

A presentation of "the fundamental concepts intended by the respective words and terms" (*Introd.*) of the Old Testament. Arranged alphabetically according to the Hebrew term. BS440.B5713

Jenni, Ernst. Theologisches Handwörterbuch zum Alten Testament ... unter Mitarbeit von Claus Westermann. München, C. Kaiser, 1976. Bd.2. **BB40**

For Bd.1 and annotation *see Guide* BB160.

Contents: Bd.2, nun–thav. (Completes the work.)

The new international dictionary of New Testament theology. [German text] Lothar Coenen, Erich Bayreuther and Hans Bietenhard, eds.; trans., with additions and revisions, from the German ... , ed. by Colin Brown. Exeter, Paternoster Pr., 1975–76. v.1–2. (v.1, £10; v.2, £14) (In progress) **BB41**

Contents: v.1–2, A–Pre.

A translation, with additions and revisions, of *Theologisches Begriffslexikon zum Neuen Testament* (Wuppertal, Brockhaus, 1970–71. 3v.).

Treats New Testament terminology of theological importance. Material from the original is rearranged in this translation so as to group related New Testament Greek terms under concepts arranged alphabetically by English word. Greek terms are treated in their classical, Old Testament and New Testament meanings. Each volume has indexes of Hebrew and Aramaic words, Greek words, and general terms. v.3 is to include an index to all volumes.

Intended as a companion volume to *The new international dictionary of the Christian church* (*Suppl.* BB21). BS2397.N48

Vigouroux, Fulcran Grégoire and **Pirot, Louis.** Dictionnaire de la Bible. ... Suppl. sous la direction de Henri Cazelles et André Feuillet. Paris, Letouzey, 1973–75. Suppl. v.9¹⁻² (fasc.48–49/50). (In progress) **BB42**

For earlier volumes and annotation *see Guide* BB166.

Contents: v.9¹⁻² (fasc.48–49/50), Psaumes–Pythagorisme.

The Wycliffe Bible encyclopedia. Charles F. Pfeiffer, Howard F. Vos and John Rea, eds. Chicago, Moody Pr., [1975]. 2v. (1851p.) il. $29.95. **BB43**

The work is comprehensive in its coverage, including every personal and place name mentioned in the Bible, important doctrines, and theological terms. "Doctrinal articles ... adhere to Christian orthodoxy, the fundamentals of the faith generally accepted by believers of conservative, evangelical persuasion."—*Pref.* BS440.W92

Patristics

Biblia patristica; index des citations et allusions Bibliques dans la littérature patristique. Paris, Éditions du Centre National de la Recherche Scientifique, 1975–77. v.1–2. (In progress) v.1, 120F; v.2, 130F. **BB44**

At head of title: Centre d'Analyse et de Documentation Patristique [Strasbourg]. Equipe de Recherche Associée au Centre National de la Recherche Scientifique: J. Allenbach [et al.].

Contents: v.1, Des origines à Clément d'Alexandrie et Tertullien; v.2, Le troisième siècle (Origène excepté).

A computer-produced index offering correspondence tables arranged according to books of the Old Testament and listing (in abbreviated form): biblical book, chapter and verse, together with relevant patristic author, work, book chapter, paragraph, page and line.

Protestant denominations

General works

Handbooks

Mead, Frank Spencer. Handbook of denominations in the United States. New sixth ed. Nashville, Abingdon Pr., [1975]. 320p. $5.95. **BB45**

5th ed. 1970 (*Guide* BB190).

Brief descriptions of more than 300 groups. BR516.5.M38

Baptist

Starr, Edward Caryl. A Baptist bibliography, being a register of printed material by and about Baptists, including works written against the Baptists. Rochester, N.Y., Amer. Baptist Historical Soc., 1974–76. v.20–25. **BB46**

For earlier volumes and annotation *see Guide* BB194.

Contents: v.20–25, Ro–Z. (Completes the set.)

Church of England

Harper, Howard V. The Episcopalian's dictionary: church beliefs, terms, customs, and traditions explained in layman's language. N.Y., Seabury Pr., [1975]. 183p. $8.95. **BB47**

Definitions intended for the layman. BX5007.H37

LeNeve, John. Fasti ecclesiae anglicanae, 1066–1300. [London], Univ. of London, Inst. of Historical Research; Athlone Pr., 1977. v.3. (In progress) **BB48**

For earlier volumes *see Guide* BB202.

Contents: v.3, Lincoln, comp. by D. E. Greenway.

——— Fasti ecclesiae anglicanae, 1541–1857. [London], Univ. of London, Inst. of Historical Research; Athlone Pr., 1974–75. v.3–4. (In progress) **BB49**

For earlier volumes *see Guide* BB204.

Contents: v.3, Canterbury, Rochester and Winchester Dioceses, comp. by J. M. Horn; v.4, York Diocese, comp. by J. M. Horn and D. M. Smith.

Lutheran

Lutheran cyclopedia. Erwin L. Lueker, ed. Rev. ed. St. Louis, Concordia, [1975]. 845p. $24.95. **BB50**

1st ed. 1954.

The previous edition was prepared under the auspices of the General Literature Board of the Lutheran Church, and drew upon materials from an earlier (1927) *Concordia cyclopedia.* This edition does not mention official church sponsorship, but the cooperation of various affiliates is noted.

Offers brief articles on important aspects of the history, thought, and teachings of the Lutheran church and various related matters. For the revised edition, the number of entries has been substantially increased, various articles have been reworked, new bibliographic references supplied, and special efforts made "to improve objectivity."—*Pref.* Although biographies of persons of various denominations and periods are included, it is understandably strong for Lutherans; for the most part, living persons are omitted. BX8007.L8.

Mennonite

Springer, Nelson P. and **Klassen, A. J.** Mennonite bibliography, 1631–1961. Scottdale, Pa., Herald Pr., 1977. 2v. $118. **BB51**

Contents: v.1, International, Europe, Latin America, Asia, Africa; v.2, North America, Indices.

Comp. under the direction of the Institute of Mennonite Studies.

Serves as a continuation of Hans J. Hillerbrand's *Bibliography of Anabaptism, 1520–1630* (Elkhart, Ind., Inst. of Mennonite Studies, 1962). Aims "to report published materials of Mennonite authorship and statements about Mennonites by non-Mennonites. These include periodicals, books, pamphlets, dissertations, festschrifts, symposia, and encyclopedia and periodical articles."—*Pref.* Topical arrangement within geographical divisions; indexes of authors, subjects, and books reviewed. More than 28,000 items. Z7845.M4S67

Methodist

The encyclopedia of world Methodism. Nolan B. Harmon, gen. ed. Prep. and ed. under the supervision of The World Methodist Council and The Commission on Archives and History. [Nashville, Tenn.], United Methodist Publ. House, [1974]. 2v. (2814p.) il. $89.50. **BB52**

Aims "to give helpful information regarding the history, doctrines, institutions, and important personages, past and present, of World Methodism."—*Pref.* Inasmuch as expenses of the project were underwritten by the United Methodist Church in America, and because that "is the largest organized body among Methodist Churches of the world," a proportionately greater part of the work is devoted to that church. Articles are signed; many include bibliographies. Very strong in biography. BX8211.E5

Shaker

Richmond, Mary L. Hurt., comp. Shaker literature: a bibliography. Hancock, Mass., Shaker Community; distr. by University Pr. of New England, 1977. 2v. $45. **BB53**

Contents: v.1, By the Shakers; v.2, About the Shakers.

About 4,000 entries. Each volume in two main parts: (1) Books, pamphlets, broadsides; (2) Periodical articles; each part is arranged by author or other main entry. Index of titles and joint authors in v.2. Z7845.S5R52

Roman Catholic church

Religious orders

Cowan, Ian Borthwick and **Easson, David E.** Medieval religious houses, Scotland: with an appendix on the houses in the Isle of Man. 2d ed. London, Longman, [1976]. 246p. £13. **BB54**

1st ed. 1957 by D. E. Easson (*Guide* BB311a).

A revision and expansion, adding new information based on recent research. BX2597.E2

Dizionario degli istituti di perfezione, diretto da Guerrino Pelliccia e da Giancarlo Rocca. [Roma], Edizione Paoline, [1974–77]. v.1–4. (In progress) L38000 per v. **BB55**

To be in 6v.

Contents: v.1–4, A–Int.

Offers signed articles ranging from a paragraph to many pages on the history and structure of about 4,000 Catholic religious orders, societies, etc., of the past and present, on monasticism of the East and West, and on religious life and institutions other than Roman Catholic. Many biographical articles on founders of religious orders, and entries on related material such as terminology of religious life, monastic architecture, etc. All but the shortest essays have bibliographies. Contributors are identified and their credentials listed. Indexes are planned.

Molette, Charles. Guide des sources de l'histoire des congrégations féminines françaises de vie active. Paris, Éditions de Paris, 1974. 477p. 96F. pa. **BB56**

"Ouvrage publié avec le concours du Centre National de Recherche Scientifique."—*t.p.*

In two main sections: (1) Introduction historique; (2) Sources et bibliographie (pp.107–379). The latter part lists nearly 400 religious congregations alphabetically by name of the order and indicates address, founding date, etc., information on the order's archives, publications, and bibliographical references to writings about an order and its members. Indexes of names, of places, and of groups (societies, congregations, etc.).

Troeyer, Benjamin de, *O.F.M.*, and **Mees, Leonide,** *O.F.M.* Bio-bibliographia franciscana neerlandica ante saeculum XVI. Nieuwkoop, B. de Graaf, 1974. 3v. il. 450 fl. **BB57**

Contents: v.1, Pars biographica (Auctores editionum qui scripserunt ante saeculum XVI), by B. de Troeyer; v.2, Pars bibliographica (Incunabula), by L. Mees; v.3, Pars bibliographica (Illustrationes incunabulorum), by L. Mees.

Includes references to manuscripts, printed works, and writings about the authors. Library locations are given for the incunabula and the manuscripts. BX3640.A1T68

BUDDHISM

Bibliography

Beautrix, Pierre. Bibliographie du bouddhisme. Premier supplément. Bruxelles, Institut Belge des Hautes Études Bouddhiques, [1975]. 119*l.* (Institut Belge des Hautes Études Bouddhiques. Sér. bibliographies, 4) **BB58**

For main volume and annotation *see Guide* BB323.

836 additional entries, following the classed order of the basic volume. Author index.

Vessie, Patricia Armstrong. Zen Buddhism: a bibliography of books and articles in English, 1892–1975. [Ann Arbor, Mich.], University Microfilms International, 1976. 81*l.* $9.50. **BB59**

"Publ. under the aegis of the East Asia Library, University of Washington."—*t.p.*

Some 760 items in classed arrangement. Lacks an index. Z7864.Z4V47

Yoo, Yushin. Books on Buddhism: an annotated subject guide. Metuchen, N.J., Scarecrow Pr., 1976. 251p. $10. **BB60**

A classed listing of some 1,300 items, with author and title indexes. Z7860.Y64

Encyclopedias

Encyclopaedia of Buddhism, ed. by G. P. Malalasekera. Colombo, Govt. Pr., 1973. v.3[3]. (In progress) **BB61**

For earlier volumes and annotation *see Guide* BB330.

Contents: v.3[3], Buddha–Burlingame.

ISLAM

Bibliography

London. University. School of Oriental and African Studies. Library. Index Islamicus. 4th supplement, 1971–75. London, Mansell, 1977. 429p. **BB62**

For main volume and earlier supplements *see Guide* BB343.

Represents a cumulation of the five annual issues for the period, plus some additions noted after those parts were published. Beginning 1977, supplemented by:

The quarterly Index Islamicus. v.1, no.1– , Jan. 1977– . London, Mansell, 1977– . Quarterly. £12.50 per yr. (Also available on microfiche) **BB63**

J. D. Pearson, ed.

Subtitle: Current books, articles and papers on Islamic studies.

Now includes citations to books as well as to periodical articles.

Encyclopedias

Encyclopaedia of Islam. New ed. . . . Leiden, Brill; London, Luzac, 1975–78. v.4[6–9] (fasc.71/72–77/78). (In progress) **BB64**

For previously published parts and annotation *see Guide* BB346.

Contents: fasc.71/72–77/78, Kārimī–Khazz. (Fasc.77/78 completes the text of v.4; preliminary matter, plus addenda and corrigenda to v.1–4 will appear as fasc.78a.)

JUDAISM

Bibliography

Bibliographical essays in medieval Jewish studies. [N.Y.], Anti-Defamation League of B'nai B'rith, [1976]. 392p. (The study of Judaism, v.2) $17.50. **BB65**

Six bibliographic essays by specialists, addressed primarily to the non-specialist. Brief contents: The Jews in Western Europe; The church and the Jews; The Jews under Islam; Medieval Jewish religious philosophy; Medieval Jewish mysticism; Minor Midrashim.

For v.1 of the series *see Guide* BB380. Z6368.B53

Brickman, William W. The Jewish community in America; an annotated and classified bibliographical guide. N.Y., B. Franklin, [1977]. 396p. $19.95. **BB66**

Aims "to present to scholars, teachers, and other interested persons a descriptively and, in part, critically annotated collection of over 800 basic and specialized writings in English, Hebrew, Yiddish, Ladino, German, French, Hungarian, Polish, and Russian" which "throw light on the Jewish experience in America from the Colonial period to the present."—*Pref.* Classified arrangement with main entry index. Appendix of reprints of documents and relevant articles. Z6373.U5B75

Brisman, Shimeon. A history and guide to Judaic bibliography. Cincinnati, Hebrew Union College Pr.; N.Y., Ktav Publ. House, 1977. 325p. (*His* Jewish research literature, v.1; Bibliographica Judaica, 7) $25. **BB67**

Concerned only with works devoted wholly to Jewish bibliography. In eight chapters: (1) General Hebraica bibliographies; (2) Catalogs of Hebraica book collections; (3) Bio-bibliographical works; (4) Subject bibliographies of Hebraica literature; (5) Judaica bibliographies; (6) Bibliographical periodicals; (7) Index to Jewish periodicals and monographs; (8) Miscellaneous Jewish bibliographical works. Indexed. Z6366.B8

Fluk, Louise R. Jews in the Soviet Union. N.Y., Amer-Jewish Committee, [1975]. 44p. $1.50 pa. **BB68**

Lists "significant and accessible" writings on Soviet Jewry appearing in English between Jan. 1967 and Sept. 1974. Z6373.R9F58

Shunami, Shlomo. Bibliography of Jewish bibliographies. Suppl. to 2d ed. enl. Jerusalem, Magnes Pr., 1975. 464p., 16p. **BB69**

Added title page in Hebrew.

For basic volume *see Guide* BB379.

About 2,000 entries, mainly publications from the 10-year period following appearance of the main volume.

Singerman, Robert. The Jews in Spain and Portugal: a bibliography. N.Y., Garland, 1975. 364p. $33. **BB70**

Lists "published materials pertaining to the Jewish presence in Spain and Portugal from antiquity to the present day" (*Introd.*), with emphasis on Jewish history and culture. More than 5,000 entries in classified arrangement. Z6373.S7S55

Dictionaries and encyclopedias

Birnbaum, Philip. A book of Jewish concepts. Rev. ed. N.Y., Hebrew Pub. Co., [1975]. 722p. $8.50. **BB71**

1st ed. 1964.

Aims "to provide in a single handy volume the essential teachings of Judaism."—*Introd.* Articles range in length from a brief paragraph to two or more pages. Arrangement is alphabetical according to the Hebrew form of the term, with an English translation or transliteration provided for each term; Hebrew and English indexes. Intended for rabbis, teachers, students and laymen. BM50.B55

Encyclopedia Talmudica; a digest of halachic literature and Jewish law from the Tannaitic period to the present time. . . . Jerusalem, Talmudic Encyclopedia Inst., [1974]. v.2. (In progress) **BB72**

For v.1, full citation and annotation *see Guide* BB389.

Contents: v.2, 'Eyn Gozrin–'Erez ha'Amin.

Everyman's Judaica: an encyclopedic dictionary. Ed. by Geoffrey Wigoder. Jerusalem, Keter Publ. House; London, W. H. Allen, [1975]. 673p. il. £12. **BB73**

Intended as a complement to the multi-volume *Encyclopedia Judaica* (*Guide* BB387); i.e., "designed as a handy reference work giving basic facts and figures."—*Introd.* Very brief entries. Numerous charts and tables; profusely illustrated. Strong in biographical entries. DS102.8E68

The new standard Jewish encyclopedia. New rev. ed., ed. by Geoffrey Wigoder. 5th ed. Garden City, N.Y., Doubleday, 1977. 2028col. il. $29.95. **BB74**

4th ed. 1970 by Cecil Roth and Geoffrey Wigoder; prior to 1970 published under title *The standard Jewish encyclopedia* (1st ed. 1959; *see Guide* BB394).

An updating of this concise encyclopedia. DS102.8.S73

Yearbooks

Encyclopaedia Judaica. Yearbook. 1973– . Jerusalem, Encyclopaedia Judaica, [1973]– . il. Frequency varies. **BB75**

1973 volume covers events of 1972, etc. Recent volumes cover two years.

In each volume a section of feature articles is followed by an alphabetically arranged section of "New facts, new entries," which offers supplementary information on matters treated in the basic work, as well as wholly new entries. The feature articles are lengthy essays by specialists on a wide range of topics, many of which are of special interest at time of publication. Indexed. DS102.8E498

B C

Linguistics and Philology

INTERNATIONAL

Bibliography

Abrahamsen, Adele A. Child language; an interdisciplinary guide to theory and research. Baltimore, University Park Pr., [1977]. 381p. $12.50. **BC1**

A topically arranged, annotated bibliography of about 1,500 items. Author and subject indexes. Z7004.C45A27

Center for Applied Linguistics. Library. Dictionary catalog of the Library of the Center for Applied Linguistics, Washington, D.C. Boston, G. K. Hall, 1974. 4v. $265. **BC2**

Reproduces the catalog cards for the Center's collection. The library maintains "a predominantly contemporary acquisitions policy with only limited retrospective purchase and limited systematic book selection."—*Introd.* Z7004.A6S46

Gazdar, Gerald, Klein, Ewan and **Pullum, Geoffrey K.** A bibliography of contemporary linguistic research. N.Y., Garland, 1978. 425p. (Garland reference library of the humanities, 119) $38. **BC3**

An author list of some 5,000 recent (i.e., 1970 and later) articles and short notes drawn from scholarly journals, conference proceedings, specialist anthologies and litho-printed books, chiefly on the central topics of linguistics: syntactic, semantic, philological and pragmatic theory. Language and subject indexes. Z7001.G38

Girke, Wolfgang, Jachnow, Helmut and **Schrenk, Josef.** Handbibliographie zur neueren Linguistik in Osteuropa. München, Wilhelm Fink Verlag, [1974]– . Bd.1– . (In progress) **BC4**

Contents: Bd.1, 1963–1965. DM240.

Table of contents and section headings in German, English, and Russian.

Nearly 6,000 items in Bd.1, mainly in the East European languages. Classed arrangement with author index. Z7001.G57

Malinskaia, B. A. and **Shabat, M. TS.** Obshchee i prikladnoe iazykoznanie. Ukaz. literatury, izd. v SSSR s 1963 po 1967 g. Moskva, "Nauka," 1972. 295p. 1.82r. **BC5**

At head of title: Akademiia Nauk SSSR. Institut Nauchnoi Informatsii i Fundamental'naia Biblioteka po Obshchestvennym Naukam.

Serves as a supplement to both the *Obshchee iazykoznanie* (1965; *Guide* BC1) and *Strukturnoe i prikladnoe iazykoznanie bibliograficheskii ukazatel' literatury* (1965; *Guide* BC4). Z7001.M33

Schaller, Helmut Wilhelm. Bibliographie zur Balkanphilologie. Heidelberg, Winter, 1977. 109p. **BC6**

A topically arranged bibliography with author and subject indexes. In addition to general studies of the Balkans as a linguistic area, includes materials on Bulgarian, Macedonian, Serbo-Croatian, Albanian, Romanian, and Modern Greek. About 1,500 items. Z2845.A2S32

Wellisch, Hans (Hanan). Transcription and transliteration; an annotated bibliography on conversion of scripts. Silver Springs, Md., Inst. of Modern Languages, [1975]. 133p. $5.95 pa. **BC7**

Arrangement follows that of the *Bibliographie linguistique* (*Guide* BC16); i.e., by language group, subdivided according to specific language. Author/title and subject indexes. Z7004.T73W44

Current

Bibliographie unselbständiger Literatur-Linguistik (BUL-L). Bearb. von Elke Suchan. Frankfurt am Main, V. Klostermann, [1976–]. Bd. 1– , 1971/75– . (Bd.1: DM240) **BC8**

Published for the Sondersammelgebiet Linguistik of the Stadt- und Universitätsbibliothek, Frankfurt am Main.

A classed bibliography of periodical articles and essays in collective works, proceedings of congresses, etc. Arrangement is by language, with detailed subject breakdown within each language section. Author and subject indexes. Concerned with Western languages only.

The 1971/75 volume lists some 13,000 entries for items drawn from 123 frequently cited journals, plus references to collective works, congress proceedings, etc. A single volume covering 1976 publications was issued 1977; thereafter the bibliography is to appear quarterly with a cumulative annual index; 5-year cumulations are also planned.

Year's work in modern language studies ... 1929/30– . London, 1931– . v.1– . Annual. **BC9**

For full information *see Guide* BC21.

With v.35 (1974) a new section, "General linguistics," is introduced at the beginning of the volume.

Language-teaching

Goldstein, Wallace L., comp. Teaching English as a second language: an annotated bibliography. N.Y., Garland, 1975. 218p. $21. **BC10**

A classed listing of 852 items, with descriptive annotations. Works are grouped under such headings as: Curriculum, Grammar, Reading, Spoken English, Teaching aids, Testing and evaluation, Texts, Writing. Key-word index and author index. Z5818.E5G64

Language teaching & linguistics: abstracts. v.8, no.1– , Jan. 1975– . London, Cambridge Univ. Pr., 1975– . 4 issues per yr. £6. **BC11**

Constitutes a change of title for *Language-teaching abstracts* (*Guide* BC23) and assumes the volume numbering of that publication. "The inclusion of *Linguistics* in the new title indicates recognition of the importance of certain areas of this field to language teaching. The journal will continue to provide objective summaries in English of selected articles taken from nearly 400 journals."—*v. 8, no. 1.*

Manuals

Allen, Charles Geoffry. A manual of European languages for librarians. [2 impression (with minor corrections)] London & N.Y., Bowker in assoc. with the London School of Economics, [1977]. 803p. £25. **BC12**

1st impression 1975.

Intended as an aid to those librarians who, "even without the necessary expert knowledge . . . must accept and deal with books" (*Introd.*) in a variety of foreign languages. Includes sections for (1) Germanic languages, (2) Latin and the Romance languages, (3) Celtic, Greek and Albanian languages, (4) Slavonic languages, (5) Baltic languages, (6) Finno-Ugrian languages, and (7) Other languages. Includes transliteration of non-Roman alphabets. P380.A4

Voegelin, Charles Frederick and **Voegelin, Florence M.** Classification and index of the world's languages. N.Y., Elsevier, [1977]. 658p. $39.50. **BC13**

"This volume is based in part upon our earlier survey of the literature, *Languages of the world,* published as twenty separate numbers of the journal *Anthropological Linguistics* (1964–66)."—*Acknowledgments.*

Arranged alphabetically by name of groups of related languages. Following a brief discussion of the language group there is a listing of generic units of the group. Bibliographic references are included in the discussions; list of references, pp. 359–83. Index of all names of groups, subgroups, languages, dialects, tribes and their alternate names which appear in the articles. P203.V6

Dictionaries and handbooks

Handbuch der Linguistik; allgemeine und angewandte Sprachwissenschaft. [München], Nymphenburger Verlagshandlung, [1975]. 584p. DM110. **BC14**

"Aus Beiträgen von Hans Arens [et al.] . . . unter Mitarbeit von Hildegard Janssen zusammengestellt von Harro Stammerjohann."—*t.p.*

Employs a dictionary arrangement and provides definitions and discussion of linguistic terms, some of the entries running to several pages and including extensive bibliographies. There is an index of names of persons mentioned in the articles and those cited in the bibliographies. P29.H33

Welte, Werner. Moderne Linguistik: Terminologie/Bibliographie. Ein Handbuch und Nachschlagewerk auf der Basis der generativ-transformationellen Sprachtheorie. [München], Max Hueber Verlag, [1974]. 2v. DM39. **BC15**

Terms are defined, with references to original and later usage. Bibliographical citations follow each entry. Arrangement is according to the German form of the term, with English and French equivalents given whenever there are corresponding terms in those languages. P29.W38

ENGLISH

Alston, Robin Carfrae. A bibliography of the English language from the invention of printing to the year 1800. A corrected reprint of volumes I–X. Ilkley, Eng., Janus Pr., 1974. lv., various pagings. £40. **BC16**

"Reproduced from the author's annotated copy with corrections and additions to 1973. Including cumulative indices."—*t.p.*

For original set and annotation *see Guide* BC47.

Scottish

Mather, J. Y. and **Speitel, H. H.** The linguistic atlas of Scotland: Scots section. Cartography by G. W. Leslie. Hamden, Conn., Archon Books, [1975–77]. 2v. maps. 28cm. $120. **BC17**

Published in London by Croom Helm.

Based on the archives of the Scots section of the Linguistic Survey of Scotland in the Faculty of Arts at the University of Edinburgh. v.2 includes an index to the 2v. set. A Gaelic section is also planned. PE2102.M3

OTHER GERMANIC LANGUAGES

Hannich-Bode, Ingrid. Germanistik in Festschriften von den Anfängen (1877) bis 1973. Verzeichnis germanistischer Festschriften und Bibliographie der darin abgedruckten germanistischen Beiträge. Stuttgart, Metzler, [1976]. 441p. (Repertorien zur deutschen Literaturgeschichte, Bd.7; London. Univ. Inst. of Germanic Studies. Publs., v.23) DM190. **BC18**

Lists and analyzes about 800 volumes of *Festschriften.* The analytical section is in nine main divisions, each with numerous subsections: (1) Allgemeines; (2) Allgemeine Sprachwissenschaft; (3) Germanische Sprachen; (4) Deutsche Sprache; (5) Allgemeine und deutsche Literaturwissenschaft; (6) Germanische Dichtung und Kultur; (7) Deutsche Literatur in einzelnen Zeitabschnitten; (8) Weltliteratur und vergleichende Literatur; (9) Nachbarwissenschaft. Indexes by author, title, broad subject, and personal names as subjects.

Scandinavian

Haugen, Einar. A bibliography of Scandinavian languages and linguistics, 1900–1970. Oslo, Universitetsforlaget, [1974]. 527p. n.kr.100. **BC19**

Aims to present "a selection of articles, brochures, monographs, books, and series relating to the scientific and practical study of the Scandinavian languages" (*Pref.*), including "all the standard and non-standard forms of Danish, Faroese, Icelandic, Norwegian, and Swedish, as well as older attested and unattested forms of these." The body of the work is an alphabetical author listing. Each entry is followed by a set of "descriptors," i.e., letters and numerals used to indicate the language or languages dealt with and the type of subject matter (grammar, syntax, language teaching, etc.). The index follows the numerical/alphabetical sequence of the descriptors. Z2555.H38

Jacobsen, Henrik Galberg. Dansk sprogrøgtslitteratur 1900–1955. København, [Gyldendal], 1974. 222p. (Dansk Sprognaevns skrifter, 7) Kr. 32.80 pa. **BC20**

A bibliography of writings appearing in periodicals, collective volumes, and *Festschriften* on Danish language and linguistics. Chronological listing with author and subject indexes. Z2575.A2J3

ROMANCE LANGUAGES

French

Bassan, Fernande, Breed, Paul F., and **Spinelli, Donald C.** An annotated bibliography of French language and literature. N.Y., Garland, 1976. 306p. $25. **BC21**

Intended as a guide for the student, the scholar, and the librarian, although emphasis is on general materials rather than scholarly studies. In three main sections: (1) General bibliographies and reference works; (2) General studies on the French language; and (3) Bibliographies and studies of literature. Items in the first section are annotated in some detail; most items in the other sections are not annotated. Nearly 1,600 entries; author/title index. Z2175.A2B38

Griffin, Lloyd W., Clarke, Jack A. and **Kroff, Alexander Y.** Modern French literature and language; a bibliography of homage studies. [Madison], Univ. of Wisconsin Pr., [1976]. 175p. $15. **BC22**

For annotation *see Suppl.* BD139.

Latin

McGuire, Martin Rawson Patrick and **Dressler, Hermigild.** Introduction to medieval Latin studies: a syllabus and bibliographical guide. 2d ed. Wash., D.C., Catholic Univ. of Amer. Pr., 1977. 406p. $16.95 pa. **BC23**

1st ed. 1964.

Aims "to give the beginning graduate student a comprehensive, solid, and up-to-date orientation" (*Pref.*) in the field. "The *Syllabus* and *Select Bibliography* are broader in scope than their titles might indicate, for they include references to, or even initial orientation in, a number of other disciplines—e.g., Classical, Patristic, Celtic, Germanic, Romance, Byzantine and Islamic Studies—insofar as these disciplines have connections with Medieval Latin Studies." Syllabus, with suggested readings, pp.1–241; Select bibliographies, pp.245–379. Indexed. PA2816.M24

GREEK

Deltion vivliographias tēs Hellēnikēs glōssēs. Bibliographical bulletin of the Greek language. 1973– . Athens, 1974– . v.1– . Annual. **BC24**

At head of title: Spoudastērion Glōssologias tou Panepistēmiou Athēnōn.

George Babiniotis, ed.

Introductory and explanatory matter in English and Greek.

Each issue is an international, classified listing (with author index) of the year's publications on "the entire Greek language (Ancient, Byzantine, Modern)."—*Pref.* Z7021.D44

SEMITIC

Bakalla, M. H. Bibliography of Arabic linguistics. [London], Mansell, 1975. 300p. £13.95. **BC25**

Introductory matter in Arabic and English.

Aims "to provide for all students of Arabic a simple but fairly comprehensive book of reference" (*Introd.*) listing books, periodical articles, and dissertations on Arabic linguistics. Separate "occidental" and "oriental" sections; listing is by author within each section. Indexes of subjects, editors, reviewers, etc. Some brief annotations. Z7052.B35

A basic bibliography for the study of Semitic languages. J. H. Hospers, ed. Leiden, Brill, 1974. v.2 (108p.). **BC26**

For v.1 *see Guide* BC120.

This volume brings together "the bibliographic material in the fields of the study of Pre-Classical, Classical and Modern Literary Arabic . . . and the Modern Arabic Dialects."—*Pref.* No index. Z7049.S5B35

B D

Literature

GENERAL WORKS

Guides

Patterson, Margaret C. Literary research guide. Detroit, Gale, [1976]. 385p. $18.50. **BD1**

Subtitle: An evaluative, annotated bibliography of important reference books and periodicals on American and English literature, of the most useful sources for research in other national literatures, and of more than 300 reference books in literature-related subject areas.

Includes sections on bibliographies of bibliographies; annual and other current bibliographies; abstracting and indexing services; English, Irish, Scottish, Welsh, Commonwealth, and American literatures; continental, comparative, and world literatures; and reference works. Most entries are annotated, many at some length. Glossary of bibliographical terms; index of authors, titles, and subjects. Z6511.P37

Bibliography

Pownall, David E. Articles on twentieth century literature: an annotated bibliography, 1954 to 1970. N.Y., Kraus-Thomson, 1974–76. v.4–5. (In progress) **BD2**

For previously published volumes and annotation *see Guide* BD15a.

Contents: v.4–5, Authors: Jabès-Pynchon.

Schwartz, Narda Lacey. Articles on women writers: a bibliography. Santa Barbara, Calif., ABC-Clio, [1977]. 236p. **BD3**

A listing of English-language articles published 1960–75 on some 600 women writers. Citations were derived from bibliographies published in about twenty journals and indexing services from the years covered. Arranged by writer's name, with index of writers and of authors of the articles. Z2013.5.W6S37

Women and literature: an annotated bibliography of women writers. 3d ed. [Cambridge, Mass.], Women and Literature Collective, [1976]. 212p. $3.50 pa. **BD4**

Ed. by Iris Biblowitz and others.

Previous ed., 1973, issued by the Sense and Sensibility Collective.

Focus is on fiction and "other forms of expressive prose" (*Introd.*) by women writers. Sections for American, British, and international (subdivided by country) writings, anthologies, and works about literature. Author and subject indexes. Z5917.W6S46

Indexes

Chicorel index series. N.Y., Chicorel Library Pub. Corp., [1970–]. v.1– . (In progress) **BD5**

For v.1–10 and a note on the series *see Guide* BD166. Additional volumes noted here expand the series well beyond the field of literature and drama.

Contents: v.11–11A, Chicorel index to abstracting and indexing services: periodicals in humanities and the social sciences (1974); v.12–12A, Chicorel index to short stories in anthologies and collections (1974, with annual supplements beginning 1977); v.13–13C,

Chicorel index to the crafts (1974); v.14, Chicorel index to reading disabilities (1974); v.14A, Chicorel index to reading and learning disabilities (1976); v.15–15A, Chicorel index to biographies (1974); v.16–16A, Chicorel index to environment and ecology (1975); v.17–17A, Chicorel index to urban planning and environmental design (1975); v.18–18A, Chicorel index to learning disorders: books (1975); v.19, Chicorel abstracts to reading and learning disabilities (annual beginning 1976); v.20–20A, Chicorel index to poetry and poets (1976); v.21, Chicorel theater index to drama literature (1975); v.22–22A, Chicorel index to film literature (1975); v.23–23B, Chicorel index to literary criticism; v.24, Chicorel index to parapsychology and occult books (1977); v.26, Chicorel index to video tapes and cassettes (1978); v.27, Chicorel index to mental health book reviews (1978).

Research methods

Thorpe, James Ernest. The use of manuscripts in literary research. N.Y., Modern Language Assoc. of America, 1974. 40p. $1.50 pa. **BD6**

A guide written from the scholar's point of view. Includes information on locating manuscripts, obtaining access to collections, permissions to photocopy and publish, and literary property rights. Z692.M28T47

Criticism

Contemporary literary criticism; excerpts from criticism of the works of today's novelists, poets, playwrights, and other creative writers. Detroit, Gale, [1975–78]. v.3–8. (In progress) **BD7**

For previously published volumes and annotation *see Guide* BD29.

Editors vary.

Each volume now lists "about 175 authors, with an average of about five excerpts from critical articles or reviews being given for the works of each author."—*Pref., v.8.* A "Cumulative index to critics" appears in each volume.

Modern black writers. Comp. and ed. by Michael Popkin. N.Y., F. Ungar, [1978]. 519p. (A library of literary criticism) $25. **BD8**

Like other volumes in the series (e.g., *Guide* BD419; *Suppl.* BD143), this is a compilation of excerpts from critical appraisals (originally published in books or periodicals) of the writers included. "The eighty writers discussed in this volume are all noted primarily for their work in either fiction, poetry, or drama."—*Introd.* Authors from some 23 countries (writing in English, French, and several African languages) are included. Index of critics, and a list of literary works mentioned. PN841.M58

Dictionaries and encyclopedias

Beckson, Karl and **Ganz, Arthur**. Literary terms; a dictionary. N.Y., Farrar, Straus and Giroux, [1975]. 280p. $10. **BD9**

A revised and enlarged edition of the same authors' *Reader's guide to literary terms* (1960; *Guide* BD31). PN44.5.B334

Cuddon, John A. A dictionary of literary terms. Garden City, N.Y., Doubleday, 1977. 745p. $17.95. **BD10**

Aims "to provide a serviceable and fairly comprehensive dictionary of those literary terms which are in regular use in the world today; terms in which intelligent people may be expected to have some interest and about which they may wish to find out something more."—*Pref.* Numerous *see* and *see also* references. PN41.C83

Elkhadem, Saad. The York dictionary of English-French-German-Spanish literary terms and their origin. Fredericton, N.B., Canada, York Pr., [1976]. 154p. $6.95. **BD11**

The main section is an English-language dictionary of terms with equivalents in the other languages and a definition in English. Indexes from the other languages. PN41.E4

Encyclopedia of world literature in the 20th century. v.4, Supplement and index, ed. by Frederick Ungar and Lina Mainiero. N.Y., Ungar, [1975]. 462p. il. **BD12**

For v.1–3, ed. by W. Fleischmann, *see Guide* BD40.

The supplement is largely made up of biographical-critical sketches of figures (from various decades of the 20th century, not merely newly established writers) not appearing in v.1–3, but also includes some new topical entries. Index to v.1–4, pp.412–62. PN774.L433

Fowler, Roger. A dictionary of modern critical terms. London, Routledge & Kegan Paul, [1973]. 208p. $10.75. **BD13**

Not a dictionary in the sense of providing brief working definitions of literary terms, this work aims "to stimulate curiosity about how literary terms work actively for us, rather than to satisfy a utilitarian desire to gain access to their traditional meanings."—*Pref.* Most entries run to a page or more, are signed with contributor's initials, and often include bibliographic references. PN41.F6

Digests

Magill's Literary annual. 1977– . Englewood Cliffs, N.J., Salem Pr., 1978– . Annual. **BD14**

1977 ed. in 2v.

Frank N. Magill, ed.

"In a sense, the new series is a continuation of the MASTERPLOTS Annuals [*see Guide* BD57]—begun in 1954 and concluded with the 1976 volume, now all collected in SURVEY OF CONTEMPORARY LITERATURE (1977) [12v.; $275]."—*Pref. 1977.*

Directories

Harmon, Gary L. and **Harmon, Susanna M.** Scholar's market: an international directory of periodicals publishing literary scholarship. Columbus, Publications Committee, Ohio State University Libraries, 1974. 703p. $14.50. **BD15**

A directory and guide for the literary scholar wishing to place a manuscript for publication in a periodical. Publications are grouped according to field of interest: e.g., periodicals devoted to a single author or group of writers, those concentrating on literature of a single country or period, those concerned with a specific literary genre, etc. Includes sections for American ethnic minorities, folklore, and film. For each periodical usually gives editorial and subscription addresses, frequency, price, circulation, notes on content, and information about submitting manuscripts (whether unsolicited manuscripts are welcomed, style requirements, length, copyright, payments, etc.). Concerned only with periodicals which publish wholly or partly in English. Indexed.

Literary awards

Literary and journalistic awards in Canada. Les prix de littérature et de journalisme au Canada. 1923–1973. Ottawa, Statistics Canada, Education, Science and Culture Div., Fine Arts and Media Section, 1976. 276p. $3.50 pa. **BD16**

"Published by authority of the Minister of Industry, Trade and Commerce."—*t.p.*

Each award is described and a list of recipients is given in chronological order. Literary and journalistic awards are listed separately, each group arranged by type of award. Alphabetical lists of the awards and of names of recipients serve as indexes.

Biographies of authors

Author biographies master index. Ed. by Dennis La Beau. Detroit, Gale, [1978]. 2v. (Gale biographical index ser., no.3) $65. **BD17**

Subtitle: A consolidated guide to biographical information concerning authors living and dead as it appears in a selection of the principal biographical dictionaries devoted to authors, poets, journalists, and other literary figures.

An index to some 413,000 entries in more than 140 biographical dictionaries and directories of writers. Much of the information in the *Children's authors and illustrators* volume of the same series is duplicated here. Z5304.A8A88

Children's authors and illustrators: an index to biographical dictionaries. Detroit, Gale, [1976]. 172p. (Gale biographical index ser., 2) $15. **BD18**

Provides an index to biographical sketches contained in 26 collections; with the exception of *Contemporary authors,* all of the publications indexed are wholly concerned with children's authors and illustrators. Employs many of the same sources indexed in *Author biographies master index* (*Suppl.* BD17). Z1037.A1C463

Havlice, Patricia Pate. Index to literary biography. Metuchen, N.J., Scarecrow Pr., 1975. 2v. $39.50. **BD19**

An index to biographical information on some 68,000 authors appearing in fifty volumes of collective biography and dictionaries of literature. Z6511.H38

Wakeman, John, ed. World authors, 1950–1970; a companion to Twentieth century authors. N.Y., Wilson, 1975. 1594p. il. $60. **BD20**

A "companion" rather than a second "supplement" to *Twentieth century authors* (*Guide* BD89) since it neither duplicates nor updates the biographical articles in that earlier work and its first supplement. Deals with 959 authors of literary importance or unusual popularity, "most of whom came to prominence between 1950 and 1970," but including "a number of writers whose reputations were made earlier, but who were absent from the previous volumes because of a lack of biographical information, or because their work was not then 'familiar to readers of English.' "—*Pref.*

As in the companion volumes, many of the authors provided autobiographical sketches; critical comment is generally fuller than in those earlier works. Bibliographies again list principal works and a selection of writings about each author. Articles are unsigned, but a list of contributors is supplied. PN451.W3

Quotations

Great treasury of Western thought; a compendium of important statements on man and his institutions by the great thinkers in Western history. Ed. by Mortimer J. Adler and Charles Van Doren. N.Y., Bowker, 1977. 1771p. $29.95. **BD21**

A collection of quotations selected on the principle that each passage quoted should be "a seminal statement about one of the great ideas in the tradition of Western thought."—*Pref.* Quotations are often long ones, the average length being about 100 words. Functions as a companion to the *Syntopicon* volumes of the *Great books of the Western world* series (*Guide* BD25). Arranged in twenty chapters (Man, Family, Love, Emotion, Mind, Knowledge, etc.) with introductory notes for each chapter and subsection. Overall subject and proper name index. PN6331.G675

Partnow, Elaine, comp. and ed. The quotable woman, 1800–1975. Los Angeles, Corwin Books, [1977]. 539p. $15. **BD22**

A book of quotations by women. Contributors were chosen on the basis of "reputation, remarkability, quotability, and availability of their work" (*Pref.*), with an attempt to be as representative of as many professions and countries as possible; "usability" was one of the principal criteria for selecting the quotations. Arrangement is chronological by birth date of the women quoted, then alphabetically within each year. Rather than keyword indexing, a "subject index" is provided which attempts "to synthesize the meaning of each quotation into one or more classifications." Occupying only pages 507–39 of the volume, this index makes for a great deal of trial and error in locating a specific remembered (or half-remembered) quotation.

What they said. 1969– . [Beverly Hills, Calif.], Monitor Book Co., 1970– . Annual. (1976: $19.50) **BD23**

Subtitle: The yearbook of spoken opinion.

Presents the statements, ideas, and opinions of persons prominent in the news during the year in question. Quotations are grouped in subject categories within three main sections: (1) National affairs; (2) International affairs; and (3) General. Indexes of speakers and of detailed subjects. For each quotation the speaker is briefly identified, the circumstances of the quotation are indicated, and (with a few exceptions) reference is given to published appearance of the statement in the newspaper or periodical press of the nation. D410.W46

Proverbs

Whiting, Bartlett Jere. Early American proverbs and proverbial phrases. Cambridge, Mass., Belknap Pr. of Harvard Univ. Pr., 1977. 555p. $20. **BD24**

Serves as a chronological predecessor to Taylor and Whiting's *Dictionary of American proverbs and proverbial phrases* (*Guide* BD156), covering the first decades of the 17th century to 1820. Although entries are derived from American sources, the compiler points out that prior to 1820, American proverbs were basically English and he states that "It is not to oversimplify to say that the contents of this book are English proverbs used by writers who happened to be in North America at the time."—*Introd.* Method of entry follows that of the Taylor/Whiting volume. Examples are drawn from the long list of works cited pp.xxiii–lxiv. PE2839.W5

Drama

Bibliography

Drury, Francis Keese Wynkoop. Drury's Guide to best plays. 3d ed. by James M. Salem. Metuchen, N.J., Scarecrow Pr., 1978. 421p. $16. **BD25**

2d ed. 1969 (*Guide* BD160).

A revised, updated, and expanded edition employing a smaller type size to permit more entries per page. In the author listing cross references have been added for joint authors, translators, authors of literary works entered under name of the person responsible for the dramatization, etc. Z5781.D8

Palmer, Helen H. European drama criticism, 1900–1975. 2d ed. Hamden, Conn., Shoe String Pr., 1977. 653p. $25. **BD26**

1st ed. (1968) and its supplements 1–2 (1970–74) by H. H. Palmer and A. J. Dyson (*Guide* BD182).

Cumulates the entries from the earlier edition and its supplements, and adds new material through 1975. Z5781.P2

Indexes

See also Suppl. BD5.

Kreider, Barbara. Index to children's plays in collections. 2d ed. Metuchen, N.J., Scarecrow Pr., 1977. 227p. $9.50. **BD27**

1st ed. 1972.

Indexes 1,450 plays appearing in collections published 1965–74. Indexing is by author, title, and subject in a dictionary arrangement. Cast analysis tables, pp.181–220. PN1627.K7

Ottemiller, John Henry. Ottemiller's Index to plays in collections: an author and title index to plays appearing in collections published between 1900 and early 1975. 6th ed., rev. and enl. by John M. Connor and Billie M. Connor. Metuchen, N.J., Scarecrow Pr., 1976. 523p. $17.50. **BD28**

5th ed. 1971 (*Guide* BD175).

190 collections added for this edition. The work now indexes 3,686 different plays in 1,237 collections. Z5781.O8

Fiction

Bibliography

Gardner, Frank M., comp. Sequels. [6th ed.] [Harrogate], Assoc. of Asst. Librarians, 1974– . v.1– . (In progress) **BD29**

Contents: v.1, Adult books. £9.

5th ed. 1967 (*Guide* BD193).

About 5,000 new adult titles have been added.

Negley, Glenn. Utopian literature; a bibliography, with a supplementary listing of works influential in Utopian thought. Lawrence, Regents Pr. of Kansas, [1977]. 228p. $15. **BD30**

An author listing of 1,232 items of Utopian literature, with indication of locations in eleven libraries in the United States, Great Britain and France (plus a few other locations for particularly rare items). The supplementary section of "influential works" lists and locates about 375 additional items. Short-title and chronological indexes. Z7164.U8N43

Walker, Warren S. Twentieth-century short story explication: interpretations 1900–1975, of short fiction since 1800. 3d ed. Hamden, Conn., Shoe String Pr., 1977. 880p. $25. **BD31**

Supersedes the 2d ed. (1967; *Guide* BD202) and its two supplements, extending the period of coverage through 1975. Now includes explications of writings by more than 850 authors, using an arrangement similar to that of the *Essay and general literature index.* Z5917.S5W33

Wilson, H. W., *firm, publishers.* Fiction catalog. 9th ed. Ed. by Estelle A. Fidell. N.Y., Wilson, 1976. 797p. $45. **BD32**

For 8th ed. and annotation *see Guide* BD200.

"This edition includes 4,734 titles selected with the assistance of staffs of a variety of public library systems . . . . Analytical entries for novelettes and composite works further enhance the value of the Catalog by insuring maximum use of a library's collections. These entries total 2,069."—*Pref.* Annual supplements. Z5916.W74

Indexes

See also Suppl. BD5.

Cook, Dorothy Elizabeth and **Monro, Isabel Stevenson.** Short story index. Supplement, 1969–1973. Ed. by Estelle A. Fidell. N.Y., Wilson, 1974. 639p. $30. **BD33**

For basic volume and earlier supplements *see Guide* BD204.

"An index to 11,561 stories in 805 collections."—*t.p.*

Cumulated fiction index, 1970–1974. Comp. by Raymond Ferguson Smith and Antony John Gordon. London, Assoc. of Asst. Librarians, 1975. 192p. £8. **BD34**

Continues the listings in the two previous volumes covering 1945/60 (entitled *Fiction index; see Guide* BD205) and 1960/69.

Ireland, Norma Olin. Index to fairy tales, 1949–1972, including folklore, legends & myths, in collections. Westwood, Mass., Faxon, 1973. 741p. (Useful reference ser., 101) $18. **BD35**

Forms a third supplement to M. H. Eastman's *Index to fairy tales* (*Guide* BD206). Indexes some 406 collections. Z5893.F17I73

Handbooks

Fisher, Margery Turner. Who's who in children's books: a treasury of familiar characters of childhood. N.Y., Holt, Rinehart and Winston, [1975]. 399p. il. $22.95. **BD36**

An avowedly personal selection of memorable characters from children's literature, "not intended primarily as a reference book."—*Pref.* Includes "as many as possible of the characters who have now become household names, together with others less familiar" whom the compiler found particularly interesting. Entries usually run to half a column or more in length, placing the character in setting and circumstances of the story, with comment on the author's technique or approach to the character. PN1009.A1F575

Freeman, William. Dictionary of fictional characters. Rev. by Fred Urquhart, with indexes of authors and titles by E. N. Pennell. Boston, The Writer, [1974]. 579p. $10. **BD37**

Published in Great Britain by J. M. Dent, 1973.

Original ed. 1963–67 (*Guide* BD69).

The revised edition adds some "1,614 new references. These references give the names and details of over 2,000 characters taken from some 360 novels and plays." Characters in many novels of the late Victorians (now little read) have been eliminated in favor of characters from works of modern authors. The author and title indexes are now bound with the dictionary itself. PR19.F7

Poetry

Indexes

See also Suppl. BD5.

Granger, Edith. Granger's Index to poetry, 1970–1977. Ed. by William James Smith. N.Y., Columbia Univ. Pr., 1978. 635p. $59.50. **BD38**

"This volume takes the place of the usual 5-year supplement to Granger's index [6th ed., 1973; *Guide* BD227]."—*verso of t.p.*

Indexes about 25,000 poems in 120 anthologies. A new feature is the designation of works recommended for priority acquisition. PN1022.G7

Index to poetry for children and young people, 1970–1975. Comp. by John E. Brewton, G. Meredith Blackburn and Lorraine A. Blackburn. N.Y., Wilson, 1978. 472p. $20. **BD39**

Subtitle: A title, subject, author, and first line index to poetry in collections for children and young people.

Forms a supplement to the 1964–69 *Index* (*Guide* BD224). Indexes "more than 10,000 poems by approximately 2,500 authors and translators" (*Introd.*) in 110 collections. PN1023.B722

Smith, Dorothy B. Frizzell and **Andrews, Eva L.** Subject index to poetry for children and young people, 1957–1975. Chicago, Amer. Lib. Assoc., 1977. 1035p. $30. **BD40**

A supplement to the 1957 edition of *Subject index to poetry for children and young people* (*Guide* BD221). Indexes 263 new anthologies, and introduces numerous new subject headings. PN1023.S6

Dictionaries

Morier, Henri. Dictionnaire de poétique et de rhétorique. [2. éd. augm. et entièrement refondue] Paris, Presses Universitaires, [1975]. 1210p. il. 350F. **BD41**

1st ed. 1961.

A dictionary of terms in modern poetry and rhetoric. Runs heavily to long, detailed articles, with numerous examples of use, and charts, diagrams, etc. to illustrate specific points. Particular attention is given to phonetics. PN1021.M6

Speech

Bibliography

Bibliographic annual in speech communication. 1970– . [Falls Church, Va.], Speech Communication Assoc., 1971– . $9 per yr., pa. **BD42**

Subtitle: An annual volume devoted to maintaining a record of graduate work in speech communication, providing abstracts of doctoral dissertations, and making available specialized bibliographies.

Continues the record previously provided by the annual "Graduate theses" lists published in *Speech monographs* (*see Guide* BD249).

Lists both master's theses and doctoral dissertations, provides abstracts of doctoral dissertations, and offers a number of specialized bibliographies in each issue. Dissertations in progress were listed only in the 1970 issue. Z5630.B48

Glenn, Robert W. Black rhetoric: a guide to Afro-American communication. Metuchen, N.J., Scarecrow Pr., 1976. 376p. $15. **BD43**

Intended as "a guide to available sources that would simplify the work of an instructor or a student interested in the content and communication of speeches and essays by Afro-Americans" (*Pref.*) from early to contemporary times. In four sections: (1) Bibliographies; (2) Anthologies; (3) History and criticism; (4) Speeches and essays. Z1361.N39G55

Indexes

Sutton, Roberta Briggs. Speech index . . . . 4th ed. Supplement, 1971–1975, by Charity Mitchell. Metuchen, N.J., Scarecrow Pr., 1977. 121p. $6. **BD44**

For 4th ed. and earlier supplement *see Guide* BD250.

Indexes speeches published in 33 anthologies from the 1971–75 period.

ENGLISH LANGUAGE

American

Guides

See also Suppl. BD1, BD82.

Gohdes, Clarence Louis Frank. Bibliographical guide to the study of the literature of the U.S.A. 4th ed., rev. and enl. Durham, N.C., Duke Univ. Pr., 1976. 173p. $8.50. **BD45**

3d ed. 1970 (*Guide* BD267).

More than 400 items have been added in the latest revision of this standard and very useful guide. Z1225.G6

Kolb, Harold H. A field guide to the study of American literature. Charlottesville, Univ. Pr. of Virginia, [1976]. 136p. $9.75. **BD46**

" . . . intended as an introduction to the most significant works currently available to the student of American literature, sufficiently annotated to indicate what they contain and how they are used."—*Introd.* Chapters for: Bibliographies; Literary history and criticism; Reference works; Editions and series; Anthologies; and Journals. The "Author, subject, and genre index" includes names of individual authors mentioned in the annotations.

A review by E. E. Chielens in *Criticism* (19:378, Fall 1977) expresses reservations about the organization and annotations, and indicates a preference for Gohdes's *Bibliographical guide* (*Suppl.* BD45) as a work for the student. Z1225.K65

Leary, Lewis. American literature; a study and research guide. With the collaboration of John Auchard. N.Y., St. Martin's Pr., [1976]. 185p. $10.95. **BD47**

"This guide attempts to chart a way through the maze of writings on American literature, most of which have appeared during the past forty years, and to point toward those earlier writings that are still useful."—*Pref.* Essentially a series of bibliographic essays on various types of sources for research and study in the field of American literature. Chapter 10 is devoted to individual major authors. Includes a section on planning and writing a research paper.

A review by E. E. Chielens in *Criticism* (19:378, Fall 1977) points out various inaccuracies and suggests that Gohdes's *Bibliographical guide* (*Suppl.* BD45) is a superior work. Z1225.L47

Bibliography

See also Suppl. BD62.

First printings of American authors; contributions toward descriptive checklists. Matthew J. Bruccoli, series ed. Detroit, Gale, [1977–78]. v.1–3. il. $140 the set. (In progress) **BD48**

To be in 4v.

" . . . planned as a field guide for scholars, dealers, librarians, researchers, students and collectors. The rationale for this work is to identify the first American printings and the first English printings of books by selected American authors."—*Introd.* About 300 authors are covered in v.1–3; selection is "admittedly impressionistic." Each list includes all separate publications wholly or substantially by the author; later printings are noted only when significant changes are incorporated. Some of the checklists are signed with initials of contributors, others were compiled by the editorial staff; some references to bibliographies and bibliocritical studies are noted; numerous illustrations. Each volume is an alphabetical sequence of checklists; v.4 is to include an index to the set. Z1231.F5F57

Jacobson, Angeline. Contemporary native American literature; a selected & partially annotated bibliography. Metuchen, N.J., Scarecrow Pr., 1977. 262p. **BD49**

Aims to list "the literary works of Native American authors which have been written and published within the years from 1960 to mid-1976."—*Introd.* Arranged by literary genre, with index of authors and a title and first-line index of poems. Z1229.I52J32

Lepper, Gary M. A bibliographical introduction to seventy-five modern American authors. Berkeley, Serendipity Books, 1976. 428p. $30. **BD50**

A series of checklists of "the writings of seventy-five American poets and novelists who have achieved literary prominence since 1945."—*Introd.* Does not include writings about the authors. The subscription books review in the *Booklist* 74:952 (Feb. 1, 1978) concludes that the volume "has only slight value for most libraries." Z1227.L46

Literary writings in America: a bibliography. Millwood, N.Y., KTO Pr., 1977. 8v. $670. **BD51**

Photoreproduction of a card file prepared at the University of Pennsylvania under the auspices of the Works Progress Administration during 1938–42. "The primary purpose of the project was to establish bibliographical controls for materials hitherto inaccessible to researchers; specifically, to construct a complete listing of creative American literature written between 1850 and 1940."—*Pref.*

Arranged alphabetically by literary author, with sections for separate works, periodical publications, biography, and criticism as applicable. "The principal sources of material used in compiling *Literary Writings* are over 2,000 volumes of magazines, more than 500 volumes of literary history and criticism, and more than 100 bibliographies."—*Pref.* Signed book reviews are entered under the name of the reviewer as well as under the name of the author of the book reviewed.

A review by the Subscription Books Committee of A.L.A. in the *Booklist* 74:1571 (June 1, 1978) notes various inconsistencies, but recommends the set as a complement to *Poole's*, early volumes of the *Reader's guide*, etc. Z1225.L58

Matthews, Geraldine O., comp. Black American writers, 1773–1949: a bibliography and union list. Boston, G. K. Hall, 1975. 221p. $16.95. **BD52**

A classed bibliography listing monographic works by more than 1,600 authors. As far as possible, locates copies in 65 libraries in the South. Author index. Z1361.N39M35

Society for the Study of Southern Literature. Committee on Bibliography. Southern literature, 1968–1975. Conflated, ed., and supplemented by Jerry T. Williams. Boston, G. K. Hall, [1978]. 271p. **BD53**

"A continuation of A Bibliographical Guide to the Study of Southern Literature ed. [by] Louis D. Rubin, Jr. [*Guide* BD277] conflated from the checklists published in the Spring issues of the Mississippi Quarterly."—*t.p.*

Cumulates the annotated entries from the *Mississippi quarterly* and adds new citations, cross references, and a name index.

Manuscripts

See also Suppl. BD6.

Robbins, John Albert, ed. American literary manuscripts; a checklist of holdings in academic, historical, and public libraries, museums, and authors' homes in the United States. 2d ed. Athens, Univ. of Georgia Pr., [1977]. 387p. $16. **BD54**

1st ed., 1960 (*Guide* BD284), comp. by the Committee on Manuscript Holdings of the American Literature Group, Modern Language Association of America. This edition sponsored by the American Literature Section of the Modern Language Association.

Follows the basic plan of the earlier edition, "adding a few new symbol categories and devising alternate modes of reporting to gain more flexibility."—*Introd.* The earlier author list was expanded from 2,350 names to nearly 2,800, and the number of libraries covered from 273 to 600. There is a separate list of "Authors for whom no holdings were reported." Z6620.U5M6

Periodicals

Chielens, Edward E. The literary journal in America to 1900; a guide to information sources. Detroit, Gale, [1975]. 197p. (American literature, English literature, and world literatures in English, v.3) $18. **BD55**

An introductory essay is followed by a series of bibliographic listings (mainly annotated) of general studies, writings on literary periodicals of specific regions (including studies of individual magazines), bibliographies and checklists, and background studies. Indexed. Z6951.C57

——— The literary journal in America, 1900–1950: a guide to information sources. Detroit, Gale, 1977. 186p. $18. **BD56**

Follows the guidelines of the author's guide for journals to 1900 (above). Includes chapters on general literary periodicals, little magazines, regional literary periodicals, politically radical literary periodicals, and academic quarterlies of scholarship and criticism. Indexed. Z6951.C572

Kirkham, Edwin Bruce and **Fink, John W.** Indices to American literary annuals and gift books, 1825–1865. New Haven, Conn., Research Publs., Inc., 1975. 627p. $49.50. **BD57**

Serves as an index to the contents of the items listed in Ralph Thompson's *American literary annuals and gift books* (*Guide* BD279) and to the microfilm edition of those books. Pt.1 lists each annual or gift book by title with a complete listing of the contents, giving editor's names, authors and titles of literary contributions, illustrations (with indication of painters and engravers), etc.; pt.2 indexes these lists by editor, publisher, city of publication, stereotypers, printers, titles of literary contributions, authors, engraving titles, painters, and engravers. AY10.T52K57

Kribbs, Jayne K. An annotated bibliography of American literary periodicals, 1741–1850. Boston, G. K. Hall, [1977]. 285p. $38. **BD58**

An alphabetical listing of literary journals published during the period indicated. Gives full title (with indication of changes), place of publication, dates of first and last issue, editor, publisher, library locations, and notes on contents with names of contributors. Chronological and geographical indexes as well as indexes of names, of editors and publishers, and of titles of tales, novels and dramas. Z1219.K75

Translations

Moscow. Vsesoiuznaia Gosudarstvennaia Biblioteka Inostrannoi Literatury. Nauchno-bibliograficheskii otdel. Proizvedeniia amerikanskikh pisatelei v perevodakh na russkii iazyk (1918–1975); bibliograficheskii ukazatel'. Moskva, 1976. 370p. 1r.,10k. **BD59**

A bibliography of Russian translations of American literary works. The main portion of the bibliography is arranged by individual author (filed according to the transliterated form of the name in the Cyrillic alphabet). Indexes of authors and of translators.

Criticism

Borklund, Elmer. Contemporary literary critics. London, St. James Pr.; N.Y., St. Martin's Pr., [1977]. 550p. $25. **BD60**

Intended as a guide to the work of 115 modern British and American critics. For each, gives a brief biographical sketch, a bibliography of works by and about the critic, and a description of the writer's critical theories and position, together with representative quotations from his works.

Curley, Dorothy Nyren, Kramer, Maurice and **Kramer, Elaine Fialka.** Modern American literature. 4th enl. ed. N.Y., Ungar, [1976]. v.4. **BD61**

For v.1–3 and annotation *see Guide* BD292.

Contents: v.4, Supplement to the fourth edition. 605p. $25.

The supplement brings up to date the criticism on about half the authors represented in v.1–3, and treats 49 additional writers. Index of critics.

History

Literary history of the United States. Eds.: Robert E. Spiller [and others]. 4th ed., rev. N.Y., Macmillan, [1974]. 2v. $19.95. **BD62**

3d ed. 1963; bibliography supplements issued 1959 and 1972 (*see Guide* BD298).

Contents: [v.1] History (1556p.); [v.2] Bibliography (1466p.).

"Again the editors have resisted the temptation to alter the main text; but new scholarship has made imperative . . . a wholly new chapter on Emily Dickinson. The chapter on the 'End of an Era,' dealing with the writers who survived World War II, has also been virtually rewritten as time has cleared perspective."—*Pref.* Section XI is now entitled merely "Mid-Century and after" and includes new subsections for poetry, drama, and fiction. The "Reader's bibliography" in v.1 has been updated, and the history volume has its own index.

The bibliography volume is a reprinting, with corrections, of the 1963 edition and the bibliography supplements of 1959 and 1972. Tables of contents of the three volumes have been combined, and a new consolidated index is supplied. PS88.L522

Biographies of authors

Rush, Theressa Gunnels, Myers, Carol Fairbanks and **Arata, Esther Spring.** Black American writers, past and present: a biographical and bibliographical dictionary. Metuchen, N.J., Scarecrow Pr., 1975. 2v. (865p.) il. $30. **BD63**

Aims to present biographical, bibliographical and critical information on about 2,000 black writers. (In some instances only a record of publications is available.) In general, a biographical sketch is followed by a list of published books, representative references to contributions to periodicals and anthologies, and references to biographical and critical studies on the writer. Z1229.N39R87

Who was who among North American authors, 1921–1939. Detroit, Gale, [1976]. 2v. (1578p.) $48. **BD64**

Represents a cumulation of the latest sketches of some 11,200 persons treated in the various volumes of *Who's who among North American authors* published 1921–39. Z1224.W6

Drama

See also Suppl. BD100.

Arata, Esther Spring and **Rotoli, Nicholas John.** Black American playwrights, 1800 to the present; a bibliography. Metuchen, N.J., Scarecrow Pr., 1976. 295p. $12. **BD65**

Arranged alphabetically by name of playwright. Lists published and unpublished works (including filmscripts, musicals, theater criticism, etc.), together with references to reviews and criticism of the writers' works. Contributions to anthologies and periodicals are noted. Title index. Z1229.N39A7

Hatch, James V. and **Abdullah, Omanii.** Black playwrights, 1823–1977: an annotated bibliography of plays. N.Y., Bowker, 1977. 319p. $17.50. **BD66**

An author listing of some 2,700 plays by approximately 900 black American playwrights. As far as possible, the following information is given for each title: date of composition or copyright, genre, brief description of theme or story line, cast (number, race, sex), length, date and place of production, publication information, library location or agent, and where to apply for permission to produce the play. Title index; various useful supplementary bibliographies and appendixes. Z1231.D7H37

Hixon, Donald L. and **Hennessee, Don A.** Nineteenth-century American drama: a finding guide. Metuchen, N.J., Scarecrow Pr., 1977. 579p. $20. **BD67**

Essentially a finding list to the "American plays, 1831–1900" portion of the Readex Corporation's microprint collection *English and American plays of the nineteenth century.* Lists about 4,500 plays, including plays of British and continental authors adapted or translated for the American stage. Author listing with three appendixes: (1) Series (which lists the contents of the many series analyzed in the main work); (2) Ethnic/racial (which lists those plays which include characters of a particular racial or ethnic origin); and (3) Subject/form (which "groups those plays dealing with particular broad subject areas, or representing specific literary and dramatic forms, into a variety of appropriate categories").—*Pref.*

Palmer, Helen H. and **Dyson, Anne Jane.** American drama criticism. Supplement II, comp. by Floyd Eugene Eddleman. Hamden, Conn., Shoe String Pr., 1976. 217p. $10. **BD68**

Updates the basic volume and its first supplement (*Guide* BD312) through the end of 1974. This supplement also lists interpretative studies of earlier plays, including increased coverage for women playwrights, black playwrights, plays by authors better known for their work in other fields, etc. Separate author and title indexes in this volume. Z1231.D7P3

Fiction

See also Suppl. BD108.

Houston, Helen Ruth. The Afro-American novel, 1965–1975; a descriptive bibliography of primary and secondary material. Troy, N.Y., Whitston, 1977. 214p. $15. **BD69**

Treats some 56 Afro-Americans who have published novels since 1964. A brief biographical note is followed by a listing of the writer's recent novels, a section of critical books by and about the author, and a listing of reviews of the post-1964 novels. Z1229.N39H68

Kirby, David K. American fiction to 1900; a guide to information sources. Detroit, Gale, [1975]. 296p. (American literature, English literature, and world literatures in English, v.4) $18. **BD70**

A brief section of general aids is followed by sections on individual authors of the period. For individual authors, lists principal works, bibliographies, biographies, and a selection of critical studies. Uneven in coverage. Z1231.F4K57

Rosa, Alfred F. and **Eschholz, Paul A.** Contemporary fiction in America and England, 1950–1970; a guide to information sources. Detroit, Gale, [1976]. 454p. (American literature, English literature, and world literatures in English, v.10) $18. **BD71**

A brief section of "Studies and reference works" is followed by a series of bibliographies of writings by and about some 136 contemporary authors. Z1231.F4R57

Woodress, James Leslie. American fiction, 1900–1950; a guide to information sources. Detroit, Gale, [1974]. 260p. (American literature, English literature, and world literature in English, v.1) $18. **BD72**

Pt.1, General bibliography, contains four brief sections: one listing general background source material; the others, specialized source materials on the novel, the short story, and interviews with authors. Pt.2 comprises 44 individual bibliographical essays on those writers "who seem in 1973 to be the most significant producers of fiction during the first half of the twentieth century. They have been selected on the basis of the critical esteem accorded them during the 23 years that have passed since 1950."—*Introd.* The bibliographical essays include notes on bibliography and manuscripts, editions and reprints, biography, and criticism. Indexed. Z1231.F4W64

Poetry

See also Suppl. BD112.

Chapman, Dorothy H. Index to black poetry. Boston, G. K. Hall, 1974. 541p. $25. **BD73**

"Black poetry is here defined in the broadest manner . . . . References are included for the work not only of black poets but also of those poets who have in some way dealt with the black experience or written within the black tradition, regardless of their racial origins."—*Foreword.* Indexes about 125 collections. A title and first line index is followed by separate author and subject indexes. PS153.N5C45

Australian and New Zealand

Lock, Fred and **Lawson, Alan.** Australian literature—a reference guide. Melbourne and N.Y., Oxford Univ. Pr., [1977]. 84p. $4.25 pa. **BD74**

A guide to sources of information for the study of Australian literature. More than 300 annotated entries in six main sections: (1) Bibliographical aids; (2) Other reference sources (e.g., encyclopedias, dictionaries, biographical dictionaries); (3) Authors (i.e., a listing of bibliographies of individual authors); (4) Periodicals; (5) Library resources; (6) Literary studies. Index of authors, and one of titles and subjects.

McNaughton, Howard Douglas. New Zealand drama; a bibliographical guide. Interim ed. [Christchurch], Univ. of Canterbury Lib., 1974. 112p. (Reference and bibliographical ser., Univ. of Canterbury Lib., 5) **BD75**

Attempts to list every New Zealand play which has been published and/or produced, of which a copy can be traced. Includes radio and television as well as stage productions. Arranged by author, with title index. Z4114.D7M3

Canadian

Canadian essay and literature index. 1973–75. Toronto, Univ. of Toronto Pr., [1975–77]. Annual. (1977: $35) **BD76**

An author-title-subject index to essays, book reviews, poems, plays and short stories appearing in anthologies, collections, and magazines published in Canada during the year of coverage. Separate sections for each genre; full lists of books and periodicals indexed at the end of the volume. The initial volume covers 91 anthologies and collections and 38 magazines.

Ceased publication. AI3.C238

Canadian essays and collections index, 1971–1972. Ottawa, Canadian Lib. Assoc., [1976]. 219p. $27.50. **BD77**

Editors: Joyce Sowby [and others].

Provides indexing of some 70 Canadian collective publications. Serves as a predecessor to *Canadian essay and literature index* (*Suppl.* BD76). Z1365.C224

Fee, Margery and **Cawker, Ruth.** Canadian fiction: an annotated bibliography. [Toronto], Peter Martin Associates, [1976]. 170p. $15; $8.95 pa. **BD78**

A bibliography of "Canadian literary prose" for the teacher, student, librarian and general reader. A section on secondary sources is followed by separate sections for "Novel annotations" and "Short story annotations." There is a title index and a "subject guide" to the novels, and separate author and title indexes for the short stories. Z1377.F4F4

Moyles, R. G. English-Canadian literature to 1900; a guide to information sources. Detroit, Gale, [1976]. 346p. (American literature, English literature, and world literatures in English, v.6) $18. **BD79**

Attempts "to provide a list of all the important primary and secondary sources necessary for a thorough study of this literature."—*Introd.* Includes general reference aids, literary histories and criticism, anthologies, plus sections for individual authors and for the literature of exploration and travel. Z1375.M68

Sedgwick, Dorothy. A bibliography of English-language theatre and drama in Canada 1800–1914. Edmonton, Alberta, 1976. 48p. (Nineteenth century theatre research. Occasional publs., 1) **BD80**

A bibliography of Canadian dramatic writings and works on the theater and dramatists of Canada. Items are grouped under the following headings: Canadian drama, Canadian dramatists, Canadian dramatic criticism, Canadian theatres, Canadian theatre history, Canadian stage-tours and visits, Reference and bibliography. Locates copies. Indexed. Z1377.D7S43

Commonwealth

New, William H., comp. Critical writings on Commonwealth literatures: a selective bibliography to 1970, with a list of theses and dissertations. University Park, Pennsylvania State Univ. Pr., [1975]. 333p. $15. **BD81**

A general section is followed by sections for Africa (East and West), Australia, Canada, New Zealand, South Africa and Rhodesia, South Asia, Southeast Asia, and West Indies. A separate "Theses and dissertations" section is also subdivided by geographic area. Includes research aids, general studies, and studies of individual major authors. United Kingdom is omitted. Index of critics, editors, translators. Z2000.9.N48

English

Guides

See also Suppl. BD1.

Bateson, Frederick Wilse and **Meserole, Harrison T.** A guide to English and American literature. 3d ed. London & N.Y., Longman, [1976]. 334p. $15. **BD82**

Previous editions had title *A guide to English literature;* 2d ed. 1967 (*Guide* BD366).

"This modest handbook is intended for the reader of any age who is entering or re-entering, the serious study of English and American literature. Here are the principal editions and commentaries that such a reader may reasonably be expected to want to know about if he is to explore at all thoroughly any of the classics or the classical areas of our literature down to the present day."—*Pref.* A general section is followed by chapters for medieval, Renaissance, Augustan, Romantic, and modern English literature, with reading lists for each of the early periods. There is a separate chapter on American literature, and one on "Literary scholarship: an introduction to research in English literature." Indexed. Z2011.B32

Bibliography

The new Cambridge bibliography of English literature. Cambridge, University Pr., 1977. v.5. $21.50. **BD83**

For v.1–4 *see Guide* BD376.

Contents: v.5, Index, comp. by J. D. Pickles. 542col.

Wider than the indexes in the individual volumes, this is "a general index to all four volumes, listing primary authors and major anonymous works, as well as certain headings from the Bibliography as a whole."—*Pref.*

Periodicals

White, Robert B. The English literary journal to 1900; a guide to information sources. Detroit, Gale, [1977]. 311p. (American literature, English literature, and world literatures in English, v.8) $18. **BD84**

Aims to present "a bibliography of what has been written since about 1890 and what is now accessible to the general reader concerning pre-1900 British literary periodicals."—*Pref.* Sections for bibliographies and general studies are followed by sections for specific periodicals, persons, and places. Indexed. Z6956.G6W47

Old and Middle English

See also Suppl. BD89.

Beale, Walter H. Old and Middle English poetry to 1500; a guide to information sources. Detroit, Gale, [1976]. 454p. (American literature, English literature, and world literatures in English, v.7) $18. **BD85**

An annotated bibliography of texts, translations, and critical writings. Z2014.P7B34

A manual of the writings in Middle English, 1050–1500. . . . New Haven, Connecticut Academy of Arts and Sciences, 1975. v.5. (In progress) **BD86**

For previously published volumes and annotation *see Guide* BD389.

Contents: v.5, Dramatic pieces (The miracle plays and mysteries, by A. J. Mill; The morality plays, by S. Lindenbaum; The folk drama, by F. L. Utley and B. Ward); Poems dealing with contemporary conditions, by R. H. Robbins.

Simms, Norman Toby. Ritual and rhetoric: intellectual and ceremonial backgrounds to Middle English literature; a critical survey of relevant scholarship. [Norwood, Pa.], Norwood Editions, 1976. 358p. $35. **BD87**

Nearly 1,500 entries grouped under such headings as: The court, The church, Schools, The city, rhetorical parts, literary genres, etc. Some annotations; no index. Z2012.S55

To 1700

Heninger, S. K. English prose, prose fiction, and criticism to 1660; a guide to information sources. Detroit, Gale, [1975]. 255p. (American literature, English literature, and world literatures in English, v.2) $18. **BD88**

Lists primary and secondary works by type (e.g., religious writings, travel literature, essays, narrative fiction, literary criticism, etc.). Nearly 800 items. Indexed. Z2014.P795H45

Manuscripts

See also Suppl. BD6.

Early English manuscripts in facsimile. Copenhagen, Rosenkilde & Bagger; Baltimore, Johns Hopkins Pr., 1974–76. v.18–19. (In progress) **BD89**

For previously published volumes and annotation *see Guide* BD410.

Contents: v.18, Old English illustrated Hexateuch, ed. by C. R. Dodwell and P. Clemoes. 1974; v.19, The Vercelli book; a late tenth century manuscript containing prose and verse (Vercelli Biblioteca Capitolare CXVII), ed. by Celia Sisam. 1976.

Stratford, Jenny. The Arts Council collection of modern literary manuscripts, 1963–1972. [London], Turret Books, 1974. 168p. £6. **BD90**

With the 1967 exhibition catalog *Poetry in the making* (ed. by Jenny Lewis; London, Turret Books, 68p.), provides a record of some of the more impressive results of the Council's efforts to collect and preserve in British repositories the manuscripts of contemporary writers. Originally restricted to poetry, the collecting policy has been extended to include prose writers. In addition to items added to the British Museum collections, this volume includes some manuscripts purchased by other libraries with Council support. Gives a brief description of each manuscript (relating it to a published version when possible) and frequently indicates where related manuscripts are to be found. Indexed. Z6611.L7S77

Criticism

Temple, Ruth Zabriskie and **Tucker, Martin.** Modern British literature. N.Y., F. Ungar, [1975]. v.4. (A library of literary criticism) **BD91**

Contents: v.4, Supplement, comp. by Martin Tucker and Rita Stein. 650p. $25.

For v.1–3 *see Guide* BD419.

"Our aim in Volume IV is twofold: first, to bring criticism up to date on approximately one-third of the authors included in the original volumes . . . ; second, to add other writers who have come to critical attention since 1965. Forty-nine of these 'new' writers are included."—*Introd.* Bibliographies have been updated. PR473.T4

Handbooks

Eagle, Dorothy and **Carnell, Hilary.** The Oxford literary guide to the British isles. Oxford, Clarendon Pr., 1977. 413p. maps. £3.95. **BD92**

In two sections: (1) List of place-names (giving location of each place and its literary associations) and (2) Index of authors (which enables the reader to follow a writer's career from place to place and to identify pertinent places in the previous section). Fictitious names of real places are entered as cross references. PR109.E18

Drama

Bibliography

King, Kimball. Twenty modern British playwrights: a bibliography, 1956 to 1976. N.Y., Garland, 1977. 289p. (Garland reference library of the humanities, v.96) $20. **BD93**

Includes contemporary playwrights such as Alan Ayckbourn, Edward Bond, Simon Gray, Joe Orton, John Osborne, Harold Pinter, together with a number of less well-known figures. Lists of the dramatists' own works (including plays staged but not published; work for television and films, etc.) are followed by annotated bibliographies of critical writings and lists of reviews. Indexed. Z2014.D7K47

Link, Frederick M. English drama, 1660–1800; a guide to information sources. Detroit, Gale, [1976]. 374p. (American literature, English literature, and world literatures in English, v.9) $18. **BD94**

In two parts, the first listing reference materials, works on the stage, and theater biography, dramatic history, and general drama criticism of the period. The second part offers brief biographical sketches of individual dramatists, with references to biographical and critical studies and editions of the plays. Z2014.D7L55

Logan, Terence P. and **Smith, Denzell S.** The popular school; a survey and bibliography of recent studies in English Renaissance drama. Lincoln, Univ. of Nebraska Pr., [1975]. 299p. $15. **BD95**

"This volume is the second in Recent Studies in English Renaissance Drama, a series which in its entirety will provide a detailed account of both the historical development and current state of scholarship on playwrights and plays from 1580 to 1642, exclusive of Shakespeare."—*Pref.* (The preceding volume of the series is *The predecessors of Shakespeare, Guide* BD443.)

Includes dramatists who wrote primarily for the open-air public theaters, and anonymous plays first performed in such theaters. Sections by contributing scholars on Thomas Dekker, Thomas Middleton, John Webster, Thomas Heywood, Anthony Munday, Michael Drayton, and the anonymous plays. Indexes of persons and of titles. Z2014.D7L82

Penninger, Frieda Elaine. English drama to 1660 (excluding Shakespeare); a guide to information sources. Detroit, Gale, [1976]. 370p. (American literature, English literature, and world literatures in English, v.5) $18. **BD96**

Intended primarily for "undergraduate and graduate students who seek direction towards editions and discussions which will enable them to initiate and pursue a study of a given area of the drama." —*Foreword.* A section of general works (bibliographies, collections and editions, general histories and studies, histories and studies of specific periods, theater and stagecraft, etc.) is followed by sections on individual dramatists. Index of authors, editors, compilers, and anonymous titles.

Thompson, Lawrence S. Nineteenth and twentieth century drama: a selective bibliography of English language works. Numbers 1–3029. Boston, G. K. Hall, [1975]. 456p. $28.50. **BD97**

"The present catalog is the first part of what will ultimately be a bibliography of the dramatic literature of the English-speaking peoples of the nineteenth century, as comprehensive as possible, and of the twentieth century selectively. While each volume will be in a separate alphabet, the numbers of the items will be consecutive, and the indexes cumulative."—*Introd.*

Author listing with title index. All material listed is available in microform from General Microfilm Co., Cambridge, Mass. Includes variant editions of some works, English translations of foreign-language plays, etc. Z2014.D7T5

Handbooks

Berger, Thomas L. and **Bradford, William C.** An index of characters in English printed drama to the Restoration. [Englewood, Colo.], Microcard Editions Books, 1975. 222p. $21. **BD98**

An index to all the characters in the plays listed in Greg's *Bibliography of English printed drama to the Restoration* (*Guide* BD437). Indexing is by name, character types, nationalities, occupations, religious proclivities, psychological states. Reference is to Greg number only; a "Finding list" provides the title, author, dates, and *STC* reference. PR1265.3.B4

Ruoff, James E. Crowell's Handbook of Elizabethan and Stuart literature. N.Y., Thomas Y. Crowell, [1975]. 468p. $13.95. **BD99**

Intended for students, teachers, and the general reader. Entries for authors, titles of literary works, and literary genres. Bibliographic notes for most articles. PR19.R8

Biographies of authors

Vinson, James, ed. Contemporary dramatists. London, St. James Pr.; N.Y., St. Martin's Pr., [1973]. 926p. £9; $30. **BD100**

Brief biographies of about 300 contemporary dramatists writing in English. Signed commentary on the writer's work (often with comment by the biographee); lists of publications. PR106.V5

Fiction

Bibliography

See also Suppl. BD71.

Cassis, A. F. The twentieth-century English novel; an annotated bibliography of general criticism. N.Y., Garland Pr., 1977. 413p. $35. **BD101**

A bibliography of general criticism on the English novel. About 2,800 items in three main sections: (1) Bibliographies and checklists; (2) Criticism (books and articles in separate listings); (3) Dissertations and theses. Indexes of novelists and of selected topics and themes. Z2014.F5C35

Dunn, Richard J. The English novel: twentieth century criticism. Chicago, Swallow Pr., [1976]- . v.1- . **BD102**

Contents: v.1, Defoe through Hardy. 202p. $20.

v.1 offers checklists of critical writings on the works of some 45 English novelists from the time of Defoe through that of Hardy. For each novelist, criticisms of individual works are followed by a section of general studies on the writer. There is also a section of general studies on the novel (pp.171–201) and a general bibliography. Z2014.F4D86

Ford, George H., ed. Victorian fiction; a second guide to research. N.Y., Modern Language Assoc. of America, 1978. 401p. $17.50. **BD103**

Intended as a companion to Lionel Stevenson's *Victorian fiction* (*Guide* BD471) which covers publications through 1962. This volume aims "to supply complete coverage from 1963 through 1974" (*Pref.*) with occasional mention of works published 1975 or later, plus chapters on Robert Louis Stevenson and Samuel Butler reviewing the scholarly writing on those two figures from the beginning through 1974. Some pre-1962 items are also mentioned. Chapters are by scholar specialists, and there has been an effort "to provide some fresh emphasis" regarding "the availability of manuscripts and the record of film versions of Victorian novels."—*Pref.* Neglected areas of research are also noted. Fully indexed.

McNutt, Dan J. The eighteenth-century Gothic novel: an annotated bibliography of criticism and selected texts. N.Y., Garland Pr., 1975. 330p. $30. **BD104**

Sections on the background, general history and specific aspects of the genre are followed by sections on the major practitioners: Horace Walpole, Clara Reeve, Charlotte Smith, Ann Radcliffe, Matthew Gregory Lewis, and William Beckford. In addition to annotations, excerpts from early reviews of individual novels are included. Z2014.F5M3

Messerli, Douglas and **Fox, Howard N.** Index to periodical fiction in English, 1965–1969. Metuchen, N.J., Scarecrow Pr., 1977. 764p. $30. **BD105**

Indexes the fiction appearing in about 400 English-language periodicals published throughout the world. Entry is by author, with title and translator indexes. Z2014.F5M475

Palmer, Helen H. and **Dyson, Anne Jane.** English novel explication. Suppl. I, comp. by Peter L. Abernethy, Christian J. W. Kloesel and Jeffrey R. Smitten. [Hamden, Conn.], Shoe String Pr., 1976. 305p. $12.50. **BD106**

For the original Palmer and Dyson bibliography *see Guide* BD470.

Emphasis is on material published 1972–74, with some earlier citations and a few 1975 publications. Z2014.F5P26

Stanton, Robert J. A bibliography of modern British novelists. Troy, N.Y., Whitston, 1978. 2v. (1123p.) $65. **BD107**

Contents: v.1, Kingsley Amis, Elizabeth Bowen, Margaret Drabble, William Golding, L. P. Hartley, Richard Hughes, Rosamond Lehmann, Doris Lessing, Brian Moore; v.2, Iris Murdoch, V. S. Naipaul, Anthony Powell, Jean Rhys, Alan Sillitoe, C. P. Snow, Muriel Spark, Angus Wilson.

For each novelist there is a list of works subdivided by genre (novels, short stories, poems, plays, "other"); a section of general secondary studies, interviews, biographical sketches and other miscellaneous items; and a list of studies and reviews of individual works. A separate section lists works referring to two or more novelists and is subdivided as (1) books and dissertations, and (2) periodical articles; cross references to this section are provided in the individual author sections.

Biographies of authors

Vinson, James. Contemporary novelists. 2d ed. London, St. James Pr.; N.Y., St. Martin's Pr.; [1976]. 1636p. £12; $30. **BD108**

1st ed. 1972 (*Guide* BD96).

Many additions in this edition; some deletions. Adds an appendix of 18 novelists "who have died since the 1950's but whose reputations are essentially contemporary."—*Pref.*

Poetry

Bibliography

See also Suppl. BD85.

Foxon, David Fairweather. English verse 1701–1750; a catalogue of separately printed poems with notes on contemporary collected editions. [London & N.Y.], Cambridge Univ. Pr., [1975]. 2v. $295. **BD109**

Contents: v.1, Catalogue; v.2, Indexes.

"The catalogue attempts to list all separately published verse written in English, as well as works written in other languages and printed in the British Isles, but it omits all works printed in America. . . . "—*Introd.* A short-title catalog by author or first word of anonymous title; includes valuable descriptive notes; locates copies. There are indexes of first lines, imprints, and subjects, plus a chronological index. Z2014.P7F69

Marcan, Peter. Poetry themes; a bibliographical index to subject anthologies and related criticism in the English language, 1875–1975. London, Bingley; Hamden, Conn., Linnet Books, [1977]. 301p. $22.50. **BD110**

Intends to index "subject anthologies which bring together poetry on one subject or a group of related subjects."—*Introd.* Includes some anthologies of poetry and prose. Critical literature (books, periodical articles, academic theses) are also listed as being useful for their bibliographies and footnote references providing sources for thematic and comparative studies. Arranged according to a classification scheme outlined pp.x–xvi, but there is no alphabetical subject index. Brief notes regarding coverage, period, emphasis, etc., frequently follow the bibliographic citations; studies and criticism are separately listed within each subject category. Index of authors and compilers. Anthologies indexed are mainly British imprints. PN1022.M3

Reilly, Catherine W. English poetry of the first World War. London, George Prior, 1978. 402p. £14.95. **BD111**

A listing of "poetry and verse on the theme of the First World War, written by English poets (i.e., poets of England, Ireland, Scotland and Wales), servicemen and civilians, who experienced the war. It is restricted to printed material in the form of book, pamphlet, card, or broadside."—*Abstract.* In two main sections: (1) Anthologies; (2) Individual authors. Title index. Supplementary list of names of war poets of other English-speaking nations. Z2014.P7

Biographies of authors

Contemporary poets. 2d ed. James Vinson, ed.; D. L. Kirkpatrick, assoc. ed. London, St. James Pr.; N.Y., St. Martin's Pr.; [1975]. 1849p. $35. **BD112**

1st ed., 1970, had title: *Contemporary poets of the English language* (*Guide* BD489).

A revised and expanded edition, representing not only augmenting and up-dating of earlier sketches, but a somewhat different selection (i.e., some poets have been dropped, and a great many new names have been added). "An appendix of entries has been included for some nineteen poets who have died since 1950 but whose reputations are essentially contemporary."—*Editor's note.* Z2014.P7C62

Diaries

Batts, John Stuart. British manuscript diaries of the nineteenth century: an annotated listing. Fontwell, Centaur Pr.; Totowa, N.J., Rowman and Littlefield, 1976. 345p. £10; $25. **BD113**

Serves as a companion to Matthews' *British diaries* (*Guide* BD508), listing unpublished diaries of the 19th century. Arranged by year, then alphabetically by diarist. Index of diarists and subject index. Z6611.B6B38

Individual authors

Chaucer

Baird, Lorrayne Y. A bibliography of Chaucer, 1964–1973. Boston, G. K. Hall, [1977]. 287p. $22. **BD114**

Intended as a continuation of W. R. Crawford's Chaucer bibliography covering 1954–63 (*Guide* BD511). Z8164.B27

Dillon, Bert. A Chaucer dictionary: proper names and allusions, excluding place names. Boston, G. K. Hall, 1974. 266p. $25. **BD115**

Names are explained, and citations to appearances in Chaucer's works are given. References to special studies relating to the names are frequently provided. Bibliography, pp.246–66. PR1903.D5

Milton

Johnson, William C. Milton criticism: a subject index. [Folkestone, Kent, Eng.], Dawson, [1978]. 450p. £17.50. **BD116**

Not a bibliography as such, but rather "a detailed and relatively complete index to subjects referred to, or covered in, a carefully selected group of 150 books of criticism pertaining to the life and writings of John Milton."—*Introd.* A computer-produced compilation based on the indexes of the selected volumes, augmented by additional entries, it enables the user to determine whether a given topic is treated in any of the critical studies without consulting the volume itself.

Shakespeare

McManaway, James Gilmer and **Roberts, Jeanne Addison.** A selective bibliography of Shakespeare: editions, textual studies, commentary. Charlottesville, pub. for the Folger Shakespeare Lib. by Univ. Pr. of Virginia, [1975]. 309p. $12.50. **BD117**

A selective bibliography of about 4,500 items which "attempts to draw attention to the best and most important publications since 1930. A scattering of representative works of earlier date is given to serve as background."—*Pref.* Almost exclusively English-language materials; cutoff date is 1970, with a few important items of later date. Topical arrangement; sections on the individual plays usually include sub-sections for editions, textual commentary, and commentary on the plays. Author index. Particularly useful for work with undergraduates. Z8811.M23

A new variorum edition of Shakespeare. Supplementary bibliographies for Henry the Fourth, part one; Henry the Fourth, part two; The tragedy of Julius Caesar; The life and death of King Richard II. [N.Y., Modern Language Assoc. of America, 1977]. 15p., 18p., 58p., 31p. $19. **BD118**

For the *New variorum edition* see *Guide* BD541.

Each bibliography is separately paged and has its own title page and index. (Each is also available in a separate, paperbound edition.) Compiled by divers hands. Period of coverage varies, the cutoff date being mainly 1972 or 1973.

Spevack, Marvin A. A complete and systematic concordance to the works of Shakespeare. Hildesheim, Olms, 1975. v.7–8. **BD119**

For previously published volumes and annotation *see Guide* BD544.

Contents: v.7, Concordances to stage directions and speech-prefixes; v.8, Concordances to the "bad" quartos and The taming of a shrew and The troublesome reign of King John.

Irish

Anglo-Irish literature; a review of research. Ed. by Richard J. Finneran. N.Y., Modern Language Assoc. of America, 1976. 596p. $18; $10 pa. **BD120**

A bibliographic survey similar to the MLA-sponsored publications by Faverty, Jordan, De Laura, etc. (*Guide* BD483, BD482, BD402).

"The primary purpose of this volume is to provide essays on writers of Anglo-Irish background whose careers have been completed and who have been the subject of a substantial body of published research. A liberal definition of 'background' accounts for the inclusion of Wilde and Shaw, whose credentials are otherwise open to some debate. The other criteria explain the lack of any detailed discussion of writers such as Beckett, Clarke, Colum, O'Faolain, and many others."—*Pref.* Includes chapters (each by a specialist) on general works, 19th-century writers, Oscar Wilde, George Moore, Bernard Shaw, W. B. Yeats, J. M. Synge, James Joyce, "Four revival figures" (Lady Gregory, A. E., Gogarty, James Stephens), Sean O'Casey, and modern drama. Indexed. PR8712.A5

CELTIC LITERATURE

Bromwich, Rachel. Medieval Celtic literature; a select bibliography. [Toronto], Univ. of Toronto Pr., [1974]. 109p. (Toronto medieval bibliographies, 5) $8.95. **BD121**

A guide for the student. Slightly more than 500 items in five main sections: (1) Introductory material; (2) Study of language; (3) Literary history and criticism; (4) Texts and translations; (5) Background material. Brief annotations; index. Z7011.B76

GERMANIC LANGUAGES

German

Bibliography

Albrecht, Günter and **Dahlke, Günther.** Internationale Bibliographie zur Geschichte der deutschen Literatur. . . . Berlin, Volk und Wissen, 1977. v.3. **BD122**

For full citation, previously published volumes, and annotation *see Guide* BD588.

Contents: v.3, Sachregister; Personen-Werk-Register.

Goedeke, Karl. Grundriss zur Geschichte der deutschen Dichtung aus den Quellen. Index bearb. von Hartmut Rambaldo. Nendeln, Liechtenstein, 1975. 393p. **BD123**

An alphabetical index of the authors treated in Bd. 1–15, 1884–1966 (3. Aufl. of Bd. 4), of the 2d ed. of Goedeke (*Guide* BD591). PT85.G72

Harvard University. Library. German literature. Cambridge, Mass., publ. by Harvard Univ. Lib., distr. by the Harvard Univ. Pr., 1974. 2v. (Widener library shelflist, 49–50) $75. **BD124**

Contents: v.1, Classification schedule; Classified listing by call number; Chronological listing; v.2, Author and title listing.

Lists "more than 46,000 titles of works on the history of German language literature, literary anthologies, and works by and about individual European authors writing in German and its dialects."—*Pref.* Z2249.H37

Melzwig, Brigitte. Deutsche sozialistische Literatur, 1918–1945: Bibliographie der Buchveröffentlichungen. Berlin, Aufbau-Verlag, [1975]. 616p. DM48. **BD125**

Lists writers' works published 1918–45, and reprints and translations through 1969. Chronological index, title index, and index of names. Z2233.3.M44

Schmitt, Franz Anselm. Stoff- und Motivgeschichte der deutschen Literatur; eine Bibliographie. 3., völlig neu bearb. und erw. Aufl. Berlin, De Gruyter, 1976. 437p. DM98. **BD126**

2d ed. 1965 (*Guide* BD600).

Adds new references to periodical articles, monographs, and dissertations published 1964–Aug. 1975. More than 300 new headings in the "Einzelne Stoffe und Motive" section. Z2231.S35

Dictionaries of authors and literature

Garland, Henry Burnand and **Garland, Mary.** The Oxford companion to German literature. Oxford, Clarendon Pr., 1976. 977p. $27.95. **BD127**

Follows the familiar plan and arrangement of the various "Oxford companions" to literature, "although exigencies of space finally made it necessary to drop such entries as conspicuous characters in literary works."—*Pref.* Covers from about 800 to the early 1970's and attempts to provide "reasonably representative" coverage of each period of the literature of each German-speaking country.

A review by S. S. Prawer in *TLS,* May 21, 1976, pp.607–8 discusses in some detail the various virtues and shortcomings of the work; similarly, the review by Roy Pascal in *Modern language review* 72:479–82 (Apr. 1977). The "collective verdict" of a group of specialists invited to review portions of the work for the *Journal of English and Germanic philology* (76:392–96, July 1977) is that the *Companion,* "while a most welcome tool, does not possess a sufficient degree of accuracy in detail and is often suspect in its emphases." PT41.G3

Kosch, Wilhelm. Deutsches Literatur-Lexikon; biographisches und bibliographisches Handbuch. 3. völlig neubearb. Aufl. hrsg. von Bruno Berger und Heinz Rupp. Bern, Francke Verlag, [1977–78]. Bd.5–6. (In progress) **BD128**

For v.1–4 and annotation *see Guide* BD623.

Contents: Bd.5–6, Filek–Gysin.

Schriftsteller der DDR. [Hrsg. Günter Albrecht u. a.] Leipzig, VEB Bibliographisches Institut, 1974. 656p. **BD129**

About 400 biographical sketches of DDR authors, mainly living persons but including some deceased persons who were still active in the last quarter century. Includes lists of publications. PT3713.S3

Stammler, Wolfgang. Die deutsche Literatur des Mittelalters: Verfasserlexikon. 2., völlig neu bearb. Aufl. Berlin, de Gruyter, [1977–]. Lfg.1– . DM68 per Lfg. (In progress) **BD130**

On cover, Lfg.1: Begründet von Wolfgang Stammler, fortgeführt von Karl Langosch . . . hrsg. von Kurt Ruh . . . Redaktion, Kurt Illing, Christine Stöllinger.

Contents: Bd.1, Lfg.1–3, A–Borgeni, Caspar.

1st ed. 1931–55 in 5v. (*Guide* BD637).

To be in 6v. of four Lfg. each, with two or three Lfg. to be published each year. This edition revised and expanded in the light of recent scholarship. Signed articles with bibliographies. Writers of antiquity and medieval Latin writers continue to be treated if they have had an impact on German literature.

Drama

Gabel, Gernot U. Drama und Theater des deutschen Barock: eine Handbibliographie d. Sekundärliteratur. Hamburg, [Selbstverlag], 1974. 182p. DM15. **BD131**

A bibliography of works about the drama and theater of the German baroque era, 1580–1700. Classed arrangement with author index. Z2232.G3

Gregor, Joseph [and others]. Der Schauspielführer. Stuttgart, Hiersemann, 1976. v.10. **BD132**

For earlier volumes and annotation *see Guide* BD643.

Contents: Bd.10, Das Schauspiel der Gegenwart von 1971 bis 1973.

Poetry

Paulus, Rolf and **Steuler, Ursula.** Bibliographie zur deutschen Lyrik nach 1945. Frankfurt am Main, Athenaion, 1974. 157p. DM22 pa. **BD133**

A bibliography of modern German poetry with a classified section of general background and critical studies followed by sections for the principal practitioners. Index of names. Z2234.P7P38

Scandinavian

Icelandic

Mitchell, Phillip Marshall and **Ober, Kenneth H.** Bibliography of modern Icelandic literature in translation, including works written by Icelanders in other languages. Ithaca, N.Y., Cornell Univ. Pr., 1975. 317p. (Islandica XL) $32.50. **BD134**

In two main sections: (1) Anthologies (grouped by language of translation), and (2) Works by individual authors (arranged alphabetically by author's name; translations of individual works are entered alphabetically by language of translation). Includes references to translations (including selections from longer works) appearing in periodicals, as parts of books, etc. Index of translators, editors and compilers. Z2551.M57

Norwegian

Næss, Harald S. Norwegian literary bibliography, 1956–1970. Red. Kaare Haukaas. Oslo, Universitetsforlaget, [1975]. 128p. (Norsk bibliografisk bibliotek, Bd. 50) **BD135**

Added title page in Norwegian: *Norsk litteraturhistorisk bibliografi.*

Meant to be looked upon as a continuation of Øksnevad's *Norsk litteraturhistorisk bibliografi 1946–1955* (*Guide* BD674). Z2601.N33

ROMANCE LANGUAGES

Belgian writers

Culot, Jean-Marie. Bibliographie des écrivains français de Belgique, 1881–1960. Bruxelles, Palais des Académies, 1972. v.4. (In progress) **BD136**

For previously published volumes and annotation *see Guide* BD697.

Contents: v.4, M–N.

Canadian writers

Barbeau, Victor and **Fortier, André.** Dictionnaire bibliographique du Canada français. Montréal, Académie Canadienne-française, [1974]. 246p. $25. **BD137**

A bibliography of the writings of French Canadian authors, together with writings on Canada by French authors. Brief biographical notes are provided in most instances. Z1365.B3

French

Bibliography

Duggan, Joseph J. A guide to studies on the *Chanson de Roland.* [London], Grant & Cutler, 1976. 133p. £5.40 pa. **BD138**

A bibliography for students and scholars, concentrating on publications of the period 1955–74. "For the period preceding 1955, items of overriding critical or historical significance have been included, as well as those which provide extensive bibliographies or outstanding surveys of the subjects to which they are devoted."—*Pref.* Includes editions of the text as well as critical studies. Classed arrangement with index of scholars and translators. Z6521.R7D83

Griffin, Lloyd W., Clarke, Jack A. and **Kroff, Alexander Y.** Modern French literature and language; a bibliography of homage studies. [Madison], Univ. of Wisconsin Pr., [1976]. 175p. $15. **BD139**

"Produced and distributed *on demand* by Xerox University Microfilms, Ann Arbor, Mich."—*verso of t.p.*

Both supersedes and extends the coverage of Golden and Simches' 1953 bibliography of the same title (*Guide* BD710). Includes references to articles pertinent to French language and literature appearing in some 588 homage volumes. Follows the arrangement of the earlier work (i.e., a listing of the *Festschriften* followed by a classified listing of the relevant contributions). Cutoff date is 1974 with some 1975 items included. The index is now a name index with reference to both authors of the articles analyzed and to literary authors as subjects (the latter designated by an asterisk). Z2175.F45G74

Talvart, Hector and **Place, Joseph.** Bibliographie des auteurs modernes de langue française (1801–1972). Paris, Éd. de la Chronique des Lettres Françaises, 1975–76. v.21–22. (In progress) **BD140**

For previously published volumes and annotation *see Guide* BD735.

Contents: v.21–22, Montherlant–Morgan, Claude; v.22 includes an "Index des illustrateurs des ouvrages décrits, tome I à XXII."

Periodicals

Place, Jean Michel and **Vasseur, André.** Bibliographie des revues et journaux littéraires des XIXe et XXe siècles. Paris, Éditions de la Chronique des Lettres Françaises, 1974–77. v.2–3. (In progress) **BD141**

For v.1 and annotation *see Guide* BD718.

v.1–2 are concerned with journals which began publication before 1900. v.3 treats a group of periodicals which began publication during the period 1915–30; it includes an index of names cited.

Translations

Bowe, Forrest. French literature in early American translation; a bibliographical survey of books and pamphlets printed in the United States from 1668 through 1820. Ed. by Mary Daniels. N.Y., Garland Pr., 1977. 528p. $60. **BD142**

The bibliography is "limited to translations of works written in French which were published in the United States from the colonial period through the year 1820. It includes books and pamphlets, as well as some broadside material. . . . In general, unless a printed text in French which served as a basis for an English translation has been located, . . . problematical works have been omitted."—*p.xxiii.* Arranged in sections according to the general subject content of the works translated (e.g., philosophy and religion, social sciences, history and biography, fiction and verse, drama, etc.); index of authors, translators and editors, and of French and English titles. Numerous descriptive and explanatory notes. Locates copies (many of the works being in the Bowe collection now at Cornell). Z1215.B66

Criticism

Modern French literature, comp. and ed. by Debra Popkin and Michael Popkin. N.Y., F. Ungar, [1977]. 2v. (A library of literary criticism) $55. **BD143**

A collection of excerpts from critical writings on 168 modern French authors considered to be "the ones who are most read, taught, and written about today in France, the United States, and Britain." —*Introd.* Excerpts are given in English, many of them translated specifically for this publication. Index to critics in v.2. Similar to other volumes in the series, e.g., *Guide* BD640. PQ306.M57

Dictionaries of authors and literature

Bonnefoy, Claude, Cartano, Tony and **Oster, Daniel.** Dictionnaire de littérature française contemporaine. Paris, Delarge, [1977]. 411p. il. **BD144**

A dictionary of selected writers of French literature who were alive as of Jan. 1, 1976, and those who, among older writers, had continued to publish new works in their late years. In most instances biographical information is very brief (sometimes minimal) and the bulk of the entry is devoted to commentary on the writer's works, themes, ideas, and place in the contemporary literary scene. A bibliography follows each entry, but this is usually limited to a list of the writer's own works. Appendixes deal with literary movements, regional literatures, and literary magazines.

The concise Oxford dictionary of French literature. Ed. by Joyce M. H. Reid. Oxford, Clarendon Pr., 1976. 669p. $15. **BD145**

An abridgement and revision of *The Oxford companion to French literature* (1959; *Guide* BD747). "Abridgement has been effected by condensation and amalgamation rather than omission. . . . Many new articles have been added, and a great many existing articles revised or expanded, in an attempt to bring the whole work more nearly up to date . . . ; a few articles have also been added to fill gaps in the coverage of earlier periods."—*Pref.* PQ41.C6

History

Histoire littéraire de la France; ouvrage commencé par des religieux bénédictins de la Congrégation de Saint Maur. . . . Paris, Impr. Nationale, 1974. v.40. (In progress) **BD146**

For full citation, previously published volumes and annotation *see Guide* BD758.

Contents: v.40, Suite du quatorzième siècle.

Fiction

Lever, Maurice. La fiction narrative en prose au XVIIème siècle: répertoire bibliographique du genre romanesque en France (1600–1700). Paris, Éditions du Centre National de la Recherche Scientifique, 1976. 645p. 160F. **BD147**

At head of title: Centre d'Étude de la Littérature française du XVIIème et du XVIIIème siècle (Paris-Sorbonne).

Interpreting "narrative fiction" as broadly as possible, the compiler aims to transcend the limitations of R. C. Williams' *Bibliography of the seventeenth-century novel in France* and to overcome the errors and deficiencies of R. W. Baldner's revision of that work (*Guide* BD776). The main listing is by title, and full bibliographic information, library locations, attribution of anonymous works, references to later editions, and the "incipit" of each work are given in that section. An author list (including pseudonyms) provides an author approach. Z5918.L47

Martin, Angus, Mylne, Vivienne G. and **Frautschi, Richard.** Bibliographie du genre romanesque français, 1751–1800. London, Mansell; Paris, France Expansion, 1977. 529p. il. $82.50. **BD148**

"Genre romanesque" is here defined as including novels, short stories, and other prose writings (such as dialogues) that embody some element of narrative fiction. In general the plan and scope of the bibliography follow that of S. P. Jones's *A list of French prose fiction from 1700 to 1750* (*Guide* BD778), except that French translations of works originally published in other languages are included herein, as are new editions of older works. Arrangement is chronological, then alphabetical by author, with an index of authors and titles. In addition to information on variant editions, serialization in periodicals, and library locations, there are often useful notes on form and content. About 6,750 entries. Z2174.F5M37

Italian

Guides

Beccaro, Felice del. Guida allo studio della letteratura italiana. [Milano], Mursia, [1975]. 350p. L7500 pa. **BD149**

A general section is followed by chapters for the literature of each century, with sub-sections for major writers of each period. Editions and studies are treated in essay form; index of names.
Z2354.C8B4

Bibliography

Harvard University. Library. Italian history and literature: classification schedule, classified listing by call number, chronological listing, author and title listing. Cambridge, publ. by Harvard Univ. Lib., distr. by Harvard Univ. Pr., 1974. 2v. (Widener Library shelflist, 51–52). $90. **BD150**

For full information *see Suppl.* DC70.

Dictionaries

Dizionario critico della letteratura italiana. Diretto da Vittore Branca. Torino, Unione Tipografico Editrice Torinese, [1973]. 3v. plates. L54000. **BD151**

A new work offering signed articles, most of them several pages in length. A high percentage of articles is biocritical in nature, but there are entries for literary terms, movements, etc. Substantial bibliographies, those for individual authors including both works by and about the writer. Cross references; index of names in v.3. PQ4057.D59

Individual authors

Dante

Enciclopedia dantesca. Roma, Istituto della Enciclopedia Italiana, [1974–76?]. v.4–5. **BD152**

For previously published volumes and annotation *see Guide* BD831.

Contents: v.4–5, N–Z. (Completes the set? The appendix promised for inclusion in v.5 does not appear therein.)

Grandgent, Charles Hall. Companion to the Divine comedy. Commentary by C. H. Grandgent as edited by Charles S. Singleton. Cambridge, Mass., Harvard Univ. Pr., 1975. 316p. il. $18. **BD153**

Intended for those "who are obliged to read their Dante in English."—*Pref.* Offers generous extracts from "those parts of Grandgent's well-known edition of the poem [i.e., *La Divina Commedia,* ed. and annotated by C. H. Grandgent, rev. by C. S. Singleton; Harvard Univ. Pr., 1972] which can be understood by a reader who has little or no Italian (and quite possibly no Latin)." PQ4464.G7

Portuguese

(including Brazilian)

Gomes, Celuta Moreira. O conto brasileiro e sua crítica. Bibliografia (1841–1974). Rio de Janeiro, Biblioteca Nacional, 1977. 2v. (654p.) **BD154**

An earlier work by the same author, *Bibliografia do conto brasileiro* (publ. 1968–69 in 2v.) covered 1841–1967.

A bibliography of the Brazilian short story, together with critical studies of the writers and their works. Arranged by literary author, with listings of their own works followed by references to critical writings. Indexes of titles and of critics.

Gonçalves, Augusto de Freitas Lopes. Dicionário histórico e literário do teatro no Brasil. Rio de Janeiro, Livraria Editora Cátedra, 1975–76. v.1–2. (In progress) **BD155**

Contents: v.1–2, A–B.

A dictionary of dramatists, actors, actresses and others in various performing arts professions, together with entries for individual theater pieces (comedies, tragedies, operas, zarzuelas, etc.).
PN2471.G6

Provençal

French XX bibliography. Provençal supplement. no.1– . N.Y., French Institute–Alliance Française and the Camargo Foundation, 1976– . (no.1: $12) **BD156**

Follows the style of the parent series (*Guide* BD740), "but because of the founding of the Félibrige in 1854 and the importance of the second half of the 19th century in the history of Provençal literature" (*Editor's note*), the period of coverage goes back to 1850; as in the main series, publications from 1940 are listed.

Spanish

Guides

Bleznick, Donald William. A sourcebook for Hispanic literature and language; a selected, annotated guide to Spanish and Spanish American bibliography, literature, linguistics, journals, and other source materials. Philadelphia, Temple Univ. Pr., [1974]. 183p. $15. **BD157**

"The guiding principle . . . was to identify essential books—occasionally articles when adequate books do not exist—and journals in those areas most central to research in Hispanic literature and language."—*Pref.* 1,075 items; brief annotations. In addition to sections for literature and linguistics, there is a section of "Other useful references in the Hispanic field" listing biographical dictionaries, encyclopedias, handbooks, etc. Indexed. Z2695.A2B55

Foster, David William and **Foster, Virginia Ramos.** Manual of Hispanic bibliography. 2d ed., rev. and expanded. N.Y., Garland Pr., 1977. 329p. $31. **BD158**

1st ed. 1970 (*Guide* BD851).

A revised and expanded edition following the plan of the earlier volume. Z2691.A1F68

Bibliography

Bibliography of Old Spanish texts. Literary texts, ed. 2. Comp. by Anthony Cárdenas [and others]. [Madison, Wis., Hispanic Seminary of Medieval Studies], 1977. 128p. $12.50. **BD159**

1st ed. 1975.

The bibliography "was originally conceived as a necessary first step in the change-over to computer-assisted techniques in the compilation of the Old Spanish dictionary, a project ongoing at the University of Wisconsin-Madison for nearly half a century."—*Introd.* Its aim is to create "an exhaustive descriptive inventory of the relevant pre-1501 Old Spanish texts" from which a selection can be made of the most lexically promising material to use in compiling the dictionary. This edition provides full citation (with indication of present location) of 1,869 items.

Simón Díaz, José. Bibliografía de la literatura hispánica. Madrid, Consejo Superior de Investigaciones Científicas, Inst. "Miguel de Cervantes" de Filología Hispánica, 1973. [Appendix]. (In progress) **BD160**

For previously published volumes and annotation *see Guide* BD858.

Contents: [Appendix], Tomos V y VI (apéndices). 314p.

This appendix volume provides interim updating of the material in v.5–6 until such time as the 2d ed. of those volumes is published, describing early editions of works which have come to light since publication of v.5–6, and indicating additional locations for rare books described in those volumes. Indexed.

——— ——— 2. ed., corr. y aum. Madrid, Consejo Superior de Investigaciones Científicas, Inst. "Miguel de Cervantes" de Filología Hispánica, 1962. v.2. (In progress) **BD161**

For previously published volumes *see Guide* BD858a.

Contents: v.2, [Bibliographies, bio-bibliographies, library catalogs, etc.].

——— Manual de bibliografía de la literatura española. 2. ed. Adiciones 1965–1970. Barcelona, G. Gili, 1972. 198p. **BD162**

On cover: Suplemento 2.
The 1963 edition of the *Manual* (*Guide* BD859) was reprinted in 1970 together with the separately-paged section of *Adiciones* for 1962–64 (originally issued separately in 1966). This new supplement carries the work forward through 1970.

Translations

Rudder, Robert S. The literature of Spain in English translation; a bibliography. N.Y., F. Ungar, [1975]. 637p. $25. **BD163**

Lists translations appearing in periodicals and in collections, as well as separately published works. Listing is by literary period (medieval, Renaissance, etc.), then by author; individual poems and stories are given separate entries. "Literature" is broadly interpreted to include historical writings, etc., of literary merit. "Spain" of the title refers to the country rather than the language, so that translations from Catalan, Basque, etc., are included, as are translations from the Latin of early Spanish writers. Indexes of authors and of anonymous works. Z2694.T7R83

Dictionaries of authors and literature

Diccionario de literatura española. Dirigido por Germán Bleiberg [y] Julián Marías. 4. ed., corr. y aum. Madrid, Ediciones de la Revista de Occidente, [1972]. 1191p., [70]p. **BD164**

1st ed. 1949; 3d ed. 1964 (*Guide* BD865).
This edition revised, expanded and updated: some new articles have been added (e.g., "lingüística"), and there is a new appendix on palaeography.

Instituto Nacional del Libro Español. Quién es quién en las letras españolas. 2a. ed. [Madrid], Instituto Nacional del Libro Español, [1973]. 546p. **BD165**

Bio-bibliographical sketches of nearly 2,000 writers. Includes journalists, essayists, and critics, as well as poets, novelists, dramatists, etc. Z2690.I55

Drama

Boyer, Mildred Vinson. The Texas collection of *comedias sueltas*: a descriptive bibliography. Boston, G. K. Hall, [1978]. 620p. $55. **BD166**

"This volume has been designed to describe The University of Texas [at Austin] holdings in Spanish dramatic literature in suelta editions prior to 1834."—*Introd.* Arranged by author, with anonymous works listed first. 1,119 items representing some 750 different titles. Indexed. Z2694.D7B7

Cambridge. University. Library. *Comedias sueltas* in Cambridge University Library: a descriptive catalog, comp. by A. J. C. Bainton. Cambridge, The Library, 1977. 281p. (Cambridge Univ. Lib. Historical bibliography ser., 2) **BD167**

Catalog of a collection of more than 900 separate editions of single plays, with full bibliographic description.

Spanish American

Bibliography

Bryant, Shasta M., comp. A selective bibliography of bibliographies of Hispanic American literature. 2d ed., greatly expanded and rev. Austin, Inst. of Latin American Studies, Univ. of Texas at Austin, 1976. 100p. (Guides and bibliographies ser., 8) $4.95 pa. **BD168**

1st ed., 1966, published by Pan American Union as its "Basic bibliography," no.3.
A guide for the student. Arranged by author or other main entry. Index of names, plus topical subjects. 662 items. Z1609.L7B77

Translations

Freudenthal, Juan R. and **Freudenthal, Patricia M.** Index to anthologies of Latin American literature in English translation. Boston, G. K. Hall, [1977]. 199p. $15. **BD169**

An index to writings in English translation of some 1,122 Spanish-American and Brazilian authors in 116 anthologies. Arranged by author, with translator and geographic indexes. Works are identified as poetry, fiction, drama, or "other." Z1609.T7F74

Shaw, Bradley A. Latin American literature in English translation; an annotated bibliography. N.Y., New York Univ. Pr., 1976. 144p. $17.75. **BD170**

"A Center for Inter-American Relations book."—*t.p.*
". . . the scope of the bibliography is limited to published books which include fiction, poetry, drama or the literary essay in English translation. . . . Periodical literature and literary criticism are not included."—*Pref.* Sections for Spanish American literature, Brazilian literature, and non-Hispanic literature of the Caribbean Islands and Guyanas, each sub-divided by genre. Indexes by author, English title, original title, and by country. Z1609.T7S47

Criticism

Foster, David William and **Foster, Virginia Ramos.** Modern Latin American literature. N.Y., Ungar, [1975]. 2v. (A library of literary criticism) $45. **BD171**

Like other volumes in the series (e.g., *Guide* BD640), these volumes present critical commentary on 20th-century Latin American authors. Commentary is drawn from book and periodical materials; about half is translated from Spanish and Portuguese sources. 137 writers are treated. Index of critics in v.2. A subscription books review in the *Booklist* 73:275 notes the omission of a number of important authors. PQ7081.F63

Drama

Lyday, Leon F. and **Woodyard, George W.** A bibliography of Latin American theater criticism, 1940–1974. Austin, Inst. of Latin American Studies, Univ. of Texas at Austin, 1976. 243p. (Texas. Univ. Inst. of Latin American Studies. Guides and bibliographies ser., 10) $5.95 pa. **BD172**

The period covered "corresponds to the establishment and development of a truly national theater movement in most areas of Latin America."—*Introd.* Author listing with subject index. 2,360 items. Z1609.D7L9

Fiction

Coll, Edna. Indice informativo de la novela hispanoamericana. [Rio Piedras], Editorial Universitaria, Universidad de Puerto Rico, 1974– . v.1– . $7.50 per v. (In progress) **BD173**

Contents: v.1, Las Antillas (1974); v.2, Centroamerica (1977); v.3, Venezuela (1978).
The completed series should offer a comprehensive bibliography of the Spanish American novel. Within each country section the listing is alphabetical by novelist's name. Most entries include a biographical note on the author, together with a list of his novels (often including a note on the character of the work) and bibliographic references to biographical and critical works. Z1609.F4C65

Foster, David William. The 20th century Spanish-American novel: a bibliographic guide. Metuchen, N.J., Scarecrow Pr., 1975. 227p. $8.50. **BD174**

Arranged by names of the novelists; cites both periodical and book materials. Index of critics. Z1609.F4F68

Individual countries

Chilean

California. University. Library. Contemporary Chilean literature in the University Library at Berkeley; a bibliography with introduction, biographical notes, and commentaries. Berkeley, Center for Latin American Studies, Univ. of California, 1975. 161p. **BD175**

Comp. by Gaston Somoshegyi-Szokol.

In three parts: (1) bibliography of selected 20th-century authors; (2) bibliographical guide to histories of Chilean literature; (3) biographical sketches of "selected contemporary Chilean writers whose works are considered to be the most significant in Chilean letters." —*Introd.* Index of authors. Z1713.C25

Colombian

Orjuela, Héctor H. Bibliografía de la poesía colombiana. Bogotá, Instituto Caro y Cuervo, 1971. 486p. (Inst. Caro y Cuervo. Publ. Ser. bibliográfica, 9) **BD176**

An author listing of the works of Colombian poets published as books, pamphlets or broadsides. Locates copies in numerous Colombian and foreign libraries. Z1744.P7

——— Bibliografía del teatro colombiano. Bogotá, [Instituto Caro y Cuervo], 1974. 312p. (Instituto Caro y Cuervo. Publ. Ser. bibliográfica, 10) **BD177**

The main section is an author listing of Colombian dramatic literature. The "Secciones complementarias," pp.209–76, offer lists of sources for the study of the Colombian theater, for the study of Latin American theater, and for the study of theater in general. Index of titles of the dramas. Many bibliographical and descriptive notes. Library locations are frequently given, including copies in selected United States libraries. Z1008.C685

Porras Collantes, Ernesto. Bibliografía de la novela en Colombia, con notas de contenido y crítica de las obras y guías de comentarios sobre los autores. Bogotá, Inst. Caro y Cuervo, 1976. 888p. (Instituto Caro y Cuervo. Publ. Ser. bibliográfica, 11) **BD178**

Based on the bibliography in A. Curcio Altamar's *Evolución de la novela en Colombia* (Bogotá, 1957). Forms a useful companion to H. H. Orjuela's bibliographies (in the same series) covering Colombian poetry and drama (*see Suppl.* BD176–BD177).

More than 2,300 entries. Arranged alphabetically by author; title and chronological indexes. Bibliographical information is very full, including details of serialization where relevant; reprints and translations are included; library locations are given (including a number of libraries outside Colombia). Numerous notes on contents, and excerpts from critical evaluations; citations to critical studies are frequently given. Z1008.C685

Ecuadorian

Barriga López, Franklin and **Barriga López, Leonardo.** Diccionario de la literatura ecuatoriana. Quito, Editorial Casa de la Cultura Ecuatoriana, 1973. 590p. S120. **BD179**

Primarily a biographical dictionary of Ecuadorian writers, with a few entries for literary societies and institutions. PQ8201.B35

Venezuelan

Cardozo, Lubio. Bibliografía de bibliografías sobre la literatura venezolana en las bibliotecas de Madrid, Paris y Londres. Maracaibo, Centro de Estudios Literarios de la Univ. del Zulia [y] Centro de Investigaciones Literarias de la Univ. de Los Andes, [1975]. 67p. **BD180**

An annotated bibliography of about 100 bibliographies. Z1911.A1C37

Diccionario general de la literatura venezolana (Autores). Mérida, Centro de Investigaciones Literarias, Univ. de Los Andes, Facultad de Humanidades y Educacion, 1974. 829p. **BD181**

Biographical sketches are followed by bibliographies—frequently extensive—which cite works by and about the authors. Foreign-born authors working in Venezuela or writing about Venezuela are included. A second volume of "Obras" is to deal with the most significant works in Venezuelan literature. PQ8534.D54

SLAVIC AND EAST EUROPEAN LANGUAGES

General works

Bibliography

Wytrzens, Günther. Bibliographische Einführung in das Studium der slavischen Literaturen. Frankfurt a. M., Klostermann, 1972. 348p. (Zeitschrift für Bibliothekswesen und Bibliographie. Sonderheft 13) DM62.50 pa. **BD182**

A bibliography of more than 5,000 items for the study of the whole range of Slavic literatures. Classified arrangement with name index and detailed table of contents. Includes works in Western European languages as well as those in the Slavic languages. Z7041.W9

Criticism

Modern Slavic literatures. Comp. and ed. by Vasa D. Mihailovich [and others]. N.Y., F. Ungar, [1976]. v.2. (A library of literary criticism) $30. **BD183**

For v.1 *see Guide* BD986.

Contents: v.2, Bulgarian, Czechoslovak, Polish, Ukrainian, and Yugoslav literatures. 720p.

Arranged alphabetically by literature, then alphabetically by author. Treats 196 writers. Index of critics. PG501.M518

Estonian

Mauer, Mare. Estonskaia literatura; rekomendatel'nyii ukazatel' literatury. Moskva, Kniga, 1975. 223p. il. 40r. **BD184**

At head of title: Gosudarstvennaia Biblioteka SSSR imeni V. I. Lenina. Gosudarstvennaia Biblioteka Estonskoi SSR imeni Fr. R. Kreitsval'da.

Bio-bibliographies of Estonian authors. Z2533.M3

Hungarian

Harvard University. Library. Hungarian history and literature: classification schedule, classified listing by call number, chronological listing, author and title listing. Cambridge, publ. by Harvard Univ. Lib., distr. by Harvard Univ. Pr., 1974. 186p. (Widener Library shelflist, 44) $25. **BD185**

For full information *see Suppl.* DC66.

Polish

Polska Akademia Nauk. Instytut Badań Literackich. Bibliografia literatury Polskiej. Nowy Korbut. Redaktor naczelny Kazimiers Budzyk. Komitet redakcyjny Ewa Korzeniewska [et al.]. [Warszawa], Państwowy Instytut Wydawniczy, [1966–73]. v.4–6², 9, 12–14. (In progress) **BD186**

For previously published volumes and annotation *see Guide* BD952.

Contents: v.4–6, Oświecenie, opracowała Elzbieta Aleksandrowska z zespołem redaktor tomo do r. 1958 Tadeusz Mikulski (1966); v.6², Oświecenie: uzupełnienia, indeksy (1972); v.9, Romantyzm (Hasła osobowe P–Z; Uzupełnienia), opracował zespół pod kierownictwem Irminy Śliwińskiej i Stanisława Stupkiewicza (1972); v.12, Józef Ignacy Kraszewski. Zarys bibliograficzny, opracowali Stanisław Stupkiewicz, Irmina Śliwińska, Wanda Roszkowska-Sykałowa (1966); v.13, Literatura pozytywizmu i młodej polski: Hasła ogólne; Hasła osobowe, A–F; v.14, Literatura pozytywizmu i młodej polski: Hasła osobowe, G–Ł, opracował zespół pod kierownictwem Zygmunte Szweykowskiego i Jarosława Maciejewskiego (1973).

Słownik terminów literackich. Michał Głowiński [et al.]. Pod red. Janusza Sławińskiego. Wrocław, Zakład Narodowy Imienia Ossolińskich, 1976. 577p. zł.190. **BD187**

A dictionary of literary terms, including terms from classical and foreign literatures. PN41.S56

Russian

Bibliography

Akademiia Nauk SSSR. Fundamental'naia Biblioteka Obshchestvennykh Nauk. Sovetskoe literaturovedenie i kritika: Russkaia sovetskaia literatura. Ukazatel' knig i statei za 1968–1970 gg. Moskva, "Nauka," 1975. 397p. 2r.,60k. **BD188**

For basic volume covering 1917–62, supplement 1963–67 and annotation *see Guide* BD967.

Moscow. Publichnaia Biblioteka. Otdel Rukopisei. Vospominaniia i dnevniki XVIII–XX vv.: ukazatel' rukopisei. Red. S. V. Zhitomirskaia. Moskva, "Kniga," 1976. 619p. 2.50r. **BD189**

For full information *see Suppl.* DC98.

Dissertations

Dossick, Jesse John. Doctoral research on Russia and the Soviet Union, 1960–1975; a classified list of 3,150 American, Canadian, and British dissertations with some critical and statistical analysis. N.Y., Garland, 1976. 345p. (Garland reference library of social science, 7) $32. **BD190**

For full information *see Suppl.* DC97.

Translations

Proizvedeniia sovetskikh pisatelei v perevodakh na inostrannye iazyki. Bibliograficheskii ukazatel', 1965/70–1971/75. Moskva, 1972–76. 2v. **BD191**

For earlier volumes and annotation *see Guide* BD990.

In two volumes: 1965/70: 225p. 1r.,58k.; 1971/75: 168p. 1r.,32k. Z2504.T7P75

Dictionaries and encyclopedias

Kratkaia literaturnaia entsiklopediia. Glav. red. A. A. Surkov. Moskva, Sovetskaia Entsiklopediia, 1975. v.8. **BD192**

For previously published volumes and annotation *see Guide* BD991.

Contents: v.8, Flober–IAshpal. Completes the set.

The modern encyclopedia of Russian and Soviet literature. Ed. by Harry B. Weber. [Gulf Breeze, Fla.], Academic International Pr., 1977–78. v.1–2. (In progress) $27.50 per v. **BD193**

Contents: v.1–2, Abaginskii–Bible, Armenian.

"The coverage envisioned for this series goes beyond writers and their works to include those aspects of Russian and Soviet cultural life which impinge in one way or another on literature in a broad sense: literary criticism, the contributions of past literary scholars (no living scholar is represented), a number of selected linguistic problems, dramatic literature (but not the theater as such), literary genres, literary movements, literary journals, and folklore. . . . The encyclopedia strives, ultimately, to arrive at a cultural profile of Russia and the Soviet Union, as revealed in Russian literature, in the many other national Soviet literatures, and in their literary traditions and literary history. This has entailed translating authoritative articles in older reference works, or combining information from many sources into a comprehensive article, or including entries by knowledgeable specialists."—*v. 1,p. vi.* Longer articles are signed; most include bibliographies. Material translated from other sources seems not to be so identified.

Timofeev, Leonid Ivanovich and **Turaev, S. V.** Slovar' literaturovedcheskikh terminov. Moskva, "Prosveshchenie," 1974. 509p. 1.53r. **BD194**

A dictionary of general literary terms. Derivation is indicated for terms of Latin, Greek, or other Western-language origin. Entries are signed; many include bibliographies. PN44.5.T5

Bio-bibliography

Russkie sovetskie pisateli. Poety. Biobibliograficheskii ukazatel'. Moskva, "Kniga," 1977– . v.1– . (In progress) **BD195**

Contents: v.1, Avramenko-Arkangelskii. 1r.,68k.

A biographical sketch of each writer is followed by a list of published works (including references for individual poems, etc.) and extensive listings of critical writings about the author.

Yugoslav

Mihailovich, Vasa D. and **Matejić, Mateja.** Yugoslav literature in English; a bibliography of translations and criticism (1821–1975). Cambridge, Mass., Slavica Publishers, [1976]. 328p. $8.95. **BD196**

Includes translations of anonymous folk literature as well as works of individual authors. The section of critical writings includes entries in reference works, books, articles, reviews, and dissertations. Indexed.

CLASSICAL LANGUAGES

Greek

Packard, David W. and **Meyers, Tania.** A bibliography of Homeric scholarship. Prelim. ed. 1930–1970. Malibu, Calif., Undena Publs., 1974. 183p. **BD197**

Cumulates into an author listing the Homer entries from *L'année philologique* of the period 1930–1970. Annotations are not included, but there is a subject index, with special sections for references to passages in the *Iliad* and the *Odyssey,* and for "Homeric words." Z8414.84.P32

Latin

Bibliography

IJsewijn, Jozef. Companion to neo-Latin studies. Amsterdam, North-Holland, 1977. 370p. $24.50. **BD198**

"Aims to pave the way to, and serve as a guide in, the immense field of Renaissance, Baroque and modern Latin" (*Pref.*) for beginners, and to provide "a compendium of basic factual and bibliographic information" for scholars in the field. "Neo-Latin" is defined as covering from about 1300 A.D. to the present. Chapters include: Classical, medieval and neo-Latin; Bibliographical aids; Historical survey of neo-Latin literature (with country subdivisions); Texts and editions; Language and style; Prosody and metrics; Literary forms and genres; Scholarly and scientific studies in neo-Latin; Historical survey of neo-Latin studies. Brief "Anthology of neo-Latin texts." Index of names. PA8020.I37

Kristeller, Paul Oskar, ed. Catalogus translationum et commentariorum: medieval and Renaissance Latin translations and commentaries. Annotated lists and guides. Wash., Catholic Univ. of America Pr., 1976. v.3. (In progress) **BD199**

For previously published volumes and annotation *see Guide* BD1044.

F. Edward Cranz is now ed. in chief.

v.3 offers further bio-bibliographies, addenda and corrigenda for v.1–2, and includes an index of manuscripts for v.1–3, an index of translators and commentators for v.1–3, and an index of ancient authors treated in v.1–3.

Individual authors

Petrarch

Cornell University. Libraries. Petrarch: catalogue of the Petrarch collection in Cornell University Library. Millwood, N.Y., Kraus-Thomson, 1974. 737p. $54. **BD200**

A revised and expanded version of the 1916 *Catalogue of the Petrarch collection* edited by Mary Fowler. However, since many of the analytic notes from the earlier work have not been carried forward (and *see* references to that work are provided), libraries holding the earlier volume will want to retain it in the reference collection. Z8676.C75

Vergil

Warwick, Henrietta Holm. A Vergil concordance. Minneapolis, Univ. of Minnesota Pr., [1975]. 962p. $45. **BD201**

A keyword-in-context concordance based on the "Oxford classical texts" edition, *P. Vergili Maronis opera,* ed. by R. A. B. Mynors (Oxford, Clarendon Pr., 1969). PA6952.W3

ORIENTAL LANGUAGES

General works

Guides

Columbia University. Columbia College. A guide to Oriental classics. . . . , ed. by Wm. Theodore De Bary and Ainslie T. Embree. 2d ed. N.Y., Columbia Univ. Pr., 1975. 257p. $9; $3.50 pa. **BD202**

1st ed. 1964.

". . . compiled as an aid to students and teachers taking up for the first time the major works of Oriental literature and thought. It is designed especially for general education, which emphasizes a careful reading of single whole works and discussion of them in a group." —*Introd.* Sections for the Islamic, Indian, Chinese, and Japanese traditions. For each of the classics considered, provides lists of English translations, selected secondary readings in English, and a list of topics for discussion; brief evaluative notes accompany most citations. Z7046.C65

Arabic

Altoma, Salih J. Modern Arabic literature: a bibliography of articles, books, dissertations, and translations in English. Bloomington, Indiana Univ., 1975. 73p. (Indiana Univ., Asian Studies Research Inst. Occasional papers, no.3) **BD203**

A guide to materials in English. Classed listing with author index; dissertations appear in a separate listing without subject approach. About 850 items.

Chinese

See also Suppl. BD202.

Bailey, Roger B. Guide to Chinese poetry and drama. Boston, G. K. Hall, 1973. 100p. $9.50. **BD204**

A bibliographic guide to works in English translation. "The bibliography addresses itself to those who are approaching the study of Chinese poetry for the first time. Individually, the annotations describe and make judgments on specific works. Taken as a whole, however, the bibliography should enable the reader to acquire as good a fundamental knowledge of Chinese poetry as is available to the English-speaking reader."—*Introd.: Poetry.* There is a separate, briefer section on the drama. Z3108.L5B34

Gibbs, Donald A. and **Li, Yun-chen.** A bibliography of studies and translations of modern Chinese literature, 1918–1942. Cambridge, Mass., East Asian Research Center, Harvard Univ.; distr. by Harvard Univ. Pr., 1975. 239p. (Harvard East Asian monographs, 61) $16; $8.50 pa. **BD205**

In three main sections: (1) Sources; (2) Studies of modern Chinese literature; (3) Studies and translations of individual authors. Concentrates on the period 1918–1942. Index of authors, translators, etc. Z3108.L5G52

Hebrew

Brisman, Shimeon. A history and guide to Judaic bibliography. Cincinnati, Hebrew Union College Pr.; N.Y., Ktav Publ. House, 1977. 325p. $25. **BD206**

For full information *see Suppl.* BB67.

Goell, Yohai. Bibliography of modern Hebrew literature in translation. Tel Aviv, Inst. for the Translation of Hebrew Literature, Ltd., 1975. 117p. **BD207**

Mainly a listing of separately-published translations, although a few translations appearing in periodicals or general anthologies have been included in cases where "special issues or sections have been devoted to modern Hebrew literature."—*Introd.* Translations are listed by language, subdivided by literary form. Appendix of monographs on modern Hebrew literature. Index of Hebrew authors, and one of translators, editors and authors of monographs. Z7070.G58

Japanese

See also Suppl. BD202.

Marks, Alfred H. and **Bort, Barry D.** Guide to Japanese prose. Boston, G. K. Hall, 1975. 150p. $12. **BD208**

A guide to Japanese literary prose available in English translation. The annotated bibliography is in two sections: (1) Pre-Meiji literature (beginnings to 1867) and (2) Meiji literature and after (1868 to present). An introductory essay places the works in their historical and literary context. Z3308.L5M37

Pronko, Leonard Cabell. Guide to Japanese drama. Boston, G. K. Hall, 1973. 125p. $9.50. **BD209**

Offers an annotated bibliography of historical and critical works available in English on the Japanese theater, and of texts of the plays available in English translation. Introductory essay on the Japanese theater, its history and traditions, and a brief chronology. Z3308.L5P76

Rimer, J. Thomas and **Morrell, Robert E.** Guide to Japanese poetry. Boston, G. K. Hall, 1975. 151p. $12. **BD210**

A "Historical sketch and bibliographic outline" is followed by an annotated bibliography of historical and critical works and of Japanese texts available in English translation. Z3308.L5R54

B E

Fine Arts

GENERAL WORKS

Guides

Ehresmann, Donald L. Fine arts: a bibliographic guide to basic reference works, histories, and handbooks. Littleton, Colo., Libraries Unlimited, 1975. 283p. $13.50. **BE1**

Identifies basic books for art reference. Inasmuch as the work was planned to complement Chamberlin's *Guide to art reference books* (*Guide* BE1), the majority of works cited were published between 1958 and 1973. Topical arrangement with author/title and subject indexes. Good annotations. Appendix: Selected list of fine arts books for small libraries, by Julia M. Ehresmann, pp.257–66.

An extensive review appears in *The booklist* 72:995–96.

Z5931.E47

Muehsam, Gerd. Guide to basic information sources in the visual arts. Santa Barbara, Calif., ABC-Clio; Oxford, Eng., Jeffrey Norton Publ., 1978. 266p. $14.95. **BE2**

A series of bibliographical essays followed by an alphabetical list of materials cited. Essays are intended for art and art history students, and discuss techniques of art research, important general art reference materials, primary sources, research materials for specific periods and forms in Western art; briefer essays are devoted to individual national schools of art (including oriental and primitive art). Name/title/subject index. N7425.M88

Bibliography

Allen, Jelisaveta S., ed. Literature on Byzantine art, 1892–1967. [London], Mansell, 1976. v.2. **BE3**

For full citation and annotation *see Guide* BE2.

Contents: v.2, By categories. 586p., $50.

In v.2 the cumulated entries are arranged topically within broad divisions on history of Byzantine art in general, and by art form (the "Iconography" section is by far the largest). For the most part, entries with a "purely regional or local orientation" have not been repeated in v.2, but this does not hold true of certain categories: the introduction spells out the policy and exceptions. Long critical annotations for entries in v.1 have not been repeated in v.2. Index of topics (including iconographic themes, museums and other owners of collections and manuscripts); index of modern authors.

Andreoli-deVillers, Jean-Pierre. Futurism and the arts: a bibliography, 1959–1973. Toronto, Univ. of Toronto Pr., [1975]. 189p. $17.50. **BE4**

A year-by-year listing of "everything of importance on or about Futurism" (*Introd.*) and other avant-garde movements as they relate to Futurism. Name and topical subject index. For earlier works on the subject see the bibliographies by M. Drudi Gambillo in *Archivi del futurismo,* v.1–2 (Rome, 1958–62). Z5936.F85A62

Buckley, Mary and **Baum, David.** Color theory: a guide to information sources. Detroit, Gale, 1975. 173p. (Art and architecture information guide ser., 2) $18. **BE5**

An annotated basic bibliography of books on color studies "in science, in psychology (especially perception of color), in chemistry, in painting, and in the artists' writings and observations."—*Introd.* Emphasis is on books that "have influenced the concepts, theories, and particularly the painting of practicing artists." Indexed.

Z7144.C7B8

Cresswell, Keppel Archibald Cameron. A bibliography of the architecture, arts, and crafts of Islam. Supplement, Jan. 1960 to Jan. 1972. [Cairo], American Univ. in Cairo Pr., 1973. 366p. **BE6**

For basic volume *see Guide* BE6.

The Frick Collection, New York. The Frick collection; an illustrated catalogue. N.Y., distr. by Princeton Univ. Pr., 1977. v.8. il. (In progress) **BE7**

For previously published volumes and annotation *see Guide* BE199.

Contents: v.8, Limoges painted enamels, Oriental rugs and English silver. $40.

German expressionism in the fine arts: a bibliography by John M. Spalek, [et al.]. Los Angeles, Hennessey & Ingalls, 1977. 272p. (Art and architecture bibliographies, 3) $39.95. **BE8**

A bibliography of more than 4,000 books, pamphlets, special journal issues, and exhibition catalogs covering the major art movements and artists in Germany, 1900–30. Includes materials in all Western languages, although most items are in German. Cutoff date is 1972. Author, gallery, and subject indexes. Z5961.G4G47

Hanks, Elizabeth Flinn. Bibliography of Australian art. Melbourne, Library Council of Victoria, 1976. 2v. **BE9**

Contents: v.1, To 1900; v.2, 1901–1925.

"Based on the holdings of the State Library of Victoria, supplemented by the collections in the Mitchell Library, Sydney and the Art Gallery of New South Wales."—*Pref.*

A bibliography of books, periodical articles, exhibition catalogs, and book illustrations relating to Australian art. Each volume includes subject and artist entries, with artist entries arranged by form (e.g., books by; books illustrated by; books about). A third volume covering publications of 1926–50 is announced as in preparation.

Z5961.A85H35

Kempton, Richard. Art nouveau: an annotated bibliography. Los Angeles, Hennessey & Ingalls, 1977– . v.1– . (Art & architecture bibliographies, 4–) (In progress) **BE10**

Contents: v.1, General, Austria, Belgium and France. $39.95.

A bibliography of books, articles, exhibition catalogs, etc., published through 1971, concerning the movement in Europe and the United States. Each section (general and national) divided by form, then by individual artists or groups. Indexed.

v.2 will include Germany, Great Britain, Italy, the Netherlands, Scandinavia, Spain, East Europe and the United States; v.3 will be supplementary, citing items omitted, theses and dissertations, and books published 1972–76. Z5936.N6K45

Kendall, Aubyn. The art and archaeology of pre-Columbian Middle America: an annotated bibliography of works in English. Boston, G. K. Hall, 1977. 324p. $25. **BE11**

An expanded edition of the same author's *The art of pre-Columbian Mexico: an annotated bibliography* . . . (Austin, Tex., 1973).

Presents more than 2,000 annotated entries for books, exhibition catalogs, and periodical articles published through Dec. 1976. Alphabetical author listing within separate sections for books and periodicals. Appendix of selected dissertation titles. Subject index.

Z1208.M4K45

New York. Metropolitan Museum of Art. Library. Library catalog. Supplement. 5th–7th. Boston, G. K. Hall, 1973–77. 4v. **BE12**

For basic set and earlier supplements *see Guide* BE20.

Supplements 5–7 represent additions to the library for the period 1970–76. In all supplements sales catalogs are listed separately.

New York. Museum of Modern Art. Library. Catalog of the Library. Boston, G. K. Hall, 1976. 14v. $1140. **BE13**

Photographic reproduction of the dictionary catalog of this library which is especially strong in the "visual arts from around 1850 to the present."—*Introd.* Includes citations to articles in periodicals not covered by the *Art index* and the *Répertoire d'art et d'archéologie;* exhibition catalogs are also represented. "Latin American ephemeral material (exhibition catalogs and artists' files)" are listed separately in v.7, as are periodical titles. Z5939.N557

New York. Public Library. Art and Architecture Division. Dictionary catalog. . . . Boston, G. K. Hall, 1975. 30v. $2950. **BE14**

Photographic reproduction of the card catalog; includes materials cataloged through Dec. 1971. Covers "painting, drawing, sculpture, and the history and design aspects of architecture and the applied arts."—*Introd.* Also lists relevant materials in the Cyrillic, Hebrew, and Oriental collections, the Local History and Rare Book divisions, and citations to periodical articles in journals in all parts of the library.

——— ——— Supplement 1974. Boston, G. K. Hall, 1976. 556p. $80.

Covers material added Jan. 1972–Sept. 1974 to the Art and Architecture Division and the Prints Division. Z5939.N56

——— Bibliographic guide to art and architecture. 1975– . Boston, G. K. Hall, 1976– . Annual. (1977: $95) **BE15**

Serves as a supplement to the Division's *Dictionary catalog* (above). In addition to the materials cataloged for the Art and Architecture Division, lists entries from Library of Congress MARC tapes. Z5939.N56a

Volz, John. Paint bibliography. Ottawa, Assoc. for Preservation Technology, 1975. 25*l*. (APT newsletter, v.4, no.1 suppl.) **BE16**

An author listing of about 450 books and periodical articles concerning "paint, its technology as well as tastes and philosophy with regard to the use of color."—*Foreword.* Based mainly on the collections at the New York Public Library and the Avery Library, Columbia University. No index.

Western, Dominique Coulet. A bibliography of the arts of Africa. Waltham, Mass., African Studies Assoc., [1975]. 123p. $10. **BE17**

Lists books, articles, and exhibition catalogs "on art, architecture, oral literature, music and dance in Sub-Saharan Africa. Each of these major categories has been subdivided into both a general listing . . . as well as broad geographical areas . . . further into ethnic groups and some nations."—*Note.* Some annotations; author index. Z5961.S85W47

Yüan, Tung Li. The T. L. Yüan bibliography of Western writings on Chinese art and archaeology. Harrie A. Vanderstappen, ed. [London], Mansell, 1975. 606p. £35. **BE18**

A subject listing, with detailed subdivisions; author index. The work was begun by T. L. Yüan and is intended as a companion volume to his *China in Western literature* (*Guide* DE96); it "now contains over 15,000 items [including reviews] of a variety of materials on Chinese art and archaeology in English, German, Dutch, Scandinavian, Slavic, and French and other Romance languages published between 1920 and 1965."—*Foreword.* Books and articles are listed in separate sections; detailed outline of each section, but no alphabetical subject index. Z5961.C5Y9

Current

Art, design, photo. 1972– . [Hemel Hempstead, Eng.], A. Davis Publ.; distr. by Somerset House, Teaneck, N.J., 1973– . Annual. £30 per yr. **BE19**

Alexander Davis, ed. and comp.

Subtitle, 1972: Annual bibliography of books, catalogues and articles on modern art, graphic design, photography, art libraries.

A current bibliography of books and essays, sale and exhibition catalogs, periodical and newspaper articles on the "late 19th and 20th century art and artists, photography and graphic design—including the decorative arts: ceramics, textiles, jewelry, fashion."—*Introd.* In two sections: (1) Artists; (2) Subjects. Each volume covers publications of the designated year, plus retrospective coverage for items received too late for inclusion in the earlier volumes. Detailed name and subject index in each volume.

May be considered a continuation of the *LOMA* bibliography (*Guide* BE27) which Davis also edited.

Artbibliographies: current titles, v.1, no.1– , Sept. 1972– . Santa Barbara, Calif., ABC-Clio, 1972– . Bi-monthly. Service rate basis. **BE20**

Provides reproductions of the table of contents from about 75 journals, museum publications, annuals and irregular serials in each issue. The serials selected are those to be indexed in *Artbibliographies modern,* with this publication serving as a current-awareness tool. Z5937.A793

Artbibliographies modern, v.4, no.1– , Spr. 1973– . Oxford, European Bibliographic Center; Santa Barbara, Calif., Clio Pr., 1973– . Semiannual. Service rate basis. **BE21**

Supersedes *LOMA: literature of modern art,* 1969–71 (*Guide* BE27) and assumes its numbering.

Offers abstracts of books, exhibition catalogs, and periodical articles dealing with art and design throughout the world from about 1800 to the present. Coverage begins with publications of 1972, and each issue will include any material currently published together with any important items omitted from earlier volumes. Alphabetical listing by topical subjects and artists' names in a single alphabet. English-language translations of foreign titles are given in parentheses following the original titles. Author index and museum/gallery index. Z5935.L64

RILA, Répertoire international de la littérature de l'art. RILA, International repertory of the literature of art. [N.Y., College Art Assoc. of America], 1975– . v.1– . 2 issues per yr. $75 per v. **BE22**

Publisher varies; frequency varies (originally annual).

Volume for 1975 preceded by a number dated 1973 (called "Demonstration issue"). v.1 issued in two parts: Abstracts, and Index; v.2– , 1976– , published in two issues per year, with each issue containing abstracts and index; no cumulative annual index has appeared to date. v.1, 1975, covers chiefly 1974 and the first half of 1975.

A major new bibliography and abstract service covering books, dissertations, museum publications, exhibition catalogs, and articles in periodicals, *Festschriften* and conference proceedings concerned with post-classical European and post-Columbian American art. Abstracts are arranged topically under broad subject headings: Reference works, General works, Medieval art, Renaissance and baroque art, Modern art, Collections, Exhibitions. (An "Exhibition list" within the latter section is a city-by-city listing of exhibits with reference to the item number in the relevant topical section where an abstract appears.) Detailed author and subject index. Z5937.R16

Indexes

Chicago. Art Institute. Ryerson Library. Index to art periodicals. First supplement. Boston, G. K. Hall, 1975. 573p. $75. **BE23**

For main set and annotation *see Guide* BE32.

Covers "indexing activity from 1961 to October, 1974."—*Pref.* Some retrospective indexing was also added.

Hewlett-Woodmere Public Library. Index to art reproductions in books. Comp. by the professional staff of the Hewlett-Woodmere Public Library [Hewlett, N.Y.] under the direction of Elizabeth W. Thomson. Metuchen, N.J., Scarecrow Pr., 1974. 372p. $12.50 **BE24**

An index to reproductions in 65 art books published 1956–71. Approach is through the artist's name, with a title index; no subject approach. N7525.H48

Smith, Lyn Wall and **Moure, Nancy Dustin Wall.** Index to reproductions of American paintings appearing in more than 400 books, mostly published since 1960. Metuchen, N.J., Scarecrow Pr., 1977. 931p. $45. **BE25**

Intended as a continuation of Monro's *Index to reproductions of American paintings* (*Guide* BE38), and similar in arrangement. "Under each artist's name, titles of his paintings are listed alphabetically and under those are placed the abbreviations for the books in which a reproduction occurs. Beside or just below the title is an abbreviation signifying the owner of a painting. Only permanent collections—no

private owners are cited."—*Pref.* Index of titles arranged by general categories (e.g., allegories, animals, architectural subjects).
ND205.S575

Dictionaries and encyclopedias

Lexikon der Kunst. . . . Hrsg. von Ludger Alscher [u.a.]. Leipzig, Seemann, 1975–77. v.3–4. il. (In progress) **BE26**

For full citation and annotation *see Guide* BE53.
Contents: v.3, Li–P; v.4, Q–S.

Myers, Bernard Samuel and **Myers, Shirley D.** Dictionary of 20th century art. N.Y., McGraw-Hill, [1974]. 440p. il. $9.95. **BE27**

Entries on art movements and artists (including graphic artists and architects) active from 1905 to the present have been drawn from the *McGraw Hill dictionary of art* (*Guide* BE55) and the brief bibliographies cumulated at the end of the present volume. Some entries have been updated. N6490.M89

Visual dictionary of art. Greenwich, Conn., New York Graphic Society, [1974]. 640p. il. $30. **BE28**

Gen. ed., Ann Hill.
A dictionary of painting and sculpture featuring concise entries and with emphasis on artists. Includes brief survey articles on the art of various periods and countries. Heavily illustrated. Name index; brief bibliography. N33.V56

Walker, John Albert. Glossary of art, architecture and design since 1945: terms and labels describing movements, styles, and groups, derived from the vocabulary of artists and critics. 2d rev. ed. London, Bingley; Hamden, Conn., Linnet Books, [1977]. 352p. $15. **BE29**

1st ed. 1973 (*Guide* BE67).
Revision includes updating of articles and of the bibliographies, plus the addition of new entries for terms which have gained currency in the four years since publication of the earlier edition. N34.W34

Directories

Abse, Joan. The art galleries of Britain and Ireland; a guide to their collections. London, Sidgwick & Jackson, 1975; Rutherford, N.J., Fairleigh Dickinson Pr., 1976. 248p. il. £5.95, $12. **BE30**

Offers descriptions of public museums and their major collections of paintings (with some attention to sculpture), together with address, telephone number, and hours of opening. Museums are listed alphabetically under name of city; index of artists and museum names. A few surprising omissions were noted (e.g., the Imperial War Museum). N1020.A27

Artist's & photographer's market '77. Eds.: Lynne Lapin, Kirk Polking and Paula Arnett Sandhage. Cincinnati, Writer's Digest, [1976]. 702p. $10.95. **BE31**

Represents a new edition of the *Artist's market* (Cincinnati, 1974).
A guide to the freelance market, with market directory listings categorized under such headings as: Advertising and public relations, Competitions and exhibitions, Craft dealers, Fine arts publishers and distributors, Galleries and art dealers, Periodicals, Photography and film, Specialized markets. Includes information on pricing, taxes, copyright, and contracts; glossary; geographical index; general index. N8600.A75

Canada. Statistics Canada. Cultural Information Section. Directory of museums, art galleries and related institutions, 1972. Répertoire des musées, galeries d'art et des établissements connexes, 1972. Ottawa, Information Canada, 1973. 216p. $1.50. **BE32**

A geographically arranged directory of museums, art galleries (noncommercial), archives, botanical gardens, zoos and aquariums, historic houses and sites, planetariums and observatories. Gives brief description, hours and dates of opening, price of admission, governing authority, but not address of institution or name of administrator. English and French in parallel columns. Institutional name index. AM21.A1D57

Filsinger, Cheryl. Locus: a cross-referenced directory of New York galleries and art sources with their current stables of artists and art; the place to find everybody's work. N.Y., Filsinger, [1975]. 192p. $10. **BE33**

The main listing is by artist's name, indicating galleries which represent or carry the artist's works (including photographs, jewelry, etc.). Galleries are listed alphabetically, giving address, hours, and artists represented; there is also a geographical listing by street. Brief directory of museums. Additions and corrections appear in *Locus 77/78 update* (N.Y., 1977. 93p. $10). N6535.N5F54

Fine arts market place 73/74– [Ed.1–]. N.Y., Bowker, 1973– . Biennial. **BE34**

3d ed. published 1977 (904p.; $19.95 pa.).
A topical listing of firms, organizations, dealers, etc., deemed useful to anyone interested in the business aspects of art. Ranges from art dealers and auction houses to suppliers of gallery equipment, restorers and conservators, art councils, and international exhibitions. Includes a section of names, addresses, and telephone numbers. N51.F55

History

Janson, Horst Woldemar and **Janson, Dora Jane.** History of art; a survey of the major visual arts from the dawn of history to the present day. 2d ed. Englewood Cliffs, N.J. Prentice-Hall; N.Y., Abrams [1977]. 767p. il. $28.50. **BE35**

For previous ed. *see Guide* BE89.
A revised and expanded edition with many new illustrations. The most extensive revision and enlargement is in the prehistoric section and in coverage of the modern period to the late 1960s. The bibliography has been expanded and updated. N5300.J3

Pelican history of art. Harmondsworth, Eng., N.Y., Penguin, 1976–77. v.39–40, 42–43. (In progress) **BE36**

For previously published volumes and annotation *see Guide* BE92; many of the volumes noted there have been issued in revised editions.
Contents: v.39, Roman art, by Donald Strong ($40); [v.40], American art, by John Wilmerding ($40); [v.42], The arts of prehistoric Greece, by Sinclair Hood ($12.95 pa.); [v.43], Etruscan art, by Otto Brendel ($15 pa.).

Biography

Bénézit, Emmanuel. Dictionnaire critique et documentaire des sculpteurs, dessinateurs et graveurs de tous les temps. . . . Nouvelle éd. ent. refondue, revue et corrigée. Paris, Gründ, 1976. 10v. port. 1500F. **BE37**

For earlier ed. *see Guide* BE95.
A complete updating and expansion of the previous edition, but using the same format and presenting the same type of information. Brief bibliography of sources at end of v.10. An unusual feature is the inclusion of tables of 20th-century rates of exchange for pounds, dollars and francs. N40.B47

Khudozhniki narodov SSSR. Biobibliograficheskii slovar' v shesti tomakh. Red. Kollegiia: T. N. Gorina [i dr.]. Moskva, Izd. Iskusstvo, 1976. v.3. (In progress) **BE38**

For v.1–2 and annotation *see Guide* BE99.
Contents: v.3, Georgadei-Elgin.

Naylor, Colin. Contemporary artists. London, St. James Pr.; N.Y., St. Martin's Pr., 1977. 1077p. il. £25; $50. **BE39**

A "bio-bibliographical reference work on the personal and professional lives of about 1300 internationally-known artists . . . who have worked as professional artists for at least 5 years, exhibited . . . in several one-man shows, . . . in museum-type survey shows and [are] represented in the permanent collections of major museums throughout the country."—*Introd.* None were deceased prior to 1930. Information for each artist includes: who's-who-type biography, lists of individual shows, selected group shows, museum collections, publications, and a short written sketch, often by the artist. N6490.C6567

Roberts, Laurance P. A dictionary of Japanese artists: painting, sculpture, ceramics, prints, lacquer. Foreword by John M. Rosenfield. Tokyo and N.Y., Weatherhill, [1976]. 299p. $22.50. **BE40**

"This dictionary limits itself to artists who were born before 1900, or, if born later, who died before 1972."—*Pref.* Entry is by the most common form of the artist's name, with an index of alternate forms and one of Japanese characters. For each artist is given: all forms of name, dates, education, career, public collections in which represented, references to items in the bibliography (pp.223–32) which provide fuller information. Brief glossary of terms. N7358.R6

United States

Cummings, Paul. Dictionary of contemporary American artists. 3d ed. N.Y., St. Martin's Pr., 1977. 545p. il. $35. **BE41**

2d ed. 1971 (*Guide* BE107).

Updated to 1976 and much expanded, the work now includes 872 American artists. Collections of papers or taped interviews in the Archives of American Art are indicated. Bibliography, pp.511–45. N6536.C8

Dawdy, Doris Ostrander. Artists of the American West; a biographical dictionary. Chicago, Swallow Pr., [1974]. 275p. $12.50. **BE42**

Lists some 1,300 artists who were born before 1900 and who painted the West, giving dates, places of residence, and references to books and articles offering fuller information. Within the listing 300 artists are accorded fuller treatment regarding career. Bibliography of directories, catalogs, books, articles, and a few manuscripts useful for obtaining further information, pp.261–74. N6536.D38

Samuels, Peggy and **Samuels, Harold.** The illustrated biographical encyclopedia of artists of the American West. Garden City, N.Y., Doubleday, 1976. 549p. il. $25. **BE43**

Treats some 1,700 artists active by 1950, who "developed Western subjects."—*Introd.* Includes some non-American painters. Gives artist's dates, price which a work has brought at auction, brief sketch of life and career, and reference to additional sources. N8214.5.U6S25

Artists' signatures

Caplan, H. H. The classified directory of artists' signatures, symbols and monograms. London, George Prior Publ., 1976; Detroit, Gale, 1977. 738p. $75. **BE44**

Intended as a comprehensive dictionary offering (1) facsimiles of artists' signatures arranged alphabetically by name; (2) facsimiles of monograms arranged alphabetically under the first or uppermost letter of the monogram, plus an unclassified section of monograms; (3) reproductions of illegible or misleading signatures arranged under the first recognizable letter, again with an unclassified section; and (4) symbols arranged by general shape, with irregular ones entered at the end of the section. N45.C36

Symbolism in art

Henkel, Arthur and **Schöne, Albrecht.** Emblemata; Handbuch zur Sinnbildkunst des XVI. und XVII. Jahrhunderts. Im Auftrage der Göttinger Akad. d. Wissenschaften. Stuttgart, J. B. Metzler, 1967 (reissued 1976). 2196col. il. DM650. **BE45**

——— ——— Supplement der Erstausgabe. Stuttgart, 1976. ccxlp. DM98.

Reproduces emblems drawn from 45 collections published during the 16th and 17th centuries. Emblems are grouped by category (e.g., macrocosm, the four elements, plants, animals); reference is given to original source. Motto Register; Bild Register; Bedeutungs-Register. The supplement is a "Bibliographie zur Emblemforschung." N7740.H53

Lexikon der christlichen Ikonographie. Hrsg. von Engelbert Kirschbaum. . . . Rom, Herder, 1974–76. v.6–8. **BE46**

For previously published volumes and annotation *see Guide* BE125.

Contents: v.6–8, Ikonographie der Heiligen: Cres–Zw. (Completes the set.)

Sill, Gertrude Grace. A handbook of symbols in Christian art. N.Y., Macmillan, 1975. 241p. il. $10.95; $5.95 pa. **BE47**

A dictionary of Christian symbols arranged under broad headings such as "Angels," "Vices and virtues," etc. Intended as a basic reference guide for museum visitors, tourists, and students, and for the home library. Indexed. N8010.S54

Vries, Ad de. Dictionary of symbols and imagery. Amsterdam, North-Holland Publ. Co., [1974]. 523p. 104fl. **BE48**

Intends to supply "associations which have been evoked by certain words, signs, etc. in Western civilization in the past, and which may float to the surface again tomorrow."—*Pref.* Includes allegories, metaphors, signs, images, etc. Emphasis is on literary, mythological, religious, and proverbial use rather than graphic representation. BL600.V74

Art reproductions

United Nations Educational, Scientific and Cultural Organization. Catalogue de reproductions de peintures 1860 à 1973. Catálogo de reproducciones de pinturas, 1860 a 1973. [10th ed.] Paris, UNESCO, 1974. 343p. il. $13.20; 40F. **BE49**

9th ed. 1969 (*Guide* BE146).

1,534 reproductions are cited in this edition. A new feature is "Fifteen projects for exhibitions."

ARCHITECTURE

Bibliography

American Association of Architectural Bibliographers. Papers. Index, v.1–10, 1965–1973. Charlottesville, Univ. Pr. of Virginia, 1975. 311p. **BE50**

Issued as v.11 of the *Papers* series (*see Guide* BE149).

Mainly an index of authors and titles of works cited in the bibliographies.

Bibliographie zur Architektur im 19 Jahrhundert; die Aufsätze in den deutschsprachigen Architektur-Zeitschriften 1789–1918. Ed., Stephen Waetzoldt; comp., Verena Haas. Nendeln, Liechtenstein, KTO Pr., 1977. 8v. 912SwFr. **BE51**

"The bibliography lists all contributions on construction projects, reconstruction, renovation, design contests, architectural theory and criticism, as well as the technical aspects of building, which appeared in the 129 most important German-language journals on architecture and the construction industry published between 1789 and 1918 in the German and Austro-Hungarian empires and in Switzerland."—*Pref.* Topically arranged by type of architecture. v.8 is an index by authors, by architects, and by places.

Columbia University. Libraries. Avery Architectural Library. Catalog. 2d ed. Suppl. 2–3. Boston, G. K. Hall, 1975–77. 7v. $715. **BE52**

For basic set and first suppl. *see Guide* BE150.

Suppl. 2 (4v.; $420) includes all books, drawings, and periodicals cataloged during the period July 1972–May 1974; Suppl. 3 (3v.; $295) covers all books and periodicals added June 1974–May 1977.

Hitchcock, Henry Russell. American architectural books; a list of books, portfolios, and pamphlets on architecture and related subjects published in America before 1895. New expanded ed., with a new introduction by Adolf K. Placzek. N.Y., DaCapo Pr., 1976. 150p. $12.50. **BE53**

Reprints the text of the 1962 ed. (*Guide* BE151), with a new introduction and "A listing of architectural periodicals before 1895" by Adolf K. Placzek, and an appendix, "Chronological short-title list of Henry-Russell Hitchcock's 'American architectural books'" comp. under the direction of William H. Jordy (originally issued as *Publication* no.4 [Oct. 1955] of the American Association of Architectural Bibliographers).

Senkevitch, Anatole. Soviet architecture, 1917–1962: a bibliographical guide to source material. Charlottesville, Univ. Pr. of Virginia, [1974]. 284p. $13.50. **BE54**

A selective bibliography listing more than 1,000 titles of books and articles on the history and theory of Soviet architecture, especially in the R.S.F.S.R. Although Western-language materials are included, the emphasis is on Russian-language publications. Topical arrangement, with names and titles index. Annotated. Especially useful is the introductory discussion of resources available in American libraries. Z5944.R9S45

Sokol, David M. American architecture and art; a guide to information sources. Detroit, Gale, 1976. 341p. (American studies information guide ser., v.2) $18. **BE55**

For the general reader. An annotated listing of books, articles, serials, and exhibition catalogs; topically arranged, with author, title, and subject indexes. Includes the decorative arts, and sections on individual artists, as well as general materials on movements, period surveys, etc. Z5961.U5S64

Wodehouse, Lawrence. American architects from the Civil War to the First World War: a guide to information sources. Detroit, Gale, [1976]. 343p. (Art and architecture information guide ser., v.3) $18. **BE56**

Intended as a continuation of Roos's *Bibliography of early American architecture* (*Guide* BE153). A general section is followed by an annotated listing of books and articles concerning individual architects active within the period. Provides a brief biography (with reference to published writings and known repositories of his drawings) for each of the 175 architects. A third section is concerned with significant architects about whom little has been written. Detailed general index; building location index. Z5944.U5W63

——— American architects from the first World War to the present; a guide to information sources. Detroit, Gale, [1977]. 305p. (Art and architecture information guide ser., v.4) $18. **BE57**

A companion to the same author's *American architects from the Civil War to the First World War* (*Suppl.* BE56).

An annotated listing of "General reference works on American architects and their architecture" is followed by an annotated bibliography for 174 American architects active since the first World War. Subject and name index; building index. Z5944.U5W635

Indexes

Columbia University. Libraries. Avery Architectural Library. Avery index to architectural periodicals. Suppl. 1–2. Boston, G. K. Hall, 1975–77. 2v. **BE58**

For basic set and annotation *see Guide* BE157.

Suppl. 1 (823p.; $115) covers the years 1973–74; Suppl. 2 covers 1975–76.

Royal Institute of British Architects, London. Comprehensive index to architectural periodicals, 1956–1970. [London, World Microfilms, 1973] 20 reels of microfilm (16mm.). $420. **BE59**

Photographic reproduction of a card file forming an international index to selected articles from some 200 architecture and planning journals of the 1956–70 period. Topical arrangement, with alpabetical listing by English-language title thereunder. The last reel contains the list of subject headings used. Much of the index was published in the quarterly issues of the *RIBA library bulletin.* For a detailed review *see* M. R. Whiteman's article in *Microform review* (3:48–50, Jan. 1974).

——— RIBA annual review, 1965/66–1971/July 1972. London, 1967–73. 7v. **BE60**

The set offers annual cumulations of the bibliography appearing in each quarterly issue of the *RIBA library bulletin.* Subject arrangement with author index. Superseded by:

Architectural periodicals index, v.1– , Aug.1972/Dec. 1973– . London, 1974– . Quarterly, the 4th issue being the annual cumulation. £35 per yr.; £30 for annual cumulation only. **BE61**

v.1 appeared quarterly with a fifth issue as the annual cumulation.

"Special fields indexed include architecture and allied arts, constructional techniques, design, environmental studies, planning."—*Pref.* Indexes some 450 journals. Classed arrangement with alphabetical listing by English-language title within subject categories; foreign-language articles carry a note as to language and presence of English summary. Name index; a geographical index is to be added beginning with the annual cumulation of v.6.

Dictionaries

Cowan, Henry J. Dictionary of architectural science. N.Y., Wiley, [1973]. 354p. il. $10.95. **BE62**

"The dictionary aims to be comprehensive within the field of architectural science proper, i.e., structures, materials, acoustics, lighting, thermal environment and building services."—*Pref.* The terms were culled from the indexes of standard textbooks, with a few terms drawn from related fields. Brief definitions; illustrations are mainly for geometry and structural terms. Appendixes include a discussion of information processing, mathematical tables, directory of organizations, and "A survey of the literature of architectural science." NA31.C64

Curl, James Stevens. English architecture, an illustrated glossary; with a foreword by Lord Muirshiel and drawings by John J. Sambrook. Newton Abbot, Eng., North Pomfred, Vt., David & Charles, [1977]. 192p. il. £9.50. **BE63**

A heavily illustrated dictionary of English (and some Scottish) terms in historical architecture. Succinct definitions; short bibliography. A related volume is Glen L. Pride's *Glossary of Scottish building* (Glasgow, Scottish Civic Trust, 1976). NA961.C87

Harris, Cyril M., ed. Dictionary of architecture and construction. N.Y., McGraw-Hill, 1975. 553p. il. $35. **BE64**

Offers "definitions of terms which are encountered in the everyday practice of architecture and construction and in their associated fields, as, for example, terms found on drawings and in specifications."—*Pref.* Includes terms relating to products and materials, tools and equipment used in the building trades, "the control of the environment in buildings," history of architecture and restoration, urban planning and landscape architecture. Definitions are brief, but the work is profusely illustrated with very helpful line drawings. NA31.H32

Historic architecture sourcebook, ed. by Cyril M. Harris. N.Y., McGraw-Hill, [1977]. 581p. il. $19.95. **BE65**

Offers brief definitions of some 5,000 architectural terms; features more than 2,000 illustrations—mainly line drawings. NA31.H56

Pevsner, *Sir* Nikolaus, Fleming, John and **Honour, Hugh.** A dictionary of architecture. Rev. and enl. ed. London, Lane, 1975. 556p. il. £10. **BE66**

1966 ed. (*Guide* BE162) and 1972 ed. had title: *Penguin dictionary of architecture.*

"Many of the entries are new, others have been expanded or revised and rewritten. Selected bibliographies have also been added to most of the entries."—*Pref.* Includes definitions of terms, brief surveys of the architectural history of individual countries, and biographical notes on leading architects. Profusely illustrated. Many of the new entries relate to non-Western architecture and are translated from the additions to a German edition of the work (*Lexikon der Weltarchitektur,* 1971). NA31.F55

Handbooks

Harvey, John Hooper. Sources for the history of houses. [London], British Records Assoc., [1974]. 61p. (Archives and the user, no.3) £1.20. **BE67**

An extremely helpful manual to guide those beginning a search into the history of English houses built before 1850; also potentially useful to researchers in more general areas of local history.

History

Fletcher, *Sir* Banister. A history of architecture. 18th ed. rev. by J. C. Palmes. N.Y., Scribner, 1975. 1390p. il. $34.50. **BE68**

For previous ed. *see Guide* BE176.

The "Comparative analysis" sections have been omitted in favor of new chapters on non-Western architectures and the "Modern movement" since World War I.

Biography

Colvin, Howard Montagu. A biographical dictionary of British architects, 1600–1840. [London], Murray, 1978. 1080p. £30. **BE69**

A completely revised edition of Colvin's 1954 dictionary (*Guide* BE183) covering 1660–1840. Includes new sketches of 250 Scottish and Welsh architects as well as 400 additional biographies of English architects. Many sketches from the earlier edition have been expanded, but some have been dropped (*see* "Appendix B").

Conservation and preservation

Rath, Frederick L. and **O'Connell, Merrilyn Rogers.** A bibliography on historical organization practices. Nashville, Tenn., American Assoc. for State and Local History, 1975–77. v.1–2. $10 per v. (In progress) **BE70**

Contents: v.1, Historical preservation, by Frederick L. Rath; v.2, Care and conservation of collections, by Rosemary S. Reese; v.3 (in press), Interpretation, by Rosemary S. Reese.

Represents a new edition of the compilers' *Guide to historic preservation, historical agencies, and museum practices* (1970; *Guide* BE175).

A selective bibliography of books, pamphlets, and periodical articles, most of them published since 1945. v.1 concentrates on five major areas: (1) Preservation law; (2) Urban development and redevelopment; (3) Preservation research and planning; (4) Preservation action; (5) Historical preservation in perspective. v.2 is arranged by type of conservation (e.g., conservation of works of art on paper), philosophy and principles, laboratories and instrumentation, training, environmental factors. Name index. Z1251.A2R35

Smith, John F. A critical bibliography of building conservation: historic towns, buildings, their furnishings and fittings. London, Mansell, 1978. £12.90. **BE71**

Comp. at the Institute of Advanced Architectural Studies, University of York, with a grant from the Radcliffe Trust.

A classed listing of books, journal articles, technical reports, and legislative documents dealing with the conservation of the "built environment" *(Foreword)*, from towns to landscaping and gardens. Emphasis is on the situation in Great Britain; cutoff date is 1976. Annotations; place name index; author index.

City planning

Council of Planning Librarians. Index to CPL exchange bibliographies. . . . [Monticello, Ill., The Council], 1975–78. 3v. (*Its* Exchange bibliography, no.716/717, 1194/1195, 1564/1565) **BE72**

The three volumes cover bibliographies no.1–715 (1958–74), no.716–1193 (1975–76) and no.1196–1563 (1977–July 1978).

The *Exchange bibliography* series ceased publication with no.1564/1565 (July 1978); it is continued by two series of *Vance bibliographies,* "Architecture series," and "Public administration series," both beginning 1978.

Land use planning abstracts. N.Y., Environment Information Center, 1974– . **BE73**

For full information *see Suppl.* CL20.

PAINTING

Bibliography

Keaveney, Sydney Starr. American painting; a guide to information sources. Detroit, Gale, [1974]. 260p. (Art and architecture information guide ser., v.1) $18. **BE74**

A selective bibliography of recent (post-World War II through July 1973) books, exhibition catalogs, and journal articles. Topical arrangement; brief annotations. Includes a directory of periodical publications, publishers, research libraries, national art organizations, and museums of importance to the researcher in the field of American painting. Well indexed. Z5949.A45K4

Waterhouse, Ellis. Roman baroque painting: a list of principal painters and their works in and around Rome, with an introductory essay. [Oxford], Phaidon Pr., [1976]. 163p. il. $45. **BE75**

Lists paintings of 79 artists "who executed commissions of some importance for the decoration of churches or palaces in Rome" (*Note*), but omitting easel pictures and painters "whose work was more domestic." Arranged alphabetically by painter's name; gives a brief note on each artist's career, a list (by location) of individual works with indication of subject and printed source of attribution, and reference to those works in the bibliography which offer further information. Topographical index. ND620.W37

Biography

Johnson, Jane and **Greutzner, A.** The dictionary of British artists, 1880–1940: an Antique Collectors' Club research project listing 41,000 artists. [Suffolk, Eng.], Antique Collectors' Club, [1976]. 567p. £17.50. **BE76**

An extension and updating of A. Graves's *Dictionary of British artists, 1760–1893* (London, 1901).

A listing of every artist (including architects and foreigners) who exhibited in any of 47 selected galleries (the selection intended to provide a representative view of art in London and across Great Britain) during 1880–1940. Gives for each: birth and/or death dates (if unknown, first and last exhibition years); towns of residence; memberships and honors; places exhibited and number of times; and, occasionally, art schools attended; an asterisk indicates that at least one picture by the artist brought more than £100 at auction during 1970–75. N6767.J63

Waters, Grant M. Dictionary of British artists, working 1900–1950. Eastbourne, Eastbourne Fine Art, 1975. 368p. £9.50. **BE77**

Offers brief biographies of some 5,500 British, Irish, and foreign-born artists active in England during the period 1900–50. Most entries give artist's dates, memberships, education, and a sentence or two about his career. N6768.W26

PRINTS AND ENGRAVINGS

(including photographs)

Bibliography

Mason, Lauris and **Ludman, Joan.** Print reference sources: a select bibliography, 18th–20th centuries. Millwood, N.Y., KTO Pr., 1975. 246p. $20. **BE78**

An extremely useful selected bibliography of catalogs, museum and dealer publications, checklists, and essays from books and periodicals concerning some 1,300 printmakers. Artists "are listed alphabetically with the references for each one arranged chronologically . . . with an average of three references under each name."—*Note.* Quality of the references varies from a catalogue raisonné to a collection with only a brief mention or with one or two relevant plates. Z5947.A3M37

New York. Public Library. Prints Division. Dictionary catalog of the Prints Division. Boston, G. K. Hall, 1975. 5v. **BE79**

Photographic reproduction of "entries for book and book-like materials, including pamphlets, clipping files, and other items of an ephemeral nature, that have been added to the collection through July 1975. Cataloging for individual prints does not appear."—*Foreword.* However, the catalog does analyze some collections of prints, scrapbooks of cartoonists, and periodicals (for biographical articles and reproductions). Z5950.N562

Handbooks

Donson, Theodore B. Prints and the print market, a handbook for buyers, collectors, and connoisseurs. N.Y., Thomas Y. Crowell, [1977]. 493p. $19.95. **BE80**

Intended to "arm the novice with enough information and savvy to venture courageously into the print market and provide the professional with fresh insights and information."—*Foreword.* Omits any consideration of Japanese woodblock prints and art photographs. Appendix provides a directory of public print institutions, print clubs and societies, print publishers in the United States and Great Britain, print conservators and restorers, print dealers and galleries, bookstores. Lexicon of French-German-English terms. NE62.D66

Shapiro, Cecile and **Mason, Lauris.** Fine prints: collecting, buying, and selling; with glossaries of French and German terms by Joan Ludman. N.Y., Harper & Row, 1976. 256p. il. $10.95. **BE81**

A good general handbook for the amateur or beginning collector of prints. Covers all aspects of the subject from how to buy and sell, to how to catalog a collection and building a reference library. The glossaries define the French and German terms most often encountered in the field. Includes a directory of museums, clubs, and dealers. NE885.S42

Directories

Evans, Hilary, Evans, Mary and **Nelki, Andrea.** The picture researcher's handbook: an international guide to picture sources—how to use them. Newton Abbot, David & Charles; N.Y., Scribner's, 1975. 365p. il. $15. **BE82**

A directory of libraries, museums, government agencies, commercial firms, and studios, providing brief descriptions of picture collections, scope, address, hours, availability, etc. Information is based on replies to questionnaires. Index of topics, names of collections, and of countries. N4000.E8

Special Libraries Association. Picture Division. Picture sources 3; collections of prints and photographs in the U.S. and Canada. N.Y., 1975. 387p. $17. **BE83**

Ann Novotny, ed.

A project of the Picture Division, Special Libraries Association, and the American Society of Picture Professionals.

2d ed., 1964, called *Picture sources* (*Guide* BE144).

This edition expanded to 1,084 entries, with about a thousand sources in the United States and more than fifty sources in Canada listed. N4000.S7

SCULPTURE

Ekdahl, Janis. American sculpture: a guide to information sources. Detroit, Gale, 1977. 260p. (Art and architecture information guide ser., v.5) $18. **BE84**

A general section of research materials is followed by chronological sections and one for individual sculptors. Annotated. "American" is taken to mean artists "who have lived and worked in the United States for a significant portion of their careers and have contributed substantially to the art of America."—*Introd.* Appended is a directory of major sculpture collections in public institutions. Author, title, and subject indexes. Z5954.U5E37

B F

Applied Arts

GENERAL WORKS

See also Suppl. BF17.

Ehresmann, Donald L. Applied and decorative arts: a bibliographic guide to basic reference works, histories, and handbooks. Littleton, Colo., Libraries Unlimited, 1977. 232p. $15. **BF1**

A classified, annotated bibliography of books in Western European languages, primarily publications from the period 1875–1975. General sections on applied and decorative arts and on ornament are followed by sections for folk art, arms and armor, ceramics, clocks, watches and automata, costume, enamels, furniture, glass, ivory, jewelry, lacquer, leather and bookbinding, medals and seals, metalwork, musical instruments, textiles, toys and dolls. Author and subject indexes. 1,240 items. Z5956.A68E47

Haslam, Malcolm. Marks and monograms of the modern movement, 1875–1930; a guide to the marks of artists, designers, retailers, and manufacturers from the period of the Aesthetic Movement to Art Deco and Style Moderne. Guildford, Eng., Butterworth; N.Y., Scribner's, 1977. 192p. il. £7.50; $12.50. **BF2**

Marks are geographically arranged under five major headings: ceramics; glass; metalwork and jewelry; graphics; furniture and textiles. A brief paragraph adjacent to each mark identifies the artist or workshop. Name index. N45.H37

The Oxford companion to the decorative arts. Ed. by Harold Osborne. Oxford, Clarendon Pr., 1975. 865p. il. $39.95. **BF3**

Aims to provide an introduction "to those arts which are made to serve a practical purpose but are nevertheless prized for the quality of their workmanship and the beauty of their appearance. The Companion includes major crafts whose origin goes back to prehistoric times such as leather-working, ceramics, textiles, costume, woodworking, metal-working, glass-making and so on; crafts which have arisen since the dawn of history such as bell-founding, paper-making, clock-making, typography, landscape gardening, photography; and specialised or luxury crafts such as arms and armour, enamels, lacquer, jewellery, toys, lace-making and embroidery."—*Pref.* Unsigned articles, some of considerable length. Bibliography, pp.851–65; references to the bibliography are indicated by numbers at the end of an article.

A review by Simon Jervis in *TLS,* Mar. 19, 1976, p.321, points out strengths and weaknesses of the work and laments the fact that it was not executed more specifically as a companion volume to the *Oxford companion to art* (*Guide* BE57), with *see* references to that work. NK30.O93

Stafford, Maureen and **Ware, Dora.** An illustrated dictionary of ornament. London, Allen & Unwin, 1974; N.Y., St. Martin's Pr., 1975. 246p. il. £9.50; $15. **BF4**

A dictionary of terms used in architecture, the decorative arts, coins, games, heraldry, etc., for *ornament,* which is defined as "an accessory to, but not the substitute of the useful . . . ; a decoration or adornment."—*Introd.* Profusely illustrated with well-produced line drawings. NK1165.S72

ANTIQUES

Bridgeman, Harriet and **Drury, Elizabeth.** The encyclopedia of Victoriana. N.Y., Macmillan, [1975]. 368p. il. $27.50. **BF5**

A topical presentation of "definitions and descriptions of Victorian artifacts and biographies of the principal designers and makers [thereof]."—*Editors' note.* For each type of material (furniture, photographs, glass, etc.) a survey of developments in Britain is followed by a survey for America, a glossary of terms, and a brief bibliography. Indexed. Illustrations are well chosen and attractively presented. NK928.B66

The complete color encyclopedia of antiques, comp. by the Connoisseur; ed. by L. G. G. Ramsey. Rev. and expanded ed. N.Y., Hawthorn Books, [1975]. 704p. il. $37.50. **BF6**

Published in London as *The Connoisseur complete color encyclopedia of antiques.*

1st ed. 1962 (*Guide* BF3).

This edition includes articles on Art Nouveau and Art Deco, "the two collecting subjects which succeeded Victoriana as the avant-garde in collecting during the 1960s."—*Pref.* The bibliography has also been updated. NK1125.R343

Mackay, James Alexander. Turn-of-the-century antiques: an encyclopedia. N.Y., Dutton, 1974. 320p. il. $18.95. **BF7**

Published in London by Ward Lock as *Dictionary of turn of the century antiques.*

Concentrates on the period 1890–1910. Dictionary arrangement of articles on movements, events, styles, furnishings, art objects, craftsmen, designers, etc., from many countries. Numerous illustrations. NK775.5.A7M32

Phipps, Frances. The collector's complete dictionary of American antiques. Garden City, N.Y., Doubleday, 1974. 640p. il. $25. **BF8**

Employs a dictionary arrangement within topical sections such as: historic periods and styles; rooms—their placement and use; crafts, trades, and useful professions; weights and measures; terms used by joiners and cabinetmakers; woods and their preferred uses; paints, dyes, finishes, varnishes, etc. A general index would have facilitated use. NK805.P52

The Random House collector's encyclopedia: Victoriana to Art Deco. N.Y., Random House, [1974]. 302p. il. $25. **BF9**

Published in London by Collins, 1974.

A companion to the *Encyclopedia of antiques* (*Guide* BF8) which covers to 1875. This volume is concerned with the period 1851 to 1939, treating decorative arts of the time and "items which are collected in the same way as antiques."—*p. 9.* Aims "to compress the maximum amount of information into the available space, employing a highly condensed style to avoid relying on abbreviations." Cross references are indicated by asterisks; numerous illustrations, many in color. Appendix of ceramic marks and silver date letters. Brief bibliography. NK775.R36

Wills, Geoffrey. A concise encyclopedia of antiques. N.Y., Van Nostrand, [1976]. 304p. il. $15. **BF10**

"The subjects discussed and illustrated are furniture, pottery and porcelain, glass, silver, and pewter and other metals, made between 1500 and 1890."—*Foreword.* Deals almost exclusively with English antiques. NK928.W53

CERAMICS

Hamer, Frank. The potter's dictionary of materials and techniques. London, Pitman; N.Y., Watson-Guptill, [1975]. 349p. il. $25. **BF11**

A work for the potter, the teacher, and the student. Articles are in dictionary arrangement according to key words and phrases, with cross references to related terms. Generously illustrated with line drawings and photographs. Appendix of tables; brief bibliography. TT919.5.H35

Savage, George and **Newman, Harold.** An illustrated dictionary of ceramics; defining 3,054 terms relating to wares, materials, processes, styles, patterns, and shapes from antiquity to the present day. N.Y., Van Nostrand, [1974]. 319p. il. $18.95. **BF12**

A dictionary of terms, with many illustrations (some in color). Includes a list of "Principal European factories and their marks." NK3770.S38

CLOCKS AND WATCHES

Distin, William H. and **Bishop, Robert.** The American clock; a comprehensive pictorial survey 1723–1900, with a listing of 6153 clockmakers. N.Y., E. P. Dutton, 1976. 359p. il. $27.50. **BF13**

About 700 photographs of American clocks arranged chronologically within sections for types of clocks (e.g., tower clocks, tall case clocks, shelf clocks, novelty clocks), with indication of kind of movement, maker (if known), place and approximate date made. The "List of clockmakers" (pp.283–347) gives location and working dates for each. Index to the illustrations. TS543.U6D57

London. Clockmakers' Company. The clockmakers' library: the catalogue of the books and manuscripts in the library of the Worshipful Company of Clockmakers, comp. by John Bromley. [London], Sotheby Parke Bernet Publs., [1977]. 136p. il. £15. **BF14**

A revised version of the catalog of the Company's library produced by G. H. Baillie in 1951.

"Today the library comprises more than one thousand printed items, mainly in the field of historical horology; unique manuscript material, including the records of the Company from its incorporation in 1631; and a small collection of prints, portraits and photographs."—*Pref.* Separate sections for printed books, for manuscripts, for portraits, and for prints, drawings, etc. Includes accessions through Sept. 1975. Z7876.L85

COSTUME

Calasibetta, Charlotte Mankey. Fairchild's Dictionary of fashion. N.Y., Fairchild, [1975]. 693p. il. $50. **BF15**

Aims to present "clothing terminology from both historical and contemporary viewpoints" (*Pref.*) and is meant to be used with *Fairchild's Dictionary of textiles* ed. by I. B. Wingate (N.Y., 1967), since "fabrics are included in this book but are not discussed in depth." Concise definitions; pronunciation is indicated when it differs "radically from a phonetic reading of the English word."—*p.xi.* Words or terms from the same basic category are grouped together and cross references made from the individual terms. Numerous line drawings and a few color plates. Following the main alphabetic arrangement there is a separate section on fashion designers grouped by country and giving brief biographical sketches; portraits and photographs of typical "designer styles" are also included. TT503.C34

Sichel, Marion. Costume reference. Boston, Plays, Inc., 1977. 6v. il. $8.95 per v. **BF16**

Contents: v.1, Roman Britain and the Middle Ages; v.2, Tudors and Elizabethans; v.3, Jacobean, Stuart and Restoration; v.4, The eighteenth century; v.5, The Regency; v.6, The Victorians.

A series of brief volumes each surveying English dress of a given period and indicating the principal trends of costume design. Includes both male and female attire, with attention to hairstyles and accessories. Illustrations in both black-and-white and in color. Indexed. The Subscription Books Committee review in the *Booklist* 74:1572 concludes that "Keeping in mind their limitations [e.g., brevity of the factual information and lack of specific detail], these volumes would be useful in a public library developing a collection on British costume. . . . " GT730.S48

FURNITURE AND INTERIOR DESIGN

Fleming, John and **Honour, Hugh.** Dictionary of the decorative arts. N.Y., Harper & Row, [1977]. 896p. il. $25. **BF17**

British ed. (1977) has title: *The Penguin dictionary of decorative arts.*

Planned as a companion to the *Penguin dictionary of architecture* (*Guide* BE162), the work is "concerned with furniture and furnishings—i.e., movable objects other than paintings and sculpture—in Europe from the Middle Ages onwards and in North America from the Colonial Period to the present day. We have gone beyond these limits of place and time only in order to include accounts of craftsmen and types of objects that have played a part in the development of the decorative arts in the West, e.g. Chinese and Japanese ceramics."—*Foreword.* Excludes articles of personal adornment, musical and scientific instruments, clocks (but not their cases), and printed books (although their bindings are considered). Cross references; bibliographic notes. NK30.F55

Paris. Bibliothèque Forney. Catalogue matières: arts-décoratifs, beaux-arts, métiers, techniques. Paris, Société des Amis de la Bibliothèque Forney, 1974. v.4. **BF18**

For v.1–3 and annotation *see Guide* BF55.

Contents: v.4, Pek–Zuy. Completes the set.

Salaman, R. A. Dictionary of tools used in the woodworking and allied trades, *c.* 1700 –1970. London, Allen & Unwin, [1975]; N.Y., Scribner, 1976. 545p. il. $47.50; £18.95. **BF19**

Tools and trades are entered alphabetically, with "families" of tools and tools of a particular trade grouped together; cross references are provided from the name of the specific tool when it is treated with tools of a trade. Many illustrations; bibliography. TT186.S24

JEWELRY

Mason, Anita Frances. An illustrated dictionary of jewellery. N.Y., Harper & Row, [1974]. 389p. il. $8.95. **BF20**

First published 1973 by Osprey Publishing, Reading, Eng.

Intended "both for those involved in the jewellery trade and for those with a less specialized interest in jewellery."—*Pref.* Attempts to cover the whole field concisely, dealing with "gemstones and their identification, with the techniques of jewellery-manufacture, with the history of jewellery, and with subjects of interest to the retail jeweller such as hallmarking." Cross references; brief bibliography. NK7304.M37

LACE

Pfannschmidt, Ernst Erik. Twentieth-century lace. London, Mills and Boon; N.Y., Scribner, [1975]. 216p. il. £4.95; $10. **BF21**

Neither a handbook of techniques nor a full history of the subject, but, rather, a series of historical notes that "point the way to recent developments that have . . . not been systematically recorded hitherto." The bulk of the book (pp.34–209) is devoted to illustrations. Indexed. NK9410.P42

RUGS

Eiland, Murray L. Oriental rugs: a comprehensive guide. Rev. & expanded ed. Boston, New York Graphic Soc., [1976]. 214p. il. $24.50. **BF22**

1st ed. 1973.

"The intention has been to include . . . all the information necessary for the reader to identify and comprehend the background of most rugs he is likely to see or be in a position to purchase. Information has been included about the peoples who make the rugs and the conditions, both geographic and cultural, under which they live."—*Introd.* Because rugs of Persia, Turkey, the Caucasus, and the Turkoman peoples are most common in the United States and Europe, the volume considers only these types; a later work is to cover rugs of India, China, Pakistan, and Morocco. Bibliographic notes; index. NK2808.E44

COINS AND CURRENCY

See also Suppl. BF29.

Friedberg, Robert. Paper money of the United States; a complete illustrated guide with valuations. 8th ed., with additions and revisions by Jack Friedberg. N.Y., Coin and Currency Institute, [1975]. 327p. il. $17.50. **BF23**

"Large size notes, fractional currency, small size notes, encased postage stamps from the first year of paper money, 1861, to the present."—*t.p.*

1st ed. 1953; 7th ed. 1972. HG591.F7

Grierson, Philip. Numismatics. London & N.Y., Oxford Univ. Pr., 1975. 211p. $11.95; $4.95 pa. **BF24**

A useful survey of the field of numismatics for the student and collector. Traces the history of coinage with attention to both Eastern and Western traditions from earliest times to the modern period. Includes a chapter on numismatic scholarship. Glossary; brief bibliography; index. CJ75.G74

Hessler, Gene. The comprehensive catalog of U.S. paper money. Chicago, Regnery, [1974]. 456p. il. $20. **BF25**

Includes both large- and small-sized notes, U.S. military payment certificates, and "all the notes circulated under U.S. authority in the districts, territories, and possessions outside the continental United States."—*Pref.* A chapter on the history of paper money, and one on types of U.S. paper money precede the catalog proper. "The values listed throughout this catalog are suggested or average prices." HG591.H47

Reinfeld, Fred and **Hobson, Burton.** Catalogue of the world's most popular coins. 9th ed. N.Y., Sterling; London, Oak Tree Pr., [1976]. 480p. il. $14.95; $9.95 pa. **BF26**

Previous ed. 1971.

Coins are listed by country or issuing region, with illustrations of both obverse and reverse sides. Prices are quoted for coins "in the condition in which the issue is usually encountered."—*p.5.*

Seaby, Herbert Allen and **Rayner, P. Alan.** The English silver coinage from 1649. [4th rev. ed.] London, Seaby, [1974]. 240p. il. £4.50. **BF27**

1st ed. 1949; 3d ed. 1968.

Aims "to provide collectors with a standard work of reference . . . , giving details of dates, varieties, comparative rarity, patterns and proofs, etc."—*Introd.* CJ2485.S4

POSTAGE STAMPS

Collectors Club, New York. Library. Philately: a catalog of the Collectors Club Library, New York City. Boston, G. K. Hall, 1974. 682p. $115. **BF28**

Contents: Author catalog; Subject catalog; Title catalog; Periodicals catalog.

Reproduction of the catalog cards for one of the world's largest philatelic collections. Z7164.P85C64

Rosichan, Richard H. Stamps and coins. Littleton, Colo., Libraries Unlimited, 1974. 404p. (Spare time guides, no.5) $13.50. **BF29**

A bibliographic guide to recently published works in the fields of numismatics and philately. Emphasis is on books, but includes information on periodicals, organizations, and libraries in the fields. Title, author, and subject indexes. Z7164.P85R56

PHOTOGRAPHY

See also Suppl. BE19, BE31, BE82–BE83.

Blaker, Alfred A. Handbook for scientific photography. San Francisco, W. H. Freeman, [1977]. 319p. il. $22.50. **BF30**

A completely revised, expanded, and reorganized edition of *Photography for scientific publication* (1965).

Contents: A review of essentials; General techniques; Solutions to problems; Related techniques; Final preparation for publication and viewing.

"Throughout the book the approach is pragmatic, being in terms of what one *needs* to know to accomplish the stated ends, rather than in terms of theory or ideal circumstances. The coverage of basic photography is skeletal, on the assumption that most readers will have some general knowledge of the field."—*Pref.* TR692.5.B55

Hedgecoe, John. The photographer's handbook; a complete reference manual of techniques, procedures, equipment and style. London, Ebury Pr.; N.Y., Knopf, 1977. 352p. il. £8.95; $16.95. **BF31**

About 600 topically arranged entries ranging from basic information about cameras and equipment to advanced techniques and special processes. Copiously illustrated with photographs and drawings. Cross references; glossary; index. TR150.H36

Photography market place. 1975/76– . N.Y., Bowker, [1975–]. Biennial. (2d ed., 1977/78: $15.50 pa.) **BF32**

Fred W. McDarrah, ed.

On cover: The complete source book for still photography.

A directory of sources, services, and potential markets in the area of still photography. In eight main sections, each with numerous subdivisions: (1) Picture buyers; (2) Technical services; (3) Equipment sources; (4) Supportive services; (5) Picture sources; (6) Publishers and publications; (7) Organizations; (8) Career opportunities. Indexed. TR12.P52

Stroebel, Leslie D. and **Todd, Hollis N.** Dictionary of contemporary photography. Dobbs Ferry, N.Y., Morgan & Morgan; London, Fountain Pr., [1974]. 217p. il. $20. **BF33**

Intended as "a record of current usage in professional and illustrative photography, cinematography (including animation), and photographic engineering and science. In addition, terms have been included from disciplines that relate to photography, such as art, electronics, photomechanical reproduction, physics, psychology, television, and applied statistics."—*Pref.* Illustrated with line drawings and photographs. TR9.S88

B G

Theater Arts

GENERAL WORKS

Guides

Whalon, Marion K. Performing arts research; a guide to information sources. Detroit, Gale, [1976]. 280p. (Performing arts information guide ser., v.1) $18. **BG1**

An annotated guide in six main sections: (1) Guides; (2) Dictionaries, encyclopedias, and handbooks; (3) Directories; (4) Play indexes and finding lists; (5) Sources for reviews of plays and motion pictures; (6) Bibliographies, indexes, and abstracts; (7) Illustrative and audiovisual sources. Author-title-subject index. Z6935.W5

Bibliography

See also Suppl. BD80, BD131, BD172.

Fordyce, Rachel. Children's theatre and creative dramatics: an annotated bibliography of critical works. Boston, G. K. Hall, 1975. 275p. $21. **BG2**

Lists some 2,269 items in a subject arrangement within three main sections: (1) Children's theatre and creative dramatics [i.e., materials covering both fields]; (2) Children's theatre; and (3) Creative dramatics. Does not include anthologies of children's plays "unless they are prefaced by or include some type of critical material."—*Pref.* Author index. Z5784.C5F67

NCTE Liaison Committee. Guide to play selection; a selective bibliography for production and study of modern plays. 3d ed. N.Y., Bowker, [1975]. 292p. $5.95. **BG3**

"Comp. by the NCTE Liaison Committee with the Speech Communication Association and the American Theatre Association, Joseph Mersand, Editorial Chairman. Distr. jointly by the National Council of Teachers of English, Urbana, Ill., and the R. R. Bowker Co., N.Y."—*t.p.*

2d ed. 1958 (*Guide* BG12).

About 850 plays are described in this edition. Three new sections have been added: (1) A guide to play production; (2) Plays by Afro-Americans; (3) Musical plays. Besides the author and title indexes, a topical index and a "player index" (arranged according to the number and sex of the players required) have been added. Z5781.N13

New York. Public Library. Research Libraries. Catalog of the theatre and drama collections. Part III: non-book collections. Boston, G. K. Hall, 1976. 30v. $3485. **BG4**

For pts.1–2 *see Guide* BG13.

Reproduction of about 744,000 cards for non-book materials such as programs, photographs of productions, portraits of theater personalities, reviews, press clippings, etc.

Separate supplements to pt.1 (Drama collection) and pt.2 (Theatre collection) were published in 1973 (pt.1: 548p., $105; pt.2: 2v., $270). Pts.1 and 2 are supplemented by:

——— Bibliographic guide to theatre arts. 1975– . Boston, G. K. Hall, 1976– . Annual. (1977: $55) **BG5**

Serves as a supplement to the Library's *Catalog of the theatre and drama collections* (Guide BG13), pts.1–2, listing materials newly cataloged by the New York Public Library, with additional entries from Library of Congress MARC tapes. Z6935.N46a

Verzeichnis der Hochschulschriften, Diplom- und Staatsexamensarbeiten der DDR zum Drama und Theater (1949–1970). [Berlin], Akademie der Künste der Deutschen Demokratischen Republik, 1973. 368p. **BG6**

Lists more than 2,000 research papers on various aspects of the theater and on dramatists of all countries and their works. Alphabetical author listing with subject index.

Indexes

Samples, Gordon. The drama scholars' index to plays and filmscripts: a guide to plays and filmscripts in selected anthologies, series and periodicals. Metuchen, N.J., Scarecrow, 1974. 448p. $12.50. **BG7**

Attempts to present a "balanced selection" of plays of all periods (including texts in foreign languages); many of the anthologies, multivolume sets, and periodicals covered here are not indexed in the standard play indexes. Full information appears under the author's name, with cross reference from the title. Z5781.S17

Reviews

Samples, Gordon. How to locate reviews of plays and films; a bibliography of criticism from the beginnings to the present. Metuchen, N.J., Scarecrow, 1976. 114p. $6. **BG8**

An annotated guide to indexes, checklists and bibliographies of reviews and critiques of plays and films. Separate sections for plays and films, subdivided by type of reference tool; within subsections the arrangement is mainly chronological by period covered. Author/title index. Unfortunately, numerous inaccuracies. Z5781.S19

Stanley, William T. Broadway in the West End; an index of reviews of American theatre in London, 1950–1975. Westport, Conn., Greenwood Pr., [1978]. 206p. $25. **BG9**

Aims to present "the essential facts of American theatrical works produced in London from 1950 through 1975" (*Pref.*), together with references to critical reviews appearing in some 17 review media. Entry is under author or adaptor of the theater piece, and for each title is given the name of the theater, inclusive dates of the run, and number of performances, followed by citations to reviews. Title index; chronology; list of longest-running American productions in London during the period, etc. Z2014.D7S77

Library resources

Performing arts resources. v.1– , 1974– . [N.Y.], Drama Book Specialists, [1975]– . Annual. (v.3, 1977: $10) **BG10**

Ed. by Ted Perry.

A series sponsored by the Theatre Library Association. "Each annual volume . . . is envisioned as a collection of articles which will enable the performing arts student, scholar, and archivist to locate, identify, and classify information about theatre, film, broadcasting, and popular entertainments."—*Pref.*

v.1 includes "Performing arts research collections in New York City" by L. A. Rachow; "Film/broadcasting resources in the Los Angeles area" by A. G. Schlosser; "The Wisconsin Center for Theatre Research" by K. Johnson; "The Motion Picture Section of the Library of Congress" by J. B. Kuiper; "Vanderbilt Television News Archive" by J. B. Pilkington, etc. Z6935.P46

Encyclopedias

The encyclopedia of world theater, with 420 illustrations and an index of play titles. N.Y., Scribner, [1977]. 320p. il. $25. **BG11**

"Based on *Friedrichs Theaterlexikon* [Hanover, Friedrich, 1969] by Karl Gröning and Werner Kliess . . . this English-language edition has been translated by Estella Schmid, and adapted and amplified under the general editorship of Martin Esslin."—*verso of t.p.*

Brief entries for actors and actresses, playwrights, directors, designers, types of drama, theatrical institutions, awards, etc. PN2035.E52

History

Wearing, J. P. The London stage, 1890–1899: a calendar of plays and players. Metuchen, N.J., Scarecrow, 1976. 2v. (1229p.) $42.50. **BG12**

Contents: v.1, 1890–1896; v.2, 1897–1899, Index.

Aims "to furnish a daily listing of the plays and players on the London stage from 1890–1899."—*Introd.* Information (in slightly abbreviated form) was gleaned from a variety of sources and is presented in the form of a series of playbills. Arrangement is chronological by date of opening night performance (by theater when there was more than one opening production on the same day). Information includes: full title, author (including details of adaptation or translation as applicable), genre of play, theater at which performed, length of run and number of performances, cast (including changes), production staff, references to reviews of first performances. Index of titles, authors, performers, theaters, managers, etc. No doubt inspired by the series of the same title covering the 1660–1800 period (*Guide* BG50). PN2596.L6W37

Biography

Kaye, Phyllis Johnson. National playwrights directory. Waterford, Conn., O'Neill Theater Center; distr. by Drama Book Specialists, [1977]. 374p. il. $15; $10 pa. **BG13**

"A project of the O'Neill Theater Center, Waterford, Conn., with the Theatre Development Fund, N.Y., N.Y."—*t.p.*

Gives brief biographical information (obtained by questionnaire) on about 400 contemporary American playwrights, including address, and (usually) agent's name and address, titles of plays with indication of productions and availability of scripts; synopses of one or more plays of a given writer are often given. Index of play titles. Uneven in amount of information provided and coverage is not comprehensive. PS129.K3

Notable names in the American theatre. [New and rev. ed.] Clifton, N.J., James T. White & Co., 1976. 1250p. $69. **BG14**

Represents a second edition of Walter Rigdon's *Biographical encyclopaedia and who's who of the American theatre* (1966; *Guide* BG66).

Contents: New York productions; Premieres in America; Premieres of American plays abroad; Theatre group biographies; Theatre building biographies; Awards; Biographical bibliography; Necrology; Notable names in the American theatre [i.e., the "who's who" section].

The section of "Theatre playbills," 1959–64, appearing in the earlier work is not carried forward to this edition. PN2285.N6

Young, William C. Famous actors and actresses on the American stage. N.Y., Bowker, 1975. 2v. (1298p.) il. (Documents of American theater history) $57.50. **BG15**

Intended as a companion to the same author's *Famous American playhouses* (*Guide* BG57).

Aims "(1) to present contemporary evaluations of the abilities of a certain actor or actress; and (2) to relate a performer's philosophy of acting and approach to certain roles."—*Pref.* 225 actors and actresses (not necessarily Americans) are treated. For each performer

there is a portrait, brief biographical data, and a number of extracts from contemporary criticism (reviews of plays, interviews, memoirs of fellow actors, etc.). Sources of the excerpts are given in full. Index of persons, plays, and characters mentioned in the extracts.
PN2285.Y6

THE DANCE

Bibliography

Kaprelian, Mary H., comp. Aesthetics for dancers, a selected annotated bibliography. Wash., Amer. Alliance for Health, Physical Education, and Recreation, [1976]. 87p. $4.50 pa. **BG16**

A bibliography of book and periodical materials topically arranged under such headings as "Aesthetic experience," "Aesthetic relevance," "Criticism and judgment," "Art and psychology." 515 items. Author index. Z5931.K34N70

New York. Public Library. Dance Collection. Dictionary catalog of the Dance Collection; a list of authors, titles, and subjects of multi-media materials in the Dance Collection of the Performing Arts Research Center of the New York Public Library. Boston, New York Pub. Lib. and G. K. Hall, 1974. 10v. $670. **BG17**

A book catalog produced by automated techniques listing materials cataloged for the collection prior to Oct. 1, 1973 (about 300,000 entries for some 96,000 items), and including entries for relevant materials in other divisions of the Research Libraries of the New York Public Library.

Supplemented by: Z7514.D2N462

——— Bibliographic guide to dance. 1st– , 1975– . Boston, G. K. Hall, 1976– . Annual. (1977: $95) **BG18**

Each annual issued in two or more volumes.

Represents an ongoing supplement to the *Dictionary catalog of the Dance Collection* (above), listing materials newly cataloged for the collection. A computer-produced catalog in dictionary form like the parent work. Z7514.D2N462a

Encyclopedias and handbooks

Balanchine, George and **Mason, Francis.** Balanchine's Complete stories of the great ballets. Rev. and enl. ed. N.Y., Doubleday, [1977]. 838p. il. $15. **BG19**

1968 ed. had title: *Balanchine's New complete stories of the great ballets* (*Guide* BG89).

Includes numerous new ballets and new photographs. The lists of ballet recordings and selected readings have been dropped from this edition. MT95.B3

The concise Oxford dictionary of ballet. [Comp. by] Horst Koegler. London & N.Y., Oxford Univ. Pr., 1977. 583p. $12.50. **BG20**

"... originally planned as an Anglo-American adaptation of the German *Friedrichs Ballett-lexikon von A–Z,* published in 1972. But while the German version can still be recognized as the point of departure, the final product has turned out to possess an individuality all of its own. Not only has matter been cut which was of interest only to German-speaking readers [but] the focus shifted towards what the Anglo-American reader might be looking for. In addition there has been a general reconsideration of the distribution of emphasis, and a considerable number of new entries have been added."—*Foreword.* Brief articles on dancers, ballets, companies, technical terms, etc., are all included. GV1585.C73

The encyclopedia of dance & ballet. Ed. by Mary Clarke & David Vaughan. N.Y., Putnam's, [1977]. 376p. il. $25. **BG21**

The title is meant "to indicate that the entries are not confined to classical ballet but record also activity in contemporary dance styles."—*Introd.* The work is, however, concerned "only with dance raised to a theatrical level as a performing art in any of the media of the twentieth century." Entries for dancers, companies, choreographers, individual ballets and types of dances. "Glossary of technical terms," pp.368–72.

Terry, Walter. Ballet guide: background, listings, credits, and descriptions of more than five hundred of the world's major ballets. N.Y., Dodd, Mead, [1976]. 388p. il. $15. **BG22**

Based in part on Terry's *Ballet, a new guide to the liveliest art* (N.Y., 1959).

Listing is alphabetical by title of the ballet. Gives choreographer, music, scenery and costume designers, company and date of first performance, principal dancers in first performance and important recreations of the roles, together with a description of the ballet. Index; glossary. GV1790.A1T47

MOTION PICTURES

Bibliography

See also Suppl. BH76–BH78, BH85.

British Film Institute, London. Library. Catalogue of the book library of the British Film Institute. Boston, G. K. Hall, 1975. 3v. $240. **BG23**

Contents: v.1, Author catalogue; Title catalogue, A–F; v.2, Title catalogue, G–Z; Script catalogue; Subject catalogue: personality index; film index; v.3, Subject catalogue: alphabetical subject index.

Reproduction of the cards from the Library's catalog. About 20,000 titles, including some 4,000 film scripts. International in scope. Z5784.M9B85

California. University. University at Los Angeles. Library. Motion pictures: a catalog of books, periodicals, screenplays, television scripts and production stills. [2d ed., rev. and expanded] Boston, G. K. Hall, 1976. 775p. $65. **BG24**

1st ed. 1972.

Reproduction of the catalog cards for this special library which aims "to acquire books, periodicals, and journals covering the historical, critical, aesthetic, biographical and technical aspects, as well as the non-book and primary source material that will provide the information and knowledge sought by scholars and researchers [in the whole range of theater arts]."—*Pref.*

This edition includes accessions through Mar. 1976. Separate sections for: (1) Books and periodicals; (2) Published screenplays; (3) Unpublished screenplays; (4) Unpublished television scripts; (5) Production stills. Z5784.M9C3

Cohen, Louis Harris. The Soviet cinema, film and photography: a selected annotated bibliography. Rev. and expanded. Edwards Air Force Base, Calif., DOETC, Air Force Flight Test Center, 1976. 492p. il. **BG25**

Preliminary ed. 1974. Based on the author's doctoral dissertation submitted at University of Southern California.

Topically arranged in chapters, with introductory notes for each chapter. Extensive annotations; numerous appendixes, including a "Dictionary of cinematography terms" which gives the Russian term in Cyrillic characters, in transliteration, and in English translation. Index of names and selected subjects. Z5784.M9C64

Dyment, Alan R. The literature of the film; a bibliographical guide to the film as art and entertainment, 1936–1970. London & N.Y., White Lion, [1975]. 398p. £15; $35. **BG26**

An annotated bibliography of English-language books on the film published since Jan. 1936 (the approximate closing date of the *Film index* [*Guide* BG121]). Classed listing with index of names and titles. About 1,300 items. Z5784.M9D9

Enser, A. G. S. Filmed books and plays; a list of books and plays from which films have been made, 1928–1974. [London], Andre Deutsch, [1975]. 549p. £8.50. **BG27**

Previous ed. 1971 (*Guide* BG112).

A cumulative edition. Z5784.M9E55

Garbicz, Adam and **Klinowski, Jacek.** Cinema, the magic vehicle: a guide to its achievement. Metuchen, N.J., Scarecrow, 1975– . v.1– . (In progress) **BG28**

Contents: v.1, The cinema through 1949. $18.50.

Attempts "to give a panoramic view of the achievement of the cinema through the 'film-by-film' approach" (*Pref.*) and "to include all films which anyone seriously interested in the cinema would consider worth seeing, wherever they come from." Chronological arrangement, with indexes of directors and of films. Screen credits and running time are given for each film, the plot is briefly outlined, and there is a critique of the film relating it to other examples of the director's work, its place in the development of a genre, etc. PN1995.G25

Sheahan, Eileen. Moving pictures; a bibliography of selected reference works for the study of film, with emphasis on holdings in the libraries of Yale University. New Haven, Yale Univ. Lib., 1973. 78p. (Yale Univ. Lib. Bibliography ser., 3) $4 pa. **BG29**

A classed, annotated bibliography with index. Covers a wide range of materials, including various items not generally considered strictly reference sources. Z5784.M9S5

Periodicals

Turconi, Davide and **Bassotto, Camillo.** Il cinema nelle riviste italiane dalle origini ad oggi. [Venezia], Edizioni Mostracinema, [1973?]. 321p. **BG30**

A chronological listing of Italian film periodicals, with full publication information and a brief descriptive note. Alphabetical title index. More than 600 entries. Z5784.M9T78

Indexes

Batty, Linda. Retrospective index to film periodicals, 1930–1971. N.Y., Bowker, 1975. 425p. $25.50. **BG31**

Indexes 14 film journals plus articles on the film appearing in the *Village voice.* Only two of the journals covered pre-date 1950. In three sections: film titles, subjects, book reviews. Z5784.M9B39

Gerlach, John C. and **Gerlach, Lana.** The critical index; a bibliography of articles on film in English, 1946–1973, arranged by names and topics. N.Y., Teachers College Pr., [1974]. 726p. $6.50 pa. **BG32**

Indexes articles from 22 American, British, and Canadian film periodicals on directors, producers, actors, critics, screenwriters, cinematographers, specific films, and on the history, aesthetics, influence, and economics of the film industry. Separate sections for names and topics; author index. About 5,000 items. Z5784.M9G47

MacCann, Richard Dyer and **Perry, Edward S.** The new film index; a bibliography of magazine articles in English, 1930–1970. N.Y., Dutton, 1975. 522p. $35. **BG33**

Intended as a supplement to the *Film index* (*Guide* BG121), although differing from that work in that only magazine articles are covered herein. Indexes some 12,000 articles arranged in 278 subject categories, with an author index. Brief annotations for most items. "Biography" section, pp.241–326, is an index to biographical articles. Does not attempt to index film reviews and book reviews. Z5784.M9M29

Reviews

See also Suppl. BG8, BG33.

Bowles, Stephen E., comp. Index to critical film reviews in British and American film periodicals, together with: Index to critical reviews of books about film. N.Y., Burt Franklin, [1974]. 3v. in 2. $35. **BG34**

Contents: v.1–2, Critical film reviews, A–Z; v.3, Critical reviews of books about film, A–Z, and indexes.

Indexes "all articles designated as 'reviews,' and includes, as well, those articles which deal with the entirety of a film (rather than a restricted aspect)" (*Introd.*) appearing in some 31 British and American film journals. In general, a full run of the journal is indexed through 1971; 1939 is the earliest publication date. Entry is by title of the film, with indexes by directors and film reviewers. The separate section of "Critical reviews of books about film" is arranged by book title, with author, reviewer, and subject indexes. Z5784.M9B64

Film review digest. v.1, no.1– , Fall 1975– . Millwood, N.Y., Kraus-Thomson, 1975– . Quarterly with annual cumulation. il. $45 per yr. **BG35**

Offers excerpts from film reviews appearing in some two dozen magazines and newspapers. Arranged by film title; full information is given on the film (director, producer, cast, running time, etc.). Citations for the reviews are to the name and date of the periodical only, not to volume and page.

The annual cumulation for 1976 (published 1977) includes reviews from the four quarterly issues of Fall 1975–Summer 1976. PN1995.F46

Hochman, Stanley, comp. and ed. American film directors. With filmographies and index of critics and films. N.Y., Ungar, [1974]. 590p. $18.50. **BG36**

At head of title: A library of film criticism.

Modeled on the volumes in the "Library of literary criticism" series (*Guide* BD419, etc.). Offers excerpts from reviews and critical writings on the work of 65 American film directors. "Filmographies," pp.531–63. Indexed. PN1995.9.P7H57

Library resources

See also Suppl. BG10.

Mehr, Linda Harris. Motion pictures, television and radio: a union catalogue of manuscript and special collections in the western United States. Boston, G. K. Hall, [1977]. 201p. $27. **BG37**

"Sponsored by The Film and Television Study Center, Inc."—*t.p.*

The work is "designed to locate, identify and describe research collections currently available for use in established institutions, libraries, museums, and historical societies in the eleven western United States: Arizona, California, Colorado, Idaho, Montana, Nevada, New Mexico, Oregon, Utah, Washington, and Wyoming." —*Foreword.* Arranged alphabetically by name of institution, with a general index and an index by occupation. Collections include production and personal papers of directors, writers, producers, actors, etc.; screenplays and scripts; advertising material and posters; photographs and stills; clipping files; scrapbooks; props, costumes and equipment, etc. Primary focus is on paper materials; collections of films, television and radio tapes are included only when part of a general collection. PN1993.4.M37

Rose, Ernest D. World film and television study resources; a reference guide to major training centers and archives. Bonn-Bad Godesberg, Friedrich-Ebert-Stiftung, 1974. 421p. **BG38**

A directory of film and television archives in 75 countries. There is usually a historical and descriptive note on film activity in each country, followed by a list of that nation's archives, institutes, etc., devoted to the film, with notes on the activities, collections, facilities, etc., of each. Arranged by continent, then by country.

Directories

American Film Institute. The American Film Institute guide to college courses in film and television. [Princeton, N.J.], Peterson's Guides for the Amer. Film Institute, [1978]. 430p. $9.75 pa. **BG39**

Editors: Dennis R. Bohnenkamp, Sam L. Grogg, Jr.

[Ed.1] 1969/70 called *Guide to college film courses.* For 1973 ed. *see Guide* BG131. 1978 issue called "6th ed."

This edition lists courses and programs in film and television at some 1,067 colleges, universities, and professional institutions in the United States.

International film guide, 1964– . London, Tantivy Pr.; N.Y., A. S. Barnes, 1963– . Annual. il. (1978: $3.95 pa.) **BG40**

Peter Cowie, ed.

Offers an annual survey of film production in countries throughout the world (50 countries in the 1978 volume), reviews of outstanding films, biographical sketches of prominent directors, directories of film festivals, archives, services, magazines, etc. Table of contents, list of films reviewed, but no general index. PN1993.3.I544

Motion picture market place, 1976/77– . Boston, Little, Brown, [1976]– . Annual? (1976/77: $12.95 pa.) **BG41**

Tom Costner, ed.

A directory which intends "to provide easy access to the people and companies involved in all phases of theatrical and telvision film production, distribution, and exhibition, as well as suppliers to the motion picture industry throughout the United States."—*Pref.* Arranged alphabetically by type of service (e.g., Advertising agencies; Animation; Costumes; Festivals; Film storage; Makeup supplies; Manuscript services; Projection equipment). Table of contents, but no index.

Dictionaries and handbooks

Aros, Andrew A. A title guide to the talkies, 1964 through 1974. (As conceived by Richard B. Dimmitt.) Metuchen, N.J., Scarecrow Pr., 1977. 336p. $12.50. **BG42**

A continuation of the Dimmitt compilation of the same title (*Guide* BG128). The producer credit has been dropped in this listing and the director's name substituted. PN1998.A6695

Halliwell, Leslie. The filmgoer's companion. 6th ed. N.Y., Hill and Wang, 1977. 825p. il. $30. **BG43**

3d ed. 1970 (*Guide* BG140); 4th ed. 1974. (The 5th ed., 1976, was a paperback issue of the 4th ed., with some slight revision.)

Revised and reset, with new illustrations used. More than a thousand new entries in this edition as well as revisions to existing articles. PN1993.45.H3

——— Halliwell's Film guide; a survey of 8000 English-language movies. London [etc.], Granada, [1977]. 897p. il. $29.95. **BG44**

May be considered a complementary volume to Halliwell's *Filmgoer's companion* (*Suppl.* BG43) inasmuch as it both elaborates the information on the approximately 800 films accorded entries there, and treats hundreds of other films omitted from that volume.

An alphabetical title listing of English-language feature-length films, indicating the compiler's rating for each, country of origin, year of release, running time, credits (production, writer, director, photography, music, etc.), cast, synopsis, assessment and notes on significance, and, for about a fifth of the items, brief comment from well-known critics. Aims "to include every film which seemed likely or worthy of remembrance by the keen filmgoer or student, whether with affection for its own sake as good entertainment, for showcasing memorable work by a particular talent, for sheer curiosity value or for box office success."—*Introd.*

The Oxford companion to film. Ed. by Liz-Anne Bawden. N.Y., Oxford Univ. Pr., 1976. 767p. il. $24.95. **BG45**

Aims "to answer any query which may occur to the amateur of film in the course of reading or film-going, and to lead him on to topics of related interest."—*Pref.* Entries for individual films, actors and actresses, directors and other motion picture personnel, film genres, and selected technical terms, etc., and brief surveys of the history of cinema art in individual countries. PN1993.45.O9

Parish, James Robert. Film actors guide: Western Europe. Metuchen, N.J., Scarecrow Pr., 1977. 606p. il. $24. **BG46**

Covers motion-picture actors and actresses "based in Western Europe exclusive of Scandinavia" (*Pref.*) who played in feature-length films. Gives name, place and date of birth, and a list of films with dates. PN1998.A2P389

Thiery, Herman. Dictionnaire filmographique de la littérature mondiale. Filmographic dictionary of world literature. Filmographisches Lexikon der Weltliteratur. Filmografisch lexicon der wereldliteratuur. [Par] Johan Daisne. Gand, E. Story-Scientia, 1971–75. 2v. il. B.Fr. 3180. **BG47**

Introduction in French, English, German, and Flemish.

Contents: v.1, A–K; v.2, L–Z.

The intention is "to illustrate how the whole of literature forms the basis of the seventh art" (*Introd.*) by identifying the works of world literature with the films derived from them. Each volume is in three parts: (1) a "filmography" arranged by author's name and giving film title, original book title if different from that of the film, country and year of production, re-makes (if any), directory, and principal cast members; (2) an extensive section of illustrations; and (3) an index of titles of both films and books. Truly international in coverage. PN1997.85.T5

Biography

See also Suppl. BG36, BG46.

Thomson, David. A biographical dictionary of film. N.Y., Wm. Morrow, 1976. 629p. $16.95; $7.95 pa. **BG48**

First published with title: *A biographical dictionary of the cinema* (London, Secker & Warburg, 1975).

Admittedly "a Personal, Opinionated and Obsessive" work which includes "the sharp expression of personal taste; jokes; digressions; insults and eulogies" (*Introd.*) along with expected factual information. PN1998.A2T55

B H

Music

GENERAL WORKS

Guides

Marco, Guy A. Information on music: a handbook of reference sources in European languages. Littleton, Colo., Libraries Unlimited, 1975–77. v.1–2. (In progress) **BH1**

Contents: v.1, Basic and universal sources. 164p. $11.50; v.2, The Americas. 296p. $18.50.

To be in 8v.

An annotated listing of books considered to be the most useful to students of music. Designed to supplement and extend Duckles (*Guide* BH2) rather than supersede that work. ML113.M33

Bibliography

Horn, David. The literature of American music in books and folk music collections; a fully annotated bibliography. Metuchen, N.J., Scarecrow Pr., 1977. 556p. $20. **BH2**

Nearly 1,500 books relating to any aspect of American musical life are cited and carefully annotated. Arrangement is chronological, then by type or form. Indexed. Based on *The literature of American music; a fully annotated catalogue of the books and song collections in Exeter University Library* (Exeter, 1972). ML120.U5H7

Hughes, Andrew. Medieval music; the sixth liberal art. Toronto, Univ. of Toronto Pr., 1974. 326p. (Toronto medieval bibliographies, 4) $20. **BH3**

A bibliography of 2,003 secondary works published as books and periodical articles, in collections of essays, dictionaries, encyclopedias, catalogs, etc., on all aspects of medieval music. Intended for the beginning student, readers without formal training in the field, and for librarians developing a collection of these materials. Topical/geographical arrangement; brief annotations; subject index and index of authors and editors. ML114.H8

Jackson, Richard. U.S. music; sources of bibliography and collective biography. Brooklyn, Inst. for Studies in Amer. Music, 1973. 80p. (ISAM monographs, no.1) $4 pa. **BH4**

An annotated listing of books which are "of practical aid to students engaged in American-music studies."—*Introd.* Arranged by broad topics (historical, regional) or by type (folk, 20th-century). Author/compiler index. ML120.U5J2

Kassel. Deutsches Musikgeschichtliches Archiv. Katalog der Filmsammlung. Kassel, Bärenreiter, 1974–77. Bd.2^{4-6}–3^{1}. (In progress) **BH5**

For previously published parts and annotation *see Guide* BH19.

Kostka, Stefan M. A bibliography of computer applications in music. Hackensack, Joseph Boonin, 1974. 58p. (Music indexes and bibliographies, no.7) $4.50. **BH6**

An author listing of 641 books, essays, periodical articles, dissertations, and mimeographed reports which discuss the application of computers to musical problems. Works cited are mainly in English, French, or German. No index. ML113.K685B5

Mathiesen, Thomas J. Bibliography of sources for the study of ancient Greek music. Hackensack, N.J., Joseph Boonin, [1974]. 59p. (Music indexes and bibliographies, no.10) **BH7**

Lists some 949 books and articles dealing with the ancient Greek theory of music. Includes material on relationship between theories of metrics and music. Author listing; no index. ML114.M3

New York. Public Library. Research Libraries. Dictionary catalog of the Music Collection. Boston, G. K. Hall, 1964. 33v. $1200. **BH8**

Photographic reproduction of the catalog cards for one of the great music collections, one particularly strong in folk song, 18th- and 19th-century librettos, full scores of operas, complete works, historical editions, Beethoven materials, Americana, music periodicals, vocal music, literature on the voice, programs, record catalogs, and manuscripts. Offers detailed cataloging for books, pamphlets, essays, periodical articles, scores and librettos; recordings are not included.

——— ——— Supplement II. Boston, G. K. Hall, 1973. 10v. $2190.

Covers all additions of the 1964–71 period and incorporates all entries from Suppl. I (published 1966).

——— ——— Supplement 1974. Boston, G. K. Hall, 1976. 559p.

Reproduces additions to the card catalog from Jan. 1972 to Sept. 1974. ML136.N5N573

——— **Music Division.** Bibliographic guide to music. 1975– . Boston, G. K. Hall, 1976– . Annual. $70 per yr. **BH9**

Serves as an ongoing supplement to the *Dictionary catalog of the Music Collection* (*Suppl.* BH8) in that it includes all publications cataloged by the Research Libraries of the New York Public Library in the field of music, but also includes additional entries from Library of Congress MARC tapes in "such areas as literature of music (bibliography, history and criticism, philosophy of music), and music instruction and study (composition, orchestration, singing and voice culture)."—*Introd., 1975.* ML136.N5N5732

Répertoire international des sources musicales. München, G. Henle, 1974–78. AI^{4-7}, $BVIII^{1}$, BIX^{2}. (In progress) **BH10**

For previously published parts and annotation *see Guide* BH20.

Contents: *Série alphabetique,* AI^{4-7}, Haack–Schreyer; *Série systematique,* $BVIII^{1}$, Das deutsche Kirchenlied, DKL: krit. Gesamtausg. d. Melodien, pt.1; BIX^{2}, Hebrew writings concerning music, its manuscripts and printed books from Geonic times up to 1800, by I. Adler.

Warfield, Gerald. Writings on contemporary music notation: an annotated bibliography. [Ann Arbor], Music Lib. Assoc., 1976. 93p. (MLA index and bibliography ser., no.16) **BH11**

Aims to be comprehensive in citing books and articles on new notation published 1950–75, but is selective in coverage of writings on music notation generally, new performance techniques, music copying, autographing and printing, ethnomusicology, and writings published 1900–50. Author arrangement, with subject index. Brief annotations.

Wenk, Arthur B. Analyses of 19th century music, 1940–1970. Ann Arbor, Mich., Music Lib. Assoc., 1975. 94p. (MLA index and bibliography ser., no.13) **BH12**

"The checklist covers some hundred fifty composers represented in 39 periodicals . . . in addition an attempt has been made to glean as many analyses as possible from biographies, book-length surveys, doctoral dissertation[s] and Festschriften."—*Pref.* Arranged by composer; author index.

——— ——— Supplement, 1970–1975. Ann Arbor, Mich., Music Lib. Assoc., 1976. 57p. (MLA index and bibliography ser., no.14) ML118.W46

Winick, Steven O. Rhythm; an annotated bibliography. Metuchen, N.J., Scarecrow Pr., 1974. 157p. $6. **BH13**

An annotated listing of almost 500 English-language books, theses, and periodical articles written during the 1900–72 period and considered useful to music educators. Topically arranged in three sections: (1) General background; (2) Psychology of rhythm; (3) Pedagogy of rhythm. Index of authors, editors and reviewers. ML128.L3W53

Periodicals

Meggett, Joan M. Musical periodical literature: an annotated bibliography of indexes and bibliographies. Metuchen, N.J., Scarecrow Pr., 1978. 116p. $6. **BH14**

"Intended primarily for college and university music students as an aid to their research through music periodical literature . . . ."—*Pref.* An annotated listing of periodical indexes and bibliographies (the latter appearing in book form or as an essay or periodical article which includes references to periodical literature) on music and music-related topics. Indexes of authors/editors/compilers, subjects, and titles. ML128.P24M43

Dissertations

Adkins, Cecil and **Dickinson, Alis.** International index of dissertations and musicological works in progress. Philadelphia, Amer. Musicological Soc., International Musicological Soc., 1977. 422p. **BH15**

"The first combined publication of Doctoral dissertations in musicology (6th cumulative ed.) and Musicological works in progress (1st cumulative ed.)."—*t.p.*

Lists 4,641 titles arranged by period, then by topic within period. Author and subject indexes. Since 1972, non-American dissertations are included, as are a few from other disciplines if the work is of a historical nature.

Mead, Rita H. Doctoral dissertations on American music: a classified bibliography. Brooklyn, Inst. for Studies in Amer. Music, 1974. 155p. (ISAM monographs, no.3) $5. **BH16**

Topically arranged within six major sections: (1) Reference and research materials; (2) Historical studies; (3) Theory; (4) Ethnomusicology; (5) Organology; (6) Related fields. Lists dissertations accepted at United States universities on American music from 1890 through 1973 (i.e., includes dissertations listed in the Fall 1973 *Journal* of the American Musicological Society and the Dec. 1973 issue of *Dissertation abstracts international*). Author and subject indexes. ML128.M8M4

Manuscript and printed music

American music before 1865 in print and on records: biblio-discography; pref. by H. Wiley Hitchcock. Brooklyn, Inst. for

Studies in Amer. Music, Brooklyn College, 1976. 113p. (ISAM monographs, no.6) $5 pa. **BH17**

This is both a "classified and annotated bibliography of pre-1865 American music . . . in print and available for purchase in 1976" and a "discography listing phonorecordings of pre-1865 American music that had been issued on 33⅓ r.p.m. discs up to 1976."—*Pref.* The bibliography is in three sections: (1) Music in performance editions; (2) Music in facsimile reprints; (3) Music in books. In all sections the arrangement is alphabetical by author or, if anonymous, by title. Index of composers, compilers, and titles for both the bibliography and the discography. ML120.U5A467

Brixel, Eugen. Klarinetten Bibliographie I. Wilhelmshaven, Heinrichshofen, [1977]. 493p. DM54. **BH18**

Clarinet music is listed by composer within sections for the instrument in various combinations (with piano, with orchestra, with a second clarinet, etc.). Bibliography of literature on the clarinet, pp.401–16. Index of composers; list of publishers. ML128.C58B74

Composium directory of new music: annual index of contemporary compositions, 1970– . Los Angeles, Crystal Record Co., 1971– . Annual. $6.95; $4.95 pa. **BH19**

Arranged by composer, giving a brief biographical sketch and a list of recent compositions (both published and unpublished); includes composer's address or name of publishing house from which copies of the works may be obtained. Ensemble and instrument listing.

Corbin, Solange, ed. Répertoire de manuscrits médievaux contenant des notations musicales. Paris, Éditions du Centre National de la Recherche Scientifique, 1965–74. 3v. **BH20**

At head of title: École pratique des hautes-études, Sorbonne. 4. section: Sciences historiques et philologiques.

Madeleine Bernard, ed.

Contents: v.1, Bibliothèque Sainte-Geneviève, Paris. 160p. 45.20F.; v.2, Bibliothèque Mazarine, Paris. 196p. 45.20F.; v.3, Bibliothèques parisiennes: Arsenal, Nationale (Musique), Universitaire, École des Beaux Arts et fonds privés. 300p. 120F.

A listing and description of each medieval manuscript containing notation of a chant. Arrangement within volumes is by type of notation (e.g., neume, square note, etc.). Indexes by manuscript numbers, by original owner of manuscript, by form of manuscript (hymnal, the offices), by type of lines on the page, and by neume. v.1–2 include a listing of manuscripts with pictures of musical instruments, though only the folio number is listed, not the name of the instrument pictured. Indexes of repositories and of incipits in v.3. M135.A2C67

Eagon, Angelo. Catalog of published concert music by American composers. 2d ed. Supplement 1–2. Metuchen, N.J., Scarecrow Pr., 1971–74. 2v. $6 per v. **BH21**

For main volume and annotation *see Guide* BH143.

The supplements bring the coverage up to Nov. 1973.

Jarman, Lynn. Canadian music, a selected checklist, 1950–1973; a selective listing of Canadian music from *Fontes artis musicae,* 1954–73 based on the catalogued entries of *Canadiana* from 1950. Toronto, Univ. of Toronto Pr., 1976. 170p. $10. **BH22**

A bibliographical project of the Canadian Association of Music Libraries.

A cumulation in classed arrangement of entries for Canadian music cited in *Fontes artis musicae.* (Items selected for inclusion in *Fontes* are those "of serious intent and of a certain length or substance."—*Pref.*) Index by composer/author, subarranged by title of works. ML120.C2J4

Newberry Library, Chicago. Bibliographical inventory of the early music in the Newberry Library, Chicago, Ill.; ed. by D. W. Krummel. Boston, G. K. Hall, 1977. 587p. $75. **BH23**

Reproduction of the relevant catalog cards from this library which is particularly strong in medieval, Renaissance, and American music. Sections for manuscripts and for printed music and treatises are followed by eight geographical sections (with subdivisions, usually chronologically arranged). Index of composers, editors, and musical subjects; index of printers, engravers, artists, copyists, and publishers. ML136.C5N43

Olmsted, Elizabeth H. Music Library Association catalog of cards for printed music, 1953–1972; a supplement to the Library of Congress catalogs. Totowa, N.J., Rowman & Littlefield, 1974. 2v. $80. **BH24**

Includes entries for printed music reported to the National Union Catalog for the period 1956–72, thus supplementing the *Library of Congress catalog—Music and phonorecords* (*Guide* BH54). Much editing was done for this publication, but cards were not retyped and a considerable number of them are virtually unreadable. Name of the library supplying the card was not included, therefore the catalog cannot be used as a tool for locating copies. ML113.O42

Keyboard instruments

Bedford, Frances and **Conant, Robert.** 20th century harpsichord music: a classified catalog. Hackensack, N.J., Joseph Boonin, [1974]. 95p. (Music indexes and bibliographies, no. 8) $8.50. **BH25**

Works for solo harpsichord are listed by composer, followed by 33 sections for combinations of other instruments with harpsichord. Each entry gives composer, title, year composed, length of performance, and source for obtaining the music. Composer index; title index; list of composers' addresses. ML128.H35B4

Chang, Frederic Ming and **Faurot, Albert.** Team piano repertoire, a manual for multiple players at one or more pianos. Metuchen, N.J., Scarecrow Pr., 1976. 184p. $8. **BH26**

An annotated listing of music available for two to four piano players, presented according to number of performers. Includes a list of recordings. ML128.P3C48

Edson, Jean Slater. Organ preludes. Supplement. Metuchen, N.J., Scarecrow Pr., 1974. 315p. $10. **BH27**

For main volume and annotation *see Guide* BH115.

Offers corrections and additions as well as updating; much new material on French *noëls* and Scandinavian music.

Faurot, Albert. Concert piano repertoire, a manual of solo literature for artists and performers. Metuchen, N.J., Scarecrow Pr., 1974. 338p. $10. **BH28**

Intended as "a comprehensive listing of piano solo literature," arranged by composer and giving a short annotation for each piece cited, together with indication of level of difficulty. "Chronology of composers," pp.325–33. Brief bibliography of books on the composers and on piano music in general. ML128.P3F39

Hinson, Maurice. Guide to the pianist's repertoire. Ed. by Irwin Freundlich. Bloomington, Indiana Univ. Pr., [1973]. 831p. $15. **BH29**

An alphabetical listing by composer, indicating available editions of the solo piano works. Anthologies and collections available are also listed by period and by country. Index of composers by nationality; lists of black composers and of women composers. Index of editors, arrangers, transcribers. ML128.P3H5

——— The piano in chamber ensemble, an annotated guide. Bloomington, Indiana Univ. Pr., [1978]. 570p. **BH30**

A listing of compositions "requiring no more than 8 instruments" but involving "the piano on an equal basis."—*Pref.* Lists mainly works written after 1700 up to and including contemporary times. Arranged by number and combinations of instruments required, then by composer; publishers are indicated. Index of composers. ML128.C4H5

Nardone, Thomas R. Organ music in print. Philadelphia, Musicdata, 1975. 262p. (Music-in-print ser., v.3) $32. **BH31**

Intended as a "comprehensive catalog of international music publishers listing the complete issues of each publisher" (*Pref.*) in the field of organ music. Composers, titles, and cross references appear in a single alphabetical arrangement. ML128.O6N37

Vocal

Edwards, J. Michele. Literature for voices in combination with electronic and tape music, an annotated bibliography. Ann Arbor, Music Lib. Assoc., 1977. 194p. (MLA index and bibliography ser., no.17) **BH32**

A listing of 400 compositions for at least three live performers who sing or speak "in combination with electronic and tape music . . . from the earliest known works through 1975 . . . . Second, the bibliography is a finding list of compositions currently available to performers."—*Pref.* Arranged by composer, with "Index by medium" (e.g., mixed choir, mixed choir and keyboard, etc.). Directory of addresses for publishers, non-score sources, foreign and hard-to-find record labels, studios. Selected bibliography of sources, pp.179–82. ML128.E4E37

Espina, Noni. Repertoire for the solo voice; a fully annotated guide to works for the solo voice published in modern editions and covering material from the 13th century to the present. Metuchen, N.J., Scarecrow Pr., 1977. 2v. (1290p.) $45. **BH33**

The solos cited are mainly based on the voice-piano editions available through the fall of 1975. Arranged by nationality, then by special forms—opera, display songs, traditional songs and spirituals. Most sections are subdivided by type of voice. "Indices of the sources of the texts and the composers." ML128.S3E8

May, James D. Avant-garde choral music; an annotated selected bibliography. Metuchen, N.J., Scarecrow Pr., 1977. 258p. $10. **BH34**

An "annotated bibliography of avant-garde choral compositions readily available from the music publishers of the United States" (*Pref.*) intended for use of high school, church, college and university choral directors. Gives full publishing information, voice requirements, accompaniment, supplementary requirements. Indexed. ML128.V7M43

Nardone, Thomas R. Classical vocal music in print. Philadelphia, Musicdata, 1976. 650p. (Music-in-print ser., v.4) $42. **BH35**

Includes all vocal music except "that which is commonly called popular music."—*Pref.* On the other hand, "many folk songs and folk song collections have been included because of their frequent demand in recital programming." Arranged by composer or anonymous title. Entries indicate vocal range and publisher's price. List of publishers with addresses. ML128.V7N335

——— **Nye, James H.** and **Resnick, Mark.** Choral music in print. Philadelphia, Musicdata, 1974. 2v. (Music-in-print ser., v.1–2) **BH36**

Contents: v.1, Sacred choral music (656p.; $45); v.2, Secular choral music (614p.; $45).

" . . . an attempt at an exhaustive listing of the music publishers throughout the world" (*Pref.*) and the choral compositions gleaned from their catalogs. In each volume the musical works are listed in a single alphabet by title and composer, with full information appearing under the author's name (or, if anonymous, under title).

——— ——— Supplement. Philadelphia, 1976. 419p. $32.

Sacred and secular compositions are again listed in separate sections. ML128.V7N33

Encyclopedias and dictionaries

Dictionnaire de la musique; publié sous la direction de Marc Honegger. [Paris], Bordas, [1970–76]. 4v. il. 320F. the set. **BH37**

Contents: v.1–2, Les hommes et leurs oeuvres; v.3–4, Science de la musique: techniques, formes, instruments.

v.1–2 form an alphabetical biographical dictionary of composers and others associated with music (e.g., music publishers, instrument makers, librettists, conductors, musicologists), both living and dead. Longer articles are signed; bibliographies are included.

v.3–4 comprise an alphabetical arrangement of survey articles on the music of individual countries, specific instruments and their development, forms of music, problems of acoustics, definitions of terms. Signed articles with bibliographies. ML100.D65

Encyclopedia of quotations about music. Comp. and ed. by Nat Shapiro. Garden City, N.Y., Doubleday, 1978. 418p. $10. **BH38**

A topical arrangement of more than 2,000 "wise, witty, and beautiful quotations about music."—*Introd.* Index of names and sources; index of keywords and phrases. ML66.E6

Musik in Geschichte und Gegenwart . . . . Kassel, Bärenreiter, 1974–78. Lfg. 148/49–154/55. (In progress) **BH39**

For full citation, earlier volumes and annotation *see Guide* BH85.

Contents: Lfg.148/49–154/55 (v.15, Suppl.), E–Rau.

Muzykal'naia entsiklopediia. Gl. red. Iurii Vsevolodovich Keldysh. Moskva, "Sov. Entsiklopediia–Sov. Kommozitor," 1973– . v.1– . il. (In progress) **BH40**

Contents: v.1, A–Oktol'. (Publ. 1973–76.)

Offers signed articles with bibliographies. Includes much biographical material. ML100.M97

Sohlmans Musiklexikon. 2 revid. och utv. uppl. [Huvudred. Hans Åastrand] [Stockholm], Sohlmans Forläg, [1975–77]. v.1–4. (In progress) **BH41**

1st ed. 1948–52 (*Guide* BH89).

Contents: v.1–4, A–Partial.

A revised edition of this major Scandinavian music encyclopedia, offering signed articles on composers, performers, institutions, works, and movements of Scandinavian music. Many bibliographies. To be in 5v. (about $225 the set).

Thompson, Oscar. International cyclopedia of music and musicians. 10th rev. ed. N.Y., Dodd., 1975. 2511p. $49.95. **BH42**

9th ed. 1964 (*Guide* BH91).

For a comparison of the 9th and 10th eds. *see* the review by the A.L.A. Subscription Books Committee in *The booklist* 72:893 which concludes that "the majority of articles in the 10th ed. are unchanged or merely dressed up with dates." ML100.T47

Dictionaries of terms

Fink, Robert and **Ricci, Robert.** Language of twentieth century music, a dictionary of terms. N.Y., Schirmer Books, 1975. 125p. $8.95. **BH43**

A dictionary offering brief definitions of "the basic terminologies of chance music, computer music, electronic music, film music, jazz, musique concrète, multimedia, rock, twelve-tone music and other more traditional styles of music composition . . . , as well as . . . a number of instruments and performance practices that have developed as composers have searched for new means of expression. Also, new tools for musical analysis have been included along with many of the important movements in contemporary plastic and graphic arts which employ techniques and aesthetic points of view similar to those found in twentieth century music."—*Pref.* Appendix: "A topical listing of terms included." Brief bibliography. ML100.F55

Picerno, Vincent J. Dictionary of musical terms. Brooklyn, Haskell House, 1976. 453p. (Studies in music, no.42) $24.95. **BH44**

Intended for the undergraduate or the interested amateur. Terms are drawn from all forms of music (jazz, electronic, classical, etc.). "A selected annotated bibliography" is appended to direct the user to further information. ML108.P57

Terminorum musicae index septum lingus redactus. Budapest, Akadémiai Kiadó, 1978. 798p. **BH45**

Title also in English: *Polyglot dictionary of musical terms.*

Horst Leuchtmann, ed. in chief.

Terms in English, German, French, Italian, Spanish, Hungarian, and Russian are given in a single alphabetical sequence, with equivalents in each of the other languages. The base word is in the language from which the word originated or, if not in one of the seven languages of the dictionary, in German; cross references are given from terms in the other languages to the base word. Separate Cyrillic alphabet section. An appendix gives equivalents in all seven languages for music notation terms and a large range of instruments through drawings and diagrams. ML108.T4

Wörterbuch Musik/Dictionary of music. Hrsg. von Horst Leuchtmann. 2. erw. Aufl. Munich, Verlag Dokumentation, 1977. 493p. DM48. **BH46**

"Englisch-Deutsch/Deutsch-Englisch; English-German/German-English."—*t.p.*

1st ed. 1964.

A dictionary of equivalent terms with separate sections for English-German and German-English. This edition expanded to include terms from music psychology and sociology, instrument-making, electronic music, acoustics, and dance as well as practical and theoretical music terms. ML108.W73

Handbooks

Berkowitz, Freda Pastor. Popular titles and subtitles of musical compositions. 2d ed. Metuchen, N.J., Scarecrow Pr., 1975. 209p. $8. **BH47**

1st ed. 1962 (*Guide* BH101).

A revised and expanded edition.

Fog, Dan and **Michelsen, Kari.** Norwegian music publication since 1800, a preliminary guide to music publishers, printers and dealers. Copenhagen, Dan Fog, 1976. 30p. Kr. 32. **BH48**

"Attempts to give in alphabetical order outlines of the history of [38 of the] more important firms—including indications appearing on title-pages which can help dating the publication."—*Introd.* Music-hire libraries of the 19th century are identified; plate numbers are indicated where known. ML112.F635N67

Hodgson, Julian. Music titles in translation: a checklist of musical compositions. London, Bingley; Hamden, Conn., Linnet Books, 1976. 370p. $17.50. **BH49**

"The list gives in one alphabetical sequence the original or English language translation followed by the translation or original as the case may be."—*Pref.* No index. ML111.H7

Krummel, Donald William. Guide for dating early published music, a manual of bibliographical practices. Hackensack, N.J., Joseph Boonin; Kassel, Bärenreiter Verlag, 1974. 267p. il., facsims. **BH50**

At head of title: International Association of Music Libraries. Commission for Bibliographical Research.

"A summary of the 'state of the art' of dating early music" (*p.15*) issued between 1700 and 1860. In two parts: (1) "Synopsis," a summary of the methodology of dating; and (2) "National reports," a country-by-country summary of music publishing therein. Index of music cited. A perceptive review by Peter Davison appears in *The library,* 5th ser., 32:75–78 (Mar. 1977). ML111.K78

Directories

British music yearbook: a summary and directory with statistics and reference articles for 1975– . London & N.Y., Bowker, 1975– . Annual. (1975: $22.50) **BH51**

Arthur Jacobs, ed.

Supersedes *Music yearbook* (London, Macmillan; N.Y., St. Martin's Pr., 1972–73).

A compilation of directory information deemed useful to the music specialist and the newcomer to the field, thus providing lists of accompanists, agents, youth orchestras, etc. Also includes survey articles such as "The musician and insurance," "New on record."

Except for topics of interest to "the young musician" (e.g., lists of appointments and awards, competitions, music publishers, places to study abroad), the international coverage of the earlier *Music yearbook* has been abandoned.

Brody, Elaine and **Brook, Claire.** The music guide to Austria and Germany. N.Y., Dodd, Mead & Co., 1975. 271p. $10. **BH52**
ML21.B77

——— The music guide to Belgium, Luxemburg, Holland and Switzerland. N.Y., Dodd, Mead & Co., 1977. 156p. $10. **BH53**
ML21.B773

——— The music guide to Great Britain: England, Scotland, Wales, Ireland. N.Y., Dodd, Mead & Co., [1975]. 240p. $10. **BH54**
ML21.B78

The above volumes are companion publications in a series which will ultimately cover 18 European countries. A summary discussion of music developments in each country is followed by notes for each major city, indicating guides and services available, opera houses and concert halls, libraries and museums, conservatories and schools, and musical organizations. Music festivals and competitions are also noted. Volumes are separately indexed.

A further addition to the series, *The music guide to Italy,* is announced for 1978 publication.

Directory of music faculties in colleges and universities, U.S. and Canada, 1976–1978. Comp. and ed. by Craig R. Short. 6th ed. [Binghamton, N.Y.], College Music Soc., [1976]. 1v., various pagings. **BH55**

Ed. 1–3 entitled *Directory of music faculties in American colleges and universities* (publ. 1967–70).

This ed. lists 20,781 music faculty members at 1,373 institutions of higher learning. In four sections: (1) alphabetical listing by state of names and addresses of colleges and universities, with list of faculty members and area of teaching interest; (2) list of faculty members by area of interest; (3) alphabetical listing by name of faculty member; (4) listing of schools by type of degree offered (e.g., M.A. in ethnomusicology). ML13.D57

Finell, Judith Greenberg. The contemporary music performance directory: a listing of American performing ensembles, sponsoring organizations, performing facilities, concert series, and festivals of 20th century music. N.Y., Amer. Music Center, [1975]. 238p. $12; $6 pa. **BH56**

Arranged geographically under the headings listed in the subtitle. Information is based on questionnaires. ML13.F48

International music guide, 1977– . London, Tantivy Pr.; Cranbury, N.J., A. S. Barnes, [1976–]. Annual. il. £2.50; $5.95 pa. **BH57**

Derek Elley, ed.

Similar to, and produced by, the same group as the *International film guide* (*Suppl.* BG40), "surveying internationally all points of interest to the modern concertgoer and general music-lover."—*Introd.* A survey of music of the year in fifteen countries and a brief review of non-classical music and recordings is followed by a directory of festivals, music magazines, music shops, and music schools.

Long, Maureen W. Music in British libraries, a directory of resources. 2d ed. London, Library Assoc., 1974. 154p. (Library Assoc. research publ., no.14) £3. **BH58**

1st ed. 1971.

An alphabetical listing of some 485 libraries in England, Scotland, Wales, and Northern Ireland with brief descriptions of their music collections.

Biography

See also Suppl. BH37, BH40–BH42, BH73.

Anderson, Ruth. Contemporary American composers, a biographical dictionary. Boston, G. K. Hall, 1976. 513p. $50. **BH59**

An alphabetical arrangement of biographical entries for about 4,000 composers who were born no earlier than 1870, have American citizenship or extended residence in the United States, and are credited with at least one original composition recorded, published, or performed in an urban setting or awarded a prize in composition. Information includes birth date, musicians with whom studied, positions held, works, current address. Addendum: listing of women composers, pp.495–510. ML390.A54

Contemporary Canadian composers, ed. by Keith Macmillan and John Beckwith. N.Y., Oxford Univ. Pr., 1975. 248p. il. $14.95. **BH60**

Sponsored by the Canadian Music Centre.

144 Canadian composers who have produced most of their works since 1920 are listed alphabetically, with a survey of their output and a list of musical works and bibliography. ML106.C3C66

International who's who in music and musicians' directory. Ed. by Ernest Kay. 7th ed.– . Cambridge, Melrose Pr. (distr. in U.S. by Rowman & Littlefield), 1975– . (7th ed.: $37.50) **BH61**

Represents a change of title for *Who's who in music and musicians' international directory* (*Guide* BH93) last published 1972. Scope has been expanded to make the work truly international. Appendixes now list professional orchestras, organizations, major competitions and awards, music libraries, conservatories, etc. ML106.G7W4

Bibliographies and indexes

Bull, Storm. Index to biographies of contemporary composers. Metuchen, N.J., Scarecrow Pr., 1964–74. 2v. (v.1, $12.50; v.2, $18.50) **BH62**

Concerned with composers who were "alive or born 1900, or later, or died in 1950 or later."—*v.1.* Information is given in columns: name, country with which the composer is identified, year of birth, country of birth (if different from the previous listing), date of death if known, indication (by abbreviation) of sources of further biographical information. About 4,000 composers listed in v.1; the second volume adds some 4,000 more names, plus further information on some of those included in v.1. ML105.B9

Moldon, David. A bibliography of Russian composers. London, White Lion Publ., [1976]; Totowa, N.J., Rowman & Littlefield, 1977. 364p. £15; $37.50. **BH63**

A bibliography of English-language books, essays, periodical articles, and some theses relating to Russian composers, i.e., "all composers born in countries comprising the present U.S.S.R."—*Pref.* Following a general section, arrangement is by name of composer, then chronologically by date of publication. Index of authors, editors and compilers, and a subject index. ML120.R8M6

Skowronski, Jo Ann. Women in American music, a bibliography. Metuchen, N.J., Scarecrow Pr., 1978. 183p. $8. **BH64**

Lists 1,305 books and periodical articles which treat any aspect of women as composers or musicians. Topical arrangement with name index. Most entries are briefly annotated. ML128.W7S6

History

New Oxford history of music. London & N.Y., Oxford Univ. Pr., 1974–75. v.5, 10. (In progress) **BH65**

For previously published volumes and annotation *see Guide* BH110.

Contents: v.5, Opera and church music 1630–1750, ed. by Nigel Fortune and Anthony Lewis; v.10, The modern age, ed. by Martin Cooper.

MUSICAL FORMS

ASCAP symphonic catalog 1977; ed. and comp. by the Amer. Soc. of Composers, Authors, and Publishers. 3d ed. N.Y., Bowker, [1977]. 522p. $25 pa. **BH66**

1st ed. 1959; 2d ed. 1966.

A listing of "26,000 symphonic, chamber orchestra, chamber ensemble (10 instruments or more) and choral works" (*Pref.*) by ASCAP members and foreign composers whose United States performances are licensed through ASCAP. Listing is by name of composer or arranger, with each entry indicating title, date, publisher, instrumentation, name of librettist if given, performance time, source of sheet music or manuscript.

Davidson, James Robert. A dictionary of Protestant church music. Metuchen, N.J., Scarecrow Pr., 1975. 349p. $12.50. **BH67**

Terms evaluated as relevant to Protestant church music are defined and treated from the historical point of view. Includes many short bibliographies; index of personal names and institutions mentioned in the text. No biographical entries. This is the first phase of a "Dictionary of church music" projected by the author. ML102.C5D33

Drone, Jeanette M. Index to opera, operetta and musical comedy synopses in collections and periodicals. Metuchen, N.J., Scarecrow Pr., 1978. 171p. $7. **BH68**

Indexes plot synopses appearing in 74 collections and four periodical series. In four sections: (1) collections indexed; (2) title index, with indication of collection or periodical in which a synopsis may be found; (3) composer index, with reference to the title section; (4) bibliography of additional sources. Intended as an extension of Rieck's *Opera plots* (*Guide* BH135). ML128.O4D76

Yeats-Edwards, Paul. English church music: a bibliography. London, White Lion Publ., [1975]. 217p. £15. **BH69**

A classed arrangement of books, pamphlets, tracts, and theses published in England, 1500–1973, and dealing with music used in the "choral worship of the church" (*Pref.*), but excluding the oratorio as dramatic music, or 'programme' music."

Represents a revision of a Library Association Fellowship thesis originally accepted 1970. ML128.C54X4

Opera

The encyclopedia of opera. Ed. by Leslie Orrey. N.Y., Scribner, 1976. 376p. il. $25. **BH70**

Offers short entries for operas and characters from opera as well as performers, composers, conductors, and designers selected for their "relevance to the contemporary scene . . . of music theater—opera, operetta, musical" (*Introd.*); emphasis, however, is on opera. Entries for music houses are found under name of the city in which located; there are also brief surveys of the history of opera in individual countries. Articles are signed with the initials of the contributor. ML102.O6E6

Northouse, Cameron. Twentieth century opera in England and the United States. Boston, G. K. Hall, 1976. 400p. $25. **BH71**

"Attempts to trace some of the basic details of the twentieth century opera subculture" (*Pref.*) by listing first performances of 1,612 20th-century English and American operas, an additional 941 operas for which complete performance information was not available, operas based on literary works, and published operas. Index of composers, librettists, opera titles, literary titles, and literary authors. ML128.O4N79

Seltsam, William H. Metropolitan opera annals. 3d suppl., 1966–1976, comp. by Mary Ellis Peltz and Gerald Fitzgerald. Clifton, N.J., publ. for the Metropolitan Opera Guild by James T. White & Co., [1978]. 208p. il. $17.50. **BH72**

Continues the record of performances and excerpts from critical reviews as found in the basic volume for 1883–1947 and its two supplements covering 1947–57 and 1957–66 (*Guide* BH129).

Who's who in opera: an international biographical directory of singers, conductors, directors, designers, and administrators. Also including profiles of 101 opera companies. Maria F. Rich, ed. N.Y., Arno Pr., 1976. 684p. $65. **BH73**

A biographical directory of opera personnel active at the time of compilation. Inclusion was according to the following criteria: "Since the beginning of the 1971–72 season: singers must have sung at least five major roles with one or more of the designated companies [i.e., some 140 opera companies and festivals in 33 countries]; conductors must have conducted at least five operas with one or more of the designated companies; stage directors/producers must have staged at least two new opera productions with one or more of the designated companies; designers must have designed sets, costumes or lighting for at least two new opera productions with one or more of the designated companies. Administrators must have been in key administrative positions with any of the designated companies. . . . "—*Pref.* Includes 2,350 biographical sketches; information is meant to be current as of the 1974–75 season. ML102.O6W5

Plots

Kobbé, Gustav. The new Kobbé's complete opera book. Ed. and rev. by the Earl of Harewood. N.Y., Putnam's, [1976]. 1694p. $20. **BH74**

1st ed. 1919; previous ed. 1972 (*Guide* BH132).

This edition (also referred to as "4th rev. ed.") reset and considerably expanded—new composers are represented, as are various operas not previously summarized.

Musical theater

Green, Stanley. Encyclopaedia of the musical theatre. N.Y., Dodd, Mead, [1976]. 488p. $17.50. **BH75**

Offers "succinct information regarding the most prominent people, productions, and songs of the musical theatre, both in New York (incl. off-Bway) and London."—*Pref.* Includes a list of awards and prizes (with recipients), a table of "long runs," a brief bibliography, and a discography. ML102.M88G7

International Music Centre, Vienna (IMZ). Music in film and television, an international selective catalogue, 1964–1974: opera, concert, documentation. Paris, UNESCO Pr., [1975]. 197p. **BH76**

Film and video-tape productions "shown between 1964–1974 at international IMZ events were taken as the basic stock . . . supplemented with representative international productions from the same period which the authors considered important."—*Pref.* In four sections: (1) music theater and opera productions; (2) concert music productions; (3) educational programs; (4) experimental programs. Indexes of titles, composers, producers, directors, performing artists, orchestra or performing groups, conductors, organizations and companies (by country), title, production company (with addresses). ML128.M7163

Pitts, Michael R. and **Harrison, Louis H.** Hollywood on record: the film stars' discography. Metuchen, N.J., Scarecrow Pr., 1978. 410p. il. $16. **BH77**

Aims to "list recorded work of motion picture performers since the introduction of the modern long-playing record in 1948."—*Introd.* Listing is by performer; no index. Limited to musical performances. ML156.4.M6P58

Woll, Allen L. Songs from Hollywood musical comedies, 1927 to the present; a dictionary. N.Y., Garland, 1976. 251p. (Garland reference library in the humanities, v.44) $25. **BH78**

" . . . provides a guide for . . . nostalgia buffs, allowing them to identify their favorite movie musical show tunes, and, if possible, find soundtrack recordings of them."—*How to use this book.* In four alphabetically arranged sections: (1) title listing of songs (with name of film); (2) title listing of musicals (with date of release, name of principal players, director, song writers, and, when available, recorded songs with name of record company and number; (3) chronological listing of musicals; (4) composers and lyricists. Name index. ML102.P66W64

Songs

Gooch, Bryan N. S. and **Thatcher, David S.** Musical settings of late Victorian and modern British literature: a catalogue. N.Y., Garland, 1976. 1112p. (Garland reference library of the humanities, v.31) $83. **BH79**

A listing of texts set to music (both published and unpublished) up to July 1975. All authors included are British or "sufficiently identified with the English literary tradition" (*Pref.*), and all were "born after 1840 and lived to 1900 or later." Arranged by literary author, with each text identified by title, first line or literary form, and date of first publication; this is followed by the composer's name, the setting and publication information thereof, vocal specifications, and accompaniment. Indexes of authors and composers. ML120.G7G66

Lowens, Irving. A bibliography of songsters printed in America before 1821. Worcester, Mass., Amer. Antiquarian Soc., 1976. 229p. $16. **BH80**

A songster is defined as "a collection of three or more secular poems intended to be sung."—*Introd.* These 650 collections are listed chronologically by title, alphabetically within each year. Geographical directory of printers, publishers, booksellers, engravers; index of compilers, authors, proprietors, and editors; title index. Locations are indicated for each collection. ML128.S3L7

Stahl, Dorothy. A selected discography of solo song: a cumulation through 1971. Detroit, Information Coordinators, 1972. 137p. (Detroit studies in music bibliography, 24) $6.50; $5 pa. **BH81**

——— ——— Supplement, 1971–1974. Detroit, 1976. 99p. (Detroit studies in music bibliography, 34) $9.50.

1st ed. publ. 1968 as *Detroit studies in music bibliography,* 13.

Provides a listing by composer, title, and first line, of recordings featuring classical songs for the solo voice. ML156.4.V7S8

Indexes

Havlice, Patricia Pate. Popular song index. Metuchen, N.J., Scarecrow Pr., 1975. 933p. $30. **BH82**

301 song books published between 1940 and 1972 have been indexed as an aid to finding both the words and music of folk songs, popular tunes, spirituals, hymns, children's songs, sea chanteys, and blues. Index by title, first line of song, and first line of chorus; index of composers and lyricists. ML128.S3H4

Jazz

Feather, Leonard G. and **Gitler, Ira.** The encyclopedia of jazz in the seventies. N.Y., Horizon Pr., [1976]. 393p. il. $20. **BH83**

Forms a companion volume to *The encyclopedia of jazz* (*Guide* BH152) and *The encyclopedia of jazz in the sixties* (*Guide* BH153), extending the coverage through the 1966–75 period, adding some new names as well as updating biographical sketches in the earlier volumes. Adds results of polls published in *Down beat* and *Swing journal,* 1965–75; lists of jazz films and recommended recordings; and a brief bibliography. ML105.F36

Jazz index: bibliography of jazz literature in periodicals and collections; Bibliographie unselbständiger Jazzliteratur. v.1, no.1– , Jan./Mar. 1977– . [Frankfurt/M., Norbert Ruecker], 1977– . Quarterly. $24 (DM48) per yr. **BH84**

Comp. by Norbert Ruecker and Christa Reggentin-Scheidt.

Introductory matter in English and German; subject headings in English only beginning with v.2.

Regularly indexes articles and reviews on jazz in more than fifty journals, with selective indexing of other journals which carry occasional articles on jazz. Beginning with v.2, record reviews were dropped, but book and concert reviews continue to be included. Articles on "blues" are listed in a separate section beginning with v.2.

Meeker, David. Jazz in the movies, a guide to jazz musicians, 1917–1977. [London], Talisman Books; New Rochelle, N.Y., Arlington House, [1977]. [286p.] $12.95. **BH85**

An alphabetical listing by movie title (including variant titles) indicating country of production and date, and including a brief note

on the jazz and jazzmen used in the film. Concerned with American and Western European films. Index of jazz musicians.
ML128.M7M38

Folk and popular music

Indiana. University. Archives of Traditional Music. A catalog of phonorecordings of music and oral data held by the Archives of Traditional Music. Boston, G. K. Hall, [1975]. 541p. **BH86**

Photoreproduction of the classified catalog for a collection of materials "transmitted in the main by performance or word of mouth," which in music features "folk music, music of non-literate societies, non-European classical or art music, and popular music. Among the verbal forms . . . are folktales, jokes, proverbs, interviews. . . . "—*Pref.* Listing is by code (i.e., classification) number, with a note for each entry indicating geographic area or culture group, name of collector and date, and HRAF number based on Murdock's *Outline of world cultures* (1969). Indexes of geographic or cultural areas, subjects, collectors, performers, informants, and recording companies. ML156.2.I53

Kinkle, Roger D. The complete encyclopedia of popular music and jazz, 1900–1950. New Rochelle, N.Y., Arlington House, [1974]. 4v. (2644p.) il. $75. **BH87**

Contents: v.1, Music year by year, 1900–1950; v.2–3, Biographies; v.4, Indexes and appendices.

v.1 offers year-by-year listings of Broadway musicals, movie musicals, and representative popular music (the last by year of greatest popularity, not by year of copyright). v.2–3 give brief career sketches (with discographies) of noted performers, lyricists and composers, bandleaders and sidemen, etc., in the field of popular music and jazz, with lesser coverage of light opera, blues, and country and western personalities. v.4 includes indexes of personal names, Broadway musicals, movie musicals, popular songs; appendices offer lists of important recordings, *Down beat* poll winners, and Academy Award winners and nominees for music, 1934–72. ML102.P66K55

McLean, Mervyn. An annotated bibliography of Oceanic music and dance. Wellington, Polynesian Soc., 1977. 252p. (Polynesian Society. Memoir, 41) $11. **BH88**

Lists nearly 2,200 books, journals, articles, reviews, record notes, theses, and manuscripts relating to music, musical instruments, song texts, and dance in Oceania (i.e., "all islands of the Pacific, together with New Guinea and nearby islands including Torres Strait"—*Introd.*). Excludes Australia, Malaysia, the Philippines, and Indonesia. Materials are in English, French, German, Italian, and Spanish. Arranged alphabetically by author; the annotation includes a geographic or cultural area code based on Murdock's *Outline of world cultures* (1963). Area index.

Sandburg, Larry and **Weissman, Dick.** The folk music sourcebook. N.Y., Knopf, 1976. 260p. il. $15; $7.95 pa. **BH89**

Sponsored by the Denver Folklore Center.

Aims to "provide the reader with information about all aspects of North American folk and folk-based music."—*Pref.* Includes an annotated listing of records, books, and other instructional materials currently in print; information on buying and caring for folk instruments; lists of important folk festivals, archives, periodicals, films, folklore centers; and a glossary. Index of names, with a few topical entries. ML19.S26

Stambler, Irwin. Encyclopedia of pop, rock and soul. N.Y., St. Martin's Pr., [1975]. 609p. il. $19.95. **BH90**

Survey articles on the history and development of rock and soul music are followed by a dictionary of names of performers and performing groups and terms current in popular music. Lists of awards; brief bibliography. ML102.P66S8

Stone, Ruth M. and **Gillis, Frank J.** African music and oral data, a catalog of field recordings, 1902–1975. Bloomington, Indiana Univ. Pr., 1976. 412p. $17.50. **BH91**

"The present catalog, based on the African Field Recordings Survey, provides concise summaries of collections of phonorecordings of music and oral data held by individuals and institutions throughout the world."—*Pref.* Information was derived from questionnaires, and the results are categorized by collector or repository, by country, and by culture group. Cross references; subject index.
ML156.4.P7S8

INSTRUMENTS

Marcuse, Sibyl. Survey of musical instruments. N.Y., Harper & Row; Newton Abbot, [Eng.], David & Charles, [1975]. 863p. il. $20; £10.50. **BH92**

Known musical instruments of all periods are discussed within appropriate "family" sections—idiophone, membranophone, chordophone, aerophone. Glossary; brief bibliography; name and topic indexes. ML460.M365S94

Music Library Association. A survey of musical instrument collections in the United States and Canada, conducted by a Committee of the Music Library Association: William Lichtenwanger, chairman and compiler. [Ann Arbor], Music Lib. Assoc., 1974. 135p. **BH93**

Through questionnaires and personal visits, 572 collections (each having at least 15 items) were identified. That number includes 334 institutions, "mostly museums and historical societies, in which musical instruments are not segregated into identifiable collections but are rather scattered amongst many other artifacts on a geographic or other non-musical basis; . . . 41 other institutions that have either a single and separate musical instrument collection . . . or a multiplicity of more-or-less separate collections; and 197 private collections." —*Pref.* Not included are collections of replicas or of phonographs.

Arranged geographically, giving for each collection: name, address, curator, hours, brief description, any finding aids or brief descriptions. Index of collectors or institutions; index of instruments and classes of instruments; index of cultural, geographical, and historical origins. ML19.M87

RECORDED MUSIC

Cooper, David Edwin. International bibliography of discographies: classical music and jazz and blues, 1962–1972; a reference book for record collectors, dealers, and libraries. Littleton, Colo., Libraries Unlimited, 1972. 272p. (Keys to music bibliography, no.2) $13.50. **BH94**

Restricted to Western classical music, jazz and blues. Lists discographies appearing in books and periodical articles published 1962–72. Arranged by period, subject or genre, composer and performer. Includes a "Summary of national discographies, catalogs and major review sources." Index of authors, titles, series, subjects.
ML113.C655I6

Gray, Michael and **Gibson, Gerald D.** Bibliography of discographies. N.Y., Bowker, 1977– . v.1– . (In progress) **BH95**

Contents: v.1, Classical music. 164p. $19.95.

An alphabetical listing of discographies of composers and performers published 1925 to 1975 in journals or as part of a monograph. v.1 includes an index of authors, compilers and editors.

To be in 5v., future volumes to cover: v.2, jazz; v.3, popular music; v.4, ethnic and folk music; v.5, general discographies, including label lists, speech, and animal sounds. ML113.G77

Halsey, Richard Sweeney. Classical music recordings: for home and library. Chicago, Amer. Lib. Assoc., 1970. 340p. $15. **BH96**

Intended as a "guide for organizations and individuals concerned with collecting and organizing, playing and caring for sound recordings."—*Pref.* The main section provides a comprehensive listing of recordings by composer and title, indicating record number, an "aesthetic significance" rating, a minimum age level, and designation of

those recordings with a high percentage of favorable reviews. A second section lists works by recording company and record number, with name of performers given. Glossary of audio terms; title index to composer list; subject, proper name and composer index.
ML111.5.H34

Rowell, Lois. American organ music on records. Braintree, Mass., Organ Literature Foundation, 1976. 105p. $6. **BH97**

A listing by composer of recordings issued 1941–75 of music written originally for the organ or transcribed for the organ by the composer. Limited to native-born composers and those who established permanent residence in the United States. Indexes by performer, organ builder and instrument location, album title, record label and number, author of program notes, series.
ML156.4O6R7

Rust, Brian. The American dance band discography, 1917–1942. New Rochelle, N.Y., Arlington House, 1975. 2v. (2066p.) $35. **BH98**

". . . seeks to list all the known recorded work of the dance bands" —(*Introd.*) issued between 1917 and 1942 (only 78 rpm issues). Arranged by band, with "Artists' index." ML156.4.P6R87

——— The complete entertainment discography from the mid-1890s to 1942. New Rochelle, N.Y., Arlington House, [1973]. 677p. $14.95. **BH99**

Attempts to list "all known records . . . of artists of the years between the beginning of commercial recording in the mid-1890s and 1942 . . . ; 'artists' means minstrel pioneers, the vaudevillians, the film stars and radio personalities, and the straight actors and actresses . . . of American birth, or of such stature that they are well-known in America . . . ."—*Introd.* Arrangement is by name of artist; a biographical note is followed by a list of recordings giving title, record number and producer, accompanist or assisting group. No index.
ML156.4.P6R88

Current

Schwann-1, records, tapes. v.27– . 1975– . Boston, Schwann Publs., 1975– . Monthly. (Also available on microfilm) **BH100**

Supersedes the *Schwann record and tape guide* (*Guide* BH191) and continues its numbering.

Reviews

Myers, Kurtz. Index to record reviews. Boston, G. K. Hall, 1978. 5v. $365. **BH101**

A cumulation of the "Index to record reviews" which appeared in the periodical *Notes* (*see Guide* BH194) from 1948 through early 1977.

C

Social Sciences

C A

General Works

GUIDES

Use of social sciences literature. N. Roberts, ed. London, Butterworth, [1977]. 326p. $19.95. **CA1**

A series of bibliographic essays by a group of British librarians and academics. Includes chapters on the literature, sources, and needs in the fields of economics, sociology, politics, social anthropology, management research, education, environmental planning, public administration, and criminology. Special chapters on use of the official publications of the United Kingdom, foreign countries, and international organizations. Index of "subjects, institutions and *types* of literature" but none of individual authors and titles. H62.U63

Walford, Albert John. Guide to reference material. 3d ed. [London], Library Assoc., [1975]. v.2. (In progress) **CA2**

For v.1 of this ed. *see Guide* EA9; for v.3. *see Suppl.* AA80.

v.2 covers philosophy, psychology, religion, the social sciences, and geography, biography and history. The number of entries has been increased to some 4,500 items, an increase of about 15% over the second edition of this volume (1968; *Guide* CA9). "Highlighted" subjects are: occultism, the less-developed countries, the European

Economic Community, international aid, Parliament, military affairs, social work, metrication, archaeology, British local history, and Latin American history.

BIBLIOGRAPHY

Comfort, A. F. and **Loveless, Christina.** Guide to government data: a survey of unpublished social science material in libraries of government departments in London. London, Macmillan, 1974. 404p. £5.95. **CA3**

Publ. for the British Library of Political and Economic Science.

For each department, provides a brief selection of published materials (especially those about departmental functions, organization, and research), followed by brief descriptions of unpublished materials produced from 1940 onwards; the latter material was originally compiled for internal use, or was prepared as ephemeral material for public distribution. Z7165.G8C72

Lu, Joseph K. U.S. government publications relating to the social sciences: a selected annotated guide. Beverly Hills, Calif., Sage, [1975]. 260p. $15. **CA4**

A detailed table of contents serves as the subject index to some 750 entries, arranged in chapters, e.g., bibliographic sources, American history, business and economics, Communism. Each entry includes the Superintendent of Documents classification number; cutoff date for entries is mid-1973. Appendixes provide brief lists of background reading and guides, order information, and a list of depository libraries. Personal name and title indexes. Z1223.Z7L8

McInnis, Raymond G. and **Scott, James William.** Social science research handbook. N.Y., Barnes and Noble, [1975]. 395p. $10; $3.95 pa. **CA5**

A bibliography of about 1,500 reference works. In two sections: pt.A defines the disciplines in the social sciences—anthropology, demography, economics, geography, history, political science, and sociology—and discusses reference sources arranged by type, and reference works on specialized subfields; pt.B follows a similar arrangement for areas of the world. A bibliography section gives full information for all titles cited in pts.A and B. Z7161.A1M3

Woronitzin, Sergej. Bibliographie der Sozialforschung in der Sowjetunion (1960–1970). Bibliography of social research in the Soviet Union (1960–1970). Pullach bei München, Verlag Dokumentation, 1973. 215p. **CA6**

Includes approximately 700 books and periodical articles published in Russian or Ukrainian, with titles also translated into German and English. Lists collected and periodically issued compilations, works on theory and methodology, and empirical research by subject area. Author index.

Periodicals

United Nations Educational, Scientific and Cultural Organization. Liste mondiale des périodiques spécialisés dans les sciences sociales. World list of social science periodicals. 4th ed. rev. and enl., prep. by International Committee for Social Science Information and Documentation. Paris, UNESCO Pr., 1976. 382p. (Services mondiaux d'information en sciences sociales. World social sciences information services, 1) $24 pa. **CA7**

For previous eds. *see Guide* CA22.

Updates listings to mid-1974. New features include: information on abstracting and review journals, periodical indexes, and current contents lists; ISSN numbers in the title index. The index of institutions is omitted. Z7163.U52

Research methods

Bunker, Barbara Benedict, Pearlson, Howard B. and **Schulz, Justin W.** A student's guide to conducting social science research. N.Y., Human Science Pr., [1975]. 120p. $3.95 pa. **CA8**

A basic guide to research methods and activities, not a bibliographic guide. H62.B84

Miller, Delbert Charles. Handbook of research design and social measurement. 3d ed. N.Y., David McKay, [1977]. 518p. $14.95; $6.95 pa. **CA9**

2d ed. 1970.

In five main parts: (1) guide to research design, including the research grant proposal; (2) collection of data in library, field, and laboratory, with a directory of social science data libraries and international social science research centers; (3) guides to statistical analysis; (4) selected sociometric scales and indexes, grouped by subject; (5) material on research budgeting, funding, and reporting in scholarly meetings and journals. Personal name index. H62.M44

Mullins, Carolyn J. A guide to writing and publishing in the social and behavioral sciences. N.Y., John Wiley, [1977]. 431p. $18.95; $9.95 pa. **CA10**

Intended "primarily for students and professionals in the social and behavioral sciences, but also for their typists, editors, and publishers."—*Pref.* Includes sections on writing outlines, first drafts, revisions; information on preparing and placing scholarly articles for journal publication; instructions for preparing a book manuscript; and information on "publishers, prospectuses, and contracts." Bibliography; illustrative examples; index. H91.M8

INDEXES AND ABSTRACT JOURNALS

Book review index to social science periodicals. [Ann Arbor, Mich.], Pierian Pr., 1978– . v.1– . (In progress) $170 the set. **CA11**

Arnold M. Rzepecki, ed.

Contents: v.1, 1964–1970 ($42.50).

To be in 4v., v.2–4 each covering reviews of a single year for the 1971–73 period. The completed set will fulfill "a commitment made in 1970 to provide book review coverage of social science journals to complement the *Index to Book Reviews in the Humanities*" (*Introd.*), thus filling "the lacuna of social science periodicals book reviews until the appearance of *Social Sciences Index* in April 1974." The term "social science" is broadly interpreted "to include not only history titles, but also archaeology and journals dealing with the sociological aspects of religion," and will therefore index reviews in the history journals dropped from *Index to book reviews in the humanities* (*see Guide* AA414, note). It should be kept in mind that *all* reviews in a given periodical are indexed, not only those on social science topics.

Public Affairs Information Service. Bulletin of the Public Affairs Information Service. **CA12**

For full information *see Guide* CA34.

Beginning with v.64, no.1 (Oct. 1, 1977), the *Bulletin* is issued semimonthly, with three quarterly cumulations and an annual bound volume with author index. The bibliographic data base is available for on-line searching from 1976 to the present.

——— Cumulative subject index to the P.A.I.S. annual bulletin, 1915–1974. Arlington, Va., Carrollton Pr., [1977–78]. v.1–9. (In progress; to be in 15v.) $1,075 the set.

Contents: v.1–9, A–M.

References listed under subject headings give reference to the years, pages, and columns of the *Bulletin* where the complete entries can be found. General, subject, and geographical sub-headings have been combined in one alphabet under the major heading, rather than listed separately as in the annual volumes. Geographical entries appear under each of the various names by which the area has been known during the sixty-year period covered.

——— Foreign language index. v.1– , 1968/71– . N.Y., 1972– . **CA13**

For full information *see Guide* CA35.

The bibliographic data base is now available for on-line searching from 1972 to the present.

DICTIONARIES

Reading, Hugo F. A dictionary of the social sciences. [London, Sociologia Publs., 1976] 231p. £3.50; £1.80 pa. **CA14**

Also published by Routledge & Kegan Paul, 1977.

Offers very brief definitions of more than 7,500 terms covering "all the social sciences with the exception of economics and linguistics." —*Pref.* Cross references are indicated by use of italics. H41.R42

Thinès, Georges and **Lempereur, Agnès.** Dictionnaire général des sciences humaines. Paris, Éditions Universitaires, [1975]. 1033p. 250F. **CA15**

"Sciences humaines" is broadly interpreted so that there are terms from anthropology, biology, criminology, demography, esthetics, linguistics, literature, mathematics, pedagogy, physiology, political science, psychiatry, psychology, sociology, statistics, etc. Field of usage is indicated for each term defined, with two or more definitions given for terms having specialized meanings in different fields. *See* and *see also* references; occasional bibliographic citations; charts and diagrams. Includes some name entries, mainly for psychologists and sociologists. BF31.T47

United Nations Educational, Scientific and Cultural Organization. Glossary of conference terms: English, French, Arabic. [Paris], UNESCO, [1974]. 121p. $4.50 pa. **CA16**

Designed to meet the needs of the ILO, FAO, and UNESCO as they gradually introduce Arabic as one of their working languages. Lists "procedural terms currently used in international organizations and conferences" (*Pref.*), with French and Arabic equivalents of the English term in parallel columns. (Separate glossaries are available with French and Arabic as the base languages.) AS6.U57

DIRECTORIES

Canadian social science data catalog. 2d ed. Downsview, Ont., York Univ., Inst. for Behavioural Research, Data Bank/Information Systems, Nov. 1976. 341p. Looseleaf. $18. **CA17**

1st ed. 1974.

A catalog of the numeric data sets at the Data Bank of the Institute for Behavioural Research which may be distributed to users outside the University; the first edition included all sets available at the Data Bank. Data set descriptions contain full summaries of the individual data sets, and are chronologically arranged; there are KWIC, principal investigator, title of study, and geographic indexes. Annual updates are planned. Z7166.C35

Levine, Herbert M. and **Owen, Dolores B.** An American guide to British social science resources. Metuchen, N.J., Scarecrow, 1976. 281p. $11. **CA18**

Organized into three chapters: (1) basic information on British information sources in the United States and the realities of British life for the American academic; (2) a description of the major British library and record office resources for the social scientist, detailing subject coverage, access, publications, and services; and (3) descriptions of relevant professional associations and political parties. Index by subject, type of material, and institution. H62.L443

University of Bath. Inventory of information resources in the social sciences. [Farnborough, Hants], Saxon House; Lexington, Mass., Lexington Books, [1975]. 239p. £6.50; $10. **CA19**

Prep. by the University of Bath for the Organisation for Economic Co-operation and Development.

J. M. Brittain and S. A. Roberts, eds.

Added title page in French; introductory matter in English and French.

In two main sections: (1) Information services and (2) Information sources. "The information services recorded are those organisations or activities, existing independently or within some other organisation, whose integral function and distinguishing feature is the management of information on given topics and the supply of that information to those who need or request it. . . . The information sources are reference or bibliographical publications providing details of the types of information potentially available to social science information users."—*Introd.* A third section, information research, contains details of research projects dealing with information activities in the social sciences. Entries are arranged by subject, and within each subject by country. General, subject, and country indexes. H61.U575

FOUNDATIONS, PHILANTHROPIC ORGANIZATIONS, AND GRANTS

Guides

Des Marais, Philip H. How to get government grants. [N.Y.], Public Service Materials Center, [1975]. 160p. $11.50 pa. **CA20**

Describes (1) how an eligible institution organizes to qualify for government funding; (2) how the institution identifies the programs and sources of government funds for which it can apply; (3) how proposals and applications for grants and contracts are developed; (4) how grants received should be managed. HJ275.D48

Hillman, Howard and **Abarbanel, Karin.** The art of winning foundation grants. N.Y., Vanguard, [1975]. 188p. $6.95. **CA21**

A step-by-step guide for grant applicants. Includes a sample proposal. HV41.H55

——— and **Natale, Kathryn.** The art of winning government grants. N.Y., Vanguard Pr., [1977]. 246p. $7.95. **CA22**

In three parts: (1) The six grant-seeking phases; (2) Where the money is (a discussion of federal, state, and local governmental and quasi-governmental agencies and their programs); (3) Information sources (both printed and institutional). Appendixes; bibliography; index. HJ275.H49

White, Virginia P. Grants: how to to find out about them and what to do next. N.Y., Plenum, [1975]. 354p. $19.50. **CA23**

In two main sections: (1) How to find out about grants and who gives them (basic sources of information; government grants; foundation grants; business and industry grants) and (2) The application (what to do before you apply; writing the proposal; how grants are awarded). Numerous appendixes; index. Q180.U5W47

Bibliography

Georgi, Charlotte, ed. Foundations, grants & fund-raising: a selected bibliography. With the assistance of Marianne Roos. [Los Angeles], Univ. of California at Los Angeles, Graduate School of Management, 1976. 67p. $5 pa. **CA24**

Includes books, government documents, newsletters and journals, reference sources, and associations; material is classed by subject (business and its social responsibilities; foundations; the Foundation Center; fund-raising; grants and grant proposals; legal and tax aspects; philanthropy; public relations). Indexed. Z7164.C4G46

Directories

Cultural directory: guide to federal funds and services for cultural activities. N.Y., Associated Councils of the Arts, [1975]. 340p. $4 pa. **CA25**

1971 ed. published under title: *Washington and the arts.*

A "guide to the art and cultural resources of the Federal Government" (*p.xi*) in three main sections: (1) Funds and services; (2) Cultural advisory groups; (3) Regulations affecting the arts. Appendixes include information on applying for government assistance, addresses of selected federal regional offices and state arts agencies, and a brief bibliography. Subject index. NX735.W3

Directory of grant-making trusts. 4th compilation. Tonbridge, Kent, Charities Aid Foundation, [1975]. 1030p. £10. **CA26**

For earlier editions *see Guide* CA55.

This edition updates the records of 1,814 trusts already in the *Directory,* adds information on 174 new trusts, and deletes 188 trusts which have been terminated or no longer qualifiy for inclusion. AS911.A2D5

Foundation Center. The Foundation Center source book. 1975/76– . N.Y., Foundation Center (distr. by Columbia Univ. Pr.), 1975– . $65 per v. **CA27**

"Documentation on large grant-making foundations: entity descriptions; policies, programs, application procedures; grants."—*t.p.*

". . . seeks to relate the needs of fund seekers to the activities of foundations and to assist foundations in making their programs known to a wider public . . . [and brings together] detailed and up-to-date information on the larger grant-making foundations in the United States operating on a regional or national basis. Fund seekers will find the essential data needed to determine if particular proposals fall within the scope of the foundation programs described."—*Introd.*

Foundations are listed alphabetically, with the following information presented for each: (1) descriptive and fiscal data (based on the entry in the *Foundation directory,* 5th ed., revised and updated as necessary); (2) statement of policy, programs, application procedures, etc.; (3) a listing of recent grants illustrating the current program. HV97.F65F67a

Foundation Center. The Foundation Center source book profiles, 1977/78– . N.Y., Foundation center, 1977– . Looseleaf. $150 per yr. **CA28**

Frequency varies: monthly, 1977/78; bi-monthly, 1978/79– . Vol. for 1977/78 called Series I; 1978/79 called Series II.

Each foundation profile includes: address, telephone number, and executive staff; background data and purpose; grant analysis by subject area, recipient, geographic distribution; a list of recent grants arranged by subject; policies, guidelines, and application procedures. About 75 profiles are included in each installment; since individual profiles are revised biennially, each volume, or series, supersedes the previous one. Focuses on foundations with national and regional grant patterns in excess of $200,000 annually. Indexes—by subject, types of support, geographic area, and foundation name—cumulate with each issue or installment.

Foundation directory. Ed. 6. Comp. by the Foundation Center. N.Y., distr. by Columbia Univ. Pr., 1977. 661p. **CA29**

Marianna O. Lewis, ed.

5th ed. 1975 (*Guide* CA56).

This edition offers entries for 2,818 non-governmental, non-profit foundations with assets of $1,000,000 or more and annual contributions of $100,000 or more. An appendix lists foundations which were included in the 5th edition but dropped from this edition for the reasons stated. Information for the current year (updated semiannually) is available through on-line searching. AS911.A2F65

Foundation grants index, 1970/71– . N.Y., 1972– . Annual. **CA30**

For full citation and annotation *see Guide* CA58

The data base used in the production of the *Index* is now available for on-line searching from 1973 to the present.

Human Resources Network. User's guide to funding resources. Radnor, Pa., Chilton, [1975]. 860p. in various pagings. $39.95 **CA31**

Subtitle: How to get money for: education, fellowships, scholarships, youth, the elderly, the handicapped, women, civil liberties, conservation, community development, arts and humanities, drug and alcohol abuse, health.

"Our intention has been to provide funding information for all fund seekers, from the largest hospital to the smallest radical-change organization. Our prejudices, however, have led us to place emphasis on the needs of individuals and grassroots community organizations."—*Introd.* General information on funding and fund-raising is followed by sections for each of the categories mentioned in the subtitle. Within each category a listing of national grant-giving foundations, organizations, institutions, etc., is followed by state listings grouped by region. Separate index for each group of related categories. HG174.H85

The international foundation directory. Consultant ed., H. V. Hodson. Detroit, Gale; London, Europa Publs., [1974]. 396p. $22. **CA32**

Intends "to present a picture of foundations as an international phenomenon and force" (*Introd.*) and, in order to be included, a foundation must operate internationally in some way. (Exceptions to the latter restriction are those institutions "of such wealth that although they may be restricted to regional or national boundaries their activities are on so great a scale as to have an international impact," and "national and international organizations serving the common purposes of institutions which themselves may figure in the list.") Arrangement is by country. Indexes by name of foundation and by activity. HV7.I57

The national directory of grants and aid to individuals in the arts, international. Ed.3– . Wash., Washington International Arts Letter, [1976]– . (Arts patronage ser., no.5) $13.95 pa. **CA33**

Ed.1–2, 1970–72, had title: *Grants and aid to individuals in the arts.*

Subtitle: Containing listings of most grants, prizes, and awards for professional work in the U.S. and abroad, and information about universities and schools which offer special aid to students.

An alphabetical listing of grant-giving organizations, institutions, etc., with brief information about type of grant, qualifications, etc. Cross references from names of grants and prizes.

Private foundations active in supporting group activity in the arts are listed in:

Millsaps, Daniel. National directory of art support by private foundations: volume 3. Wash., Washington International Arts Letter, 1977. 264p. (Arts patronage ser., no.6) $45 pa. **CA33a**

A revised version of Millsaps's 1974 publication, *Private foundations & business corporations active in arts/humanities/education: vol. 2.* NX711.U5M53

Wilson, William K. and **Wilson, Betty L.** Directory of research grants, 1975– . [Phoenix], Oryx Pr., [1975]– . Annual. (1977/78: $35.75) **CA34**

Place of publication varies.

Aims to offer "up-to-date information about grant, contract and fellowship support programs available for Federal and State governments, private foundations, associations, and corporations for research, training and innovative efforts."—*Pref.* A few programs sponsored by countries other than the United States are also included. Arrangement is alphabetical by subject field, "Accident prevention" through "Water resources and pollution." Indexes of grant names and of sponsoring bodies. LB2338.W55

ASSOCIATIONS, SOCIETIES, AND ACADEMIES

International

Directory of European associations. Répertoire des associations européennes. Handbuch der europäischen Verbände. 1971– . Beckenham, Eng., CBD Research; Detroit, Gale, 1971– . **CA35**

Contents: Pt. 1 National industrial, trade and professional associations [*see Guide* CA64]; Pt. 2 [first publ. 1975: $45], National learned, scientific and technical societies.

Pt. 2 is a classed directory of voluntary associations in the natural sciences, technology, engineering and architecture, economics, finance, management, medicine, social sciences, law, history, archaeology, literature and the arts. Indexed by subject, abbreviation, and name of organization. Subsequent volume(s) will cover the arts, sports, social welfare, and other activities. AS98.D55

World guide to scientific associations and learned societies. Verbände und Gesellschaften der Wissenschaft. Ein internationales Verzeichnis. 2d ed. Michael Zils, ed. N.Y., Bowker; München, Verlag Dokumentation, 1978. 510p. $49.50. **CA36**

Prefatory matter and headings in English and German.

1st ed., 1974, had title: *World guide to scientific organizations.*

A directory of more than 11,000 national and international associations and societies in various fields of science, technology, the humanities, and the social sciences. Information on each association includes founding date, address, name of executive head and secretary, and number of members. Arranged by continent, then by country; indexed by subject.

United States

Greenfield, Stanley R. National directory of addresses and telephone numbers. N.Y., Nicholas Pub. Co./Bantam Books, [1977]. 386p., 233p. $9.95 pa. **CA37**

In two sections: (1) Classified; (2) Alphabetical. Gives addresses and telephone numbers of some 50,000 companies, agencies, foundations, government departments, associations, etc., throughout the United States. E154.5.G73

Washington information directory. 1975/76– . [Wash.], Congressional Quarterly Inc., 1975– . Annual. $18 per yr. **CA38**

Subject chapters (e.g., Congress and politics; employment and business; energy) list executive agencies, congressional committees and subcommittees, and private organizations as information sources. Each entry gives address, telephone number, director, and brief description of the agency. Appendixes give directory information for Congress, executive agencies, foreign embassies, national labor unions, religious organizations, state and local officials, and regional federal information sources. Subject and agency indexes. A very useful handbook. F192.3.W33

Canada

Directory of associations in Canada. Répertoire des associations du Canada. Prep. under the direction of Brian Land. [2d ed.] [Toronto], Univ. of Toronto Pr., [1975]. 550p. **CA39**

Introductory and explanatory matter in English and French.

1st ed. 1974.

Gives brief directory information on non-governmental, non-profit organizations. Detailed subject index to specialized interests of the associations. Lists about 9,300 associations. AS40.A7D57

France

France. Comité des Travaux Historiques et Scientifiques. Liste des sociétés savantes et littéraires. Paris, 1975. 114p. **CA40**

Revision and updating of an edition which appeared in 1958.

Geographical listing of French societies with indexes by title of publication, name of society, broad subject, and area (for local history societies). AS158.F72

Germany

Domay, Friedrich. Handbuch der deutschen Wissenschaftlichen Akademien und Gesellschaften, einschliesslich zahlreicher Vereine, Forschungsinstitute und Arbeitsgemeinschaften in der Bundesrepublik Deutschland. Mit einer Bibliographie deutscher Akademie- und Gesellschafts-publikationen. 2., völlig neu bearb. u. erw. Aufl. Wiesbaden, F. Steiner Verlag, 1977. 1209p. DM240. **CA41**

Represents a new and greatly expanded edition of Domay's *Handbuch der deutschen wissenschaftlichen Gesellschaften* (1964; *Guide* CA77). In addition to added information for scientific academies as noted in the title, there are new sections for information science and documentation and for the arts. Indexed.

BIOGRAPHY

American men and women of science: Social and behavioral sciences. 13th ed., ed. by the Jaques Cattell Pr. N.Y., Bowker, 1978. 1545p. $69.95. **CA42**

For other volumes of the 13th ed. *see Suppl.* EA38.

This volume "covers the twelve areas of the social and behavioral sciences not included in the major compendium [i.e., the 7v. set published 1976]; namely administration and management, area studies, economics, environmental studies, futuristics, international studies, political science, psychology and sociology."—*Pref.* About 24,000 biographical sketches are included, and there are discipline and geographic indexes.

C B

Education

GENERAL WORKS

Guides

Berry, Dorothea M. A bibliographic guide to educational research. Metuchen, N.J., Scarecrow Pr., 1975. 150p. $6. **CB1**

Intended "as a concise guide to assist the student in education courses to make effective use of the resources of the library of his college or university."—*Pref.* An annotated listing of about 500 items arranged by type (periodicals, research studies, government publications, reference materials, etc.), with author, title, and subject indexes. Z5811.B39

Humby, Michael. A guide to the literature of education. 3d ed. London, Univ. of London, Inst. of Education Lib., 1975. 142p. (Education libraries bulletin. Suppl. 1) £1 pa. **CB2**

Based on *A guide to the literature of education* by S. K. Kimmance (2d ed. 1961).

Aims "to give selected examples of the various types of printed material to be found in an education library."—*Introd.* 572 annotated entries arranged by type: guides to the literature of education, bibliographies, encyclopedias, dictionaries, directories and yearbooks, periodicals, biographies, statistics, etc. Indexed. Z5811.H85

Bibliography

General

Columbia University. Teachers College. Library. Dictionary catalog of the Teachers College Library. 1st–3d supplements. Boston, G. K. Hall, 1971–77. 17v. **CB3**

For main set *see Guide* CB4.
1st suppl. (1971), 5v., $390; 2d suppl. (1973), 2v., $240; 3d suppl. (1977), 10v., $875.
Cover materials added to the Library for the period 1970–76.

Higson, Constance Winifred Jane. Supplement to Sources for the history of education. [London], Library Assoc., 1976. 221p. £12.50; $27.50. **CB4**

Subtitle: A list of materials added to the libraries of the institutes and schools of education, 1965–1974, together with works from certain university libraries.
For basic volume *see Guide* CB7. Z5811.H5

McCarthy, Joseph M. An international list of articles on the history of education published in non-educational serials, 1965–1974. N.Y., Garland, 1977. 228p. (Garland reference library of the social sciences, 33) $24. **CB5**

More than 2,800 items in a geographical arrangement with author index. Z5813.M18

Higher education

Altbach, Philip G. Comparative higher education abroad: bibliography and analysis. N.Y., Praeger, [1976]. 274p. $15. **CB6**

"Publ. in cooperation with the International Council for Educational Development."—*t.p.*
A bibliography of more than 1,700 items (books, articles, and dissertations, mainly from 1974) is followed by a section of "Book notes" on significant books of 1974, and two bibliographic essays on aspects of higher education. The bibliography is arranged by continent, then by country. A "cross reference index" offers a broad subject approach. Z5814.U7A39

——— and **Kelly, David H.** Higher education in developing nations: a selected bibliography, 1969–1974. N.Y., Praeger, [1975]. 229p. $15. **CB7**

"Publ. in cooperation with the International Council for Educational Development."—*t.p.*
2,400 items supplementing Altbach's 1970 work of similar title (*Guide* CB27). Arranged by country; "cross reference index."
Z5814.U7A42

Beach, Mark. A bibliographic guide to American colleges and universities, from colonial times to the present. Westport, Conn., Greenwood Pr., 1975. 314p. $17.50. **CB8**

". . . an effort to bring together in one source citations to major books, articles and dissertations relating to the history of specific institutions of higher learning."—*Introd.* Listing is by state, with general works followed by histories of specific institutions. Subject index. 2,806 entries. Z5815.U5B4

Bibliographie internationale de l'histoire des universités. Genève, Droz, 1973– . v.1– . (Études et documents publiés par la Section d'histoire de la Faculté des lettres de l'Université de Genève, 9 [etc.]; Commission internationale pour l'histoire des universités. Études et travaux, 2 [etc.]) (In progress) **CB9**

Contents: v.1, Espagne, Louvain, Copenhague, Prague (1973; 24Sw.Fr. pa.); v.2, Portugal, Leiden, Pécs, Franeker, Basel (1974; 32Sw.Fr.).
A project of the Commission Internationale pour l'Histoire des Universités. "The original purpose of the project was, first, to complete and bring up to date the bibliographical references given in the new edition of H. Rashdall *The Universities of Europe in the Middle Ages* by F. M. Powicke and A. B. Emden (Oxford: Oxford University Press, 3 volumes [1936]); second to list publications related to the history of universities during the 16th, 17th and 18th centuries."—*Pref., v.2.*
Represents contributions of various scholars toward a comprehensive international bibliography of the history of universities. The general plan proposed for each national section groups the citations as: (1) sources (archives, etc.); (2) general histories; (3) administrative history; (4) social history; (5) intellectual history; (6) iconography and topography of the universities. Individual contributions exhibit certain variations from this scheme.
Related publications sponsored by the Commission (e.g., the Gabriel and Hassinger bibliographies listed below, *Suppl.* CB10, CB11) are cited in the prefaces to v.1 and 2. Z5814.U7B483

Gabriel, Astrik Ladislas. Summary bibliography of the history of the universities of Great Britain and Ireland up to 1800, covering publications between 1900 and 1968. Notre Dame, Ind., Mediaeval Inst., Univ. of Notre Dame, 1974. 154p. (Texts and studies in the history of mediaeval education, 14) $18.95. **CB10**

About 1,500 items. Sections on the history of education in Europe and in England to 1800 are followed by sections on the history of universities in England, Scotland, Wales and Ireland. Author and subject indexes. Z5815.G5G3

Hassinger, Erich, ed. Bibliographie zur Universitätsgeschichte; Verzeichnis der im Gebiet der Bundesrepublik Deutschland 1945–1971 veröffentlichen Literatur. Bearb. von Edwin Stark. Freiburg, Verlag Karl Alber, [1974]. 316p. DM64. **CB11**

More than 3,200 items. A general classified section is followed by studies on individual universities arranged alphabetically by city. Author and subject indexes. Z5814.U7H35

Moscow. Universitet. Biblioteka. Universitetskoe obrazovanie v SSSR i za rubezhom. [Moskva], Izdat. Moskovskogo Universiteta, 1974. vyp.2. **CB12**

Added title page in English: University studies in the USSR and abroad. Pt.II, Bibliography of Russian and foreign literature (1961–1967).
For vyp.1 and annotation *see Guide* CB12.
Contents: vyp.2, Ukazatel' russkoi i inostrannoi literatury za 1961–1967. 475p. 2r.,5k.
Continued by: Z5814.U7M6

Sovetskie i zarubezhnye universitety: annotirovanni ukazatel' literatury, 1968–1972. Moskva, Izd-va Moskovskogo Universiteta, 1975. 298p. 1r.,14k. **CB12a**

Eds., E. A. Nersesova and G. G. Tolstikova.
At head of title: Moskovskii gosudarstvennyi universitet imeni M. V. Lomonosova. Kafedra nauchnoi informatsii.
Added title page in English: Soviet and foreign universities: annotated bibliography.
Prefatory matter, section headings, etc., in Russian and English.
Serves as a continuation of the preceding item, listing books and articles on various aspects of Soviet and foreign universities. Separate sections for the USSR and for foreign universities, with author/editor indexes for each. Z5814.U7S68

Minorities and disadvantaged

Brooks, Ian R. and **Marshall, A. M.** Native education in Canada and the United States: a bibliography. [Alberta], Office of Educational Development, Indian Students University Program Services, Univ. of Calgary, [1976]. 298p. $7.25. **CB13**

A classed, annotated bibliography of about 3,000 references on the pedagogy, psychology, sociology, and politics of Native education, written during the period 1900–75. Author index.
Z1209.2.N67B76

Chambers, Fredrick. Black higher education in the United States: a selected bibliography on Negro higher education and historically black colleges and universities. Westport, Conn., Greenwood Pr., [1978]. 268p. $19.95. **CB14**

Materials are grouped according to type: (1) Doctoral dissertations, 1918–1976; (2) Institutional histories, 1867–1976; (3) Periodical literature, 1857–1976; (4) Masters' theses, 1922–1974; (5) Selected books and general references; (6) Miscellaneous. Subject index. Z5814.B44C45

Occupational education

Resources in vocational education. 1977– . Columbus, Ohio State Univ., Center for Vocational Education, 1977– . Bimonthly. $34 per year. **CB15**

A continuation of *AIM/ARM abstracts of instructional and research materials in vocational and technical education* (1974–76) which was formed by the merger of *Abstracts of research and related materials in vocational and technical education* (*Guide* CB46) and *Abstracts of instructional materials in vocational and technical education* (*Guide* CB45).

Other special topics

Apanasewicz, Nellie Mary. Education in the U.S.S.R.; an annotated bibliography of English-language materials, 1965–1973. [Wash.], U.S. Dept. of Health, Education, and Welfare, [1974]. 92p. $1.35 pa. **CB16**

An earlier bibliography by Apanasewicz and S. M. Rosen, *Soviet education: a bibliography of English-language materials,* was published 1964. The present work serves as a supplement to that volume and "lists 347 titles indexed in 224 subject categories."—*Foreword.* Z5815.R9A76

A bibliography of American educational history: an annotated and classified guide. Ed. by Francesco Cordasco and William W. Brickman. N.Y., AMS Pr., [1975]. 394p. $15. **CB17**

Listings of general bibliographies, encyclopedic works, collections of source materials, and comprehensive histories are followed by sections on elementary, secondary, and vocational education; education in the individual states; higher education; school books and instructional materials; the teaching profession; church, state and education; the federal government and education; education of women; biographies of American educators; foreign influences; contemporary issues; and separate sections for specific periods in American education. Sections have been contributed by various scholars. Author index. Z5814.U5B5

Burnett, Jacquetta H. Anthropology and education; an annotated bibliographic guide . . . with the collaboration of Sally W. Gordon and Carol J. Gormley. New Haven, HRAF Pr. for the Council on Anthropology and Education, 1974. 159p. $8; $3.50 pa. **CB18**

Concentrates on "anthropological research on formal and informal education" with only highly selective coverage of psychological anthropology, linguistics, and comparative education."—*Foreword.* Author listing without index.

Kept up to date by listings in the *Newsletter* of the Council on Anthropology and Education. Z5811.B867

Cantwell, Zita M. and **Doyle, Hortense A.** Instructional technology: an annotated bibliography. Metuchen, N.J., Scarecrow Pr., 1974. 387p. $12.50. **CB19**

An annotated bibliography of English-language materials (mainly publications of the 1960–73 period), arranged by author, with a subject index. "Emphasis in the selection has been given to studies of the actual use of an aspect of Instructional Technology in a learning situation."—*Introd.* 958 items. Z5814.A85C35

Laubenfels, Jean. The gifted student: an annotated bibliography. Westport, Conn., Greenwood Pr., [1977]. 220p. (Contemporary problems of childhood, no.1) $15. **CB20**

A classified, annotated bibliography of about 1,300 items (including books, periodical articles, government publications, and dissertations). Emphasis is on publications "of the past fifteen years since the 1961 publication of John Gowan's *Annotated Bibliography on the Academically Talented Student.*"—*Pref.* Appendixes: (A) Some individuals and organizations concerned with the gifted; (B) List of instruments useful in identifying the gifted; (C) Audio-visual materials for professional use. Indexed. LC3993.L35

Taggart, Dorothy T. A guide to sources in educational media and technology. Metuchen, N.J., Scarecrow Pr., 1975. 156p. $6. **CB21**

An annotated bibliography for teachers and students, particularly concerned with providing the basis for a "well-balanced and up-to-date collection for the university library in the field of educational media and technology."—*Pref.* Topically arranged, with author and title indexes. Z5814.V8T33

Teichler, Ulrich and **Voss, Friedrich.** Bibliography on Japanese education: postwar publications in Western languages. Pullach, Verlag Dokumentation, 1974. 294p. DM36. **CB22**

Title also in German; preface and section headings in English and German.

A bibliographic record of the literature for non-Japanese-speaking persons; publications listed are mainly in English, with some in German and a few in other Western languages. Classed arrangement, with index of authors and institutions; detailed table of contents, but no subject index. Includes books, periodical articles, and doctoral dissertations. Z5815.J3T44

Von Klemperer, Lily. International education: a directory of resource materials on comparative education and study in another country. [Garrett Park, Md., Garrett Park Pr., 1973] 202p. $6.95 pa. **CB23**

A bibliography in two main sections: (1) Description and comparison of education systems of the world, and (2) International exchange of persons. Author index; annotations. Z5814.C76V66

Dissertations

Kirschner, Charlene D., Mapes, Joseph L. and **Anderton, Ray L.** Doctoral research in educational media, 1969–1972. [2d ed.] Stanford, Calif., ERIC Clearinghouse on Information Resources, Stanford Center for Research and Development in Teaching, School of Education, Stanford Univ., 1975. 96p. $5 pa. **CB24**

1970 ed. had title: *Doctoral research in library media.*

An annotated listing of dissertations from the 1969–72 period, topically arranged within categories such as "Audio," "Audiovisual," "Computers in instruction," "Library," etc. No index. LB1028.5.K535

Parker, Franklin. American dissertations on foreign education; a bibliography with abstracts. Troy, N.Y., Whitston, 1972–77. v.3–10. (In progress) **CB25**

For v.1–2 and annotation *see Guide* CB72.

Contents: v.3, Japan; v.4, Africa; v.5, Scandinavia; v.6, China (in 2v.); v.7, Korea; v.8, Mexico; v.9, South America; v.10, Central America.

Periodicals

Arnold, Darlene Baden and **Doyle, Kenneth O.** Education/psychology journals: a scholar's guide. Metuchen, N.J., Scarecrow Pr., 1975. 143p. $6. **CB26**

A listing of 122 journals "of professional interest to many psychologists, educationists, educational psychologists, and educators."—*Introd.* Intended "to help these people decide which journals to read and subscribe to and to which to submit their professional manuscripts." In addition to directory information, gives a description of content, indication of typical disciplines served, intended audience, criteria for accepting articles, style requirements for manuscripts, etc. LB1051.A732

Camp, William L. and **Schwark, Bryan L.** Guide to periodicals in education and its academic disciplines. 2d ed. Metuchen, N.J., Scarecrow Pr., 1975. 552p. $19.50. **CB27**

1968 ed. (*Guide* CB76) had title: *Guide to periodicals in education.*

This edition "contains information obtained from editors and publishers of 602 nationally distributed education and education-related periodicals issued in the United States."—*Pref.* Z5813.C28

Krepel, Wayne J. and **DuVall, Charles R.** Education and education-related serials: a directory. Littleton, Colo., Libraries Unlimited, 1977. 255p. $15. **CB28**

Offers directory information and descriptions of "501 journals and newsletters, all related in some way to the field of education" (*Introd.*), and whose contents deal with teaching and learning. Entries include information about submitting articles for publication, style requirements for manuscripts, etc. Appendix lists indexing and abstracting services in the field. Z5813.K74

Indexes and abstracts

Education index, Jan. 1929– . . . . N.Y., Wilson, 1932– . **CB29**

For full information *see Guide* CB83.

The *Guide* entry CB83 failed to note the restoration of author entries to this index. From v.20 (July 1969–) author entries are again provided in the *Index* and the subtitle reads: "A cumulative author subject index to a selected list of educational periodicals, proceedings, and yearbooks."

Resources in education. v.10, no.1– , Jan. 1975– . [Wash., U.S. Dept. of Health, Education, and Welfare, Nat. Inst. of Education], 1975– . Monthly. $42.70 per yr. **CB30**

Supersedes *Research in education* (*Guide* CB85) and continues its numbering. Follows the plan of the earlier title (i.e., documents are listed in numerical order by ED number, with subject, author, and institution indexes in each issue); indexes cumulate semiannually. Z5813.R4

Dictionaries and encyclopedias

Anderson, Scarvia B., Ball, Samuel and **Murphy, Richard T.** Encyclopedia of educational evaluation. San Francisco, Jossey-Bass, 1975. 515p. il. $17.50. **CB31**

Attempts to present the major concepts and techniques for evaluating education and training programs in a single alphabetical arrangement of articles "and in terms that are generally comprehensible to program administrators, funding agents, and students coming new to the field, as well as to the social scientists and measurement specialists who have tended to dominate it."—*Pref.* Bibliographic references; charts and diagrams; index. LB2823.A65

Educational Resources Information Center. Thesaurus of ERIC descriptors. 7th ed. N.Y., Macmillan Information, [1977]. 451p. **CB32**

Consists of three main sections: "Descriptors," an alphabetical list of all terms existing in the *Thesaurus* file in June, 1977, including the number of postings in *Current index to journals in education* (*Guide* CB81) and *Resources in education* (*Guide* CB85); "Rotated descriptor display," an alphabetical index to all significant words that form descriptors; and the "Two-way hierarchical display," showing the broader-narrower relationships of all main terms. Z695.1.E3E34

The international encyclopedia of higher education. Asa S. Knowles, ed. in chief. San Francisco, Jossey-Bass, 1977. 10v. $400. **CB33**

Contents: v.1, Contents, contributors, acronyms, glossary; v.2–9, [Entries] A–Z; v.10, Indexes.

A new work representing the contributions of an international roster of scholars (listed with their current positions in v.1, pp. 119a–79a). Entries are presented in an alphabetical arrangement, but with some grouping of materials in order to "reduce duplication of data and give readers easier access to related subjects."—*Pref.* Types of entries may be broadly categorized as: (1) national systems of higher education; (2) topical essays; (3) fields of study; (4) educational associations; (5) research centers and institutes; (6) reports on higher education; (7) documentation centers; plus the sections for acronyms and glossary of terms in v.1. No biographical entries are included. Articles are signed and bibliographies are appended. Intended for the layman as well as the specialist, with basic information in each article meant to be understandable to the non-specialist. *See* and *see also* references in addition to the name and subject indexes in v.10. LB15.I57

Page, G. Terry, Thomas, John Bernard and **Marshall, Alan R.** International dictionary of education. London, Kogan Page; N.Y., Nichols, [1977]. 381p. il. $20. **CB34**

More than 10,000 entries covering expressions and terms, international organizations, major national institutions and associations, educators, etc. Appendixes list abbreviations for associations and organizations, as well as United States honor societies, fraternities and sororities. LB15.M3

Handbooks

Goodman, Steven E., ed. Handbook on contemporary education. Comp. and ed. in association with Reference Development Corp. N.Y., Bowker, [1976]. 622p. $37.50. **CB35**

A collection of papers by specialists on contemporary topics in education, each paper "designed to provide the user with needed 'state-of-the-art' information as well as further sources of information."—*Pref.* In eight sections: (1) Educational change and planning; (2) Administration and management of education; (3) Teacher/faculty issues; (4) Education and training of teachers and administrators; (5) Students and parents; (6) Special interest groups; (7) Teaching and learning strategies; (8) Some alternatives and options in education. Indexed. LB17.H27

United Nations Educational, Scientific and Cultural Organization. World guide to higher education; a comparative survey of systems, degrees, and qualifications. [Epping, Eng.], Bowker; [N.Y.], Unipub, [1976]. 302p. £8.50; $18. **CB36**

Essentially an English-language version of its predecessors [i.e., the 1973 ed. of Marcel de Grandpré's *Les études supérieures: presentation comparative*. . . and Rafael Torrella's Spanish edition, *Estudios superiores*), "drastically amended and updated, extending coverage to 135 territories."—*Introd.* LA183.U52

Yearbooks

Educational media yearbook. 1973– . N.Y., Bowker, [1973]– . Annual. $19.95. **CB37**

James W. Brown, ed.

Ed.3 covered 1975/76 (publ. 1975).

Aims "to bring together significant information pertaining to educational media activities that would be useful to professional personnel in the interrelated disciplines of instructional-educational technology, librarianship, information science, and telecommunications."—*Pref., 1977.*

1977 ed. in three main sections: (1) "The year in review"; (2) "Mediagraphy: print and nonprint sources"; (3) "Guide to organizations, training programs, and funding sources." Appendix: "Directory of producers, distributors, and publishers." Indexed. LB1028.3.E37

Sourcebook of equal educational opportunity. Ed.2– . Chicago, Marquis, 1977– . il., maps. (Ed.2: $34.50) **CB38**

1st ed. (1976) entitled *Yearbook of equal educational opportunity.*

Intends "to present a comprehensive picture of the current status of equal opportunity in education. It contains statistical and narrative data gathered from a variety of government and private sources tracing from historical roots the struggle for equal access and quality education."—*Pref.* Ed.2 has a general section followed by sections for specific groups: American Indian/Native Alaskan, Asian American/Pacific Islander, Black, Hispanic, Women. Subject and geographic indexes. LC213.2.S6

Yearbook of adult and continuing education. Ed.1– , 1975/76– . Chicago, Marquis, [1975]– . (Ed.3: $34.50) **CB39**

Each edition offers "government and private agency statistics and general information on a variety of problems related to adult basic, adult continuing and career-related adult education."–*Introd., 2d ed.* Subject and geographical indexes.

Yearbook of special education. Ed.1– , 1975/76– . Chicago, Marquis, 1975– . Annual. (1977/78: $34.50) **CB40**

The 1st ed. "presented government and private agency statistics on a variety of educational problems within the field of special education. The second edition is intended to complement the first by offering evaluative studies related to the various handicaps, current status reports of federal and state legislation, and listings of on-going research. Included are programs and associations of interest to professionals and families of people requiring special educational assistance and data on career education."—*Introd.,2d ed.* Includes sections for the mentally retarded, speech and hearing handicapped, physically handicapped, blind and visually impaired, gifted and talented. Indexed. LC4001.Y4

Directories

International

Garraty, John Arthur, Von Klemperer, Lily and **Taylor, Cyril J. H.** The new guide to study abroad: summer and full-year programs for high-school students, college and university students, and teachers: 1976–1977 ed. N.Y., Harper & Row, [1976]. 451p. il. $11.95; $4.95 pa. **CB41**

For 1971/72 ed. *see Guide* CB121. 1974/75 ed. publ. 1974.
A revised and updated edition. LB2376.G33

World guide to universities. Internationales Universitäts-Handbuch. 2d ed. N.Y., Bowker; München, Verlag Dokumentation, 1976. 2pts. in 4v. pt.1, $120; pt.2, $95. **CB42**

Contents: pt.1, v.1–2, Europe; index; pt.2, v.1, America; pt.2, v.2, Africa, Asia, Oceania; index.
Ed. by Michael Zils.
1st ed. 1971–72.
Prefatory matter and textual headings in German and English.
Within continental sections, presents information country-by-country, then by university, on universities and other institutions of higher education. For each institution gives: address, telephone, founding date, enrollment, principal administrative officers, address of library and name of director, faculties or departments (with affiliated schools and institutes), names of academic staff members (with indication of subject field). Subject and personal name indexes for each part.

United States

General

School universe data book. Library edition. 1976/77– . [Denver], Curriculum Information Center, 1977– . Annual. $325. **CB43**

1976/77 ed. in 5v. (Also available in a "Marketing edition" of 51v. for the individual states.)
Offers "a complete reference file, in printed form, of all the information about schools stored in the computer bank created and maintained by the Curriculum Information Center ... [providing] comprehensive, verified data about public schools, Catholic schools, and other independent schools in all 50 states and the District of Columbia."—*Introd.* A state-by-state compilation, giving names of state and district-level administrators, street addresses and phone numbers of school districts, data on enrollment, statistical summaries by county and district, etc. L901.S473

U.S. Office of Education. Education directory. . . . **CB44**

In view of various changes in designation of the component parts and addition of another section to the *Directory* (*see Guide* CB136), Library of Congress has recataloged the individual sections (now no longer numbered), entering each part separately by title:
Education directory: colleges and universities, 1975/76– (previously entitled *Education directory: higher education);*
Education directory: education associations, 1969/70– ;
Education directory: public school systems, 1969/70– ;
Education directory: state education agency officials, 1976/77– ;
Education directory: state governments, 1969/70– .

Higher education

Bayerl, Elizabeth. Interdisciplinary studies in the humanities: a directory. Metuchen, N.J., Scarecrow Pr., 1977. 1091p. $35. **CB45**

"The programs in the directory are intended to be inclusive of the main kinds of formal academic programs in colleges and universities in the United States fitting within the context of interdisciplinary studies in the humanities. . . ."—*Foreword.* Program descriptions are drawn mainly from college catalogs. In two main sections: (1) Senior institutions; (2) Two-year colleges. Listing in each section is by state, then by name of institution. Index by names of formal curricular offerings. AZ183.U5B29

Cass, James and **Birnbaum, Max.** Comparative guide to two-year colleges and career programs. N.Y., Harper & Row, [1976]. 549p. $17.50; $6.95 pa. **CB46**

Describes, state-by-state, about 1,740 institutions in terms of admission requirements, programs and degrees offered, and costs. Indexed by field of study and religious affiliation of church-related institutions. Makes a special attempt to identify programs related to those occupations which promise to offer above-average job opportunities in the foreseeable future.

Continuing education: a guide to career development programs. [Syracuse, N.Y.], Gaylord in assoc. with Neal-Schuman Publ., [1977]. 704p. $39.95. **CB47**

A directory of institutions and organizations offering programs in continuing education. Information is based on "questionnaires, catalogs, brochures, and announcements submitted by the nearly 2500 institutions and organizations that are included."—*Pref.* Institutions are grouped by state; organizations are listed alphabetically by name in a separate section. A "Guide to career areas" provides a subject approach to the programs; index of institutions and organizations. L901.C835

Livesey, Herbert B. and **Doughty, Harold.** Guide to American graduate schools. 3d ed., rev. and updated. N.Y., Viking, [1975]. 437p. $17.50. **CB48**

Previous ed. 1970 (*Guide* CB150).
". . . describes more than six hundred institutions throughout the United States providing graduate and professional study. All have been surveyed once again for this third edition. . . ."—*Pref.* L901.L5

Specialized education

Gollay, Elinor and **Bennett, Alwina.** The college guide for students with disabilities. Cambridge, Mass., Abt Publs.; Boulder, Colo., Westview Pr., [1976]. 545p. $30; $18.50 pa. **CB49**

Subtitle: A detailed directory of higher education services, programs, and facilities accessible to handicapped students in the United States.
Provides information on college-based, state, and national resources. Brief chapters cover legal rights, handbooks and directories, financial aid, and private, federal, and state agencies relevant to the disabled. College summary tables and individual college descriptions are followed by accessibility tables on over 7,000 buildings surveyed. Index of colleges. L901.G68

Canada

Directory of Canadian universities. Répertoire des universités canadiennes. 1977– . Ottawa, Statistics Canada, 1978– . Annual. $5.25 pa. **CB50**

Represents a change of title from *Universities and colleges of Canada* (*Guide* CB166). Published jointly by the Association of Universities and Colleges of Canada and Statistics Canada.
"Those familiar with the Handbook will find many changes in this edition. . . . The comprehensive listing of senior academic and administrative staff has been removed and is now being made available in a separate booklet prepared by the AUCC. Other sections which do not appear in this edition include an article about community colleges in Canada and a listing of these institutions, a list of Canadian associations related to higher education and a list of degree abbreviations."—*Pref., 1977.* Includes a list of "Undergraduate and graduate diploma and degree programs at Canadian universities" which indicates the institutions and levels at which the programs are offered. L905.D5

Statistics

Hamilton, Malcolm C. Directory of educational statistics: a guide to sources. Ann Arbor, Mich., Pierian Pr., 1974. 71p. il. $6.95. **CB51**

99 bibliographic sources are grouped by subject—general, public elementary and secondary schools, public school expenditures and revenues, salaries, nonpublic schools, higher education, degrees and enrollment, international education, education in Great Britain, miscellaneous. The entry for each source gives a brief description and publication history. Title and subject indexes.

Biography

Biographical dictionary of American educators. Ed. by John F. Ohles. Westport, Conn., Greenwood Pr., [1978]. 3v. (1666p.) $95. **CB52**

Aims "to provide a ready source of biographical information about those people who have shaped American education from colonial times to the American bicentennial of 1976. Because education in the United States developed on the state level, leaders in education in the states have been included, as well as national figures and those who have been leaders in subject matter fields. Basic criteria for selection were persons who had been engaged in education, were eminent, and had reached the age of sixty, had retired, or had died by January 1, 1975."—*Pref.* Signed articles, averaging about a page in length, are mainly by educators and concentrate on the biographee's education, employment, contributions to the field of education, and participation in professional associations and activities. Bibliographic sources are cited. General index in v.3. Appendixes include lists of biographees by place of birth, by state of major service, by field of work, and by year of birth. LA2311.B54

Leaders in education. 5th ed. Ed. by Jaques Cattell Pr. N.Y., Bowker, 1974. 1309p. $52.50. **CB53**

1st ed. 1932.

About 17,000 biographical sketches. "... includes officers and deans of accredited institutions of higher learning, professors of education, directors and staff of educational research institutes, state and provincial commissioners of education and certain members of their staffs, leading figures in the public and private school fields, officers of foundations concerned with education, officials of the Office of Education and major educational associations, and authors of important pedagogical books."—*Pref.* This edition includes a new "specialty" index to biographees, as well as a geographic index.

National faculty directory. [8th ed.] 1978. Detroit, Gale, [1977]. 2v. $115. **CB54**

For earlier eds. *see Guide* CB182a.

Since 5th ed., 1975, has included name, departmental affiliation, and institutional addresses for teaching faculties at Canadian institutions "using instructional materials primarily in English."—*Introd. note.* L901.N34

GUIDANCE

Bibliography

Career education: a dissertation index. Ann Arbor, Mich., University Microfilms International, 1976. 333p. $31. **CB55**

The main portion of the work is a keyword index to "career education titles accepted by North American universities between 1972 and 1975."—*Introd.* About 2,700 titles; all are abstracted in *Dissertation abstracts international* (and citations to that publication are included along with information for ordering copies from University Microfilms). The author index repeats the full citation. Expands and updates Edwin G. York's *1900 doctoral dissertations on career education* (1975).

Handbooks

The encyclopedia of careers and vocational guidance. William E. Hopke, ed.-in-chief. 3d ed. Chicago, J. G. Ferguson, [1975]. 2v. il. $39.50. **CB56**

Rev. ed. 1972 (*Guide* CB189).

Contents: v.1, Planning your career; v.2, Careers and occupations.

Intended for junior and senior high school students, their parents, teachers and counselors. v.1 presents general information on choice of vocation and finding a job, etc., followed by chapters (arranged alphabetically by occupational field) contributed by leaders in various professions, industries, and occupations, and offering information about career opportunities and the type of work involved. v.2 now follows the classification system of the 3d ed. of the *Dictionary of occupational titles* (*Guide* CH501) and presents more specific information about the particular career or branch of a profession. HF5381.E52

FELLOWSHIPS AND SCHOLARSHIPS

The college blue book: scholarships, fellowships, grants, and loans. M. Lorraine Mathies, ed.; Elizabeth I. Dixon, assoc. ed. N.Y., Macmillan Information, [1975]. 506p. $35. **CB57**

Awards are grouped as (1) General, (2) Humanities, (3) Social sciences, (4) Sciences, (5) Health and medical sciences, (6) Area studies, (7) Specialized programs, with numerous subdivisions in categories 2–7. Within categories, listing is by name of agency giving the award; information is quite full. Indexed. LB2338.C58

Searles, Aysel. Guide to financial aids for students in arts and sciences for graduate and professional study. Rev. ed. [by] Anne Scott. N.Y., Arco, [1974]. 107p. $3.95 pa. **CB58**

1st ed. 1971.

On cover: Scholarships, loan funds, subsidies, fellowships and traineeships, teaching and research assistantships, funds available to members of minority groups, awards for study abroad.

Aids are listed by subject field or profession, with special sections for study abroad, minority groups, and unrestricted aids. Includes information on application for advanced study, and a bibliography. Indexed. LB2338.S4

ACADEMIC CUSTOMS

Prizes and awards

Hohenberg, John. The Pulitzer Prizes; a history of the awards in books, drama, music, and journalism, based on the private files over six decades. N.Y., Columbia Univ. Pr., 1974. 434p. $14.95. **CB59**

A history of the prizes, with appendixes listing members of the advisory board and terms of service, and recipients of the awards in chronological order. Indexed. AS911.P8H83

Wasserman, Paul and **McLean, Janice W.** Awards, honors, and prizes. 3d ed. Detroit, Gale, 1975. 2v. **CB60**

Subtitle: An international directory of awards and their donors recognizing achievement in advertising, art, business, government, finance, science, education, engineering, literature, technology, sports, religion, public affairs, radio and television, politics, librarianship, fashion, medicine, law, publishing, international affairs, transportation, architecture, journalism, motion pictures, music, photography, theatre and performing arts.

2d ed. 1972 (*Guide* CB212).

Contents: v.1, United States and Canada ($38); v.2, International and foreign ($48).

Coverage has been expanded by the inclusion in v.2 of international prizes and honors, and national awards given in 61 countries; international awards supported by agencies based in the United

States and Canada are included in both volumes. Provides details for about 3,000 awards. v.1 of the 4th ed. was scheduled for publication in late 1978. AS8.W38

RECREATION AND SPORTS

Bibliography

Belch, Jean, comp. Contemporary games. Detroit, Gale, [1973–74]. 2v. $93. **CB61**

Subtitle: A directory and bibliography covering games and play situations or simulations used for instruction and training by schools, colleges and universities, government, business and management.

Contents: v.1, Directory (560p.; $48); v.2, Bibliography (408p.; $45).

". . . a collection of current and retrospective games and simulations, comprising in all more than 900 decision-making or problem-solving exercises having sufficient intellectual content to be used for educational purposes. . . ."—*Introd.*

The alphabetical listing of games with their descriptions in v.1 is preceded by a guide to subject areas (which lists the game names by subject category) and an age and grade level breakdown. In the bibliography volume a general section is followed by sections on games in the classroom, business games and management simulations, conflict resolution, etc. Author, game, and institution indexes.

Lovell, Eleanor Cook and **Hall, Ruth Mason.** Index to handicrafts, model-making and workshop projects. Suppl. 5, 1968–1973. Pearl Turner, comp. Westwood, Mass., Faxon, [1975]. 629p. (Useful reference ser., 102) $18. **CB62**

For main volume and previous supplements *see Guide* CB220.

Indexes about 1,000 books and 15 periodicals published from 1968 to 1973; none of the periodicals is indexed in the *Readers' guide to periodical literature.* Excludes the fine arts and needlework.

Nunn, Marshall E. Sports. Littleton, Colo., Libraries Unlimited, 1976. 217p. (Spare time guides, no.10) $11.50. **CB63**

A classed, annotated bibliography of 649 books on American sports, such as baseball, football, hockey, golf, self-defense, motorcycling, tennis, equestrian sports, the Olympics, etc.; within each subject chapter there are reference and non-reference sections. Also gives an annotated listing of 93 sports periodicals arranged by subject, and lists of associations and publishers. The "Spare time guide" series is designed "to provide sufficient information to enable librarians and hobbyists to distinguish between books of varying quality."—*Pref.* A review in the *Booklist* (73:1596, June 15, 1977) treats this volume and no.9 in the series, R. G. Schipf's *Outdoor recreation* (1976; 278p.), which performs a similar bibliographic service for non-competitive sports. Z7511.N86

Shields, Joyce F. Make it: an index to projects and materials. Metuchen, N.J., Scarecrow Pr., 1975. 477p. $15. **CB64**

". . . an index to hand-crafted projects described in 475 English language volumes published between January 1, 1968 and January 1, 1974."—*p.v.* The first part of the work is an alphabetical index by specific type of project or craft; the second section provides an index by materials from which the projects are crafted. Z7911.S54

Dictionaries and encyclopedias

Diagram Group. Rules of the game. [N.Y. & London], Paddington Pr., [1974]. 320p. il. $15.95. **CB65**

"The complete illustrated encyclopedia of all the sports of the world."—*t.p.*

Attempts to explain through diagrams and drawings the features of each game and its official international rules. GV731.D52

——— The way to play; the illustrated encyclopedia of the games of the world. N.Y., Paddington Pr., [1975]. 320p. il. $15.95. **CB66**

A companion to *Rules of the game* (*Suppl.* CB65).

Covers "family games and social games, games played for fun, and games played for profit" (*Foreword*), including games from foreign countries and from ancient times. Gives a note on the history or origin of each game, concise rules, players and equipment needed. Games are grouped by type, such as race board games, general card games, target games, dice games, word and picture games, children's party games, etc. Indexed. GV1201.D48

Encyclopedia of physical education, fitness, and sports. Thomas K. Cureton, Jr., series ed.; sponsored by the American Alliance for Health, Physical Education, and Recreation. Reading, Mass., Addison-Wesley, [1977]– .v.1– . il. **CB67**

Contents: [v.1], Sports, dance, and related activities, ed. by R. B. Frost.

v.1 is in three sections as suggested by the volume's title, with sections 1 and 3 comprising chapters by contributing editors on specific sports (archery, badminton, baseball, etc.) and related activities (angling and casting, backpacking, boating, etc.); the "Dance" section is written by a single editor. Provides information on the origin and development of individual sports, rules, equipment, basic skills, etc. GV567.E49

Hickok, Ralph. New encyclopedia of sports. N.Y., McGraw-Hill, [1977]. 543p. il. $27.50. **CB68**

Intends to provide information "about all North American competitive sports."—*Pref.* Entries are mainly for specific sports, but some terms applicable to or encompassing a number of sports (e.g., handicap, Olympic Games) are also used as entries. Articles for individual sports usually include notes on the history of the sport, a summary of its rules, and a list of results and records; some include biographical sections for outstanding athletes, and glossaries.

A Reference and Subscription Books Committee review in the *Booklist* (74:1699, July 1, 1978) concludes: "Libraries that have acquired Frank Menke's *The Encyclopedia of Sports,* 5th ed., 1975, and John Arlott's *Oxford Companion to World Sports and Games,* 1975, may have sufficient coverage to serve their clientele." GV567.H52

Menke, Frank G. The encyclopedia of sports. 6th rev. ed. Revisions by Pete Palmer. South Brunswick, N.J., A. S. Barnes, [1978]. 1132p. $30. **CB69**

5th ed. 1975; *see Guide* CB230.

In general, records, etc., have been updated through 1976.

The Oxford companion to world sports and games. Ed. by John Arlott. London & N.Y., Oxford Univ. Pr., 1975. 1143p. il. £8.50; $29.95. **CB70**

Aims to provide an introduction to sports and games "which are the subject of national or international competition" (*Pref.*), but omits blood sports and board and table games. Intends "to help the reader to understand a sport when he watches it for the first time. The descriptive section explains how it is played—as distinct from how to play it." Does not print the rules of each game, but provides a digest thereof, together with a diagram of the playing field, etc., as applicable. Entries for individual sports figures and champions, and for specific sporting events and competitions. Articles are unsigned, but a list of contributors is provided. Cross references; occasional bibliographic citations. GV207.O93

Directories

Contemporary crafts market place, 1975/76– . N.Y., Bowker, 1975– . Ed.1– . (2d ed. 1977/78: $13.95 pa.) **CB71**

American Crafts Council, comp.

A directory in nine sections: suppliers (classed by product); shops and galleries; services; organizations; periodicals and newspapers; audiovisual materials; events; courses; reference books (grouped by type of craft). Indexed. HD2346.U5C56

Glassman, Judith. National guide to craft supplies. N.Y., Van Nostrand Reinhold, [1975]. 224p. $12.95; $6.95 pa. **CB72**

Identifies about 600 sources of supply by craft area, e.g., basket and seat weaving, ceramics, dolls, yarn, etc. Under each craft area suppliers are listed by state. Each entry includes address, description and cost of catalogs, purchase requirements, shipping information, etc. Also has sections on bookstores, societies, galleries and museums, instruction, fairs, periodicals. Subject bibliography of about 800 titles. Indexed. TT153.7.G48

Jaques Cattell Press. The big book of halls of fame in the United States and Canada: sports. Comp. and ed. by Paul Soderberg and Helen Washington. N.Y., Bowker, 1977. 1042p. $29.95. **CB73**

Arranged alphabetically by particular fields of sport ("Angling" through "Wrestling," plus a separate section for "Special fields"). Entries include directory and general information about each hall of fame, followed by a list of members with a biographical sketch of each intended to give enough information to indicate why the biographee was worthy of inclusion in the hall of fame. Indexed. CT215.J36

Individual sports and games

Baseball

The baseball encyclopedia: the complete and official record of major league baseball. Bicentennial ed. [3d ed.] N.Y., Macmillan; London, Collier Macmillan, [1976]. 2142p. $25. **CB74**

1st ed. 1969 (*Guide* CB233).

An introductory section on the history of the game is followed by sections on special achievements, records, and awards; lifetime major league rosters; all-time leaders; the teams and their players; registers by national association, manager, player, and pitcher; the World Series; all-star games.

Grobani, Anton. Guide to baseball literature. Detroit, Gale, [1975]. 363p. il. $15. **CB75**

A classed bibliography of works on various aspects of the game—histories, instructional manuals, rule books, record books, team histories, biographies of individual players, etc.—including lists of periodicals, anthologies of writings on the sport, fiction and other literary treatments. Z7514.B3G76

Turkin, Hy and **Thompson, S. C.** The official encyclopedia of baseball. 9th rev. ed. South Brunswick, N.J., A. S. Barnes, [1977]. 668p. il. $14.95. **CB76**

Revisions by Pete Palmer.

Chapters on the history of the game and its major leagues are followed by chapters on: register of all players and their records since 1871, World Series records, special records, honored players, umpires, administration, miscellany, and stadium diagrams.

Chess

Betts, Douglas A. Chess; an annotated bibliography of works published in the English language, 1850–1968. Boston, G. K. Hall, 1974. 659p. $35. **CB77**

Lists and annotates English-language works on the game of chess published 1850–1968. Classed arrangement with index of authors, titles, and subjects. Z5541.B47

Sunnucks, Anne. The encyclopaedia of chess. 2d ed. London, Hale; N.Y., St. Martin's Pr., 1976. 619p. il. £9.50; $17.95. **CB78**

1st ed. 1970.

Provides information on chess as played throughout the world, lists of national champions, results of major international tournaments, biographies of leading players, etc. A Subscription Books Committee review in the *Booklist* (74:1573, June 1, 1978) terms the work "an excellent informational source . . . appropriate for all types of libraries." Some information in the 1st ed. was not carried over into the new work. GV1314.5.S93

Football

Grobani, Anton. Guide to football literature. Detroit, Gale, [1975]. 319p. il. $15. **CB79**

A bibliography of works on all aspects of the sport, arranged by categories such as: general works, early British works, record books, general histories, team histories, biographies, anthologies, periodicals, yearbooks, rule books, dictionaries and spectators' guides, etc. Indexed. Z7514.F7G76

NFL's Official encyclopedic history of professional football. [2d ed.] N.Y., Macmillan, 1977. 512p. il. $19.95. **CB80**

1st ed. 1973.

Based on official records of the National Football League. Includes individual team histories and rosters, team standings and records, records of championship and bowl games, etc. GV954.N37

Treat, Roger L. The encyclopedia of football. 15th rev. ed.; revisions by Pete Palmer. South Brunswick, N.J., A. S. Barnes, [1977]. 702p. il. $15.95. **CB81**

1st ed. 1952.

In five main sections: (1) The story of the game; (2) Year-by-year history from 1919 to the present; (3) The players (with lists of individual and championship game records); (4) The coaches; (5) The teams (with lists of records, etc.). No index. GV954.T7

Golf

The encyclopedia of golf, ed. by Donald Steel and Peter Ryde. N.Y., Viking, [1975]. 480p. il. $30. **CB82**

The main portion of the work is an alphabetical arrangement of entries for players, terms, courses, clubs and associations, tournaments and championships, etc. Tables of results of championships and cup matches, pp.427–73. GV965.E5

Mountaineering

Unsworth, Walter. Encyclopaedia of mountaineering. London, Robert Hale; N.Y., St. Martin's Pr., [1975]. 272p. il. $12.95. **CB83**

An alphabetical arrangement of entries for places (i.e., "all the important mountain areas of the world and most of the lesser ones" —*Pref.*), people (about 400 climbers from various countries and periods), techniques and equipment, terms, and topics from other fields which have some bearing on mountain climbing. Indexed. GV199.85.U57

Tennis

Robertson, Maxwell. The encyclopedia of tennis. N.Y., Viking, [1974]. 392p. il. $22.50. **CB84**

In three main sections: (1) background information on the history and development of the game, rules and their interpretation, courts and equipment, playing the game; (2) an alphabetical arrangement of entries for individual players, developments in specific countries, terms, championships, etc.; (3) tables of records of championships and cup matches. GV990.R62

C C

Sociology

GENERAL WORKS

Guides

Bart, Pauline and **Frankel, Linda.** The student sociologist's handbook. 2d ed. Morristown, N.J., General Learning Pr., [1976]. 264p. $4.50 pa. **CC1**

1st ed. 1971.

Some brief notes on the study of sociology are followed by sections on writing a sociology paper; doing library research; periodical literature of the field; guides, indexes, bibliographies, and other reference sources; governmental and non-governmental data sources; and a glossary of statistical terms. Indexed. HM68.B37

Mark, Charles. Sociology of America: a guide to information sources. Detroit, Gale, 1976. 454p. (American studies information guide series, v.1) $18. **CC2**

A classed listing of almost 1,900 English-language books on the sociological study of American life. Most titles were published since 1960, and most are annotated. Chapters 1–3 deal with bibliographic resources, general reference works, and journal titles; remaining chapters list empirical studies on various subjects. Author, title, subject, and periodical title indexes. Z7164.S66M37

Bibliography

Latin, Howard A. Privacy: a selected bibliography and topical index of social science materials. South Hackensack, N.J., F. B. Rothman, 1976. 93p. $7.50 pa. **CC3**

Sponsored by the Earl Warren Legal Institute, University of California.

An author listing of books, essays, symposia proceedings, and scholarly journal articles from social science disciplines relevant to the study of privacy. Topical subject index, without cross references. Z7161.L38

Nandan, Yash. Durkheimian school: a systematic and comprehensive bibliography. Westport, Conn., Greenwood Pr., [1977]. 457p. $29.50. **CC4**

A classified list of over 7,000 entries divided into three parts: (1) bibliographies of the periodicals produced by the Durkheimian school; (2) bibliography of members' works published outside of the *Année sociologique;* and (3) bibliography of works on the Durkheimian school. Within most of these divisions the arrangement is chronological. Includes all available English translations. Appendixes. Author index to pt.I. Z7164.S68N36

Current

Bibliography of society, ethics and the life sciences. Hastings-on-the-Hudson, N.Y., Inst. of Society, Ethics and the Life Sciences, 1973– . Annual. (1976–77: $4 pa.) **CC5**

Less comprehensive and not as well indexed as the *Bibliography of bioethics* (*Suppl.* CC6), but coverage is more up-to-date and some annotations are provided. Classified subject arrangement; author index. Z5322.B5B52

Walters, LeRoy. Bibliography of bioethics. Detroit, Gale, [1975]– . v.1– . Annual. **CC6**

Issued by the Center for Bioethics, Kennedy Institute, Georgetown University.

A subject bibliography listing English-language books, essays in books, journal and newspaper articles, court decisions, bills or laws, films, and audio cassettes. Concerned with ethical aspects of health care, contraception, abortion, population, reproductive technologies, genetic intervention, mental health therapies, human experimentation, artificial and transplanted organs or tissues, death and dying, etc. v.3 (publ. 1977) indexes materials issued during the 1973–76 period, concentrating on 1975 publications. Title and author indexes. Z6675.E8W34

Dissertations

Sociology theses register. Ed.1– . [London?], Social Science Research Council [and] British Sociological Assoc., [1976–]. Annual. £1.50 per yr. **CC7**

Frances Wakeford, ed.

A pilot issue, *Register of post-graduate theses,* was published 1974.

Lists research "using a sociological perspective" in progress for higher degrees at United Kingdom institutions, mainly in departments of sociology, education, social administration and management studies. Classified listing with subject index.

Periodicals

Sussman, Marvin B. Author's guide to journals in sociology & related fields. N.Y., Haworth Pr., [1978]. 214p. $14.95. **CC8**

For more than 350 journals listed in *Sociological abstracts* and the "Sociology" section of *Ulrich's International periodicals directory,* provides a profile which includes: manuscript and subscription addresses, price, frequency, indexing/abstracting sources; general interest areas, and appropriate and inappropriate topics; style sheet, review period, publication lag, acceptance rates, reprint policy, etc. Subject, title, and keyword index. Z7163.S87

Dictionaries and encyclopedias

Baüml, Betty J. and Baüml, Franz H. A dictionary of gestures. Metuchen, N.J., Scarecrow Pr., 1975. 249p. il. $11. **CC9**

Describes "culturally transmitted (semiotic) gestures" *(Introd.)* which are depicted in verifiable printed or artistic sources. Entries are by parts of the body, under which are given the significance of the gesture, its geographical identification, and its source of verification. Source list (bibliography) and list of art works cited. More illustrations would have been helpful. BF591.B3

Encyclopedia of sociology. Guilford, Conn., Dushkin Publishing Group, [1974]. 330p. il. $5.95 pa. **CC10**

Brief definitions or descriptions (some signed) of "the language of sociology, the full range of its theories, the institutions of society, and the leading figures in both historical and contemporary sociology." —*Pref.* More than 1,300 articles, ranging in length from 25 to 2,500 words. Classified bibliography of approximately 700 recent publications for "nonprofessionals in the field." HM17.E5

Lexikon zur Soziologie. Hrsg. von Werner Fuchs [et al.]. Opladen, Westdeutscher Verlag, 1973. 783p. DM45. **CC11**

Brief definitions of sociological terms; most entries are signed with the initials of the contributors. Equivalent English terms are given in many instances. HM17.L483

Handbooks

Handbook of contemporary developments in world sociology. Ed. by Raj P. Mohan and Don Martindale. Westport, Conn., Greenwood Pr., 1975. 493p. (Contributions in sociology, 17) $25. **CC12**

Analyzes, on a regional and an individual country basis, the status of post-World War II sociology. Each article, written by a scholar in the field, discusses historical and intellectual background of the discipline, teaching and research, methodology, and fields of specialization; some articles also treat organizations, research centers, and periodicals in the field. Bibliographical notes. HM19.H23

SOCIAL CONDITIONS AND SOCIAL WELFARE

Bibliography

Blackstone, Tessa. Social policy and administration in Britain: a bibliography. London, F. Pinter, 1975. 130p. £4.95; £1.50 pa. **CC13**

Designed for undergraduate students of social policy, as a work complementary to *Modern British society* by John Westergaard and others (*Suppl.* CC26). Emphasizes British books on the current status of social services. Subject classification with detailed table of contents; no index. Z7165.G8B56

Chaloner, William Henry and **Richardson, R. C.** British economic and social history; a bibliographical guide. [Manchester], Manchester Univ. Pr.; [Totowa, N.J.], Rowman and Littlefield, [1976]. 129p. £8.50; $17.50. **CC14**

A select bibliographic guide to books and periodical articles in English. A brief general section is followed by four main chronological sections (1066–1300; 1300–1500; 1500–1700; 1700–1970), each with appropriate subdivisions. Index of authors and editors. Detailed table of contents, but no alphabetical subject index. More than 4,200 items; some brief annotations. Z7165.G8C46

Emezi, Herbert O. Nigerian population and urbanization, 1911–1974; a bibliography. Los Angeles, African Studies Center, Univ. of California, 1975. 145p. (Calif. Univ. at Los Angeles. African Studies Center. Occasional paper, 10) $3. **CC15**

More than 1,600 items arranged under headings such as urbanization, settlement, migration, population, family planning, etc. Author index. DT1.C12 no.10

Hoerder, Dirk. Protest, direct action, repression: dissent in American society from colonial times to the present; a bibliography. München, Verlag Dokumentation, 1977. 434p. **CC16**

A classed bibliography of English-language books, periodical articles, and doctoral dissertations. In three parts, with appropriate topical and chronological subdivisions: (1) General literature on direct action and social change; (2) Social protest and repression in mainstream American history; (3) Minorities in the United States, rebellion against discrimination and oppression. Chronological register of events cited (with references to bibliographic citations); author index. An earlier bibliography by Hoerder is *Violence in the United States, riots, strikes, protest and suppression* (Berlin, 1973). Z7165.U5H63

International Development Research Centre. Migration Task Force. Social change and internal migration; a review of research findings from Africa, Asia, and Latin America. [Ottawa, IDRC, 1977] 128p. **CC17**

Alan Simmons, Sergio Diaz-Briquets, Aprodício A. Laquian, comps.

Literature reviews for the three areas mentioned in the title cover determinants of migration, migrant characteristics, consequences of migration, and policy implications. Text citations refer to a bibliography (pp.113–28) for complete information. HB2121.I57

Key, Mary Ritchie. Nonverbal communication: a research guide & bibliography. Metuchen, N.J., Scarecrow Pr., 1977. 439p. $17.50. **CC18**

A companion volume (providing the complete bibliography) to the same author's *Paralanguage and kinesics (nonverbal communication): with a bibliography* (1975). Aims to be "fairly complete . . . on the communicative aspects of paralanguage and kinesics, together with contributing features in proxemics, tactile behavior, silence. . . . It is not complete in areas which are disciplines in themselves" (*p.140*), such as dance, psychology, and education. Text of 140 pages, although more thorough treatment of ideas is in the earlier work. Bibliography includes books, articles, some unpublished papers. Author listing with subject index. P99.5.K4

Lange, Peter. Studies on Italy, 1943–1975. [Turin], Fondazione Giovanni Agnelli, [1977]. 183p. $5.50. **CC19**

Subtitle: Select bibliography of American and British materials in political science, economics, sociology and anthropology.

A classed bibliography of books, chapters in books, periodical articles, government documents, doctoral dissertations, and research in progress. Future volumes are planned to include materials in Italian, French, German, and East European languages. Author "index" repeats the citations.

Litman, Theodor J. Sociology of medicine and health care: a research bibliography. San Francisco, Boyd & Fraser, [1976]. 664p. $30. **CC20**

Chapters arranged by broad topics (e.g., the family and health care; political aspects of health care) are further subdivided (the rural family; Medicare and national health insurance) and include English-language books, periodicals, and doctoral dissertations published from the early 1920s to 1971. Drug addiction, family planning, social gerontology, sexual deviancy, and mental illness are not included. Author and subject indexes.

Manning, Diana Helen. Disaster technology: an annotated bibliography. N.Y., Pergamon, 1976. 282p. $15. **CC21**

For full information *see Suppl.* EK3.

Marien, Michael. Societal directions and alternatives: a critical guide to the literature. LaFayette, N.Y., Information for Policy Design, [1976]. 400p. $16.50 pa. **CC22**

A classed bibliography of more than 1,000 English-language books and articles intended "to identify, categorize, and comment upon much of the contemporary literature addressing four central . . . questions: Where are we? Where are we headed? What kind of society could we have? What are the possible strategies for achieving the desirable society?"—*Introd.* Annotations are lengthy, critical, and indicate audience level. Nine indexes: author, organization, chronological book title, titles for our present society, evolutionary stage theories, alternative societies, selected proposals, selected criticism, selected subjects and ideas. Z5579.M36

Recent immigration to the United States: the literature of the social sciences. Wash., Smithsonian Institution Pr., 1976. 112p. (RIIES bibliographic studies, 1) $2.75 pa. **CC23**

Prep. for the Research Institute on Immigration and Ethnic Studies, Smithsonian Institution, by Paul Meadows, Mark LaGory, Linda Leue and Peter Meadows.

A bibliography on post-World War II immigration to the United States, emphasizing the themes of general migration theory, world immigration trends, the impact of immigration on the home country and on the United States, immigration policy in countries of origin and settlement, the settlement process, and comparison of the "old" and "new" immigrants. No index. An extract from this work was published as a special essay in *Sage race relations abstracts,* v.2, no.3 (June 1977), pp.1–30. Z7164.I3R38

Simonis, Heide and **Simonis, Udo E.** Lebensqualität: Zielgewinnung und Zielbestimmung. Quality of life: methods and measurement. Kiel, Bibliothek des Instituts für Weltwirtschaft, 1976. 312p. (Kieler Schrifttumskunden zu Wirtschaft und Gesellschaft, Bd.21) DM65 pa. **CC24**

Introductory matter in German and English.

Lists 2,064 published and unpublished materials on the methodological and empirical research on the quality of life and social indicators. In two parts: (1) materials located at the Library of the Kiel Institute for World Economy; (2) materials not located at the library. Within each part, citations are listed by author; there are personal and corporate author indexes. Lack of subject approach hampers effective use.

Wehler, Hans-Ulrich. Bibliographie zur modernen deutschen Sozialgeschichte (18.–20. Jahrhundert). Göttingen, Vandenhoeck & Ruprecht, [1976]. 269p. (Arbeitsbücher zur Modernen Geschichte, Bd.1) DM14.80 pa. **CC25**

A classed bibliography in 50 subject sections. Includes reference works and secondary sources on the theory of social history, its subject themes, and its application to specific historical periods and events. Covers books, chapters in collective works, and periodical articles; international in scope. No index. Z7165.G3W44

Westergaard, John H., Weyman, Anne and **Wiles, Paul.** Modern British society; a bibliography. N.Y., St. Martin's Pr., [1977]. 199p. $16.95. **CC26**

A revised and updated edition of a work by the same authors and with the same title published in London, 1974. Classed arrangement with author index. Detailed table of contents, but no subject index. Mainly books, with relatively few periodical articles listed.
Z7165.G8W48

Current

Floyd, Mary K. Abortion bibliography for 1970– . Troy, N.Y., Whitston, 1972– . Annual. (1975: $15) **CC27**

Books and government documents are entered by author, periodical articles by title, in separate listings. A "subject index" repeats the full citation under specific subject headings. Author index.
Z6671.2.A2F57

Directories

The futures directory. Comp. by John McHale and Magda Cordell McHale with Guy Streatfield and Laurence Tobias. [Guildford, Surrey, Eng.], IPC Science and Technology Pr.; [Boulder, Colo.], Westview Pr., [1977]. 396p. $38.50. **CC28**

Subtitle: An international listing and description of organizations and individuals active in future studies and long-range planning.

Presents results of survey studies carried out at the Center for Integrative Studies, State University of New York at Binghamton, in cosponsorship with the United Nations Institute for Training and Research. Provides information on orientation of work, methods used, time range of work, funding sources, for whom work is done, etc. Separately indexed for organizations and individuals by geographic location, method, and subject. CB158.F87

World Future Society. The future: a guide to information sources. Wash., World Future Society, [1977]. 603p. $17.50 pa. **CC29**

"This directory provides information on some 450 individuals, 230 organizations, 116 research projects, 400 books and reports, 107 periodicals, 354 films, [various other audiovisual resources], and more than 200 courses and programs offered by educational institutions."—*Introd.* Glossary; geographical and subject indexes.

Social Work

Bibliography

Li, Hong-Chan. Social work education: a bibliography. Metuchen, N.J., Scarecrow Pr., 1978. 341p. $15. **CC30**

A classed bibliography, listing more than 3,000 books, periodicals, proceedings, reports, government documents, ERIC materials, and doctoral dissertations. International in scope, but limited to English-language materials, principally from 1960 to the present. Author index. Z7164.C4L49

Social work research & abstracts. v.13, no.2– , Summer 1977– . N.Y., Nat. Assoc. of Social Workers, 1977– . Quarterly. **CC31**

Supersedes *Abstracts for social workers* (*Guide* CC25) which ceased with v.13, no.1 (Spr. 1977), and continues its numbering.

Each issue presents five or six research papers, followed by abstracts of articles grouped within six main sections: (1) fields of service; (2) social policy and action; (3) service methods; (4) the profession; (5) history; (6) related fields of knowledge. Quarterly author and subject indexes cumulate annually.

Inasmuch as doctoral dissertations were included in *Abstracts for social workers* beginning 1975 and are continued in the new title, the annual listing of dissertations in *Social service review* (*see Guide* CC31) was discontinued after the Dec. 1974 issue (v.48, no.4).

Directories

National directory of private social agencies. Queens Village, N.Y., Social Service Publications, [1977–78]. Looseleaf. **CC32**

Helga B. Croner, comp.; Ruth Sutera, managing ed.

For earlier ed. *see Guide* CC37.

Pt.1 is an index of services offered, referring the user to pt.2, the address list arranged by state and then by city. Kept up to date by monthly supplements.

Social service organizations. Ed.-in-chief, Peter Romanofsky. Westport, Conn., Greenwood Pr., [1978]. 2v. (843p.) $59.50. **CC33**

A dictionary arrangement of historical sketches of nearly 200 national and local voluntary social service agencies, particularly those that have been listed in the *Encyclopedia of social work* (*Guide* CC32) and the *Social work year book.* Sketches run three to five pages in length, and mention archives, publications, and scholarly secondary sources. Appendixes provide: (1) list of religiously affiliated social service organizations; (2) chronology of founding dates; (3) subject index of agency functions; (4) "genealogy" of name changes, mergers, dissolutions, etc. Indexed. HV88.S59

Stickney, Patricia J. and **Resnick, Rosa Perla.** World guide to social work education. N.Y., Internatl. Assoc. of Schools of Social Work, [1974]. 297p. **CC34**

This volume "describes the major features of 79 schools of social work, illustrates programs of social work education in 65 countries, and provides general information on 19 national associations of schools of social work, three regional associations, and the International Association of Schools of Social Work."—*Pref.*

Aging

Cohen, Lilly and **Oppedisano-Reich, Marie.** National guide to government and foundation funding sources in the field of aging. Garden City, N.Y., Adelphi Univ. Pr., [1977]. 175p. $13.50. **CC35**

In three main sections: (1) federal programs applicable to funding in the field of aging, listed by broad subject; (2) private philanthropy and foundation funding, by source and subject; (3) state listings for foundations offering program support. Bibliography. Appendixes provide glossary, list of abbreviations, and various related directories. Indexed by government agency and foundation.

DeLuca, Lucy, McIlvaine, B. and **Mundkur, Mohini.** Aging: an annotated guide to government publications. Storrs, Conn., Univ. of Connecticut Library, 1975. 68p. (*Its* Bibliography ser., 3) **CC36**

Selective coverage of federal, state, foreign and international documents for the period 1960–74. Classed by broad subject, with title and series indexes. SuDocs classification numbers are provided.
Z7164.O4D44

Handbook of aging and the social sciences. Editors, Robert H. Binstock [and] Ethel Shanas. N.Y., Van Nostrand Reinhold, [1976]. 684p. il. $33.50. **CC37**

A review of research, organized in broad sections. Chapters by specialists cover the social aspects of aging; aging and social structure (including the status of the aged in various societies); aging and social systems; aging and interpersonal behavior; aging and social intervention. Extensive bibliographies for each chapter, with author index and subject index.

Other titles in the publisher's "Handbooks of aging" series are *Handbook of the biology of aging* by Caleb L. Finch and Leonard Hayflick (1977; $33.50) and *Handbook of the psychology of aging* by James E. Birren and K. Warner Schaie (1977; $23.50).
HQ1061.H336

Norback, Craig T. and **Norback, Peter G.** The older American's handbook. N.Y., Van Nostrand Reinhold, [1977]. 311p. $8.95 pa. **CC38**

Subtitle: Practical information and help on ... medical and nursing care, housing, recreation, legal services, employment, in-home services, food associations and organizations, transportation, mental health and counseling ... for older and retired Americans.

Bernard E. Nash, consulting ed.

A subject listing of agencies, programs, and publications serving the areas mentioned in the subtitle. Stresses the "do-it-yourself" approach for older Americans who wish to take care of themselves. No index. HQ1064.U5N58

Sourcebook on aging. Chicago, Marquis Academic Media, [1977]. 662p. il. $34.50. **CC39**

A compilation of reprinted source materials arranged in ten subject sections: aging (general); health; economic status; housing; employment; education; transportation; leisure and retirement; special concerns/problems; government programs. Subject and geographic indexes. Particularly useful for statistical and tabular data. HQ1064.U5S63

United Nations. Dept. of Economic and Social Affairs. International directory of organizations concerned with the aging. N.Y., United Nations, 1977. 54p. $4 pa. **CC40**

Contains information on 117 international, regional, and national institutions. Gives name, address, executive officer, brief description of the organization, its structure, personnel, and programs. Includes a list of periodicals. HV1451.U55

Alcoholism

See also Suppl. CC54.

Gold, Robert S., Zimmerli, William H. and **Austin, Winnifred K.** Comprehensive bibliography of existing literature on alcohol, 1969 to 1974. Dubuque, Ia., Kendall/Hunt, [1975]. 470p. $12.95 pa. **CC41**

Intends to list materials both of research and general periodical nature. Separate sections for periodical articles, books, pamphlets, and dissertations. Classed arrangement within each section. Author index and a "subject index" which offers a list of titles to be found under each topical category. Z7721.G64

Children and youth

Child abuse and neglect research: projects and publications. Feb. 1976– . Wash., U.S. Dept. of Health, Education, and Welfare, Office of Human Development, Office of Child Development, Children's Bureau, Nat. Center on Child Abuse and Neglect, 1976– . Irregular. $25 per yr. **CC42**

Frequency varies; May 1978 issue indicates annual publication.

Identifies and describes current research projects and about 700 publications, dated 1965 to 1977, selected from journals, books, and other "readily accessible" sources. Projects and publications are listed in separate sections, alphabetically by investigator and author; projects are indexed by investigator, organization, financial sponsor, and subject; publications are indexed by author and subject. A companion publication, *Child abuse and neglect programs* (1976; $11) identifies about 2,000 private and public agencies with programs in the field; it is arranged geographically, with program director, organization, and subject index. Both are produced from the National Center on Child Abuse and Neglect's data base, *Child abuse and neglect,* which covers 1965 to date and is available for on-line searching. HV741.C456

Garoogian, Andrew and **Garoogian, Rhoda.** Child care issues for parents and society: a guide to information sources. Detroit, Gale, [1977]. 367p. (Social issues and social problems information guide ser., 2) $18. **CC43**

An annotated guide to "books and periodicals of a nontechnical nature, ... audiovisual aids, sources of free and inexpensive materials, and organizations ... that have emerged in the field of child care during the past five years [1970–75]."—*Introd.* Organized by subject, with books, pamphlets, audiovisual materials, etc., listed by form under each subject. Author, title, organization, and subject indexes. Z7164.C5G37

Kalisch, Beatrice J. Child abuse and neglect: an annotated bibliography. Westport, Conn., Greenwood Pr., [1978]. 535p. (Contemporary problems of childhood, 2) $27.50. **CC44**

Includes more than 2,000 English-language sources (most of them from the 1960–77 period) in classed arrangement. Introductory section is followed by broad subject sections, subdivided as necessary, on: prediction, detection, and prevention; causative factors; manifestations; treatment; sexual abuse; legal issues. Appendixes note bibliographic tools, selected organizations, and text of the Child Abuse Prevention and Treatment Act. Author and keyword subject indexes. Z7164.C5K34

Urban Information Interpreters. The national children's directory: an organizational directory and reference guide for changing conditions for children and youth. Ed. by Mary Lee Bundy and Rebecca Glenn Whaley. College Park, Md., Urban Information Interpreters, [1977]. 303p. $39.95. **CC45**

Identifies about 700 national and local groups organized toward improving conditions for children and youth in the United States. Each entry describes objectives, activities, publications, background and membership. National groups are listed alphabetically; local groups by state. Title and classified subject indexes. Includes sections on "alternative" children and youth programs, and federal government activities in this area. Classed, annotated bibliography of about 300 items. HV741.U7

van Why, Elizabeth Wharton. Adoption bibliography and multi-ethnic sourcebook. Hartford, Conn., Open Door Soc. of Connecticut, [1977]. 320p. $7.50 pa. **CC46**

Consists of (1) a bibliography including articles, books, audiovisual materials, periodicals, and bibliographies; (2) a "multi-ethnic" sourcebook describing organizations and their available materials; and (3) appendixes. The bibliography is indexed by geographic locations, peoples, and languages. Z7164.A23V35

Death and dying

Comprehensive bibliography of the thanatology literature. Ed. by Martin L. Kutscher [and others]. N.Y., MSS Information Corp., [1975]. 285p. $13.50. **CC47**

An author listing of 4,844 books, periodical articles, essays, reports, government documents, and unpublished materials. The broad subject terms used in the index (e.g., death, hospitals, children) impair the usefulness of the work. Z5725.C65

Miller, Albert Jay and **Acri, Michael James.** Death: a bibliographical guide. Metuchen, N.J., Scarecrow Pr., 1977. 420p. $16. **CC48**

Nearly 3,850 items in classed arrangement, with author and subject indexes. Sections for general works, education, humanities, medical profession and nursing experiences, religion and theology, science, social sciences, and audiovisual media. Brief annotations. Includes suicide. Z5725.M54

Poteet, G. Howard. Death and dying; a bibliography (1950–1974). Troy, N.Y., Whitston, 1976. 192p. $12.50. **CC49**

Concentrates "almost exclusively on the psychology of death" *(Pref.),* omitting materials on suicide, legal interpretations of death, and most materials on euthanasia. Books are separately listed in an author arrangement; periodical articles appear in an alphabetical subject listing. Author index. Z7204.D4P68

Prentice, Ann E. Suicide: a selective bibliography of over 2,200 items. Metuchen, N.J., Scarecrow Pr., 1974. 227p. $8. **CC50**

Separate sections for books, theses and dissertations, articles in books, articles in religious journals, articles in medical and scientific journals, etc. Separate author and subject indexes. Z7615.P73

Sell, Irene L. Dying and death: an annotated bibliography. N.Y., Tiresias Pr., [1977]. 144p. $9. **CC51**

506 annotated items are grouped in three sections: (1) 328 articles in journals or collected papers; (2) 71 books; (3) 53 audiovisual aids. Within each section items are arranged by author. Author and title indexes. The bibliography "was prepared primarily for nursing practitioners, educators, and students involved with providing care for dying patients."—*Pref.* Z6675.T4S44

Strugnell, Cécile. Adjustment to widowhood and some related problems; a selective & annotated bibliography. N.Y., Health Sciences Publ. Corp., 1974. 201p. $6.50 pa. **CC52**

English-language materials (books, parts of books, periodical articles) on bereavement, widowhood (general and cross-cultural), the elderly widowed, children's bereavement, loneliness, etc., are listed and annotated. Lacks an index. Z7961.S78

Triche, Charles W. and **Triche, Diane Samson.** The euthanasia controversy, 1812–1974; a bibliography with select annotations. Troy, N.Y., Whitston, 1975. 242p. $18. **CC53**

About 1,350 items; includes book materials, periodical articles, and newspaper accounts. Subject arrangement of the periodical literature: author index. Z6675.E95T74

Drug abuse

Andrews, Theodora. A bibliography of drug abuse, including alcohol and tobacco. Littleton, Colo., Libraries Unlimited, 1977. 306p. $15. **CC54**

An annotated listing of 725 works, mostly English-language books published during the last ten to fifteen years. Pt.I lists general reference sources, including periodical titles. Pt.II is a classed list of source material by subject area, e.g., psychology, education, the law, medical aspects, religion, hallucinogens, marihuana, stimulants. The sections on alcohol and tobacco cover thirty pages. Prices, LC card numbers, and ISBN numbers have been provided for many entries. Author/title and subject indexes. Z7164.N17A52

Iiyama, Patti, Nishi, Setsuko Matsunaga and **Johnson, Bruce D.** Drug use and abuse among U.S. minorities; an annotated bibliography. N.Y., Praeger, [1976]. 247p. $18.50. **CC55**

Outgrowth of "a document originally prepared by Patti Iiyama of the Metropolitan Applied Research Center (MARC), as source material for the National Conference on Drug Abuse (Washington, December 1972), which focused on narcotics addiction among minorities" *(Pref.)* — i.e., blacks, Asian Americans, Mexican Americans, Puerto Ricans, and Native Americans. As used here, "drug abuse" refers "primarily to opiate, in the main heroin, addiction." Entries are grouped by minority. Lengthy annotations. Name and subject indexes. Z7164.N17I37

National Institute on Drug Abuse. Findings of drug abuse research. Rockville, Md., The Institute, 1975. 2v. (762p.) (*Its* Research monograph ser., 1) v.1, $7; v.2, $5.05. **CC56**

"An annotated bibliography of NIMH and NIDA-supported extramural grant research 1967–74. . . ."—*t.p.*

v.1 "offers three sections of entries pertaining to the methodology of drug abuse research and findings of basic research into the chemical and metabolic characteristics of drugs and their mechanisms of action."—*Introd.* v.2 "includes entries on the behavioral and clinical aspects of drug abuse research including results of studies of adverse effects, prevention and treatment systems and the literature on human and psychosocial factors of drug abuse research." Author/editor and subject/drug indexes for each volume. Heavy biomedical emphasis. Z7164.N17N38

Handicapped

See also Suppl. CB49.

Bauman, Mary Kinsey. Blindness, visual impairment, deaf-blindness: annotated listing of the literature, 1953–75. Philadelphia, Temple Univ. Pr., [1976]. 537p. $25. **CC57**

Serves as a supplement to Helga Lende's *Books about the blind* (*Guide* CC52). About 3,750 items in classed arrangement, with author and analytical subject indexes. Includes a directory of associations and agencies.

Kept up to date by a semiannual bibliography of the same title: Z5346.B38

Blindness, visual impairment, deaf-blindness: semiannual listing of current literature. v.1, no.1– , Summer 1976– . Philadelphia, Nevil Interagency Referral Service, 1976– . Semiannual. $5. **CC58**

An author listing of English-language material of "professional relevance," excluding medical literature. Annotations. Analytical subject index, cumulative within each year. Z5346.A2B54

Directory of national information sources on handicapping conditions and related services. Wash., U.S. Dept. of Health, Education and Welfare, Office for Handicapped Individuals, Clearinghouse on the Handicapped, 1976. 405p. (DHEW publ. no.: (OHD)77–22003) **CC59**

Identifies and describes 270 federal and private organizations providing information or direct service relevant to handicapped individuals (mental health, alcoholism and drug abuse are not fully represented). Each entry describes the organization's activities, clientele, and services in terms of user eligibility, fees, etc. In two sections: national organizations; federal information sources. Indexed by disorder, special "target" populations, and subject areas in which organizations have information relative to handicaps.

Fellendorf, George W. Bibliography on deafness: *The Volta review,* 1899–1976, *American annals of the deaf,* 1847–1976. [Rev. ed.] [Wash., Alexander Graham Bell Assoc. for the Deaf, 1977] 272p. $10 pa. **CC60**

1st ed. 1966; supplement 1973.

A subject listing of articles and research reports printed in these journals during the periods indicated. Under each topic articles from the journals are listed separately, in chronological order. Author index. Z5721.F4

U.S. Library of Congress. National Library Service for the Blind and Physically Handicapped. Address list, regional and subregional libraries for the blind and physically handicapped. Wash., Govt. Prt. Off., 1978. 27p. **CC61**

Lists by state the addresses, telephone numbers, and names of librarians in charge of each of the regional and subregional libraries in the network which provides free delivery of books and magazines in recorded form or in braille, and which lends phonographs and cassette players to borrowers of talking books.

U.S. Office for Handicapped Individuals. Federal assistance for programs serving the handicapped. Wash., U.S. Dept. of Health, Education, and Welfare, Office of the Asst. Secretary for Human Development, Office for Handicapped Individuals, 1977. 333p. (DHEW publ.; no.(OHD) 77–22001) $5 pa. **CC62**

First issued 1976.

Describes about 200 programs and activities for people with disabilities, including programs to alleviate the problems of alcoholism and drug abuse; information on the majority of programs was derived from the *Catalog of federal domestic assistance* (*Guide* CH205), augmented by surveys conducted by the Office for Handicapped Individuals. Does not include general programs for the financially disadvantaged or aged persons. Program descriptions include restrictions, eligibility requirements, application procedure, contacts, enabling legislation, appropriations. Indexed by agency, subject, and applicant eligibility. Appendixes include related programs, resource centers and bibliography, and state agencies serving the handicapped. HV3001.A1O36

Marriage and the family

Aldous, Joan and **Dahl, Nancy.** International bibliography of research in marriage and the family, volume II, 1965–1972. [Minneapolis], Univ. of Minnesota Pr., [1974]. 1530p. $35. **CC63**

Publ. in association with the Institute of Life Insurance for the Minnesota Family Study Center.

For earlier volume *see Guide* CC63.

A computer-produced bibliography of 12,870 citations for books, pamphlets, bulletins, collective works, and journal articles, including some 3,292 citations for the period 1900–64.

Continued by: Z7164.M2A48

Inventory of marriage and family literature. 1973/74– . St. Paul, Minn., Family Social Science, Univ. of Minnesota, 1975– . Annual beginning with vol. covering 1975. $35 per yr. **CC64**

1973/74 designated as "Volume III."

Designed as an ongoing supplement to the *International bibliography of research in marriage and the family* (*Guide* CC63). The *Inventory* "provides an annual listing of all relevant articles published in professional journals, and is not restricted to research or theory articles."—*Introd.*

McKenney, Mary. Divorce: a selected annotated bibliography. Metuchen, N.J., Scarecrow Pr., 1975. 157p. $6. **CC65**

About 600 items in classed arrangement; subject and author indexes. Most entries are briefly annotated. 1972 cutoff date, with a few later publications noted. Appendixes for relevant organizations and state divorce laws. Z7164.M2M34

Milden, James Wallace. The family in past time; a guide to the literature. N.Y., Garland, 1977. 200p. $19. **CC66**

An annotated bibliography of English-language materials published prior to Dec. 31, 1975, including books, articles, unpublished papers and theses. Classified arrangement with author index. Sections for methodology and theory; family in European history, in American history, and in non-Western history; and family history projects. Z5118.F2M54

Population planning

Bilsborrow, Richard E. Population in development planning: background and bibliography. Chapel Hill, N.C., Laboratories for Population Statistics-Technical Information Service, Univ. of North Carolina, 1976. 216p. (TIS bibliography ser., 11) **CC67**

A classed bibliography of the published literature dealing with "relationships between population factors and social and economic factors, particularly in developing countries."—*Pref.* Chapters cover macroeconomic models and capital formation and the main themes in planning: regional, labor, agricultural, educational, health, and housing. Author index. Z7164.D3B54

Freedman, Ronald. The sociology of human fertility; an annotated bibliography. N.Y., Irvington Publishers, [1975]. 283p. $14.95. **CC68**

An earlier compilation by the same author appeared as "The sociology of human fertility: a trend report and annotated bibliography" in *Current sociology,* v.10/11, no.2, 1961–62. "The present work consists mainly of an annotated and classified bibliography of the literature on fertility published since 1961. It also includes a reworking of that portion of the original essay which dealt with the basis for the recent interest in the sociology of human fertility and a descriptive model of the classes of variables that affect fertility."—*Pref.* More than 1,650 English-language items, plus an appendix of some 430 additional recent publications listed alphabetically by author and without annotation. Geographical index only. Z7164.D3F7

International family-planning programs, 1966–1975: a bibliography. Ed. by Katherine Ch'iu Lyle, Sheldon J. Segal. University, Ala., Univ. of Alabama Pr., [1977]. 207p. $10.75. **CC69**

". . . covers sociological, medical and behavioral literature, including books, chapters of books, conference papers, and journal articles."—*p.ix.* Arrangement is by country, with an introductory section on general aspects; within each country section entries are listed alphabetically by author. Subject and author indexes. Z7164.B5I57

Konoshima, Sumiye, Radel, David and **Buck, Elizabeth Bentzel.** Sources of information on population/family planning: a handbook for Asia. Honolulu, East-West Communication Institute, 1975. 263p. $3.75 pa. **CC70**

"This Handbook contains profiles of sixty-four national, regional, and international information sources. . . . The profile . . . describes its general activities, its information and materials services, its resource base, and the subject and geographical coverage."—*Abstract.* Six indexes: classed subject, keyword subject, institutional name, geographical location, geographic area as subject, audiovisual services. HQ766.K66

Trzyna, Thaddeus C. Population: an international directory of organizations and information resources. Claremont, Calif., Public Affairs Clearinghouse, 1976. 132p. (Who's doing what ser., 3) $18.75 pa. **CC71**

Aims to provide "in convenient reference form a central source of information about organizations concerned with population and family planning, their programs and activities, key personnel, publications, and other information resources."—*Introd.* HB850.T79

Poverty

Cameron, Colin. Attitudes of the poor and attitudes toward the poor: an annotated bibliography. [Madison], Inst. for Research on Poverty, Univ. of Wisconsin–Madison, [1975]. 182p. **CC72**

Emphasis is on recent literature, particularly publications of the 1965–73 period. Classed arrangement. Author and subject indexes. Z7164.U5C34

Human resources abstracts. v.10, no.1– , Mar. 1975– . Beverly Hills, Calif., Sage Publs., 1975– . Quarterly. **CC73**

Represents a change of title for *Poverty and human resources abstracts* (*Guide* CC71) which ceased with v. 9 (1974). HD4802.H85

Sex and sexual behavior

An annotated bibliography of homosexuality. Vern L. Bullough [and others]. N.Y., Garland, 1976. 2v. $75. **CC74**

Sponsored by the Institute for the Study of Human Resources, Los Angeles.

"The . . . aim has been to bring together representative entries from a multidisciplinary point of view."—*p.xv.* More than 12,700 citations are classed under broad subject headings, e.g., behavioral sciences, education and children, law and its enforcement, novels, the homophile movement, transvestism and transsexualism. Author index and index of pseudonyms for each volume, but no detailed subject approach. Despite the title, annotations are few and exceedingly brief. Z7164.S42A66

Astin, Helen S., Parelman, Allison and **Fisher, Anne.** Sex roles: a research bibliography. Rockville, Md., Nat. Inst. of Mental Health, [1975]. 362p. $3.30 pa. **CC75**

About 450 entries in classed arrangement, with author and subject indexes. Covers publications of 1960–72. Abstracts are provided. Emphasis is on psychological and sociological attitudes of contemporary "developed" nations. BF692.A87

Barnes, Dorothy L. Rape: a bibliography, 1965–1975. Troy, N.Y., Whitston, 1977. 154p. $15. **CC76**

In three main sections: (1) books, arranged by author; (2) periodical articles, arranged by title; and (3) periodical articles, arranged by subject and repeating the complete entries from the previous section. English-language material only. Author index. Z5703.4.R35B37

A bibliography of prostitution. N.Y., Garland, 1977. 419p. $30. **CC77**

Ed. by Vern Bullough, Barrett Elcano, Margaret Deacon, Bonnie Bullough.

Includes more than 6,400 books and periodical articles arranged by broad topics such as anthropology, area studies (subdivided by country or region), biography, fiction, law, males, war, etc. No detailed subject approach. Author index. Z7164.P95B52

Friedman, Leslie. Sex role stereotyping in the mass media: an annotated bibliography. N.Y., Garland, 1977. 324p. $31. **CC78**

Concerns sex role stereotyping in the American mass media. Arranged by broad topic, with more detailed subdivisions. Covers the mass media in general, advertising, broadcast media, film, print media, popular culture (music, humor, comic strips and books, science fiction, pornography), media image of minority group women, media image of men, children's media, impact of media stereotypes on occupational choices. Author and subject indexes. Z7164.S42F74

Henley, Nancy and **Thorne, Barrie.** She said/he said; an annotated bibliography of sex differences in language, speech, and nonverbal communication. Pittsburgh, Know, Inc., [1975]. p.205–311. $3. **CC79**

First published as the bibliography to the authors' *Language and sex* (Rowley, Mass., Newbury House, 1975).

About 150 items in classed arrangement with author index. Almost exclusively English-language materials, but with some reference to other languages; includes manuscript papers as well as published materials.

Indiana. University. Institute for Sex Research. Library. Catalog of the social and behavioral sciences monograph section of the Library of the Institute for Sex Research, Indiana University, Bloomington, Indiana. Boston, G. K. Hall, 1975. 4v. $300. **CC80**

Reproduces about 36,500 cards representing some 30,000 books cataloged through Sept. 1973. The Institute was founded in 1947 by Alfred C. Kinsey, and the library contains principally Western-language works from the 19th and 20th centuries in such areas as marriage, women's rights, sex education, sex ethics and religion, abortion, contraception, venereal disease, etc.

Continued and complemented by:

——— Catalog of periodical literature in the social and behavioral sciences section, . . . including supplement to monographs, 1973–1975. Boston, G. K. Hall, 1976. 4v. $350. **CC81**

Reproduces about 68,800 cards in dictionary arrangement, giving citations to some 14,000 journal and reprint articles, 200 doctoral dissertations, and 1,000 monographs (these last added to the collection 1973–75). Subject headings are taken from the Institute's *Sexual nomenclature: a thesaurus,* comp. by JoAnn Brooks and Helen C. Hofer (Boston, G. K. Hall, 1976. 403p. $70).

Kemmer, Elizabeth Jane. Rape and rape-related issues: an annotated bibliography. N.Y., Garland, 1977. 174p. $18. **CC82**

Includes literature on rape published in English for the period 1965–76. Author arrangement; subject index. Z7164.S44K45

Parker, William. Homosexuality bibliography: supplement, 1970–1975. Metuchen, N.J., Scarecrow Pr., 1977. 337p. $12.50. **CC83**

For main volume *see Guide* CC23.

Lists more than 3,100 entries by type—books (non-fiction), pamphlets and documents, theses and dissertations, etc.—with subject and author indexes. Appendixes list: movies; television programs; audio-visual aids; American laws applicable to consensual adult homosexuals. Z7164.S42P35 suppl.

Urban problems

See also Suppl. DC1

Bell, Gwen, Randall, Edwina and **Roeder, Judith E. R.** Urban environments and human behavior, an annotated bibliography. Stroudsburg, Pa., Dowden, Hutchinson & Ross, [1973]. 271p. (Community development ser., 2) $15. **CC85**

Lists a selection of books, essays, and periodical articles which discuss behavior and urban forms in terms of: (1) the design viewpoint; (2) the social science viewpoint; and (3) parts of the urban environment, from a room to a new town. International in scope; English-language materials only. Author and subject indexes. Z5942.B35

Hoover, Dwight W. Cities. N.Y., Bowker, 1976. 231p. $15.50. **CC86**

More than 1,000 items in classed arrangement, with author and title indexes. "The basic criteria for inclusion . . . were contemporaneity and availability of materials."—*Pref.* Includes books, films, filmstrips, and other media. Annotated. Z7164.U7H66

Ross, Bernard H. and **Fritschler, A. Lee.** Urban affairs bibliography; an annotated guide to the literature in the field. 3d ed. Wash., School of Govt. and Pub. Admin., College of Pub. Affairs, American Univ., 1974. 85p. $4.95 pa. **CC87**

1st ed. 1969.

Limited to books. Classed arrangement; no index. Z7165.U5F74

Sage urban studies abstracts. v.1, no.1– , Feb. 1973– . Beverly Hills, Calif., Sage Publs., 1973– . Quarterly. $60 to institutions; $36 to individuals. **CC88**

Each issue offers some 250 abstracts of English-language books, periodical articles, reports, and documents. A section for "related citations" includes similar materials (some in foreign languages) without annotations. Author and subject indexes. HT51.S24

CRIMINOLOGY

Guides

Wright, Martin. Use of criminology literature. [Hamden, Conn.], Archon Books; [London, Butterworth, 1974]. 242p. $13.50. **CC90**

A guide to the major literature and reference tools, with chapters by specialists on: search methodology; sociological aspects; criminological aspects of psychology; alcoholism and crime; drug dependence; treatment of offenders; criminal law and the administration of criminal justice; police; statistics; prisons and penal practices; illustrations; and official publications. Subject index. Z5118.C9W74

Bibliography

Felkenes, George T. and **Becker, Harold K.** Law enforcement: a selected bibliography. 2d ed. N.Y., Scarecrow Pr., 1977. 329p. $12.50. **CC91**

1st ed. 1968.

A classed list of more than 6,900 books and periodical articles arranged in five main groups, with appropriate subdivisions: (1) police personnel administration; (2) police functions and practices; (3) criminal law; (4) criminal evidence; (5) administration of justice. Brief annotations for most entries. Detailed table of contents; author index. KF9201.F44

Prostano, Emanuel T. and **Piccirillo, Martin L.** Law enforcement: a selective bibliography. Littleton, Colo., Libraries Unlimited, 1974. 203p. $10. **CC92**

Covers English-language books, pamphlets and audiovisual materials published between 1967 and 1972, with a section listing serial titles. Subject arrangement using such headings as alcoholism, behavioral and social science, civil rights, etc. 250 starred titles are highly recommended. Author and title indexes. Z7164.P76P74

Radzinowicz, Leon and **Hood, Roger.** Criminology and the administration of criminal justice: a bibliography. Westport, Conn., Greenwood Pr., [1976]. 400p. $29.95. **CC93**

Nineteen chapters list books, periodical articles, and government reports chronologically within subject area. "Focus on criminology has been predominantly sociological rather than psychiatric and . . . in criminal justice and penology more concerned with issues of policy and the results of research than with day-to-day practical matters." —*Introd.* Primarily literature of the period 1954–74, with a supplement updating to Feb. 1976. Author index. Z5118.C9R3

Rank, Richard. The criminal justice systems of the Latin-American nations: a bibliography of the primary and secondary literature. South Hackensack, N.J., Rothman, 1974. 540p. (New York Univ. Criminal Law Education and Research Center. Publ., 11) $45. **CC94**

A classed list of about 9,000 items covering Central and South America, Cuba, the Dominican Republic, Haiti, and Puerto Rico. Arranged by country, with subsections on general works, criminal law, criminal procedure, criminology, and military criminal law. For some countries, state or provincial material is also included. No index.

Wolfgang, Marvin E., Figlio, Robert M. and **Thornberry, Terence P.** Criminology index: research and theory in criminology in the United States, 1945–1972. N.Y., Elsevier, 1975. 2v. $60. **CC95**

Sponsored by the Center for Studies in Criminology and Criminal Law, University of Pennsylvania.

A bibliography and citation source on theoretical and empirical work in criminology, composed of three main sections: (1) the "Source document index," or bibliography, divided into two sections, (a) articles, and (b) books, dissertations, and reports; (2) the "Subject index," a paired keyword-in-title listing; (3) the "Criminology citation index," a list of all works cited by authors appearing in the "Source document index," divided into anonymous works, general works, and legal documents. Does not include works on the administration of justice, police, courts, and corrections, or doctoral dissertations done before 1968. There is an addendum to the "Source document index." Z5118.C9W64

Current

Criminal justice abstracts. v.9, no.1– , Mar. 1977– . Hackensack, N.J., Nat. Council on Crime and Delinquency, 1977– . Quarterly. $40 per yr. **CC96**

Supersedes *Crime and delinquency literature* and continues its numbering. Coverage and format remain the same as in the earlier publication, the name having been changed "to reflect more accurately the nature of the contents."—*v.9,no.1,p.1.*

Criminal justice periodical index, 1975– . Ann Arbor, Indexing Services, University Microfilms, 1975– . 3 issues per yr., the 3d issue being the annual cumulation. $60 per yr. **CC97**

Offers separate author and subject indexes to the contents of about seventy English-language periodicals, with special attention to those issued by professional or research organizations active in the areas of police administration, corrections, juvenile delinquency, criminal law, and security. Entries are repeated in both indexes. Z5118.C9C74

Dictionaries

Rush, George Eugene. Dictionary of criminal justice. Boston, Holbrook Pr., [1977]. 374p. $13.95; $9.50 pa. **CC98**

Covers terms, cases, names, and places in the areas of law enforcement, courts, probation, parole, and corrections. Many definitions have been reprinted from 25 sources, and are identified by an abbreviated reference to the source. HV6017.R87

Directories

Newton, Anne, Perl, Kathleen Yaskiw and **Doleschal, Eugene.** Information sources in criminal justice; an annotated guide to directories, journals, newsletters. [Hackensack, N.J.], Information Center, Nat. Council on Crime and Delinquency, 1976. 164p. $15 pa. **CC99**

Includes 57 directories, 185 criminal justice journals, and 254 newsletters; each of these three types of publication is organized by subject, then alphabetically by organization and title. No index.

O'Brien, Kevin E., Boston, Guy and **Marcus, Marvin.** Directory of criminal justice information sources. [Wash.], Nat. Inst. of Law Enforcement and Criminal Justice, Law Enforcement Assistance Admin., 1976. 159p. $2.35 pa. **CC100**

"The organizations included in this directory were chosen because of their particular information resources, such as computerized literature search services, interlibrary loan programs, reference services, or technical assistance provisions that are available to criminal justice professionals."—*Introd.* An alphabetical arrangement of more than 150 organizations; information on each includes notes on information services and resources, user restrictions, cost, and publications. Subject index. HV8138.O37

Szabo, Denis. Criminology in the world. Montreal, International Centre for Comparative Criminology, Université de Montréal, 1977. xvii, 49a [i.e., 63] *l.* $3.50 pa. **CC101**

In two parts: (1) "Criminology teaching and research" surveys the field of study and its levels and programs, and lists principal reference sources and a general bibliography; (2) "Research organizations and teaching establishments" is an international directory, arranged by country.

RACE RELATIONS AND MINORITIES

Bibliography

See also Suppl. CC23, CH7.

Allworth, Edward. Soviet Asia, bibliographies: a compilation of social science and humanities sources on the Iranian, Mongolian, and Turkic nationalities, with an essay on the Soviet-Asian controversy. N.Y., Praeger, [1975]. 686p. $37.50. **CC102**

Lists about 5,200 bibliographies, in book and periodical format, published in Czarist Russia and the Soviet Union between 1850 and 1970. Classified by five geographical divisions, and further subdivided into national groups, entries are listed under broad subject categories. Annotations indicate: language of the book, main languages of the entries and number of entries, period covered and dates within which the entries are published, and pagination. Z3414.M54A44

Buenker, John D. and **Burckel, Nicholas C.** Immigration and ethnicity: a guide to information sources. Detroit, Gale, [1977]. 305p. (American government and history information guide ser., 1) $18. **CC103**

A selected, annotated bibliography of more than 1,400 English-language books, periodical articles, and doctoral dissertations, emphasizing post-1945 imprints. Excludes Afro-Americans and Native Americans, fiction, autobiographical and audiovisual material. Topical arrangement includes general accounts, "old" and "new" immigration, Orientals, "recent" ethnics after the 1920s, acculturation and restriction, private centers and federal government information sources. Author and subject indexes. Z7165.U5B83

Cashman, Marc and **Klein, Barry.** Bibliography of American ethnology. Rye, N.Y., Todd Publs., [1976]. 304p. $17.50. **CC104**

In four main sections: (1) General ethnology; (2) American Indians; (3) Black Americans; (4) Other minorities. Each section has numerous subdivisions (e.g., Assimilation, Civil rights, Culture, Education), including individual tribes and specific ethnic groups (Japanese-Americans, Jewish Americans, etc.). Lists about 4,500 in-print books. Publisher index, but none of authors and titles. Brief descriptive annotations for many entries. The subscription books review in the *Booklist* 73:52 points out numerous short-comings of the compilation. Z1361.E4C37

Cordasco, Francesco. Italian Americans: a guide to information sources. Detroit, Gale, [1978]. 222p. (Ethnic studies information guide ser., 2) $18. **CC105**

Some 2,000 English- and Italian-language sources are grouped under five main headings: (1) General reference works; (2) Social sciences; (3) History and regional studies; (4) Applied sciences; (5) Humanities. Two separate chapters deal with newspapers and periodicals, and fraternal, professional, and religious organizations. A very brief appendix treats audiovisual materials. Locations are indicated for rare items.

Cordasco is the author of two earlier, related publications: *Italians in the United States: a bibliography* (N.Y., Oriole, 1972) and *The Italian American experience: an annotated and classified bibliographical guide* (N.Y., B. Franklin, 1974). Z1361.I8C659

Gakovich, Robert P. and **Radovich, Milan M.** Serbs in the United States and Canada: a comprehensive bibliography. [Minneapolis], Immigration History Research Center, Univ. of Minnesota, 1976. 129p. il. (IHRC ethnic bibliography, no.1) **CC106**

A bibliography and partial union catalog for nearly 800 archival collections, books, pamphlets, and articles; also lists current and historical newspapers and periodicals. Author index. Z1361.S4G34

Jerabek, Esther. Czechs and Slovaks in North America: a bibliography. N.Y., Czechoslovak Soc. of Arts & Sciences in America; Chicago, Czechoslovak Nat. Council of America, 1976. 448p. $17.50 pa. **CC107**

A classed bibliography of more than 7,600 items relating to Czechs and Slovaks in North America. Useful list of periodicals and newspapers, pp.314–64. Fully indexed.

Johnson, Harry Alleyn. Ethnic American minorities: a guide to media and materials. N.Y., Bowker, 1976. 304p. $16.50. **CC108**

"The primary purpose of this book . . . is . . . to present a highly documented, annotated source of instructional materials and media on four major minorities—Afro-Americans, Asian Americans, Native Indian Americans, and Spanish-speaking Americans."—*Pref.* Chapters by a specialist on each minority conclude with annotated entries for multimedia resources, classed by type. A fifth chapter treats other ethnic minorities. Directory of producers and distributors. Title index for media, as well as a general index. E184.A1J58

Kinton, Jack F. American ethnic groups and the revival of cultural pluralism: evaluative sourcebook for the 1970's. 4th ed. [Aurora, Ill., Social Science & Sociological Resources], 1974. 206p. $9.95; $7.25 pa. **CC109**

Lists books and articles in a classed arrangement. No index. Z1361.E4K55

Miller, Wayne Charles [and others]. Comprehensive bibliography for the study of American minorities. N.Y., New York Univ. Pr., 1976. 2v. (1380p.) $85. **CC110**

A classified, briefly annotated bibliography of approximately 29,300 entries; mainly monographs are cited, with articles and pamphlets included for those ethnic groups with less coverage (exceptions being made for American Indian artists and the black American civil rights movement). Good coverage of many ethnic groups not represented elsewhere. Includes other bibliographies, periodicals and indexes, as well as works in social sciences and humanities. Historical-bibliographical essays preceding each group have been reprinted in Miller's *Handbook of American minorities* (*Suppl.* CC119). Author and title indexes. Z1361.E4M529

Minnesota. University. Immigration History Research Center. Hungarians in the United States and Canada: a bibliography. Holdings of the Immigration History Research Center of the University of Minnesota. [Minneapolis], The Center, 1977. 113p. (IHRC ethnic bibliography, no.2) $6 pa. **CC111**

Comp. and ed. by Joseph Széplaki.

Based on the holdings of the Immigration History Research Center, but including some particularly useful items to be found in the University of Minnesota's Wilson Library. Classed arrangement with name index. Separate sections for serials and manuscripts. About 900 items. Z1361.H84M56

Oaks, Priscilla. Minority studies: a selective annotated bibliography. Boston, G. K. Hall, [1975]. 303p. $22. **CC112**

A section of general studies is followed by sections (with appropriate subdivisions by type of material and subject) on Native Americans, Spanish Americans, Afro-Americans, and Asian Americans. Author/title index. Includes popular as well as scholarly materials. 1,800 items. Z1361.E4O24

Pap, Leo. The Portuguese in the United States: a bibliography. [N.Y.], Center for Migration Studies, 1976. 80p. $7.50 pa. **CC113**

A classed bibliography of books, periodical articles, master's theses, doctoral dissertations, and federal government publications. 800 items; no index. Z1361.P65P36

Schlachter, Gail A. and **Belli, Donna.** Minorities and women: a guide to reference literature in the social sciences. Los Angeles, Reference Services Pr., 1977. 349p. $19.50. **CC114**

Descriptive annotations for over 800 English-language reference materials on minorities and women in America. Divided into information sources (fact-books, biographies, documentary sources, directories, and statistical materials) and citation sources (bibliographies, indexes, abstracts, etc.). Further subdivided by group: minorities, American Indians, Asian Americans, black Americans, Spanish Americans, and women. Author, title, and subject indexes.

Tolzmann, Don Heinrich. German-Americana: a bibliography. Metuchen, N.J., Scarecrow Pr., 1975. 384p. $15. **CC115**

A classed bibliography of more than 5,300 entries on German-American history, language and literature, press and book trade, religious and cultural life, business and industry, radicalism, biography, and genealogy. Includes books, newspaper and periodical articles, pamphlets, dissertations, government documents, and audiovisual materials, most of them produced since 1941. Also includes many directory entries. Indexed. Z1361.G37T64

Current

Ethnic studies bibliography. v.1– , 1975– . [Pittsburgh], Univ. Center for Internatl. Studies, Univ. of Pittsburgh, [1977]– . Annual. (1977: $50 pa.) **CC116**

Published in conjunction with the Pennsylvania Ethnic Heritage Studies Center.

A spin-off from the data base used for *United States political science documents* (*Suppl.* CJ23). v. 2, 1976, included abstracts for 565 articles from 393 United States social science journals. Five indexes (author, subject, geographic area, proper name and journal) precede the abstracts, which also note tabular material and cited persons.

Sage race relations abstracts. v.1, no.1– , Nov. 1975– . London & Beverly Hills, Calif., Sage, 1976– . Quarterly. $50 per yr. **CC116a**

Published on behalf of the Institute of Race Relations, London. Supersedes *Race relations abstracts* (*Guide* CC110).

Abstracts European and American periodical literature on immigration and race relations, with some books, essays, and "grass-roots and other fugitive literature" included. Some British emphasis. Each issue contains a bibliographical essay, e.g., "The Netherlands as a multi-racial society." Author and subject, but no geographical, indexes. HT1521.S15

Directories and handbooks

Directory of special programs for minority group members: career information services, employment skills banks, financial aid. 1974– . [Garrett Park, Md., Garrett Park Pr.], 1974– . Annual. $8.50 per yr. **CC117**

Includes information on general employment and educational assistance programs, federal aid programs, women's programs, college and university awards. HD5724.D56

Handbook of major Soviet nationalities. Zev Katz, ed. N.Y., Free Pr., [1975]. 481p. $25. **CC118**

Groups 17 Soviet nationalities by geographical and/or cultural area: the Slavs, the Baltics, the Transcaucasus, Central Asia, and other nationalities (Jews, Tatars, and Moldavians). The chapter on each nationality includes general information (territory, economy, history, demography, culture, external relations), media (language, media, and educational institutions), and national attitudes. Each chapter is written by a specialist and includes bibliography. Appendix of comparative tables for the nationalities. Subject index. DK33.H35

Miller, Wayne Charles. A handbook of American minorities. N.Y., New York Univ. Pr., 1976. 225p. $15. **CC119**

Reprints the essays which introduce the sections for individual ethnic groups in Miller's *Comprehensive bibliography for the study of American minorities* (*Suppl.* CC110). "The essays contained in this volume are designed to provide basic historical overviews of many American minorities and to provide bibliographical introductions to some of the most useful sources for the study of them."—*Introd.* Minorities are treated according to country or region of origin within six main sections: (1) From Africa and the Middle East; (2) From Europe; (3) From Eastern Europe and the Balkans; (4) From Asia; (5) From the Islands; (6) Native Americans. Lacks an index. Z1361.E4M53

U.S. Bureau of Labor Statistics. Directory of data sources on racial and ethnic minorities. Wash., Govt. Prt. Off., 1975. 83p. (U.S. Bureau of Labor Statistics. Bulletin 1879) $1.50 pa. **CC120**

"Data sources covered in this directory include recent Federal Government publications presenting the social and economic characteristics of minority groups for the Nation and selected areas based primarily on household surveys. These include reports from the 1970 Census of Population and Housing and from monthly Current Population Surveys. In addition, there are references to program and establishment reports prepared by the Equal Employment Opportunity Commission, the Civil Service Commission, and selected publications prepared by other Federal agencies."—*Gen. Introd.* Classed by racial or ethnic group (black Americans, persons of Spanish ancestry, races other than black, ethnic groups other than Spanish) and subdivided by report source (census, *Current population survey,* other data sources). Introduction, appendixes, subject and report series indexes.

Wasserman, Paul and **Morgan, Jean.** Ethnic information sources of the United States. Detroit, Gale, 1976. 751p. $45. **CC121**

Subtitle: A guide to organizations, agencies, foundations, institutions, media, commercial and trade bodies, government programs, research institutes, libraries and museums, religious organizations, banking firms, festivals and fairs, travel and tourist offices, airlines and ship lines, bookdealers and publishers' representatives, and books, pamphlets and audiovisuals on specific ethnic groups.

Sections on more than 100 ethnic peoples are arranged alphabetically by group name, with information sources indicated in the subtitle grouped under 26 major headings within each group. Blacks, American Indians, and Eskimos are not included. Organization and publication indexes. E184.A1W27

Wynar, Lubomyr R. Encyclopedic directory of ethnic organizations in the United States. Littleton, Colo., Libraries Unlimited, 1975. 414p. $19.50. **CC122**

Aims "to identify major ethnic organizations in terms of their objectives, publications, and activities."—*Pref.* Lists 1,475 organizations arranged under 73 categories representing separate ethnic groups. Indexed. E184.A1W94

Afro-Americans

Bibliography

See also Suppl. AE6.

Abajian, James. Blacks and their contributions to the American West; a bibliography and union list of library holdings through 1970. Boston, G. K. Hall, 1974. 487p. $29.50. **CC123**

"Compiled by James de T. Abajian for the Friends of the San Francisco Public Library in cooperation with the American Library Association."

A classed list of some 4,300 items with detailed author/subject index. Z1361.N39A27

Brignano, Russell Carl. Black Americans in autobiography; an annotated bibliography of autobiographies and autobiographical books written since the Civil War. Durham, N.C., Duke Univ. Pr., 1974. 118p. $7.75. **CC124**

In two main sections: (1) Autobiographies ("volumes describing appreciable spans of the authors' lives") and (2) Autobiographical books (diaries, journals, collections of essays, eyewitness accounts of important events, etc.). Locates copies. Occupational, institutional, and title indexes. Z1361.N39B67

Davis, Lenwood G. The black family in the United States: a selected bibliography of annotated books, articles, and dissertations on black families in America. Westport, Conn., Greenwood Pr., [1978]. 132p. $11.95. **CC125**

More than 380 annotated entries are grouped by type (books, articles, dissertations), and subdivided by subject (slavery, poverty, economic status, religion, education, health, sex, etc.). There are author and "selective" keyword subject indexes. Z1361.N39D355

——— The black woman in American society; a selected annotated bibliography. Boston, G. K. Hall, [1975]. 159p. $17. **CC126**

Entries are grouped according to type: books, articles, general reference works, etc. Author and subject index. Includes a directory of selected black periodicals, lists of pertinent national organizations, elected officials, etc., and some brief tables of statistics on black women. Z1361.N39D36

Dunmore, Charlotte. Black children and their families: a bibliography. San Francisco, R & E Research Associates, 1976. 103p. $9 pa. **CC127**

Lists published materials on the black American child in sections on adoption, education, health, family life, ghetto life, mental health, sex and family planning. Separate sections include bibliographies and reference works, a periodicals directory, source directory for films and filmstrips, and a list of selected library collections. No index. Z1361.N39D898

Fisher, William Harvey. Free at last; a bibliography of Martin Luther King, Jr. Metuchen, N.J., Scarecrow Pr., 1977. 169p. $7. **CC128**

A bibliography of primary and secondary sources, arranged in four sections: (1) works written by King, including manuscript collections; (2) books, articles, dissertations, documents and manuscript collections primarily about King; (3) similar materials about his family, associates, and death; (4) reviews of books by King. Some entries are briefly annotated. Author index. Z8464.44.F57

Helmreich, William B. Afro-Americans and Africa: black nationalism at the crossroads. Westport, Conn., Greenwood Pr., 1977. 74p. (African Bibliographic Center. Special bibliographic ser., n.s., no.2) $12.95. **CC129**

An annotated list of about 400 books and articles (including some newspaper pieces) from the period 1960–73. Also provides a general bibliography of works on Afro-Americans and Africans in which further titles are grouped by subject. Introductory essays review the literature of African and black nationalism both historically and in a social science context. Subject index. Z3501.Af852 no.2

Jenkins, Betty Lanier and **Phillis, Susan.** Black separatism: a bibliography. Westport, Conn., Greenwood Pr., [1976]. 163p. $11. **CC130**

A classified, annotated list of books and articles arranged in two parts: (1) The separatism vs. integration controversy; (2) Institutional and psychological dimensions. Pt.I is organized historically; pt.II by subject (identity, education, politics, economics, and religion). Name and title indexes. Z1361.N39J45

Miller, Joseph C. Slavery: a comparative teaching bibliography. [Waltham, Mass.], Crossroads Pr., [1977]. 122p. $12 pa. **CC131**

Designed as an introductory bibliography for students, listing secondary literature relating to slavery. More than 1,600 entries are grouped by broad geographic or subject area (French North America, the Muslim world, the slave trade, etc.), with author and geographical keyword indexes. Z7164.S6M5

New York. Public Library. Schomburg Collection of Negro Literature and History. Dictionary catalog. Supplement [3], 1974. Boston, G. K. Hall, 1976. 580p. $80. **CC132**

For main set and earlier supplements *see Guide* CC121.

Includes bibliographic data for materials added Jan. 1972–Sept. 1974. Catalog cards are no longer reproduced, but this supplement retains the dictionary format for main and added entries. Materials processed after 1974 appear in:

Schomburg Center for Research and Black Culture. Bibliographic guide to black studies, 1975– . Boston, G. K. Hall, 1976– . Annual. (1977: $45) **CC133**

The 1975 volume covers materials acquired by the New York Public Library's Schomburg Collection between Sept. 1974 and Sept. 1975. Later volumes include some additional entries from Library of Congress MARC tapes. Dictionary catalog arrangement; employs some subject headings developed especially for the Schomburg Collection. Z1361.N39S373a

Obudho, Constance E. Black-white racial attitudes: an annotated bibliography. Westport, Conn., Greenwood Pr., 1976. 180p. $11.50. **CC134**

An annotated, classified bibliography of books and periodical articles published between 1950 and 1974 on attitude formation and change and associated factors in the United States. Articles include doctoral dissertation abstracts in *Dissertation abstracts international.* Author and subject indexes. Z1361.N39O28

Partington, Paul G. W. E. B. DuBois: a bibliography of his published writings. Whittier, Calif., P. G. Partington, 1977. 202p. $10 pa. **CC135**

A classed, partially annotated listing of more than 2,300 items, including periodicals edited by DuBois; newspaper, magazine and newsletter contributions; translations; book reviews; books; and miscellaneous contributions. No index. Z8244.9.P37

Smith, Dwight LaVern. Afro-American history; a bibliography. Santa Barbara, Calif., ABC-Clio, [1974]. 856p. (Clio bibliography ser., 2) $55. **CC136**

For full information *see Suppl.* DB8.

Walton, Hanes. The study and analysis of black politics; a bibliography. Metuchen, N.J., Scarecrow Pr., 1973. 110p. $6. **CC137**

A classed listing of more than 1,000 books and articles on the American black political experience. Each of 13 subject chapters begins with a brief introduction, then lists materials by type. Treats political parties and candidates, voting patterns, international politics, urban politics, the Supreme Court, etc. Author index. Z1361.N39W29

Westmoreland, Guy T. An annotated guide to basic reference books on the black American experience. Wilmington, Del., Scholarly Resources Inc., [1974]. 98p. $12.50. **CC138**

A classified, annotated guide to reference works "which deal primarily or completely" with the black American experience. Author, title, and subject indexes. Z1361.N39W528

Williams, Ora. American black women in the arts and social sciences: a bibliographic survey. Rev. and expanded ed. Metuchen, N.J., Scarecrow Pr., 1978. 197p. il. $8. **CC139**

1st ed. 1973.

Pt.1, "Comprehensive listing," includes reference works, autobiographies and biographies, anthologies, literature, feminist issues, miscellaneous subjects, art (including art and musical works), and audiovisual material. Pt.2, "Selected individual bibliographies," includes portraits, and primary and secondary works. Pt.3, "Ideas and achievements of some American black women," is followed by a list of black periodicals and publishing houses. Indexed. Z1361.N39W56

Dissertations

Peebles, Joan B. A bibliography of doctoral research on the Negro, 1967–1977. Ann Arbor, Mich., University Microfilms Internatl., [1978?]. 65p. Free. pa. **CC140**

Cover title: *Black studies: a dissertation bibliography.*

Supplements E. H. West's *Bibliography of doctoral research on the Negro, 1933–1966* (*Guide* CC130) and supersedes an earlier supplement covering 1967–69. Retains the classified arrangement and provides similar information as in the West volume. E29.N393

Handbooks

The black American reference book. Ed. by Mabel M. Smythe. Englewood Cliffs, N.J., Prentice-Hall, 1976. 1026p. $35. **CC141**

Sponsored by the Phelps-Stokes Fund.

A revised and updated edition of *The American Negro reference book* edited by J. P. Davis (1966; *Guide* CC133). E185.D25

Ploski, Harry A. and **Marr, Warren.** The Negro almanac; a reference work on the Afro American. 3d rev. ed. N.Y., Bellwether, [1976]. 1206p. il. $59.95. **CC142**

2d ed. 1971 (*Guide* CC135).

Updated, revised and reset. Arrangement remains much the same, with some section headings altered slightly, and several new chapters added (e.g., Black capitalism, Blacks in colonial and revolutionary America, Black classical musicians, Prominent black Americans). E185.P55

Directories

Black list. [2d ed.] N.Y., Black List, [1975]. 2v. $50 pa. **CC143**

Subtitle: The concise and comprehensive reference guide to black journalism, radio and television, educational and cultural organizations in the USA, Africa and the Caribbean.

Contents: v.1, Afroamerica (USA); v.2, Africa, the Caribbean, Latin America.

1st ed. 1970.

Lists television and radio networks, cable television networks, newspapers, magazines, and educational and cultural institutions, with address and person in charge. P88.B6

Directory of African and Afro-American studies in the U.S. 1976– . Waltham, Mass., African Studies Assoc., 1976– . Annual. $25 per yr. **CC144**

Continues the *Directory of African studies in the U.S.,* 1971–1974/75.

1976 ed. comp. by Mitsue Frey and Michael Sims.

Offers brief descriptions and lists of courses for 623 colleges and universities offering at least one course in relevant areas. Lists an additional 295 institutions known to offer pertinent courses, but which failed to answer the questionnaire. Indexes by institution, discipline, language, and faculty. DT19.9.U5D561

Asian-Americans

Bibliography

Matsuda, Mitsugu. The Japanese in Hawaii; an annotated bibliography of Japanese Americans. Rev. by Dennis M. Ogawa with Jerry Y. Fujioka. Honolulu, Social Sciences and Linguistics Inst., Univ. of Hawaii, [1975]. 304p. (Hawaii ser., no. 5) $7 pa. **CC145**

Publication supported by the Japanese American Research Center (JARC).

Matsuda's original bibliography covering 1868–1967 was published 1968.

An author listing of more than 750 published English-language items, plus a list of newspapers and periodicals and a separate section of Japanese materials. Subject index to the English-language materials. Intended for undergraduate student use. Z4708.J3M3

Norell, Irene P. Literature of the Filipino-American in the United States: a selective and annotated bibliography. San Francisco, [R and E Research Associates], 1976. 84p. $8 pa. **CC146**

Classed arrangement; no index. Includes books, periodical articles, and academic theses. E184.F4N67

Rj Associates. Asian American reference data directory. [Wash.], U.S. Dept. of Health, Education, and Welfare, Office of Special Concerns, Office for Asian American Affairs, 1976. 482, [93]p. $9.25 pa. **CC147**

Canta Pian, project director.

Focuses on data developed by federal and state agencies, universities and individuals on topics "relevant to the Department" (*Introd.*), such as the current health, education, and social welfare of the Asian American population. Most of the 480 abstracts cover material produced within the past five years. Indexed by subject area, ethnic group, and author. Z1361.O7R57

Saito, Shiro. Filipinos overseas: a bibliography. N.Y., Center for Migration Studies, 1977. 156p. $8.95 pa. **CC149**

An updating and expansion of the author's "Bibliographic considerations and research status of the overseas Filipinos," a working paper submitted at the first Conference on International Migration from the Philippines, June 10–14, 1974. Entries are arranged according to the conference agenda: Demographic overview of migration; U.S. immigration policy; Views from the barrios; The brain drain; and Destinations of migration, with a section on each area. Includes published and unpublished English-language materials. Appendixes list papers presented at the first and second Conferences on International Migration from the Philippines, relevant dissertations and theses done at the University of Hawaii, and a list of Filipino newspapers and periodicals published in Hawaii and located in the University of Hawaii Library. Author index. Z3298.I3S24

Dissertations

Ong, Paul M. and **Lum, William Wong.** Theses and dissertations on Asians in the United States, with selected references to other overseas Asians. Davis, Calif., Asian American Studies, Dept. of Applied Behavioral Sciences, Univ. of California, 1974. 113p. **CC150**

A major revision and expansion of Lum's *Asians in America* (1970; *Guide* CC139). Lists 1,372 items in topical arrangement, with keyword and author indexes. Z1361.O7L84

Indians

Bibliography

California State University, Northridge. Libraries. Native Americans of North America: a bibliography based on collections in the Libraries of California State University, Northridge. Comp. by David Perkins and Norman Tanis. Metuchen, N.J., Scarecrow Pr., 1975. 558p. il. $12. **CC151**

"This book was first published by California State University, Northridge."—*verso of t.p.*

A classed bibliography of books, with author/title and series indexes. About 3,400 items. Z1209.2.N67C34

Hodge, William H. A bibliography of contemporary North American Indians. Selected and partially annotated with study guide. N.Y., Interland Publ., 1976. 310p. $27.50. **CC152**

Materials included must meet one or more of the following criteria: "(1) They have not been published, e.g., state and federal reports such as committee hearings, position papers, procedural guides, tribal government documents, etc.; (2) For one or a combination of reasons, they have not been widely circulated; (3) They contain significant amounts of ethnographic data which also have immediate implications for important theoretical questions now current within the society sciences; (4) Their chief focus is upon current Indian activity."—*Introd.* Intended to complement rather than supplant existing guides and bibliographies of the subject. Separate study guides for "Indian life prior to 1875" and "Contemporary American Indians" are followed by topical sections such as "History—overview," "Social organization," "Migration patterns," "City living," "Anthropology of development," "Religion," "Health-disease-poverty." Author index; subject index is limited to entries for geographic areas and names of tribes. Z1209.2.N67H6

Huntington Free Library and Reading Room, New York. Dictionary catalog of the American Indian collection. Boston, G. K. Hall, 1977. 4v. $350. **CC153**

Photoreproduction of the catalog cards for the collection which serves as the library for the Museum of the American Indian, Heye Foundation, New York City. Represents more than "35,000 volumes relating to the anthropology, art, history and current affairs of all the Native Peoples of the Western Hemisphere."—*Introd.* Z1209.H85

Indians of the United States and Canada; a bibliography. Ed., Dwight L. Smith. Santa Barbara, Calif., ABC-Clio, [1974]. 453p. (Clio bibliography ser., 3) $40. **CC154**

Nearly 1,700 annotated entries drawn from *America: history and life,* 1954–72. Regional and tribal sections within four main divisions: (1) Pre-Columbian Indian history; (2) Tribal history, 1492–1900; (3) General Indian history, 1492–1900; (4) The Indian in the twentieth century. Index of authors and subjects; list of periodicals abstracted. Z1209.2.N67I52

Johnson, Steven L. Guide to American Indian documents in the Congressional serial set: 1817–1899. N.Y., Clearwater Publ. Co., [1977]. 503p. $30. **CC155**

"A project of the Institute for the Development of Indian Law." —*t.p.*

Lists some 10,649 documents relating to Indian affairs "which were located in the Serial Set volumes from 1817 through 1899."—*p.xv.* A chronological section lists the documents sequentially, giving title and date, citation to the Serial Set, and a brief description of the contents of the document. A subject index, organized mainly by tribal headings, is intended as "an index to the listings and not to the contents of the documents." KF8201.A1J63

Jones, Dorothy Miriam and **Wood, John R.** An Aleut bibliography. [Fairbanks], Inst. of Social, Economic and Govt. Research, Univ. of Alaska, [1975]. 195p. in various pagings. maps. (ISEGR report ser., 44) $15 pa. **CC156**

A selective, annotated survey of English-language materials on Aleut cultural and social life. In four sections: (1) alphabetical list of Aleut literature by author; (2) complete bibliographic information, including annotation; (3) list of literature arranged by time of observation (precontact and aboriginal period, Russian administration to 1867, American administration, 1867 to 1940, contemporary); (4) list organized by broad subject and type of publication. Z1210.A4J6

Laird, W. David. Hopi bibliography, comprehensive and annotated. Tucson, Univ. of Arizona Pr., [1977]. 735p. $13.50; $7.95 pa. **CC157**

An alphabetical listing of over 2,900 published books, articles, and government and church reports on all aspects of Hopi life; excludes book reviews, newspaper articles, audiovisual materials, and most foreign-language publications. Title index and subject index; the latter refers to entries which include in their title the subject named, not necessarily to content of the items listed. Z1210.H6L33

Newberry Library, Chicago. Center for the History of the American Indian. The Newberry Library Center for the History of the American Indian bibliographical series. [Chicago, 1976–] [v.1–] $3.95 per v., pa. (In progress?) **CC158**

Contents: Native American historical demography, by Henry F. Dobyns (1976. 95p.); The Indians of California, by Robert F. Heizer (1976. 68p.); The Indians of the Subarctic, by June Helm (1976. 91p.); The Plains Indians, by E. Adamson Hoebel (1977. 75p.); The Navajos, by Peter Iverson (1976. 64p.); The Ojibwas, by Helen Hornbeck Tanner (1976. 78p.); The Apaches, by Michael E. Melody (1977. 86p.); United States Indian policy, by Francis Paul Prucha (1977. 54p.).

Subtitle: A critical bibliography.

Each volume has two main parts: a bibliographical essay and an alphabetical list of all works cited. There are also two sets of recommended titles: (1) books for beginners; (2) books for a basic library collection. The alphabetical list of all works cited is keyed as to level of suitability, and includes books and periodical articles.

Prucha, Francis Paul. A bibliographical guide to the history of Indian-white relations in the United States. Chicago, Univ. of Chicago Pr., [1977]. 454p. $17.50; $6.95 pa. **CC159**

"A publication of the Center for the History of the American Indian of the Newberry Library."—*t.p.*

A classed bibliography of about 9,700 items; author/subject index. "Emphasis is on United States history, but British colonial Indian affairs have been included."—*Pref.* In two parts: (1) Guides to sources (i.e., reference works on archives, government documents, manuscripts, and similar materials); (2) Classified bibliography of published works through 1974. Z1209.2.U5P67

Sutton, Imre. Indian land tenure: bibliographical essays and a guide to the literature. N.Y., Clearwater, [1975]. 290p. il. $18; $6.95 pa. **CC160**

Presents a series of bibliographical essays in seven areas; (1) Aboriginal occupancy and territoriality; (2) Land cessions and the establishment of reservations; (3) Land administration and land utilization; (4) Aboriginal title and land claims; (5) Title clarification and change; (6) Tenure and jurisdiction; (7) Land tenure and culture change. A final essay compares the Native American experience with that of other post-colonial indigenous groups. Chapter bibliographies refer to the main bibliography, pp.221–76; this is indexed by tribal and geographical indexes. Subject index to the essays. Z1209.2.U5S95

Whiteside, Don. Aboriginal people: a selected bibliography concerning Canada's first people. Ottawa, Nat. Indian Brotherhood, [1973]. 345p. $6.50 pa. **CC161**

Emphasizes unpublished speeches, reports, conference proceedings, newspaper articles, works by aboriginal people (indicated by an asterisk in the author index), and includes a section on the philosophy of aboriginal resistance. A classed list, with author and subject indexes. Z1209.2.C2W46

Wolf, Carolyn E. and **Folk, Karen R.** Indians of North and South America: a bibliography based on the collection at the Willard E. Yager Library-Museum, Hartwick College, Oneonta, N.Y. Metuchen, N.J., Scarecrow Pr., 1977. 576p. $22.50. **CC162**

A main-entry list of over 4,000 books, periodical articles or issues, essays, and analyzed series published before late spring 1976, together with a description of the Yager collection of newspaper clippings. Title, series, and subject indexes. Z1209.W82

Dissertations

Dockstader, Frederick J. and **Dockstader, Alice W.** The American Indian in graduate studies; a bibliography of theses and dissertations. N.Y., Museum of the American Indian, Heye Foundation, 1973–74. 2v. (Museum of the American Indian, Heye Foundation. Contributions, v.25, pts.1–2) $18 pa. **CC163**

Pt.1 of the bibliography was originally published 1957 (*Guide* CC144). It was reprinted 1973 in a 2d ed. omitting the "Addenda," pp.362–64 and the index. Pt.2 covers the period 1955–70; it continues the item numbering from the main section of pt.1 (i.e., beginning with item 3660) and incorporates the addenda from the original volume into the alphabetical author sequence of pt.2. A new index to both volumes is provided. The total number of entries is now 7,446. Dissertations known to be available from University Microfilms are marked with an *M* following the citation. Z1209.D62

North American Indians: a dissertation index. Ann Arbor, Mich., University Microfilms Internatl., 1977. 169p. $28. **CC164**

A keyword index listing over 1,700 doctoral dissertations written between 1904 and 1976, with an author index; both parts supply full bibliographic information. References to abstracts in *Dissertation abstracts international* and order information for dissertations available from University Microfilms are provided. Z1209.N67N67

Encyclopedias and handbooks

Klein, Barry. Reference encyclopedia of the American Indian. 3d ed. Rye, N.Y., Todd Publs., [1978]. 2v. $25. **CC165**

1st ed. 1967 (*Guide* CC151); 2d ed. 1973.

v.1 is a classified directory listing relevant government agencies and associations, museums, and cultural institutions, reservations and tribal councils, educational courses and materials, and an extensive bibliography (arranged by author and subject). v.2 offers biographical sketches of individuals named in the first volume—American Indians prominent in Indian affairs, business, the arts and professions, and non-Indians active in fields related to the study of American Indians. E76.2.R8

Marquis, Arnold. A guide to America's Indians; ceremonials, reservations, and museums. Norman, Univ. of Oklahoma Pr., [1974]. 267p. il. $9.95; $4.95 pa. **CC166**

A brief reference guide to many aspects of American Indian life. Useful maps, tables of tribes and reservations, etc. Bibliography; index. E76.2.M37

Spanish-speaking Americans

Bibliography

Pino, Frank. Mexican Americans; a research bibliography. [East Lansing], Latin American Studies Center, Michigan State Univ., 1974. 2v. $10. **CC167**

The work "is intended as an interdisciplinary guide to the study of the Mexican American" and "includes materials ranging from the early Spanish settlements to the present day activities of the Hispano, Mexican-American and Chicano."—*p.ix.* Lists books, monographs, master's theses, doctoral dissertations, articles in journals, and government publications. Arranged in 35 subject categories, with extensive cross-referencing. Author index, but no detailed subject index. Z1361.M4P55

Talbot, Jane Mitchell and **Cruz, Gilbert R.** A comprehensive Chicano bibliography, 1960–1972. Austin, Tex., Jenkins Publ. Co., 1973. 375p. $9.50. **CC168**

A classed bibliography (books, articles, theses and dissertations, government documents, reports) with author index and a "cross index" indicating materials which relate to other topics in addition to the category in which the citation is placed. Includes audiovisual materials and children's literature. Z1361.M4T34

Trejo, Arnulfo D. Bibliografía chicana; a guide to information sources. Detroit, Gale, [1975]. 193p. (Ethnic studies information guide ser., 1) $18. **CC169**

An annotated guide to more than 300 publications concerning Chicano life and experience. Subject arrangement with author and title indexes. Includes directories of relevant newspapers, periodicals, and publishers. Z1361.M4T73

Woods, Richard D. Reference materials on Mexican Americans: an annotated bibliography. Metuchen, N.J., Scarecrow Pr., 1976. 190p. $7.50. **CC170**

Lists separately published bibliographies and reference-type works (dictionaries, collective biographies, etc.) on Mexican Americans in the United States. 387 entries in classed arrangement, with author, subject, and title indexes. E84.M5W66

WOMEN

Guides

Lynn, Naomi B., Matasar, Ann B. and **Rosenberg, Marie Barovic.** Research guide in women's studies. Morristown, N.J., General Learning Pr., [1974]. 194p. $3.95 pa. **CC171**

A basic guide, mainly at the undergraduate level. Only four chapters deal specifically with women's studies and courses; the remaining six deal with general reference works and subjects such as how to research and write a paper, how to use statistics, etc. Subject index. HQ1206.L96

McKee, Kathleen Burke. Women's studies; a guide to reference sources. Storrs, Conn., Univ. of Connecticut Lib., [1977]. 112p. (Bibliography ser., no.6) $5 pa. **CC172**

"With a supplement on feminist serials in the University of Connecticut Library's Alternative Press Collection, by Joanne V. Akeroyd."—*t.p.*

Arranged by type of publication (guides; library catalogs; handbooks; directories; statistics; indexes, abstracts and bibliographies) with topical subdivisions as appropriate. Author, title, and subject indexes. Based on the collection at the University of Connecticut Library, Storrs. 364 items with annotations. Z7965.M33

Bibliography

See also Suppl. CC114.

Arthur and Elizabeth Schlesinger Library on the History of Women in America. The manuscript inventories and the catalogs of manuscripts, books and pictures. Boston, G. K. Hall, 1973. 3v. $235. **CC173**

Contents: v.1, Book catalog, A–L; v.2, Book catalog, M–Z, Etiquette, Periodicals; v.3, Manuscript catalog, Manuscript inventories, Picture catalog.

Reproduces the subject, title, and author cards for some 12,000 volumes, over 200 collections of personal papers, and 31 archives of women's organizations located at Radcliffe College; books from the Widener Library at Harvard are also listed. Z7965.A78

Bickner, Mei Liang. Women at work; an annotated bibliography. Los Angeles, Manpower Research Center, Inst. of Industrial Relations, Univ. of California, [1974–77]. 2v. $15 pa. **CC174**

A selective bibliography intended "primarily for persons who teach, conduct research, or are serious students in the general area of working women."—*Introd.* Classed arrangement of books, journal articles, government documents, reports, and court decisions; author, title, classed category, and subject indexes. Special attention is paid to minority women, women employed outside the professions, and relevant legal developments. v.1 includes material published 1959–73 ($6); v.2 covers the literature from 1973 to 1975 ($9). Z7963.E7B52

Equal Rights Amendment Project. The equal rights amendment: a bibliographic study. Westport, Conn., Greenwood Pr., [1976]. 367p. $19.95. **CC175**

About 5,800 items arranged by type of media, with author and organization indexes. Provides references to pertinent materials in the microfilm series *Herstory* and *Women and the law* (reel 1). KF4758.A1E6

Frank, Geneviève and **Gaudier, Maryse.** Les implications sociales d'un nouvel ordre économique international: bibliographie sélective. [Geneva, Internatl. Inst. for Labour Studies, 1976] 101p. 10Sw.Fr. pa. **CC176**

Title (*The social implications of a new international economic order: selective bibliography*) and supporting materials also in English.

Prep. for the World Symposium on the Social Implications of a New International Economic Order, Algiers, Jan. 19–23, 1976.

About 1,000 books, articles, and documents in English and French classed by subject: establishment of a new international economic order, development strategies, employment, science and technology, social policy, international organizations and international action. Author index. Z7164.E15F7

Goodwater, Leanna. Women in antiquity: an annotated bibliography. Metuchen, N.J., Scarecrow Pr., 1975. 171p. $7. **CC177**

"Intended as a guide to the political, social, legal, and literary achievements and treatment of women in antiquity . . . specifically ancient Greece and Rome, . . . the Minoans, Etruscans, the Hellenistic kingdoms, and some provinces of the Roman Empire" (*Pref.*), this work omits material on women in Africa or the Near East, as well as Cleopatra, Christian saints, and literary material on Sappho. Its two main sections cover (1) ancient sources by and about women and women authors and (2) modern works. Indexes by personal names of classical women, and by authors, editors, and translators. Z7961.G66

Haber, Barbara. Women in America: a guide to books, 1963–1975. Boston, G. K. Hall, [1978]. 202p. $18. **CC178**

Intended for "college teachers not familiar with recent literature on women's issues who would like to incorporate such material into introductory courses; librarians interested in building a core collection in women's studies; undergraduate students, and general readers who might welcome some guidance in structuring independent reading programs."—*Introd.* Excludes literary works and reference books. Broad subject arrangement; all entries are annotated. Name/title index. Z7964.U49H3

Harrison, Cynthia. Women's movement media: a source guide. N.Y., Bowker, 1975. 269p. $14.95 pa. **CC179**

". . . includes approximately 550 descriptions of organizations, arranged by function, type or main interest of the group, which supply books, periodicals, films, tapes, records, services, and information on and for women."—*Pref.* Sections for: (1) Publishers, distributors, news services, and products; (2) Women's research centers and library research collections; (3) Women's organizations and centers; (4) Governmental and quasi-governmental organizations and agencies; (5) Special interests. Geographic index; media title index; name index of groups; subject index of groups. Z7964.U49H37

Hughes, Marija Matich. The sexual barrier: legal, medical, economic and social aspects of sex discrimination. Wash., Hughes Pr., [1977]. 843p. $40. **CC180**

A revised and enlarged ed. of the author's earlier volumes of similar title (San Francisco, 1970; Suppl. 1–2, 1971–72). It groups more than 8,000 English-language books, articles, pamphlets and documents of the 1960–75 period into 17 subject chapters which are further subdivided by specific topic and/or geographic region. Many brief annotations. Principal strength is the comprehensive treatment of legal issues affecting women; the detailed listing of materials on women in specific occupations is another distinctive and useful feature. KF4758.A1H83

Jacobs, Sue-Ellen. Women in perspective; a guide for cross-cultural studies. Urbana, Univ. of Illinois Pr., [1974]. 299p. $8.95; $3.45 pa. **CC181**

An extensive and important bibliography of book and periodical materials, dissertations, etc. In two main sections: (1) Geographical topics and (2) Subject topics, the first section subdivided by country or region, the second by specific subject. Author index and detailed table of contents, but no subject index. Z7961.J33

Knaster, Meri. Women in Spanish America: an annotated bibliography from pre-conquest to contemporary times. Boston, G. K. Hall, [1977]. 696p. $38. **CC182**

More than 2,500 items in classed arrangement, with author and subject indexes. Unpublished doctoral dissertations and master's theses are separately listed without annotations. A geographic index would have been helpful. Z7964.L3K525

Kratochvil, Laura and **Shaw, Shauna.** African women: a select bibliography. Cambridge, Eng., African Studies Centre, [1974]. [74p.] £1.25 pa. **CC183**

A classed list of more than 1,200 items. International in scope. Items are keyed as to regions covered. Regional and author indexes. Z7964.A3K7

Krichmar, Albert. The women's movement in the seventies; an international English-language bibliography. [With the assistance of] Virginia Carlson Smith and Ann E. Wiederrecht. Metuchen, N.J., Scarecrow Pr., 1977. 875p. $30. **CC184**

Lists some 8,600 "English-language publications concerning the status of women in nearly 100 countries.... The emphasis is on change, attempted change, and continuing problems confronting women in the countries in which they live."—*Introd.* Includes doctoral dissertations, books, pamphlets, research reports, periodical articles, and government documents published or reprinted 1970–75," plus some 1976 publications. Geographical arrangement, with topical subdivisions under those countries or areas about which there is a considerable quantity of literature. Author and subject indexes; numerous annotations. Z7961.K57

Phelps, Ann T., Farmer, Helen S. and **Backer, Thomas E.** New career options for women: a selected annotated bibliography. N.Y., Human Sciences Pr., [1977]. 144p. $9.95. **CC185**

A classed bibliography of 240 English-language books, journal articles and government reports published since 1970, designed to complement *New career options for women; a counselor's sourcebook* (N.Y., Human Sciences Pr., 1977). Stresses information useful to career counselors for women, covering topics such as types of work (professional, part-time, crafts, management), education and apprenticeship programs, effects on children of a working mother, other social, biological and psychological factors, and legal issues. Author and title indexes. Z7164.V6P48

al-Qazzaz, Ayad. Women in the Middle East and North Africa: an annotated bibliography. Austin, Center for Middle Eastern Studies, [1977]. 178p. (Middle East monographs, no.2) $5 pa. **CC186**

Includes English-language books, essays in books, periodical articles, conference reports, pamphlets, and unpublished papers. Author listing with country and subject indexes. Z7964.N42Q38

Rosenberg, Marie Barovic and **Bergstrom, Len V.** Women and society: a critical review of the literature with a selected annotated bibliography. Beverly Hills, Sage Publs., [1975]. 345p. **CC187**

The "Introduction: a selective review of the literature" is a 20-page survey of classic books on women in history, women at work, and women in politics; the remainder of the volume cites 3,600 books, articles, documents, periodicals and newspapers, and women's collections and libraries grouped into large subject areas; most chapters have more detailed subject breakdowns. Brief annotations. Indexed by authors, journal issues devoted to women, persons, places, subjects.

Continued by: Z7961.R67

Een, JoAnn Delores and **Rosenberg-Dishman, Marie B.** Women and society, citations 3601 to 6000: an annotated bibliography. Beverly Hills, Sage Publs., [1978]. 275p. $17.50. **CC188**

Retains the basic organization of the preceding work while adding sections on the political status of women and women's handbooks and almanacs, and omitting sections on women's collections and libraries and women's periodicals and newspapers. Indexed by authors, places and topics, with a special index of journal issues or sections devoted to women. Z7961.E4

Soltow, Martha Jane and **Wery, Mary K.** American women and the labor movement, 1825–1974: an annotated bibliography. Metuchen, N.J., Scarecrow Pr., 1976. 247p. $8. **CC189**

A revised edition of *Women in American labor history* (East Lansing, Mich., 1972).

Classed arrangement under the following main headings: (1) Employment; (2) Trade unions; (3) Working conditions; (4) Strikes; (5) Legislation; (6) Worker education; (7) Labor leaders; (8) Supportive efforts. Author and subject indexes. Z7963.E7S635

Stanwick, Kathy and **Li, Christine.** The political participation of women in the United States: a selected bibliography, 1950–1976. Metuchen, N.J., Scarecrow Pr., 1977. 160p. $6.50. **CC190**

Comp. by Center for the American Woman and Politics, Eagleton Institute of Politics, Rutgers–The State University of New Jersey.

Expansion and updating of the Center's *Women and American politics; a selected bibliography, 1965–1974* (New Brunswick, N.J., 1974). More than 1,500 entries grouped by type, with biographical and author indexes, but no topical subject approach. Includes substantial amounts of unpublished material and research in progress. Z7961.S74

Wheeler, Helen Rippier. Womanhood media supplement: additional current resources about women. Metuchen, N.J., Scarecrow Pr., 1975. 482p. $15. **CC191**

For the basic volume *see Guide* CC166.

"... continues the media and other resource parts of the 1972 volume, i.e., its Part III, 'A Basic Book Collection,' IV, 'Non-Book Resources,' and V, 'Directory of Sources.' "—*Introd.* Z7961.W48

Women in medicine; a bibliography of the literature on women physicians. Comp. and ed. by Sandra L. Chaff [and others]. Metuchen, N.J., Scarecrow Pr., 1977. 1124p. $35. **CC192**

"This work provides citations to literature which documents [the] increasing involvement of women in medicine, and examines the causes and future course of this trend. It includes, also, material about the lives of specific women physicians and helps provide insight into how the careers of most women physicians have differed from those of their male colleagues."—*Introd.* About 4,000 entries in classed arrangement, representing literature from the 18th century through 1975. International in scope. Author, subject, and personal name indexes. Z7963.M43W65

Handbooks and directories

Directory of Indian women today. Chief ed., Ajeet Cour; ed., Arpana Cour. [New Delhi], India Internatl. Publs., [1976]. various paging. il. R.125. **CC193**

Brief biographies and photographs of more than 6,000 living Indian women, arranged by professions, with a name index. A "Facts and views" section includes essays on Indian women in various professions; "Social welfare organisations" is a directory arranged by state. HQ1742.A3D55

Handbook of international data on women. [By] Elise Boulding [and others]. [Los Angeles], Sage Publs.; N.Y., Halsted Pr., [1976]. 468p. $25. **CC194**

Presents data derived from the United Nations and the Institute of Behavioral Science, University of Colorado, on: general economic activity; economic activity by status; economic activity by industry; economic activity by occupation; literacy and education; migration; marital status; life, death, and reproduction; political and civic participation; and a world overview of national statistics. For much of the data 1968 is the mean year. HQ1115.H36

Rutgers University, New Brunswick, N.J. Center for the American Woman and Politics. Women in public office: a biographical directory and statistical analysis. N.Y., Bowker, 1976. 455p. $19.95. **CC195**

Comp. by Center for the American Woman and Politics, Eagleton Institute of Politics, Rutgers–The State University of New Jersey.

The first edition of what is intended to be an ongoing series. Provides a directory of "women holding public office in the United States during 1974 and the first half of 1975."—*Introd.* Includes the following offices: U.S. Congress, state executive offices, state cabinet offices, state legislatures, state boards and commissions, state appellate and trial courts of general jurisdiction, county commissions, townships, mayoralties, city councils. Arranged by state, with the higher offices listed first. Name index. Introductory matter includes state summaries of numbers of women in office, and a profile of women holding office. HQ1391.U5R88

Schlachter, Gail Ann. Directory of financial aids for women. Los Angeles, Reference Service Pr., [1978]. 200p. $15.95. **CC196**

Subtitle: A listing of: scholarships, fellowships, loans, grants, internships, awards and prizes designed primarily or exclusively for women; women's credit unions; sources of state educational benefits; and reference sources on financial aids.

Aids are listed according to the categories mentioned in the subtitle; the "reference sources" section is an "Annotated bibliography of general financial aids directories," pp. 157–92. Subject index. HQ1381.S36

U.S. Bureau of the Census. A statistical portrait of women in the U.S. [Wash.], 1976. 90p. (Current population reports: special studies: ser. P–23, no.58) $2.10 pa. **CC197**

Offers a wide range of statistical information drawn from U.S. government sources. Chapters on: population; longevity, mortality and health; residence and migration; marital and family status; fertility; education; labor force participation; occupation and industry; work experience; income and poverty status; voting and public office holding; crime and victimization; black women; Spanish women. Detailed table of contents, but no index. HQ1420.A52

U.S. Women's Bureau. Handbook of facts on women workers. [Wash.], 1948– . (*Its* Bulletin 225–) (1975 ed.: $4.70 pa.) **CC198**

The 1975 ed. (*Bulletin* 297; 435p.) is in three parts: (1) women in the labor force, their occupations, income, and training; (2) laws governing women's employment and status; (3) national and international organizations interested in the advancement of women. HD6093.A35

Who's who and where in women's studies. Ed. by Tamar Berkowitz, Jean Mangi and Jane Williamson. [Old Westbury, N.Y.], Feminist Pr., 1974. 308p. $12.50; $7.50 pa. **CC199**

A directory of American colleges and universities with information on their course offerings in women's studies is followed by a faculty list with address and titles of courses taught. There is also a list of courses by academic department. Information is updated periodically in *Women's studies newsletter.* HQ1181.U5W48

C D

Anthropology and Ethnology

BIBLIOGRAPHY

General

Divale, William Tulio. Warfare in primitive societies: a bibliography. [Rev. ed.] Santa Barbara, Calif., ABC-Clio, [1973]. (War/peace bibliography ser., 2) $4.95 pa. **CD1**

1st ed. 1971.

Pt.I is divided into sixteen theoretical or topical sections (biological factors, demographic factors, scalping, war ceremonies, etc.); pt.II comprises sections on seven major geographical regions (four of which are further subdivided by area), and lists sources on the warfare of the various peoples of these regions. Author and tribal name indexes. Z5118.W3D57

Favazza, Armando R. and **Oman, Mary.** Anthropological and cross-cultural themes in mental health; an annotated bibliography, 1925–1974. Columbia, Univ. of Missouri Pr., 1977. 386p. $30. (Univ. of Missouri studies, v.65) **CD2**

Includes over 3,600 English-language periodical articles. Chronological arrangement, with author and subject indexes. The introduction provides a most interesting review of the cultural areas and specific themes included. RC455.4.E8F38

Harvard University. Peabody Museum of Archaeology and Ethnology. Library. Catalogue: authors. Supplement 3. Boston, G. K. Hall, 1975. 3v. **CD3**

——— Catalogue: subjects. Supplement 3. Boston, G. K. Hall, 1975. 4v.

For main set and earlier supplements *see Guide* CD5.

These supplements to the author and subject catalogs include more than 130,000 entries, representing about 27,000 volumes added 1971–75.

Jones, J. Owen and **Jones, Elizabeth A.** Index of human ecology. London, Europa Pub., [1974]. 169p. $19. **CD4**

"The purpose of the Index . . . is to provide a convenient, compact tool for cross-disciplinary literature search and retrieval in human ecology."—*p.10.* Pt.I lists for each related discipline the principal "secondary journals," i.e., abstract journals and indexes. Pt.II describes these sources and their "complementary services," e.g., review articles, regular special features, translation services, computerized retrieval services. Selection criteria for titles included are: world coverage, English-language, inclusion of abstracts. Consolidated subject index. Z5861.J65

Kemper, Robert V. and **Phinney, John F. S.** The history of anthropology: a research bibliography. N.Y., Garland, 1977. 212p. $20. **CD5**

A classed bibliography of more than 2,400 entries arranged in five major sections: (1) general sources; (2) background (largely pre-1900); (3) modern anthropology; (4) related social sciences; (5) bibliographical sources. Each major section is further subdivided by subject, geographic area, and personality. Author index. Z5111.K44

Lapointe, François H. and **Lapointe, Claire C.** Claude Lévi-Strauss and his critics: an international bibliography of criticism (1950–1976) followed by a bibliography of the writings of Claude Lévi-Strauss. N.Y., Garland, 1977. 219p. $23. **CD6**

Pt.I lists books, reviews and unpublished theses and dissertations on Lévi-Strauss, works giving a "general presentation," titles devoted to a single work of Lévi-Strauss, materials comparing him with other figures, and works arranged by subject. Pt.II is a chronological bibliography of his writings, including translations. Covers through June 1975. Author and name index. Z8504.35.L36

Rosenstiel, Annette. Education and anthropology: an annotated bibliography. N.Y., Garland, 1977. 646p. $55. **CD7**

An international bibliography of 3,435 books, periodical articles, dissertations, papers, reprints, etc., "reflecting (1) historical influences, (2) current trends, (3) theoretical concerns, and (4) practical methodology at the interfaces of these two disciplines."—*Introd.* Author arrangement, with English translations provided for foreign-language titles. Covers the literature from 1689 to 1976. Topical subject and name indexes. Z5814.E2R67

Dissertations

See also Suppl. CD18.

McDonald, David R. Masters' theses in anthropology: a bibliography of theses from United States colleges and universities. New Haven, HRAF Pr., 1977. 453p. **CD8**

A list of more than 3,700 titles, arranged by broad subjects—social/cultural anthropology, archaeology, physical anthropology, linguistics. Indexed by subject, ethnic group, geographical area, cross-cultural studies, author, and educational institution. Z5111.M26

Manuscripts and archives

Smithsonian Institution. National Museum of Natural History. Department of Anthropology. Catalog to manuscripts at the National Anthropological Archives. Boston, G. K. Hall, 1975. 4v. $310. **CD9**

A photographic reproduction of catalog cards representing documents collected by the Bureau of American Ethnology between 1879 and 1965. In three divisions: (1) an alphabetical file on the Indians of North America north of Mexico; (2) a smaller geographical file on peoples of Mexico, Central America, and non-North American areas; (3) a numerical file indicating the subject under which cards have been filed in the other two divisions. Subject approach is by tribe, linguistic group, or name of individual.

The Americas

See also Suppl. CC104, CC151–CC166.

Murdock, George Peter and **O'Leary, Timothy J.** Ethnographic bibliography of North America. 4th ed. New Haven, Human Relations Area Files Pr., 1975. 5v. $175. **CD10**

Contents: v.1, General North America; v.2, Arctic and subarctic; v.3, Far West and Pacific coast; v.4, Eastern United States; v.5, Plains and Southwest.

3d ed. 1960 (*Guide* CD28).

Computer produced; contains about 40,000 entries for books and articles on the native ethnic groups of North America. This edition shows an expanded number of ethnic group bibliographies (especially for the North Mexican area) which have been added to correspond to the *Handbook of North American Indians* (*Suppl.* CD25). New bibliographies on Pan-Indianism, urban Indians, Canadian Indians, and United States and Canadian government relations with the native peoples. The "General introduction" supplies excellent discussion of sources of materials not included: government publications, ERIC documents, theses and dissertations, manuscripts and archives, nonprint materials and maps, and general bibliographic sources. Z1209.2.N67M87

Storck, Peter L. A preliminary bibliography of early man in eastern North America, 1839–1973. [Toronto], Royal Ontario Museum, [1975]. 110p. (Archaeology monograph, 4) $3 pa. **CD11**

"This bibliography contains 1242 . . . journal articles, reviews, monographs, and books dealing in whole or in part with the subject of Early Man in eastern North America" (*Introd.*), i.e., early and late Palaeo-Indian and possible antecedent cultures in Canadian provinces east of Manitoba and the United States east of the Mississippi River. Author listing, with geographic, subject, and site-locality indexes. Z1208.N6S77

Africa

Anthropology of southern Africa in periodicals to 1950: an analysis and index. Comp. under direction of N. J. van Warmelo. Johannesburg, Witwatersrand Univ. Pr., 1977. 1484p. map. R.60. **CD12**

A chronological list of periodical articles, from 1795 to 1950; each entry gives bibliographic citation and list of subjects, tribes and ethnic groups, place-names, and persons covered, with coded notation as to fullness of information. Indexed by linguistic group, place-name, and author; the linguistic group index is further subdivided by subject, tribe and group, and person. "The field covered by indices is the history, anthropology, and linguistics of the Bantu ethnic groups of Southern Africa (South Africa, Botswana, Lesotho, and Swaziland), whilst only bibliographies [Pt.4 of the book] cover the adjacent areas."—*Introd.* Z5113.A56

Armer, Michael. African social psychology: a review and annotated bibliography. N.Y., Africana Publishing Co., [1975]. 321p. (African bibliography ser., 2) $30. **CD13**

863 abstracts are grouped in five broad subject divisions: (1) Attitudes, values, and aspirations [covering such areas as occupation, education, politics, health, the family, religion]; (2) Personality types, traits, and abnormalities; (3) Personality development, change, and adjustment [acculturation, modernization, etc.]; (4) Psychological structures and processes; (5) Methods, techniques, and bibliographies. Author, country, and cross-classification (i.e., cross reference) indexes. Z7165.A4A75

Baldwin, David E. and **Baldwin, Charlene M.** The Yoruba of Southwestern Nigeria: an indexed bibliography. Boston, G. K. Hall, [1976]. 269p. $25.50. **CD14**

Lists, alphabetically by author, articles, books, and other publications on Southwestern Nigeria of "geographical, geological, agricultural, zoological, biological, sociological, and anthropological" interest. Literary works by Yoruba authors are also included. Subject index. Z3597.B34

Neser, L. Zulu ethnography: a classified bibliography. [KwaDlangezwa], publ. for the KwaZula Documentation Centre by the Univ. of Zululand, 1976. 92*l.* (Publications, Univ. of Zululand: Ser.3, Specialized publications, 18) $3.50. **CD15**

Includes books, articles, chapters in books, theses, dissertations and manuscripts. Author index. Z3608.E85N47

Asia

Bibliography of anthropology of India (including index to current literature). Ed. by N. C. Choudhury; comp. by Shyamal Kumar Ray. Calcutta, Anthropological Survey of India, [1976]– . v.1– . (In progress) (v.1: R.29.) **CD16**

Contents: v.1, 1960–1964.

An international classed bibliography of books and articles, largely in the English language, published during the period indicated. Broad subject arrangement, with items listed alphabetically by author within classes. Four indexes: author, ethnic or population group, geographical or Indian state, and regional (pertaining to more than one state). Further volumes are planned.

Kanitkar, Helen A. An anthropological bibliography of South Asia . . . together with a directory of anthropological field research comp. by Elizabeth von Fürer-Haimendorf. The Hague, Mouton, [1976–]. New ser., v.1– . **CD17**

Contents: v.1, 1965–1969 ($38).

The continuation of a work with the same title by E. von Fürer-Haimendorf (*Guide* CD42), now compiled and edited in the School of Oriental and African Studies, University of London. Arrangement remains the same, but physical anthropology and prehistoric archaeology have been dropped; tribal welfare and problems, urbanization and industrialization, values and attitudes, political sociology and sociolinguistics have been added. Appendixes on social and cultural anthropology of South Asians overseas, and ethnology of India as depicted in literature to 1750 A.D. Author and field research indexes. Z5115.K35

Australia, New Zealand, and Oceania

See also Suppl. CD28.

Coppell, William George. World catalogue of theses and dissertations about the Australian Aborigines and Torres Strait Islanders. Sydney, Sydney Univ. Pr., [1977]. 113p. $12.50. **CD18**

A provisional edition appeared in the Australian Institute of Aboriginal Studies *Newsletter,* n.s., no.2:32–52 (1974).

"The catalogue is very largely confined to works presented at universities, except that several diploma theses presented at other tertiary education institutions have been included, where they are of particular interest in the field of Aboriginal studies."—*Introd.* Author listing with subject index; cutoff date is June 1976. Z5116.C66

Hays, Terence A. Anthropology in the New Guinea highlands: an annotated bibliography. N.Y., Garland, 1976. 238p. $23. **CD19**

Entries are grouped into broad subject chapters: (1) general, including reference works, surveys, and material by non-anthropologists; (2) social and cultural anthropology; (3) linguistics; (4) prehistory; (5) physical anthropology; (6) physical environment. Includes books, scholarly articles, master's theses, and doctoral dissertations completed through 1974. Author and ethnolinguistic group indexes. Z5116.H38

Marshall, Mac and **Nason, James D.** Micronesia 1944–1974; a bibliography of anthropological and related source materials. New Haven, HRAF Pr., 1975. 337p. $15. **CD20**

An author listing of book and periodical materials, with a "Guide to topics and areas" serving as a topical index. The Gilbert Islands (because British-controlled rather than part of the Trust Territory administered by the United States) are omitted from the compilers' definition of Micronesia. Includes some unpublished papers and doctoral dissertations, but no government documents. Z5116.M37

Potter, Michelle. Traditional law in Papua New Guinea: an annotated and selected bibliography. Canberra, Australian Nat. Univ., Dept. of Law, Research School of Social Sciences, 1973. 132p. maps. $3.95 pa. **CD21**

An author arrangement of 283 periodical articles. Each entry contains a brief summary and shows which groups and subjects are discussed. Indexed by group, alphabetic subject, and systematic subject. All indexes are divided into "Index A," dealing with traditional law in general, and "Index B," dealing with changes in the traditional law as a result of outside influences. Cutoff date is 1970.

Europe

O'Leary, Timothy J. and **Steffens, Joan.** Lapps ethnographic bibliography. New Haven, Human Relations Area Files, 1975. 2v. $20.25 pa. **CD22**

A computer-produced list of more than 1,421 books, periodical articles, and chapters from collected works. Each entry is composed of three parts: (1) the standard bibliographic citation; (2) coded descriptive notes on bibliography, cataloging source, format, language; (3) content analysis relative to dates covered, Lapps regional and cultural types discussed, geographic area and site, date of fieldwork, social unit involved, primary or secondary nature of data, author's background, and language used. Indexed by *Outline of cultural materials* (OCM); by author, sub-group, geographic location; by field date and bibliography date.

Sanders, Irwin Taylor, Whitaker, Roger and **Bisselle, Walter C.** East European peasantries: social relations; an annotated bibliography of periodical articles. Boston, G. K. Hall, [1976]. 179p. $12. **CD23**

"Titles included . . . refer to periodical articles collected and bound in thirty volumes by countries . . . in Mugar Library at Boston University."—*Introd.* Geographical arrangement, with annotations. No index. Z7165.E82S26

DICTIONARIES AND ENCYCLOPEDIAS

Encyclopedia of anthropology. Ed. by David E. Hunter and Phillip Whitten. N.Y., Harper & Row, [1976]. 411p. il. $7.95 pa. **CD24**

Intended for the student and instructor in anthropology. About 1,400 entries "ranging in length from 25 to 3,000 words."—*Pref.* Many articles are signed by the contributors; some have brief bibliographies appended. Includes biographies, but no ethnographic articles on cultural groups. GN11.E52

HANDBOOKS

Handbook of North American Indians. Wash., Smithsonian Institution, 1978– . v.8. il., maps. (In progress) **CD25**

William C. Sturtevant, gen. ed.

Contents: v.8, California, Robert F. Heizer, vol. ed. (800p., $13.50).

v.8 is the first published part of a 20v. set planned to give "an encyclopedic summary of what is known about the prehistory, history, and cultures of the aboriginal peoples of North America who lived to the north of the urban civilizations of central Mexico."—*Pref.* The volume consists of 44 chapters by scholars on individual tribes or groups of closely related tribes, and 25 chapters on historical research, archaeology, linguistics, intergroup conflict, arts and crafts, religion and mythology, societal roles and organization, treaties and litigation, and 20th-century secular movements. Tribal sketches are followed by a brief list of sources; the bibliography is pp.721–68. Indexed.

Other volumes are to cover: [1] Introduction, methodology, sources, and continental summaries; [2] Indian and Eskimo communities in the twentieth century; [3] Environmental and biological backgrounds, physical anthropology, and earliest prehistoric cultures; [4] History of Indian-white relations; [5–7] and [9–15] will deal with major culture areas other than California; [16] Technology and the visual arts; [17] Native languages; [18–19] Biographical dictionary; [20] Cumulative index. E77.H25

Muslim peoples; a world ethnographic survey. Richard V. Weekes, ed.in-chief. Westport, Conn., Greenwood Pr., [1977]. 546p. $35. **CD26**

An alphabetical arrangement of brief survey articles on some 300 ethnic groups throughout the world which have been identified as wholly or partly Muslim. Articles are signed, and each carries a bibliography of English-language materials. The work is "designed primarily for the English-speaking nonspecialist, whether academician or layman."—*Introd.* Bibliographic entries are " 'recent,' that is, since 1945," and the bibliographies "concentrate on works related to current patterns of living—the theme of this survey." DS35.625.A1M87

Sixty cultures: a guide to the HRAF probability sample files. Robert O. Lagacé, ed. Appendix by David Levinson. New Haven, Human Relations Area Files, 1977– . Pt.A– . (In progress; Pt.A: $20) **CD27**

Pt.A consists of profiles of each of the sixty cultural groups which constitute the HRAF Probability Sample Files. Each profile includes a summary of information on the culture, a general review of the sources processed for that file (usually with evaluative comments), a bibliographic list of sources processed, and a list of other sources cited which have not been processed for the file. Pt.B will include an additional sixty cultures. Subject index. GN307.S59

Tindale, Norman Barnett. Aboriginal tribes of Australia: their terrain, environmental controls, distribution, limits, and proper names. Berkeley, Univ. of California Pr., 1974. 404p. il., maps. $35. **CD28**

"The principal theme of this book . . . , after first giving an outline picture of these people and their ways of life, is focused on telling as much as has been learned of the distribution, size, composition, and dynamics of the Australian tribes and the history of the aborigines. . . ."—*Introd.* Includes a lengthy bibliography. Appendix on Tasmanian tribes by Rhys Jones. GN665.T56

C E

Mythology

GREEK AND ROMAN

Harnsberger, Caroline Thomas. Gods and heroes: a quick guide to the occupations, associations and experiences of the

Greek and Roman gods and heroes. Troy, N.Y., Whitston, 1977. 396p. $20. **CE1**

The main body of the work is arranged alphabetically by terms denoting occupations, characteristics, attributes, etc., with the names of gods and goddesses associated with the term listed thereunder, together with a brief explanation of the association. An index of the names of the deities and heroes refers to the term associated with each.

Kravitz, David. Who's who in Greek and Roman mythology. N.Y., C. N. Potter; distr. by Crown, [1976]. 246p. il. $10; $3.95 pa. **CE2**

Published 1975 by New English Library, London, under title: *The dictionary of Greek & Roman mythology.*

A dictionary of very brief definitions of characters, places, themes, etc., associated with Greek and Roman mythology. Emphasizes the family relationships of its subjects, sometimes providing tables of "lovers" and "children of the union." For major deities, includes epithets, iconography, associations, festivals, and places of worship. BL715.K7

Peradotto, John Joseph. Classical mythology; an annotated bibliographical survey. Urbana, Ill., Amer. Philological Assoc., 1973. 76p. $2.50 pa. **CE3**

A "bibliographical survey, which is offered as a set of possible tools—for whatever kind of mythology course (even at the graduate level)."—*Introd.* Presented as a series of brief, evaluative essays on selected works covering various aspects of the study of mythology. Works are rated according to a code indicating suitability for college-level courses.

C F

Folklore and Popular Customs

GENERAL WORKS

Guides

Brunvand, Jan Harold. Folklore; a study and research guide. N.Y., St. Martin's Pr., [1976]. 144p. $10.95; $3.95 pa. **CF1**

Intended as a guide "for the beginner, chiefly the college undergraduate."—*Introd.* In three main sections: (1) The subject in context; (2) Reference guide; (3) The research paper. The "Reference guide" is a bibliographic essay on the tools for folklore research. Glossary; index. Z5981.B78

Bibliography

Cornell University. Libraries. Catalogue of the Witchcraft Collection in the Cornell University Library. Millwood, N.Y., KTO Pr., 1977. 644p. $95. **CF2**

Introduction by Rossell Hope Robbins; ed. by Martha J. Crowe; index by Jane Marsh Dieckmann.

Reproduces approximately 12,000 catalog cards for the 2,900 printed works and manuscripts in the collection. "The main topics included are demonic possession, theological and legal disputation, witchcraft trials, and torture. Not included in the collection are materials dealing largely or solely with alchemy, astrology, cabala, magic, the occult, prophecies, and superstition."—*Pref.* Author/title list, with separate subject index. Z6878.W8C67

Dundes, Alan. Folklore theses and dissertations in the United States. Austin, Tex., publ. for the Amer. Folklore Soc. by the Univ. of Texas Pr., [1976]. 610p. (Publs. of the Amer. Folklore Soc., bibliographical and special ser., 27) $15. **CF3**

A chronological listing of doctoral dissertations and master's theses from 1860 through 1968. Indexed by author, subject, and institution. Z5981.D85

Current

Folklore bibliography for 1973– . Bloomington, Ind., Folklore Institute, Indiana Univ., 1975– . Annual. (Folklore Inst. monograph ser., 28–) **CF4**

Volumes for 1973 and 1974 (publ. 1975–77) comp. by Merle E. Simmons. Continues the annual bibliography formerly published in *Southern folklore quarterly* (*Guide* CF13).

Dictionaries and handbooks

Briggs, Katharine Mary. Encyclopedia of fairies, hobgoblins, brownies, bogies, and other supernatural creatures. N.Y., Pantheon Books, [1976]. 481p. il. $12.95. **CF5**

First published under title: *A dictionary of fairies.*

For the most part, treats fairies of the British Isles, with mention of foreign fairies "for comparison or elucidation."—*Pref.* Numerous cross references. Bibliography; index of types and motifs to the folktales recounted in the text. GR549.B74

Gordon, Lesley. Green magic: flowers, plants & herbs in lore & legend. N.Y., Viking Pr., [1977]. 200p. il. $14.95. **CF6**

Narrative chapters on such topics as: Christian flower legends; herbals and herbalists; plants of love, hate and blood; a few flowers from Shakespeare; political and historical flowers. Provides a cross-register for plants and the sentiments they express. Bibliography; index. GR780.G67

THE AMERICAS

Flanagan, Cathleen C. and **Flanagan, John T.** American folklore: a bibliography, 1950–1974. Metuchen, N.J., Scarecrow Pr., 1977. 406p. $16. **CF7**

Concerned "only with verbal folklore: more specifically ballads, folk songs, myths, legends, tales, superstitions, beliefs, cures, proverbs, riddles, and the like."—*Pref.* Sections for "Festschriften, symposia, collections," "Bibliography, dictionaries, archives," "Folklore: study and teaching," and "General folklore" are followed by sections arranged by type of material treated. Author index, but none of detailed subjects. About 3,600 items. Supplements Haywood's *Bibliography of North American folklore and folksong* (*Guide* CF24). Z5984.U6F55

Fowke, Edith. Folklore of Canada. [Toronto], McClelland and Stewart, [1976]. 349p. $10.95. **CF8**

An anthology of fairy-tales, legends, jokes, myths, tall tales, riddles, and songs, grouped by ethnic source: native peoples, Canadians, Anglo-Canadians, and other groups. Sources are noted. Extensive bibliography. Indexed by tale types; motifs; contributors and informants; general index. GR113.F67

Heisley, Michael. An annotated bibliography of Chicano folklore from the Southwestern United States. Los Angeles, produced for and distr. by the Center for the Study of Comparative Folklore and Mythology, Univ. of California, [1977]. 188p. **CF9**

A classed bibliography with author, geographical, and subject indexes. Each subject section is subdivided as (1) published works and (2) theses and dissertations. Slightly more than 1,000 items. Z5984.U6H45

Reader's Digest. American folklore and legend. Pleasantville, N.Y., Reader's Digest Assoc., [1978]. 448p. il. $14.95. **CF10**

Anthology of popular stories, poems, songs, and folklore following a chronological arrangement. Also gives a state-by-state calendar of folk events in America, with brief description and source of further information. Indexed.

EUROPE

Hole, Christina. British folk customs. London, Hutchinson, [1976]. 232p. il., map. £6.95. **CF11**

An alphabetical arrangement of brief articles on customs chosen on the basis of intrinsic interest, importance, length of their history, etc. Some articles have bibliographical references, and there is also a select bibliography. A calendar groups events by dates, and a map shows locations mentioned in the text, whether historic or contemporary. Index.

Lockwood, Yvonne R. Yugoslav folklore: an annotated bibliography of contributions in English. San Francisco, [R and E Research Associates], 1976. 82p. $8 pa. **CF12**

An author listing of about 600 items. Indexes of genres and of ethnic groups. Z5984.Y8L6

AFRICA

Coughlan, Margaret N. Folklore from Africa to the United States: an annotated bibliography. Wash., Lib. of Congress, 1976. 161p. il. $4.50. **CF13**

A selective listing of folklore collections, linguistic, ethnological, and anthropological studies, travel accounts and government reports containing tales. The arrangement is geographical, from general sub-Saharan Africa through regions of Africa to the West Indies and the United States; within each region, the material is grouped as studies and collections for adults, and collections for children. Lengthy annotations. Author-title index. Z5984.A35C68

HOLIDAYS

Festivals sourcebook. Paul Wasserman, managing ed. Detroit, Gale, 1977. 656p. $45. **CF14**

Subtitle: A reference guide to fairs, festivals and celebrations in agriculture, antiques, the arts, theater and drama, arts and crafts, community, dance, ethnic events, film, folk, food and drink, history, Indians, marine, music, seasons, and wildlife.

Covers events in the United States and Canada. Arranged according to the categories mentioned in the subtitle, then by state and province. Includes a chronological listing of events, an event name index, geographic index, and subject index. GT4802.F47

Gregory, Ruth Wilhelme. Anniversaries and holidays. 3d ed. Chicago, Amer. Lib. Assoc., 1975. 246p. $10.50. **CF15**

"A revision of the work by Mary Emogene Hazeltine."—*t.p.*

2d ed. by M. E. Hazeltine publ. 1944 (*Guide* CF49).

"The 1975 edition includes 1,690 full or partial holidays and special-observance days.... The total number of entries in the third edition is 2,736 as compared with 1,764 in the second edition. These entries identify anniversaries and holidays in 152 countries."—*Pref.* In three sections: (1) Calendar of fixed dates; (2) Calendar of movable days; and (3) Books relating to anniversaries and holidays. Index to pts.1–2. Includes brief information about the origin or method of celebrating the holiday, or identification or significance of the person or event commemorated. GT3930.H38

ETIQUETTE

McCaffree, Mary Jane and **Innis, Pauline B.** Protocol: the complete handbook of diplomatic, official, and social usage. Englewood Cliffs, N.J., Prentice-Hall, [1977]. 414p. il. $14.95. **CF16**

"The purpose of this book is to help the newcomer to official life . . . to learn and understand the rules of protocol and to serve as a reference for the person whose life is governed . . . by the practices and policies of protocol."—*Pref.* Stresses everyday usage of protocol in the United States, covering order of precedence, titles and forms of address, calling and calling cards, invitations and replies, official entertaining and private parties, places to entertain, table seating arrangements, White House entertaining, the diplomatic corps, ceremonies, flag etiquette, and women in public and official life. Bibliography. Subject index. BJ1853.M23

C G

Statistics

GENERAL WORKS

Guides and bibliographies

United Nations. Statistical Office. Directory of international statistics, [1973–]. N.Y., United Nations, 1975– . (*Its* Statistical papers, ser. M, no.56, etc.) $12.50 pa. **CG1**

Supersedes the Office's *A list of statistical series collected by international organizations* (1951, rev. 1955) and its *Directory of international standards for statistics* (1945, rev. 1960).

In four parts: pt.1 outlines the organization, statistical responsibilities, and statistical publications of the United Nations, its specialized agencies, and selected organizations outside the U.N. system; pt.2 is a classed list of the statistical series published by the U.N. system, detailing issuing agency, source, frequency, and whether the series is in machine readable form; pt.3 lists methodological concepts, classifications, standards and recommendations, with references to the publications in which they can be found (the publications are described in an ensuing bibliography); pt.4 is an inventory of data bases and their organization in the system.

COMPENDIUMS

International

Demographic yearbook; Annuaire démographique, 1948– . N.Y., 1949– . Annual. **CG2**

For full information and annotation *see Guide* CG35.

The 1976 volume contains a cumulative subject index covering all previous issues.

Sovet ekonomicheskoi vzaimopomoshchi. Sekretariat. Statistical yearbook of member states of the Council for Mutual

Economic Assistance, 1976– . London, IPC Industrial Pr., [1977–]. Annual. $55 per yr. **CG3**

A translation of the Council's *Statisticheskii ezhegodnik stranchlenov.*

The 1976 yearbook covers Bulgaria, Cuba, Czechoslovakia, the German Democratic Republic, Hungary, Mongolia, Poland, Romania, and the Soviet Union. Includes figures for 1960, 1965, 1970–75 on area and population, cultural activities, public health and social security, and aspects of the national economy.

Statistical Office of the European Communities. ACP: statistical yearbook. ACP: annuaire statistique, 1970/76– . Luxembourg-Kirchberg, 1977 [i.e., 1978]– . 300BFr. pa. **CG4**

On cover: Eurostat.

In English and French.

Presents a selection of the main demographic, economic, and social indicators relating to those 52 countries which are signatories to the Lomé Convention (called the ACP countries); a smaller section provides data on similar topics for all developing countries (ACP and others). HA12.5.S73a

United Nations. Statistical Office. Statistical pocketbook. Ed. 1– . N.Y., United Nations, 1976– . Annual. $3.95 pa. (*Its* Statistical papers, ser. V, no.1–) **CG5**

Pt.1 provides basic statistical information (area, population density and growth rate, national accounts, education, etc.) for each member country of the United Nations. Pt.2 presents demographic, economic, and social statistics by subject, for the world as a whole, selected regions, and major countries. Data in the 1977 edition refer to 1960, 1965, 1970, and 1975.

——— Supplement to the Statistical yearbook and the Monthly bulletin of statistics; methodology and definitions. Issue 2, 1972. N.Y., United Nations, 1974. 424p. $14. **CG6**

For "1st issue" *see Guide* CG48a.

"The descriptive notes given in the *Supplement* relate to the tables published in the 1972 edition of the *Statistical Yearbook* and the March-June 1973 issues of the *Monthly Bulletin of Statistics.* New series and major revisions introduced in the *Bulletin* after June, 1973, are described in annex IV of each issue of the *Bulletin.*"—*Introd.*

U.S. Central Intelligence Agency. Handbook of economic statistics, 1975– . Wash., 1975– . Annual? (*Its* Research aid) **CG7**

Prep. by the Agency's Office of Economic Research.

Provides statistics for selected non-Communist countries and all the Communist countries on national accounts, foreign trade, foreign aid, energy, minerals and metals, agriculture, transportation, manufacturing, construction, communication, etc. Tables arranged by topic, with subject index.

World tables 1976, from the data files of the World Bank. Baltimore, Johns Hopkins Univ. Pr., [1976]. 552p. $22.50. **CG8**

Mimeographed ed. issued 1971.

Presents statistics for developing countries and industrialized market economies that are World Bank members. In three main sections: (1) basic economic data presented by country, utilizing 1950–73 as a time series; (2) comparative economic data, arranged by subject; (3) comparative social indicators for 1960 and 1970. Derived from the data files of the World Bank; notes and sources for all tables. HC59.W67

Guides and bibliographies

Statistics sources. Ed. by Paul Wasserman and Jacqueline Bernero. 5th ed. Detroit, Gale, [1977]. 976p. $58. **CG9**

4th ed. 1974 (*Guide* CG52).

". . . there has been an expansion of subjects covered, particularly insofar as international coverage is concerned . . . and the bibliography has been increased approximately fifty percent."—*Pref.*

Inter-American

Harvey, Joan M. Statistics America: sources for market research (North, Central & South America). Beckenham, Kent, Eng., CBD Research, [1973]. 225p. £6; $22.50. **CG10**

For each country, gives description of central statistical office, other major organizations publishing statistics, principal libraries of statistical material, libraries and information services abroad, bibliographies of statistics, and descriptions of major statistical publications arranged in the following groups: general, production, external trade, internal distribution, population, and standard of living. Title and organization indexes. Z7554.A5H37

United States

Guides and bibliographies

Research Publications, Inc. Bibliography and reel index: a guide to the microfilm edition of United States decennial census publications, 1790–1970. Woodbridge, Conn., Research Publs., 1975. 276p. $45. **CG11**

Serves both as a bibliography of U.S. decennial census publications and a reel index to the microfilm edition thereof. Final reports are taken from the *Catalog of United States census publications, 1790–1945* (*Guide* CG60) and the *Bureau of the Census catalog of publications, 1946–1972* (*Suppl.* CG12) and arranged according to the numbering system used in the *International population census bibliography* (*Guide* CG13). Z7554.U5R47

U.S. Bureau of the Census. Bureau of the Census catalog of publications, 1790–1972. [Wash.], The Bureau, 1974. 320p., 591p. $7.10 pa. **CG12**

The first part of the volume is a reprint of the 1790–1945 catalog published 1950 (*Guide* CG60). The second section covers the period 1946–1972 and is based primarily on the annual issues of the Bureau's *Catalog* (*Guide* CG59) for those years. Each section has its own index.

Kept up-to-date by: Z7554.U5U58

——— Bureau of the Census catalog. Wash., 1973– . Quarterly with monthly suppl. and annual cumulation. (1976: $14.40 pa.) **CG12a**

Continues the Bureau's *Catalog of United States census publications* (*Guide* CG59).

Each quarterly issue is in two parts: I, Publications; II, Data files and special tabulations. Z7554.U5U32

——— Guide to recurrent and special governmental statistics. Wash., Govt. Prt. Off., 1976. 205p. (State and local government special studies, no.78) $3.20 pa. **CG13**

The *Guide* "summarizes the tabular presentations produced as part of the Census Bureau's program of State and local government statistics. It is divided into two sections, one for recurrent reports and the other for special studies. Within these sections are chapters referring to the most recent issue of the various reports published in this statistical series. Each chapter is essentially a synthesis of the original report, and contains the title, table of contents, and a sample of every table published in the original report."—*Pref.*

Compendiums

Columbia Broadcasting System, Inc. CBS News. The CBS news almanac, 1977– . Maplewood, N.J., Hammond Almanac Inc., 1976– . il., maps. Annual. $5.95; $3.25 pa. **CG14**

Continues *The official Associated Press almanac* (1973–75), which in turn continued *The New York times encyclopedic almanac.*

A handbook of miscellaneous information, beginning with a survey of the year's events by CBS news correspondents, and a chronology. Chapters arranged by broad topics present information on United States history and government, taxes and expenditures, finance, travel, population and social services, crime, civil rights, health, geography, the universe, science, states of the United States and world nations, diplomatic and military affairs, education, communication, biography, the arts, prizes, religion, sports, and obituaries. Indexed. AY67.N5T55

The people's almanac. Ed. by David Wallechinsky and Irving Wallace. N.Y., Doubleday, 1975. 1478p. il. $14.95; $7.95 pa. **CG15**

In endeavoring to produce "a reference book to be read for pleasure," the editors admit to sacrificing "a small degree of comprehensiveness for detail."—*p.xv.* A general almanac with a good deal of unusual and out-of-the-way information. Contributions are signed (some material is reprinted from indicated sources); suggestions for further reading are sometimes given. Indexed. AG106.P46

Social indicators 1976; selected data on social conditions and trends in the United States. [Wash.], U.S. Dept. of Commerce, Office of Federal Statistical Policy and Standards, and Bureau of the Census, 1977. lxxxiii, 564p. il. $7 pa. **CG16**

An earlier ed. appeared in 1973.

Presents maps, charts, and tables illustrating statistical measures of well-being and public perception in eleven major social areas, such as population, the family, social security and welfare, health and nutrition, public safety, etc. Each chapter on these major areas contains: (1) introductory text and charts; (2) statistical tables, with source references; and (3) technical notes and definitions, with a brief bibliography. International comparisons are presented for each social area. "For lengthier and more authoritative interpretations, the reader is advised to consult the following publication: The American Academy of Political and Social Science, "America in the Seventies: some social indicators." *The Annals,* volume 435 (January 1978). The entire issue is devoted to a number of articles based on the chapters of *Social Indicators, 1976.*"—*Introd.* HN52.S6

U.S. Bureau of the Census. County and city data book, 1949– . Wash., Govt. Prt. Off., 1952– . (Irregular) **CG17**

For full information *see Guide* CG70.

The 1977 volume gives statistical data for each country in the United States, 277 standard metropolitan statistical areas, and 910 incorporated cities having 25,000 inhabitants or more in 1975. Comparable totals are shown for states, census divisions and regions, standard federal administrative regions, and the United States.

——— Historical statistics of the United States, colonial times to 1970. Bicentennial ed. Wash., U.S. Dept. of Commerce, for sale by Supt. of Docs., 1975. 2v. (House document, 93d Congress, 1st session, no.93–78) $26. **CG18**

Represents a complete revision of the Bureau's *Historical statistics ... colonial times to 1957* and its *Continuation to 1962* (*Guide* CG71). Maintains the broad subject arrangement of the previous edition and includes almost all of its time series, plus about 4,500 new series. Reinstates the time series index which first appeared in *Historical statistics of the United States, 1789 to 1945;* the index indicates which statistics for particular subjects begin in the specified 10- or 20-year time segment. HA202.B87

Indexes

American statistics index ... A comprehensive guide and index to the statistical publications of the U.S. government, 1973– . Wash., Congressional Information Service, 1973– . Annual, with monthly supplements. **CG19**

For full information *see Guide* CG76.

The 1974 "Annual and retrospective edition" covered federal government statistical publications in print, as well as significant publications issued since the early 1960s; in the case of serial publications, only the format and contents of the most recent edition were described, with notes characterizing any major changes throughout the years. The 1974 "Annual" supersedes the initial 1973 edition, which was limited to social statistics. Supplementary "Annual" editions cumulate coverage of publications originally provided by the monthly supplements from 1974 to date. Indexed by: subjects and names; categories (geographic, economic, demographic, and standard classification systems); titles; agency report numbers.

The "ASI Microfiche Library" includes almost all publications abstracted and indexed in *American statistics index;* it is available in a variety of purchase possibilities. The bibliographic data base used in the compilation of the *Index* is available for on-line searching from 1973 to the present.

Directories

Stemmons, John D. The United States census compendium: a directory of census records, tax lists, poll lists, petitions, directories, etc. which can be used as a census. Logan, Utah, Everton Publ., [1973]. 144p. **CG20**

Listing is by state, then by county, with indication of date of census or other type of record and a coded reference to source. Both printed and manuscript sources are considered. While the references to materials appearing in periodicals and special materials will be useful, there is a preponderance of references to National Archives and Records Service sources. The introduction fails to explain fully the source references. Z1250.S83

U.S. Bureau of the Census. Directory of federal statistics for local areas: a guide to sources, 1976. [Wash., Govt. Prt. Off.], 1978. 359p. $5.50 pa. **CG21**

Updates the 1966 volume of the same title (*Guide* CG77). "Provides table-by-table descriptions of statistical reports on areas smaller than States . . . ; to be included, a table must provide statistics on a type of local area for the entire United States."—*p.[v].* Arranged alphabetically by broad topic (agriculture, banking and finance, commerce and trade, etc.). Within each topic, information is presented in a five-column tabular format covering: subject; data items included; areas to which data apply; frequency; bibliographic source. Appendixes describe sources of unpublished data, give population and rank of SMSAs and of cities of 100,000 or more by rank (1970 and 1975), and list data sources for federal and municipal statistics. Bibliography; subject index. HB2175.U54

Atlases

U.S. Bureau of the Census. Urban atlas; tract data for standard metropolitan statistical areas. [Wash., Govt. Prt. Off., 1974–] maps. (In progress) (GE80–no.240 [etc.]) Prices vary. **CG22**

Prep. in cooperation with the Labor Department, Manpower Administration.

Contents: no.240, Allentown, Bethlehem, Easton; no.520, Atlanta; no.720, Baltimore; no.1000, Birmingham; no.1120, Boston; no.1280, Buffalo; no.1600, Chicago; no.1640, Cincinnati; no.1680, Cleveland; no.1920, Dallas; no.2000, Dayton; no.2080, Denver; no.2160, Detroit; no.3120, Greensboro, Winston-Salem, High Point; no. 3360, Houston; no. 3760, Kansas City; no.4480, Los Angeles, Long Beach; no.4920, Memphis; no.5120, Minneapolis, St. Paul; no.5600, New York; no.5640, Newark; no.5720, Norfolk, Portsmouth; no.5880, Oklahoma City; no.5920, Omaha; no.6160, Philadelphia; no.6280, Pittsburgh; no.6760, Richmond; no. 6840, Rochester; no.7040, St. Louis; no.7280, San Bernardino, Riverside, Ontario; no.7320, San Diego; no.7360, San Francisco, Oakland; no.7400, San Jose; no.8160, Syracuse; no.8280, Tampa, St. Petersburg; no.8400, Toledo.

Provides a graphic presentation of selected census tract statistics for the 65 largest SMSAs existing at the time of the 1970 census of population and housing. Each atlas contains twelve maps illustrating, by census tract, percentages, ratios, or medians for: population density; population under 18 years of age; population over 65 years of age; black population; high school graduates; median family income; interrelationship of family income and educational attainment; blue-collar labor force; median housing value; median contract rent; housing units which are owner occupied; occupied units built during 1960–70.

Africa

Harvey, Joan M. Statistics Africa: sources for social, economic, and market research. 2d ed., rev. and enl. Beckenham, Kent, Eng., CBD Research; [Detroit, Gale, 1978]. 374p. $60. **CG23**

1st ed. 1970.

A section on Africa as a whole precedes sections on individual countries. Each section contains: (1) information on the central statistical office and other organizations collecting or publishing statistical material; (2) principal libraries inside the country with statistical collections open to the public; (3) libraries and information services in other countries (particularly English-speaking countries) where the country's statistical publications are available; (4) statistical bibliographies; (5) the major statistical publications (grouped as general, production, external trade, internal distribution and service trades, population, social, finance, transport and communications). Indexed by organization, title, and subject. Z7554.A34H37

Arab countries

Cairo. Ma'had al-Takhṭīṭ al-Qawmī. Dalīl al-maṣādir al-iḥṣā' īyah fī al-bilād al-'Arabīyah. Cairo, al-Ma'had, 1975. 416p. **CG24**

A country-by-country listing of statistical sources of Arab countries, with subject subdivisions. Western-language sources are included. Indexed. Z7554.A6A2

Asia

Harvey, Joan M. Statistics Asia & Australasia: sources for market research. Beckenham, Kent, Eng., CBD Research, [1974]. 238p. £8; $26.50. **CG25**

Describes the main statistical information sources for each country, including: directory information on the central statistical office and other statistics-gathering organizations; principal libraries with statistical sources open to the public; libraries and information services in other countries (usually English-speaking) where such materials are available; current statistical bibliographies; and major statistical publications. Indexes of titles and organizations. HA37.A775H37

Australia

Australia. Bureau of Statistics. Official year book of Australia. no.59– , 1973– . Canberra, 1973– . Annual. il., maps. **CG26**

Represents a change of title for the *Official year book of the Commonwealth of Australia* (*Guide* CG87) of which v.58, 1972, was the last issue published; format and general content remain the same. HA3001.B52

Bolivia

Bolivia en cifras, 1972– . [La Paz], Instituto Nacional de Estadística, [1973–]. Annual. il., maps. (1973: $5) **CG27**

A statistical compendium of general data and the principal statistical series on demography, economics, and social conditions. No index or detailed list of tables; no bibliographical sources cited. HA965.B65

Canada

Colombo, John Robert. Colombo's Canadian references. Toronto, Oxford Univ. Pr., 1976. 576p. $17.50. **CG28**

Aims to provide "a single wide-ranging source of information on Canadian subjects that would combine facts that were already available in various publications with material that was virtually inaccessible to the general reader."—*Pref.* About 6,000 entries for personal and place names, terms, organizations and agencies, etc. No citations to sources. F1006.C6

Perspective Canada; a compendium of social statistics. Prep. in the Office of the Senior Adviser on Integration, Statistics Canada. [Ottawa, Information Canada, 1974] 321p. il., maps. $8.10 pa. **CG29**

Publ. under the authority of the Minister of Industry, Trade and Commerce.

Presents selected statistics in the areas of population and the family, health, education, leisure, work, income and expenditure, quality of the environment, housing, bilingualism, native peoples, ethnicity, and criminal justice. List of sources and further readings for each chapter. HN104.P47

Canada. Statistics Canada. Perspective Canada II: a compendium of social statistics, 1977. Ottawa, Minister of Supply and Services, 1977. 335p. il. $11 pa. **CG30**

Prep. in the Office of the Senior Advisor on Integration, Statistics Canada.

Intended both to update and to complement the material in *Perspective Canada* (above), this volume includes new chapters on urbanization and on the older population. Lists of sources and further readings, and a subject index.

China

Statistical yearbook of the Republic of China, 1975– . [Taipei], Directorate-General of Budget, Accounting & Statistics, Executive Yuan, Republic of China, [1975–]. Annual. **CG31**

Pt.I consists of statistical tables which are, in numbering and format, identical to those used in the United Nations *Statistical yearbook* (*Guide* CG48); comparative figures for the period from 1946 are given as appropriate. Pt.II contains definitions of terms, sources of data, statistical procedures used in censuses and surveys, etc. HA1710.5.A183a

Europe

Mitchell, Brian R. European historical statistics, 1750–1970. N.Y., Columbia Univ. Pr., 1975. 827p. $50. **CG32**

For full information *see Suppl.* DC6.

Bibliography

Harvey, Joan M. Statistics Europe; sources for social, economic and market research. 3d ed., rev. and enl. Beckenham, Kent, Eng., CBD Research; [Detroit, Gale, 1976] 467p. $40. **CG33**

2d ed. 1972.

Information presented for each country includes: directory information on the central statistical office and other major organizations publishing statistical information; principal libraries inside and outside the country where its statistical materials are available; current bibliographies and sales lists of statistics; list of the major statistical publications, arranged as general, production, external trade, internal distribution and service trades, population, social, finance, transport and communications (with appropriate subdivisions for most groups). Organization, title, and subject indexes. Z7554.E8H35

France

Paroisses et communes de France. Dictionnaire d'histoire administrative et démographique. Paris, Éditions du Centre National de la Recherche Scientifique, 1974– . [v.1–] il. (In progress) **CG34**

Ed. by Jacques Dupâquier and others.

Contents: [v.1] Région parisienne; [v.7] Ardèche; [v.10] Aube; [v.49] Maine-et-Loire; [v.60] Oise; [v.62] Pas-de-Calais (in 2v.); [v.67] Bas-Rhin. (Price per v. varies)

An attempt to provide parish-by-parish demographic statistics from the 17th century to 1968. Includes bibliographic references. JS5112.P37

Germany

Basisdaten: Zahlen zur sozio-ökonomischen Entwicklung der Bundesrepublik Deutschland. Bearb. von Roland Ermrich. Bonn-Bad Godesberg, Verl. Neue Gesellschaft, [1974]. 648p. il. DM25 pa. **CG35**

A handbook of social indicators relating to population, employment, economy, raw materials, education, health, housing, working conditions, income and expenditure, leisure, mass media, political participation, etc. Most time series cover 1950–70. Sources indicated for all tables. Bibliography; list of tables; subject index.
HC286.6.B27

Soziologischer Almanach: Handbuch gesellschaftspolitischer Daten und Indikatoren für die Bundesrepublik Deutschland. Frankfurt and N.Y., Herder & Herder, [1975]. 531p. (SPES-Projekt, Bd.5) DM38 pa. **CG36**

A compendium of socioeconomic statistics for West Germany, in the areas of population, production, institutions, family, leisure, specific social groups, inequality, labor, crime, political participation, mass communications, taxation and public expenditure. Tables show historical data for the last 100 years, and comparative figures for other countries. HN445.S6

Great Britain

Feinstein, C. H. Statistical tables of national income, expenditure, and output of the U.K., 1855–1965. Cambridge, Eng., Cambridge Univ. Pr., [1976]. 141p. £4.75. **CG37**

First published as part of *National income, expenditure and output of the United Kingdom, 1855–1965* (1972); issued separately, with a new introduction, 1976.

Presents 65 tables of "estimates of national income, expenditure and output at current and constant prices . . . [and] series for the capital stock, population, employment and unemployment, prices and wages."—*Introd.* Original explanatory text from the 1972 edition has not been included. HC260.I5F42

Bibliography

Maunder, W. F., ed. Reviews of United Kingdom statistical sources. London, Heinemann, [1974–76]. 5v. **CG38**

Publ. for the Royal Statistical Society and the Social Science Research Council.

Contents: v.1, [pt.1] Personal social services, by B. P. Davies; [pt.2] Voluntary organisations in the personal social service field, by G. J. Murray (£3.25); v.2, [pt.3] Central government routine health statistics, by M. Alderson; [pt.4] Social security statistics, by F. Whitehead (£4.50); v.3, [pt.5] Housing in Great Britain, by S. Farthing; [pt.6] Housing in Northern Ireland, by M. Fleming (£5.); v.4, [pt.7] Leisure, by F. M. M. Lewis and S. R. Parker; [pt.8] Tourism, by L. J. Lickorish (£6); v.5, [pt.9] General sources of statistics, by G. F. Lock (£3).

Constitutes a revised and expanded edition of *The sources and nature of the statistics of the United Kingdom,* ed. by Maurice Kendall (2v., 1952–57; *Guide* CG137). HA37.G7M38

Pickett, Kathleen G. Sources of official data. [London], Longman, [1974]. 158p. £2.75. **CG39**

Aims "to provide a guide to some principal sources of [British] statistical data which are published on a regular basis."—*Foreword.* Chapters on (1) Population and the census; (2) Other census topics; (3) The labour force; (4) Education; and (5) Sampling frames.
HA37.G7P5

India

India; a statistical outline. [Ed.1–] Bombay, Indian Oxygen Ltd., 1965– . Irregular. **CG40**

For full information *see Guide* CG142.

Ed.5, 1976, is based on the final figures from the 1971 census. There are new sections on foreign investment, foreign collaboration, industrial licensing, and industrial finance.

Israel

Israel. ha-Lishkah ha-merkazit li-statistikah. Society in Israel: selected statistics. 2d ed., ed. by U. O. Schmelz. Jerusalem, 1976. liv, 172, 42p. I£40. **CG41**

In English and Hebrew.

A compendium of statistics for the period from 1950 to the present, in the areas of population and vital statistics, immigration, households, employment, income and expenditure, social security, housing, health, education, leisure, and public order. Statistical data are preceded by explanatory chapters which include lists of published sources. Subject index. HA1932.L57

Latin America

Anuario estadístico de América Latina. Statistical yearbook for Latin America, 1973– . Santiago, Chile, United Nations Economic Commission for Latin America, 1974– . **CG42**

Supersedes the Commission's *Boletín estadístico de América Latina; Statistical bulletin for Latin America.*

In English and Spanish.

Each issue consists of a number of parts: (1) statistical series for region and regional associations (e.g., Latin American Free Trade Association, Andean Group, Central American Common Market, and Caribbean Free Trade Association); (2–4) statistical series for Latin American and Caribbean countries arranged alphabetically by country. Includes population, national accounts, agriculture, industry, transport, trade, prices, balance of payments, and social statistics.

Statistical abstract of Latin America. Supplement [3–7]. [Los Angeles, Univ. of California at Los Angeles, Center of Latin American Studies], 1973–77. 5v. **CG43**

For basic work and earlier supplements *see Guide* CG170.

Contents: [no.3] Statistics and national policy (publ. 1974); [no.4] Urbanization in 19th century Latin America: statistics and sources (publ. 1973); [no.5] Measuring land reform (publ. 1974); [no.6] Quantitative Latin America studies: methods and findings (publ. 1977); [no.7] Money and politics in Latin America (publ. 1977).

With ed. 17 (1976) of the main work several changes in content and format were made: (1) "Non-Latin American countries" (Barbados, Jamaica, Guyana, Trinidad and Tobago) were excluded; (2) a time-series dimension was added, rather than simply presenting material for the most current year; (3) the twenty Latin American countries are presented in alphabetical order in each table; (4) a cartogram series has been added to show the spatial extent of political units in terms of population size; (5) series which have not changed significantly since the previous edition, or which are scheduled for updating in the next edition, are not published.

Union of Soviet Socialist Republics

USSR: facts and figures annual. v.1– , 1977– . Gulf Breeze, Fla., Academic International Pr., 1977– . Annual. il. (v.1: $31.50) **CG44**

Presents statistical and factual data on various areas of Soviet life: government, Communist Party, republics, demography, armed forces, economy, agriculture, foreign trade and aid, health, education and welfare, communications, transportation, institutions, labor, and special topics. Data are derived from Soviet, American, and international sources; bibliographic references are noted for all data. "Future annual editions are planned as revised continuation volumes to UFFA/1977 rather than another year of the same information."—*Introd., v.1.* A very useful compendium.

C H

Economics

GENERAL WORKS

Guides

Helppie, Charles E., Gibbons, James R. and **Pearson, Donald W.** Research guide in economics. Morristown, N.J., General Learning Pr., [1974]. 166p. il. $3.95 pa. **CH1**

An introductory guide for the novice researcher. Discusses research formats, functional analytical approaches, methodological assumptions, use of library resources, primary reference sources and information services, statistical sources and techniques of quantitative analysis, together with information on how to write the research paper and on research trends. Glossary; index of annotated sources. H62.H3767

Bibliography

Amstutz, Mark R. Economics and foreign policy: a guide to information sources. Detroit, Gale, [1977]. 179p. (International relations information guide ser., v.7) $18. **CH2**

An annotated bibliography of over 750 English-language books and articles on the political economy of international relations, grouped into chapters on international political economy and economic relations, politics and trade, regional integration, politics and the international monetary system, politics and foreign aid, foreign private investment, imperialism, and the economics of war and defense. Final chapter covers bibliographies and journals. Author, title, and subject indexes. Z7164.E17A48

Annotated bibliography on the economic history of India (1500 A.D. to 1947 A.D.). Pune, Gokhale Inst. of Politics and Economics; New Delhi, Indian Council of Social Science Research, 1977– . v.1–2. (In progress) **CH3**

Half-title: Economic history of India: a bibliography.

Contents: v.1 (pts.1–4), Selections from records; Survey and settlement reports; Gazetteers; Acts and regulations; v.2 (pts.5–6), British Parliamentary papers; Reports of committees and commissions.

A classified arrangement of English-language printed sources; each part has an introduction, as well as subject, region, and author indexes. v.3 will include census reports and serials; v.4 will cover books, articles, and theses. Particular attention has been given to statistical material on economic history. A major bibliography.

Birkos, Alexander S. and **Tambs, Lewis A.** East European and Soviet economic affairs; a bibliography (1965–1973). Littleton, Colo., Libraries Unlimited, 1975. 170p. $10. **CH4**

A selective bibliography of English-language books and articles from the period 1965–73. Classed arrangement within country divisions. About 1,200 items. Author, title, and periodical/publisher indexes. Z7165.E8B55

Dick, Trevor J. O. Economic history of Canada: a guide to information sources. Detroit, Gale, [1978]. 174p. (Economics information guide ser., 9) $18. **CH5**

A classed bibliography of materials grouped in five chapters, with appropriate topical, geographical, and chronological subdivisions: (1) Interpretive and bibliographic sources; (2) From colonial times to the present; (3) The colonial period to 1867; (4) Confederation (1867) to 1920; (5) From 1920 to the present. Brief evaluative comments on the sources precede each subdivision. Author, title, and subject indexes. Z7165.C2D5

Frank, Geneviève. Women at work and in society; a selected bibliography, 1970–1975. Geneva, International Institute for Labour Studies, [1976]. 44p. 10Sw.Fr. pa. **CH6**

Prep. for the research symposium on "Women and decision-making: a social policy priority," organized by the International Institute for Labour Studies, Nov. 17–19, 1975.

Title and prefatory material also in French.

Over 500 English- and French-language books, periodical articles, symposia proceedings, and documents grouped by topic: labor force participation, work and family, sexual division of work, education and training, women's role in the economy, etc. Author index.

Gagala, Kenneth L. The economics of minorities: a guide to information sources. Detroit, Gale, [1976]. 212p. (Economics information guide ser., 2) $18. **CH7**

An annotated bibliography of English-language sources, most of them published from 1965 to 1974, on the economic conditions of nonwhite peoples in the United States. Ten chapters deal with topics related to the black American: education, urbanization, housing, consumption, labor, economic development and inequality, governmental law and policy. Two chapters are devoted to American Indians and Spanish-Americans. Author, title, and subject indexes. Z1361.N39G26

Goldsmiths'-Kress library of economic literature: a consolidated guide to Segment I of the microfilm collection. Woodbridge, Conn., Research Publs., 1976–77. v.1–2. (In progress.) $575 the 4v. set. **CH8**

To be complete in 4v.

Contents: v.1, Through 1720; v.2, 1721–1776.

Primarily an access tool to the microfilm collection published by Research Publications. Segment I of the collection is to include the pre-1801 holdings (about 3,000 titles) of the Goldsmiths' Library of Economic Literature at the University of London and the Kress Library of Business and Economics at the Harvard Graduate School of Business.

Arranged chronologically, with topical headings within years.

See also Suppl. CH14. Z7164.E2G64

Hughes, Catherine A. Economic education: a guide to information sources. Detroit, Gale, [1977]. 267p. (Economics information guide ser., 6) $18. **CH9**

Presents a selection of the books and media that are available to the teacher of economics, arranged within broad subject chapters and keyed by grade level (primary through high school). Also includes textbooks, teachers' materials, tests, games, periodical titles, pamphlet series, and a directory of suppliers. Author, title, subject, and audiovisual titles indexes. Z7164.E2H8

Hutchinson, William Kenneth. History of economic analysis: a guide to information sources. Detroit, Gale, [1976]. 243p. (Economics information guide ser., 3) $18. **CH10**

A "sourcebook for the neophyte" (*Introd.*), dealing with the period 1600–1940. Each chapter is devoted to a particular school of thought—the forerunners of classical economics, classical economics, inductivists, marginalists, American economists, and 20th-century British economic thought—and consists of introduction, major contributions, commentaries on the major contributions, and contributions of lesser importance; the last are not annotated. List of relevant journals and organizations. Author, title, and subject index. Z7164.E2H87

Kazmer, Daniel R. and **Kazmer, Vera.** Russian economic history; a guide to information sources. Detroit, Gale, [1977]. 520p. $18. **CH11**

A classified, annotated listing of books, pamphlets, and periodicals in English, with many references to Russian-language source material. Subject classification approximates arrangement used in *Index of economic articles* (*Guide* CH43); chapters are subdivided into general materials or works dealing with the periods up to 1860; from 1860 to 1917; and post-1917. Author and title indexes. Z7165.R9K34

Killick, Tony. The economies of East Africa. Boston, G. K. Hall, [1976]. 150p. $12.50. **CH12**

An annotated bibliography of English-language materials published since 1963 on the economics of Kenya, Tanzania, and Uganda.

Material is classed by topic (e.g., international trade, agriculture, industrial and service sectors, population, manpower, technologies). Indexed by subject, place, and author. Z7165.A42K54

Latin America; a guide to economic history, 1830–1930. Roberto Cortés Conde and Stanley J. Stein, eds. Berkeley, Univ. of California Pr., 1977. 685p. $35. **CH13**

"Sponsored by the Joint Committee on Latin American Studies of the American Council of Learned Societies and the Social Science Research Council and by the Consejo Latinoamericano de Ciencias Sociales."—*t.p.*

A cooperative effort of an international group of scholars. A section for general bibliography is followed by separate sections for Argentina, Brazil, Chile, Colombia, Mexico, and Peru. Each country section begins with an interpretive essay, and the ensuing bibliography for each is topically subdivided under ten major headings: (1) General and reference works; (2) Demography, manpower, and living conditions; (3) Structures and institutions; (4) Macroeconomic growth and fluctuation; (5) Foreign trade and investment; (6) Regional economy; (7) Agriculture, ranching, forestry; (8) Industry: factory and artisan; (9) Extractive industry; (10) Transport, public utilities and services. Introductory essays and annotations are in the language of the contributor. Indexes of authors and of periodicals. Z7165.L3L32

London. University. Library. Goldsmiths' Company's Library of Economic Literature. Catalogue of the Goldsmiths' Library of Economic Literature. Comp. by Margaret Canney, David Knott and Joan M. Gibbs. [Cambridge], Cambridge Univ. Pr. for the Univ. of London Lib., 1975. v.2. £30. **CH14**

Contents: v.2, Printed books, 1801–1850.

For v.1 *see Guide* CH22.

"The arrangement of the second volume of the catalogue follows that of the first, but there is one major change in the material to be found in it: British Parliamentary Papers, as printed for the two Houses of Parliament, have been excluded after the year 1801."—*Pref.* Includes entries no.18114–37258. Z7164.E2L65

Mossé, Robert. Bibliographie d'économie politique . . . [Suppl.4–5] 1969/71, 1972/74. [Paris, Conseil International de la Langue Française, 1973–76] 2v. (194p.; 313p.) **CH15**

For full citation, earlier supplements and annotation *see Guide* CH26.

Suppl. 4 covers 1969–71, Suppl. 5, 1972–74. Both supplements are limited to works in the French language. After Mossé's death in 1973, the work has been edited by Nicole Clerc-Péchiné.

O'Relley, Z. Edward. Soviet-type economic systems: a guide to information sources. Detroit, Gale, [1978]. 228p. (Economics information guide ser., 12) $18. **CH16**

A selective bibliography of English-language sources (including translations) on theories, models, and processes of the economies of Bulgaria, Czechoslovakia, East Germany, Hungary, Poland, Romania, and the Soviet Union. Material is arranged by category (e.g., planning theory, efficiency and productivity, sectoral problems and accomplishments), with very brief annotations. Author, title, and subject indexes. Z7164.E2O66

Orsagh, Thomas, ed. The economic history of the United States prior to 1860; an annotated bibliography. Santa Barbara, [Amer. Bibliog. Ctr.–Clio Pr., 1975]. 100p. $7.95. **CH17**

About 800 entries. Brief annotations for most items. Classed arrangement; author and subject indexes. Z7165.U5O77

Sources of European economic information. [Epping, Eng.], Gower Pr.; N.Y., Bowker, [1974]. 343p. £12.50. **CH18**

In English, French and German.

Intended "as a practical aid for those concerned with identifying and collating economic data across Western Europe. It does not provide the economic data *per se* but rather gives clear and precise signposts to the existence and availability of such material."—*Foreword.* Country-by-country arrangement, with alphabetical list of publications cited. Z7165.E8S68

Zaremba, Joseph. Mathematical economics and operations research: a guide to information sources. Detroit, Gale, [1978]. 606p. (Economics information guide ser., 10) $22. **CH19**

An annotated bibliography of more than 1,600 English-language books published before 1975 which have substantial portions of their analysis in terms of a well-defined branch of mathematics (differential calculus, matrix algebra, set theory, etc.) or which undertake analysis in terms of established analytical techniques (linear programming, dynamic programming, etc.). In three main sections, subdivided by topic—mathematics, economics, operations research—with appendixes on methodology and miscellaneous topics. Annotations are quite full; they include predicted audience, mathematical prerequisites for comprehension, presence of exercises, problems, references, and summaries. Author, title, and subject indexes. Z7164.E2Z37

Current

Bibliographic guide to business and economics, 1975– . Boston, G. K. Hall, 1975– . Annual. (1977 in 3v.: $190) **CH20**

A dictionary catalog of all materials cataloged during the year by the Research Libraries of the New York Public Library, with additional entries from the Library of Congress MARC tapes. Full bibliographic information is given in the main entry, with abbreviated or condensed citations for added entries, titles, series, and subject headings. Includes print and non-book materials in the following major subject areas: economic theory, population, demography, economic history, land and agriculture, industry and labor, transportation and communication, commerce, business administration, finance, foreign exchange, insurance, revenue and taxation, and public finance.

Economic books; current selections. v.1– , Mar. 1974– . Clifton, N.J., Kelley, 1974– . Quarterly. $26 per yr. **CH21**

A publication of the Dept. of Economics and the University Libraries of the University of Pittsburgh.

Continues in part *Economics selections* (*Guide* CH37) which ceased publication in 1973. Annotates English-language books, and indicates suitability for libraries of various sizes. Classed subject arrangement; author index.

A companion publication is: Z7164.E2E2

Economics selections: an international bibliography. v.21– , Jan. 1976– . N.Y., Gordon and Breach, 1976– . Quarterly. $22.50 per yr. **CH22**

Subtitle: Annotations on new titles in economics, business and finance.

Issued by the Dept. of Economics and Finance, Baruch College, City University of New York.

Continues in part the University of Pittsburgh publication of the same title (*Guide* CH37), and assumes its numbering. Z7164.E2E252

——— Cumulative bibliography, series I and II, 1963–1970. N.Y., Gordon and Breach, [1974]. 393p. $64. **CH23**

Continues *Economics library selections,* ser. 1–2, 1954–62 (publ. 1965), which contained the citations, without annotations, from *Economics library selections* issued by Johns Hopkins University, Dept. of Political Economy (*see Guide* CH37).

The 1963–70 volume "consists of the books classified during the years 1963 through 1970 for the journal "Economics selections: an international bibliography [Series I: New books in economics]."—*Pref.* Uses the same classification system as *Economics selections* (*Guide* CH37), but omits annotations and titles listed in its section on related fields. Z7164.E2E256

Indexes and abstract journals

Economic titles/abstracts. v.1– , Jan. 1974– . The Hague, Nijhoff, 1974– . Semimonthly. 787.50gldr. **CH24**

Comp. by the Library and Documentation Center of the Economic Information Service (Ministry of Economic Affairs), The Netherlands.

Contains information taken from approximately 2,000 journals, as well as books and reports. Each issue consists of about 600 entries arranged by the Universal Decimal Classification. Entries consist of bibliographic data, English keywords, and brief abstract in the original language of the publication. Annual subject index.

Key to economic science. v.23– , Jan. 1, 1976– . The Hague, Nijhoff, 1976– . Semimonthly. 84gldr. **CH25**

Subtitle varies: 1976–77, Review of abstracts on economics, finance, trade, industry, foreign aid, management, marketing, labour; 1978– , Key to economic science and managerial sciences.

Comp. by the Library and Documentation Center of the Economic Information Service (Ministry of Economic Affairs), The Netherlands.

Supersedes *Economics abstracts* (*Guide* CH42), which ceased with v.22, no.24, Dec. 15, 1975.

Offers a selection from the abstracts of books, reports, and scholarly journal articles which were originally published in *Economic titles/abstracts* (*Suppl.* CH24). Classed arrangement with annual author and subject indexes.

Book reviews

Wall Street review of books. v.1– , Mar. 1973– . Pleasantville, N.Y., Redgrave Publ. Co., 1973– . Quarterly. $22 per yr. **CH26**

Each issue contains from 15 to 20 signed reviews of current books in all fields relevant to business and economics. HG1.W28

Dictionaries

Ammer, Christine and **Ammer, D. S.** Dictionary of business and economics. N.Y., Free Pr.; London, Collier Macmillan, [1977]. 461p. il. $19.95. **CH27**

Offers fairly lengthy entries for terms, associations, abbreviations, and economists, ranging "from economic theory of the past and present to its numerous applications in the world of business firms and consumers, from price and income theory to real estate, insurance, business law and accounting, from public finance and labor economics to the world of the small investor."—*Pref.* Bibliography. HB61.A53

Anderla, Georges and **Schmidt-Anderla, Georgette.** Dictionnaire des affaires anglais-français, français-anglais; Delmas business dictionary English-French, French-English. [Paris], J. Delmas, [1972]. 587p. F185. **CH28**

Cover title: Delmas dictionnaire des affaires; Harrap business dictionary.

Consists of about 70,000 English or French phrases and their equivalents in the other language, with a separate section for abbreviations. Includes an appendix of basic weights, measures, and conversion coefficients.

Moffat, Donald W. Economics dictionary. N.Y., Elsevier, [1976]. 301p. il. $14.95; $9.75 pa. **CH29**

Brief definitions, with extensive cross references and some repetition of the shorter definitions. Criteria for length of entry are: "for expressions found in the popular and trade press, but not in textbooks, give a full explanation; for expressions involved in controversy, give a summary of what both sides are saying; ordinary economics expressions found in textbooks should be included, but with only a brief explanation."—*Pref.* HB61.M54

Handbooks

An introduction to the sources of European economic history, 1500–1800. Ithaca, Cornell Univ. Pr., [1977]. 256p. il. $17.50. **CH30**

Ed. by Charles Henry Wilson and Geoffrey Parker.

A team of international economic historians have compiled the chapters herein, covering: Italy, Spain, Portugal, the Low Countries, the British Isles, France and Germany. The narrative of each chapter follows the same format: the country's population, agriculture, industry, trade and transport, currency and finance, prices and wages, and wealth and social structure. Numerous charts, graphs, and tables. Bibliographic notes and references; indexed. HC240.I68

The organization and retrieval of economic knowledge. Ed. by Mark Perlman. Boulder, Colo., Westview Pr., [1977]. 520p. $38.50. **CH31**

Proceedings of a conference held by the International Economic Association at Kiel, West Germany.

Presents 26 papers by economists, data retrieval specialists and librarians discussing library resources and technology, their uses for economic research, and the information needs of researchers in various areas of economics. Indexed. Z675.E2O73

Annuals

Dow Jones–Irwin. Dow Jones–Irwin business almanac. Ed. by Sumner N. Levine. Homewood, Ill., Dow Jones–Irwin, 1977– . il. Annual. $15; $9.95 pa. **CH32**

A quick-access source to a variety of current information in business, investment, finance, and economics. The 1978 almanac has new sections on executive recruiting organizations, advertising, financial statements for various industries in ratio form, and business communications services, with expanded stock market, labor, and commodities sections. Emphasis on American domestic and international business. Index. HF5003.D68a

ACCOUNTING

Bibliography

Commerce Clearing House. Accounting articles, 1971–1974. Descriptions of accounting articles published in accounting and business periodicals, books and pamphlets for the years 1971–1974. Chicago, [1975]. 1v., various pagings. **CH33**

For earlier volume and annotation *see Guide* CH73.

Articles described in this volume were originally covered in the current monthly reports of *Accounting articles,* which continues to report accounting articles for 1975 and subsequent years.

Institute of Chartered Accountants in England and Wales, London. Library. Historical accounting literature. [London], Mansell, 1975. 360p. £24.25. **CH34**

Subtitle: A catalogue of the collection of early works on bookkeeping and accounting in the Library of the Institute of Chartered Accountants in England and Wales, together with a bibliography of literature on the subject published before 1750 and not in the Institute Library. Z7164.C81I43

Dictionaries

Kohler, Eric Louis. A dictionary for accountants. 5th ed. Englewood Cliffs, N.J., Prentice-Hall, [1975]. 497p. il. $19.95. **CH35**

4th ed. 1970 (*Guide* CH81).

About 200 new entries have been added in this edition. HF5621.K6

Handbooks

Ameiss, Albert P. and **Kargas, Nicholas A.** Accountant's desk handbook. Englewood Cliffs, N.J., Prentice-Hall, [1977]. 501p. il. $24.95. **CH36**

A sourcebook in four main parts: (1) external and internal reporting; (2) computer systems, procedures, and management information reporting; (3) auditing standards and procedures; (4) profit planning. Many illustrative examples and forms. Bibliographic references. HF5635.A474

Encyclopedia of accounting systems. Rev. and enl. ed. Gen. ed., Jerome K. Pescow. Englewood Cliffs, N.J., Prentice-Hall, [1976]. 3v. (1859p.) il. $79.50. **CH37**

1st ed. 1958.

Each chapter, written by a specialist, covers the accounting system for a particular industry and discusses the following topics: the industry in brief, the accounting system, account classifications and books of account, data processing procedures, cost system, time and payroll system, plant and equipment records and depreciation, the reporting system, data processing applications, and time-saving techniques. HF5635.E54

Handbook of modern accounting. Sidney Davidson, ed.; Roman L. Weil, assoc. ed. 2d ed. N.Y., McGraw-Hill, [1977]. 1372p. in various pagings. il. $29.95. **CH38**

1st ed. 1970 (*Guide* CH80).

Offers 47 chapters by specialists on various accounting topics. New material includes use of the computer in accounting. Chapters have brief bibliographies. Appendix provides compound interest, annuity, and bond tables. Indexed. HF5635.H23

The modern accountant's handbook. Homewood, Ill., Dow Jones–Irwin, [1976]. 1203p. il. $30. **CH39**

Ed. by James Don Edwards and Homer A. Black.

A compendium of current knowledge on practical accounting policies. Chapters written by authorities are organized into eight parts: (1) objectives of corporate financial accounting; (2) realization and measurement of earnings; (3) special problems in accounting measurement; (4) special problems in administering corporate resources; (5) publication of financial information; (6) accounting policy and corporate liability; (7) accounting standards for special enterprises; (8) planning and control. HF5635.M757

ADVERTISING

Lipstein, Benjamin and **McGuire, William J.** Evaluating advertising: a bibliography of the communications process. N.Y., Advertising Research Foundation, 1978. 362p. $95 pa. **CH40**

A classified bibliography of more than 7,000 books and periodical articles published since 1960 on "the creation and evolution of persuasive communications" (*p.xxvii*), in terms of source, audience, policy, theory, media employed, etc. Arranged alphabetically by author; indexed by "access words" keyed to the relevant class number in the "Topic index" which lists item numbers of relevant entries. Z7164.C81L734

Tatham-Laird & Kudner. Dictionary of advertising terms. Ed. by Laurence Urdang. [Chicago], Tatham-Laird & Kudner, [1977]. 209p. il. $19.95. **CH41**

Over 4,000 very brief explanations of specialized terms, special meanings of ordinary words, names of devices, services and organizations, with cross references for abbreviations, acronyms, and synonyms. HF5803.T37

BUSINESS

Guides

See also Suppl. AB34.

Brown, Barbara E. Canadian business & economics: a guide to sources of information. Economiques et commerciales canadiennes: sources d'informations. Ottawa, Canadian Lib. Assoc., [1976]. 636p. $35 Can. **CH42**

In English and French.

A comprehensive work, with many annotations, arranged by nation and then by region and province; within each province, entries are listed by type (bibliography, directory, etc.) and subject. Omits trade journals, most annual reports of government agencies, and most publications listed in the Statistics Canada catalogs. English and French indexes by author, title, corporate author, and, occasionally, series. Z7165.C2B76

Daniells, Lorna M. Business information sources. Berkeley, Univ. of California Pr., [1976]. 439p. $14.95. **CH43**

"Although this was begun as a revision of Edwin T. Coman's *Sources of Business Information* (2d ed., University of California Press, 1964) [*Guide* CH93] . . . and covers some of the same material, it is, in fact, a completely different work."—*Pref.*

Intended as a guide for the businessman, the business student, and the librarian. Offers a selected, annotated list of business books and reference sources arranged under such chapter headings as: Methods of locating facts; Basic time-saving sources; Locating information on companies, organizations and individuals; Basic U.S. statistical sources; Industry statistics; Investment sources; U.S. business and economic trends; Management; Computers and management information systems; Corporate finance and banking; Insurance and real estate; International management; Personnel management and industrial relations. Fully indexed. Z7164.C81D16

Encyclopedia of business information sources. 3d ed. Paul Wasserman, managing ed. Detroit, Gale, 1976. 667p. $42. **CH44**

Subtitle: A detailed listing of primary subjects of interest to managerial personnel, with a record of sourcebooks, periodicals, organizations, directories, handbooks, bibliographies, and other sources of information on each topic.

[2d ed.] 1970 (*Guide* CH94).

This edition covers about 1,300 specific subjects, with information revised and updated through the end of 1975. HF5353.E9

Use of management and business literature. Ed., K. D. C. Vernon. London, Butterworths, [1975]. 327p. il. £10.80. **CH45**

In three parts: (1) The literature, the library and the bibliographic tools; (2) Business information in three different forms [research materials, statistical publications, and company information]; (3) Subject surveys of the literature. The first part "is written specifically for users of libraries" (*Pref.*) and emphasizes British publications and library practices. Pts.2 and 3 comprise contributions by a number of subject and information specialists. Index is primarily of subjects. HD30.36.U5U74

Bibliographies and indexes

Jones, Donald G. Business ethics bibliography, 1971–1975. Charlottesville, Va., Univ. Pr. of Virginia, [1977]. 207p. $13.95. **CH46**

Sponsored by the Center for the Study of Applied Ethics, Colgate Darden Graduate School of Business Administration, University of Virginia.

Continues in part D. L. Gothie's *Selected bibliography of applied ethics in the professions* (*Guide* BA11), but selects only those books, essays, and articles dealing with management of particular services, issues relevant to the social responsibilities of business, theory, and religion and business ethics. Annotated. Z7164.C81J59

Current

Business books and serials in print. 1977– . N.Y., Bowker, 1977– . Annual. (1977: $37.50; Suppl., $24) **CH47**

Represents a change of title for *Business books in print* (*Guide* CH105).

Author, title, and subject lists of U.S. books in economics, industry, finance, business, management, industrial psychology, and vocational guidance make up the bulk of the volume. A separate section includes information on serials and is reprinted from the various Bowker sources (i.e., *Ulrich's; Irregular serials and annuals; Ulrich's quarterly*). An annual midyear supplement entitled *Business books and serials in print supplement* (the first issue covering 1977/78) is a new complementary volume, similar in format, which lists new titles and updates information from the basic volume when necessary. Publishers' addresses are provided.

Canadian business periodicals index. v.1, no.1– , July 1975– . Toronto, Information Access, 1975– . Monthly with annual cumulation. $175 per yr.; $125 annual cumulation only. **CH48**

An index to about 150 Canadian magazines, as well as the *Financial post, Financial times,* and the *Globe and mail.* In three sections: subject (topical, geographical, political); corporate name; personal name (including personal subjects and authors of indexed articles). Book reviews are entered under that heading, as well as under appropriate subject and under author's name.

Management contents. Fall, 1975– . Skokie, Ill., Management Information Services, G. D. Searle & Co., 1975– . Biweekly. $40 per yr. **CH49**

Contains tables of contents of current issues of approximately 200 English-language journals, grouped by broad subject. The bibliographic data base from which it is compiled is available for on-line searching.

Predicasts. no.1– , Oct. 1960– . Cleveland, Predicasts, Inc., 1960– . Quarterly. $450 per yr. **CH50**

Volumes for 1960–66 published by Economic Index & Survey, Inc.

Gives short- and long-term statistical projections for United States basic economic indicators and products (by SIC number). For each statistic, gives bibliographic reference to the source, periodical article, government document, or private study. The *Predicasts terminal system* is available for on-line searching. HC101.P7

——— World product casts. Dec. 15, 1964?– . Cleveland, 1964?– . Quarterly. **CH51**

Issued in four looseleaf binders called: P-1, General economics, utilities & services; P-2, Agriculture, mining, forestry, food, textiles, wood & paper; P-3, Chemicals, polymers, drugs, oil, rubber, stone, clay & glass; P-4, Primary metals, machinery, electronics, transportation equipment. Titles vary. HC1040.P74

——— World regional casts. Dec. 15, 1964?– . Cleveland, 1964?– . Quarterly. **CH52**

Issued in four looseleaf binders called: R-1, Common Market; R-2, Other Europe (incl. U.S.S.R.); R-3, Americas (excluding U.S.A.); R-4, Africa, Asia & Oceania. Titles vary.

The two titles above are supplementary to *Predicasts;* the complete service is available at $900 per year. The latter provides short- and long-term projections for basic economic and industrial statistics for countries other than the United States. Indicates periodical article, government document, or other source from which the statistics are derived. Available for on-line searching as part of *Predicasts terminal system.* HF1040.P75

Periodicals

Ledbetter, William and **Denton, Lynnard Wayne.** A directory of American business periodicals. [Columbus, Ohio, Grid, Inc., 1974] 167p. $7.95 pa. **CH53**

"Intended to aid the writer in making a more intelligent publishing choice by providing pertinent information on nearly 300 periodicals in Business and related fields."—*Pref.* Includes scholarly journals and trade publications; for each, provides information on publication, article topics preferred, manuscript submission, copyright and payment. Subject index. HF5001.L33

Business services

Directory of business and financial services. 7th ed. Ed. by Mary McNierney Grant and Norma Cote. N.Y., Special Libraries Assoc., 1976. 232p. $18.80. **CH54**

6th ed. 1963 (*Guide* CH108).

Revised and updated to include 1,051 publications representing 421 publishers. Arranged by title of service, with publisher and subject indexes. HF5003.H19

Dictionaries

Gullberg, Ingvar Emanuel. Svensk-Engelsk fackordbok för näringsliv, förvaltning, undervisning och forskning. Andra rev. uppl. med suppl. Stockholm, Norstedt, [1977]. 1722p. K.575. **CH55**

1st ed. 1964. (*Guide* CH126).

Reprints the earlier edition and adds a supplement, pp.1249–1718.

Moore, Norman D. Dictionary of business, finance and investment. Dayton, Ohio, Investor's Systems, 1975. 543p. il. $14.95. **CH56**

A layman's dictionary offering brief, clear discussions of basic terms and phrases, with lists of related terms. Much paper and expense could have been saved with greater use of cross references, and less repetition of material (e.g., identical entries under abbreviations and full names). HF1001.M76

Handbooks

Corporate profiles for executives and investors, 1976–77 ed. Chicago, Rand McNally, [1976]. unpaged. $14.95; $9.95 pa. **CH57**

1975 ed. had title: *The executive's corporate handbook* (publ. by Joseph Lloyd Corp.).

Includes a five-year review of sales, earnings, and dividends, and a two-year statement of assets, liabilities, and stock market performance for American publicly-held corporations with more than $75 million in sales. Other sections list corporations geographically, by principal industrial activity, and by SIC code number.

Human Resources Network. Handbook of corporate social responsibility: profiles of involvement. [2d ed.] Radnor, Pa., Chilton Book Co., [1975]. 629p. $40. **CH58**

1st ed. (1972) had title: *Profiles of involvement.*

An introductory survey gives comparative data on social programs sponsored by corporations, in terms of size of company, sponsoring department and personnel, budget, etc. The corporate profiles section contains brief descriptions of these programs classified in 27 topical areas. Indexed by corporation, subject, and geographical location. HD60.5.U5H85

Troy, Leo. Almanac of business and industrial financial ratios. Englewood Cliffs, N.J., Prentice-Hall, 1972– . Annual beginning 1974. (1978: $16 pa.) **CH59**

For 1972 ed. *see Guide* CH131. Now issued annually.

For the industry as a whole and for corporations of similar size as measured by assets, gives comparative figures, percentages, and ratios for factors such as net sales, total receipts, cost of operations, compensation of officers, taxes, interest, depreciation, amortization, pensions and benefit plans, etc. 1978 edition is the first to show separate tables for each total industry and for those operating at a profit. Indexed by field of activity. HF5681.R25T68

Directories

Angel, Juvenal Londoño. Directory of inter-corporate ownership: (who owns whom in America). [N.Y.], Simon and Schuster, [1974]. 2v. $75. **CH60**

v.1 lists, in alphabetical order, all parent companies, their addresses, and the names and addresses of firms they own or control; v.2 is an alphabetical index of the approximately 90,000 entries in the first volume, including American companies owned or controlled by foreign firms operating in the United States. HG4057.A156

Dun & Bradstreet, Inc. Principal international businesses, 1974– . N.Y., Dun & Bradstreet, 1974– . Annual. $500. **CH61**

Subtitle: A world marketing directory.

Introductory matter in English, French, German and Spanish.

Section I lists companies by country, providing for each: sales volume, indication of whether it exports or imports, number of employees, SIC and DUNS numbers, description of field of activity, and name and title of senior operating officer. Section II lists businesses by SIC number, and Section III lists them by name.

Europe's 5000 largest companies, 1975– . Oslo, etc., A. S. Økonomisk Literatur, Bowker, 1975– . Annual. $35. **CH62**

Title also in German and French. Text in English, German, and French.

Publisher varies: 1977, A. S. Økonomisk Literatur, Dun & Bradstreet International.

For Western Europe, ranks companies within these categories: (1) the 5,000 largest industrials; (2) the 500 largest industrials by profit; (3) the 250 most profitable industrials; (4) the money losers; (5) the largest industrials by activity group; (6) the largest industrials by country; (7) the 1,000 largest trading companies; (8) the 100 largest transport companies; (9) the 100 largest banks. Appropriate statistics are provided for each company. Indexed.

World guide to trade associations. N.Y., Bowker; Pullach/München, Verlag Dokumentation, 1973. 2v. (Handbook of international documentation and information, 12) $52.50. **CH63**

Michael Zils, ed.

Contents: v.1, Europe; v.2, Africa, America, Asia, Oceania.

Prefatory matter in English and German.

Presents addresses and telephone numbers for about 26,000 national and international chambers of commerce, professional organizations, consumer organizations, employers' and employees' groups. Arranged by continent, country, and name of association. Indexed by subject. HD2421.W67

Bibliography

Guide to American directories. 9th ed. Bernard Klein, ed. Coral Springs, Fla., Rye, N.Y., B. Klein Publs., [1975]. 496p. $35. **CH64**

For earlier editions *see Guide* CH140.

"This ... edition contains complete information on over 5,200 directories ... [with] over 1,500 new directories, including many new categories."—*Pref.* Z5771.G8

Statistics

Edwards, Bernard. Sources of economic and business statistics. London, Heinemann, [1972]. 272p. £3.75. **CH65**

Introductory chapters on statistical collection and classification and the development of British government statistical services are followed by chapters discussing the origin, uses, and publication of several types of statistics: manpower and wages, production and industry, distribution, transport, GNP, overseas trade and balance of payment, family expenditure. Also discusses various indexes. Only British sources are considered. Indexed. HA37.G7E4

Statistics on American business abroad, 1950–1975. [N.Y.], Arno Pr., 1976. about 300p. $23. **CH66**

Consists of a number of detailed statistical articles reprinted from the *Survey of current business* (*Guide* CH148). HG4538.S74

U.S. Bureau of the Census. 1972 Census of retail trade. [Wash., Govt. Prt. Off.], 1976. 3v. in 7. il., maps. $106.50. **CH67**

Continues in part the Bureau's *Census of business* (*Guide* CH152).

Contents: v.1, Summary and subject statistics; v.2, Area statistics: pt.1, Alabama–Indiana; pt. 2, Iowa–North Carolina; pt.3, North Dakota–Wyoming; v.3, Major retail center statistics [in 3 pts. as for v.2]. HF5429.3.U535

——— 1972 Census of selective service industries. [Wash.], Govt. Prt. Off., 1976. 2v. in 4. il., maps. $67. **CH68**

Continues in part the Bureau's *Census of business* (*Guide* CH152).

Contents: v.1, Summary and subject statistics; v.2, Area statistics: pt.1, U.S. summary, Alabama–Indiana; pt.2, Iowa–North Carolina; pt.3, North Dakota–Wyoming. HD9981.4.U54

——— 1972 Census of wholesale trade. [Wash., Govt. Prt. Off.], 1976. 2v. il., maps. $37. **CH69**

Continues in part the Bureau's *Census of business* (*Guide* CH152).

Contents: v.1, Summary and subject statistics; v.2, Area statistics. HF5421.U6

Yearbook of industrial statistics, 1974– . N.Y., United Nations, 1976– . Annual. $62. **CH70**

Continues *The growth of world industry* (*Guide* CH151) issued by the United Nations Statistical Office.

Issued in 2v. per year: v.1, General industrial statistics; v.2, Commodity production data.

Presents (1) national surveys for about 200 countries or areas on various indicators of industrial activity, classified by ISIC code, with a selection of indicators to measure global and regional trends in industrial productivity and employment, and (2) production statistics on more than 527 industrial commodities. HA40.I6Y4

History

Dallas. Public Library. Business and Technology Division. Business history collection: a checklist. Dallas, Tex., 1974. 236p. $5.40 pa. **CH71**

A listing of histories of particular firms, American and foreign, arranged by the name of the firm. No index.

Biography

Business people in the news; over 300 articles from newspapers and magazines. Ed. by Barbara Nykoruk. v.1– . Detroit, Gale, [1976–]. Annual? (Biography news library) $24 per v. **CH72**

Subtitle: A compilation of news stories and feature articles from American newspapers and magazines covering people in industry, finance, and labor.

Presents reproductions of biographical articles drawn from more than fifty newspapers and magazines. v.1 offers articles on about 300 personalities, some of which previously appeared in the publisher's now defunct *Biography news.* Alphabetically arranged by name. HC102.5.A2B8

Atlases

Business atlas of western Europe. [Epping, Essex, Eng., Gower Pr., 1974] 144p. il., maps. £8.85. **CH73**

Text in English, French, German, and Spanish.

In four parts: (1) Basic market information (politics, population, labor, finance and trade); (2) Major industries of Europe, with comparative data for seven key industrial sector groupings, and indicating competing companies; (3) The European consumer, in terms of incomes, expenditure, housing, education, and press circulation; (4) Surveys of the national economies. G1801.G1B8

BUSINESS MANAGEMENT

Bibliography

Administration and management: a selected and annotated bibliography, by William G. Hills [and others]. Norman, Univ. of Oklahoma Pr., [1975]. 182p. $8.95. **CH74**

A selection of readily available works chosen for their practical utility to public human-service administrators. Classed arrangement in six parts: (1) Development, scope, and emphasis; (2) The organization; (3) The administrative process; (4) Personnel; (5) The administrative environment; (6) Comparative administration. Appendixes list relevant journals and reference works. Author and title indexes. Z7164.O7A35

American Management Association. Index to AMA resources of the seventies, 1970–1976. N.Y., AMACOM, [1977]. 162p. $12 pa. **CH75**

Elizabeth A. Keegan, comp.

A subject arrangement of all books, periodical articles, reports, studies and services published by the AMA during this period. Title-series and author indexes. Z7164.O7A49

Bakewell, K. G. B. Management principles and practices: a guide to information sources. Detroit, Gale, [1977]. 519p. (Management information guide ser., 32) $18. **CH76**

A selective, briefly annotated bibliography of books, periodical titles and articles, and audiovisual materials on management in general and its various functional areas. Appendixes provide directories of organizations, periodicals, and publishers/distributors. Proper name, title, and subject index. Z7164.O7B25

Franklin, Jerome L. Organization development: an annotated bibliography. Ann Arbor, Mich., Univ. of Michigan, Inst. for Social Research, Center for Research on Utilization of Scientific Knowledge, [1973]. 104p. $8. **CH77**

An alphabetical author listing of books and articles dealing with the improvement of organizational performance, with the emphasis on the social aspects of organizational functioning. Author and subject indexes. Z7164.C81F65

Hanson, Agnes O. Executive and management development for business and government: a guide to information sources. Detroit, Gale, [1976]. 357p. (Management information guide ser., 31) $18. **CH78**

An annotated bibliography, principally of English-language books; selected sources emphasize "development of conceptual approaches and skills, imagination, and judgment, factors that contribute to flexibility and adaptability, rather than techniques, methods, and procedures."—*Pref.* The final three chapters list relevant reference sources, periodical titles, and organizations. Author, title, subject, and proper name indexes. Z7164.O7H275

Hollander, Stanley C. Management consultants and clients. East Lansing, Div. of Research, Grad. School of Business Admin., Michigan State Univ., 1972. 541p. $12. **CH79**

1st ed. (1963) had title: *Business consultants and clients.*

An annotated bibliography of over 1,200 entries on the client-consultant relationship in the United States and abroad. Classed arrangement with author index. Z7164.C81H6

Stogdill, Ralph Melvin. Leadership abstracts and bibliography, 1904 to 1974. Columbus, College of Administrative Science, Ohio State Univ., 1977. 829p. (College of Administrative Science monograph, no.AA10) $29.50. **CH80**

When the author's *Handbook of leadership* (N.Y., Free Pr., 1974; $19.95) was published, *The booklist* review (71:1093) suggested that the most useful section for reference purposes was the bibliography. The abstracts of more than 3,000 books and journal articles from that bibliography are provided here; arrangement is alphabetical by author, with author and subject indexes. Z7164.S68S86

Periodicals

Tega, Vasile. Management and economics journals: a guide to information sources. Detroit, Gale, [1977]. 370p. (Management information guide, 33) $18. **CH81**

A selection of over 160 journals, "academic and business oriented, [which] are internationally prestigious and generally regarded as 'core' journals."—*Introd.* Entries follow an alphabetical title arrangement, and provide publication information, a description of scope, purpose, and content, editorial policy on manuscript submission, notes on registers of doctoral dissertations and current research, and details of special issues published since 1960. An appendix lists by subject journals which include lists of doctoral dissertations and research in progress. Periodicals subject index; special issues subject index; and index of journals which deal with single attributes of top companies (e.g., *Business week's* "Highest paid executives" annual issue). Z7164.O7T23

Dictionaries

French, Derek and **Saward, Heather.** Dictionary of management. N.Y., International Publications Service, [1975]. 447p. $17.50. **CH82**

First published by Gower Pr., Epping, Essex, Eng., 1975.

Brief explanations of about 4,000 terms, including abbreviations, associations, and foreign expressions. Variations between American and British usage are noted. HD19.F73

Johannsen, Hano and **Page, G. Terry.** International dictionary of management: a practical guide. [London], Kogan Page, [1975]. 416p. il., maps. $25. **CH83**

Provides explanations and definitions for about 5,000 words, abbreviations, concepts, and institutions, with addresses given for the institutions. Abundant use of cross references. Appendixes include information on units of measure, names of the world's currencies, time zones, and directory information on the world stock exchanges.

Handbooks

The chief executive's handbook. Ed. by John Desmond Glover and Gerald A. Simon. Homewood, Ill., Dow Jones–Irwin, 1976. 1106p. il. $35. **CH84**

An attempt to provide a practical handbook for corporate chief executive officers, with chapters by specialists on organization, motivation, strategy, research and development, production, marketing, finance, international business, public relations, etc. Bibliographical footnotes. HD31.C47

Craig, Robert L. Training and development handbook: a guide to human resource development. 2d ed. N.Y., McGraw-Hill, [1976]. 859p. in various pagings. il. $24.50. **CH85**

Sponsored by the American Society for Training and Development.

A series of chapters by specialists on continuing education and training for work. New material includes: behavioral sciences applications to management practices and development training; the use of systematic and quantitative methods; instructional methods and media; training of specific employee groups (minority, international, secretarial and clerical); new concepts such as organization development. Most chapters include references and bibliography. HF5549.5.T7C7

The Dartnell office administration handbook. Ed. by Robert S. Minor and Clark W. Fetridge. 5th ed., rev. and enl. Chicago, Dartnell, [1975]. 1087p. il. $39.50. **CH86**

4th ed. 1967 (*Guide* CH184).

A comprehensive treatment of the managerial, psychological, and physical aspects of office administration, with expanded coverage of personnel administration and computer/electronic technology. Appendix includes a glossary. HF5547.D251

Directories

Directory of internships, work experience programs, and on-the-job training opportunities. Ed.1– . Thousand Oaks, Calif., Ready Reference Pr., [1976]– . (Ed.1: $45) **CH87**

Subtitle: A guide to internship, work experience, and on-the-job training opportunities sponsored by governmental agencies, business and industry, professional associations, foundations, and various social and community organizations.

Listing is alphabetical by sponsoring body, with program title, geographic, and subject indexes.

Wasserman, Paul, ed. Consultants and consulting organizations directory. 3d ed. Detroit, Gale, 1976. 1034p. $78. **CH88**

Janice W. McLean, assoc. ed.

2d ed. 1973 (*Guide* CH206).

This edition has expanded coverage of about 5,314 firms, individuals, and organizations. Branch offices and foreign firms have been included in the subject listings for the first time.

Kept up-to-date by: HD69.C6W37

New consultants. no.1– , June 1976– . Detroit, Gale, 1976– . Looseleaf. Semiannual. $65 for 4 issues. **CH89**

Wasserman, Paul and **Palmer, Marlene A.** Training and development organizations directory. Detroit, Gale, 1978. 614p. $45. **CH90**

Subtitle: A reference work describing firms, institutes, and other agencies offering training programs for business, industry, and government.

Presents data on 985 organizations offering training for managerial personnel through workshops and non-degree courses. Alphabetical arrangement by organization; entries include staffing, areas of specialization, description and cost of programs. Four indexes: geographic, by state and city; broad subject, by state and city; detailed subject; individual personnel. HD30.42.U5W37

Weiner, Richard. Professional's guide to public relations services. 3d ed. [N.Y., R. Weiner, Inc., 1975] 301p. il. $30. **CH91**

1st ed. 1968.

More than 700 companies and services are listed in 30 functional categories—broadcast monitoring, clipping bureaus, mailing services, literary services, research, translations, etc. Each category begins with a description of the service, and concludes with descriptions of individual services—name and address, fee, background, names of personnel, branch offices, etc. Indexed. HD59.W38

Who's who in consulting; a reference guide to professional personnel engaged in consultation for business, industry, and government. 2d ed. Detroit, Gale, [1973]. 1011p. $45. **CH92**

Paul Wasserman, managing ed.

1st ed. 1968.

Supplements and serves as a companion to *Consultants and consulting organizations* (3d ed., *Suppl.* CH88) by offering biographical and career information on more than 7,500 individuals. Section I is the main body of the text, providing the biographical listings; Section II is a subject index of consultants arranged within field of activity by state, city, and consultant. HD69.C6W52

COMMERCE

Commercial products and commodities

Crowley, Ellen T. Trade names dictionary. Detroit, Gale, 1976. 2v. $65. **CH93**

Subtitle: A guide to trade names, brand names, product names, coined names, model names, and design names, with addresses of their manufacturers, importers, marketers, or distributors.

A preliminary edition was published 1974.

Contains some 106,000 entries for consumer products, manufacturers, and distributors. Product entries provide trade name, name of producer, and code indicating source of information.

Kept up-to-date by: T223.V4A22

——— New trade names, 1976– . Detroit, Gale, 1977– . (1977: $45 pa.) **CH94**

Guide to world commodity markets. London, K. Page; N.Y., Nichols Pub. Co., [1977]. 308p. il., map. $25. **CH95**

Consultant ed., Brian Reidy; Editorial adviser, John Edwards; Editor, Ethel de Keyser.

In three parts: pt.1, The role and function of commodity markets (a series of descriptive essays); pt.2, Commodities (providing statistical information on the trading of major commodities—cocoa, coffee, copper, cotton and wool, grains, lead, rubber, silver, sugar, tin, and zinc); pt.3, Commodity market data (providing detailed information on the markets, using a geographical arrangement). Appendix 1 offers directory information for trading members of the futures markets. HG6046.G84

Wasserman, Paul and **Kemmerling, Diane.** Commodity prices: a source book and index. Detroit, Gale, [1974]. 200p. $15. **CH96**

Subtitle: A source book and index providing references to wholesale and retail quotations for more than 5,000 agricultural, commercial, industrial, and consumer products.

An updated and revised ed. of *Sources of commodity prices* (1959; *Guide* CH209). Z7164.P94W33

Woy, James B. Commodity futures trading: a bibliographic guide. N.Y., Bowker, 1976. 206p. $19.95. **CH97**

The main text defines various commodity trading methods and related topics, and annotates information available on each subject in collected works, monographs, and periodical articles; the full bibliographic citation is included in the "Bibliography" section. Lists relevant federal government reports and periodicals. Author and subject indexes. Z7164.C83W69

Consumerism

Consumer Help Center of WNET/NYU Law School. The consumer help manual: a reference book for consumer complaint centers. Helen D. Johnson, ed. [N.Y., 1976] 430p. il. Looseleaf. **CH98**

"A project of the Consumer Help Center of WNET/NYU Law School . . . and the New York State Consumer Protection Board."—*t.p.*

An earlier version appeared in 1975.

Provides information on procedures to follow regarding consumer complaints, organizations and agencies to consult, etc.

Consumer protection directory. 2d ed. Chicago, Marquis Academic Media, 1975. 466p. $44.50. **CH99**

Subtitle: A comprehensive guide to consumer protection organizations in the United States and Canada.

Eds., Sally R. Osberg and Thaddeus C. Trzyna.

1st ed. published 1973 as part of the *Directory of consumer protection and environmental agencies* (*Guide* CH217).

Gives addresses of organizations, names of chief administrative officers and, frequently, a statement of purpose or function. A "User's guide" is provided "to help readers identify organizations concerned with a specific area of interest, such as insurance or food and nutrition."—*Introd.* Subject index, organization index, personnel index, publication index. HC110.C63C635

Consumers index to product evaluations and information sources. v.1, no.1– , Winter 1974– . Ann Arbor, Mich., Pierian Pr., 1973– . Quarterly, with annual cumulation. (1978: $39.50) **CH100**

A broad subject index to the contents of about 100 periodicals, intended for the consumer, library, business office, and educational instructor. Each item is briefly annotated; if specific products are included, the entry is coded to indicate description, evaluation, or test. A similarly classed section treats books, pamphlets, and consumer aids.

David, Nina. Reference guide for consumers. N.Y., Bowker, 1975. 327p. $16.50. **CH101**

In three parts: (1) "Multimedia materials," providing fairly lengthy annotations for more than 500 books, pamphlets, periodical titles and films published between 1960 and 1974; (2) "Organizations," giving directory information for United States federal, state, county and city agencies, private organizations, and Canadian national and provincial agencies; (3) "Newspapers," listing American and Canadian newspapers with consumer features, and syndicated columnists. Author, title, and subject indexes. Z5776.C65D4

Dorfman, John. A consumer's arsenal. N.Y., Praeger, [1976]. 270p. $10. **CH102**

In three main parts: (1) a "tactics manual," describing ten basic steps that should be taken in a complaint procedure; (2) a state-by-state evaluation of consumer agencies and laws, suggesting how good the consumer's chances of redress are; (3) a dictionary arrangement of common consumer complaints, with advice on their solutions. HF5415.5.D66

Porter, Sylvia Field. Sylvia Porter's Money book: how to earn it, spend it, save it, invest it, borrow it—and use it to better your life. Garden City, N.Y., Doubleday, [1975]. 1105p. $14.95; $5.95 pa. **CH103**

A basic book in personal and family finance for the layperson. Advice on personal expenditure, the cost of marriage, children, divorce, funerals, and estates, money management and investment, consumer and other economic rights. HG179.P57

Rosenbloom, Joseph. Consumer complaint guide, 1978. N.Y., Macmillan Information, 1977. 485p. $10.95; $4.95 pa. **CH104**

First published 1971.

"The purpose of this book . . . is to aid the consumer in finding the right person or agency to help with his particular consumer problem. Part I, 'The Consumer in the Marketplace,' offers some advice for the buyer to consider prior to making a purchase. Part II, 'How and to Whom to Complain,' discusses how to make a consumer complaint, and how to find the right person or agency for help. Part III, 'Who's Who in the Marketplace,' lists companies engaged in providing consumer products or services."—*Introd.* T12.R66

——— Consumer protection guide, 1977. N.Y., Macmillan Information, [1976]. $10.95; $4.95 pa. **CH105**

Attempts "to identify the proper person or agency who will listen to and can do something about grievances over inadequate services." —*Pref.* Material is arranged by profession or service activity. Information on each profession includes: a brief description of the profession, its training and qualifications, complaint procedures, directories of state licensing boards and professional associations. Service activities which do not involve licensing or professional associations are treated more generally. HC110.C63R67

Wasserman, Paul and **Morgan, Jean.** Consumer sourcebook. 2d ed. Detroit, Gale, 1978. 2v. (1662p.) $48. **CH106**

Subtitle: A directory and guide to government organizations; associations, centers and institutes; media services; company and trademark information; and bibliographic material relating to consumer topics, sources of recourse, and advisory information.

1st ed. 1974.

Offers directory and descriptive information arranged according to the categories indicated in the subtitle. The review in *Library journal* (103:2227) concludes that "the listings and bibliographies have been updated; the number of entries has been expanded greatly; some new sources are covered—public utility commissions, safety organizations, syndicated newspaper columns, and network radio and television programs on consumer issues; and many more telephone numbers are provided. However, much of this information is available elsewhere; over half the book is merely a directory of companies; and there is still no subject index. Useful only for those who found a need for the first edition." HC110.C63W37

Foreign trade

Bibliography

Brooke, Michael Z., Black, Mary and **Neville, Paul.** International business bibliography. N.Y., Garland, 1977. 480p. $25. **CH107**

First published by Macmillan Pr., London, 1977.

Produced by the International Business Unit of the University of Manchester Institute of Science and Technology.

An author listing of books published in the last twenty years and articles and papers published in the last five years; brief summaries of many entries. Indexed by geographic area and broad subject; more specific subject indexing should have been provided and will be a necessary improvement in the proposed continuation. Directory of journals, book publishers, and institutions. "The next volume will also include a list of scholars and centers of research . . . and information on current work. . . ."—*Introd.* Z7164.C81B86

European Centre for Study and Information on Multinational Corporations. Multinational corporations; the E.C. S.I.M. guide to information sources. Comp. and ed. by Joseph O. Mekeirle. Brussels, ECSIM, 1977. 454p. 1600BFr. **CH108**

Title and prefatory material also in French and German.

In three main parts: (1) Primary information sources (i.e., commercial book publishers, research sources and organizations, periodicals and special periodical issues); (2) Secondary information sources (i.e., bibliography of bibliographies, company information sources, current bibliographies, data bases); (3) Indexes (author, title, periodical title, organizational, subject). Many annotations. Z7164.T87E95

Hernes, Helga. The multinational corporation: a guide to information sources. Detroit, Gale, [1977]. 197p. (International relations information guide ser., 4) $18. **CH109**

An annotated bibliography of English-language books and periodical articles emphasizing the social aspects of multinational corporations, grouped into three parts: (1) the multinational corporation as a large organization; (2) the multinational corporation and the nation; (3) the role of the multinational corporation in the international system. Introductory bibliographic essays. Cutoff date is apparently 1974. Author, title, and subject indexes. HD2755.5.H47

Lall, Sanjaya. Foreign private manufacturing investment and multinational corporations: an annotated bibliography. N.Y., Praeger, [1975]. 196p. $18.50. **CH110**

Includes English-language publications on the manufacturing sector, written mostly between 1965 and 1973, and arranged in chapters by topic. One chapter deals specifically with Marxist and "dependence" school analysis of foreign investment, another with area studies. Cross references, but no subject index. Author index. Z7164.F5L34

Saqafi-nizhad, Taqi and **Belfield, Robert.** Transnational corporations, technology transfer, and development: a bibliography. Philadelphia, Worldwide Institutions Research Group, Wharton School, Univ. of Pennsylvania, 1976. [181*l*.] **CH111**

English-language books, periodicals, dissertations and documents are listed in eight chapters: (1) The setting: science and technology in development; (2) The international technology gap; (3) Transnational corporations and international trade in technology; (4) The anatomy of corporate technology transfer: modes, costs, management; (5) Impact of technology transfer on host countries: appropriateness, *dependencia,* sovereignty; (6) Sectoral analysis: case studies; (7) Technology transfer and the home country; (8) Regulating technology transfer; codes of conduct and institutional mechanisms. Author index.

Dictionaries

Kohls, Siegfried. Dictionary of international economics: German, Russian, English, French, Spanish. Leiden, Sijthoff; Berlin, Verlag Die Wirtschaft, 1976. 619p. 70.70 fl.; $27.75. **CH112**

Prefatory material in the five languages covered.

Originally published as *Ökonomisches Wörterbuch Aussenwirtschaft.*

The alphabetically arranged main section gives about 6,500 German terms and phrases with their equivalents in the other four languages; indexes from each of the other languages. Emphasizes terms of commerce, commercial law, payments system, carrying trade, and customs administration; largely exclusive of monetary systems, industrial and trade terminology. HF1002.K6613

Handbooks and yearbooks

Concise guide to international markets, 1966– . London, Internatl. Advertising Assoc., United Kingdom Chapter, 1966–. il., maps. Irregular. (3d ed. 1977/78) **CH113**

Leslie Stinton, ed.-in-chief.

Provides marketing information for 110 countries, grouped by continent or region. Profile of each country includes statistical information on income, expenditure, retail and wholesale outlets, advertising agencies and expenditure, regulations, available media, market research and public relations facilities, and advertising reference books.

East-West trade: a sourcebook on the international economic relations of socialist countries and their legal aspects. Comp. and ed. by Dietrich André Loeber. Dobbs Ferry, N.Y., Oceana, 1976. 4v. $37.50 per v. **CH114**

Contents: v.1, Background material. Organization of international economic relations. Equality and discrimination in international economic relations; v.2, Foreign trade system. Foreign trade contracts; v.3, Industrial cooperation. Intellectual property; v.4, Financial relations. Transport. Dispute settlement.

Assembles international agreements, national statutes, administrative regulations, and documents of regional and international organizations dealing with the international economic relations of the Soviet Union, socialist East European countries, China, Mongolia, North Korea, North Vietnam, and Cuba. Bibliography of secondary literature and indexes of persons, subjects, and countries in the final volume. HF1411.E14

European Data Index Ltd. European advertising & marketing handbook: a Eurodatex special report. [Ed.1–] [London, European Data Index Ltd., 1973–] maps. **CH115**

2d (1975/76) ed. publ. 1975 (237p.; £25 pa.).

Profiles of thirteen Western European nations (excluding Eire, Greece and Portugal) offer statistical data on age and structure of the population, size of households and their income, education, ownership of consumer durables, consumer spending, and employment. Detailed information on advertising conditions in each country is also supplied. HF5813.E79E84

Foreign trade marketplace. George J. Schultz, ed. Detroit, Gale, 1977. 662p. $48. **CH116**

Introductory chapters cover the operations aspects of international trade from the standpoint of American companies. The main text consists of 35 chapters providing directory information on exporting and importing, United States and foreign government agencies and organizations, marketing, advertising, transportation, communication, and regulations. Indexed by subject and by geographic area. HF1010.F67

Jonnard, Claude M. Exporter's financial and marketing handbook. 2d ed. Park Ridge, N.J., Noyes Data Corp., 1975. 308p. $18. **CH117**

1st ed. 1973.

A textbook and basic methods manual, with chapters on the United States position in international trade, the mechanics of exporting, statistics, financing, federal government export expansion programs, international agencies, distribution, licensing, free trade zones, etc. Brief bibliography. No index. HF1009.5.J65

Middle East annual review, 1975– . Saffron Walden, Essex, Eng., Middle East Review Co., Ltd., 1974– . il., maps. Annual. (1978: £11.50; $20.50 pa.) **CH118**

Also issued in an Arabic ed.

Distributed in the United States by Rand McNally.

In two main sections: (1) a series of introductory chapters by British and American journalists and researchers on various topics in areas of trade, industry, civil engineering and construction, services, finances, etc.; (2) a country-by-country survey contributed by individual authors; these surveys include politics, foreign relations, social conditions, development plans, budget, foreign investment, balance of payments, etc., and provide factual and analytical information. "Middle East" is defined to include North Africa, Somalia, and the Sudan. Similar volumes cover other geographic regions: *Africa guide, Latin America annual review and the Caribbean, Asia & Pacific annual review.*

United Nations. Statistical Office. Yearbook of international trade statistics, 1950– . N.Y., 1951– . Annual. **CH119**

For a note on the series *see Guide* CH239.

The 25th ed. (1976; publ. 1977) is in 2v.: v.1, Trade by country, contains detailed data for 156 countries, with summary tables on trade relations of each with its region and the world; v.2, Trade by commodity [and] commodity matrix tables, shows the total economic world trade of certain commodities analysed by region and country.

Directories

Arpan, Jeffrey S. and **Ricks, David A.** Directory of foreign manufacturers in the United States. Atlanta, Georgia State Univ., School of Business Administration, Publishing Services Division, 1975. 151p. $11.95; $7.50 pa. **CH120.**

Lists about 1,200 foreign-owned United States companies, with address, SIC product classification numbers, major products, and parent company name and address. Arranged alphabetically by American subsidiary, and indexed by parent company, home country of parent company, state of location, and SIC product classification number. HD9723.A76

Money

McCusker, John J. Money and exchange in Europe and America, 1600–1775; a handbook. Chapel Hill, Univ. of North Carolina Pr. for Inst. of Early Amer. History and Culture, Williamsburg, Va., [1978]. 367p. il. $25.95. **CH121**

"Aims to provide sufficient information of a technical and statistical nature to allow the reader to convert a sum stated in one money into its equivalent in another."—*p.[3].* HG219.M33

Rock, James M. Money, banking, and macroeconomics; a guide to information sources. Detroit, Gale, 1977. 281p. (Economics information guide ser., 11) $18. **CH122**

An introductory, annotated survey of the literature on macromonetary economics and its main fields; financial intermediation and commercial banking; macro-monetary theory; central banking; and stabilization policy. Concentrates on recent, widely available, English-language books and periodical articles. Author, title, and subject indexes. Z7164.F5R63

Transportation

Bibliography

Davis, Bob J. Information sources in transportation, material management, and physical distribution: an annotated bibliography and guide. Westport, Conn., Greenwood Pr., [1976]. 715p. $35. **CH123**

Materials are organized under 67 subjects, and within each subject, by type: book and pamphlet (including government publications); periodical titles (including directories, guides, and services); organizations; education (awards, libraries, programs, courses, scholarships, certification); and miscellaneous (analyses and statistics, atlases and maps). Indexed. An impressive compilation based in part on *An annotated bibliography of books, periodicals, films, and organizations of the oil pipeline industry* (1972) and *An annotated bibliography of the motor carrier industry* (1976). Z7164.T8D25

Rakowski, James P. Transportation economics: a guide to information sources. Detroit, Gale, [1976]. 215p. (Economics information guide ser., 5) $18. **CH124.**

An annotated bibliography of the most widely available book and article literature produced between 1960 and 1974 on transportation economics and business logistics. Sources are arranged by the industry discussed—railroads, highways, air, water, and urban transportation. Books and articles are listed separately for each industry; book titles are annotated; articles are subdivided by topic and listed without annotation. Final chapter covers reference sources, periodical titles, private and government sources of information. Author, title, and subject indexes. Z7164.T8R34

Encyclopedias

Rand McNally and Company. The Rand McNally encyclopedia of transportation. Chicago, Rand McNally, [1976]. 256p. il. $16.95. **CH125**

Geoffrey Crow, ed.

Offers brief definitions and discussions of modes of travel, mechanics of engines, personalities, specific ships and planes, and other topics involved in or associated with transportation. Dictionary arrangement, with numerous cross references and illustrations. TA1009.R36

Aviation

International encyclopedia of aviation. N.Y., Crown, [1977]. 480p. il. $30. **CH126**

David Mondey, gen. ed.

A heavily illustrated encyclopedia on the history of aviation, rocketry, and space flight. Chapters by individual specialists are grouped in seven sections: origins and development; military aviation; civil and maritime aviation; lighter-than-air; specialized aircraft; rocketry and space exploration; facts, feats and records (including flying feats, air crimes, air disasters, aviation law, biographical sketches, chronology, and international directory of air museums). Indexed.

Wragg, David W. A dictionary of aviation. [Reading, Berkshire, Eng.], Osprey, [1973]; N.Y., F. Fell, 1974. 286p. £4.45; $9.95. **CH127**

Intended for the layperson. Provides brief definitions of terms and concepts, events and personalities, major airlines, guided weapons, aircraft, and aircraft manufacturers. "Aviation" is broadly defined to include lighter-than-air flight and space flight, to a lesser degree. Individual air forces and air arms are not treated in any detail. TL509.W67

Railroads

Morris, James Oliver. Bibliography of industrial relations in the railroad industry. Ithaca, New York State School of Industrial and Labor Relations, Cornell Univ., [1975]. 153p. (Cornell industrial and labor relations bibliography ser., 12) $5. **CH128**

Attempts to identify published source material on the work environment, its influences, and its consequences within the intercity and interstate rail transportation system. Materials are categorized into sections by type, including: bibliographies; manuscripts, books and theses; periodical literature; government serial publications. Books, periodical literature, and government documents are further organized by topic and chronological period. No index. Z7164.T7M67

Ships

The Oxford companion to ships & the sea. London, Oxford Univ. Pr., 1976. 971p. il., maps. $35; £12. **CH129**

Peter Kemp, ed.

"The field to be covered is immense, ranging from the ships and the men who first opened up the world with their voyages into the unknown, through the struggles of nations as they developed and recognized that power and prosperity depended on the exercise of sea power, to those who wrote about, and painted, the sea scene."—*Pref.* Brief entries for personal, place, and ship names, nautical terms (including seamen's slang). Good illustrations. Cross references V23.O96

Communications

Postal guides

United States Postal Service. Postal service manual. [Wash., Govt. Prt. Off.], 1970– . Looseleaf. $33. **CH130**

Supersedes the *Postal manual* of the U.S. Post Office Dept. (*Guide* CH298).

Contents: (1) Domestic mail (including Instructions for mailers); (2) Organization and administration; (3) Postal procedures; (4) Personnel; (5) Transportation; (6) Facilities.

Mass media

Bibliography

Communication abstracts. v.1, no.1– , Mar. 1978– . Beverly Hills, Calif., Sage, 1978– . Quarterly. $60 per yr. **CH131**

Publ. with the cooperation of the School of Communications and Theater, Temple University.

Each issue offers about 250 abstracts of articles from about 100 journals and 50 recent books. Topically arranged, using headings such as: general communication, advertising, communication theory, mass communication, public communication, journalism, etc. Author and subject indexes in each issue cumulate annually. P87.C578

McCavitt, William E. Radio and television: a selected, annotated bibliography. Metuchen, N.J., Scarecrow Pr., 1978. 229p. $10. **CH132**

An annotated listing of some 1,100 "selected books on broadcasting."—*Introd.* A topical listing (under such headings as: surveys, history, regulation, programming, production, criticism, audience, cable television, broadcasting careers) with author index. Z7221.M23

Mass communication in India; an annotated bibliography. Comp. at Indian Institute of Mass Communication. Singapore, Asian Mass Communication Research and Information Centre, [1976]. 216p. (Asian mass communications bibliography ser., 2) S$18. **CH133**

A subject-classed, annotated list of over 800 English-language materials. Includes published materials (books, collections, conference reports, and government publications) from 1945 to 1973, and unpublished sources (M.A. and Ph.D. theses, seminar papers) from 1960 to 1973. Lists periodical titles but not articles. Author/title index. Z5630.M38

Richstad, Jim and **McMillan, Michael.** Mass communication and journalism in the Pacific islands: a bibliography. Honolulu, Univ. Pr. of Hawaii, [1978]. 299p. $15. **CH134**

"An East-West Center book from the East-West Communication Institute."—*t.p.*

For each nation or territory, lists materials in the following areas: reference works; newspapers; periodicals; biographies; government and international agency reports; divisions of the media (cinema, the press, radio, television); and related topics (news agencies, legal issues, printing, labor relations, etc.). Most entries are briefly annotated; indexed. Includes Hawaii. P92.I78R5

Dictionaries and encyclopedias

Brown, Les. The New York Times encyclopedia of television. [N.Y.], Times Books, [1977]. 492p. il. $20. **CH135**

Brief articles on multiple aspects of television: stars and programs, history, technology, special language, personnel, laws, networks, ratings, public and cable television, foreign broadcasting systems, etc. Short bibliography. PN1992.18.B7

Diamant, Lincoln. The broadcast communications dictionary. N.Y., Hastings House, [1974]. 128p. $6.95. **CH136**

Provides very brief definitions of some 2,000 technical, common, and slang terms; cross references are italicized. Not intended as a technical dictionary. A revised and enlarged edition was published 1978 ($9.95). P87.5.D48

Ellmore, R. Terry. Illustrated dictionary of broadcast—CATV—telecommunications. Blue Ridge Summit, Pa., Tab Books, [1977]. 396p. il. $14.95; $8.95 pa. **CH137**

A dictionary of words, phrases, acronyms and initials directly related to radio, television, and cable television. Brief definitions, with extensive use of cross references. "Advertising, production, and regulation . . . are covered extensively. The coverage of film, lighting and news is centered around the terms' relationship to radio, television and cable television."—*Introd.* Engineering terms are defined for the non-engineer. About 8,000 definitions. TK6634.E37

Terrace, Vincent. The complete encyclopedia of television programs, 1974–1976. South Brunswick, N.J., A. S. Barnes, [1976]. 2v. il. $29.95. **CH138**

An alphabetical title listing of television serials and shows televised on a continuing basis. Gives a description of the show format or summary of the principal action of a series, performers (with indication of character played), playing time, inclusive dates when televised, music credits, etc. No cross references and no index. A 2d, rev. ed. was scheduled for publication in late 1978 ($29.95).
PN1992.3.U5T46

Handbooks and directories

Television factbook, 1946– . Wash., Television Digest, Inc., [1946–]. no.1– . Annual. $74.50 per yr. **CH139**

Subtitle: The authoritative reference for the advertising, television and electronics industries.

Frequency varies. Title varies (1946–50 called *TV directory*).

Now published in two volumes per year: the "Services" volume covers all data other than stations; the "Stations" volume includes United States, Canadian, and international stations. TK6540.T453

World communications; a 200-country survey of press, radio, television and film. [5th ed. Epping, Eng., and N.Y.], Gower Pr., Unipub, [1975]. 533p. $21. **CH139a**

4th ed. 1964 (*Guide* CH312).

"The purpose of this, as of previous editions, is to describe the situation of the four principal media (press, radio, television, film) in the various countries and territories of the world, indicating, with statistical support, the general structure, facilities, output, distribution and coverage of each. . . ."—*Pref.* New categories on space communications and professional training and association. Index of news agencies and a brief bibliography. P90.W64

FINANCE AND BANKING

Bibliography

Brealey, Richard A. and **Pyle, Connie.** A bibliography of finance and investment. Cambridge, Mass., MIT Pr., [1973]. 361p. $18.50. **CH140**

A classed bibliography of more than 3,600 books, periodical articles, dissertations, and unpublished papers, most appearing after 1962. Within each subject area materials are chronologically arranged. The author "index" repeats the full citation.
Z7164.F5B77

Dictionaries, encyclopedias, and handbooks

Baughn, William Hubert and **Walker, Charles E.** The bankers' handbook. Rev. ed. Homewood, Ill., Dow Jones–Irwin, [1978]. 1205p. il. $35. **CH141**

1st ed. 1966.

Presents a series of 87 essays by experts in the field, grouped into broad sections, e.g., organization, personnel, information and data systems, planning, investments and securities markets, credit, international banking. Indexed. HG2491.B3

Levine, Sumner N. Financial analyst's handbook. Homewood, Ill., Dow Jones–Irwin, 1975. 2v. il. $60. **CH142**

Contents: v.1, Methods, theory, and portfolio management; v.2, Analysis by industry.

A series of chapters written by specialists as "a comprehensive guide to the principles and procedures necessary for successful investment management."—*Pref.* v.1 provides a discipline oriented coverage of investments, covering investment vehicles, special investment vehicles, the analysis of financial reports, economic analysis and timing, mathematical aids, and portfolio management and theories. v.2 provides analyses of specific industries, and includes a section on information sources, with an essay by Sylvia Mechanic on "Key references sources" (pp.859–82) and a subject guide to industry publications (pp.833–926). Overall index in both volumes.
HG4521.L625

Munn, Glenn Gaywaine. Glenn G. Munn's Encyclopedia of banking and finance. 7th ed., rev. and enl. by F. L. Garcia. Boston, Bankers Pub. Co., 1973. 953p. **CH143**

6th ed. 1962 (*Guide* CH328).

Entries and bibliographies have been revised, expanded, and updated. "The sole test of admissibility has been whether the term finds a place in the actual vocabulary of bankers, investors, financiers and brokers."—*Pref., 1st ed.* HG151.M8

Prentice-Hall, Inc. Corporate treasurer's and controller's encyclopedia, revised. Englewood Cliffs, N.J., Prentice-Hall, [1975]. 2v. (1050p.) il. $54.50. **CH144**

Rev. by Sam R. Goodman.

Previous editions ed. by Lillian Doris (*see Guide* CH326).

A practical manual, with many illustrations of forms and procedures. No bibliography. HG4061.P74

Thomson, William. Thomson's Dictionary of banking. 12th ed. [London], Pitman, [1974]. 669p. il. £10. **CH145**

F. R. Ryder, legal ed.; D. B. Jenkins, gen. ed.

1st ed. 1912.

More a one-volume encyclopedia than a dictionary. Deals with the business of banking as practiced in England; appendixes treat Scottish banking and Northern Ireland land laws relating to banking. Articles include sections from relevant laws, results of law cases, and law reports, if appropriate; historical development is usually traced. List of abbreviations; numerous tables and cross references.
HG151.T38

Thorndike, David. The Thorndike encyclopedia of banking and financial tables. Yearbook, 1975– . Boston, Warren, Gorham & Lamont, 1975– . Annual. (1976: $24.75 pa.) **CH146**

Prep. in conjunction with editorial staffs of the *Bankers magazine* and the *Banking law journal.*

For the *Encyclopedia see Guide* CH330.

Designed to supplement the main volume through the addition of tables and other materials reflecting changing economic conditions. Pt.I is made up of tables; pt.II is a narrative and tabular discussion of new developments in finance, investment, laws and regulations, etc. Indexed. HG1626.T49

Treasurer's handbook. Ed. by J. Fred Weston and Maurice B. Goudzwaard. Homewood, Ill., Dow Jones–Irwin, [1976]. 1181p. il. $30. **CH147**

More than fifty contributing authors have supplied chapters on current theory and practices written for the practicing treasurer. Most chapters include selected reading lists. Appendix of compound interest tables. HG4026.T73

Statistics

Fisher, Lawrence and **Lorie, James Hirsch.** A half-century of returns on stocks and bonds; rates of return on investments in common stocks and on U.S. Treasury securities, 1926–1976. Chicago, Univ. of Chicago Grad. School of Business, 1977. 174p. **CH148**

Presents 51 tables showing annual estimates of rates of return on investments in portfolios of common stocks listed on the New York Stock Exchange, and on investments in U.S. Treasury securities. Rates are presented in current dollars and adjusted for changes in the Consumer Price Index. Based on a machine-readable data file at the Center for Research in Security Prices. HG4915.F47

U.S. Board of Governors of the Federal Reserve System. Banking and monetary statistics, 1914–1941. Pt. I. Wash., [1976]. 682p. $5 pa. **CH149**

——— Banking and monetary statistics, 1941–1970. Wash., [1976]. 1168p. $15 pa. **CH150**
HG2493.U54

——— Annual statistical digest, 1971/75– . Wash., [1976–]. Annual. $5. **CH151**

The 1914–41 volume is a reprint of pt.1 of the original 1943 edition (*Guide* CH 346) and includes "data on the condition and operation of all banks . . . , statistics of bank debits, bank earnings, bank suspensions, branch, group, and chain banking, currency, money rates, security markets, Treasury finance, production and movement of gold, and international financial developments."—*Pref.* Some statistical series predate 1914. (Pt.II, detailing member bank statistics for each Federal Reserve district, was not reprinted.) This basic volume is amended and updated by the 1941–70 volume and by the *Annual statistical digest.* The latter also contains data previously published in the *Federal Reserve bulletin,* and which will no longer appear in that publication.

Directories and annuals

European financial almanac, 1974/75– . N.Y., Bowker, 1975– . Biennial. $50. **CH152**

Editions available in English, French, German, and Italian.

Includes information on the countries of the European Economic Community and Switzerland, Austria, Sweden and Norway. Pt.I consists of appraisals by specialists of the finance markets in each country. Pt.II is a directory of the major financial organizations grouped by country. Pt.III is a biographical dictionary. Indexes of organizations, persons listed by organization, and persons listed by country.

International stock & commodity exchange directory, 1974/75 ed. Canaan, N.H., Phoenix Publishing, [1974]. 340p. $30. **CH153**

Peter Wyckoff, comp.

A listing by country and city of the major stock and commodity exchanges. Information provided for each includes officers, hours, regulatory laws, issues traded and volume, unit of trading, memberships, commissions, and historical background. Section on related information has time zone designations, glossary; indexes by person, commodity, and name of exchange.

——— 1976 supplement. Canaan, N.H., [1976]. 53p.

Notes changes since the 1974/75 edition. HG4512.I5

Key figures of European securities, Jan. 1966– . Brussels, Investment Research Group of European Banks International, 1966– . 3 nos. a year. Free. **CH154**

In English. *Handbook for the use of Key figures of European securities* (annual) also available in French, German, or Dutch.

Provides concise information on European shares and securities. Arrangement is by country and then by firm, with figures on share capital, assets and liabilities, financing, sales, field of activity, adjusted figures per share. Indexed by industry. The *Handbook* summarizes regulations, notes on taxation, and regulations on international security transactions.

Who is where in world banking, 1975/76– . London, Banker Research Unit, [1975–]. (1976/77: £9 pa.) **CH155**

Subtitle: A guide to the overseas representation of the world's major banks classified by financial centre.

Eds., Philip Thorn and Jean Lack.

A list by country and then by city of the overseas offices of the world's leading banks, providing name, status, and address.

A companion volume is: HG1536.W48

Who owns what in world banking, 1975/76– . London, Banker Research Unit, [1975–]. Annual. (1976/77: £19 pa.) **CH156**

Subtitle: A guide to the subsidiary and affiliated interests of the world's major banks.

Eds., Philip Thorn and Jean Lack.

An alphabetical list of major individual and consortia banks. For each bank, domestic and international subsidiaries and affiliates are given, with percentage figures for the parent bank holdings. Index for all banks.

Biography

Who's who in world banking, 1975/76– . London, Financial Times, 1975– . Annual. £12; $36 per yr. **CH157**

J. B. Bonham, ed.

A biographical dictionary of more than 2,500 executive officers. Arrangement is by name, with an index arranged by country and by banks in each country.

INSURANCE

Bibliographies and indexes

Insurance periodicals index. 1963– . Boston, Special Libraries Assoc., Insurance Div., 1964– . Annual. $25 per yr. **CH158**

Place of publication varies.

For an earlier note on the index *see Guide* CH374.

Since Jan. 1969 the monthly indexes have appeared in *Best's review.* More than 40 periodicals are now indexed; a geographic index was added with the 1976 cumulation.

International Social Security Administration. Documentation Service. Recueil documentaire. Documentation series. Genève, 1963– . no.1– . Irregular. **CH159**

Title and prefatory matter in French, English, Spanish, and German.

Contents: no.1, Liste universelle des périodiques de sécurité sociale (1963); no.2, Bibliographie universelle de sécurité sociale, 1960–1963 (1964); no.3, Liste universelle des périodiques de sécurité sociale [2d ed.] (1966); no.4, Aspects économiques de la sécurité sociale, recherche en matière de sécurité sociale, bibliographie (1971).

Nelli, Humbert O. and **Ewedemi, Soga.** A bibliography of insurance history. 2d ed. Atlanta, Publishing Services Division, School of Business Administration, Georgia State Univ., 1976. 115p. (Research monograph, School of Business Admin., Georgia State Univ., no.70) $10. **CH160**

Comp. from the Insurance History Collection at the Center for Insurance Research, Georgia State University.

A wide variety of types of material—company histories, periodicals, clippings, photographs, policies, etc.—is arranged by broad topic: fire insurance, life insurance, marine insurance, general insurance, friendly societies, guilds, notarial activities. International in scope; no index. Z7164.I7N37

Handbooks

Callund, David. Employee benefits in Europe: an international survey of state and private schemes in 16 countries. [Epping, Essex, Eng.], Employment Conditions Abroad/ Gower Economic Publs., [1975]. 260p. Looseleaf. £19.95. **CH161**

Describes social security and employee benefit plans existing in Western European countries. Pt.I is a comparative analysis of the principles and evolution of social security systems, employee benefit plans, and private supplementary arrangements; pt.II is a country-by-country survey. An appendix offers a directory of relevant government offices and private associations. HD7166.C26

Gregg, Davis Weinert and **Lucas, Vane B.** Life and health insurance handbook. 3d ed. Homewood, Ill., Richard D. Irwin, 1973. 1336p. il. $35; text ed. $15.50. **CH162**

2d ed. 1964.

A series of chapters by specialists on all major phases of life and health insurance, including pensions, profit sharing, and estate planning. Most chapters have selected bibliographic references. HG8769.G7

LABOR AND INDUSTRIAL RELATIONS

Bibliography

Bibliographie zur Geschichte der deutschen Arbeiterbewegung. Jahrg. 1– , 1976– . Bonn-Bad Godesberg, Verlag Neue Gesellschaft GmbH., 1976– . Quarterly. DM58 per yr. **CH163**

Hrsg.: Bibliothek des Archivs der Sozialen Demokratie (Friedrich-Ebert-Stiftung).

A current international bibliography of writings (both book and periodical materials) on the German workers' movement. Classed arrangement with author and subject indexes. Citations are printed on perforated pages so that thev can be re-arranged as a 3X5 card file or kept in bound-volume form.

Dwyer, Richard E. Labor education in the U.S.: an annotated bibliography. Metuchen, N.J., Scarecrow Pr., 1977. 274p. $12. **CH164**

A listing, with very brief annotations, of periodical articles, parts of conference proceedings and ERIC materials produced from 1914 to 1976 on the three stages of labor education: (1) worker's education (1900–1940s); (2) labor education (post-World War II to the late 1960s); (3) labor studies (late 1960s to the present). Also lists archival and oral history collections. Author and subject indexes. Z5184.A24D95

Ente per la Storia del Socialismo e del Movimento Operaio Italiano. Bibliografia del socialismo e del movimento operaio italiano. Roma, Edizioni E.S.S.M.O.I., 1975–76. v.2 suppl. in 2v. **CH165**

For previously published volumes and annotation *see Guide* CH401.

Contents: v.2, Libri, opuscoli, articoli almanacchi, numeri unici (Supplemento 1953–67). In two parts: I, A–L; II, M–Z.

Continues the alphabetical arrangement—by author or title—of items published 1953–67; gives locations in Italian libraries.

Fink, Gary M. State labor proceedings: a bibliography of the AFL, CIO, and AFL-CIO proceedings, 1885–1974, held in the AFL-CIO Library. Westport, Conn., Greenwood Pr., [1975]. 291p. $35. **CH166**

Mary Mills, comp.

A guide to the publisher's microfiche collection of the proceedings (which will be updated and made available on a continuing basis). Pt.1 of the guide provides brief chronological surveys of each state labor movement, with annotations of the types of issues discussed in convention proceedings. Pt.2 is the bibliography of convention proceedings, yearbooks, minutes of executive board meetings, etc., listed alphabetically by state. HD8055.A6F55

Hepple, B. A., Neeson, J. M. and **O'Higgins, Paul.** A bibliography of the literature on British and Irish labour law. [London], Mansell, 1975. 331p. £9.75. **CH167**

Attempts to cover "all the relevant literature concerned with the legal relationships of people at work" (*Introd.*) in England, Wales, Scotland, Northern Ireland and the Republic of Ireland. Includes "the individual relationship between worker and employer . . . , the payment of wages, hours, holidays and other conditions of employment . . . ; protective legislation . . . ; compensation for accidents and diseases . . . ; training and vocational education . . . ; unemployment . . . ; collective bargaining . . . ; industrial conflict . . . ; organisation of employers and workers . . . ; and certain international aspects of direct relevance to Great Britain and Ireland."—*Introd.* Classed arrangement with author and subject indexes. Mainly English-language materials (books and periodical articles) from the 18th century through the end of 1972. More than 4,500 items; library locations are given for books and pamphlets. KD3001.H46

McBrearty, James C. American labor history and comparative labor movements; a selected bibliography. Tucson, Univ. of Arizona Pr., [1973]. 262p. $7.50. **CH168**

Pt.I, "Books," subdivides American labor history by chronological period and by topic, and comparative labor movements by country; pt.II, "Articles," follows the same format. There is a separate section for novels. Limited to English-language materials. Author index. Z7164.L1M15

Microfilming Corporation of America. American labor unions' constitutions and proceedings: a guide to the microform edition. Part I: 1836–1974. Glen Rock, N.J., Microfilming Corp. of America, 1975. 72p. $75. **CH169**

Independently useful as a bibliography of constitutions and proceedings of American labor unions as well as serving as a key to the microform collection. Arranged by broad subject groups (e.g., clothing, transportation, communications, etc.), with keyword index. Z7164.L1M62

U.S. Dept. of Labor. Library. United States Department of Labor library catalog. Boston, G. K. Hall, 1975. 38v. $3,560. **CH170**

A dictionary catalog representing more than 535,000 volumes, including books, periodicals, government reports, labor union publications, microforms, and cassettes. The collection deals with "the history of the labor movement; labor economics and industrial relations; arbitration, conciliation and mediation; labor laws; employment and unemployment; labor force and labor market; unemployment insurance; workmen's compensation; apprenticeship and training; wages and hours; working conditions; women's employment; industrial hygiene and safety; wholesale and retail prices; cost of living, productivity and other related subjects."—*Pref.* Extensive use of analytics. Z7164.L1U55

Woodbridge, Mark E. American Federation of Labor and Congress of Industrial Organizations pamphlets, 1889–1955: a bibliography and subject index to the pamphlets held in the AFL-CIO Library. Westport, Conn., Greenwood Pr., [1977]. 73p. $15. **CH171**

For each of the two unions, pamphlets are listed chronologically and alphabetically by title within the year; subject index covers both collections. Includes more than 1,300 pamphlets. Z7164.L1W66

Current

Work related abstracts, 1972– . Detroit, Information Coordinators, 1972– . Looseleaf. Monthly. $235 per yr. **CH172**

Continues *Employment relations abstracts* (*Guide* CH420), but provides abstracts for periodical articles only.

Periodicals

Harrison, Royden John, Woolven, Gillian B. and **Duncan, Robert.** The Warwick guide to British labour periodicals 1790–1970; a check list. [Hassocks, Eng.], Harvester Pr.; [Atlantic Highlands, N.J.], Humanities Pr., [1977]. 685p. $45. **CH173**

"By a *Labour periodical* we understand one which falls into one or other of the following three categories: First, one which was produced by an organised body consisting wholly or mainly of wage-earners or collectively dependent employees. . . . Second, . . . all periodicals which were produced in the avowed interest of the working class. . . . Third, . . . those which were produced for wage-earners by members of other social classes who sought to improve them, instruct them, or entertain them."—*Introd.*

An alphabetical listing of some 4,125 titles, giving (as far as the information was available) dates of publication, volumes or issues published, sponsoring body, library locations, a code letter indicating character of the journal, and often, a descriptive or explanatory note.

Subject index (which includes names of sponsoring agency or organization) and index of dates. Z7164.L1H37

Encyclopedias and handbooks

Labor unions. Ed.-in-chief, Gary M. Fink. Westport, Conn., Greenwood Pr., [1977]. 520p. (Greenwood encyclopedia of American institutions, 1) $27.50. **CH174**

Offers "historical sketches of more than two hundred national unions and labor federations that have been part of the American labor movement."—*Pref.* Selection criteria included "longevity, historical significance, size and economic power, and the influence a particular union had in the development of organized labor in America. An effort was also made to include unions representative of most minority groups, trades and industries, chronological time periods, and ideological movements."—*Pref.* Includes bibliographic references. HD6508.L234

Vetter, Betty M. and **Babco, Eleanor L.** Professional women and minorities: a manpower resource service. Wash., Scientific Manpower Commission, 1975. 668p. Looseleaf. il. $40. **CH175**

Detailed statistical information on the education, participation and availability of women and minorities. General information on enrollment, degrees, professions, workforce, and academic workforce is followed by information on specific subject fields. Recruitment resources lists registers of women and minority members in each subject field. Bibliography and index. Kept up-to-date by semiannual supplements ($20 per yr.). HD6278.U5V47

Biography

Fink, Gary M., ed. Biographical dictionary of American labor leaders. Westport, Conn., Greenwood Pr., [1974]. 559p. $25. **CH176**

About 500 biographies. "It was determined that each individual included . . . should have had a substantial impact on the American labor movement in one way or another. . . . It was also considered important to include a broad sampling of leaders from different eras, from as many different industries, crafts and trades as possible, and from among those women, Afro-Americans, and Chicanos whose contributions to the labor movement were largely ignored until recently. Although the emphasis was on leaders of the trade-union movement, an effort was made to include a representative group of labor-oriented radicals, politicians, editors, staff members, lawyers, reformers, and intellectuals."—*Pref.* Bibliographical sources are cited; many of the sketches are signed. Appendixes include lists by union affiliation, religious preference, place of birth, and major public offices, plus tables indicating formal education and political preference. Indexed. HD8073.A1F56

Who's who in labor. Ed.1– . N.Y., Arno Pr., 1976– . (Ed.1: $65) **CH177**

An earlier work with the same title, ed. by Marian Dickerman and Ruth Taylor, was published 1946 (*Guide* CH451).

Ed.1 (807p.) presents biographical sketches of leaders "currently active in the labor movement" (*Pref.*), including persons involved in industrial relations as neutrals or government officials. In addition to the biographies, there are sections offering information on: (1) AFL-CIO and other federations; (2) National unions and employee associations; (3) Government offices serving labor; (4) Labor studies centers. There are also a glossary of labor terms, a bibliography of labor periodicals, and an index by organization. About 3,800 biographies. HD8073.A1W5

MARKETING

Bibliography

Thompson, Ralph B. and **Faricy, John H.** A selected and annotated bibliography of marketing theory. 2d rev. ed. Austin, Bureau of Business Research, Univ. of Texas at Austin, [1976]. 86p. (Bibliography ser., 18) $3 pa. **CH178**

1st rev. ed. 1970.

A classified list stressing material relevant for theorists or students of marketing, with emphasis on behavioral sciences concepts. Each section is on a particular theory (e.g., consumer behavior) and is subdivided by format (i.e., books and articles). No index. Z7164.C81T4 no.18

Handbooks

Britt, Steuart Henderson. The Dartnell marketing manager's handbook. Chicago, Dartnell, [1973]. 1135p. il. $39.50. **CH179**

Chapters written by professors and marketing executives treat marketing management, organization and staffing, research, planning, consumer products and services, industrial products, promotion, international marketing, and program evaluation. Brief bibliographies.

Dartnell Corporation. The Dartnell sales promotion handbook. 5th ed. Ovid Riso, ed. Chicago, Dartnell, [1973]. 1206p. il. $37.50. **CH180**

5th ed. 1966 (*Guide* CH490).

A desk-reference book detailing techniques and tools of sales promotion, distribution channels, evaluation of effectiveness, equipment, mail order selling, the role of computers, etc.

Ferber, Robert. Handbook of marketing research. N.Y., McGraw-Hill, [1974]. 1v., various paging. il. $34.50. **CH181**

Consists of chapters by specialists arranged in four sections: (1) Introduction, focusing on the history, function, and operations of marketing research; (2) Techniques, covering quantitative methods such as surveys, sampling, model building, and computer techniques; (3) Behavioral science techniques; (4) Major areas of application, subdivided by major types of marketing—new products, sales, advertising, industrial, international. Indexed. HF5415.2.F419

Directories

Directory of U.S. and Canadian marketing surveys and services. Ed. by Valerie Kollonitsch and Kathleen DiCioccio. Fairfield, N.J., Charles H. Kline & Co., [1976]. 115p. $75 pa. **CH182**

An alphabetical list of nearly 1,000 marketing reports and syndicated continuing services available from 85 American, Canadian, and European consulting firms. Each entry lists the firm's name, its syndicated services, individual surveys under $1,000, and individual surveys over $1,000. Subject index.

OCCUPATIONS

Clapp, Jane. Professional ethics and insignia. Metuchen, N.J., Scarecrow Pr., 1974. 851p. il. $27.50. **CH183**

205 United States professional organizations, in categories from accountants to zoologists, are listed with address, corresponding officer, and one or more of the following items: code of ethics, conduct, standards, or rules; emblem; accreditation program. Includes a few international organizations. HD6504.A194

Dickhut, Harold W. and **Davis, Marvel J.** Professional resume/job search guide. 3d ed. Chicago, Management Counselors, Inc., [1975]. 254p. il. $14.95. **CH184**

1st ed. 1972; 2d ed. 1973.

A guide to preparing the resumé; numerous sample resumés and cover letters. Index. A 4th ed. was scheduled for late 1978 publication ($16.95). HF5383.D47

Peck, Theodore P. Occupational safety and health: a guide to information sources. Detroit, Gale, [1974]. 261p. (Management information guide, 28) $18. **CH185**

Sec. 1–5 describe federal and state agency programs, training programs, research centers, and professional societies and trade associations. Sec. 6, 7 and 11 list bibliographic materials (by subject and format), media resources, and library collections. Sec. 8, 9, 10 and 12 cover information sources on standards, safety equipment suppliers, related legislation and codes, and international information sources. Indexed. Z6675.I5P4

REAL ESTATE

Bibliography

MacBride, Dexter D. The bibliography of appraisal literature. Wash., American Soc. of Appraisers, 1974. 769p. $30. **CH186**

English-language sources (principally books and periodical articles) selected by specialists and arranged in fifteen subject chapters, each with sub-categories. Includes real property, personal property, intangibles, utilities, machinery and equipment, technical evaluation, appraisal administration. Author index. Z7164.V3M3

Paulus, Virginia. Housing: a bibliography, 1960–1972. N.Y., AMS Pr., [1974]. 339p. $25. **CH187**

A classed list of 3,625 entries on housing concerns in the United States, excluding architecture, vacation homes, and new towns. A wide variety of materials is grouped into six major categories or "frameworks": economic; legal; social/political; demographic; informational (i.e., reference works); and general works and anthologies. Detailed table of contents. Author index and "subject finding guide." Z7164.H8P38

Dictionaries

Boyce, Bryl N. Real estate appraisal terminology. Cambridge, Mass., Ballinger Pub. Co., [1975]. 306p. $12.50. **CH188**

Sponsored jointly by the American Institute of Real Estate Appraisers and the Society of Real Estate Appraisers.

Based on the Institute's *Appraisal terminology and handbook* (5th ed. 1967; *Guide* CH502) and the Society's *Real estate appraisal principles and terminology* (2d ed. Chicago, 1971), with new and expanded terminology in the areas of investment analysis, statistics, mathematics, and computers. HD1387.B69

Dumouchel, J. Robert. Dictionary of development terminology. N.Y., McGraw-Hill, [1976]. 278p. $9.95. **CH189**

Subtitle: The technical language of builders, lenders, architects and planners, investors, real estate brokers and attorneys, appraisers, land taxing and zoning authorities, government officials, community organizers, housing managers, urban renewal specialists.

Very brief definitions of terms used in urban renewal and the housing industry, e.g., "Fannie Mae," Capehart-Wherry housing, New Community Development Program. List of abbreviations and acronyms precedes the definitions. HT108.5.D84

Handbooks and statistical sources

The McGraw-Hill construction business handbook: a practical guide to accounting, credit, finance, insurance, and law for the construction industry. Ed. by Robert F. Cushman. N.Y., McGraw-Hill, [1978]. various pagings. il. $32.50. **CH190**

Presents 52 chapters by individual specialists in areas such as: organization, accounting, taxes, and record-keeping; financing, insurance, and bonding; contract analysis and procurement; government regulations; contract performance and rights; collection procedures. Bibliographic footnotes; indexed. HD9715.A2M27

U.S. Bureau of the Census. 1970 census of housing. [Wash., Govt. Prt. Off., 1973] v.6–7. **CH191**

For v.1–5 *see Guide* CH509.

Contents: v.6, Plumbing facilities and estimates of dilapidated housing; v.7, Subject reports [on such topics as housing of senior citizens and selected racial groups, mobile homes, cooperative and condominium housing].

C J

Political Science

GENERAL WORKS

Guides

Holler, Frederick L. The information sources of political science. [2d ed.] Santa Barbara, Calif., ABC-Clio, [1975]. 5v. $28.25. **CJ1**

1st ed. 1971 (*Guide* CJ3).

Contents: v.1, General reference sources; v.2, Social sciences, political sciences, history, anthropology, sociology, psychology, economics, geography; v.3, Federal government, state government, local government, political behavior, public law, international law; v.4, International relations, international organization, comparative and area studies of politics & government; v.5, Public administration, political theory.

A revised and greatly expanded edition: new titles have been added, annotations expanded, and the classification scheme altered. The author, title, and subject indexes to the full set are repeated in each volume. Z7161.H64

Pfaltzgraff, Robert L. The study of international relations: a guide to information sources. Detroit, Gale, [1977]. 155p. (International relations information guide ser., v.5) $18. **CJ2**

An annotated bibliography of English-language books (most published since 1945) on the theory and methodology of international relations. General introductory chapters on the nature of the discipline and approaches to it are followed by chapters listing works on the international system, diplomacy, power and theories of conflict, military strategy and theories of deterrence, and integration and alliance theories. Annotated list of important journals, and list of recommended books for the small library. Author, title, and subject indexes. Z6461.P53

Bibliographies and indexes

Beaufays, Jean. Le féderalisme, le régionalisme: bibliographie. Liège, Département de Science Politique, Université de Liège et Centre Universitaire de Droit Publique, 1976. 280*l.* (Études et recherches—Université de Liège, Département de science politique, no.10) 280F. pa. **CJ3**

An author listing of more than 2,300 books and periodical articles, indexed by geographic area and subject. Z7164.F4B4

Bibliographies françaises de sciences sociales. Guides de recherches. Paris, Colin, 1972–75. v.4–6. (In progress) **CJ4**

For earlier volumes *see Guide* CJ7.

Contents: v4, Henri Ménudier. L'Allemagne après 1945 (1972);

v.5, Denis Martin. L'Afrique noire (1973); v.6, Guy Feuer. Le Moyen-Orient contemporain (1975).

——— Répertoires documentaires. Paris, Fondation, 1971. v.4.

For earlier volumes *see Guide* CJ7.

Contents: v.4, Supplément au Catalogue général des périodiques reçus par La Fondation Nationale des Sciences Politiques.

Blackey, Robert. Modern revolutions and revolutionists. Santa Barbara, Calif., Clio Books, [1976]. 257p. $15.75. (War/peace bibliography ser.) **CJ5**

The series was developed in cooperation with the Center for the Study of Armament and Disarmament, California State Univ., Los Angeles.

A list of 2,400 English-language books and articles. Materials on the concepts and aspects of revolution are arranged topically (sociology of revolution, counter-revolution, violence, etc.); remaining materials follow a geographical arrangement (North America: American Revolution, New Left, Herbert Marcuse, Student rebellions, Black revolution). Index. Z7161.B65

Blackstock, Paul W. and **Schaf, Frank L.** Intelligence, espionage, counterespionage, and covert operations: a guide to information sources. Detroit, Gale, [1978]. 255p. (International relations information guide ser., 2) $18. **CJ6**

A highly selective, annotated bibliography, limited mainly to books and articles in the English language. Concentrates on the post-1945 period, with some attention to historical treatments. Author and title indexes. Z6724.I7B55

Böttcher, Winfried. Britische Europaideen, 1940–1970: eine Bibliographie. Düsseldorf, Droste, [1971–]. Bd.1– . (In progress) **CJ7**

Contents: Bd.1, Bücher und Broschüren; Bd.2, Zeitschriften.

Title also in English and French: *Great Britain and Europe; La Grand Bretagne et l'Europe.* Text in German, English, and French.

Bd.1 is a chronological list of books and brochures published in Britain on European integration; within each year, titles are arranged alphabetically by author. Person and subject index. Bd.2 follows a similar arrangement, but includes more material from British periodicals on conditions within individual European countries. Indexed by author, and by subject (Europe, individual country, and person). Bd.3 is projected as a bibliography, index, and analysis of speeches on Europe and European integration in the House of Commons. Z2000.B64

Bracher, Karl Dietrich, Jacobsen, Hans-Adolf and **Funke, Manfred.** Bibliographie zur Politik in Theorie und Praxis. Aktualis. Neuaufl. Düsseldorf, Droste, 1976. 574p. (Bonner Schriften zur Politik und Zeitgeschichte, 13) DM62. **CJ8**

1st ed. 1970 (*Guide* CJ9). Ergänzungsband Auswahl aus der von Juni 1969 bis Oktober 1972 erschienenen Literatur und Nachträge (Düsseldorf, Droste, 1973. 207p.; Bonner Schriften zur Politik und Zeitgeschichte, 8).

A substantial revision and expansion of the first edition to some 7,900 entries. More emphasis on reference tools, methodology, the developing world, and political economy. Classed table of contents is more detailed, and there is an author/personal name index. The country index has been omitted, possibly because of the added geographical breakdown in the table of contents. Z7161.A2B73

Britain and Europe since 1945. A bibliographical guide. Comp. by James Hennessy. [Brighton, Eng.], Harvester Pr., 1973. 98p. £12.50. **CJ9**

Subtitle: An author, title and chronological index to British primary source material on European integration issued since 1945.

A guide to the publisher's microfiche collection of the same title, which reproduces 26,000 pages of literature produced by British pressure groups and other organizations on the topic of British integration into Europe. Participating organizations are briefly described. Includes material produced through 1972. The collection is updated annually and issued with: HC241.25.G7B675

Britain and Europe during 1973– ; a bibliographical guide. [Hassocks, Eng.], Harvester Pr., 1974– . Annual. (1977: £4.50) **CJ9a**

Subtitle: An author, title and chronological index to British primary source material on European integration issued during 1973– .

1975 volume is entitled *Britain and Europe during 1975—year of the Referendum.*

The combined retrospective index set to journals in political science, 1886–1974. Wash., Carrollton Pr., 1977. 8v. $750. **CJ10**

At head of title: C.R.I.S.

Annadel N. Wile, exec. ed.

Contents: v.1, International law, international organizations, international relations, international trade and economics; v.2, Methodology and theoretical approaches, political behavior and process, political ideologies, political systems, political thought; v.3, Administration in general, economics in general, financial administration, management in general, organization, departments and functions; v.4–5, Organization, departments and functions (cont'd.); v.6, Organization, departments and functions, personnel, population. v.7–8, Author indexes.

More than 115,000 articles from 179 English-language political science journals have been assigned to one or more of 95 subject categories, then computer-sorted by keyword and chronological coverage under each subject category. Each entry provides keyword, brief title, author's name, year, volume and code number for journal title, and beginning page.

The publisher also offers a *Combined retrospective index to journals in sociology, 1895–1974,* covering about 105,000 articles from 118 English-language sociology journals (6v., $550).

Hawley, Willis D. and **Svara, James H.** The study of community power: a bibliographic review. Santa Barbara, Calif., ABC-Clio, [1972]. 123p. $12.75; $5.50 pa. **CJ11**

Emphasizes English-language materials published since 1920 on "the structure or pattern of community-wide decision making that is intended to authoritatively allocate significant privilege or resources among various institutions, groups and/or individuals" (*Pref.*), thus excluding studies of specific interests or subcommunities. Chapters on history of the field, field studies in communities, methodology, and secondary analysis. Annotations; reviews are noted. Author index. Z7164.C842H38

International relations theory: a bibliography. Ed. by A. J. R. Groom and Christopher Mitchell. London, Frances Pinter; N.Y., Nichols, [1978]. 222p. $20. **CJ12**

". . . the aim has been to reflect and comment upon the present state of the literature in International Relations in . . . its theoretical and conceptual aspects and to point to both likely and desirable future directions."—*Introd.* Chapters by individual scholars compare English-language sources in areas such as methodology, research methods, strategy, foreign policy analysis, etc.; each essay concludes with a list of titles mentioned. Z6461.I49

Kujath, Karl. Bibliographie zur Europäischen Integration: mit Anmerkungen. Bonn, Europa Union, [1977]. 777p. DM150. **CJ13**

Title and prefatory matter also in French and English.

A major international bibliography, concentrating on monographs and periodical titles, arranged within a detailed subject classification. Covers international organizations, European unification and integration in general, and each of the intergovernmental and supranational European organizations. Personal name index. Z2000.K85

LaBarr, Dorothy F. and **Singer, Joel David.** The study of international politics: a guide to the sources for the student, teacher and researcher. Santa Barbara, Calif., Clio Books, [1976]. 211p. $17.95. **CJ14**

A bibliography of English-language materials grouped into eight main sections: (1) Approaches to the study and teaching; (2) Texts and general treatises; (3) American and comparative foreign policy; (4) Journals and annuals; (5) Special series; (6) Abstracts and book reviews; (7) Data sources and handbooks; (8) Bibliographies. The sections are subdivided by type, e.g., authored volumes, articles, edited volumes; contents of edited volumes are listed. Excludes material on international law and international organizations. Author index includes individual authors within the edited volumes. Z6461.L3

Leif, Irving P. Community power and decision-making: an international handbook. Metuchen, N.J., Scarecrow Pr., 1974. 170p. $6. **CJ15**

A classed bibliography of books, articles, dissertations, theses, and conference papers; chapters on theory, methodology, community power as a discipline, American community power studies (subdivided by topical issues such as education, labor, urban planning), and international community power studies. Author index. A selection from this bibliography, with annotations, was published as part of "Community power and decision-making; a trend report and bibliography" by Leif and T. N. Clark in *Current sociology* 20, no. 2 (1972). Z7164.C842L43

Menendez, Albert J. Church-state relations: an annotated bibliography. N.Y., Garland, 1976. 126p. $14. **CJ16**

A topically arranged listing of English-language books; brief annotations; author index. Emphasis is on developments in the United States and Great Britain. Z7776.72.M45

Mikolus, Edward F. Annotated bibliography on transnational and international terrorism. [Wash.], U.S. Central Intelligence Agency, 1976. 225p. **CJ17**

"Designed to provide . . . a comprehensive survey of non-journalistic literature dealing with . . . transnational or international terrorism . . . it does not include domestic incidents having no international connection, nor does it deal with terrorist groups based in the United States or incidents within the United States."—*Note.* Deals with aspects of terrorism in general, and in specific regions. Subject arrangement; no index.

U.S. Air Force Academy. Library. Terrorism. [Comp. by Betsy Coxe. Colorado Springs, Colo.], U.S. Air Force Academy Lib., 1977. 47p. (Special bibliography ser., no.57) **CJ18**

A selection from the library's holdings "acquired during the last five years."—*Introd.* Arranged by geographical region, with sections on terrorism in general, global terrorism, and nuclear terrorism; within each region, entries are classed by type, e.g., books, periodical (and newspaper) articles, government publications, and report literature (AD reports and Rand material). No index. Z5703.4.T47U54

Wright, Moorhead, Davis, Jane and **Clarke, Michael.** Essay collections in international relations; a classified bibliography. N.Y. & London, Garland, 1977. 172p. $21. **CJ19**

"This bibliography details original material on international relations since 1870 written in English and appearing in non-recurrent multi-author works published between 1945 and 1975."—*Introd.* Selective inclusion of materials in "peripheral" areas of international economics, international law, and diplomatic history, and concentration on theoretical, analytical, and historical work rather than current events reporting. Main text is a classified bibliography of individual essays, referring to the list of essay collections for full bibliographic information. Author and subject indexes. Z6461.W7

Current

ABC pol sci . . . [Santa Barbara, Calif., ABC-Clio, 1969–] **CJ20**

For full citation and annotation *see Guide* CJ28.

Beginning 1977, published six times a year. Since 1973 has included monthly indexes to laws and to court decisions and cases, cumulating in the final issue of the year.

Canadian review of studies in nationalism. Revue canadienne des études sur le nationalisme. Annual bibliography of works on nationalism: a regional selection. v.1– , 1974– . (Suppl. to the semiannual periodical *Canadian review of studies in nationalism*) $9 per yr. **CJ21**

A selective guide to the contemporary (1970 to the present) literature on nationalism. Each section by an individual scholar includes a brief "state of the scholarship" survey on particular regions or cultures; entries for books and periodical articles are annotated. Volume for 1976 includes review articles such as "Sociological perspectives on Québec nationalism, 1945–1969." No index. Z7164.N2C3

Fondation Nationale des Sciences Politiques. Bibliographie courante d'articles de périodiques postérieurs à 1944 sur les problèmes politiques, économiques, et sociaux. Supplement 5–8. Boston, G. K. Hall, 1973–77. 8v. (price varies: 8th suppl., $230) **CJ22**

For main set and earlier supplements *see Guide* CJ14.

United States political science documents. v.1– , 1975– . Pittsburgh, Univ. of Pittsburgh, Univ. Center for International Studies, 1976– . Annual. (v.1, pts.1–2: $120) **CJ23**

Contents: pt.1, Indexes; pt.2, Document descriptions.

"Published by University Center for International Studies, University of Pittsburgh, in conjunction with the American Political Science Association."—*t.p.*

An abstracting service for more than 120 American journals in the political, social, and policy sciences. Pt.1 includes five indexes: Author/Contributor, Subject, Geographic area, Proper name, and Journal; all give complete bibliographic citations and reference to the abstract printed in pt.2. (The parts are available separately.) Abstracts in pt.2 are 100–200 words in length. Subject and geographic area indexes are based on descriptors from the *Political science thesaurus* by Carl Beck and others (*Suppl.* CJ24). The data base established for *USPSD* has also been used for a number of "derivative publications": *Comparative studies documents, Ethnic studies bibliography, Intercultural studies reference guide, International studies documents, Public policy studies documents, Strategic studies documents, Russian and East European studies bibliography,* and *Asian studies bibliography.* JA51.U55

Dictionaries and encyclopedias

Beck, Carl, Dym, Eleanor D. and **McKechnie, J. Thomas.** Political science thesaurus. Wash., Am. Pol. Sci. Assoc., [1975]. 463p. $30; $25 pa. **CJ24**

The "terminology control device" for the United States Political Science Information System, developed by the American Political Science Association in cooperation with the University of Pittsburgh. (For a description of the system and its elements, including *United States political science documents* [*Suppl.* CJ23], see Carl Beck and Thomas McKechnie, "United States Political Science Information System up and running," *PS* 10,no.1:40–42, Winter 1977.) The thesaurus is divided into three sections: (1) the "Thesaurus of terms" lists 5,721 main entry terms and geographical/political area terms; (2) the "Permuted index" lists every significant word in the terms used in the "Thesaurus of terms," to indicate word order and specific, rather than general terms; and (3) the "Hierarchical index" gives "the position of membership of a term in an overall family of descriptors."—*p.10.* Z695.1.P63B4

Countries of the world and their leaders. [Ed.1–] Detroit, Gale, 1974– . Irregular. maps. (4th ed., 1978: $24) **CJ25**

Ed. 1 called *Countries of the world.*

Subtitle: The U.S. Department of State's report on Status of the world's nations, combined with its series of Background notes. . . . Includes Central Intelligence Agency's List of chiefs of state and cabinet ministers of foreign governments.

Gathers together and reprints the current *Background notes, Status of the world's nations, Chiefs of state and cabinet ministers of foreign governments,* and the *International organizations* series on CENTO, OAU, NATO, OECD, and the European Communities. Alphabetical and chronological lists of newly independent nations. G122.C67

Diplomaticheskii slovar'. V 3-kh t. Gl. red. A. A. Gromyko [i dr. Pererad. i dop. izd.]. Moskva, Politizdat, 1973. v.3. **CJ26**

For full information *see Guide* CJ36.

Contents: v.3, R-IA; Register of current diplomatic officers and index by country. Completes the set.

Dizionario di politica. Diretto da Noberto Bobbio e Nicola Matteucci. [Turin], UTET, [1976]. 1097p. L.32,000. **CJ27**

Lengthy, signed articles by an international group of scholars stress the variant definitions of political concepts and their historical development. Most articles have brief bibliographies. JA64.I8D59

The encyclopedia of U.S. government benefits. 2d ed. Union City, N.J., Wm. H. Wise, 1975. 1013p. il. $17.95. **CJ28**

Subtitle: A complete, practical and convenient guide to United States government benefits available to the people of America. Written by a group of government experts; ed. by Roy A. Grisham, Jr., and Paul D. McConaughy.

1st ed. 1965 (*Guide* CJ47).

A considerably revised edition. While a good deal of the material remains unchanged, information has been updated as necessary and numerous new articles inserted. Various entries of marginal interest for a work of this kind (e.g., entries for the individual national parks) have been dropped. JK424.E55

Greenstein, Fred I. and **Polsby, Nelson W.** Handbook of political science. Reading, Mass., Addison-Wesley, [1975]. 9v. **CJ29**

Contents: v.1, Political science: scope and theory; v.2, Micropolitical theory; v.3, Macropolitical theory; v.4, Non-governmental politics; v.5, Governmental institutions and processes; v.6, Policies and policy-making; v.7, Strategies of inquiry; v.8, International politics; v.9, Cumulative index.

A collection of review articles by scholars representing the major areas of political science, similar in concept to the Gardner Lindzey and Elliot Aronson *Handbook of social psychology* (2d ed., 1968–69. 5v.). Each essay concludes with extensive references. Author and subject index. Extensive reviews of each volume appears in *American political science review* 71:1621–36 (Dec. 1977). JA71.G752

Haensch, Günther. Wörterbuch der internationalen Beziehungen und der Politik, systematisch und alphabetisch; Deutsch, Englisch, Französisch, Spanisch. [München], Max Hueber Verlag, [1975]. 781p. **CJ30**

1st ed. 1965 (*Guide* CJ39).

Title also in English (*Dictionary of international relations and politics*), French, and Spanish.

A revised and updated edition. The section of "Names of states, territories, etc." has been omitted. JX1226.H283

Laqueur, Walter Ze'ev, ed. A dictionary of politics. Rev. ed. N.Y., Free Pr., [1974]. 565p. $14.95. **CJ31**

1st ed. 1971 (*Guide* CJ41).

This edition includes references to events and new developments through early 1973. D419.L36

Spuler, Bertold. Rulers and governments of the world. London & N.Y., Bowker, [1977]. v.2–3. (In progress) $45 per v. **CJ32**

Gen. ed., C. G. Allen.

Contents: v.1 [to be publ. late 1978], Earliest times to 1941; v.2, 1492 to 1929; v.3, 1930 to 1975.

v.2 and 3 are based on the 2d ed. of v.3–4 of Spuler's *Regenten und Regierungen der Welt* (Würzburg, Ploetz, 1962–64), the 1964/65 appendix to v.4 (publ. 1966), and v.5, "Neueste Zeit 1965–1970" (publ. 1972). Material for the 1971–75 period was compiled for this edition by Charles Geoffry Allen and Neil Saunders. v.1 is to be entirely new in the English edition.

For each state, entry begins with a brief note on its origin (self-government or independence), followed by names and dates of heads of state, representatives of the home country for colonies and dominions, and list of members of governments (prime ministers, foreign ministers, and cabinets of major countries in the modern era). Name index in each volume. D11.5.R67

Worldmark encyclopedia of the nations. Ed. and publ., Moshe Y. Sachs. 5th ed. N.Y., Worldmark Pr., 1976. 5v. $99.50. **CJ33**

4th ed. 1971 (*Guide* CJ45).

Contents: v.1, United Nations; v.2, Africa; v.3, Americas; v.4, Asia and Australasia; v.5, Europe.

Includes 18 new articles on new nations, revised histories and demographic information, and expanded bibliographies. G63.W67

Handbooks

Cook, Chris and **Paxton, John.** European political facts, 1918–73. [London, Macmillan]; N.Y., St. Martin's, [1975]. 363p. $14.95; £10. **CJ34**

Offers statistical tables, lists and statements of fact concerning political, economic, and social affairs of European countries "from the Atlantic to the Urals."—*Pref.* Includes sections for international organizations, heads of state, parliaments, ministers, elections, political parties, justice, defense and treaties, dependencies, population, economics, trade unions, education, and press. Indexed. JN12.C64

Herman, Valentine. Parliaments of the world; a reference compendium. Prep. . . . with the collaboration of Françoise Mendel. Berlin & N.Y., DeGruyter, [1976]. 985p. $70. **CJ35**

At head of title: Inter-Parliamentary Union.

Data on 56 parliaments as they existed Sept. 1, 1974, are presented in a series of 70 comparative tables. "Each table should not only enable the reader to ascertain the essential similarities and differences between various parliamentary systems in respect of a given question, but also to find detailed information concerning one or more individual Parliaments."—*Introd.* Tables are preceded by textual surveys of the matter in question. Indexed. JF501.H45

Mackie, Thomas T. and **Rose, Richard.** The international almanac of electoral history. N.Y., Free Pr., [1974]. 434p. $15. **CJ36**

"The purpose of this book is to provide a complete and accurate compilation of election results in Western nations since the beginning of competitive elections."—*Introd.* An introductory note precedes the statistical tables for each country. "The starting point chosen for each country is the first election in which the great majority of seats for the national parliament were contested and most candidates fought under common cross-local labels." JF1001.M17

Directories

American Political Science Association. Directory of members, January 1977. Supplement to the APSA biographical directory. Wash., Assoc., [1977]. 137p. $3 pa. **CJ37**

For the *Biographical directory* which this supplements *see Guide* CJ59. Affiliations and addresses of members are given, but no biographical information.

Murphy, Dennis D. Directory of conservative and libertarian serials, publishers, and freelance markets. [Tucson, Ariz., Author], 1977. 64p. $3.50 pa. **CJ38**

For full information *see Suppl.* AE10.

Yearbooks

Political handbook of the world. 1975– . N.Y., McGraw-Hill, 1975– . Annual. Price varies (1977: $24.95, or $17.50 by subscription) **CJ39**

Arthur S. Banks, ed.

Publ. for the Center for Social Analysis of the State University of New York at Binghamton and for the Council on Foreign Relations.

Subtitle [varies]: Governments, regional issues and intergovernmental organizations. . . .

Supersedes the *Political handbook and atlas of the world* (*Guide* CJ66).

The atlas section has been dropped, the information on intergovernmental organizations expanded, and a new section added for regional issues.

GOVERNMENT

United States

Guides

Simpson, Antony E. Guide to library research in public administration. N.Y., John Jay College of Criminal Justice, Center for Productive Public Management, [1976]. 210p. il. $5.95 pa. **CJ40**

Chapters on the field of public administration, and the definition of the research problem and search strategy, are followed by chapters on types of reference works, computer searches, archival resources, and suggestions on writing the research paper. Indexed. Z7164.A2S5

Vose, Clement E. A guide to library sources in political science: American government. Wash., Amer. Pol. Sci. Assoc., [1975]. 135p. il. (Instructional resource monograph, no.1) $6.50; $4 pa. **CJ41**

A guide for students in three main sections: (1) American national government, discussing government publications, indexes, and reference sources for research relating to various branches of the government and their activities; (2) General reference books of interest to the research worker in political science; (3) The political scientist in the library, discussing basic library techniques, plus information on the use of manuscripts and archives. No index. Z7165.U5V67

Bibliography

Filler, Louis. Progressivism and muckraking. N.Y., Bowker, 1976. 200p. $15.95. **CJ42**

For full information *see Suppl.* DB28.

Kaid, Lynda Lee, Sanders, Keith R. and **Hirsch, Robert O.** Political campaign communication: a bibliography and guide to the literature. Metuchen, N.J., Scarecrow Pr., 1974. 206p. $6.50. **CJ43**

A listing of over 1,500 books, articles, pamphlets, federal documents, and unpublished materials on political campaign communication in the United States between 1950 and 1972. Also includes a French- and German-language supplement, an annotated list of fifty "seminal" books on the topic, and a guide to the literature to keep the user abreast of research. Subject index. Z7165.U5K34

Manheim, Jarol B. and **Wallace, Melanie.** Political violence in the United States, 1875–1974: a bibliography. N.Y. & London, Garland, 1975. 116p. $16. **CJ44**

A classed list of over 1,500 entries: books, articles, doctoral dissertations, and government documents covering strikes, race riots, gun control, assassinations, anarchism and terrorism, vigilantism, police violence, etc. Author index but no detailed subject approach. Z7165.U5M27

Millett, Stephen M. A selected bibliography of American constitutional history. Santa Barbara, Calif., ABC-Clio, [1975]. 116p. $9.75. **CJ45**

A brief discussion of primary sources is followed by a list of more than 1,000 secondary works topically arranged: surveys; historical origins of the Constitution; particular articles and sections; the Bill of Rights and Amendments; case histories; judicial biographies; and extrajudicial events which have affected constitutional history. List of pertinent journals and addenda. Author index. KF4546.M54

Registers

Directory of registered lobbyists and lobbyist legislation. Ed. 2– . Chicago, Marquis Academic Media, 1975– . **CJ46**

Continues the *Directory of registered federal and state lobbyists* (*Guide* CJ74). JK1118.D561

Directory of Washington representatives of American associations & industry; who does what for whom in the nation's capital. [v.1–] Wash., Columbia Books, [1977–]. Annual. $30 pa. **CJ47**

Craig Colgate, Jr., ed.; Halvor O. Ekern, asst. ed.

Subtitle: A compilation of Washington representatives of the major national associations, labor unions and U.S. companies, registered foreign agents (nation-wide), lobbyists, lawyers, law firms and special interest groups, together with their clients and areas of legislative and regulatory concerns.

The main "Representative index" provides name, address, telephone number, background, date registered as lobbyist (if applicable), and list of organizations represented. "Organization index" lists those concerns with Washington offices or representatives. "Subject index" refers to concerns listed in the "Organization index."

U.S. Congress. The United States Congressional directories, 1789–1840. Ed. by Perry M. Goldman and James S. Young. N.Y., Columbia Univ. Pr., 1973. 417p. $22.50. **CJ48**

Collates information provided in the early Congressional directories, including names and addresses of state delegations, members of standing and select committees, and the boardinghouse groups (or fraternities) of Congressional members. The cutoff date of 1840 was chosen because "most . . . libraries possess a complete series of the *Congressional Directories* from 1840 on, and . . . the earlier directories are rare items." No personal names index or biographical material; the user is referred to the *Biographical directory of the American Congress* (*Guide* CJ69) for material on the state delegations. JK1011.U53

United States government manual. Supplement to the 1977/78 . . . manual. [Wash., 1978] 156p. $2.75 pa. **CJ49**

For a note on the *Manual see Guide* CJ72.

Indicates changes in personnel and organization which have occurred since May 1, 1977, especially programs and activities of the Department of Energy and the Office of Administration within the Executive Office of the President.

Executive branch

Greenstein, Fred I., Berman, Larry and **Felzenberg, Alvin S.** Evolution of the modern presidency; a bibliographical survey. Wash., Amer. Enterprise Inst. for Public Policy Research, [1977]. unpaged. (AEI studies, 153; Studies in political and social processes) $4.75 pa. **CJ50**

A classed listing of about 2,500 items; author index. Brief annotations for most entries. Emphasis on developments during the administrations of Franklin D. Roosevelt through Gerald Ford. Z7165.U5G74

Kane, Joseph Nathan. Facts about the presidents; a compilation of biographical and historical data. 3d ed. N.Y., Wilson, 1974. 407p. $15. **CJ51**

2d ed. 1968 (*Guide* CJ77).

This edition covers to Dec. 1973. "Hail to the chiefs" (19p.) deals with Nixon, Ford, and Carter. The publisher offers free supplements to update the volume. E176.1.K3

Newcomb, Joan I. John F. Kennedy: an annotated bibliography. Metuchen, N.J., Scarecrow, 1977. 143p. $6. **CJ52**

A listing of English-language books arranged in nine major categories: writings of Kennedy; biographies of the Kennedy family; books on his campaigns and elections; books on the Kennedy administration; the assassination; and tributes, poetry, fiction, and juvenile literature. Most entries have very brief annotations. Author and title indexes. Z8462.8.N48

Sobel, Robert. Biographical directory of the United States executive branch, 1774–1977. [2d ed., rev.] Westport, Conn., Greenwood Pr., [1977]. 503p. $29.95. **CJ53**

Represents an updated edition of the 1971 volume covering 1774–1971 (*Guide* CJ76). E176.B576

Tracey, Kathleen. Herbert Hoover—a bibliography; his writings and addresses. Stanford, Hoover Inst. Pr., [1977]. 202p. (Hoover bibliographical ser., 58) $15. **CJ54**

A listing of 1,245 published books, collections, contributions to books and pamphlets, contributions to periodicals and the press, reports, testimonies, and addresses. Excludes messages to Congress, executive proclamations and orders, and some presidential publications included in readily available sources. Arrangement is chronological within sections. Subject/name index and author/title index to books and collections. Z8414.97.T7

Vexler, Robert I. The vice-presidents and cabinet members: biographies arranged chronologically by administration. Dobbs Ferry, N.Y., Oceana, 1975. 2v. $50. **CJ55**

Biographical sketches are followed by bibliographic citations to sources of further information. Name index in v.2. E176.V48

Congress

Congressional Information Service. CIS/Five-year cumulative index, 1970–1974. Wash., 1975. 2v. $385. **CJ56**

Contents: v.1, Subject index, A–L; v.2, Subject index, M–Z; Supplementary indexes.

Revises and supersedes the *CIS annual* index volumes (*see Guide* CJ83) issued for 1970 through 1974, and is designed to be used with the *CIS annual* abstract volumes. Subject index includes subjects and names; supplementary indexes cover titles; bill, report, and document numbers; and committee and subcommittee chairmen.

The bibliographic data base of the *CIS index* (*Guide* CJ83) is now available for on-line searching.

Congressional Quarterly, Inc. Congressional Quarterly's Guide to Congress. 2d ed. [Wash., 1976] 721, 293–Ap. $52.50. **CJ57**

1st ed. 1971 (*Guide* CJ86).

Retains the basic organization of the first edition, adding new material on Watergate and its consequences, the control of foreign policy, efforts to reform campaign finance and the federal budgetary process, and Congressional reorganization. Footnotes have been added; bibliographies and factual material in the appendix have been updated. JK1021.C56

Congressional sourcebook series, 1976– . Wash., Program Analysis Div., General Accounting Office, 1976– . Annual? **CJ58**

1977 issue called 2d ed.

The series consists of three volumes per issue, each being "an indexed directory and guide, addressing the following areas: (1) *Requirements for Recurring Reports to the Congress*—describes the various requirements for recurring reports to the Congress from the executive, legislative, and judicial branches of the Federal Government. (2) *Federal Information Sources and Systems*—describes approximately 1,400 Federal sources and systems maintained by 91 executive agencies, which contain fiscal, budgeting, and program-related information. (3) *Federal Program Evaluation*—contains an inventory of program evaluation reports produced by and for most of the departments, agencies, and various commissions of the Federal Government."—*Foreword.*

Issued in paperback, the volumes may be purchased separately: 1: $5.75; 2: $6.75; 3: $9.

U.S. Congress. Senate. Senate Historical Office. The United States Senate: a historical bibliography. [Wash., Govt. Prt. Off.], 1977. 78p. il. $2.20 pa. **CJ59**

A classed bibliography of approximately 1,000 books, articles, and dissertations on the Senate, its practices, customs, and former members. Includes a reference section for primary materials, directories, indexes, etc. State index of senators for the biographical section; index of authors and editors.

Elections

Congressional Quarterly. Congressional Quarterly's Guide to U.S. elections. Wash., Congressional Quarterly, 1975. 1103p. maps, il. $49.50. **CJ60**

A narrative section on the history of the party system and nominating conventions is followed by four main sections listing popular vote returns: since 1824 for presidential, gubernatorial and House elections, since 1913 for Senate elections, and since 1919 for southern primaries. Also supplies biographical material for presidential and vice-presidential candidates, and lists of governors and senators since 1789. General index and special candidate indexes. An impressive compilation. JK1967.C66

——— Congressional Quarterly's Guide to 1976 elections: a supplement to CQ's Guide to U.S. elections. Wash., Congressional Quarterly, 1977. 66p. $5.25 pa. **CJ61**

Follows the format of the parent work (above), presenting material on the 1976 elections. Narrative section on political party conventions is followed by sections giving voting statistics for presidential, gubernatorial and senatorial, and House elections. Lists corrections to the *Guide*. Bibliography; candidates index. JK1968 1976.C65

Political parties

Johnson, Donald Bruce and **Porter, Kirk H.** National party platforms, 1840–1972. [5th ed.] Urbana, Univ. of Illinois Pr., [1973]. 889p. $20. **CJ62**

For earlier eds. *see Guide* CJ105.

A collection of all the platforms of the major parties, and of the principal minor parties. A 6th, or "revised," ed. was scheduled for publication in late 1978 in 2v., covering 1840 to 1956 and 1960 to 1976 ($30).

Biography

Morris, Dan and **Morris, Inez.** Who was who in American politics. N.Y., Hawthorn Books, [1974]. 637p. $29.95. **CJ63**

Subtitle: A biographical dictionary of over 4,000 men and women who contributed to the United States political scene from colonial days up to and including the immediate past.

Includes some living persons no longer active in politics. E176.M873

Political profiles. Ed., Nelson Lichtenstein; assoc. ed., Eleanora W. Schoenebaum. N.Y., Facts on File, [1976–77]. v.2–4. $45 per v. (In progress) **CJ64**

Contents: [v.2], The Eisenhower years; v.3, The Kennedy years; v.4, The Johnson years.

Each volume contains about 500 signed biographies, ranging from 400 to 2,000 words, of the most politically influential persons in each presidential administration. Includes officeholders, journalists, intellectuals, economic leaders, civil rights activists, etc. Figures with long political careers may be found in several volumes, with the text focusing on the person's activity during the period covered. Short bibliographies for some entries. Each volume has a chronology, appendixes of officeholders, general bibliography, and index. E840.6.P64

State and local government

See also Suppl. AJ15.

Bibliography

Browne, Cynthia E. State constitutional conventions, from Independence to the completion of the present Union, 1776–1959: a bibliography. Westport, Conn., Greenwood Pr., [1973]. 250p. $15. **CJ65**

A bibliography of the "publications of state constitutional conventions, commissions, and legislative or executive committees, and all publications for or relating to these conventions and commissions issued by other agencies of state government."—*Pref.* Entries are arranged chronologically within each state.

Continued by: KF4501.B76

Yarger, Susan Rice. State constitutional conventions, 1959–1975; a bibliography. Westport, Conn., Greenwood Pr., [1976]. 50p. $10. **CJ66**

"Included in this collection are [citations for] all publications of state constitutional conventions, commissions, and legislative or executive committees, and all special studies prepared for the convention or commission bodies. The documents selected ... were generally of an official, noninterpretive nature, such as, enabling legislation, proceedings, journals, resolutions and rules, public hearings, the proposed constitution, and the constitution as revised and implemented by the electorate. Exception to 'noninterpretive' materials was made for the many special studies commissioned by the various conventions."—*Pref.* Includes Arkansas, Connecticut, Florida, Hawaii, Illinois, Louisiana, Maryland, Michigan, Montana, New Hampshire, New Jersey, New Mexico, New York, North Dakota, Pennsylvania, Rhode Island, Tennessee, and Texas.

Supplemented in part by: KF4501.Y37

Canning, Bonnie. State constitutional conventions, revisions, and amendments, 1959–1976; a bibliography. Westport, Conn., Greenwood Pr., [1977]. 47p. $10. **CJ67**

Subtitle: A supplement to State constitutional conventions, from Independence to the present Union, 1776–1959, comp. by Cynthia E. Browne, and State constitutional conventions, 1959–1975, comp. by Susan Rice Yarger.

Cites official published and unpublished materials for states holding constitutional conventions and those revising their constitution through other procedures. Includes California, Delaware, Florida, Kentucky, Louisiana, New Jersey, Texas, Washington, and Wisconsin, and supplements Yarger (*Suppl.* CJ66) for Louisiana, Texas, Florida, and New Jersey. Subject index. KF4501.B76 Suppl.

Council of State Governments. State blue books and reference publications (a selected bibliography). Rev. and annotated ed., March 1974. Lexington, Ky., The Council, [1974]. 86p. $4 pa. **CJ68**

1st ed. 1972 (*Guide* CJ111).

Lists state blue books (or nearest equivalent), legislative manuals and rules, digests of legislative action, etc., on a state-by-state basis. Only the blue books are annotated (by descriptive coding), but the list is useful as a directory (with addresses and price information) of a wide variety of other state publications. Z7165.U5C68

Hutcheson, John D. and **Shevin, Jann.** Citizen groups in local politics: a bibliographic review. Santa Barbara, Calif., Clio, 1976. 275p. $19.75. **CJ69**

"Focuses on the organization, activities, strategies, and impacts of citizen groups attempting to influence local governmental decision-making processes in the United States."—*Introd.* Chapters present reviews of the literature of topics such as "Citizen groups in planning and community development," citing books, articles, reports, and doctoral dissertations written in English between 1950 and 1975; some book reviews are indicated. Author index. Z7165.U5H87

Murphy, Thomas P. Urban politics: a guide to information sources. Detroit, Gale, [1978]. 248p. (Urban information guide ser., 1) $22. **CJ70**

A selective, annotated bibliography of English-language books and periodicals (most of them published since 1970), on American urban governmental structure, political parties and leaders, community participation, socio-ethnic politics, public policy issues, the reorganization of metropolitan governments and adjacent areas, and federal urban relations. Appendixes list bibliographies, abstracts and indexes, other reference books, textbooks, periodical titles, and associations. Author, title, and subject indexes. Z7165.U5M85

White, Anthony G. Reforming metropolitan governments: a bibliography. N.Y., Garland, 1975. 116p. $15. **CJ71**

Treats reform in its literal sense, as the changing of form to deal with jurisdictional problems, mostly in relation to consolidated city-counties. The first section of the book includes survey and census data on this type of metropolitan area. The second section is an annotated bibliography of more than 580 sources, grouped by type: (1) books, documents, pamphlets; (2) periodicals, major news articles; (3) legal documents, decisions. Subject and author indexes. Z7164.L8W47

Handbooks and yearbooks

The county year book. v.1– . Wash., Nat. Assoc. of Counties [and] Internatl. City Management Assoc., [1975–]. Annual. $17.50 per yr. **CJ72**

Subtitle: The authoritative source book on county governments.

Similar in format and purpose to the *Municipal year book* (*Guide* CJ118a), this work presents survey chapters analyzing general and comparative data on administrative and legislative trends, management structure, administrative functions and services. A directory section provides information on associations, agencies and officials, and sources of information (a selected bibliography for major areas of county administration). JS301.C67

Directory of recognized local governments, 1977. Wash., Internatl. City Management Assoc., [1977]. 90p. $5 pa. **CJ73**

Identifies cities, counties and councils of government in the United States and Canada which are recognized by the I.C.M.A. "as having established an appointed position of overall professional management."—*p.5.* Statistical tables on council-manager and general management counties and municipalities. Directory section arranged by state and then by municipality, with population, legal basis, form and year of recognition, executive, year of appointment. Directories of related agencies include state municipal leagues, provincial associations and unions, and state and provincial agencies for local affairs.

Glashan, Roy R. American governors and gubernatorial elections, 1775–1975. [Stillwater, Minn., Croixside Pr., 1975] 370p. **CJ74**

Offers chronological lists of the governors of each state, together with election statistics on each gubernatorial contest. Bibliography; no index.

Lukowski, Susan and **Grayson, Cary T.** State information book. Wash., Potomac Books, [1977]. 306p. maps. $14.50. **CJ75**

1973 and 1975 eds. had title: *State information and federal region book.*

For each state, provides names of state executive and legislative officers, justices, and Washington representatives, together with addresses of major state departments and federal agencies located in the state. Gives similar information for the District of Columbia, Puerto Rico, the Virgin Islands, American Samoa, Guam, the Trust Territory of the Pacific Islands, and the Northern Mariana Islands. Also gives addresses for the Federal Regional Councils. JK2443.L84

Municipal year book, 1934– . Chicago, 1934– . Annual. **CJ76**

For full information *see Guide* CJ118a.

Beginning 1973 includes data and articles on Canadian municipalities.

The national directory of state agencies, 1974/75– . Wash., Information Resources Pr., 1974– . Biennial. $55. **CJ77**

Comp. by Matthew J. Vellucci, Nancy D. Wright and Gene P. Allen.

In two main parts, the first listing the states and the District of Columbia, and for each identifying all agencies concerned with a particular function (administration, aging, etc.), giving title of administrator, name of agency and name of overall department, address and telephone number. The second section organizes the information by function, and under that provides identical information listed by state. Appendix lists associations of state officials by function. JK2443.N37

State administrative officials classified by functions. 1977– . Lexington, Ky., Council of State Governments, 1977– . Biennial. (1977: $10 pa.) **CJ78**

State elective officials and the legislatures. 1977– . Lexington, Ky., Council of State Governments, 1977– . Biennial. (1977: $10 pa.) **CJ78a**

The above two items supersede the biennial supplements (last published 1975) to the *Book of the states* (*Guide* CJ118).

Public opinion

Gallup, George Horace. The Gallup poll: public opinion 1972–1977. Wilmington, Del., Scholarly Resources, 1978. 2v. (1334p.) $95. **CJ79**

Contents: v.1, 1972–75; v.2, 1976–77.

A continuation of the volumes covering 1935–71 (*Guide* CJ119). Presents, in chronological order, the results of all the public opinion polls conducted by the American Institute of Public Opinion. Each volume begins with a chronology of the years covered. Indexed. HN90.P8G32

National governments

Bibliography

Bloomfield, Valerie. Commonwealth elections, 1945–1970: a bibliography. Westport, Conn., Greenwood Pr., [1976]. 306p. $32. **CJ80**

"This bibliography developed out of the library and research activities of the Institute of Commonwealth Studies, University of London."—*Introd.* References to some 760 elections have been provided in some 5,600 citations. "Originally it was intended to restrict the survey to elections and referenda at the national level, but in response to suggestions from political scientists coverage has been extended to state and provincial elections as well." Includes unpublished sources, official reports, electoral studies, and political party documents. Academic theses are excluded. Author and name index. Z7164.R4B55

Palic, Vladimir M. Government organization manuals: a bibliography. Wash., Lib. of Congress, 1975 [i.e., 1976]. 105p. $1.40 pa. **CJ81**

"This bibliography is essentially a list of manuals and other publications that outline, in more or less detail, the organization of national governments."—*Pref.* Owing to the rarity of detailed and current manuals, there are also included "works of a more general scope that describe the history and often the legislative background of government agencies and bibliographies which may lead the researcher to other sources of information on governmental organization." General, regional, and individual country listings. Index. Z7164.A2P33

Africa

See also Suppl. CJ128.

Annuaire de l'Afrique du Nord. Tables décennales, 1962–1971. Paris, Éditions du Centre National de la Recherche Scientifique, 1978. 135p. maps. 85F. **CJ82**

For series entry and annotation *see Guide* CJ128.

Contents: Table des auteurs; table des comptes rendus; table des sigles; table des documents [listed by country and then by topic]; table analytique [by subject, subdivided by country].

Asiedu, Edward Seth. Public administration in English-speaking West Africa: an annotated bibliography. Boston, G. K. Hall, [1977]. 365p. $50. **CJ83**

Includes books, pamphlets, surveys, reports, theses, and periodical articles published between 1945 and 1969 on Gambia, Ghana, Liberia, Nigeria, and Sierra Leone; an addenda section covers materials published 1970–75. The bibliography "includes anything on the subject of the institutions of government at all levels, i.e., Federal, Regional, and local, and also anything on the process of administering public policy."—*Pref.* Indexed. Z7165.A48A83

A bibliography for the study of African politics. [s.l.], Crossroads Pr., 1977– . v.1– . (In progress?) (v.2: $15 pa.) **CJ84**

v.1 was previously issued in 1973 as a monograph by R. B. Shaw and R. L. Sklar under the same title used for the series (*see Guide* CJ132). v.2, by Alan C. Solomon, is designed as a supplement and covers the 1971–75 period. Its more than 3,900 entries (mostly English-language materials) are grouped as: (1) general works, subdivided by form and subject; and (2) works on specific regions and states. Indexed. Z3508.P6B52

Drabek, Anne Gordon and **Knapp, Wilfrid.** The politics of African and Middle Eastern states: an annotated bibliography. Oxford & N.Y., Pergamon, [1976]. 192p. $14; $7 pa. **CJ85**

A geographical listing of principally English-language books on post-independence political development and international politics; within each region, titles are further classed as dealing with: (A) Political history; (B) Political systems, government; (C) Political parties, interest groups and ideologies; (D) Biographies, memoirs, speeches, writings by political leaders; (E) External relations. No index. Z3508.P6D7

Duic, Walter Zwonimir. Africa administration; directory of public life, administration and justice for the African states. N.Y. & Paris, K. G. Saur; München, Verlag Dokumentation Saur, 1978– . v.1– . maps, il. (In progress) DM398 the set; DM148 per v. **CJ86**

Contents: v.1, Zaïre, Ivory Coast, Benin, Gabon, Guinea-Bissau, Ghana, Upper Volta, Liberia, Guinea, Senegal, Cameroon, Togo, Gambia, Sierra Leone, Nigeria, Zambia. 1285p.

In English, German, French, Spanish, Italian, and Serbo-Croatian.

A systematically arranged directory providing data on state and regional government, public life, commerce, the judicial system, social affairs, education, and religion; gives addresses, telephone and telex numbers, and names of executive officers. Numerous country and city maps locate about 20,000 cities and towns. Similar in concept and format to Duic's *Europa administration* (*Suppl.* CJ97). To be in 3v. DT2.D84

Albania

U.S. Central Intelligence Agency. Directory of officials of the People's Socialist Republic of Albania. [Wash.], Central Intelligence Agency, 1970– . (*Its* Reference aid CR70-11 [etc.]) **CJ87**

Revised periodically (e.g., Reference aid CR77-10848, Mar. 1977).

Supersedes the *Directory of Albanian officials* issued by the U.S. Dept. of State, Bureau of Intelligence and Research (*Guide* CJ133).

Identifies by office the officials of the national and district government, the Communist party, and other prominent public organizations. Name index. JN9684.U54

Asia

Ferguson, Anthony. Far Eastern politics: China, Japan, Korea, 1950–1975. Paris, International Political Science Abstracts, 1978. 250p. $12.50 pa. **CJ88**

This is a special index to *International political science abstracts* (*Guide* CJ32), v.1–25. Each entry provides full bibliographic information and the original abstract number for access to the *IPSA* volumes. Titles of articles in languages other than English have been translated. Arrangement is by country, subdivided by topic; author and detailed subject indexes. JA36.I5 Suppl.

Australia

Australian government directory, 1973– . Canberra, Australian Govt. Pub. Service, 1973– . Irregular. (1975: $5.50 Austral. pa.) **CJ89**

Subtitle: A guide to the Office of the Governor General, the Parliament, the executive government, the judiciary, departments and authorities.

Supersedes the *Commonwealth of Australia directory . . .* (*Guide* CJ134) last published 1972.

Kept up-to-date by an annual "Names supplement" to coincide with the new sittings of Parliament.

The Australian political handbook. Canberra City, Internatl. Public Relations Pty., 1974. 210p. maps. $15 (Austral.) pa. **CJ90**

Subtitle: A handbook listing the executive structures of Australia's major political parties, trade union organisations and other politically important groups, with complete lists of federal and state parliamentarians, and federal and state electoral maps.

Identifies, with brief biographical information for major figures, the organization and executives of political parties and trade unions, both federal and state. Also lists federal and state cabinets and members of Parliament.

Mayer, Henry, Bettison, Margaret and **Keene, Judy.** A research guide to Australian politics and cognate subjects (ARGAP). [Melbourne], Cheshire, [1976]. 329p. $35 (Austral.). **CJ91**

An annotated bibliography of bibliographies, with notes on standard works and yearbooks, together with mention of journal articles, mimeographed material, etc. Classed by type of publication and by subject; "cognate subjects" include the economy, domestic affairs, society, biography, and research. Both the main text and "Supplement 1" (pp. 269–310) have author and title indexes. Checklist of relevant Australian periodicals, with index or abstracting source, and list of Australian newspaper indexes, 1800–1973. Z7165.A8M35

Rydon, Joan. A biographical register of the Commonwealth Parliament, 1901–1972. Canberra, Australian Nat. Univ. Pr., 1975. 229p. (Australian parliaments: Biographical notes, 5) $7.95 (Austral.) pa. **CJ92**

An alphabetical arrangement of entries which include personal biography, career outside Parliament, political career, and sources of further information. Details of ministries and dates of parliaments have been excluded, as they are available in the *Parliamentary handbook* (*Guide* CJ135). JQ4054.R93

Bulgaria

U.S. Central Intelligence Agency. Directory of officials of the Bulgarian People's Republic. [Wash., Central Intelligence Agency], 1975– . charts. (*Its* Reference aid A(CR)75–38 [etc.]) **CJ93**

Revised periodically.

Supersedes the *Directory of Bulgarian officials* (1972), issued by the U.S. Dept. of State, Bureau of Intelligence and Research.

Lists officeholders of the central and regional governments, political parties, diplomatic posts, major public organizations, and mass media. Name index.

Canada

Campbell, Colin. Canadian political facts 1945–1976. Toronto, [etc.], Methuen, [1977]. 151p. $9.95 pa. **CJ94**

A miscellaneous collection of statistical tables, lists of office holders, etc., grouped under such headings as: The executive, Parliament, Elections, Political parties and pressure groups, The Canadian economy, Population and language. Lacks an index. JL65 1977.C35

Heggie, Grace F. Canadian political parties, 1867–1968; a historical bibliography. [Toronto], Macmillan, [1977]. 603p. $75. **CJ95**

An annotated bibliography on federal Canadian politics, with approximately 8,850 entries, including books, essays, historical societies' publications, theses, and journal articles. Pt.I, "The federal political parties of Canada," is arranged by chronological period and individual party; pt.II, "Government and political institutions," lists works on Dominion-Provincial relations, the constitution, government organization and administration, the executive, Parliament, and the judiciary. Appendixes list reference sources and periodicals. Author and subject indexes. Z7165.C2H34

China

Chūka Jimmin Kyōwakoku Soshikibetsu Yōjin Meibo, 1977. China directory, 1977. [Tokyo], Radiopress, [1977]. lv., various paging. Y14,400 pa. **CJ96**

In Japanese and English.

An earlier ed. appeared in 1975. Contains approximately 6,000 names of leading Chinese figures, classified by organization, as of Sept. 1976, with diplomatic list from the end of that year. Names were gleaned from official Chinese information organs, publications, and radio. Central Committee and revolutionary committees, party and revolutionary committees, PLA provincial commands, trade union councils are represented. Name index.

Europe

Duic, Walter Zwonimir. Europa-Administration: Handbuch der Verwaltung und Justiz für die Europäischen Gemeinschaften. München, Verlag Dokumentation, 1976. 1161p. maps. DM180. **CJ97**

In German, French, Dutch, English, Italian, and Serbo-Croatian.

Entries for all member states of the European Communities (Germany, France, Italy, the Netherlands, Belgium, the United Kingdom, Denmark, Republic of Ireland, Grand Duchy of Luxembourg, and the European Communities as such) have been standardized by identifying all comparable institutions concerned with the same subject area with the same code number; each entry provides name, address, telephone number, and name of executive officer. Includes more than 16,000 entries from national to county level. Covers state, regional, and local administrative institutions, police, judiciary, labor authority, social affairs, finance administration, transport, building construction and public works, commerce, tourism, education, and defense. JN94.A12D84

France

Dictionnaire des parlementaires français. . . . Publié sous la direction de Jean Jolly. . . . Paris, Presses Universitaires de France, 1977. v.8. **CJ98**

For earlier volumes and annotation *see Guide* CJ152.

Contents: t.8, Biographical sketches, R–Z. Completes the set.

Dioudonnat, Pierre-Marie and **Bragadir, Sabine.** Dictionnaire des 10,000 dirigeants politiques français. Paris, SEDOPOLS, [1977]. 755p. 180F. **CJ99**

Subtitle: Décrivant la carrière politique de toutes les personnes qui ont joué un rôle depuis 1967 (les candidats à l'Assemblée nationale, au Sénat et à la présidence de la République, les dirigeants des partis politiques, les membres des gouvernements et des cabinets ministériels et précédé d'un dictionnaire des organisations politiques, groupes parlementaires et étiquettes électorales.

Information in the biographical sketches is limited to the subject's political career. Entries for political and parliamentary groups provide history, dates of conferences, statistics on electoral results, membership, and lists of periodical publications. Useful appendixes on such topics as current political documents, composition of the government, the Senate, the Assemblée Nationale, and other subjects.

The Gallup international public opinion polls, France, 1939, 1944–1975. George H. Gallup, gen. ed. N.Y., Random House, [1976]. 2v. (1257p.) $70. **CJ100**

Contents: v.1, 1939, 1944–1967; v.2, 1968–1975.

A compilation of the tabular data resulting from the French Gallup reports, chronologically arranged. Subject index. HN440.P8G35

Germany

Geschichtliche Grundbegriffe; historisches Lexikon zur politischsozialen Sprache in Deutschland. . . . Stuttgart, Ernst Klett Verlag, [1975]. v.2. (In progress) **CJ101**

For v.1 and annotation *see Guide* CJ158.

Contents: Bd.2, Ehre-Grundrechte.

Wahlstatistik in Deutschland: Bibliographie der deutschen Wahlstatistik, 1848–1975. Bearb. von Nils Diederich, Niedhard Fuchs, Irene Kullack und Horst W. Schmollinger. München, Verlag Dokumentation, 1976. 206p. (Berichte und

Materialen des Zentralinstituts für sozialwissenschaftliche Forschung (ZI6) der Freien Universität Berlin, Bd.4) DM36. **CJ102**

Sources are arranged geographically by state (plus the city of West Berlin), then by type of election—Bundestag, Landtag, municipal, town, etc., for the period since 1945. A second section treats historical elections for the German Empire, Prussia, Bavaria, Hamburg, and other states. Z7164.R4W33

Germany, East

DDR Handbuch. Hrsg. vom Bundesministerium für innerdeutsche Beziehungen; wissenschaftliche Leitung Peter Christian Ludz, unter Mitwirkung von Johannes Kuppe. Köln, Verlag Wissenschaft und Politik, [1975]. 992p. il. DM29.50 pa. **CJ103**

A dictionary arrangement of fairly lengthy articles on all major aspects of East German society, politics, economy, foreign policy, and legal system. Classified bibliography, pp.975–92.

U.S. Central Intelligence Agency. Directory of officials of the German Democratic Republic. [Wash.], 1975– . (*Its* Reference aid A(CR)75–44 [etc.]) **CJ104**

Supersedes the *Directory of East German officials* (*Guide* CJ162).

Germany, West

Bermbach, Udo. Hamburger Bibliographie zum parlamentarischen System der Bundesrepublik Deutschland 1945–1970. Opladen, Westdeutscher Verlag, 1973. 629p. DM88. **CJ105**

A comprehensive bibliography in topical arrangement. Index of authors and personal names, and of subject categories.

——— ——— Ergänzungslieferung 1–3. Opladen, 1974–77.

Contents: no.1, 1971–1972. 154p.; no.2, 1973–1974. 256p.; no.3, 1975–1976. 170p.

Great Britain

Registers

The civil service year book, 1974– . London, H.M.S.O., 1974– . Annual. (1977: £4 pa.) **CJ106**

Supersedes the *British imperial calendar and civil service list* (*Guide* CJ170) which ceased with the issue for 1973.

In five chapters: (1) The royal households and offices; (2) Parliamentary offices; (3) Ministers and departments: England; (4) Libraries, museums and galleries, research councils and other organisations: England; (5) Departments and other organisations [separately listed for Northern Ireland, Scotland, and Wales]. Includes salary tables and indexes to officers and to departments and organizations. Kept up to date in part by the quarterly *Her Majesty's ministers and senior staff in public departments* (£1.50 per yr.).

The diplomatic service list. 1966– . London, H.M.S.O., 1966– . Annual. (1977: £5.25 pa.) **CJ107**

Issued by the Diplomatic Service Administration Office.

Continues in part the *Foreign Office list and diplomatic and consular year book* (*Guide* CJ174) last published 1965.

In four parts: (1) Home departments (the Foreign and Commonwealth Office); (2) British missions overseas; (3) Chronological lists from 1957 of Secretaries of State, Ministers of State, Permanent Under-Secretaries, Ambassadors, and High Commissioners; (4) Biographical notes and lists of staff. JX1783.A22

Directories

Bazlinton, Chris and **Cowen, Anne.** The Guardian directory of pressure groups & representative associations. Detroit, Gale, [1977]. 265p. $18. **CJ108**

First publ. London, Wilton House, 1976.

"A pressure group . . . is an association of individuals joined together by a common interest, belief, activity or purpose that seeks to achieve its objectives, further its interests and enhance its status in relation to other groups, by gaining the approval and co-operation of authority in the form of favourable policies, legislation and conditions."—*Introd.*

A directory of British organizations in classed arrangement (e.g., political, trade unions, consumer groups, women's organizations, etc.) with an alphabetical index. JN329.P7B39

Handbooks

Butler, David and **Sloman, Anne.** British political facts, 1900–1975. 4th ed. N.Y., St. Martin's Pr., [1975]. 432p. $19.95. **CJ109**

1st ed. 1963; 3d ed. 1969 (*Guide* CJ176).

"This book was first compiled at the beginning of the 1960s. It has been checked, updated and modified through successive editions in response to the reactions of its readers."—*Introd.* Includes some early 1975 data. JN231.B8

Cook, Chris. Sources in British political history, 1900–1951. N.Y., St. Martin's Pr., 1975–78. 5v. **CJ110**

For full information *see Suppl.* DC53.

——— and **Keith, Brendan.** British historical facts, 1830–1900. [London, Macmillan, 1975] 279p. £15. **CJ111**

For full information *see Suppl.* DC55.

Sainty, John Christopher. Office-holders in modern Britain. London, Athlone Pr. [for] Univ. of London, Inst. of Historical Research, 1975–76. v.4–6. **CJ112**

For full information *see Suppl.* DC57.

Parliament

Craig, Fred W. S. A handbook of parliamentary election results, 1974–1977. [Chichester, Eng.], Parliamentary Research Services, [1977]. 273p. (Britain votes, 1) £5.50 pa. **CJ113**

The first volume in a new series planned to supplement the compiler's previously published *British parliamentary election results,* 1832–1885 (*Suppl.* CJ114), *1885–1918* (*Suppl.* CJ115), *1918–1949* (2d ed., *Suppl.* CJ116), and *1950–1970* (*Guide* CJ183). Its presentation is identical to that of the earlier volumes. New editions will be published following each British general election. JN1037.C723

——— British parliamentary election results, 1832–1885. [London, Macmillan, 1977] 692p. £16. **CJ114**

JN1037.C67

——— British parliamentary election results, 1885–1918. [London, Macmillan, 1974] 698p. £9.50. **CJ115**

This and the preceding item are companion volumes to the same author's compilations for the 1918–70 period (*Guide* CJ182–CJ183). Arranged by constituency, then by date of the election; indexes of candidates and constituencies. Numerous useful tables and appendixes. JN1037.C68

——— British parliamentary election results, 1918–1949. Rev. ed. [London, Macmillan, 1977] 785p. £9. **CJ116**

1st ed. 1969 (*Guide* CJ182).

This edition has been "updated against new sources of information" and includes "analysis of the voting in the two-member constituencies and the detailed figures of the single transferable vote elections in the multi-member University constituencies."—*Pref.*

JN1037.C7

——— Minor parties at British parliamentary elections, 1885–1974. [London, Macmillan, 1975] 147p. £6. **CJ117**

Serves as a companion to the compiler's several volumes of *British parliamentary election results* (*Guide* CJ182–CJ183, *Suppl.* CJ114–CJ116). Entries are arranged by name of party, outlining history, policy, sources of information, and electoral activity. Statistical summary. Party and personal name indexes. JN1037.C725

Dissension in the House of Commons: intra-party dissent in the House of Commons' division lobbies, 1945–1974. Comp.

and ed. by Philip Norton. [London, Macmillan, 1975] 643p. £25. **CJ118**

Attempts to record "all cross-votes and other occasions of intra-party dissent which have taken place in the House of Commons' division lobbies from 1945 to 1974. Each occasion in which Members of either the Conservative or Labour parties in Parliament entered a lobby against their party Whip, or, in exceptional cases, against the clearly expressed wishes of their Front Benches, is recorded. In each case, the names of those Members who voted against the Whip are listed, preceded by a short *précis* of the debate upon which the vote occurred, with particular emphasis upon the views (if any) by those who subsequently cast the dissenting votes."—*Introd.* JN675 1975.D57

Stenton, Michael. Who's who of British Members of Parliament. [Hassocks, Sussex, Eng.], Harvester Pr.; [Atlantic Highlands, N.J.], Humanities Pr., [1976]– . v.1– . (In progress) **CJ119**

Contents: v.1, 1832–1885 (£25); v.2, 1886–1918 (£28.50).

"A biographical dictionary of the House of Commons based on annual volumes of 'Dod's Parliamentary companion' and other sources."—*t.p.*

The editor has selected "the fullest and most useful entries that Dod [*Guide* CJ173] provides on each MP's parliamentary career" (*Pref.*) and rounded them out with additional information such as the reason for leaving Parliament, highlights of subsequent career, death date.

A review of v.1 in *TLS* Feb. 18, 1977, p.185, notes various shortcomings of the work. JN672.S73

Public opinion

The Gallup international public opinion polls, Great Britain, 1937–1975. George H. Gallup, gen. ed. N.Y., Random House, [1976]. 2v. (1578p.) $70. **CJ120**

Contents: v.1, 1937–1964; v.2, 1965–1975.

Statistical data from all British Gallup Poll reports; editorial and interpretive material has been omitted. Subject index. HN400.P8G34

Hungary

U.S. Central Intelligence Agency. Directory of officials of the Hungarian People's Republic. [Wash., Central Intelligence Agency], 1971– . charts. (*Its* Reference aid A71–18 [etc.]) **CJ121**

Revised periodically (e.g., Reference aid A(CR)75–1, 1975).

Supersedes the *Directory of Hungarian officials* issued by the U.S. Dept. of State, Bureau of Intelligence and Research (*Guide* CJ196).

Lists officials of national and regional governments, Communist party, and major public organizations. Name index.

Ireland

Ford, Percy and **Ford, Grace.** A select list of reports of inquiries of the Irish Dáil and Senate, 1922–72. [Dublin], Irish Univ. Pr., [1974]. 64p. (Southampton, Eng. Univ. Studies in parliamentary papers) £4. **CJ122**

Aims "to help students to follow the development of thought on Eire's main lines of domestic policy since the foundation of the State."—*Scope.* Lists reports and papers on policy in constitutional, economic, social and legal matters. Classed arrangement; index based on keywords in title, with addition of names of personal authors and chairmen. Z7165.I68F67

Ireland: a directory and yearbook, 1976– . Dublin, Inst. of Public Administration, [1976–]. Annual. **CJ123**

A specially prepared reference edition of the *Administration yearbook and diary* published by the Institute of Public Administration. Basic information on Irish government, associations, finance, communications, higher education, religion, and Northern Ireland's governmental structure. Yearbook section provides statistics on population, commerce, labor, trade, banking, agriculture, social services, etc. Also includes general information on maps, taxes, etc. Index. JN400.I68

Italy

Pallotta, Gino. Dizionario politico e parlamentare italiano. [Rome], Newton Compton, [1976]. 302p. (Paperbacks società d'oggi, 6) L.2,500 pa. **CJ124**

Offers brief definitions of political terms, abbreviations, organizations, movements, with longer articles on political parties and changes in the government. Includes tables of election statistics and lists of the Councils of Ministers. JA64.I8P34

Ivory Coast

Les élites ivoiriennes: who's who in Ivory Coast; qui est qui en Côte d'Ivoire. [Ed.1–]. Paris, Ediafric, 1976– . 324F. pa. **CJ125**

Cover title: Numéro special du Bulletin de l'Afrique noire.

A register and biographical directory of the principal political figures of the Ivory Coast. DT545.82.A2E43

Korea, North

U.S. Central Intelligence Agency. National Foreign Assessment Center. Directory of officials of the Democratic People's Republic of Korea. [Wash., The Center], 1978– . (*Its* Reference aid CR78–11396 [etc.]) **CJ126**

Supersedes the Agency's *Directory of North Korean officials* (1972).

Identifies persons holding "key positions in the Korean Workers Party; national, provincial, and municipal governments; legislative bodies; military organizations; the diplomatic service; and selected mass, cultural and scientific organizations."—*Pref.* Name index.

Mexico

Camp, Roderic Ai. Mexican political biographies, 1935–1975. Tucson, Univ. of Arizona Pr., [1976]. 468p. $27.50; $8.95 pa. **CJ127**

"Contains the biographies of public men, living or deceased, who have been prominent in Mexican political life from 1935 to early 1974."—*p.ix.* The appendixes supply lists of Supreme Court justices, federal senators, directors of federal departments, governors, party executives, union executives, etc. List of sources consulted and selective bibliographical essay. F1235.5.A2C35

Near and Middle East

See also Suppl. CJ85.

Schulz, Ann. International and regional politics in the Middle East and North Africa: a guide to information sources. Detroit, Gale, [1977]. 244p. $18. **CJ128**

Chapters begin with an essay on the literature, then list English-language books, with annotations. Concentrates on post-1945 situation, with chapters on regional issues, foreign policies of individual states, external powers, Arab-Israeli conflict, petroleum. Reference materials are listed in a separate chapter. Author, title, and subject indexes. Z6465.N35S38

Poland

U.S. Central Intelligence Agency. Directory of officials of the Polish People's Republic. [Wash., Central Intelligence Agency], 1977– . (*Its* Reference aid CR 77–13209 [etc.]) **CJ129**

Supersedes the *Directory of Polish officials* (*Guide* CJ212).

Lists prominent personalities in the national, provincial and municipal governments; political parties; mass, cultural, and economic organizations; diplomatic service; mass media. Name index.

Rhodesia

Cary, Robert and **Mitchell, Diana.** African nationalist leaders in Rhodesia: who's who. Bulawayo, Books of Rhodesia, 1977. 310p. $32.50 **CJ131**

In two main sections: (1) biographies of the principal nationalists (arranged chronologically according to when each individual made his appearance on the political scene) and (2) biographies of military leaders and other prominent persons connected with the guerrilla war. DT962.76.A2C37

Romania

U.S. Central Intelligence Agency. National Foreign Assessment Center. Directory of officials of the Socialist Republic of Romania. [Wash.], The Center, 1976– . (*Its* Reference aid CR 76–12905 [etc.]) **CJ132**

Revised periodically (e.g., CR 77–15215, Nov. 1977). Ed. for 1976 published by the Central Intelligence Agency.

Supersedes the *Directory of Romanian officials* (*Guide* CJ213).

Lists by office or organization the major officials of the national and local governments, the Romanian Communist party and its organizations, and other major public associations. Name index. JN9627.U55

South Africa

Wynne, Susan G. South African political materials: a catalogue of the Carter-Karis collection. Bloomington, Southern African Research Archives Project, 1977. 811p. $32.55 **CJ133**

A classified catalog of mainly primary material collected in Southern Africa and used in preparing *From protest to challenge: a documentary history of African politics in South Africa, 1882–1964* (Stanford, Hoover Inst. Pr., 1977. 4v.). Also serves as a reel guide to the microfilm copy of the collection available through the Cooperative Africana Microfilm Project. Name index.

Union of Soviet Socialist Republics

Hodnett, Grey and **Ogareff, Val.** Leaders of the Soviet Republics, 1955–1972; a guide to posts and occupants. Canberra, Dept. of Pol. Sci., Research School of Social Sciences, Australian Nat. Univ., 1973. 454p. $8.50 (Austral.) pa. **CJ134**

A listing by republic and office of officials in republic-level party positions, positions in the republic Council of Ministers, and other high-ranking republic-level positions. Within each position category, the arrangement is chronological, indicating service dates of each official. Name index. JN6521.H62

U.S. Central Intelligence Agency. Directory of Soviet officials. [Wash., Central Intelligence Agency], 1975. v.3. **CJ135**

For historical note *see Guide* CJ228.

Contents: v.3, Union republics. (Reference aid A(CR)75–18)

Identifies officials in selected party, government and public organizations of the 14 republics other than the R.S.F.S.R. (v.1 dealt with officials of national organizations; v.2 with officials of the R.S.F.S.R) and completes the series. Name index.

Vietnam

U.S. Central Intelligence Agency. Council of ministers of the Socialist Republic of Vietnam. [Wash.], 1977. 103p. il. (*Its* Reference aid CR 77–10004). **CJ136**

Offers biographical material on the 38 members of the council. Each biography provides a photograph, current positions and previous posts, and miscellaneous information on party membership, family, education, etc.

Yugoslavia

U.S. Central Intelligence Agency. Directory of officials of the Socialist Federal Republic of Yugoslavia. [Wash., Central Intelligence Agency], 1976– . charts. (*Its* Reference aid CR76–10408 [etc.]) **CJ137**

Revised periodically.

Supersedes the Agency's *Directory of Yugoslav officials* (1972).

Lists by office and organization the major personalities of federal and local governments; political parties; mass organizations; international relations, commercial, academic, and religious organizations; and the mass media. Name index.

Parliamentary procedure

Deschler, Lewis. Deschler's Rules of order. Englewood Cliffs, N.J., Prentice-Hall, [1976]. 221p. $10. **CJ138**

A system of parliamentary procedure based on the author's experience as parliamentarian of the U.S. House of Representatives. "In preparing this book, I have taken the approach that the House parliamentary system is readily adaptable to any membership organization that needs some form of parliamentary procedure. I have simplified and generalized that system in such a way that it will be applicable to any membership organization, large or small, legislative or nonlegislative."—*Pref.* JF515.D45

Keesey, Ray E. Modern parliamentary procedure. Boston, Houghton Mifflin, [1974]. 176p. $5.95 pa. **CJ139**

"This is a textbook and manual of simplified parliamentary procedure, entirely compatible with accepted parliamentary principles but free of the traditional mysterious jargon of the professional parliamentarian."—*Pref.* Intends to simplify the conduct of meetings and to make for easier participation by members of a group. JF515.K395

Communism and socialism

Bibliography

Eubanks, Cecil L. Karl Marx and Friedrich Engels: an analytical bibliography. N.Y., Garland, 1977. 163p. $20. **CJ140**

Intended to be "a comprehensive bibliography of those writings by and about Marx and Engels either written or translated into English, including books . . . , articles, chapters from books and doctoral dissertations . . . . Marx and Engels, not Lenin, not Mao and not the history of various communist revolutions were the primary focus of attention."—*Introd.* Introductory bibliographic essay, pp.ix–lxii. Primary materials include individual and collected works of Marx, Engels, and Marx and Engels. Secondary literature is arranged by type—books, articles, and doctoral dissertations. No index. Z8551.67.E94

Kehde, Ned. The American left, 1955–1970: a national union catalog of pamphlets published in the United States and Canada. Westport, Conn., Greenwood Pr., [1976]. 515p. $25. **CJ141**

A main-entry listing of some 4,000 pamphlets, with index of subjects, joint authors, and publishers. Includes pamphlets in the Labadie Collection of the University of Michigan, the Bancroft Library of the University of California, the Kansas Collection of the University of Kansas, the Tamiment Library of New York University, and the Division of Archives and Manuscripts of the State Historical Society of Wisconsin, as well as pamphlet entries from the *National union catalog* and the New York Public Library card catalogs. Selection criteria extend to "any pamphlet written by an individual or a political or social organization advocating a liberal to radical position."—*Introd.* Z7165.U5K43

Phan Thien Chau. Vietnamese communism; a research bibliography. Westport, Conn., Greenwood Pr., [1975]. 359p. $19.95. **CJ142**

"An attempt to present a systematic assessment of research materials available in North America as of June 1974 on Vietnamese nationalism, communism and revolution."—*Introd.* A classed, computer-produced list of books and articles in Vietnamese, English, and French. The "Introductory bibliographic guide" (pp.3–19) critically annotates major primary and secondary sources. Author and title indexes. Z7165.V5P48

Sharma, Jagdish Saran. Indian socialism; a descriptive bibliography. Delhi, Vikas, [1975]. 349p. R.65. **CJ143**

A classed list with author index. Intends to document the growth and development of Indian socialism, the role of national leaders and statesmen, etc. Books, periodical and newspaper articles, pamphlets, government documents, etc., are included. Some entries are briefly annotated. Z7164.S67S44

Spiers, John, Sexsmith, Ann and **Everitt, Alastair.** The Left in Britain: a checklist and guide. [Hassocks, Sussex, Eng.], Harvester Pr., [1976]. 168p. £12.50. **CJ144**

Subtitle: With historical notes to 37 left-wing political movements and groupings active in Britain between 1904–1972 whose publications comprise the Harvester/Primary Sources Microfilm Collection.

A checklist of the publications of about forty groups, which also serves as a guide to the 71,000 pages reproduced by the publishers in microform. Although the collection goes back to 1904 (largely based on materials from the Socialist Party of Great Britain), most of the material is from the 1950s to date. The background of each group is briefly sketched before the main text of the checklist, which is divided into four parts; each part has, when appropriate, an author, title, and chronological index, and consolidated author and title indexes are also provided. While a number of Marxist, Leninist, Trotskyist and Maoist groups are represented, the Communist party of Great Britain is not included. Z7165.G8S65

Whetten, Lawrence L. Current research in comparative communism; an analysis and bibliographic guide to the Soviet system. N.Y., Praeger, [1976]. 159p. $17.50. **CJ145**

Pt.I is a discussion of research design, methodology, evolution of themes in Communism, and problem areas involving domestic change and reform. Pt.II is a selected bibliography on change in domestic policy in the USSR and East European states (excluding Albania). The bibliography is a classed list of English-language books and periodical articles published 1965–75 on topics such as economic development, social change, Communist elites and interest groups, ideology, censorship, law, and agriculture. Entries are keyed to audience and nature of item (general, statistical, technical, conceptual). No index. Z7164.S67W47

Periodicals

Shaffer, Harry G. Periodicals on the socialist countries and on Marxism: a new annotated index of English-language publications. N.Y., Praeger, [1977]. 133p. $16.50. **CJ146**

A 1971 edition had title: *English language periodic publications on Communism.*

The "annotated index" of the subtitle might better read "annotated bibliography"; the volume offers a list of English-language periodicals which "concentrate on subject matter of concern to students of communism whose interest lies in the social sciences, in the humanities, or in related fields" *(Pref.)*, together with descriptions of their contents and publishing information. Arrangement is alphabetical by title, with a "geographic reference index." Z7164.S67S35

Armed forces

Bibliography

Aimone, Alan C. Bibliography of military history; a selected and annotated history of reference sources. 3d ed. West Point, N.Y., U.S. Military Academy, 1978. 68p. (U.S.M.A. Library bulletin no. 14A) **CJ147**

Previous eds. 1969 and 1975.

A classed bibliography of reference sources on the various aspects of military history. Author, title, subject index.

Anderson, Martin and **Bloom, Valerie.** Conscription: a select and annotated bibliography. Stanford, Hoover Inst. Pr., 1976. 453p. (Hoover bibliographical ser., 57) $15. **CJ148**

Over 1,385 entries organized into 17 chapters representing major subjects; within most chapters writings are classified as books, unpublished manuscripts, articles, pamphlets, reprints, speeches, and government documents. Emphasis is on U.S. experience, "particularly from the viewpoint of public policy recommendations" *(Introd.)*, but material relevant to England and other foreign countries is included. Separate chapter on bibliographies. Author and title indexes. Z6724.C63A53

Martin, Michel L. L'armée et la société en Afrique: essai de synthèse et d'investigation bibliographique. [Bordeaux, France], Centre d'Études d'Afrique Noire, 1975. 241*l*. 200F. **CJ149**

A selection of more than 1,700 items on the history and structure of African military institutions, civil-military relations, the role of the army in the development process, etc.; includes material on these subjects pertaining to other Third World countries. Z6725.A4M37

U.S. Dept. of the Army. National security, military power & the role of force in international relations; a bibliographic survey of literature. [Wash., Govt. Prt. Off.], 1976. 177p. $2.55 pa. **CJ150**

Abstracts for some 850 books, periodical articles, reports, papers, and documents are grouped in broad subject divisions, with topical and geographical subdivisions. Concerned with the post-World War II period. No index. Z6721.U542

Dictionaries and encyclopedias

Dupuy, Richard Ernest and **Dupuy, Trevor N.** The encyclopedia of military history; from 3500 B.C. to the present. Rev. ed. N.Y., Harper & Row, [1977]. 1464p. il. $20. **CJ151**

1st ed. 1970 (*Guide* CJ269).

Incorporates "minor corrections, and a few substantial revisions" *(Pref.)* in addition to extending the coverage of the final chapter (now retitled "Superpowers in the nuclear age") through 1975. Includes a separate index of wars. D25.A2D8

Parkinson, Roger. The encyclopedia of modern war. N.Y., Stein and Day, [1977]. 226p. maps. $15. **CJ152**

An attempt to cover "battles . . . weapons [and] personalities, plus . . . conceptual topics such as strategy, tactics and various theories and principles."—*Pref.* Dictionary arrangement of brief entries covering the period 1793 to the present. Numerous cross references; index. U24.P37

Sanderson, Michael W. B. Sea battles: a reference guide. Middletown, Conn., Wesleyan Univ. Pr., [1975]. 199p. maps, il. $9.95. **CJ153**

Offers concise accounts of more than 250 battles "fought between considerable forces in the open sea . . . [but] naval bombardments, combined operations, inland-water engagements and single-ship actions have been excluded."—*Foreword.* Covers 494 B.C. to 1944 A.D. Chronology precedes the text. D27.S34

Sovetskaia voennaia entsiklopediia: [V 8-mi t./In-t voen. istorii]; Gl. red. komis., Marshal Sov. Soiuza A. A. Grechko (pred.) . . . [i dr.]. Moskva, Voenizdat, 1976– . v.1– . il., maps. (In progress) **CJ154**

On leaf preceding t.p., v.1– : Ministerstvo oborony SSSR.

Contents: v.1–4, A–Lineinyi. (21.20r.)

Emphasizes post-revolutionary military history, biography, theory, and technology. Many articles are signed; brief bibliographies. To be in 8v. U24.S72

Wedertz, Bill. Dictionary of naval abbreviations. 2d ed. Annapolis, Md., Naval Institute Pr., 1977. 352p. $9.95 **CJ155**

1st ed. 1970 (*Guide* CJ275).

Over 20,000 abbreviations "commonly used by the naval establishment and . . . unavailable in standard dictionaries . . . . All medical, chemical, educational, and religious abbreviations have been deleted, as have abbreviations dealing with computers and computer languages, foreign organizations, state and city designations, and the aerospace industry."—*Pref.* V23.W43

Handbooks

Reference handbook of the armed forces of the world. 4th ed. Ed. by Robert C. Sellers. N.Y. & London, Praeger, 1977. 278p. $20. **CJ156**

For previous eds. *see Guide* CJ276.

Organizational information and special notes section have been expanded. New material includes data on national flag, official language, and combat effectiveness evaluation for each country, and appendixes on U.S.–Third World security assistance funding, Middle East procurements since 1971, and U.S.–U.S.S.R. military posture. UA15.R43

Biography

Martell, Paul and **Hayes, Grace P.,** eds. World military leaders. N.Y., Bowker; Dunn Loring, Va., T. N. Dupuy Associates, [1974]. 268p. $25. **CJ157**

Trevor N. Dupuy, exec. ed.

Intends to provide biographical sketches "of military and civilian personnel in senior positions in military establishments in all nations of the world."—*Pref.* Includes a list of "Military leaders by nation." U51.M35

Atlases

Banks, Arthur. A world atlas of military history. N.Y., Hippocrene Books, [1973–]. v.1– . il., maps. 26cm. (In progress) **CJ158**

First publ. in London by Seeley Service and Co.

Contents: v.1, To 1500 ($12.95); v.3, 1861–1945 (publ. 1978; $22.50).

Black-and-white maps with notes printed on the maps. Some general maps in addition to those for wars, particular battles, defense systems, etc. Indexes of battles, individuals, groups of peoples, and places. G1030.B27

Arms control and peace research

Burns, Richard Dean. Arms control and disarmament: a bibliography. Santa Barbara, Calif., ABC-Clio, [1977]. 430p. (War/peace bibliography ser., no.6) $32.50. **CJ159**

The series was developed in cooperation with the Center for the Study of Armament and Disarmament, California State University, Los Angeles.

Over 8,000 primary and secondary English-language sources on the theory and practice of arms control and disarmament, both historical and contemporary. Cutoff date appears to be 1976. Subject and author indexes. Z6464.D6B87

United Nations. Department of Political and Security Council Affairs. United Nations disarmament yearbook. v.1– , 1976– . N.Y., United Nations, 1977– . (v.1: $15) **CJ160**

Prep. by the United Nations Centre for Disarmament.

"The approach adopted is . . . to cover each question in the field of disarmament and arms control which was dealt with by the General Assembly during . . . 1976."—*Introd.* Future volumes will include reports on the status of existing disarmament agreements, chronologies of events, and factual information on military expenditures, arms trade, armed forces, etc. Appendixes include documents, lists of resolutions, activities of U.N.-related organizations. Detailed table of contents, but no index. JX1974.U372

United States

Bibliography

A guide to the sources of United States military history. Ed., Robin Higham. Hamden, Conn., Archon Books, 1975. 559p. $27.50. **CJ161**

For full information *see Suppl.* DB4.

Paszek, Lawrence J. United States Air Force history: a guide to documentary sources. Wash., Off. of Air Force History, 1973. 245p. il. $2.45 pa. **CJ162**

Locates and describes more than 700 collections of primary and secondary documents on the Air Force. In five sections: (1) official Air Force depositories; (2) National Archives, Federal Records Centers, and presidential libraries; (3) university collections; (4) Library of Congress, federal and local government depositories and historical societies; (5) other sources on astronautics and aviation in general. Index to depositories and general index. CD3034.5.P37

Smith, Myron J. Navies in the American Revolution: a bibliography. Metuchen, N.J., Scarecrow Pr., 1973. 219p. (American naval bibliography, 1) $7.50. **CJ163**

An author listing of approximately 1,600 items, including monographs, articles, papers, master's theses and doctoral dissertations. Subject index. This is the only volume of the series which includes foreign-language material. Z1238.S54

——— The American Navy, 1789–1860; a bibliography. Metuchen, N. J., Scarecrow Pr., 1974. 489p. (American naval bibliography, 2) $15. **CJ164**

About 4,000 entries. A section of general works is followed by separate sections for (1) 1789–1815; (2) 1815–1860; and (3) government documents. Subject index. Z6835.U5S6

——— American Civil War navies: a bibliography. Metuchen, N. J., Scarecrow Pr., 1972. 347p. (American naval bibliography, 3) $11. **CJ165**

Lists over 2,800 English-language items alphabetically by author, with a subject index. Z1242.S63

——— The American Navy, 1865–1918: a bibliography. Metuchen, N.J., Scarecrow Pr., 1974. 372p. (American naval bibliography, 4) $12.50. **CJ166**

Roughly 3,500 entries alphabetically arranged in six sections: (1) General works; (2) 1865–1898: From the old Navy to the new; (3) 1898: The war with Spain; (4) 1898–1917: The "bully" years; (5) 1917–1918: The First World War; (6) Government documents. Subject index. Z6835.U5S62

——— The American Navy, 1918–1941: a bibliography. Metuchen, N. J., Scarecrow Pr., 1974. 429p. (American naval bibliography, 5) $15. **CJ167**

More than 4,700 entries in an alphabetical arrangement; government documents have been included on a selective basis and are listed chronologically in a separate section. Subject index. Z6835.U5S63

Ships

U.S. Naval History Division. Dictionary of American naval fighting ships. Wash., 1976. v.6. (In progress) **CJ168**

For previous volumes and annotation *see Guide* CJ305.

Contents: v.6, Historical sketches, R-S; Appendices: Submarine chasers (SC), Eagle-class patrol craft (PE). 751p. $13.

Biography

Webster's American military biographies. Springfield, Mass., G. & C. Merriam, 1978. 548p. $12.95. **CJ169**

Presents more than 1,000 biographies of persons important to the military history of the nation, including "not only the battlefield heroes and great commanders, but also the frontier scouts, nurses, Indian leaders, historians, explorers, shipbuilders, and inventors. . . ."

—*Introd.* Biographies average 450 words and cover the entire career. Bibliographies are not provided. Addenda section offers lists of chief service officers, and chronological lists of wars, battles, expeditions, etc., for the Army, Navy, and Marine Corps. U52.W4

Great Britain

Bibliography

Bruce, Anthony Peter Charles. An annotated bibliography of the British Army, 1660–1914. N.Y., Garland, 1975. 255p. $23. **CJ170**

Books, periodical articles, government documents, and unpublished official and personal papers are grouped in five broad subject chapters: (1) Bibliographies, guides and indexes; (2) General works; (3) Organization, management and personnel; (4) Military theory, tactics, drill and equipment; (5) Military campaigns and foreign stations of the army. Each chapter is subdivided by type of material, subjects, or chronological period. Indexed. Z6725.G7B78

Greenwich, Eng. National Maritime Museum. Guide to the manuscripts in the National Maritime Museum. Ed. by R. J. B. Knight. London, Mansell, [1977–]. v.1– . (In progress) **CJ171**

Contents: v.1, The personal collections ($21.50).

v.1 offers 300 short biographies of individuals, with a description of the papers of each. The second volume is to cover all other manuscript holdings in the Museum's collection. Chronological, general, and ship indexes in v.1.

Handbooks

Carman, W. Y. A dictionary of military uniform. N.Y., Scribner's, [1977]. 140p. il. $12.50. **CJ172**

Brief entries for items of military dress, badges, etc. Many illustrations. "Unless otherwise stated the description refers to the British Army although possibly it could apply to other nations."—*Note.* UC480.C27

C K

Law

GENERAL WORKS

Guides

See also Suppl. AB35.

Cohen, Morris L. Legal research in a nutshell. 3d ed. St. Paul, West Pub. Co., 1978. 415p. il. **CK1**

2d ed. 1971 (*Guide* CK2).

An updated edition of this now standard work.

How to find the law. Morris L. Cohen, gen. ed. 7th ed. St. Paul, West Pub. Co., 1976. 542p. il. $11.95. **CK2**

6th ed. 1965 (*Guide* CK3).

New material includes chapters on social science materials, foreign and comparative law, international law, English and Canadian sources, and use of computers, audiovisual materials and microforms. Designed as a text, and thus less useful for bibliographic reference work. KF240.H6

Jacobstein, J. Myron and **Mersky, Roy M.** Fundamentals of legal research. Mineola, N.Y., Foundation Pr., 1977. 660p. il. $15. **CK3**

Serves as a successor to E. H. Pollack's *Fundamentals of legal research* (4th ed., 1973; *Guide* CK6).

Intended as an aid to students learning to do legal research, but summary and citation sections of each chapter are useful for reference purposes. Most useful for Anglo-American law. New material includes chapter on computers and microforms in legal research. Available in an abridged version as *Legal research illustrated* (Mineola, N.Y., Foundation Pr., 1977. 450p.). KF240.J3

Bibliography

Akademie für Staats- und Rechtswissenschaft der DDR. Informationszentrum Staat und Recht. Katalog iuridicheskikh dokumentatsionnykh istochnikov sotsialisticheskikh stran. Register of legal documentation of socialist states. Potsdam-Babelsberg, [Informationszentrum Staat und Recht], 1976– . v.1– . (Spezialbibliographien zu Frage des Staates und des Rechts, Heft 16) (In progress) **CK4**

Contents: v.1, Union of Soviet Socialist Republics, German Democratic Republic; v.2, Hungary, Poland; v.3, Yugoslavia, Romania.

Prefatory material in Russian, German, English and French.

For each country lists: (1) published texts of the constitution, codes and laws in force, collections of laws in various subjects, and collections of court decisions; (2) legal journals, bibliographies, and dictionaries; (3) directory information on juridical research and teaching institutions.

Bibliography of translations of codes and other laws of private law. [2d ed.] Strasbourg, Council of Europe, 1975. 314p. $20.30. **CK5**

In French, English, and German.

1st ed. 1967.

Chapters for each of 27 countries are subdivided into sections listing sources of translations (French, English, and German) relating to civil law, commercial law, civil procedure, and special legislative texts. Limited to European countries, with the following exceptions: Brazil, the United States, Israel, Japan, Egypt, and Turkey.

Columbia University. Libraries. Law Library. Dictionary catalog. Second supplement. Boston, G. K. Hall, 1977. 4v. $480. **CK6**

For main set and 1st suppl. *see Guide* CK10.

Represents titles cataloged (and recataloged) from the middle of 1972 through 1975—more than 50,000 cards. This is to be the final supplement.

Duggan, Michael A. Law and the computer; a KWIC bibliography. N.Y., Macmillan Information; London, Collier Macmillan, [1973]. 323p. $9.95. **CK7**

An alphabetically arranged list of more than 6,000 sources on "the impact of the law on computing and vice versa, as well as particular areas of the law where computer-spawned techniques are having a noticeable effect."—*Pref.* Emphasis is on "the societal effects of the computer and the law." KWIC and author indexes. KF242.A1D8

Hamburg. Max-Planck-Institut für Ausländisches u. Internationales Privatrecht. Aufsatzdokumentation zur Privatrechtsvergleichung, Privatrechtsvereinheitlichung sowie zum internationalen Privatrecht und ausländischen Privatrecht. Eine Bibliographie der Jahre 1968–1972. Tübingen, Mohr (Siebeck), 1975. 1133p. DM230. **CK8**

Hrsg. vom Max-Planck-Institut für ausländisches und internationales Privatrecht.

Added title page in English: *Bibliography of articles on comparative private law, unification of private law, and on private international law and foreign private law. A bibliography of the years 1968–1972.*

In German and English.

Lists about 9,600 articles from periodicals, *Festschriften* and other collected works in a detailed classification scheme within each of the four legal areas noted in the title. Indexed by author, geographic area, and subject. For a detailed review, *see International journal of law libraries,* 4:257–60 (Nov. 1976).

Lansky, Ralph. Handbuch der Bibliographien zum Recht der Entwicklungsländer. Handbook of bibliographies on the laws of developing countries. Hamburg, 1977. 469p. DM30. pa. **CK9**

"Übersee-Dokumentation im Verbund der Stiftung Deutsches Übersee-Institut in Zusammenarbeit mit der Arbeitsgruppe Auslandsrecht der Arbeitsgemeinschaft für juristisches Bibliotheks- und Dokumentationswesen."—*t.p.*

In German, English, French and Spanish.

An annotated bibliography of about 700 bibliographies and other legal reference books supplying bibliographic information on the law of developing countries. Classed first by region and country, then by date of publication. Works of special importance are marked with an asterisk. Indexed. Supplement of additional materials. K38.L36

Szladits, Charles. Bibliography on foreign and comparative law; books and articles in English. 1966–1971. Dobbs Ferry, N.Y., Oceana, 1975. 2v. **CK10**

For earlier volumes and annotation *see Guide* CK17.

Cumulates material listed in the annual supplements for 1966–70, with material for 1971, plus some articles of special importance published after that date.

Annual supplements covering 1972– continue to be published.

Current

Bibliographic guide to law, 1975– . Boston, G. K. Hall, 1975– . Annual. (1977 in 2v.: $75) **CK11**

Serves as a successor to the *Law book guide* (*Guide* CK22), last published 1974.

Includes all material cataloged by the Library of Congress within each year specified, in the subject areas of U.S. law, international law, international arbitration, treaties, and foreign law; all unclassified works assigned to the Law Library of the Library of Congress are also identified. Dictionary arrangement; accessible through main and added entries, title, series, and subjects. Includes full cataloging information. KF38.B52

Jacobstein, J. Myron and **Pimsleur, Meira G.,** eds. Law books in print: books in English published throughout the world and in print through 1974. Dobbs Ferry, N.Y., Glanville, 1976. 4v. **CK12**

For previous edition and annotation *see Guide* CK20.

Contents: v.1–2, Author/title list; v.3, Subject list [including series]; v.4, Publishers list.

New features include listings of new periodical titles which began publication in 1973 or later, and of reprints, microfilms, and cassettes. LC card numbers are indicated when available.

Periodicals

Hein, William S., Marmion, Kevin M. and **Hein, Ilene N.** Hein's Legal periodical check list. Buffalo, W. S. Hein, 1977– . v.1– . Looseleaf. (In progress) $47.50. **CK13**

Contents: v.1, A–L.

For each Anglo-American title listed in the June 1976 (v.69, no.9) issue of the *Index to legal periodicals,* the work correlates volume and issue number with appropriate date, and notes any misprints, title changes, issue variations, cumulative indexes available, current publishing address, etc. Alphabetical index notes all title changes. v.2 will contain titles M–Z; supplements are planned. K36.H43

Wypyski, Eugene M. Legal periodicals in English. Dobbs Ferry, N.Y., Glanville, 1976– . v.1– . Looseleaf. (In progress) $60 per v. **CK14**

Contents: v.1, Alphabetical index, cumulative (covering items 1–1100), Items 1 through 400; v.2, Items 401 through 800, and 1978 supplement to v.1–2; v.3, Items 801 through 1100, subject index, geographic index.

For each title, reproduces Library of Congress printed card or "original" catalog card, with information on title, publishing address, frequency, variations in title, subjects treated, indexing source, reprint editions, where cited in "Shepard's Citations." Attempts to "expand and restructure" *(Pref.)* L. W. Morse's *Checklist of Anglo-American periodicals* (Dobbs Ferry, N.Y., Glanville, 1962). A fourth volume is anticipated.

United States

Klein, Fannie J. The administration of justice in the courts; a selected annotated bibliography. Dobbs Ferry, N.Y., Oceana, 1976. 2v. (1152p.) $75. **CK15**

Publ. for the Institute of Judicial Administration and National Center for State Courts.

Updates and expands the author's *Judicial administration and the legal profession* (1963; *Guide* CK25).

Contents: v.1, The courts; v.2, The administration of criminal justice in the courts.

A classed bibliography of more than 5,000 items, dealing with court systems, the judge, the administration and operation of courts, the trial process, the appellate process, the criminal justice system, the criminal trial, sentencing procedures, etc. "Selected bibliographies, guidebooks, and handbooks," pp.939–79. Table of cases. Personal name and subject indexes. KF8700.A1K39

National Indian Law Library. Catalogue; an index to Indian legal materials and resources. v.1– , 1973/74– . [Boulder, Colo.], 1974– . Looseleaf. **CK16**

Cumulative eds. issued at irregular intervals. Each cumulative ed. has four cumulative supplements.

Publ. with the Native American Rights Fund.

The 1976 cumulative ed. includes about 1,900 items relating to "tribal existence, protection of tribal resources, promotion of human rights, advancement of tribal self-determination; and to the accountability of the dominant society."—*Introd.* A subject section, plaintiff/defendant, defendant/plaintiff table, and author/title table refer user to the numerical listing where complete bibliographic and file contents information are given. KF8201.A1N38

Schwartz, Mortimer D. Environmental law: a guide to information sources. Detroit, Gale, 1977. 191p. (Man and the environment information guide ser., 6) $18. **CK17**

Includes English-language monographs, U.S. Congressional materials, proceedings, and periodical titles dealing with environmental law "as a field intended to protect, preserve, or rehabilitate the physical environment."—*Pref.* Three main sections cover: (1) The legal process; (2) Pollution control; and (3) Conservation of resources. Existing bibliographies are noted for each topic discussed. Annotations are brief. Author, title, and subject indexes. KF3775.A1S35

Great Britain

Raistrick, Donald and **Rees, John.** Lawyers' law books; a practical index to legal literature. [Abingdon, Oxon, Eng.], Professional Books, 1977. 576p. £9. **CK18**

A bibliography of United Kingdom legal literature. Under detailed subject headings, lists encyclopedic statutory references, specialized reports and journals, and books. Bibliographic information is as minimal as possible for correct identification. Author and short title index.

Japan

Coleman, Rex and **Haley, John.** An index to Japanese law: a bibliography of Western language materials, 1867–1973. [Tokyo, Univ. of Tokyo Pr.], 1975. 167p. **CK19**

On cover: *Law in Japan; an annual,* special issue, 1975.

A classed bibliography of Western-language translations of Japanese legal materials, as well as secondary literature in book, pamphlet, and article form. No index. Updates Coleman's *Index to Japanese law 1868–1961* (Cambridge, Mass., 1961).

Latin America

American Association of Law Libraries. Committee on Foreign and International Law. Basic Latin American legal materials, 1970–1975. Eds., Juan F. Aguilar [and] Armando E. Gonzalez. South Hackensack, N.J., Rothman, 1977. 106p. (AALL publ. ser., 13) $8.78 pa. **CK20**

Updates K. Wallach's *Union list of basic Latin American legal materials* (1971; *Guide* CK45). Lists, by country: constitutions, major codes, laws in specific subject areas, and secondary monographs published 1971–75.

Peru

Valderrama, David M. Law & legal literature of Peru: a revised guide. Wash., Library of Congress, 1976. 296p. $7.30. **CK21**

Original ed. by H. L. Clagett publ. as *A guide to the law and legal literature of Peru* (*Guide* CK47).

A major revision, representing a reorganization of the contents, updating of previous entries, and addition of new topics such as Indians, agrarian reform, territorial waters, etc. Covers legislative history from 1821 to 1972.

Union of Soviet Socialist Republics

Butler, William Elliott. Russian and Soviet law: an annotated catalogue of reference works, legislation, court reports, serials, and monographs on Russian and Soviet law (including international law). Zug, Switz., InterDocumentation, [1976]. 122p. (Bibliotheca slavica, 8) 38.50Sw.Fr. **CK22**

Serves as the catalog of the publisher's microfiche collection of more than 1,100 titles. Within sections on Russian, Soviet, foreign, and international law, entries are arranged by form (reference works, legislation, periodicals, official gazettes, etc.), and then by subject if appropriate. "The collection does not aspire to 'completeness' nor to the inclusion of 'basic' materials; its object is to supply at modest cost whatever legal materials in this field scholars or libraries deem desirable or advisable to have available."—*Introd.*

Dictionaries

Egbert, Lawrence Deems and **Morales-Macedo, Fernando.** Multilingual law dictionary: English-Français-Español-Deutsch. Alphen aan den Rijn, Sijthoff; Dobbs Ferry, N.Y., Oceana; Baden-Baden, Nomos, 1978. 551p. $45; $39 pa. **CK23**

For English legal terms and phrases, provides equivalents in French, German and Spanish, with indexes from each of those languages. Appendixes: (1) list of brief definitions of English legal terms and phrases; (2) bibliography of law dictionaries; (3) selective guide to legal literature; (4) list of member countries of the United Nations, and a list of U.N. organs and related agencies. K54.E3

Jowitt, William Allen Jowitt, *1st Earl.* The dictionary of English law. 2d ed. by John Burke. London, Sweet & Maxwell, 1977. 2v. (1935p.) £45. **CK24**

1st ed. 1959 (*Guide* CK58).

Changes in this edition reflect the exclusion of Scottish legal terms, reorganization of the court system, remodelling of local and central government, etc. KD313.J6

Stroud, Frederick. Stroud's Judicial dictionary of words and phrases. 4th ed., by John S. James. London, Sweet & Maxwell, 1974. v.4–5. **CK25**

For v.1–3 and annotation *see Guide* CK60.

Contents: v.4–5, P–Z. Completes the set.

Encyclopedias

American jurisprudence; a modern comprehensive text statement of American law, state and federal. 2d ed. . . . Rochester, N.Y., Lawyers Co-operative, 1974–78. v.74–85. **CK26**

For full citation and earlier volumes *see Guide* CK77.

——— General index. Rochester, N.Y., 1977–78. 8v. KF154.A42

——— New topic service. Rochester, N.Y., Lawyers Co-operative; San Francisco, Bancroft-Whitney, 1973– . **CK26a**

Introduces material on rapidly changing or new topics; issued in pamphlet form or bound volumes, which are further supplemented by annual cumulative pamphlets (e.g., *New topic service: Federal rules of evidence.* 1975. 585p.; kept up-to-date by supplements).

Halsbury's Laws of England. 4th ed. London, Butterworth, 1973–78. v.1–20, 25. (In progress) **CK27**

3d ed. (*Guide* CK81) had title *The laws of England.*

Contains new titles on capital gains taxation, administrative law, foreign relations law, leasehold enfranchisement, European Communities, etc. Cumulative interim indexes are issued after every tenth volume; the master index will be the final two volumes of the set. Kept up-to-date by a monthly service and an annual cumulative supplement. A new feature is the *Monthly review,* which offers digests of reports and statutes, notices of white papers and similar documents, and references to articles published on legal topics; these are consolidated each year in the *Annual abridgment,* thus providing an annual record of the development of English law.

International encyclopedia of comparative law. Tübingen, Mohr (Siebeck); The Hague, Mouton, 1971– . v.1– . (In progress) 7,905 Dfl. **CK28**

Prep. under the auspices of the International Assoc. of Legal Science.

Contents: v.1, National reports, V. Knapp, ed.; v.2, The Legal systems of the world, D. René, ed.; v.3, Private international law, K. Lipstein, ed.; v.4, Persons and family, M. Rheinstein, ed.; v.6, Property and trust, F. H. Lawson, ed.; v.7, Contracts in general, A. T. von Mehren, ed.; v.8, Specific contracts, K. Zweigert, ed.; v.11, Torts, A. Tunc, ed.; v.12, Law of transport, R. Rodière, ed.; v.13, Business and private organizations, A. Conard, ed.; v.14, Copyright and industrial property, E. Ulmer, ed.; v.15, Labour law, O. Kahn-Freund, ed.; v.16, Civil procedure, M. Cappelletti, ed.; v.17, State and economy, B. T. Blagojevic, ed.

A major enterprise, intended to be complete in 17v. (about 17,000 pages). Chapters in each volume are being issued in fascicles; v.1 will incorporate a detailed description of the legal system of about 140 nations; the remaining 16v. will offer comparative analyses of the main issues in civil and commercial law throughout the world. Each section is by an individual scholar, and is provided with extensive footnotes and bibliography.

Handbooks

Alexander, Shana. Shana Alexander's State-by-state guide to women's legal rights. Barbara Brudno, legal consultant. Los Angeles, Wollstonecraft, distr. by Price/Stern/Sloan Publishers, [1975]. 224p. $12.95; $5.95 pa. **CK29**

Marriage, children, adoption, abortion, divorce, rape, widowhood, work, crime, and legal age are covered in chapters with introductory essays and state-by-state summaries of the legal situation. Glossary. KF478.Z95A4

Environment regulation handbook. N.Y., Environment Information Center, 1973– . 3v. Looseleaf. il., maps. $275 per yr. with monthly updating service. **CK30**

Arranged by subject—air pollution, land use, mobile sources, National Environmental Policy Act, etc. Each section has an introductory summary of relevant laws, regulations, and court decisions; this is followed by the texts of important laws, federal regulations, notices, policy guides, etc. Subject index. Although most sources are federal in origin, some chapters have summaries of state laws, and these laws pertaining to specific or local jurisdictions can be ordered from the publisher.

Environmental legislation: a sourcebook. Ed. by Mary Robinson Sive. N.Y., Praeger, 1976. 561p. $35. **CK31**

Provides "a sampling of environmental laws at the federal and state levels, plus some state constitutional provisions, presidential executive orders, and administrative regulations."—*Introd.* Legislative excerpts are grouped in subject chapters, with brief introductions; criteria for inclusion are: (1) in force as of 1975; (2) historically significant; (3) have stringent requirements and sanctions; (4) regulate rather than simply promote study. Appendixes include: directory of organizations, government agencies, and public interest law firms; brief discussion on finding the law; index to legal excerpts by title and detailed subject; bibliography. KF3775.E54

Professional responsibility of the lawyer; the murky divide between right & wrong. Dobbs Ferry, N.Y., Oceana, 1977. 815p. $35. **CK32**

Proceedings of a series of symposia sponsored by the Association of the Bar of the City of New York. Nina Moore Galston, ed.

The most useful sections of this work for reference purposes are the appendixes: (1) the Code of Professional Responsibility and other texts related to legal ethics; (2) "The Canons and Code construed: a selection of judicial decisions and bar association opinions applying the Canons of Professional Ethics and the Code of Professional Responsibility"; (3) bibliography, pp.777–800. Tables of cases and opinions. KF306.A5P76

Robinson, Joan. An American legal almanac. Law in all states: summary and update. Dobbs Ferry, N.Y., Oceana, 1978. 439p. charts. $21. **CK33**

A popular statement of contemporary law in the areas of: family relationships, including marriage, divorce, inheritance, and estate planning; commercial law and laws governing workers and labor relations; laws for special groups—home owners and tenants, consumers, juvenile law, environmental law, women and the law; civil rights and duties, and criminal law. Numerous charts comparing state laws relevant to these topics. Also serves as an update to seventy numbers of the publisher's "Legal almanacs" series. KF387.R55

Ross, Martin J. New encyclopedic dictionary of business law —with forms. Englewood Cliffs, N.J., Prentice-Hall [1975]. 289p. il. $19.95. **CK34**

Offers definitions of commonly used legal terms, with examples of their uses in different contexts. Illustrations are given of typical situations, and more than forty specimen legal forms are reproduced. KF887.R67

World Peace Through Law Center. Law and judicial systems of nations. 3d rev. ed. Ed. by Charles S. Rhyne. Wash., World Peace Through Law Center, 1978. 919p. $35. **CK35**

1st ed. 1968.

Various legal scholars and practitioners have provided narrative sketches of the legal systems of 144 countries, covering the legal profession and organization of the bar, legal education, courts of justice, and the legal system. Tables of statutes index the sources mentioned in the text and footnotes; there is a bibliography. K583.W64

Indexes

Anderman, Nancy. United States Supreme Court decisions: an index to their locations. Metuchen, N.J., Scarecrow Pr., 1976. 316p. $12. **CK36**

Intends "to provide locations for reprints of Supreme Court decisions, whether abridgments or complete decisions."—*Pref.* Includes citations to *United States reports.* Cases are listed chronologically, with indexes by case name and by subject. Of little use in the law library, but likely to have utility in libraries with limited holdings of legal materials. KF101.6.A5

The consolidated index to the I.L.O. legislative series, 1919–1970. Ed. by Mina Pease. N.Y., UNIFO Pub.; Oxford, Oxford Microform Pub., 1975. 264p. £15. **CK37**

Covers the legislation published in the International Labor Office's *Legislative series* which is still in force, excluding international treaties and agreements. Chronological and subject indexes. Also serves as an index to the microfiche collection, *The ILO legislative series (1919–1970),* covering translated texts of labor and social security legislation from 140 countries.

Index to Canadian legal periodical literature. 1971–1975. Montreal, [1977]. 1v., various pagings. **CK38**

A quinquennial cumulation of materials from the annual volumes for the period (*see Guide* CK93).

In 1977, frequency of the *Index* changed to quarterly, with each issue cumulating all previous material for that year through the usual annual cumulation. Now indexes articles, case comments, and book reviews from about sixty Canadian periodicals; also includes relevant cassettes and essays published in book form.

Index to periodical articles related to law. Five-year cumulation, volumes 11–15 (1969–1973). Dobbs Ferry, N.Y., Glanville, 1974. 408p. **CK39**

For earlier information *see Guide* CK92.

Cumulates the entries from the annual volumes for the years noted. Continues the policy of selecting "substantive and relevant articles in English from all fields of publication," *(Introd.),* excluding periodicals cited in the *Index to legal periodicals* or the *Index to foreign legal periodicals.* Another five-year cumulation covering 1974–78 is planned.

Schultz, Jon S. Comparative statutory sources. [Buffalo, N.Y., W. S. Hein, 1973] 63p. $18. **CK40**

A subject index to publications containing comparative statutory studies which are revised or supplemented annually or more frequently and those which are published in loose-leaf services. . . ." —*Introd.* Sources indexed include various CCH and BNA reporters, *Constitutions of the United States, Book of the states,* various almanacs, etc. HF1.S35

U.S. Library of Congress. Hispanic Law Division. Index to Latin American legislation. Supplement 3. Boston, G. K. Hall, 1978. 2v. **CK41**

For main set and earlier supplements *see Guide* CK100.

This supplement covers the period 1971–75.

Directories

Lawyer's register by specialties and fields of law; a national directory of lawyers listed by fields of law and including a list of corporate counsel. Cleveland, Lawyer to Lawyer Consultation Panel, 1978– . Annual. $35 pa. **CK42**

Under each of 158 fields of law, lists (by state and city) the lawyers specializing in that field, with name of affiliated firm and biographical information; there is a listee index by state and personal name. The corporate counsel section lists the corporate counsel for 1,020 counties, with a personal name index.

Tseng, Henry P. The law schools of the world. Buffalo, N.Y., William S. Hein, 1977. 419p. $47.50. **CK43**

Pt.I is a country-by-country survey of legal education systems; pt.II is a similarly arranged directory of law schools, providing name of school, address, telephone, degree offered, whether foreign students are admitted, language of instruction, names of admissions officer, dean, and law librarian. K100.A4T76

World legal directory. 2d ed. Wash., World Peace Through Law Center, 1974. 431p. $35.82. **CK44**

Subtitle: A comprehensive computerized directory of judges, lawyers, teachers of law, courts, law schools, law libraries, and bar associations in 145 countries.

1st ed. 1969 (*Guide* CK110).

This edition includes the first selective listing of members of law firms in the United States and Canada; this feature is to be expanded in future editions.

Biography

The American bench: judges of the nation. Ed.1– , 1977– . Minneapolis, R. B. Forster & Associates, 1977– . Annual. (1977: $80) **CK45**

Mary Reincke, exec. ed.

Offers biographical information on "judges from all levels of federal and state courts with jurisdictional and geographical information on the courts they serve."—*Foreword, 1977.* Arranged in fifty-two sections, one for the United States courts, and one for each of the fifty states and the District of Columbia. Each section includes descriptive information on each court in the state, followed by maps of the judicial divisions and subdivisions, then an alphabetically arranged series of biographies of the judges. An alphabetical name index at front indicates title, court and state of each judge.

Biographical dictionary of the federal judiciary. Comp. by Harold Chase [and others]. Detroit, Gale, [1976]. 381p. $38. **CK46**

Offers biographical sketches of United States federal judges, 1789–1974. Includes judges of the Supreme Court, U.S. Circuit Court, U.S. District Courts, U.S. Court of Claims, etc.; only judges with lifetime tenure were selected for inclusion. Biographies appearing in *Who's who in America* and *Who was who in America* are reproduced here; when no sketch was available in those works, one was compiled from other sources. KF353.B5

Who's who in American law. Ed.1– . Chicago, Marquis, 1978– . $52.50. **CK47**

The 1st ed. provides "biographical information on approximately 18,000 lawyers, judges, and educators. Included are attorneys for federal and state agencies; United States attorneys; presidents and key committee heads of federal, state and local bar associations; general counsel to America's largest corporations; and partners and members of major law firms. Among the judicial population are federal and supreme court justices; chief judges of each federal court; Judge Advocate Generals from each branch of the armed services; and hundreds of judges from state and local courts throughout the United States. Listed also are educators—deans and professors from America's foremost law schools."—*Pref.*

STATUTES

United States

U.S. Laws, statutes, etc. United States code. 1976 ed. Wash., Govt. Prt. Off., 1977– . v.1– . (In progress) **CK48**

For 1970 ed. and annotation *see Guide* CK116.

Contains the general and permanent laws of the United States in force on Jan. 3, 1977; titles 1 through 42 available through late 1978.

Great Britain

Great Britain. Laws, statutes, etc. Halsbury's Statutes of England. 3d ed. Consolidated tables and index for volumes 1–45. London, Butterworth, 1977. 1432p. **CK49**

For the main set *see Guide* CK128.

Covers the basic set, an additional volume on European Communities laws, and the annual continuation volumes for 1968 through 1975.

CANON LAW

Caes, Lucien and **Henrion, R.** Collectio bibliographica operum ad ius romanum pertinentium. Bruxelles, Office Internat. de Librairie, 1973–75. Ser.I, v.22–24. (In progress) **CK50**

For previously published parts and annotation *see Guide* CK9.

INTERNATIONAL LAW

Bibliography

Bermes, Annick and **Lévy, Jean-Pierre.** Bibliographie du droit de la mer. Bibliography on the law of the sea. Paris, Éditions Techniques et Économiques, [1974]. 138p. 25F. pa. **CK51**

Prefatory matter and chapter headings in French and English.

A "very selective" international bibliography of recent books and articles in a classed subject arrangement, with author index. Z6464.M2B47

Doimi di Delupis, Ingrid. Bibliography of international law. London & N.Y., Bowker, [1975]. 670p. $36. **CK52**

Concentrates on books published between 1920 and 1974, but includes many journal articles as well. "Important" sections begin with an introduction which mentions particularly significant works in that section. The detailed classification scheme is outlined in the table of contents. Author index. Typography does not meet the usual Bowker standard, and a highly critical review appeared in the *International journal of law libraries* 4:160–62; however, the work includes a broad range of materials. Z6461.D63

Grieves, Forest L. International law, organization, and the environment; a bibliography and research guide. Tucson, Univ. of Arizona Pr., [1974]. 131p. (Institute of Government Research. International studies, 4) $3.50 pa. **CK53**

Selects, classes by broad topic, and briefly annotates English-language books, periodical articles, and documentary materials "not so much [to serve] as recommended reading, but rather as a vehicle for surveying the range of materials available."—*Introd.* Includes lists of relevant periodical titles and international organizations. Covers general materials, the seas and other waters, polar areas, air space and outer space, nuclear and thermal issues, resources and land uses, overpopulation.

Heere, Wybo P. International bibliography of air law: supplement 1972–1976. Leyden, Sijthoff, 1976. 169p. 60.30fl. **CK54**

For main volume *see Guide* CK133.

Maintains the classified arrangement and selection criteria of the main volume, with name and subject indexes. A looseleaf, computer-produced future edition with annual supplements is planned. Z6464.A4H43

Kavass, Igor I. and **Blake, Michael J.** United States legislation on foreign relations and international commerce: a chronological and subject index of public laws and joint resolutions of the Congress of the United States. Buffalo, N.Y., W. S. Hein, 1977– . v.1– . (In progress?) **CK55**

Contents: v.1, 1789–1899; v.2, 1900–1929; v.3, 1920–1949; v.4, 1950–1969.

Based on texts published in the *Statutes at large,* and thus includes repealed and superseded legal provisions, as well as those in effect as presented in the *Revised statutes* and the *United States code.* The main text of each volume consists of a chronological index, with short summaries of each statute or joint resolution, followed by a subject index.

Kurdiukov, Gennadii Irinarkhovich. Mezhdunarodnoe pravo. Bibliografiia 1917–1972gg. Moskva, IUridicheskaia Literatura, 1976. 598p. 1r.,97k. pa. **CK56**

A selective bibliography of about 8,000 entries for books and periodical articles written by Soviet scholars on international law; updates V. N. Durdenevskii's *Sovetskaia literatura po mezhdunarodnomu pravu, 1917–1957* (Moscow, 1959). Arranged in 19 broad subject sections, with author index. Reviews of the most important works are noted. Z6461.K87

Li, Kuo Lee. World wide space law bibliography. Toronto, Carswell Co., distr. by ICASL, McGill University, Montreal, 1978. 700p. **CK57**

At head of title: Institute and Center of Air and Space Law, Institut et Centre de Droit Aérien et Spatiel.

Organizes a wide variety of materials in a detailed subject classification, including works on astronautics, astropolitics, space telecommunications, and socio-economic aspects of space. Makes a special effort to identify United Nations documents and international agreements. Author and subject indexes. Z6464.S62L48

Miller, William. International human rights: a bibliography, 1970–1976. Notre Dame, Ind., Center for Civil Rights, Univ. of Notre Dame Law School, 1976. 118p. $2 pa. **CK58**

Covers English-language materials. Publications are grouped by type (i.e., periodical articles listed by author; anonymous articles; monographs; documents), with subject index. Supplements listing documents of the United Nations and human rights organizations are planned. K3236.M34

Schutter, Bart de and **Eliaerts, Christian.** Bibliography on international criminal law. Leiden, Sijthoff, 1972. 423p. 58fl. **CK59**

A classed bibliography listing more than 5,000 books, essays in collective works, periodical and newspaper articles, and official documents of international organizations. Treats such topics as extraterritorial jurisdiction, extradition, war crimes, genocide, piracy, slavery, humanitarian law, etc. Author and subject indexes. Z6464.C8S38

Current

Checklist of human rights documents. v.1, no.1/5– . Austin, Tex., Tarlton Law Library, Univ. of Texas School of Law, 1976– . Monthly. $25 per yr. **CK60**

Publ. in cooperation with the United States Institute of Human Rights, New York.

Continues in part a journal with the same title published by the United States Institute of Human Rights and the Charles B. Sears Law Library of the State University of New York at Buffalo, but with an expanded scope. Current issues list documents of: (1) international and regional organizations, national governments, and non-governmental organizations; and (2) commercial publications, subdivided as yearbooks, monographs, journals, and journal articles. Separate sections for ratifications and accessions, and for current announcements. No index.

Public international law, a current bibliography of articles. v.1, no.1– , 1975– . Berlin [etc.], Springer-Verlag, 1976– . Semiannual. (1978: DM49) **CK61**

A classed listing of periodical articles and essays from collected works, selected from some 1,000 journals and collective volumes. Case notes and book reviews are selectively included. International in scope. Author and subject index in each issue, cumulating annually.

Digests and collections

Digest of commercial laws of the world. George Kohlik, ed. Rev. ed. Dobbs Ferry, N.Y., Oceana, 1975– . Looseleaf. **CK62**

Publ. for the National Association of Credit Management.

For previous ed. *see Guide* CK140.

Contents: v.1–2, Patents and trademarks.

A country-by-country survey. Each quarterly supplement supersedes the previous one; original pamphlets will be revised and reissued periodically.

Digest of United States practice in international law, 1973– . [Wash., U.S. Govt. Prt. Off.], 1974– . Annual. (U.S. Dept. of State. Publ. 8756 [etc.]) (1976: $9.50) **CK63**

Continues M. M. Whiteman's *Digest of international law* (*Guide* CK143) and is updated by the section "Contemporary practice of the United States relating to international law" in each quarterly issue of the *American journal of international law.*

Human rights: a compilation of international instruments. [3d ed.] N.Y., United Nations, 1978. 132p. ([Document] United Nations; ST/HR/1/Rev. 1) $9 pa. **CK64**

Prep. by the Division of Human Rights of the United Nations Secretariat.

1st ed. 1968.

Includes the texts of conventions, declarations, and recommendations on human rights adopted by the United Nations up to Dec. 31, 1977. Arranged by broad topic, with a chronological listing. JX1976.A49XIV.H882

Annuals and current surveys

American foreign relations; a documentary record, 1971– . N.Y., New York Univ. Pr., 1976– . Annual (1976 publ. 1978). **CK65**

Ed. by Richard P. Stebbins and Elaine P. Adam.

"Continuing the series of foreign policy surveys initiated by the Council of Foreign Relations in 1931 under the title *The United States in World Affairs,* the volume also maintains the service provided for more than three decades by the separate *Documents on American Foreign Relations* series [*Guide* CK147]" (*Pref.,* 1975), thus combining narrative with documentation. Appendix lists principal sources. Indexed.

Directories

Human rights organizations & periodicals directory, 1973– . Berkeley, Calif., Meiklejohn Civil Liberties Inst., 1973– . (1977: $6.75 pa.) **CK66**

3d ed., 1977, ed. by David Christiano.

Intended as "a referral list for people seeking information or assistance in human rights cases; as a guide for teachers, students, and researchers seeking hard-to-find sources of information; and as a resource for attorneys concerned with human rights cases."—*Introd., 2d ed.* In two parts: (1) Alphabetical guide and (2) Subject index. KF4741.H84

TREATIES

General

Grenville, John Ashley Soames. The major international treaties, 1914–1973; a history and guide with texts. N.Y., Stein and Day, [1974]. 575p. maps. $25. **CK67**

Each section begins with a brief history and analysis of circumstances leading up to the treaties, and concludes with versions of the treaties edited to remove formal legal materials and focus on the important articles. Arrangement is chronological through World War II, then regional. Source references are given for the full texts of treaties included. Indexed. JX171.G86

Parry, Clive, ed. The consolidated treaty series. Dobbs Ferry, N.Y., Oceana, [1969–78]. v.76–170. (In progress) **CK68**

For earlier volumes and annotation *see Guide* CK157.

Contents: v.76–170, 1825–1888.

Rohn, Peter H. Treaty profiles. Santa Barbara, Calif., ABC-Clio, [1976]. 256p. $30. **CK69**

A quantitative inventory and survey of national, regional, and global treaty patterns from 1946 to 1965. Offers a standard, one-page profile of the treaty pattern of every country and treaty-making international organization. Tabular format lists treaty partners in descending order, with total number of treaties and mutual treaties between the two countries; for the latter category, presents information on number signed within specific time periods, topics, international organizations referred to in the text, etc. Covers more than 12,000 treaties. JX171.R62

——— World treaty index. Santa Barbara, Calif., ABC-Clio, [1974]. 5v. (3053p.) $400. **CK70**

Contents: v.1, League of Nations treaty series; v.2, United Nations treaty series: ser. 1, nos.1–6485; v.3, United Nations treaty series, ser. 1, nos.6486–10841; ser. 2, nos.1–657; National treaty collections; v.4, Chronological, party, international organization and *UNTS* self-index sections; v.5, Topic section.

An inventory and index to more than 23,000 bilateral and multilateral treaties appearing in *LTS, UNTS,* and the national treaty collections of 25 countries. Full bibliographic citations appear in the main entry section (v.1–3) and provide: name of instrument and whether uni- , bi- , or multilateral; series or source citation; date of signature and entry into force; registrant; number of articles; languages; title keywords; topics; reference to international government organizations; reference to other treaties; procedural references; names of parties; annex information from *LTS/UNTS.* Index sections in v.4–5 refer to date, parties, topical subjects and classed subjects. The set is a product of the data base maintained by the Treaty Research Center at the University of Washington, which offers individual research consultations and computer print-outs. JX171.R63

Treaties and alliances of the world: an international survey covering treaties in force and communities of states. [Rev. and updated ed.] N.Y., Scribner's; Bonn, etc., Siegler, [1974]. 235p. il., maps. $15. **CK71**

1st ed. 1968 (*Guide* CK159).

Surveys the major treaties in effect as of Jan. 1, 1973, with a supplement updating the contents to Sept. 30, 1973. A new chapter treats East-West treaties of 1970–72. Citations to *Keesing's Contemporary archives* provide additional information, and in many cases the full text of the document. Separate indexes to text and supplement. JX4005.T72

Vambery, Joseph T. and **Vambery, Rose V.** Cumulative list and index of treaties and international agreements registered or filed and recorded with the Secretariat of the United Nations, December 1969–December 1974. Dobbs Ferry, N.Y., Oceana, 1977. 2v. $50. **CK72**

Lists some 4,000 international agreements registered or filed and recorded with the Secretariat for the period 1969–74, as well as ratifications, accessions, prorogations, corrections and additions made during these years to agreements registered or filed and recorded before Dec. 1, 1969. The chronologically arranged entries note date and method of entry into force of the agreement, date of registration, and language of text. Subject and parties indexes. JX171.V35

United States

Kavass, Igor I. and **Michael, Mark A.** United States treaties and other international agreements cumulative index 1776–1949. Buffalo, N.Y., W. S. Hein, 1975. 4v. $225. **CK73**

Subtitle: Cumulative index to United States treaties and other international agreements 1776–1949 as published in Statutes at large, Malloy, Miller, Bevans, and other relevant sources.

Contents: v.1, In numerical order of TS, EAS, TIAS and AD numbers . . . (and a list of United States postal agreements 1844–1949); v.2, Chronological index; v.3, Country index; v.4, Subject index.

Lists about 2,600 treaties and international executive agreements, either bilateral or multilateral, entered into by the United States with foreign countries and international organizations; excludes treaties with American Indians.

Continued by: JX231.K4

——— and **Sprudzs, Adolf.** UST cumulative index 1950–1970; cumulative index to United States treaties and other international agreements 1950–1970: 1 UST-21UST, TIAS nos. 2010–7034. Buffalo, N.Y., W. S. Hein, 1973. 4v. $270. **CK74**

Contents: v.1, In numerical order of TIAS numbers, 2010–7034; v.2, Chronological index; v.3, Country index; v.4, Subject index.

Indexes and arranges in appropriate lists some 5,000 treaties and agreements included in *UST* for this period.

Continued by: JX231.K38

——— UST cumulative index 1971–1975: a cumulative index to United States treaties and other international agreements 1971–1975: 22 UST–26 UST, TIAS nos. 7035–8224. Buffalo, N.Y., W. S. Hein, 1977. 593p. $62.50. **CK75**

Divided into sections corresponding to the volumes of the previously mentioned sets: (1) Numerical list of documents, arranged by TIAS number; (2) Chronological index; (3) Country index, subdivided by bilateral and multilateral treaties and agreements; (4) Subject index.

Unperfected treaties of the United States of America, 1776–1976. Dobbs Ferry, N.Y., Oceana, 1976–77. v.1–3. (In progress) $40 per v. **CK76**

Ed. and annotated by Christian L. Wiktor.

Contents: v.1, 1776–1855; v.2, 1856–1882; v.3, 1883–1904.

Presents, in chronological order, the texts of all international agreements concluded by the United States which have failed to go into force (excluding Indian treaties and postal agreements). Each text is preceded by a note giving: the name of the party or parties, short title, place and date of signature, Senate action, location in the treaty file of the National Archives, source of printed text, and history. Each volume is provided with a list of works cited, a table of contents listing the treaties, and an index; there will be a cumulative index in the final volume. JX236 1776.U56

Great Britain

Gt.Brit. Foreign Office. British and foreign state papers, 1812– , with which is incorporated Hertslet's Commercial treaties. London, Stat. Off., 1976–77. (In progress) **CK77**

For annotation *see Guide* CK175.

The following general indexes have been published: v.165, indexes v.139–64 (1935–60); v.170, indexes v.166–69 (1961–68).

Parry, Clive and **Hopkins, Charity.** An index of British treaties, 1101–1968. London, H.M.S.O., 1970. 3v. £14. **CK78**

"Comp. and annotated under the auspices of the International Law Fund and the British Institute of International and Comparative Law."—*t.p.*

"One of the main purposes of this work is to serve as a complete consolidated index to the *Treaty Series* of the United Kingdom, which began in 1892 [*Guide* CK174]."—*Pref.* In four parts: (1) Index of multilateral treaties by subject; (2) Index of bilateral treaties by country, etc.; (3) Index of bilateral treaties by subject; (4) Chronological list. JX636 1892 Index

Korea

Ginsburgs, George and **Kim, Roy U. T.** Calendar of diplomatic affairs, Democratic People's Republic of Korea, 1945–1975. [Moorestown, N.J.], Symposia Pr., 1977. 275p. $27.50. **CK79**

"Sponsored by the Social Science Research Council."—*t.p.*

Entries are arranged chronologically and identified as to nature of the item (unilateral, bilateral, etc.), agents, place signed, and subject. Identifies source where text of each document can be located, and secondary information thereon. Indexes by country and plurilateral treaties. Appendix provides a list of Korean ambassadors. DS935.5.G56

CONSTITUTIONS

Collections

Blaustein, Albert P. and **Blaustein, Eric B.** Constitutions of dependencies and special sovereignties. Dobbs Ferry, N.Y., Oceana, [1975–]. 6v. Looseleaf. $75 per v. **CK80**

Contents: v.1, United States [and] United Kingdom; v.2, British dependent territories; v.3, British associated states; v.4, In association with the British crown, Australian overseas territories, New Zealand territories; v.5, French overseas departments, French overseas territories, Scandinavian territories, Soviet territories with recognized sovereignty, Democratic Arab Republic of the Sahara, Macao, Netherlands Antilles, Palestine, Turkish Federated State of Cyprus, Vatican City State; v.6, Republic of South Africa, homelands.

Serves as a companion to Blaustein and Flanz's *Constitutions of the countries of the world* (*Guide* CK182). For each associated state, dependent territory, and area of special sovereignty, a pamphlet provides an outline of constitutional status, a copy of the constitution in English, and a briefly annotated bibliography.

——— and **Flanz, G. H.** Constitutions of the countries of the world. . . . Permanent ed. Supplement, 1975– . Dobbs Ferry, N.Y., Oceana, 1975– . Irregular. Looseleaf. **CK81**

For the main set and annotation *see Guide* CK182.

Records additions to the constitutional chronologies, texts, and bibliographies until the next full revision of the country pamphlets.

As of Dec. 1977, the main set offers material on 158 countries in 15 looseleaf binders.

United States

Columbia University. Legislative Drafting Research Fund. Constitutions of the United States, national and state. 2d ed. Dobbs Ferry, N.Y., Oceana, 1974–78. 6v. Looseleaf. $69 per v. **CK82**

1st ed. 1962 (*Guide* CK191).

Current texts and amendments of the United States Constitution, the state constitutions, the constitution of Puerto Rico, and the constitutions and acts of possessions and territories of the United States are all included. KF4530.C6

Swindler, William Finley, ed. Sources and documents of United States constitutions. Dobbs Ferry, N.Y., Oceana, 1974–78. v.3–7. (In progress) **CK83**

For v.1–2 and annotation *see Guide* CK193.

Contents: v.3–7, Hawaii–Ohio. KF4530.S94

U.S. Constitution. The Constitution of the United States of America: analysis and interpretation. Annotations of cases decided by the Supreme Court of the United States to June 29, 1972. [Rev. ed.] Wash., Govt. Prt. Off., 1973. 1961p. (92d Cong., 2d Sess. Senate doc. no. 92–82) $20.50. **CK84**

Prep. by the Congressional Research Service, Library of Congress; Lester S. Jayson, supervising ed.

For earlier editions *see Guide* CK190.

The "Historical note" reprints PL91-589, which calls for cumulative pocket supplements to be issued every two years (also as Senate documents) until the next edition, which is scheduled for 1982 publication. KF4527.J39

INTERNATIONAL ORGANIZATIONS

Bibliography

Atherton, Alexine L. International organizations: a guide to information sources. Detroit, Gale, [1976]. 350p. $18. **CK85**

Classed listing, primarily of 20th-century English-language books, with a few articles, doctoral dissertations, and U.S. government reports. Pt.I is a guide to reference sources in the field; pt.II is a bibliography, with annotations for the more significant titles. A guide primarily for the beginner. Author, title, and subject indexes. Z6464.I6A74

British Library. Lending Division. BLL conference index 1964–1973. Boston Spa, 1974. 1220p. £15. **CK86**

For full information *see Suppl.* EA31.

Gesamtverzeichnis der Kongress-Schriften in Bibliotheken der Bundesrepublik Deutschland einschliesslich Berlin (West). Schriften von und zu Kongressen, Konferenzen, Kolloquien, Symposien, Tagungen, Versammlungen und dergleichen vor 1971 mit Besitznachweisen Stand: 1976. München, Verlag Dokumentation, 1976. 2v. DM220. **CK87**

Added title page in English: *Union list of conference proceedings in libraries of the Federal Republic of Germany including Berlin (West).*

A companion publication to the *Gesamtverzeichnis ausländischer Zeitschriften und Serien (GAZS)* and its supplements (*Guide* AE145), listing conference proceedings not already registered in *GAZS.* Most foreign proceedings are listed after 1959, and international conference proceedings after 1967. Listing is by name of conference or sponsoring body; v.2 is a keyword index of the names of conferences and corporate bodies.

Current

New York. Public Library. Research Libraries. Bibliographic guide to conference publications: 1975– . Boston, G. K. Hall, [1976]– . Annual. $101 per yr. **CK88**

Each volume is a bibliography in the form of a dictionary catalog (i.e., main entries plus added entries as applicable for editors, titles, series, and subject headings). Covers publications cataloged by the Research Libraries of NYPL together with additional entries from Library of Congress MARC tapes. "Included are works in all languages and all forms—non-book materials as well as books and serials."—*Pref.* (Coverage is of works *cataloged* during the year in question, so that each volume includes many publications of earlier date.)

A volume from the same publisher, *Conference publications guide: 1974,* Gerald L. Swanson, ed., is derived solely from MARC data and lists main entries, subject entries, "area studies entries," series, and titles in separate sections. Although announced as an annual, this title is evidently superseded by the *Bibliographic guide* series. Z5056.N47a

Dictionaries

Paxton, John. A dictionary of the European Economic Community. N.Y., Facts on File, [1977]. 287p. $17.50. **CK89**

Brief entries for acronyms and abbreviations, persons, places, and topics relevant to the EEC. Longer articles on treaties and other important documents summarize rather than quote. Entries for countries belonging to the EEC give brief data on area, population density, vital statistics, labor force, international and EEC trade, and standard of living. Select bibliography of books, pp.285–87. HC241.2.P378

Abbreviations

Buttress, F. A. World guide to abbreviations of organizations. 5th ed. Detroit, Gale, [1974]. 470p. $24. **CK90**

4th ed. 1971 (*Guide* CK212).

Expanded to about 18,000 entries, of which over 5,000 are continental European. AS8.B8

League of Nations

Birchfield, Mary Eva. Consolidated catalog of League of Nations publications offered for sale. Dobbs Ferry, N.Y., Oceana, 1976. 477p. $50. **CK91**

Consolidates the entries from the League's *Catalog of publications, 1930–35* and its supplements, and includes additional material from Carroll's *Key to League of Nations documents* (*Guide* CK224). Arrangement is by category (e.g., Assembly, Council, Library, Health, Social Questions, Legal, etc.), then chronologically unless some other arrangement is dictated for ease of use. Indexes by official number, sales number, and subject/title. Z6479.Z9B57

Reno, Edward A., ed. League of Nations documents, 1919–1946; a descriptive guide and key to the microfilm collection. New Haven, Conn., Research Publs., [1974–75]. v.2–3. **CK92**

For v.1 and annotation *see Guide* CK226.

Contents: v.2, Subject categories V through VII; C.P.M. documents; Minutes and reports of the Permanent Mandates Commission; and 19/F/– , 19/6/– , 20/6/– , 21/6/– , Documents; v.3, Subject categories VIII through General, serial publications reel index, Minutes of the Directors' meetings reel index.

Subject categories included are: V, Legal questions; VIA, Mandates; VIB, Slavery; VII, Political questions; VIII, Communications and transit; IX, Disarmament; X, Financial administration of the League of Nations; XI, Traffic in opium and other dangerous drugs; XIIA, Intellectual cooperation; XIIB, International Bureaux; XIII, Refugees; G, General. v.3 includes a consolidated index for subject categories IA through G, "followed by separate listings for the Permanent Mandates Commission (C.P.M.) Documents, the Minutes and Reports of the Permanent Mandates Commission, and the collection of Secretariat communications known as the 19/F/– , 19/6/– , 20/6/– , and 21/6/– Series."—*p. v.*

United Nations

Guides and handbooks

A comprehensive handbook of the United Nations: a documentary presentation in two volumes. Comp. and ed. by Min-chuan Ku. [N.Y.], Monarch Pr., [1978]. 2v. il. $42.50 per v. **CK93**

v.1 covers background material, organizational documents and procedural rules of the principal organs of the United Nations; v.2 treats the specialized agencies, nongovernmental organizations having relations with the United Nations, trusteeship agreements, regional agencies, and General Assembly resolutions. Bibliography; indexed. JX1977.C6123

Bibliography

Hüfner, Klaus, and **Naumann, Jens.** The United Nations system, international bibliography. Das System der Vereinten Nationen, internationale Bibliographie. München, Verlag Dokumentation, 1976– . v.1– . (In progress) **CK94**

A publication of the Research Unit of the German United Nations Association, Bonn/Berlin.

Prefatory matter and headings in English and German.

Contents: v.1, The United Nations system; an international bibliography . . . 1945–65 (1976. 519p. DM98); v.2A, Learned journals, 1965–70 (1977. 286p. DM78); v.2B, Learned journals, 1971–75 (1977. 436p.).

A bibliography of secondary literature published in English, German, and French on the United Nations and its specialized agencies. v.1 is a reprint of Hüfner's *Zwanzig Jahre Vereinte Nationen . . . 1945–1965* (*Guide* CK235). v.2 covers articles produced between 1965 and 1975 in about 360 journals. The classification scheme organizes 8,342 articles in four sections: (1) The United Nations as part of the empirical solutions for four main functional problems of world society [polity, adaptation, normative integration, cultural problems]; (2) The United Nations system and its internal structures and processes; (3) The United Nations system—institutional and organizational arrangements; (4) The United Nations system—actual and potential areas of activity. Detailed table of contents; author index. v.3 is to cover books and essays in collected works of the 1965–75 period. Z6481.H83

League of Nations & United Nations Monthly list of selected articles; cumulative 1920–1970. Dobbs Ferry, N.Y., Oceana, 1974–75. v.4–6. (In progress) **CK95**

For previously published volumes and annotation *see Guide* CK236.

Contents: v.4, Economic questions: economic conditions—petroleum, miscellaneous industries; v.5, Economic questions: commercial policy; v.6, Economic questions: economic policy.

Publications

United Nations. Secretary-General. Public papers of the Secretaries-General of the United Nations. Andrew W. Cordier, Wilder Foote, and Max Harrelson, eds. N.Y., Columbia Univ. Pr., 1969–77. v.1–8. $225 the 8v. set; price per v. varies. **CK96**

v.1–3 were noted in *Guide* CK246n.

Contents: v.1, Trygvye Lie, 1946–1953; v.2, Dag Hammarskjöld, 1953–56; v.3, Dag Hammarskjöld, 1956–57; v.4, Dag Hammarskjöld, 1958–60; v.5, Dag Hammarskjöld, 1960–61; v.6, U Thant, 1961–64; v.7, U Thant, 1965–67; v.8, U Thant, 1968–71.

Includes reports, statements, speeches, diplomatic correspondence, and press conferences, with source of original publication indicated. Each volume has its own index.

Biography

Who's who in the United Nations and related agencies. 1st ed. N.Y., Arno Pr., 1975. 785p. $65. **CK97**

Table of contents in English, French, Spanish, Russian, Chinese and Arabic.

A biographical directory of delegates and senior personnel, past presidents of the General Assembly, and principal officials of the UN media correspondents' association, the World Federation of UN Associations, and non-governmental organizations accredited to the United Nations. An organizational roster lists office-holders by their posts, and other material includes a directory of UN agencies in each country, a list of member states as of the end of 1974, addresses of the permanent missions in New York and Geneva, a list of General Assembly Presidents 1946–74, names of the principal office-holders from 1946–74, a directory of the World Federation of United Nations Associations, and a list of United Nations depository libraries. Index by nationality. JX1977.W467

C L

Geography

GENERAL WORKS

Guides

Josuweit, Werner. Studienbibliographie Geographie: Bibliographie und Nachschlagewerke. Wiesbaden, Steiner, 1973. 122p. il. DM12. **CL1**

A briefly annotated guide to serials and basic reference sources for geography and its subfields. Book reviews are cited. Author/title and publisher indexes. Z6001.J67

Lock, Clara Beatrice Muriel. Geography and cartography; a reference handbook. 3d ed. rev. and enl. London, Bingley; Hamden, Conn., Linnet Books, [1976]. 762p. $32.50. **CL2**

A combined and revised edition of *Geography: a reference handbook,* first published 1968 (2d ed. 1972; *Guide* CL3), and of *Modern maps and atlases,* first published 1969 (*Guide* CL166). It constitutes an enlarged edition of the *Geography* handbook with "additional extended articles" and includes "some of the updated cartographical material that would otherwise appear in a revised *Modern maps. . . .*" —*Foreword.*

The review in *RQ,* 16:259 (Spr. 1977) concludes that "for libraries having the second edition [of *Geography: a reference handbook*], the purchase of *Geography and Cartography* is not recommended due to the large amount of duplicate information present and to the high price." G63.L6

Bibliography

Aiyepeku, Wilson O. Geographical literature on Nigeria, 1901–1970: an annotated bibliography. Boston, G. K. Hall, 1974. 214p. map. $19.50. **CL3**

Includes 1,441 English-language books, journal articles, essays, conference papers, master's theses and doctoral dissertations classified by subject categories developed by the Association of American Geographers. Lists of core authors, periodical titles, and bibliographies consulted. Author, place, and subject indexes. Z3597.A657

American Geographical Society of New York. Research catalogue. Supplement. Boston, G. K. Hall, 1972–74. 4v. **CL4**

For main set *see Guide* CL6.

Contents: [pt.1] Regional (2v., $230); [pt.2] Topical (2v., $235).

This first supplement covers materials added to the library from 1962 to 1971, thus cumulating the citations first published in *Current geographical publications* (*Guide* CL23), v. 25–34.

Bederman, Sanford Harold. Africa, a bibliography of geography and related disciplines: a selected listing of recent literature published in the English language. 3d ed. Atlanta, Publ. Serv. Div., Sch. of Bus. Admin., Georgia State Univ., 1974. 334p. $6.95 pa. **CL5**

1st–2d eds. (1970–72) published under title: *A bibliographic aid to the study of the geography of Africa.*

A geographically classified list of over 3,600 English-language citations (principally periodical articles). The general and regional sections each have a topical index, and there is also a country index subdivided into topics. Author index. Z3501.B4

Blotevogel, Hans H. and **Heineberg, Heinz.** Bibliographie zum Geographiestudium. Paderborn, Schöningh, [1976]. 2v. **CL6**

Contents: Teil 1, Fachtheorie. Didaktic der Geographie. Arbeitsmethoden. Physische Geographie/Geoökologie (239p.; DM15.80); Teil 2, Kulturgeographie. Sozialgeographie. Raumplanung. Entwicklungsländerforschung. Statistische Quellen (352p.; DM19.80).

A classed, annotated bibliography of books, articles, and essays, mainly in German and English. Important introductory works have been noted typographically. Both volumes have personal name indexes; v.2 has a regional index covering both volumes. Z5814.G34B56

Harris, Chauncy Dennison. Bibliography of geography. Chicago, 1976. pt.1. (Chicago. Univ. Dept. of Geography. Research paper no. 179) (In progress) **CL7**

Contents: pt.1, Introduction to general aids. 276p. $6 pa.

"This part includes only general bibliographical aids and does not cover bibliographies or bibliographical series limited to individual systematic fields of geography or to regions."—*Pref.* Does not intend to fully supersede Wright and Platt (*Guide* CL5) for, although "many items in Wright and Platt are out of date or superseded by later or better works, yet the essential core of older works of enduring value published up to 1946, carefully selected and expertly annotated, remains recorded there and does not need to be repeated."—*Pref.* Chapters on bibliographies of bibliographies (guides, comprehensive retrospective and current bibliographies of geography, specialized bibliographies) are followed by sections for bibliographies of books, serials, government documents, dissertations, photographs, maps and atlases, gazetteers, place name dictionaries, dictionaries, encyclopedias, statistics, and methodology.

In each chapter, introductory remarks are followed by carefully annotated lists of bibliographies. The sections on the comprehensive current and retrospective bibliographies are particularly precise and detailed. Appendix 1 lists "Gazetteers of the U.S. Board on Geographic Names"; Appendix 2 is an annotated list comprising "A small geographical reference collection." Indexed.

"Bibliographical sources for the systematic fields of geography, both physical and human, and for regional geography are planned for later treatment but no publication date is predicted."—*Pref.* H31.C514, no.179

——— Guide to geographical bibliographies and reference works in Russian or on the Soviet Union. Chicago, Univ. of Chicago, Dept. of Geography, 1975. 478p. maps. (Chicago. Univ. Dept. of Geography. Research paper, no.164) $5 pa. **CL8**

"Annotated list of 2660 bibliographies or reference aids."—*t.p.*

Intended as an aid to individuals outside the Soviet Union who wish to become informed on "the corpus of serious scientific work in geography and related disciplines published in Russian or in other languages of the Soviet Union or dealing with the geography of the Soviet Union."—*Pref.* Classed arrangement with author-title-subject index. Primarily non-Western language materials; entries are given in transliteration, with an English translation of the title. H31.C514 no.164

Morrison, Denton E., Hornback, Kenneth E. and **Warner, W. Keith.** Environment: a bibliography of social science and related literature. Prep. for Office of Research and Monitoring, U.S. Environmental Protection Agency. Wash., Govt. Prt. Off., 1974. 860p. (Socioeconomic environmental studies series, EPA-600/5-74-011) $7.45 pa. **CL9**

A comprehensive, unannotated bibliography of "nearly 5,000 items covering literature in and related to the fields of anthropology, communications, economics, education, design, geography, history, human ecology, landscape architecture, management, planning, politics and government, population, psychology, public administration, recreation, social psychology and sociology. The emphasis is on literature that is substantively, methodologically or theoretically relevant to man and his activities in relationship to natural environments."—*Abstract.* Author listing with a "subject-title index" which lists the titles within 42 subject categories. Z7161.M56

Owings, Loren C. Environmental values, 1860–1972; a guide to information sources. Detroit, Gale, 1976. 324p. (Man and the environment information guide ser., v.4) $18. **CL10**

"The theme of this bibliography is the historical development of attitudes toward, and concern for, nature in the United States."—*Introd.* Chapters cover general works, travel reports, landscape painting, national parks, conservation and the idea of wilderness, conservation and the ecological ethic, nature study, camping, "Back to Nature" movement, and general reference works. Annotated. Author-title-subject index. Z5861.O93

Paylore, Patricia. Desertification: a world bibliography. Tucson, Univ. of Arizona, Office of Arid Lands Studies, [1976]. 644p. **CL11**

1st ed., 1973, had title: *World desertification: cause and effect.*

A computer-produced, annotated bibliography on desertification rather than simply arid lands. Includes books, chapters of books, articles, reports, proceedings, and government documents. Geographical arrangement, with introduction and author-keyword indexes for each region (except for the Soviet Union, which has a more detailed subject breakdown within its section). Primarily literature of the past decade. Z6004.D4P35

Sanguin, André Louis. Géographie politique: bibliographie internationale. Montréal, Presses de l'Université du Québec, 1976. 232p. **CL12**

An attempt to distinguish political geography from geopolitics. Subject-classed list of works on cultural geography; the nation and the state; the frontier; territorial conflicts; oceans and international rivers; space; military, administrative, and electoral geography; international affairs and regionalism; and colonialism. Within each topic, citations are usually arranged by general or regional content, with subdivisions by book or article format. Author index. Z6004.P7S3

Sukhwal, B. L. South Asia: a systematic geographic bibliography. Metuchen, N.J., Scarecrow Pr., 1974. 827p. $27.50. **CL13**

More than 10,300 entries. Within geographic divisions (South Asia, India, Pakistan, Bangladesh, Sri Lanka, Tibet, Kingdom of

Nepal, Kingdoms of Bhutan and Sikkim, Indian Ocean and islands), materials are listed in classed arrangement. Author index. Z3185.S94

West, Henry W. and **Sawyer, Olive Hilda Matthew.** Land administration: a bibliography for developing countries. Cambridge, Cambridge Univ. Pr., 1975. 292p. £2.50. **CL14**

English-language books, periodical articles, papers and conference proceedings (published 1960–73) on land ownership, policy, tenure and law are grouped first by continent, then by country. Author index. Z7164.L3W47

Wisconsin. University-Madison. Land Tenure Center. Library. Agrarian reform in Latin America: an annotated bibliography. Madison, The Center, 1974. 2v. in 1. (Land economics monographs, 5) $20; $7.50 pa. **CL15**

"Published . . . under the sponsorship of *Land Economics.*"—*t.p.*

A guide to book, journal, pamphlet, and unpublished material on land tenure, land reform, and problems of the small farmers. Entries are grouped by region (Latin America, Central America, the Caribbean), then by individual country. Items of particular interest or importance are specially coded. Personal and corporate author indexes, classified subject index. Z7164.L3W56

——— Land tenure and agrarian reform in Africa and the Near East: an annotated bibliography. Boston, G. K. Hall, [1976]. 423p. $22. **CL16**

Entries for books, articles, pamphlets, and unpublished materials are grouped by region (Africa, Near East and North Africa) and then by country. Author, corporate author, and classified subject index. A similar volume for Asia is projected. Z7164.L3W56

Current

Bibliographie géographique internationale, 1891– . Paris, Centre National de la Recherche Scientifique, 1894– . v.1– . **CL17**

For full information *see Guide* CL24.

With v.82 (1977) became a quarterly publication. The classed arrangement remains basically the same, but the annotations have increased significantly in number and length. Each issue has subject, place, and author indexes which cumulate in an annual index issue. Because the items are now stored on computer tapes, the Centre offers an SDI (Selective Dissemination of Information) service for users wishing a bibliographic data base literature search.

Dokumentation zur Raumentwicklung. Jahrg. 1974/75– , Heft 1– . Bonn-Bad Godesberg, Bundesforschungsanstalt für Landeskunde und Raumordnung, 1975– . Quarterly, with annual index. DM120 per yr. **CL18**

Subtitle: Vierteljahreshefte zur Literaturdokumentation aus Raumforschung, Raumordnung, Regionalforschung, Landeskunde und Sozialgeographie/A current and annotated bibliography of regional science, regional planning and social geography.

Supersedes *Documentatio geographica; Vierteljahreshefte zur Literatur-Dokumentation aus Landeskunde, Raumordnung, Regionalforschung, Landeskunde und Sozialgeographie* (*Guide* CL25).

Published in 2v. per year: T.1, Titelband (comprising 4 quarterly issues); T.2, Registerband (issued annually in publisher's binding).

A classed bibliography, with author, subject, and regional indexes. Z7164.R33D64

Geo abstracts. [Norwich, Eng., Univ. of East Anglia], 1972– . **CL19**

For prior information *see Guide* CL27.

Beginning 1974, section *D: Social and historical geography* supersedes the earlier section *D: Social geography and cartography,* and a new section is added, *G: Remote sensing and cartography.* A new annual index series (v.1– , 1974–) covers pts. A, B, E and G.

Land use planning abstracts. N.Y., Environment Information Center, 1974– . Annual? $85 per yr. **CL20**

Subtitle, 1974: A select guide to land and water resources information since 1970.

1975 ed. covers publications of 1974–75; 1977 (called "3d ed.") covers 1976–77; intended to be an annual thereafter?

The volume covering 1976–77 offers abstracts of about 1,800 journal articles, conference papers, government hearings, and special studies grouped under 21 main headings (e.g., air pollution, chemical and biological contamination, energy). Subject index. A "Review" section at the beginning of each volume presents essays on the state of land use planning and policy. Z7164.O7L3

Sahel bibliographic bulletin. East Lansing, Sahel Documentation Center, Michigan State Univ., 1977– . v.1– . Quarterly. Free. **CL21**

Text in English or French.

Books, articles, papers and documents dealing with agricultural and economic development in the Sahel (Cape Verde, Chad, Gambia, Mali, Mauritania, Niger, Senegal, and Upper Volta) are listed by country, with a subject index. Also includes notes on research projects, information centers and services and bibliographies on special subjects. Z3684.S23S23

Dictionaries and encyclopedias

DeSola, Ralph. Worldwide what & where: geographic glossary & traveller's guide. Santa Barbara, Calif., ABC-Clio, [1975]. 720p. $23.50. **CL22**

A miscellany of geographical facts, abbreviations, places, names, etc., in dictionary arrangement. For many localities lists "scenic spectacles," cities ranked by population (without figures), unusual place names. Addenda include list of capital cities, ferry routes, festivals, museums, and abbreviations. G63.D47

Monkhouse, Francis John and **Small, Ronald John.** A dictionary of the natural environment. N.Y., Wiley, [1978]. 320p. il. $19.50; $6.95 pa. **CL23**

Based in part on the revisions prepared for a new edition of *A dictionary of geography* (*Guide* CL41), with 465 new definitions, line diagrams, and photographs. Emphasizes terms used by physical geographers and environmental scientists. GB10.M64

Bibliography

Meynen, Emil. Bibliography of mono- and multilingual dictionaries and glossaries of technical terms used in geography as well as in related natural and social sciences. Wiesbaden, Franz Steiner Verlag, 1974. 246p. **CL24**

Title page and all explanatory material in English and French.

Comp. and ed. by the International Geographical Union Commission, "International Geographical Terminology."

A selective, classed list of dictionaries and glossaries published from 1920 to date in monographic and periodical article format. Excludes gazetteers of geographical names and dictionaries of regional data, with the more comprehensive treatment given to multilingual, rather than monolingual works. Includes bibliographical references and a supplement. Author index includes titles if they are the main entry. Each citation indicates languages used in the work. Z6004.D5M48

Directories

Environmental protection directory. 2d ed., ed. by Thaddeus C. Trzyna, with the assistance of Sally R. Ogsberg. Chicago, Marquis Academic Media, [1975]. 526p. $44.50. **CL25**

Publ. for the Center for California Public Affairs.

1st ed. publ. 1973 as part of the *Directory of consumer protection and environmental agencies* (*Guide* CH217).

Subtitle: A comprehensive guide to environmental organizations in the United States and Canada.

A "User's guide" is arranged topically "to help readers identify organizations concerned with a specific area of interest, such as water quality or fish and wildlife."—*Introd.* Remainder of the text follows geographic arrangement. Subject, organization, personnel, and publication indexes. TD171.E57

Paylore, Patricia. Arid lands research institutions; a world directory. Rev. and updated ed. Tucson, Univ. of Arizona Pr., 1977. 317p. $7.50 pa. **CL26**

1st ed. 1967 (*Guide* CL53).

Format and arrangement follow that of the 1st ed.; information is derived from direct correspondence with the institutions, and several institutions have been dropped. Name and subject indexes. GB841.P38

Biography

Geographers: biobibliographical studies. v.1– . Ed. by T. W. Freeman, Marguerita Oughton and Philippe Pinchemel. [London], Mansell, 1977– . il. (v.1: $21.50 pa.) (In progress) **CL27**

Published on behalf of the International Geographical Union Commission on the History of Geographical Thought.

v.1 presents 18 studies on deceased figures important in the history of geography. The biographical section of each study deals with personal background, career development, and contribution to the field; the bibliographies are selective, usually including primary, secondary, and archival sources. International in scope. Indexed. Z6001.G42

Henze, Dietmar. Enzyklopädie der Entdecker und Erforscher der Erde. Graz, Akademische Druck u. Verlagsanstalt, 1975– . Lfg.1– . (In progress) (Lfg.1: 460sch.) **CL28**

Contents: Lfg.1, A.

Offers biographical articles on explorers and discoverers. Entries include bibliographies of primary and secondary writings. Scope encompasses persons from ancient to modern times. G200.H37

GAZETTEERS

General

Paxton, John. The statesman's year-book world gazetteer. N.Y., St. Martin's Pr.; [London, Macmillan, 1975]. 733p., 24p. maps. $15; £6.95. **CL29**

Intended as a companion to *The statesman's year-book* (*Guide* CG45). Gives brief information on places of size and importance. Some statistical tables and a glossary of about 800 statistical terms are supplied. G103.5.P38

U.S. Board on Geographic Names. Gazetteer. no.130–[142]. Wash., Govt. Prt. Off., 1974–77. Irregular. **CL30**

For previously published volumes and annotation *see Guide* CL59.

Contents: 130, Surinam. 1974; [131], British Solomon Islands Protectorate and Gilbert and Ellice Islands Colony. 1974; [132], Fiji, Tonga, and Nauru. 1974; [133], New Caledonia and dependencies and Wallis and Futuna. 1974; [134], New Hebrides. 1974; [135], Republic of China. 1974; [136], Bahrain, Kuwait, Qatar, and United Arab Emirates. 1976; [137], Bangladesh. 1976; [138], Guyana. 1976; [139], Oman. 1976; [140], Peoples Democratic Republic of Yemen. 1976; [141], Yemen Arab Republic. 1976; [142], Gazetteer of conventional names. 1977.

The following revised editions have also appeared: 22, Mainland China, v.1, A–L. 2d ed., 1976; 25, Nicaragua. 2d ed., 1976; 106, Liberia. 2d ed., 1976.

Brazil

Dicionário de geografia do Brasil, com terminologia geográfica. Organização geral, Departamento Editorial das Edições Melhoramentos; redação de temas e verbetes, Erasmo d'Almeida Magalhaes [et al.]. [2. ed. São Paulo], Edições Melhoramentos, [1976]. 544p. Cr $200. **CL31**

Combines gazetteer information on major cities and states, and definitions of geographical terms and concepts, with emphasis on Brazilian aspects. Supplementary list of cities with more than 20,000 people is based on 1970 census figures. Bibliography. F2504.D48

Dicionário geográfico brasileiro, com numerosas ilustrações, inclusive mapas dos estados e territórios. 2. ed. Pôrto Alegre, Editôra Globo, [1972]. [621p.] il., maps. Cr$60 pa. **CL32**

1st ed. 1966.

Offers far more detailed gazetteer information on a greater number of geographical features, cities, towns, states, and territories in Brazil than does the *Dicionário de geografia do Brasil* (above). Provides population figures based on 1970 census estimates. Bibliography. F2504.D5

Canada

Canada. Permanent Committee on Geographical Names. Gazetteer of Canada. Ottawa, 1952– . (In progress) **CL33**

For prior information *see Guide* CL131.

The following additional volumes have been published: Alberta (2d ed., 1974); Ontario ([2d ed.] 1975); Yukon Territory (4th ed., 1976); Northwest Territories (3d provisional ed., 1971).

Great Britain

Bartholomew (John) and Son, Ltd. Bartholomew gazetteer of Britain. [Edinburgh], Bartholomew, [1977]. xlviii, 271p., 128 pl. maps. 30cm. £9.50. **CL34**

Oliver Mason, comp.

An earlier work by John G. Bartholomew was first published 1904 as *Survey gazetteer of the British Isles* and in 1966 as *Gazetteer of the British Isles* (*Guide* CL86). This edition updates statistical sections in accordance with the 1971 census, with provisional figures for 1975. Area covered is England, Scotland, Wales, and the Isle of Man. DA640.B24

India

Gazetteer of India: Indian Union. [Delhi], 1973–75. v.2–3. (In progress) **CL35**

For v.1, full citation and annotation *see Guide* CL93.

Contents: v.2, History and culture, ed. by P. N. Chopra (1973. 807p.); v.3, Economic structure and activities, ed. by P. N. Chopra (1975. 1278p.).

Iran

Adamec, Ludwig W. Historical gazetteer of Iran. Graz, Austria, Akademische Druck- und Verlagsanstalt, 1976– . v.1– . maps. (In progress) **CL36**

Contents: v.1, Tehran and northwestern Iran.

This volume adds to and updates material originally presented in the General Staff of British India's *Gazetteer of Persia* (1914; republished 1918); the text has been reprinted, with new entries and passages added. Includes geographical features, villages and towns, ethnographic groups, etc., arranged alphabetically, plus a glossary, index of subtribes, and a map section. Statistics are based on the 1966 census. DS253.A54

El Salvador

Salvador. Instituto Geográfico Nacional. Diccionario geográfico de El Salvador/Ministerio de OO.PP.[Obras Públicas], Instituto Geográfico Nacional. [San Salvador], El Instituto, 1970 [i.e., 1971–76]. 4v. il. $45 pa. **CL37**

A gazetteer, with detailed historical, geographical, and statistical information on 24,519 names. Each volume contains data on a number of "departamentos": v.1, Ahuachapán, Santa Ana and Sonsonata; v.2, La Libertad, Chalatenango, San Salvador, and

Cuscatlán; v.3, La Paz, Cabañas and San Vicente; v.4, Usulután, San Miguel, Morazán, and La Unión. No consolidated index.
F1482.S35

GEOGRAPHICAL NAMES AND TERMS

General works

Harder, Kelsie B. Illustrated dictionary of place names, United States and Canada. N.Y., Van Nostrand Reinhold, [1976]. 631p. il. $18.95. **CL38**

"The names of all provinces, states, provincial and state capitals, counties and county seats are listed. An attempt is also made to include a comprehensive selection of the most viable and interesting United States cities and towns, based on current census reports and ZIP code directories."—*Introd.* Major geographical features are also covered. Illustrations depict persons for whom places were named, the site named, or a historical event related to the site. Bibliography.
E155.H37

Bibliography

Raper, P. E. Bronnegids vir toponimie en topologie. Source guide for toponymy and topology. Pretoria, S. A. Naamkundesentrum, Raad vir Geesteswetenskaplike Navorsing, 1975. 478p. (Naamkundereeks, 5) R15. **CL39**

A bibliography for "the study of places and place names."—*Pref.* Includes books, pamphlets, periodical and newspaper articles, and theses. In two sections, the first arranged by subject or place name; the second by author. Full information is given in both sections.

United States

Carlson, Helen S. Nevada place names; a geographical dictionary. Reno, Univ. of Nevada Pr., 1974. 282p. map. $15. **CL40**

Entries include counties and county seats, post offices, state and national parks and monuments, railway stations, all present-day cities, towns, and settlements, former settlements, mining camps, Pony Express stops, and natural features. Entries are keyed to bibliography, maps cited, and railroads. F839.C37

Pukui, Mary Kawena, Elbert, Samuel H. and **Mookini, Esther T.** Place names of Hawaii. Rev. and enl. ed. Honolulu, Univ. Pr. of Hawaii, [1974]. 289p. maps. $9.50; $4.95 pa. **CL41**

1st ed. 1966.

About 4,000 entries, including names in English as well as Hawaiian. Extensive appendixes and references. DU622.P79

Canada

Hamilton, William B. The Macmillan book of Canadian place names. Toronto, Macmillan of Canada, [1978]. 340p. $18.60. **CL42**

Begun as a revision of G. H. Armstrong's *Origin and meaning of place names in Canada* (1930; *Guide* CL129), but in effect a new work. Selection criteria included: (1) size (i.e., "major centres of population and the most important physical features."—*Pref.*); (2) historical significance; and (3) human interest. Bibliography, pp.333–40. F1004.H35

Germany

Historisches Ortsnamenbuch von Bayern. München, Kommission für bayerische Landesgeschichte, 1973–77. (In progress) **CL43**

For previously published parts *see Guide* CL138.

Contents: *Oberfranken:* Bd.3, Rehau-Selb, von Reinhard Höllerich (1977).

Oberpfalz: Bd.1, Stadt- und Landkreis Amberg, von Hans Frank (1975).

Schwaben: Bd.6, Stadt- und Landkreis Lindau, von Heinrich Löffler (1973); Bd.7, Landkreis Sonthofen, von Richard Dertsch (1974).

Great Britain

English Place-Name Society. [Survey of English place-names] Cambridge, Univ. Pr., 1974–77. v.50–52. (In progress) **CL44**

For previously published volumes and annotation *see Guide* CL143.

Contents: v.50–51, The place-names of *Berkshire,* pts.2 and 3, nos.1 and 2, by Margaret Gelling (1974–76. 2v.); v.52, The place-names of *Dorset,* pt.1, by A. D. Mills (1977).

ATLASES

Guides

See also Suppl. AB33a.

Alexander, Gerard L. Guide to atlases supplement: world, regional, national, thematic. Metuchen, N.J., Scarecrow Pr., 1977. 362p. $14. **CL45**

"An international listing of atlases published 1971 through 1975 with comprehensive indexes."—*t.p.*

Includes some entries from the 1950–70 period overlooked in the basic volume (*Guide* CL165). Indexed by publisher and by author/cartographer/editor. Z6021.A43

Guide to U.S. government maps: geologic and hydrologic maps. 1975– . McLean, Va., Documents Index, [1976–]. Annual. (1976: $55) **CL46**

Issue for 1975, called "Preliminary edition," was accompanied by a location index which was a reprint of the index of the *National atlas of the United States of America,* published by the U.S. Geological Survey in 1970 (*Guide* CL230). Issue for 1976 (publ. 1977) also called "Preliminary edition," updated through Aug. 1976. The "third edition" will bring coverage through 1977, be published in 1978, and will begin this title's official annual publication. Covers maps published by the U.S. Geological Survey; entries and annotations were taken from the Survey's *Publications* lists. Arrangement is by series, with area, subject, and coordinate indexes. Brief descriptive annotations for some entries. A list is included following each section showing maps currently available and their prices.
Z6034.U49A53

International maps and atlases in print. Ed. by Kenneth L. Winch. 2d ed. N.Y. & London, Bowker, [1976]. 866p. il., maps. $42.50. **CL47**

1st ed. 1974.

Classed arrangement by the world, region, and country notation of the Universal Decimal System. Within each area, the publications are divided into maps and atlases, and each of these types is subdivided by subject (general, town plans, official surveys, political and administrative, etc.); arrangement within the subject groups is by scale. Index diagrams of multi-sheet series have been reproduced to show publication status. Full bibliographic details for each publication. Index of countries, regions, and islands. Very useful.
Z6021.I596

Bibliography and indexes

American Geographical Society of New York. Map Dept. Index to maps in books and periodicals. Second supplement. Boston, G. K. Hall, 1976. 568p. $85. **CL48**

For main set and first supplement *see Guide* CL168.

This supplement covers the period 1972–75; format remains the same.

British Library. Catalogue of printed maps, charts and plans. Ten-year supplement, 1965–1974. [London], British Museum Publications, [1978]. 1380 cols. £45. **CL49**

For the main set *see Guide* CL169.

Contains entries for "(a) maps, atlases, globes and related materials, including literature on them, acquired by the Map Library during 1965–1974, and (b) the more important cartographic materials in other collections of the Department of Printed Books and of the Department of Oriental Manuscripts and Printed Books of the British Library Reference Division catalogued during the same period." —*Pref.* The first in a projected series of ten-year supplements.

Z6028.B86

U.S. Library of Congress. Map Division. A list of geographical atlases in the Library of Congress, with bibliographical notes. Wash., Govt. Prt. Off., 1974. v.8. **CL50**

For earlier volumes and annotation *see Guide* CL185.

Contents: v.8, Index to v.7 (Titles 10255–18435).

Current

Bibliographia cartographica. no.1– , 1974– . Pullach bei München, Verlag Dokumentation, [1974–]. Semiannual. DM36 per yr. **CL51**

Supersedes *Bibliotheca cartographica* (*Guide* CL193).

Issued by Staatsbibliothek Preussischer Kulturbesitz in cooperation with the Deutsche Gesellschaft für Kartographie.

Except for structural publishing changes and a new section on school cartography, this is a continuation of the *Bibliotheca cartographica.* Author index. Z6021.B48

Directories

World directory of map collections. Comp. by the Geography and Map Libraries Sub-Section; ed. by Walter W. Ristow. München, Verlag Dokumentation, 1976. 326p. (IFLA publs., 8) DM48. **CL52**

Lists by country some 285 map and chart collections in 46 countries, with information on size and type of collection, reference services, reproduction facilities, and publications. Only selected entries for countries with existing directories of map collections (Canada, German Federal Republic, France, the United States).

GA192.W67

General

Bartholomew (John) and Son, Ltd. The Times atlas of the world, comprehensive ed. [5th ed., reprinted with revisions. London], Times Books, [1977]. xl, 224p., [64] leaves of plates. il. 46cm. £29.50. **CL53**

For earlier editions *see Guide* CL201.

A review in *The booklist* (72:1632) concluded that this "is a beautifully produced, well-balanced, and authoritative general world atlas. . . . Its maps are current and accurate, clearly drawn and printed, and effectively locate a diversity of man-made and natural features. The index-gazetteer [about 200,000 entries] is an extremely well-designed key to the atlas' contents."

National Geographic Society, Washington, D.C. Cartographic Division. National Geographic atlas of the world. 4th ed. Wash., Nat. Geographic Soc., 1975. 330p. il., maps. 48cm. $23.90. **CL54**

Melville Bell Grosvenor, ed.-in-chief; Gilbert M. Grosvenor, ed.; William T. Peele, chief cartographer; Jules B. Billard, atlas text.

3d ed. 1970 (*Guide* CL211).

Some sections have been rearranged, and maps seem more legible because of changes in color printing. Information on population figures, etc., has been updated to 1974. G1019.N28

Oxford University Press. The new Oxford atlas. Prep. by the Cartographic Dept. of the Oxford Univ. Pr. [London], Oxford Univ. Pr., [1975]. 202p. il., maps. 39cm. $19.95. **CL55**

1st ed., 1951 (frequently reprinted with revisions), entitled *The Oxford atlas.*

Termed "a development rather than a straightforward second edition" (*Pref.*), the work "retains the scales, projections, sheet lines, and general colouring of its topographic maps, whilst incorporating complete revision of all information liable to change and a re-styling of certain elements of map design in the interests of greater clarity. Its thematic or special subject maps, which are particularly concerned with the basic aspects of physical geography and demography, incorporate the results of modern research and latest available information and are presented by newly-evolved cartographic techniques." Index of towns and topographical features shown on the maps (plus, in italics, some historical place-names not shown but located by reference to places shown on the maps). G1019.O872

Rand McNally concise atlas of the earth. N.Y., [etc.], Rand McNally in assoc. with Mitchell Beazley, London, [1976]. 240p. il., maps. 37cm. $19.95. **CL56**

In three main sections: (1) "The good earth" (providing textual and graphic description of the earth's geology and climate, as well as its resources); (2) "Maps" (offering physical maps of the continents and regional and country maps); (3) "City maps" (covering United States cities in far greater detail than foreign cities). Geographical index-gazetteer. Many of the maps are derived from the publisher's *International atlas* (1969) and *The earth and man* (1976).

G1021.R3

National and regional

United States

Adams, John S. A comparative atlas of America's great cities: twenty metropolitan regions. [Minneapolis], Univ. of Minnesota Pr., [1976]. 503p. il., maps. 34cm. $95. **CL57**

Editor, Ronald Abler; text, John S. Adams and Ronald Abler; chief cartographer, Ki-Suk Lee.

A product of the Comparative Metropolitan Analysis Project of the Association of American Geographers, Cambridge, Mass., which published two companion volumes: *Contemporary metropolitan America: twenty geographical vignettes* and *Urban policymaking and metropolitan dynamics: a comparative geographical analysis* (1976).

The atlas is in four parts: (1) Introduction; (2) Current patterns in American cities (with comparative maps for housing, the people, socio-economic characteristics, and topics of special interest for each city or Standard Metropolitan Statistical Area); (3) Metropolitan problems (offering maps showing aspects of metropolitan physical environment, open space for metropolitan leisure-time use, housing, transportation and communication, metropolitan growth, education, public health, socio-economic segregation, employment and poverty, urban renewal); and (4) Policy requisites for American metropolitan regions. Glossary; index/gazetteer. G1201.A1A3

Andriot, John L. Township atlas of the United States; named townships. McLean, Va., Andriot Associates, 1977. 724p. maps. $40. **CL58**

"The purpose of this volume is to provide a handy atlas showing the named townships which exist today, their relative size and location within the county, and a detailed index to the 22,000 townships. . . ."—*Foreword.* Each section on a particular state contains a state map showing all counties with a county location index, and a state name index of all incorporated places and unincorporated places of 1,000 or more population, giving the name of the county where each is located; within each state section, county maps are alphabetically arranged. The township index concludes the volume. Map and state location indexes have been reproduced from material generated by the U.S. Bureau of the Census for the 1970 census of population. G1201.F7A5

Austria

Akademie der Wissenschaften, Vienna. Kommission für Raumforschung und Wiederaufbau. Atlas der Republik Österreich. Vienna, 1974–77. Lfg. 6^{1-3}. (In progress) **CL59**

For full citation and annotation *see Guide* CL234.

Teil 1–3 of Lfg.6 includes some 15 looseleaf maps.

Canada

Canada. Surveys and Mapping Branch. Geography Division. The national atlas of Canada. 4th ed. (rev.). Toronto, Macmillan, 1974. 254p. maps. 38cm. **CL60**

1st ed. 1906. 1st–3d eds. publ. under title *Atlas of Canada;* 1st– 2d eds. issued by the Dept. of the Interior; 3d ed. issued by the Geographical Branch.

The 4th ed. (1970–73; *Guide* CL237) was first issued in a small press run of loose sheets. The bound volume supersedes those sheets. G1115.C55

China

Chang, Chi-yun, ed. National atlas of China. 1st–2d ed. Taiwan, National War College, 1962. v.4–5. **CL61**

For v.1–3 and annotation *see Guide* CL238.

Contents: v.4, South China; v.5, General maps of China.

The general maps illustrate communications, climate, soils, vegetation and forestry, agriculture, fishing, livestock, minerals, population, and major languages.

The Times atlas of China. [London], Times Books; [N.Y.], Quadrangle/New York Times Book Co., [1974]. xlp., 144p., 27p. il., maps. 38cm. $75. **CL62**

Editors and chief contributors: P. J. M. Geelan, D. C. Twitchett; Cartographic consultant, John C. Bartholomew & Son, Ltd.

Offers maps and explanatory text representing a variety of historical, economic, and physical topics, maps of the provinces of China, and a section of city plans. Wade-Giles system of transcription of Chinese names is used on the maps. In the index names are arranged alphabetically by Wade-Giles transcription with the Pinyin transcription following; cross references are provided from the old Post Office spellings. It is clearly stated in the Introduction that some of the information is fairly tentative since "detailed geographical and particularly statistical information at the time of writing is, by Western standards, hard to come by." G2305.T47

Europe

Bartholomew/Scribner atlas of Europe: a profile of Western Europe. Edinburgh, Bartholomew; N.Y., Scribner's, [1974]. 128p. il., maps. 30cm. $14.95. **CL63**

Presents economic and social information on 18 countries through maps, graphs, diagrams, and tabulations. Data presented is for the 1960–70 period. Most illustrations show data for all 18 countries; individual country maps and statistical profiles are also included. Glossary, list of sources, and subject and individual country map indexes.

Japan

Kokusai Kyōiku Jōhō Sentā. Atlas of Japan: physical, economic, and social. 2d [rev.] ed. Tokyo, Internatl. Soc. for Educational Information, 1974. 64p., 64p. maps. 37cm. **CL64**

Prep. under the joint guidance of Akira Ebato and Kazuo Watanabe.

1st ed. 1970.

Text in English, French, and Spanish.

64 map plates illustrating land forms, weather, cities, population, agriculture and land use, mineral resources, manufacturing industries, cultural elements, and transportation, are followed by 64 pages of explanatory notes. Figures have been updated for the 1970–73 period. Map of Japan in pocket. G2355.K65

Mexico

Atlas of Mexico. [2d ed.] Stanley A. Arbingast [and others], eds. [Austin], Bureau of Business Research, Univ. of Texas at Austin, [1975]. 164p. il., maps. 28X37cm. $15. **CL65**

1st ed. 1970 (*Guide* CL255).

An updated and expanded edition. G1545.A9

New Zealand

New Zealand atlas. Ed. by Ian Wards. Wellington, A. R. Shearer, Govt. Printer, 1976. 291p. il., maps. 32cm. **CL66**

Although undertaken as a revised edition of *A descriptive atlas of New Zealand* ed. by A. H. McLintock (*Guide* CL256), only two maps are carried over from that work; the rest of the compilation, cartographic and textual, is new.

"The aim has been an even balance between cartographic exposition, textual explanation and photographic illustration, each complementary to the other."—*Introd.* In addition to topographic maps (including numerous maps of urban areas), there are maps showing discovery and settlement, population distribution, climate, geology, forests, fauna, fishing, mineral resources, etc. Index gazetteer. Beautifully illustrated. G2795.N4

Philippines

Fund for Assistance to Private Education. Philippine atlas. Manila, The Fund, 1975. 2v. (304p., 125p.) il. maps. **CL67**

Contents: v.1, A historical, economic and educational profile of the Philippines; v.2, Directory of schools, assistance groupings, and index.

v.1 surveys the situation of the Philippines in the world in terms of land area, population and education; describes, through text, maps, and illustrations, the physical geography, history, culture, population, and economy; and describes the educational structure. v.2 gives descriptive data on 695 higher education institutions, identifies public and private sources of educational funding, and includes name/place and general index. G2391.G1F8

GUIDEBOOKS

Bibliography

Nueckel, Susan. Selected guide to travel books. N.Y., Fleet Pr. Corp., [1974]. 117p. $10.50. **CL68**

Works are grouped under such headings as: Backpacking and hiking, Bicycling, Camping, Countries, Currency conversation, Foreign language aids, Mountaineering, etc. About 700 items; brief anotations; subject index. Z6011.N83

Travel Reference Center. Travel research bibliography: a bibliography of the holdings of the Travel Reference Center. Comp. by C. R. Goeldner, Karen Dicke and Susan Behrends. Boulder, Colo., Business Research Div., Graduate School of Business Admin., Univ. of Colorado, in cooperation with the Travel Research Assoc., [1976]. 213*l*. **CL69**

In five sections: (1) Periodicals and reports: (2) Bibliographies; (3) National (i.e., works dealing with travel in the United States or specific regions thereof); (4) State publications (dealing with individual states of the U.S.); and (5) International publications. Subject index. Z6004.T6T72

D

History and Area Studies

D A

General History

GENERAL WORKS

Guides

Walford, Albert John. Guide to reference material. 3d ed. [London], Library Assoc., 1975. v.2. (In progress) **DA1**

For full information *see Suppl.* CA2.

v.2 is devoted to the social and historical sciences, philosophy and religion.

Historical method

Barzun, Jacques and **Graff, Henry F.** The modern researcher. 3d ed. N.Y., Harcourt Brace Jovanovich, [1977]. 378p. $12.95; $6.95 pa. **DA2**

2d ed. 1970 (*Guide* DA5).

A thorough revision of the text, with much new illustrative material. The checklist of historiographical materials (pp.329–51) has also been updated. D13.B334

Bibliography

Stanford University. Hoover Institution on War, Revolution and Peace. The library catalogs of the Hoover Institution.... 1st–2d supplement. Boston, G. K. Hall, 1972–77. **DA3**

For the main set and annotation *see Guide* DA20.

Contents: Suppl. 1, Catalog of the Western language collection (5v., $650), Chinese collection (2v., $260), Japanese collection (1v., $120); Suppl. 2, Western language collections (6v., $780), Chinese collection (2v., $260), Japanese collection (1v., $130).

Covers materials cataloged July 1969–June 1973. Unlike the main set, the supplements do not include government documents, society publications, Western-language serials and newspapers, and archives and manuscripts.

Current

Index to book reviews in historical periodicals, 1972– . Metuchen, N.J., Scarecrow Pr., 1976– . Annual. (1975 publ. 1977: $22.50) **DA4**

John W. Brewster and Joseph A. McLeod, comps.

An index to book reviews appearing in 90-odd English-language historical periodicals. Works in disciplines other than history are included, as are reviews of foreign-language books if the review is in English. Entry is by author, with a title index.

Recently published articles. v.1, no.1– , Feb. 1976– . Wash., Amer. Historical Assoc., 1976– . 3 issues per yr. $8. **DA5**

The classified, current bibliography formerly published as part of the regular issues of the *American historical review.* The United States section cumulates into the annual volumes of *Writings on American history* (*Suppl.* DB12).

Dissertations

Doctoral dissertations in history. v.1– , Jan./June 1976– . [Wash.], Amer. Historical Assoc., Institutional Services Program, 1976– . v.1– . Semiannual. **DA6**

v.1, no.1 preceded by an unnumbered issue dated July/Dec. 1975. With the July–Dec.1976 issue the issue number is included in the numbering (i.e., v.1, no.2–).

For earlier series *see Guide* DA27.

Each issue follows a chronological (Ancient, Medieval, Modern)/ geographical arrangement, with the United States section broken down by subject. Within each section "in progress" listings precede the completed dissertations. Author index. Beginning with the Jan./ June 1976 issue a précis supplied by the author is included with the listing. Z6205.D6

Jacobs, Phyllis M. History theses 1901–70: historical research for higher degrees in the universities of the United Kingdom. [London], Univ. of London, Inst. of Historical Research, 1976. 456p. £4.50. **DA7**

An attempt to provide a comprehensive list of theses "completed and approved for the degree of B.Litt. and for doctor's and master's degrees in universities of the United Kingdom."—*Introd.* More than 7,600 entries; classed arrangement with author and subject indexes. Unfortunately, it is "not a list of theses which are necessarily available for consultation, since in nearly all British universities it is only in relatively recent years that students have been required to place a copy of their work on deposit."

Although regularly published lists of research for university degrees have been issued by the Institute of Historical Research from 1920 to date (*Guide* DC187), the compiler went beyond a mere cumulation of the printed lists, attempting to verify citations, correct errors, and winnow out theses which may have been listed as completed but which were, in fact, never approved. Z6201.J23

Historiography

Berding, Helmut. Bibliographie zur Geschichtstheorie. Göttingen, Vandenhoeck & Ruprecht, 1977. 331p. (Arbeitsbücher zur modernen Geschichte, Bd.4) **DA8**

A classed bibliography of book and periodical materials on the theory and writing of history. Includes sections for interdisciplinary materials (e.g., history and sociology; history and psychology). Lacks an index. Z6201.A2B47

Birkos, Alexander S. and **Tambs, Lewis A.** Historiography, method, history teaching; a bibliography of books and articles in English, 1965–1973. [Hamden, Conn.], Linnet Books, 1975. 130p. $7.50. **DA9**

In four main sections: (1) Research methods in history; (2) Teaching of history; (3) Historiography and philosophy of history; (4) Historiographical studies by area. Author index. The bibliography "is designed not only to aid university, college and high school historians in their teaching, research and publication, but also to facilitate their awareness of new and often conflicting trends in current historiography."—*Pref.* Z6208.H5B57

Day, Alan Edwin. History; a reference handbook. London, Clive Bingley; Hamden, Conn., Linnet Books, [1977]. 354p. £5.50. **DA10**

Intends to provide a guide to reference works—dictionaries, bibliographies, atlases, biographical works, etc.—in the field of history and, "at the same time, to indicate the main purposes and features of the equally varied forms of historical publications and standard textbooks, monographs and large scale cooperative histories, collections of texts and primary source material, learned and popular historical journals."—*Foreword.* Entries are mainly for titles of books or series (e.g., Texts and calendars; The Ford lectures), with some personal and institutional names (e.g., American Historical Association; School of Oriental and African Studies; Halévy, Elie). Index. Z2016.D38

Stephens, Lester D. Historiography: a bibliography. Metuchen, N.J., Scarecrow Pr., 1975. 271p. $9. **DA11**

In four main sections: (1) Theories of history; (2) Historiography; (3) Historical methods; (4) Reference works. Nearly 2,300 items; many brief annotations; index. Z6208.H5S73

Fellowships, grants, etc.

Fellowships and grants of interest to historians. 1976/77– . [Wash.], Amer. Historical Assoc., Institutional Services Program, [1977]– . Annual? (1976/77: $2.50) **DA12**

Listing is by name of the fund or the grant-giving agency. Indicates requirements for eligibility, amount and term of the grant, application deadline, etc.

Dictionaries, outlines, tables

Freeman-Grenville, Greville Stewart Parker. Chronology of world history; a calendar of principal events from 3000 BC to AD 1973. [Totowa, N.J.], Rowman & Littlefield, 1975. 753p. $40. **DA13**

Events and developments are presented in tabular form, six columns on facing pages. The first five columns are devoted to politico-historical matters arranged under geographical headings (with variations in the headings to reflect shifting emphasis); the sixth column is headed "Religion & culture" and chronicles developments in all geographical areas. Index of persons, places, events, etc. D11.F75

Grun, Bernard. The timetables of history; a horizontal linkage of people and events. Based on Werner Stein's *Kulturfahrplan.* N.Y., Simon and Schuster, [1975]. 661p. $24.95. **DA14**

Contemporary names and events in various fields are presented in parallel columns: (A) History, politics; (B) Literature, theater; (C) Religion, philosophy, learning; (D) Visual arts; (E) Music; (F) Science, technology, growth; (G) Daily life. Much of the material is directly translated from Werner Stein's *Kulturfahrplan,* first published 1946. D11.G78

Langer, William Leonard. The new illustrated encyclopedia of world history. N.Y., H. N. Abrams, [1975]. 2v. (1368p.) il. $65. **DA15**

A Subscription Books Committee review in the *Booklist* (73:276) indicates that the text is the same as that of the 1972 edition of

Langer's encyclopedia (*Guide* DA42) except for correction of a few errors in the index; the illustrations are new. D21.L276

Annuals and current surveys

Facts on file. Five-year index, 1971–1975. N.Y., Facts on File, Inc., 1976. 983p. $70. **DA16**

For a note on the series *see Guide* DA51.

Atlases

Gilbert, Martin. Jewish history atlas. 2d ed. London, Weidenfeld & Nicolson, [1976]; N.Y., Macmillan, [1977]. 121p. maps. 26cm. £4.25; £3 pa.; $3.95 pa. **DA17**

1st ed. 1969 (*Guide* DE142).

Mainly single-page maps in black-and-white tracing "the worldwide Jewish migrations from ancient Mesopotamia to modern Israel."—*Pref.* Some maps have been revised and expanded, and the number of maps in this edition increased to 121 (from 112). The index of the earlier edition was dropped, but the bibliography has been retained and enlarged.

Lloyd, Christopher. Atlas of maritime history. [Feltham, Middlesex, Eng.], Country Life; N.Y., Arco Publ. Co., [1975]. 144p. il., maps. 34cm. £10; $35. **DA18**

Maps and explanatory text "aim at displaying the entire maritime history [i.e., economic and political as well as naval aspects] of the western nations from the time of the Greeks and the Phoenicians to that of the Americans and the Russians of the present day."—*Pref.* Index to the maps and diagrams. G1060.L65

ARCHAEOLOGY AND PREHISTORY

Bibliography

Battersby, Harold R. Anatolian archaeology: a bibliography. New Haven, Human Relations Area Files, Inc., 1976. 2v. (Anatolian studies, 1) $18. **DA19**

5,169 articles, essays, books, and periodical titles are listed in two alphabetical author sequences, with index by topic or excavation site. Z2857.A67B38

Jerusalem. École Biblique et Archéologique Française. Bibliothèque. Catalogue . . . (Catalog of the Library of the French Biblical and Archeological School, Jerusalem). Boston, G. K. Hall, 1975. 13v. $1240. **DA20**

Lists both books and periodical articles in the collection of the École Biblique. Strong in Old and New Testament studies, Judaism, Christian antiquity, papyrology, linguistics, epigraphy, numismatics, archaeology, Assyriology, Egyptology, geography, Oriental history, biblical theology, etc. Materials are listed by author and by subject in a single alphabet. Subject headings in French. Z7770.J36

Sovetskaia arkheologicheskaia literatura; bibliografiia, 1963/67. Leningrad, Nauka, 1975. 471p. **DA21**

For earlier volumes and annotation *see Guide* DA68.

This volume edited by T.N. Zadnieprovskaia.

Encyclopedias and handbooks

Encyclopedia of archaeological excavations in the Holy Land; rev. tr. Entsiklopedyah la-hafirot arke'ologiyot be-Erets Yisrael. Ed., English ed., Michael Avi-Yonah. Englewood Cliffs, N.J., Prentice-Hall, 1975–78; London, Oxford Univ. Pr., 1976–78. v.1–3. il., maps, tables. (In progress) $100. **DA22**

Contents: v.1–3, A–N.

A translation of the Hebrew edition (Jerusalem, 1970. 2v.) with updating to the end of 1971. The completed work will present a comprehensive summary of excavated sites in Palestinian archaeology. Selected bibliography at the end of each entry; v.4 will include a glossary of Hebrew terms. DS111.A2E5

Reallexikon der Assyriologie. . . . Berlin, de Gruyter, 1975–77. v.4^{4-7}–$5^{3/4}$. (In progress) **DA23**

For previously published parts and annotation *see Guide* DA77. Contents: v.4^{4-7}–$5^{3/4}$, Hazga–Kalhu.

Atlases

Whitehouse, David and **Whitehouse, Ruth.** Archaeological atlas of the world, with 103 maps drawn by John Woodcock and Shalom Schotten. London, Thames and Hudson; San Francisco, W. H. Freeman, [1975]. 272p. $19; $9.50 pa. **DA24**

Small maps, with explanatory notes, "pinpointing some 5,000 pre- and proto-historic sites."—*Introd.* Suggestions for further reading accompany the notes. Index with map grid references. G1046.E15W5

Directories

Archaeologists' yearbook, 1973– ; an international directory of archaeology and anthropology. [Christchurch, Hants], Dolphin Pr.; [Park Ridge, N.J.], Noyes Pr., [1973]– . Biennial. (1973: £4) **DA25**

A directory of "museums, universities, associations and other institutions whose activities cover the fields of archaeology (including industrial), anthropology, ethnology and folk-life studies."—*Foreword.* Sections are divided as "British" and "International," with the latter subdivided by country. Name index. CC120.A67

Dawson, Warren Royal and **Uphill, Eric Parrington.** Who was who in Egyptology. 2d rev. ed. London, Egypt Exploration Soc., [1972]. 315p. £7.75. **DA26**

1st ed. 1951.

Subtitle: A biographical index of Egyptologists; of travellers, explorers, and excavators in Egypt; of collectors of and dealers in Egyptian antiquities; of consuls, officials, authors, benefactors, and others whose names occur in the literature of Egyptology, from the year 1500 to the present day, but excluding persons now living.

This edition considerably revised and enlarged. PJ1063.D3

CLASSICAL ANTIQUITIES

Bibliography

Christ, Karl. Römische Geschichte, eine Bibliographie. Darmstadt, Wissenschaftliche Buchgesellschaft, 1976. 544p. DM100. **DA27**

A guide to recent (i.e., 20th-century) books, articles, and some dissertations on the history of the Roman world through the 5th century A.D. Topical arrangement with subject index. Z2340.C49

Harvard University. Library. Ancient history. Classification schedule, classified listing by call number, chronological listing, author and title listing. Cambridge, Mass., publ. by Harvard Univ. Lib.; distr. by Harvard Univ. Pr., 1975. 363p. (Widener Library shelflist, 55) $40. **DA28**

For a note on the series *see Guide* AA111.

"This volume . . . lists more than 11,000 titles concerning the history, civilization, government, economic and social conditions, and geography of the Mediterranean region and Western Asia down to the Barbarian invasions in Europe and the Arab conquest in Asia and Africa. Also included are works on Egyptian and Assyro-Babylonian literatures and on the archaeology of Assyria and Babylonia. In general, archaeological works and works on prehistoric times are excluded."—*Pref.* Z6202.H37

Dissertations

Thompson, Lawrence Sidney. A bibliography of dissertations in classical studies: American, 1964–1972; British, 1950–1972; with a cumulative index, 1861–1972. [Hamden, Conn.], Shoe String Pr., 1976. $22.50. **DA29**

This is "somewhat more than a supplement to *A Bibliography of American Doctoral Dissertations in Classical Studies* . . .[*Guide* DA87]" (*Pref.*) since, in addition to listing American doctoral studies of the 1964–72 period (as well as some earlier ones omitted from the previous compilation), it lists British master's theses and doctoral dissertations for 1950–72. The cumulative index serves both volumes. Z7016.T482

Manuals, dictionaries, and handbooks

Illustrated encyclopaedia of the classical world [by] Michael Avi-Yonah and Israel Shatzman. N.Y., Harper & Row, [1975]; Maidenhead, Sampson Low, 1976. 509p. il. $20; £10. **DA30**

Intended "to satisfy the requirements of those who have no direct training in the classical disciplines, but who, for one reason or another, are interested in the classical world, and want clear, concise and reliable information about it."—*Foreword.* Comprises about 2,300 articles "comprehending the main themes, persons and places of Greek and Roman history, classical mythology and religion, philosophy and thought, together with the most important writers, artists and statesmen, the chief sites, the topography and the social background of the ancient world." Some brief bibliographical citations. Index of names, terms and subjects which are not entries in the main body of the encyclopedia. DE5.I44

Pauly, August Friedrich von. Paulys Real-Encyclopädie der classischen Altertumswissenschaft. . . . Munich, Alfred Druckenmüller, 1974–78. Suppl. 14–15. (In progress) **DA31**

For the main set and earlier supplements *see Guide* DA93.

Each *Supplementband* is an alphabetical A–Z arrangement of articles.

Der kleine Pauly; Lexikon der Antike. . . . Munich, Alfred Druckenmüller, 1975. v.5. **DA32**

For earlier volumes and annotation *see Guide* DA94.

Contents: v.5, Schaf–Zythos; Nachträge.

Includes a section of corrigenda and addenda to all five volumes. Completes the set.

The Princeton encyclopedia of classical sites. Richard Stillwell, ed. Princeton, Princeton Univ. Pr., 1976. 1019p. plates, maps. $125. **DA33**

Aims "to provide a one-volume source of information on sites that show remains from the Classical period."—*Pref.* (The "Classical period" is understood to cover from about 750 B.C. to the 6th century A.D.) In general, entry is under the form of the name of the site as it was known in classical times, with the modern name, when it differs, following. Location and historical notes are given, together with dates of excavation expeditions and a general summary of the extent of the work done. Bibliographical references are provided and indication is made of those works which include site maps, plans, or illustrations. Some corrections and additions are included in Charles Delvoye's review in *L'antiquité classique,* XLVI (1977), pp.345–47. DE59.P7

General history

Cambridge ancient history. 3d ed. London, Cambridge Univ. Pr., 1975–77. v.2,pt.2; plates to v.1 & 2. (In progress) **DA34**

For previously published parts *see Guide* DA104.

Contents: v.2,pt.2, History of the Middle East and the Aegean region c1380–1000 B.C., ed. by I. E. S. Edwards [and others], $39.50; plates to volumes 1 and 2, [called "New ed."] ed. by I. E. S. Edwards [and others], $25.

MEDIEVAL AND RENAISSANCE

Guides

Medieval studies; an introduction. Ed. by James M. M. Powell. [Syracuse], Syracuse Univ. Pr., 1976. 389p. $24; $9.95 pa. **DA35**

Designed to offer the student "a convenient orientation in the field."—*Introd.* Essays by various authors on all aspects of medieval studies. Bibliographical footnotes and/or substantial bibliographies at the end of each chapter. Includes paleography, diplomatics, chronology, literature, music, etc., as well as history. D116.M4

Bibliography

Caenegem, R. C. van. Guide to the sources of medieval history. With the collaboration of F. L. Ganshof. Amsterdam, etc., North-Holland Publ. Co., 1978. 428p. (Europe in the Middle Ages. Selected studies, v.2) 110fl. **DA36**

Earlier versions appeared in Dutch (*Encyclopedie van de Geschiedenis der Middeleeuwen.* Ghent, 1962) and German (*Kurze Quellenkunde des west-europäischen Mittelalters.* Göttingen, 1964); this is a revised and expanded edition, not merely a translation.

In five main sections: (1) Typology of the sources of medieval history; (2) Libraries and archives (i.e., repositories of medieval manuscripts); (3) Great collections and repertories of sources; (4) Reference works for the study of medieval texts; (5) Bibliographical introduction to the auxiliary sciences of history. Each section consists of a number of explanatory or bibliographic chapters citing and describing a wide range of sources for the many aspects of medieval studies. Detailed table of contents; index of names and anonymous titles. D117.C2213

Dumbarton Oaks. Dictionary catalogue of the Byzantine Collection of the Dumbarton Oaks Research Library, Harvard University. Boston, G. K. Hall, 1975. 12v. $1335. **DA37**

Photographic reproduction of the card catalog of one of the most important libraries for Byzantine studies. Includes major collections in related cultures—Islamic, medieval Eastern European, and late classical. Z6207.B9D85

Dissertations

Monumenta Germaniae Historica. Hochschulschriften zur Geschichte und Kultur des Mittelalters 1939 bis 1972/74 (Deutschland, Österreich, Schweiz), zusammengestellt von Mitarbeiten der Monumenta Germaniae Historica. München, 1975. 3v. (1051p.) (*Its* Hilfsmittel, 1) DM40 pa. **DA38**

A classed listing of some 8,400 dissertations, both published and unpublished. Author and subject indexes in v.3. Z5579.M66

Dictionaries and compendiums

Lexikon des Mittelalters. Redaktion: Liselotte Lutz [et al.]. München, Artemis Verlag, [1977–]. Bd.1, Lfg.1– . DM32 per Lfg. (In progress) **DA39**

Contents: Bd.1, Lfg.1–2, Aachen–Almohaden.

To be in 5v. plus index.

A new work with signed contributions by an international roster of scholars. Entries for persons, places, terms, etc. Bibliographies. Covers the period 300–1500 A.D., concentrating on Europe.

MODERN

Bibliography

See also Suppl. CJ2, CJ5, CJ12, CJ14, CJ19.

Foreign affairs bibliography; a selected and annotated list of books on international relations, 1962–1972. N.Y., publ. for the Council on Foreign Relations by R. R. Bowker, 1976. 921p. $45. **DA40**

Comp. by Janis A. Kreslins.

For earlier volumes of the series *see Guide* DA138.

Concerned only with works on the historical period since the outbreak of World War I. "Of the approximately 1100 titles included in the present volume, a little less than half were listed in the Recent Books section of the *Foreign Affairs* quarterly."—*Pref.*

The World Wars

Guides

Bayliss, Gwyn M. Bibliographic guide to the two World Wars; an annotated survey of English-language reference materials. London & N.Y., Bowker, [1977]. 578p. $30. **DA41**

Undertakes "to describe the most important published aids available" *(Introd.)* for the study of the two World Wars. Arranged by form or type of reference work: general guides, bibliographies, periodical directories and library catalogs, dictionaries and encyclopedias, periodicals, biographies, etc. Author, title, regional/country, and subject indexes.

Bibliography

Bloomberg, Marty and **Weber, Hans H.** World War II and its origins: a select annotated bibliography of books in English. Littleton, Colo., Libraries Unlimited, 1975. 311p. $13.50. **DA42**

Aims "to help provide a selected body of literature on the origins of World War II and on the military, political, social, cultural, and technological events of the war years, from 1939 to 1945."—*Introd.* Limited to books originally published in English or translated into English. About 1,600 items in classed arrangement, with "Author-title-biographee" index. Z6207.W8B58

Enser, A. G. S. A subject bibliography of the Second World War: books in English 1939–1974. Boulder, Colo., Westview Pr.; London, Deutsch, [1977]. 592p. $28.75; £11.95. **DA43**

Intended as a guide for "both the general reader and the researcher."—*Pref.* Subject categories are in alphabetical order; author index. Most entries "have been taken from the *Cumulative Book Index,* the *British National Bibliography* and *Whitaker.*" Z6207.W8E57

Smith, Myron J. World War II at sea: a bibliography of sources in English. Metuchen, N.J., Scarecrow Pr., 1976. 3v. $35 the set. **DA44**

Contents: v.1, The European theater ($12.50); v.2, The Pacific theater ($15); v.3, pt.1, General works, naval hardware, and the All hands chronology (1941–45), pt.2, Home fronts and special studies ($20).

Nearly 10,500 items (books and periodical articles) in classed arrangement. Some annotations. Volumes 1 and 2 each have their own author and name indexes; v.3 has comprehensive author and name indexes to all volumes. Z6207.W8S57

Manuscripts

Mayer, Sydney L. and **Koenig, William J.** The two World Wars: a guide to manuscript collections in the United Kingdom. London & N.Y., Bowker, [1976]. 317p. $27.50. **DA45**

"The primary material covered . . . concentrates on military and naval records in the public domain as well as the diplomatic and political records which impinge directly on the course of the wars themselves. With one or two exceptions, material still in private ownership has not been included."—*Introd.* Intended as an introductory tool to identify repositories and the nature of their contents rather than as a comprehensive guide. Arranged by place, then by repository. Subject index.

Atlases

Banks, Arthur. A military atlas of the First World War, with commentary by Alan Palmer. N.Y., Taplinger; London, Heinemann Educational, [1975]. 338p. maps. 26cm. $29.95; £8.50. **DA46**

Black-and-white maps, together with diagrams and brief notes. General index of names and topics; "Armed forces index" by country and unit. G1037.B3

Chronology

Williams, Neville. Chronology of the modern world, 1793–1965. Rev. ed. Harmondsworth, Eng., Penguin, 1975. 1020p. £1.95. **DA47**

1st ed. 1967 (*Guide* DA149); "2d ed." 1969.

The text has been revised for errors and omissions, and entries have been updated to take account of deaths, changes of title, etc.

D B

The Americas

GENERAL WORKS

Bibliography

New York. Public Library. Reference Dept. Dictionary catalog of the History of the Americas Collection. First supplement. Boston, G. K. Hall, 1974. 9v. $800. **DB1**

For main set and annotation *see Guide* DB7.

Reproduces cards for all materials added to the collection through Dec. 31, 1971. After that date additions appear in the *Dictionary catalog of the Research Libraries* (*Guide* AA112).

UNITED STATES

Bibliography

American studies bibliography, 1974– . [London], Univ. of London, Inst. of United States Studies, 1975– . Microfiche. Monthly with annual cumulation. £23 per yr. **DB2**

The bibliography for 1974 was issued only as an annual cumulation; beginning Jan. 1975, issued monthly with annual cumulation. Each section of the bibliography can be purchased separately.

In four sections: (1) Author; (2) Title; (3) Subject; (4) Dewey classified. Each entry in all sections provides full bibliographic information for any book, pamphlet, government document, or conference proceedings relevant to the study of the United States. For a full description *see Microform review* 5:194–95 (July 1976).

Cassara, Ernest. History of the United States of America: a guide to information sources. Detroit, Gale, [1977]. 459p. (American studies information guide series, v.3) **DB3**

An annotated listing of nearly 2,000 works on American history. Sections on "Aids to research" and "Comprehensive histories" are followed by chronological sections. "The selection is made up of a mixture of narrative histories and monographs. Most can be labelled scholarly, but there is a good sprinkling of so-called popular books." —*Introd.* Indexed. Z1236.C33

Guide to the sources of United States military history, ed. by Robin Higham. Hamden, Conn., Archon Books, 1975. 559p. $27.50. **DB4**

Offers bibliographical essays by historians; surveys the field of U.S. military history, with sections on specific wars, periods, or topics (e.g., military and naval medicine). Each chapter indicates important general references or histories, documents, journals, primary sources, specialized articles and books, and suggests areas for further research; full bibliographic citations appear at the end of each chapter. Materials are judiciously selected with no intention of being comprehensive. No index. Z1249.M5G83

Millett, Stephen M. A selected bibliography of American constitutional history. Santa Barbara, Calif., Clio Books, [1975]. 116p. $9.75. **DB5**

About 1,000 entries in classed arrangement, with author index. KF456.M54

Minnesota. University. Library. James Ford Bell Collection. The James Ford Bell collection; a list of additions, 1970–1974, comp. by John Parker and Carol Urness. Minneapolis, James Ford Bell Lib., 1975. 165p. **DB6**

For main volume and earlier supplements *see Guide* DB14–DB15.

Okinshevich, Leo. United States history & historiography in postwar Soviet writings, 1945–1970. Santa Barbara, Calif., [Clio Pr., 1976]. 431p. $27.50. **DB7**

A bibliography of nearly 3,700 items. Arrangement is mainly by historical period (with topical subdivisions), but there are additional sections for United States cultural history; church and religion; history of particular regions and dependencies; and Soviet evaluation and criticism of American studies. Separate indexes for Soviet authors, non-Soviet authors, and subjects. Titles are given in transliteration, with an English translation supplied. Occasional explanatory notes. List of periodicals cited, pp.377–88. Z1236.O44

Smith, Dwight L. Afro-American history: a bibliography. Santa Barbara, Calif., ABC-Clio, [1974]. 856p. (Clio bibliography ser., 2) $55. **DB8**

Essentially a "spin-off" from *America: history and life* (*Guide* DB29), reprinting the relevant abstracts from v.1–10 (1964–72) and v.0 (1954–63) of that series. Brings together some 2,274 abstracts in classed arrangement, with author/subject index. Z1361.N39S56

U.S. Library of Congress. General Reference and Bibliography Division. A guide to the study of the United States of America. . . . Supplement, 1956–65; prep. under the direction of Roy P. Basler by Oliver H. Orr, Jr., and the staff of the Bibliography and Reference Correspondence Section. Wash., 1976. 526p. $12. **DB9**

For the basic volume *see Guide* DB28.

A few pre-1956 titles are included, but most works cited were published 1956–65. A second supplement covering 1966–75 is in preparation.

Current

America: history and life. Five year index, v.6–10, 1969–1973. Santa Barbara, Calif., ABC-Clio, 1977. 473p. $135. **DB10**

For the main set and annotation *see Guide* DB29.

Writings on American history, 1962-73; a subject bibliography of articles. James J. Dougherty, comp.-ed. Wash., Amer. Historical Assoc.; Millwood, N.Y., KTO Pr., 1976. 4v. $275. **DB11**

Contents: v.1, Chronological; v.2, Geographical; v.3, Subjects; v.4, Subjects [cont.]; Author index.

Designed to fill the gap between the National Historical Publications Commission's final volume of the same series title (*Guide* DB31; volume for 1961 not yet published) and the first volume of a further series edited by Dougherty and covering 1973/74 (*see* below). Only periodical articles are included: some 33,000 citations from 510 journals. Each volume is appropriately subdivided (though categories tend to be very broad) to facilitate searching, but there is no detailed subject index.

Note: The Library of Congress enters this set and the new series beginning 1973/74 under the compiler-editor's name.

——— 1973/74– ; a subject bibliography of articles. James J. Dougherty, comp.-ed. Millwood, N.Y., Kraus-Thomson [for] Amer. Historical Assoc., 1974– . Annual. $15 per yr. **DB12**

The first volume of this new series covers the period June 1973–June 1974, and subsequent annual volumes follow that pattern. Listings are derived from the "Recently published articles" section of the *American historical review* (now separately published; *see Suppl.* DA5), with the addition of supplementary material. Topical subject arrangement with author index. Lacks a detailed subject index.

Manuscripts and archives

Guide des sources de l'histoire des États-Unis dans les archives françaises. Madeline Astorquia [et al.], comp. Paris, France Expansion, 1976. 390p. 160F. **DB13**

A survey of documents in the Archives Nationales, Services d'Archives de la Guerre et de la Marine through 1940, and through 1929 for the Ministère des Affaires Étrangères relating to American history. Includes: 16th–17th centuries, America in general; 18th century–1815, North America and the Caribbean; after 1815, only the United States. For the most part, the papers in the municipal libraries are pre-20th century. No indexes. CD1192.A2G84

Meckler, Alan M. and **McMullin, Ruth.** Oral history collections. N.Y., Bowker, 1975. 344p. $22.50. **DB14**

In two main sections: (1) name and subject index, and (2) directory of oral history centers (subdivided as United States and foreign centers). The index includes both the names of persons interviewed and those prominently mentioned in the interviews. The compilers plan future editions with the hope of achieving a "comprehensive annotated listing of oral history collections located in libraries, oral history centers, and archives. The names of those whose memoirs are included comprise a list of the people most active in recent and contemporary history."—*Foreword.* AI3.M4

U.S. National Archives and Records Service. Guide to the National Archives of the United States. Wash., for sale by Supt. of Docs., 1974. 884p. $12.30. **DB15**

Previous ed., 1948, had title *Guide to the records in the National Archives* (*Guide* DB46).

Lists and briefly describes the various collections of official records accessioned as of June 30, 1970, regardless of where the records are located. "Collectively, these records document the history of the Government from its establishment through the mid-20th century." —*Introd.* Arranged by branch of government, then by bureau or agency; subject index. CD3023.U54

American Revolution

Bibliography

Clark, David Sanders. Index to maps of the American Revolution in books and periodicals illustrating the Revolutionary War and other events of the period 1763–1789. Westport, Conn., Greenwood Pr., [1974]. 301p. $15. **DB16**

An index to maps in monographs, journals, general histories, textbooks and standard reference books which portray any part of the United States, Canada, the Caribbean and West Indies of the period 1763–89. Although the maps are largely military and naval, many show population, roads and boundaries, towns, etc. Geographical arrangement; extensive subject and name index. Z6027.U5C57

Coakley, Robert W. and **Conn, Stetson.** The War of the American Revolution: narrative, chronology, and bibliography. Wash., D.C., United States Army, Center of Military History, 1975. 257p. il. $3.15 pa. **DB17**

In three parts, as indicated in the subtitle: (1) a brief narrative, pp.1–83; (2) a chronology, pp.85–137; and (3) a select bibliography, pp. 141–244. Indexed. E320.C62

Era of the American Revolution; a bibliography. Dwight L. Smith, ed. Santa Barbara, Calif., ABC-Clio, [1975]. 381p. (Clio bibliography ser., 4) $35. **DB18**

A classified arrangement of some 1,400 entries, with abstracts, derived from *America, history and life* (*Guide* DB29). Author/subject index. Z1238.E7

Shy, John. The American Revolution. Northbrook, Ill., AHM Publ. Corp., [1973]. 134p. $2.95 pa. **DB19**

A selective bibliography of books, articles, dissertations on the period 1763–83, topically arranged. Author index; *see also* references used in the text. Z1238.S45

Manuscripts and archives

Koenig, William J. and **Mayer, Sydney L.** European manuscript sources of the American Revolution. London & N.Y., Bowker, [1974]. 328p. $29.95. **DB20**

"It is not our intention to provide a comprehensive guide to the documentary material [on the American Revolution] in Europe, but rather to offer the scholar, particularly the graduate student, an introduction to the source material in Europe so that research can be more effectively planned. This volume is really a *point d'appui* and time saver, a tool which the scholar can use to identify repositories, with summaries of their contents and notices of relevant bibliography."—*Gen.Introd*. Arranged by country, then by city and repository; general index. Provides references to published descriptions of the collections, of individual manuscripts, etc. CD1002.K63

U.S.Library of Congress. American Revolution Bicentennial Office. Manuscript sources in the Library of Congress for research on the American Revolution. Wash., Lib. of Congress, 1975. 372p. $8.70. **DB21**

Comp. by John R. Sellers, Gerald W. Gawalt, Paul H. Smith, and Patricia Molen van Ee.

"In the preparation of this guide virtually every collection in the Library's Manuscript Division, Rare Book Division, and Law Library was surveyed for documents from the Revolutionary era [1763 to 1789]."—*Introd*. Includes photostats, transcripts, and microfilms as well as original manuscripts. In two main sections: (1) Domestic collections, and (2) Foreign reproductions. Descriptive notes vary according to the specific item or collection in question: "Collections that are extremely large and uniform in content may receive more cursory treatment than smaller collections containing a variety of documents." Index to repositories and a detailed subject index. Z1238.U57

Dictionaries and handbooks

Dupuy, Trevor Nevitt and **Hammerman, Gay M.** People & events of the American Revolution. N.Y., Bowker; Dunn Loring, Va., Dupuy Associates, 1974. 473p. $12.95. **DB22**

In two main sections: a chronology of events 1733–83, and an alphabetical section of names with short biographies. Index covers events listed in the chronology. E209.D86

Stember, Sol. The bicentennial guide to the American Revolution. N.Y., Saturday Review Pr. [distr. by Dutton], 1974. 3v. maps. **DB23**

Contents: v.1, The war in the North ($12.95; $4.95 pa.); v.2, The Middle Colonies ($8.95; $3.95 pa.); v.3, The war in the South ($8.95; $3.95 pa.).

On cover: Touring guide to Revolutionary War sites.

Sites are considered area by area, and as much in chronological sequence of the war as is feasible without constant back-tracking over the same region. E230.S74

Atlases

Atlas of early American history: the Revolutionary era, 1760–1790. Lester J. Cappon, ed.-in-chief. [Princeton, N.J.], publ. for the Newberry Lib. and the Inst. of Early American History and Culture by Princeton Univ. Pr., 1976. 157p. 47cm. $125. **DB24**

An impressive new historical atlas containing 74 pages of colored maps of varying size, followed by extensive explanatory text and a detailed index. "The basic framework . . . is chronological, conceived as a work of history rather than one of historical geography. Three periods are easily recognized in the table of contents: (1) the colonial years before 1776; (2) the War of the American Revolution; and (3) the postwar years of Confederation period."—*Introd*. G1201.S3A8

Nebenzahl, Kenneth. Atlas of the American Revolution; map selection and commentary by Kenneth Nebenzahl; narrative text by Don Higginbotham. Chicago, Rand McNally, [1974]. 218p. il. maps. 39cm. $35. **DB25**

Reproductions of 18th-century maps with commentary and narrative text. Indexed. G1201.S3N4

19th century

Bibliography

Aimone, Alan Conrad. The official records of the American Civil War: a researcher's guide. [2d ed.] [West Point, N.Y.], U.S. Military Academy, [1978?]. 50p. (U.S.M.A. Library bulletin no.11A) **DB26**

1st ed. 1972.

Offers information on the background, content, accuracy, and omissions in the compilations of official records. Appendix A is a "Diagram, map, picture, and sketch index to the N[aval] O[fficial] R[ecords] and the O[fficial] R[ecords]."

Dictionaries and handbooks

Warner, Ezra J. and **Yearns, W. Buck.** Biographical register of the Confederate Congress. Baton Rouge, Louisiana State Univ. Pr., [1975]. 319p. il. $15. **DB27**

Biographical sketches of the 267 members of the Confederate Congress. Includes some bibliographical notes. Appendixes: (1) Sessions of the Confederate Congress: (2) Standing committees of the Confederate Congresses; (3) Membership of the Congresses [by state]; (4) Maps of occupied Confederate territory. JK9663.W3

20th century

Filler, Louis. Progressivism and muckraking. N.Y., Bowker, 1976. 200p. (Bibliographic guides for contemporary collections) $15.95. **DB28**

Comprises a series of brief bibliographic essays grouped in four main sections: (1) A meaning for modern times; (2) Progressivism; (3) Progressivism: second phase; (4) Search for values. A bibliography, pp.121–68, lists the books cited in the essays. Subject and title index. Z7164.S66F54

Regional

New York. Public Library. Local History and Genealogy Division. Dictionary catalog of the Local History and Genealogy Division. Boston, G. K. Hall, 1974. 20v. $1540. **DB29**

For full information *see Suppl.* AK8.

U.S. Library of Congress. United States local histories in the Library of Congress: a bibliography. Ed. by Marion J. Kaminkow. Baltimore, Magna Carta Book Co., 1975. 4v. $250. **DB30**

Contents: v.1–2, Atlantic States; v.3, Middle West, Alaska, Hawaii; v.4, The West.

". . . includes all the books cataloged and classified under the local history portion of the Library of Congress classification schedule (F1–975) for which cards had been filed in the Library's shelflist by mid-1972."—*Pref.* Arrangement is by classification number (which provides a state-by-state listing). For each state a classification schedule is given, as is a "Supplementary index of places." There is no general index. Z1250.U59

Periodicals

Crouch, Milton and **Raum, Hans.** Directory of state and local history periodicals. Chicago, Amer. Lib. Assoc., 1977. 124p. $5.50 pa. **DB31**

A state-by-state listing of "state and local history periodicals currently being published in the United States" *(Introd.)*, with title index. Information on published or unpublished indexes is included with the citation. Z1250.C76

New England

Committee for a New England Bibliography. Bibliographies of New England history. Boston, G. K. Hall, 1976–77. v.1–2. (In progress) **DB32**

Contents: v.1, Massachusetts: a bibliography of its history, ed. by John Haskell. 583p. $30; v.2, Maine: a bibliography of its history, ed. by John D. Haskell. 279p. $25.

For a description of the project and guidelines for compilation *see* the *New England quarterly* 43:523–26 (Sept. 1970).

Books, collected series, journal articles are arranged alphabetically within a geographical framework. Cutoff date for Massachusetts is generally Dec. 1972; for the Maine volume, 1975. If no location is indicated in the *National union catalog* or the printed catalog of the Library of Congress, a location symbol is given. Indexes cite authors, editors, subjects, and geographical places (including variant names and extinct places).

Besides volumes for other states, future plans include publication of guides to manuscripts and official publications as well as a final volume on New England as a whole.

The South

Ross, Charlotte T. Bibliography of Southern Appalachia; a publication of the Appalachian Consortium, Inc. Boone, N.C., Appalachian Consortium Pr., [1976]. 235p., 16p. **DB33**

A union list of the books, monographs and films relating to Southern Appalachia held by the thirteen libraries of the Appalachian Consortium. Author/main entry listing with subject index; separate section for films.

The West

California. University, Berkeley. Bancroft Library. Catalog of printed books. Supplements 1–2. Boston, G. K. Hall, 1969–74. Suppl. 1, 6v., $490; Suppl. 2, 6v., $660. **DB34**

For the main set *see Guide* DB77.

These two supplements cover materials added 1964–68 and 1969–73 dealing with western North America from Alaska through Panama. Of special interest is the acquisition of a collection of Mexican political pamphlets from the 1880s to the 1960s.

The reader's encyclopedia of the American West. Ed. by Howard R. Lamar. N.Y., T. Y. Crowell, [1977]. 1306p. il. $24.95. **DB35**

"Historically the term *American West* has meant either any part of the continental United States in its formative or frontier period or the entire trans-Mississippi West from the time of first exploration to the present. The editor has employed both these approaches. Thematically the *Encyclopedia* embraces the story of Indian-white relations; the diplomacy of American expansion; the overland trails experience; the era of the fur trader, the miner, the cowboy, and the settler; and those western subcultures we call Texas and Mormon." —*Pref.* Includes entries for persons, places, organizations, events, terms, etc. About 2,400 entries by some 200 contributors. Articles are signed with initials; many include bibliographic references. F591.R38

Dictionaries and encyclopedias

Dictionary of American history. Rev. ed. N.Y., Scribner's, [1976]. 8v. $359. **DB36**

Louise Bilebof Ketz, managing ed.

1st ed. 1940 (*Guide* DB89).

A thorough revision of this standard work. All entries were reviewed and articles revised, updated, or completely rewritten as necessary; some entries were deleted, and some 500 new articles were added. (There are 7,200 entries in the revised edition, with revisions and new entries representing the work of some 800 contributors.) In addition to general revision and updating, special attention was given to strengthening coverage of science and technology, history of the arts, Native Americans, and Afro-Americans. An analytical index constitutes v.8. E174.D52

Encyclopedia of American foreign policy; studies of the principal movements and ideas. Ed., Alexander De Conde. N.Y., Scribner's, 1978. 3v. (1201p.) $99. **DB37**

Offers some 95 well-written and researched "essays of original scholarship . . . [which] explore concepts, themes, large ideas, theories, and distinctive policies in the history of American foreign relations."—*Pref.* Conventional accounts of major episodes are excluded. Brief, but judiciously selected bibliographies are appended; cross references to related essays are provided. A biographical dictionary, pp.995–1138, is based on information from the *Concise dictionary of American biography* (*Suppl.* AJ17) and the 5th suppl. to the *Dictionary of American biography* (*Suppl.* AJ16). Extensive name and subject index. JX1407.E53

Morris, Richard B., ed. Encyclopedia of American history. Bicentennial edition. Jeffrey B. Morris, assoc. ed. N.Y., Harper & Row, [1976]. 1245p. $25. **DB38**

Previous ed. 1970 (*Guide* DB95).

Revised, enlarged, and updated to include events to Jan. 1, 1974 (with some updating to press time). Additional coverage for minorities, ethnic groups, and women; a new section on "Mass media" and new subsections for film and dance. The biographical section has been expanded to include 500 sketches of notable Americans. E174.5.M847

Atlases

Atlas of American history. Rev. ed. Kenneth T. Jackson, ed.; James Truslow Adams, ed. in chief, original ed. N.Y., Scribner's, [1978]. 294p. maps. 22x28cm. $40. **DB39**

1st ed. 1943 (*Guide* DB100).

Retains all the maps from the earlier edition and adds 51 new maps to the original 147. "Most of the new maps deal with twentieth-century developments or with other subjects [e.g., major Utopian experiments, universal male suffrage, woman's suffrage, abolition of slavery, various general economic developments] that were considered only slightly or not at all by Adams and his co-workers. . . . A third of the new maps are essentially demographic in nature."—*Introd.* New table of contents and revised index.

CANADA

Bibliography

Granatstein, J. L. and **Stevens, Paul.** Canada since 1867; a bibliographical guide. 2d ed., completely rev. Toronto, Hakkert; Sarasota, Fla., S. Stevens, 1977. 204p. $9.95; $4.95 pa. **DB40**

1st ed. 1974.

A series of bibliographic essays on: national politics, foreign and defense policy, business and economic history, social and intellectual history, the West, Ontario, French Canada, and Atlantic Canada. Mainly book materials, but some important periodical articles are cited. Subject index, but none of authors. Z1385.G7

Page, Donald M. Bibliography of works on Canadian foreign relations, 1945–1970. [Toronto], Canadian Inst. of Internatl. Affairs, [1973]. 441p. $6.75. **DB41**

More than 6,000 books, pamphlets, documents, periodical articles, and dissertations appearing since 1945 are listed by broad topics and geographical areas, with detailed subject and author indexes. Sec. VI is a "Chronological list of statements and speeches issued by the Department of External Affairs," followed by an "Index to the Monthly report on Canadian external relations and International Canada, 1962–1970." Z6465.C2P33

——— ——— Supplement 1971–1975. [Toronto, 1976] 300p. $9.25.

Follows the arrangement of the basic volume and adds materials issued 1971–75.

Manuscripts and archives

Canada. Public Archives. General inventory: manuscripts. . . . Ottawa, 1974–77. v.2–3, 7–8. (In progress) **DB42**

For previously published parts and annotation *see Guide* DB122.

Contents: v.2, MG11–16: Public Record Office, London: Colonial Office, Admiralty, War Office, Audit Office, Treasury, Foreign Office; v.3, MG17–21: Archives religieuses, Documents antérieurs à la cession, Fur trade and Indians, Hudson's Bay Company archives, Transcripts from papers in the British Museum; v.7, MG29: Nineteenth century post-Confederation manuscripts; v.8, MG80: Manuscripts of the first half of the twentieth century ("accessions completed before 1 April 1976").

Union list of manuscripts in Canadian repositories. Rev. ed. Ottawa, Public Archives, 1975. 2v. (1578p.) $50. **DB43**

"Joint project of the Public Archives of Canada and the Humanities Research Council of Canada."—*t.p.*

Title also in French; text in English or French.

1st ed. 1968.

Represents about 27,000 collections in 171 repositories. Arranged by name of the collection with an index of names, subjects, and cross references. An added feature is a "Catalogue-by-repositories" which brings together the names of all collections in a given repository. CD3622.A2U54

——— Supplement 1976. Ottawa, Public Archives, 1976. 322p. $9 ($7.50 in Canada).

Adds some 5,000 new entries for materials received by repositories Jan.31, 1974–Mar. 31, 1976, plus about 1,000 entries inadvertently omitted from the 1975 edition. Three annual supplements are planned, with a new edition scheduled for 1980.

Regional

Artibise, Alan F. J. Western Canada since 1870; a select bibliography and guide. Vancouver, Univ. of British Columbia Pr., [1978]. 294p. il. **DB44**

A selective bibliography of books, pamphlets, periodical articles, theses and dissertations on any area of Western Canadian studies (i.e., Manitoba, Saskatchewan, Alberta, British Columbia). Topical arrangement; author index. Select subject index for ethnic groups and political parties and politicians. Z1365.A78

Morley, William F. E. Ontario and the Canadian North. Toronto, Univ. of Toronto Pr., [1978]. 322p. il. (Canadian local histories to 1950, a bibliography, v.3) $25. **DB45**

A companion to the volumes on Quebec (*Guide* DB125) and the Atlantic Provinces (*Guide* DB129).

Lists more than 1,000 titles of local histories published before 1950. In two parts: (1) Ontario; (2) Yukon and Northwest Territories. Within each part arrangement is alphabetical by regions, counties and districts; cities, towns and settlements. Annotated; Canadian library location given for each item. Geographical name and personal name indexes. Z1392.O6M67

General histories

The Canadian centenary series. A history of Canada. . . . Toronto, McClelland & Stewart, 1971–74. v.2, 14, 16, 18. (In progress) **DB46**

For previously published volumes and annotation *see Guide* DB136.

Contents: v.2, The beginnings of New France, 1524–1663, by Marcel Trudel (1973; $12.50); v.14, Canada, 1896–1921; a nation transformed, by Robert Craig Brown and Ramsey Cook (1974; $12.50); v.16, The opening of the Canadian North, 1870–1914, by M. Zaslow (1971; $14.95); v.18, The forked road: Canada 1939–1957, by D. Creighton (1976; $14.95).

v.2 is mainly a condensation of v.1–3 of Trudel's *Histoire de la Nouvelle-France* (Montreal, 1963–75).

Atlases

Kerr, Donald Gordon Grady. An historical atlas of Canada. 3d rev. ed. [Don Mills, Ont.], Nelson, [1975]. 100p. 32cm. il. maps. $10.95. **DB47**

2d ed. 1966 (*Guide* DB138).

Much revision is evident, especially in pt.6, "Main economic and political trends since 1867." A few maps from the earlier edition were dropped or combined. G1116.S1K4

LATIN AMERICA

General works

Bibliography

Dorn, Georgette Magassay. Latin America, Spain and Portugal, an annotated bibliography of paperback books. 2d rev. ed. Wash., Lib. of Congress, 1976. 322p. (Hispanic Foundation bibliography ser., no.14) $1.50 pa. **DB48**

1964 ed. by D. H. Andrews had title: *Latin America, a bibliography of paperback books.*

Lists 2,200 titles in three sections: Latin America; Spain and Portugal; Dictionaries, grammars, readers, and textbooks. Subject index. Z1601.D

Markman, Sidney David. Colonial Central America; a bibliography, including materials on art and architecture, cultural, economic, and social history, ethnohistory, geography, government, indigenous writings, maps and plans, urbanization, bibliographic and archival documentary sources. Tempe, Arizona State Univ., Center for Latin Amer. Studies, [1977]. 345p. $15. **DB49**

2,250 items in classed arrangement, with an "Index of authors, people, places and subjects." Brief annotations. Z1437.M37

Texas. University at Austin. Library. Latin American Collection. Catalog of the Latin American collection. Boston, G.

K. Hall, 1971–77. Suppl.1–4. (Suppl.1, 5v. $410; Suppl.2, 3v. $325; Suppl.3, 8v. $890; Suppl.4, 3v. $220) **DB50**

For main set and annotation *see Guide* DB161.

Covers materials processed for the collection 1969–74. Suppl. 1 includes cards for "Hilea–Hispanidad A" which were omitted from the 1969 catalog. Suppl.3–4 include a number of pre-1970 imprints from the cataloging backlog.

Wilgus, Alva Curtis. Latin America, Spain and Portugal: a selected and annotated bibliographical guide to books published in the United States, 1954–1974. Metuchen, N.J., Scarecrow Pr., 1977. 910p. $20. **DB51**

A selection made from the compiler's quarterly list, "Doors to Latin America," which has appeared in various forms and in various publications over the years. Arranged in nine main sections, with topical/geographical subdivisions as appropriate: (1) Mexico and related parts of the United States; (2) Central America; (3) Caribbean and West Indies; (4) South America; (5) Latin America; (6) Latin America related; (7) Iberia; (8) Adult fiction; (9) Children's books. Index of names. Z1601.W687

Dissertations

Deal, Carl W. Latin America and the Caribbean, a dissertation bibliography. [Ann Arbor, Mich.], University Microfilms Internatl., [1978]. 164p. free. **DB52**

More than 7,200 dissertation titles accepted through 1977 are arranged by broad subject areas, subdivided by country. Includes only those dissertations available from University Microfilms. Author index.

Hanson, Carl A. Dissertations on Iberian and Latin American history. Troy, N.Y., Whitston, 1975. 400p. $20. **DB53**

In addition to United States and Canadian dissertations on Latin America completed in history departments, the bibliography includes studies on: "Iberia and its non-Latin American holdings; other European possessions, past and present, on the perimeter of Latin America; dissertations completed in British and Irish universities and colleges; and titles from disciplines other than history."—*Introd.* Geographical/chronological arrangement. Author index. More than 3,500 entries. Z1601.H32

Guides to records

Guide to the sources of the history of nations. A. Latin America. Zug, Switz., Inter Documentation, 1967–1976. Microfiche. **DB54**

For previously published volumes with the same series title *see Guide* DB171.

A microfiche series assembled by Inter Documentation which reproduces inventories available on paper from other publishers. Other volumes in the series include: *Guide des sources de l'histoire d'Amérique Latine conservées en Belgique* by L. Liagre (Brussels, 1967. 132p.); *Übersicht über die Quellen zur Geschichte Lateinamerikas in Archiven der D.D.R.* comp. at the Staatliche Archivverwaltung of the German Democratic Republic (Potsdam, 1971. 122p.); *Führer durch die Quellen zur Geschichte Lateinamerikas in der Bundesrepublic Deutschland*, v.2,pt.1, by R. Hauschild-Thiessen (Bremen, 1972. 437p.); *A guide to the manuscript sources for the history of Latin America and the Caribbean in the British Isles* by P. A. Walne (*Guide* DB170); *Guida delle fonti per la storia dell'America latina esistenti in Italia* by E. Lodolini (Rome, 1976. 403p.); *Fuentes para la historia de Ibero-América: Escandinavia* by M. Mörner (Stockholm, 1968. 105p.); *Guide to materials on Latin America in the National Archives* comp. at the U.S. National Archives (*see Suppl.* DB56); *Guida delle fonti per la storia dell'America Latina negli archivi della Santa Sede e negli archivi ecclesiastici d'Italia* by L. Pásztor (Vatican, 1970. 665p.).

Naylor, Bernard, Hallewell, Laurence and **Steele, Colin.** Directory of libraries and special collections on Latin America and the West Indies. [London], Athlone Pr., 1975. 161p. (London. Univ. Inst. of Latin Amer. Studies. Monographs, no.5) £3.50. **DB55**

Concentrates on collections of printed materials in British repositories and is therefore complementary to the *Guide to manuscript sources for the history of Latin America and the Caribbean in the British Isles* (*Guide* DB170). Z1601.N37

U.S. National Archives & Records Service. Guide to materials on Latin America in the National Archives of the United States. By George S. Ulibarri and John P. Harrison. Wash., Nat. Archives & Records Serv., 1974. 489p. $7.85. **DB56**

"This guide supersedes the *Guide to Materials on Latin America in the National Archives* (vol. I, 1961 [*Guide* DB114]), compiled by Dr. John P. Harrison, and includes the records descriptions contained in that guide. In addition, it includes descriptions of pertinent records of the executive, legislative, and judicial branches of the Government that were not included in the earlier guide."—*Introd.* The 1961 guide was intended to be in 2v.; the present work results from a decision to present the earlier material in revised form together with much new information. CD3023.U54

Historiography

Wilgus, Alva Curtis. The historiography of Latin America: a guide to historical writing, 1500–1800. Metuchen, N.J., Scarecrow Pr., 1975. 333p. $15. **DB57**

Provides an account of the principal individual historians and their works. Separate sections for the 16th, 17th, and 18th centuries. Within each section a "Historical note" and several pages of "Lifecharts" (indicating birth and death dates of the historians and their relative periods of activity) precede the "Authors" section, which is subdivided by country; a supplementary list of writers is given for each century. "Selected references," pp.280–311. Index of names. F1409.7.W54

Dictionaries and encyclopedias

Encyclopedia of Latin America. Ed. by Helen Delpar. N.Y., McGraw-Hill, [1974]. 651p. il. $33.30. **DB58**

Intended as a "comprehensive yet concise reference book offering authoritative information on the history, economy, politics, arts, and other aspects of Latin America."—*Introd.* Treats "the eighteen Spanish-speaking republics plus Brazil, Haiti, and Puerto Rico," with a survey article included for each of these countries. Emphasis is on the national period, but attention is given to important colonial figures and institutions. Employs an alphabetical arrangement, with numerous *see* and *see also* references. Articles are signed; the longer ones include bibliographical citations. Statistical appendix, pp.644–47; select bibliography of bibliographies, pp.649–51. F1406.E52

Latin American historical dictionaries. Gen ed., A. Curtis Wilgus. Metuchen, N.J., Scarecrow Pr., 1973–77. v.9–16. (In progress) **DB59**

For earlier volumes and annotation *see Guide* DB178.

Contents: v.9, Puerto Rico and the U.S. Virgin Islands, by Kenneth R. Farr (1973. $6); v.10, Ecuador, by Albert Bork and Georg Maier (1973. $7); v.11, Uruguay, by Jean Willis (1974. $9); v.12, British Caribbean, by William R. Lux (1975. $9); v.13, Honduras, by Harvey K. Meyer (1976. $15); v.14, Colombia, by Robert H. Davis (1977. $11); v.15, Haiti, by Roland I. Perusse (1977. $6); v.16, Costa Rica, by Theodore S. Creedman (1977. $10).

Argentina

Matijevic, Nicolás and **Matijevic, Olga H. de.** Bibliografía patagónica y de las tierras australes. Bahía Blanca, Centro de Documentación Patagónica, Univ. Nacional del Sur, 1973– . v.1– . (In progress) **DB60**

Contents: v.1, Historia.

v.1 includes more than 2,800 entries in topical arrangement, with index. Sections for archaeology, voyages and chronicles, mythology and legends, general history, and a special section on Argentinian-Chilean boundary questions.

Further volumes are to cover: (2) Geografía; (3) Indígenas; (4) Botánica y zoología; (5) Geología y paleontología; (6) Recursos naturales y desarrollo. Z1634.P58M38

Brazil

Grande enciclopédia portuguesa e brasileira. 2. parte: Brasil. Lisboa, Editorial Enciclopédia, 1974. v.3[1-2]. (In progress) **DB61**

For previously published parts and annotation *see Guide* DC310.

Contents: v.3, pts.1–2, Gelbecke, José–Guaranésia.

U.S. Library of Congress. Catalog of Brazilian acquisitions of the Library of Congress, 1964–1974. Comp. by William V. Jackson. Boston, G. K. Hall, 1977. 751p. $95. **DB62**

Added title page in Portuguese; introductory matter in English and Portuguese.

"This book contains cataloging information for all publications relating to Brazil, or with Brazilian imprints, acquired and cataloged by the Library of Congress from mid-1964 through 1974."—*Introd.* Classed arrangement with author and subject indexes. Z1699.U54

Chile

Fuentes, Jordi [and others]. Diccionario historico de Chile. 5. ed. rev., adicionada y puesta al día. Santiago de Chile, [1978]. 669p. **DB63**

Previous ed. 1966 (*Guide* DB200) by Jordi Fuentes and Liá Cortés.

A revised and expanded edition.

Williams, Lee H. The Allende years; a union list of Chilean imprints, 1970–1973, in selected North American libraries, with a supplemental holdings list of books published elsewhere for the same period by Chileans or about Chile or Chileans. Boston, G. K. Hall, 1977. 339p. $24. **DB64**

The Chilean holdings of fourteen United States libraries are cited in three main sections: (1) Chilean monographs published 1970–73; (2) Books published outside Chile, 1970–73, about Chile or by Chileans; (3) Serial publications issued in Chile, 1970–73. The first two sections are subdivided by topic. Personal and corporate name index. Z1701.W55

Mexico

Enciclopedia de México. Ciudad de México, Instituto de la Enciclopedia de México, 1973–77. v.7–12. **DB65**

For earlier volumes and annotation *see Guide* DB217.

Contents: v.7–12, Honor–Zurita.

Venezuela

Lombardi, John V., Carrera Damas, Germán and **Adams, Roberta E.** Venezuelan history; a comprehensive working bibliography. Boston, G. K. Hall, [1977]. 530p. $20. **DB66**

Intended as "a starting place for the study of Venezuelan history." —*Pref.* More than 4,600 entries arranged under the following main headings: (1) General reference; (2) History; (3) Bolivar; (4) Church; (5) Civilization; (6) Education; (7) Geography; (8) Petroleum; (9) Population; (10) Urbanization. There is an author index, but none of detailed subjects. Z1911.L64

ISLANDS OF THE CARIBBEAN AND WEST ATLANTIC

General works

Bibliography

Comitas, Lambros. The complete Caribbeana, 1900–1975; a bibliographic guide to the scholarly literature. Millwood, N.Y., KTO Pr., [1978]. 4v. $170. **DB67**

Prep. under the auspices of the Research Institute for the Study of Man.

Contents: v.1, People; v.2, Institutions; v.3, Resources; v.4, Indexes.

Based on the same author's *Caribbeana 1900–1965* (1968; *Guide* DB231), but representing a thorough revision thereof, expanding the geographical coverage to include Bermuda and the Bahamas, and extending the period of coverage through 1975. Now lists "over seventeen thousand complete references to authored publications such as monographs, readers, conference proceedings, doctoral dissertations, master's theses, journal articles, reports, pamphlets, and other miscellaneous works."—*Pref.* v.1–3 are each divided into three main sections with numerous subdivisions: v.1, Introduction to the Caribbean; The past; The people; v.2, Elements of culture; Health, education and welfare; Political issues; v.3, Socio-economic activities and institutions; The environment and human geography; Soils, crops and livestock. Separate author and geographical indexes. Library location indicated for most items. Z1595.C63

Miami, University of, Coral Gables, Fla. Cuban and Caribbean Library. Catalog. . . . Boston, G. K. Hall, 1977. 6v. $400. **DB68**

"Books chosen for inclusion are those whose subject headings or titles indicate content specifically within the scope of the Catalog; books by known authors important to the Caribbean, Cuban, Dominican, Puerto Rican literature, history, art, music, etc., as could be determined by classification in our shelf list."—*Introd.* Government publications and periodicals are not included. Geographic areas covered are Cuba, the Antilles, Guyanas, Venezuela, Mexico, Colombia, and all of Central America except San Salvador. Z1595.M5

Dissertations

Commonwealth Caribbean Resource Centre. Theses on the Commonwealth Caribbean, 1891–1973. London, Ont., Office of Internatl. Education, Univ. of Western Ontario, [1974?]. 136p. **DB69**

An author listing of dissertations accepted mainly in British, United States, and Canadian universities. "Geographical index of countries studied," but no topical index. Useful for supplementing and updating the Baa compilation (*Guide* DB234), though not as complete nor as accurate. Z1502.B5C65

Cuba

Perez, Louis A. The Cuban revolutionary war, 1953–1958: a bibliography. Metuchen, N.J., Scarecrow Pr., 1976. 225p. $9. **DB70**

A classed bibliography of nearly 2,500 items. Author index. Z1525.P43

Jamaica

Ingram, Kenneth E. Sources of Jamaican history, 1655–1838; a bibliographical survey with particular reference to manuscript sources. Zug, Switz., Inter Documentation Co., [1976]. 2v. (1310p.) **DB71**

Revision of the author's thesis, University of London, 1970.

A survey of manuscript collections in British and Jamaican repositories, with some attention to European and North American archives. The only printed sources included are newspapers, almanacs, legislative documents, etc., and these are listed chronologically with library locations. A supplement, pp.1124–93, adds materials discovered since 1970 when the survey was originally made. Extensive index of names and subjects. Z1541.I53

Netherlands Antilles

Nederlandse Stichting voor Culturele Samenwerking met Suriname en de Nederlandse Antillen. Bibliografie van de Nederlandse Antillen. Amsterdam, De Stichting, [1975]. 271p. **DB72**

A classed bibliography of writings about the Netherlands Antilles —social, economic and cultural affairs, natural resources, etc. Z1502.D7N42

Puerto Rico

La gran enciclopedia de Puerto Rico. Madrid, [Ed. R, 1976]. 14v. il. **DB73**

Vincente Baez, ed.

Contents: v.1, Historia; v.2, Politica; v.3, Poesia; v.4, Cuento; v.5, Novela; v.6, Teatro; v.7, Musica; v.8, Artes plasticas; v.9, Arquitectura leyes; v.10, Educacion, flora, fauna, economia; v.11, Deportes; v.12, Folklore; v.13, Municipios; v.14, Diccionario historico-biografico.

A heavily illustrated general encyclopedia. Each volume is made up of essays by specialists on the topics covered; v.14 is a biographical dictionary. Name index and brief bibliography in each volume. F1954.G72

Surinam

Encyclopedie van Suriname. Hoofdredactie, C. F. A. Bruijning, J. Voorhoeve; Samensteller, W. Gordijn. Amsterdam, Elsevier, 1977. 716p. il. **DB74**

A national encyclopedia with articles relating to the immediate area (natural and political history, physical features, flora, fauna, places, personalities, etc.).

D C

Europe

GENERAL WORKS

Bibliography

Guide international d'histoire urbaine. Paris, Klincksieck, 1977– . v.1– . (In progress) **DC1**

At head of title: Commission Internationale pour l'Histoire des Villes.

Contents: v.1, Europe, préparé ... sous la direction de Philippe Wolff. 544p. 196F.

Brief sections on "La ville antique" and "La ville byzantine" are followed by entries for the individual countries of Europe in alphabetical sequence. Each country section begins with a brief historical introduction, followed by a review of the principal sources, published and unpublished, for urban history research (with attention to archives and their organization), a list of institutes and periodicals concerned with urban history, and a selected bibliography.

International Committee of Historical Sciences. Commission internationale d'histoire ecclésiastique comparée, British sub-commission. The bibliography of the Reform, 1450–1648, relating to the United Kingdom and Ireland for the years 1955–70. Ed. by Derek Baker. Oxford, Blackwell, 1975. 242p. £7.50. **DC2**

Serves as a companion to the *Bibliographie de la réforme* (*Guide* DC4).

In three main sections: (1) England and Wales; (2) Scotland; and (3) Ireland. Within each section, items are grouped as books, periodical articles, reviews, and theses. Author listing within subsections. No subject index. Z7830.I522

Current

Archiv für Reformationsgeschichte. Beiheft: Literaturbericht, v.1– . Gütersloh, G. Mohn, 1972– . Annual. ($13 per yr. for suppl. only; $19 for the journal plus suppl.) **DC3**

Added title page: Archive for Reformation history, an international journal concerned with the history of the Reformation and its significance in world affairs. Supplement: Literature review.

Published under the auspices of the Verein für Reformationsgeschichte and the American Society for Reformation Research.

A selective bibliography of books, collections of essays, and periodical articles arranged topically or by geographic area. Brief abstracts; no index. Z7830.A7

Guides to records

Thomas, Daniel H. and **Case, Lynn M.** The new guide to the diplomatic archives of Western Europe. [Philadelphia], Univ. of Pennsylvania Pr., [1975]. 441p. $10. **DC4**

1st ed. 1959 (*Guide* DC10).

A revised and updated edition. New chapters on Finland, Greece, and Luxemburg have been added, and there are new subsections for the International Labour Organisation and the International Telecommunication Union. CD1001.T4

Handbooks and histories

Cambridge economic history of Europe. Cambridge, Cambridge Univ. Pr., 1977. v.5. $38.50. (In progress) **DC5**

For previously published volumes *see Guide* DC12.

Contents: v.5, The economic organization of early modern Europe, ed. by E. E. Rich and C. H. Wilson.

v.7, The industrial economies: capital, labour and enterprise, ed. by P. Mathias and M. M. Postan, was listed as "in press" in 1978. Recent volumes have title: *Cambridge economic history.*

Mitchell, Brian R. European historical statistics, 1750–1970. London, Macmillan; N.Y., Columbia Univ. Pr., 1975. 827p. £24; $60. **DC6**

Official and unofficial statistical sources were used to provide comparative data for the 26 European countries treated. The 75 tables are arranged in 11 sections: Climate; Population and vital statistics; Labour force; Agriculture; Industry; External trade; Transport and communications; Finance; Prices; Education; National accounts. Understandably, coverage is uneven, but the editors have tried to complete the information provided by a given country's statistical office. HA1107.M5

EASTERN AND SOUTHEASTERN EUROPE

Bibliography

Akademiia Nauk SSSR. Fundamental'naia Biblioteka Obshchestvennykh Nauk. Sovetskoe slavianovedenie. . . . Sost. I. A. Kaloeva. Moskva, 1973–76. 2v. **DC7**

For main volume and annotation *see Guide* DC13.

Supplementary volumes covering 1963–68 and 1969–73 have been issued in seven parts per volume.

Hunter, Brian. Soviet-Yugoslav relations, 1948–1972; a bibliography of Soviet, Western and Yugoslav comment and analysis. N.Y., Garland, 1976. 223p. (Garland reference library in social science, v.18) $20. **DC8**

In three sections: (1) The Soviet view; (2) The Western view; (3) The Yugoslav view. Arrangement is chronological within sections. Author, subject, and periodical indexes. Many brief descriptive notes. Z2517.R4H85

Johann Gottfried Herder-Institut, Marburg. Bibliothek. Alphabetischer Katalog. First supplement. Boston, G. K. Hall, 1971. 2v. $195. **DC9**

For main set and annotation *see Guide* DC28.

Covers new material cataloged through 1970, including a gift of a specialized library on Polish and Baltic history.

Kanet, Roger E. Soviet & East European foreign policy; a bibliography of English- & Russian-language publications 1967–1971. Santa Barbara, Calif., ABC-Clio, [1974]. 208p. $18.25. **DC10**

An author listing of more than 3,200 items (books and periodical articles), with subject index. "The selection of items for this bibliography is as inclusive as possible and all non-Soviet items published in English noted by the editor are included. All of the Russian-language and Soviet-published English materials that concern Soviet or East European foreign policy directly have been included. In addition, there is a selection of Soviet books and articles which deal primarily with such general topics as developing countries and imperialism and also concern Soviet or East European foreign policy."—*Pref.* Russian-language titles are given in transliteration, with a translation supplied in brackets. Not annotated. Z2510.K3

New York. Public Library. Slavonic Division. Dictionary catalog of the Slavonic collection. . . . 2d ed., rev. and enl. Boston, G. K. Hall, 1974. 44v. $2900. **DC11**

1st ed. 1959 (*Guide* DC29).

This edition (which supersedes the 1959 edition) "contains approximately 724,000 cards. Both roman and non-roman alphabet language materials published in 1971 or earlier are included."—*Foreword.* In recent years "increasing attention" has been given to science, technology, and economics. Z881.N59

Nowak, Chester Michael. Czechoslovak-Polish relations, 1918–1939: a selected and annotated bibliography. Stanford, Hoover Inst. Pr., 1976. 219p. (Hoover Inst. bibliographical ser., 55) $10. **DC12**

Based on the author's thesis, Boston Univ., 1971.

Offers an "annotated selection of books, pamphlets, articles, and press reports necessary, or useful, for the study of Czechoslovak-Polish relations during 1918–1939 . . . [including] some basic materials showing Polish-Czech contacts during the years 1914–1918."—*Introd.* Name index. Z2138.R4N68

Südosteuropa-Bibliographie. . . . München, Oldenbourg, 1976. Bd.5, T.2. (In progress) **DC13**

For earlier volumes and annotation *see Guide* DC21.

Contents: Bd.5, 1966–70: T.2, Albanien, Bulgarien, Jugoslawien.

Terry, Garth M. A bibliography of Macedonian studies. Nottingham, Nottingham Univ. Lib., 1975. 121p. £1.25 pa. **DC14**

A classed bibliography of more than 1,600 items. Name index. Macedonia is considered to be "historic Macedonia (i.e., the pre-1912 area), Yugoslav or Vardar Macedonia (1913–1944), or the Socialist People's Republic of Macedonia."—*Introd.* Includes a brief section on Pirin and Aegean Macedonia (post-1912). Z2957.M3T47

Current

ABSEES: Soviet and East European abstracts series, v.8– , Sept. 1977– . Oxford, Oxford Microform Publs., 1977– . 3 issues per yr. **DC15**

Sponsored by the National Association for Soviet and East European Studies in collaboration with the Centre for Russian and East European Studies, University of Birmingham.

Continues *ABSEES: Soviet and East European abstracts series* published by the University of Glasgow (*Guide* DC24) and assumes its numbering.

Each number is now issued as a printed pamphlet which includes microfiche in pockets interleaved with printed pages. Arrangement and coverage are much the same in the new format, i.e., classed listing within country divisions for citations to periodical and newspaper articles. Each citation is followed by a very brief abstract; for most citations a longer abstract appears on the accompanying microfiche. The latter abstracts are very full, even reproducing statistical tables from the articles; occasionally the entire text is reproduced. Topical index for each issue.

Library resources

Budurowycz, Bohdan. Slavic and East European resources in Canadian academic and research libraries. Ottawa, Collections Development Branch, Resources Survey Division, Nat. Lib. of Canada, 1976. 595p. (Research collections in Canadian libraries, II: Special studies, no.4) $6. **DC16**

A survey of 67 Canadian libraries, reporting for each the extent and nature of the collections of printed materials, microforms, and manuscripts in whatever language originating in or dealing with the following countries: Albania, Bulgaria, Czechoslovakia, Hungary, Poland, Romania, the USSR (including Estonia, Latvia and Lithuania), and Yugoslavia. Extensive index.

East Central and Southeast Europe, a handbook of library and archival resources. Paul L. Horecky, chief ed. Santa Barbara, Calif., Clio Pr., 1976. 466p. (Joint Committee on Eastern Europe. Publ. ser., no.3) $35.75. **DC17**

A survey of "the essential collections available in major libraries, archives, and research institutions in the U.S. and Canada, . . . outlining the profiles of these collections and offering broad guidance to their subject and area contents. The focus is on the humanities and the socioeconomic and political sciences."—*Foreword.* Forty-three institutions are described; there is a geographical breakdown within each entry. Area and subject index.

A careful review by Patricia Grimsted appears in *Slavic review* 37:146–48 (Mar. 1978). Z2483.E2

Dictionaries and handbooks

Südosteuropa-Handbuch. Hrsg. Klaus-Detlev Grothusen in Verbindung mit dem Südosteuropa-Arbeitskreis der Deutschen Forschungsgemeinschaft. Göttingen, Vandenhoeck u. Ruprecht, 1975–77. v.1–2. (In progress) **DC18**

Contents: Bd.1, Jugoslawien (DM140); Bd.2, Rumänien (DM175).

Title also in English: *Handbook on South Eastern Europe.*

Articles contributed by authorities from Germany, the United States, Yugoslavia, etc., survey the political and legal structure, the economic system, social and cultural life. Each volume includes an extensive bibliography and a brief biographical dictionary of contemporary politicians of the country.

ALBANIA

Jubani, Bep. Bibliografi e arkeologjisë dhe historisë së lashtë të shqipërisë (1945–1971). Tiranë, 1972. 222p. **DC19**

At head of title: Universiteti i Tiranës. Instituti i Historisë. Sektori i Arkeologjisë e Historisë Lashtë të Shqipërisë.

Added title page in French: Bibliographie de l'archéologie et de l'histoire antique de l'Albanie.

Introduction in Albanian and French.

An annotated author listing of about 700 items. Entries are first given in the original language, with annotations in Albanian, then repeated in a second section with titles translated into French and with annotations in French.

ARMENIA

Avakian, Anne M. Armenia and the Armenians in academic dissertations. Berkeley, Calif., Professional Pr., 1974. 38p. **DC20**

An author listing of some 260 dissertations and master's essays completed through 1972 at foreign as well as American universities. Topical index. Z3461.A85

Nersessian, V. An index of articles on Armenian studies in Western journals. London, Luzac, [1976]. 95p. £3.50. **DC21**

A classed bibliography without index. Includes religion and theology, history, numismatics, mythology and folklore, palaeography, philology and linguistics, and the arts. Z3461.N5

AUSTRIA

Behrmann, Lilly-Ralou, Proché, Peter and **Strasser, Wolfgang.** Bibliographie zur Aussenpolitik der Republik Österreich seit 1945. (Stand: 31. Dez. 1971). Wien, W. Braunmüller, 1974. 505p. (Schriftenreihe der österreichischen Gesellschaft für Aussenpolitik und internationale Beziehungen, Bd. 7) 588sch. **DC22**

Lists books, pamphlets, periodical articles, and essays in a chronological/topical arrangement with author index; country breakdown within chronological sections.

BELGIUM

Winkler Prins encyclopedie van Vlaanderen. [Brussels], Elsevier Sequoia, 1974. v.4–5. **DC23**

For earlier volumes and annotation *see Guide* DC57.

Contents: v.4–5, La–Zw.

v.4 begins with introductory essays on Flemish art; v.5 with essays on Flemish literature, language, music, and science. v.5 also includes supplementary articles updating introductory essays throughout the set.

BULGARIA

Lazarov, Mikhail. Bulgariia na balkanite, 1944–1974: bibliografiia. Sofiia, 1975. 371p. 2.64 leva. **DC24**

At head of title: Bulgarska Akademiia na Naukite. Institut za Balkanistika.

Title also in English: *Bulgaria in the Balkans.*

A classified listing of books, essays, articles, and reviews published in Bulgaria "which directly refer to the Balkans, individual Balkan countries and the relations of the People's Republic of Bulgaria with them and such as treat problems of the Danube, the Black Sea, etc." —*Notes.* In addition to historical, economic, and political studies, materials on art, the cinema, the press, religion and atheism, linguistics, etc., are also cited. Z2831.L39

Sofia. Narodna Biblioteka. 1300 godini Bulgariia; tematichna prepor'chitelna bibliografiia. [By G. G. Draganov et al.] Sofiia, 1973. 363p. 1.83 leva. **DC25**

A classed bibliography of more than 2,500 items. Author index. Z2896.S69

DENMARK

Bruun, Henry. Dansk historisk Bibliografi, 1913–1942. København, Rosenkilde og Bagger, 1977. v.6. **DC26**

For earlier volumes and annotation *see Guide* DC67.

Contents: v.6, Registre. (Completes the set.)

This final volume includes a list of corrections and additions, indexes of authors, titles, *Festschriften,* periodicals indexed, and topical headings used.

GERMANY

Bibliography

Dahlmann, Friedrich Christoph and **Waitz, Georg.** Quellenkunde der deutschen Geschichte; Bibliographie der Quellen und der Literatur zur deutschen Geschichte. 10. Aufl. . . . Stuttgart, A. Hiersemann, 1974–78. Lfg. 23/24–32. (In progress) **DC27**

For full citation and annotation *see Guide* DC121.

Following the appearance of Lfg.3 (1966), publication of the bibliography has proceeded mainly according to the overall sequence outlined for the work rather than in sequence of completion of individual sections as originally announced. Thus, Lfg.1 (introduction and abbreviations) and 4–11 comprise Bd.1 (Abschnitt 1–38); Lfg. 12–20 make up Bd.2 (Abschnitt 39–57). Lfg.21–23/24 (Abschnitt 58–107) belong to the still incomplete Bd.3 (i.e., Abschnitt 108–157 not yet published) which will finish Pt.A, "Allgemeiner Teil." Pt.B, "Die einzelnen Zeitalter," begins with Lfg.25. Lfg.2–3 (Abschnitt 394–402; publ. 1965–66) begin coverage of the period 1914 and after.

Goguel, Rudi. Antifaschistischer Widerstand und Klassenkampf; die faschistische Diktatur 1933 bis 1945 und ihre Gegner. Bibliographie deutschsprachiger Literatur aus den Jahren 1945 bis 1973. Unter bibliographischer Mitarbeit von Jutta Grimann, Manfred Püschner, Ingrid Volz. [Berlin], Militärverlag der Deutschen Demokratischen Republik, [1976]. 567p. **DC28**

A classed listing of some 4,700 items, with author and subject indexes.

Merritt, Anna J. and **Merritt, Richard L.** Politics, economics, and society in the two Germanies, 1945–75; a bibliography of English-language works. Urbana, Univ. of Illinois Pr., [1978]. 268p. $12. **DC29**

A computer printout listing more than 8,500 titles of books and periodical articles published before mid-1976 and relating to the post-war Germanies. Arrangement is by subject within six major divisions: (1) general (including the historical and demographic background); (2) the Occupation; (3) political systems; (4) economic systems; (5) social systems; and (6) foreign policy issues. Each item is cited only once in the bibliography. Author index. Z7165.G3M47

Price, Arnold Hereward. The Federal Republic of Germany: a selected bibliography of English-language publications. 2d rev. ed. Wash., Lib. of Congress, 1978. 116p. **DC30**

1st ed. 1972 (*Guide* DC136).

A "substantially enlarged and revised edition, which, with its mostly new entries, reflects developments that have occurred over the last ten years."—*Pref.* Z2240.3.P75

Stachura, Peter D. The Weimar era and Hitler, 1917–1933. Oxford, Clio Pr., [1977]. 276p. $43.25. **DC31**

A topically arranged bibliography of Western-language books, pamphlets, *Festschriften,* theses, and other secondary materials published mainly between May 1945 and early 1975. Aims to be comprehensive, but critical annotations distinguish the more useful from the slighter studies. Author and subject indexes.

Wattenbach, Wilhelm. Deutschlands Geschichtsquellen im Mittelalter: Vorzeit und Karolinger. Bearb.: Wilhelm Levison und Heinz Löwe. Weimar, Böhlaus, 1973–76. Heft 5 and Beiheft. (In progress) **DC32**

For previously published parts and annotation *see Guide* DC130.

Contents: Heft 5, Die Karolinger vom Vertrag von Verdun bis zum Herrschaftsantritt der Herrscher aus dem sächsischen Hause das Westfränkische Reiche. 155p.; Beiheft: Das Rechtsquellen. 87p.

——— and **Schmale, Franz-Josef.** Deutschlands Geschichtsquellen im Mittelalter vom Tode Kaiser Heinrichs V. bis zum Ende des Interregnum. Darmstadt, Wissenschaftliche Buchgesellschaft, 1976– . v.1– . (In progress) **DC33**

The first volume of this new series supersedes the second half of the second volume of the 6th ed. of Wattenbach's *Deutschlands Geschichtsquellen im Mittelalter* (publ. 1894).

Guides to records

American Historical Association. Committee for the Study of War Documents. Guide to German records microfilmed at Alexandria, Va. Wash., Nat. Archives and Records Service, 1974–78. Pts.67–75. (In progress) **DC34**

For previously published parts and annotation *see Guide* DC142.

U.S. Dept. of State. Historical Office. A catalog of files and microfilms of the German Foreign Ministry archives, 1920–1945. Stanford, Calif., Hoover Inst. Pr., 1972. v.4. (Hoover Inst. publ. 120) **DC35**

For earlier volumes and annotation *see Guide* DC145.

"The availability of new materials, specifically the files from various German missions and consulates in Europe as well as from some of the overseas offices, necessitated publication" (*Pref.*) of this final volume of the series.

Dictionaries and handbooks

Lexikon der deutschen Geschichte: Personen, Ereignisse, Institutionen, von der Zeitwende bis zum Ausgang des 2. Weltkrieges. Unter Mitarbeit von Historiken und Archivaren hrsg. von Gerhard Taddey. Stuttgart, Alfred Kröner Verlag, [1977]. 1352p. DM125. **DC36**

Brief, signed articles on persons, events, institutions important in German history. Bibliographic references accompany many entries.

Reallexikon der germanischen Altertumskundes. Begründet von Johannes Hoops. 2. völlig neu bearb. und stark erw. Aufl. Hrsg. Herbert Jankuhn [et al.]. Berlin, de Gruyter, 1976–78. v.2–3. (In progress) **DC37**

For Bd.1 and annotation *see Guide* DC152.

Contents: Bd.2–3, Bake–Brunichilde.

Snyder, Louis Leo. Encyclopedia of the Third Reich. N.Y., McGraw-Hill, [1976]. 410p. il. $19.95. **DC38**

Entries for persons, places, terms, events, etc. "The major area covered is the period from the rise of National Socialism to the fall of the Third Reich in 1945. There are selected entries from the time of the Weimar Republic, which preceded Hitler, and from the Bonn Republic, which succeeded him. . . . The names of the biographees selected are those that would be recognized by most historians of the Third Reich as of some significance."—*Pref.* Brief bibliographies appended to many articles (English translations are cited in preference to the German originals); general bibliography, pp.389–410. Terms are entered under the German form with cross references from the English equivalent. DD256.5.S57

GREAT BRITAIN

Bibliography

Harvard University. Library. British history. Classification schedule, classified listing by call number, chronological listing. Cambridge, Mass., publ. by Harvard Univ. Lib., distr. by Harvard Univ. Pr., 1975. 2v. (Widener Library shelflist, 53–54) $85. **DC39**

For a note on the series *see Guide* AA111.

Lists "more than 45,000 titles of works on the history of the British Isles."—*Pref.* Z2016.H37

Early

A bibliography of English history to 1485, based on The sources and literature of English history from the earliest times to about 1485 by Charles Gross. Ed. by Edgar B. Graves. Oxford & N.Y., Clarendon Pr., 1975. 1103p. £20; $52. **DC40**

"Issued under the sponsorship of the Royal Historical Society, the American Historical Association and the Mediaeval Academy of America."—*t.p.*

Like Gross's *Sources and literature of English history* (*Guide* DC165), this edition is planned as "a systematic survey of the printed materials relating to the political, constitutional, legal, social, and economic history of England, Wales and Ireland down to 1485."—*Pref.* Older standard or seminal works have been retained and recent writings added, "especially those which set forth new or controversial interpretations or include modern specialized bibliographies." Includes works published through Dec. 1969 for the pre-1066 period; through Dec. 1970 for the period 1066–1485. The sections for economic and cultural and social history are considerably expanded. Extensive index. Z2017.B5

Bonser, Wilfrid. A prehistoric bibliography; extended and ed. by June Troy. Oxford, Blackwell, 1976. 425p. £25. **DC41**

About 9,000 items in classed arrangement with an author/subject index. In five main sections: (1) Men and methods in archaeology; (2) Field archaeology; (3) Specific sites; (4) Material finds; (5) Culture. Followed chronologically by the same author's *Romano-British bibliography* (*Guide* DC162) and his *Anglo-Saxon and Celtic bibliography* (*Guide* DC161). Z2007.A67B65

Medieval

Guth, DeLloyd J. Late-medieval England, 1377–1485. Cambridge & N.Y., Cambridge Univ. Pr., for the Conference on British Studies, [1976]. 143p. (Conference on British Studies bibliographical handbooks) £3.95; $10. **DC42**

Classified arrangement listing some 2,500 printed materials published through Dec. 1974 and dealing with England and Wales (plus a few references to Scotland and Ireland), 1377–1485. Some annotations. Index of editors, authors, and translators. Z2017.G87

Wilkinson, Bertie. The high Middle Ages in England, 1154–1377. Cambridge, Cambridge Univ. Pr. for the Conference on British Studies, [1978]. 130p. $9.95. **DC43**

A select bibliography for the student and scholar. Classed arrangement, with author index. Includes books and periodical articles. 2,259 items. Z2017.W54

18th and 19th centuries

Batts, John Stuart. British manuscript diaries of the nineteenth century: an annotated listing. Fontwell, Centaur Pr.;

Totowa, N.J., Rowman and Littlefield, 1976. 345p. £10; $25. **DC44**

For full information *see Suppl.* BD113.

Brown, Lucy M. and **Christie, Ian R.** Bibliography of British history, 1789–1851. Oxford, Clarendon Pr., 1977. 759p. **DC45**

"Issued under the direction of the American Historical Association and the Royal Historical Society of Great Britain."—*t.p.*

Forms an unnumbered volume in the *Bibliography of British history* series (*Guide* DC155), filling the gap between the Pargellis and Medley (*Guide* DC181) and Hanham (*Suppl.* DC46) compilations, and following the plan of other volumes of the series. Very selective in its inclusiveness. "The various sections and subsections have been prepared with the object of providing, first, a representative sample of the more prolific forms of contemporary imprints, such as pamphlets and essays; secondly, an outline of each field as treated in the literature concerned with it, drawing attention to leading features and/or personalities; thirdly, reference, where this is possible, to up-to-date authoritative treatment; and fourthly, an indication of further immediate guidance to be found, for instance, in specialist bibliographies, in reading lists of books, or by reference to specialist journals or series."—*Pref.* Cutoff date appears to have been approximately 1973, with some items as late as 1975 noted. Z2019.B76

Hanham, Harold John. Bibliography of British history, 1851–1914. Oxford, Clarendon Pr., 1976. 1606p. £35. **DC46**

"Issued under the direction of the American Historical Association and the Royal Historical Society of Great Britain."—*t.p.*

Forms an unnumbered volume in the *Bibliography of British history* series (*Guide* DC155), being the chronological successor to the Brown and Christie compilation (*Suppl.* DC45), and following the plan of other volumes of the series. Aims "to list the major works which a student is likely to wish to consult, a selection of other works which makes clear the scope of contemporary printed materials, and a selection of biographies and autobiographies."—*Pref.* Cutoff date was generally 1970, but some publications as late as 1973 have been included. The principal sections are: (1) General; (2) Political and constitutional history; (3) External relations; (4) The armed forces; (5) The legal system; (6) The churches; (7) Economic history; (8) Social history; (9) Intellectual and cultural history; (10) Local history; (11) Wales; (12) Scotland; (13) Ireland. Author and subject index, pp.1239–1606. Z2019.H35

Harrison, John Fletcher Clews and **Thompson, Dorothy.** Bibliography of the Chartist movement, 1837–1976. Hassocks, Sussex, Eng., Harvester Pr.; Atlantic Highlands, N.J., Humanities Pr.,[1978]. 214p. £12.50. **DC47**

". . . intended as a modest tool for working scholars and as a survey of the state of Chartist scholarship to date."—*Introd.* Aims to include known Chartist items in local and national archives of Britain, together with materials in important Chartist collections abroad. In five main sections: (1) Bibliographies; (2) Manuscript sources; (3) Contemporary printed sources; (4) Unpublished secondary material; (5) Published secondary material. Manuscript materials are listed by repository; library locations are given for the less usual printed items. Indexed.

20th century

Havighurst, Alfred F. Modern England, 1901–1970. Cambridge & N.Y., Cambridge Univ. Pr. for the Conference on British Studies, [1976]. 109p. (Conference on British Studies bibliographical handbooks) £3. **DC48**

". . . a bibliographical handbook designed as a ready book of reference for the scholar, for the teacher, for the student, and for the general reader."—*Pref.* Classified arrangement; index of authors, editors, translators. Z2020.H38

Current

Annual bibliography of British and Irish history. Publications of 1975– . [Hassocks, Eng.], Harvester Pr. for the Royal Historical Soc., [1976–]. Annual. £10. **DC49**

"Auxiliary" and "General" sections are followed by chronological sections for England/Britain, Medieval Wales, Scotland before the Union, and Ireland, each with appropriate subdivisions (e.g., Politics, External affairs, Religion, Social structure and population). Separate author and subject indexes. Items covering more than one category are entered only once, with cross references from the other sections.

Bindoff, Stanley Thomas and **Boulton, James T.** Research in progress in English and history in Britain, Ireland, Canada, Australia, and New Zealand. London, St. James Pr.; N.Y., St. Martin's Pr., [1976]. 284p. £5; $15. **DC50**

Represents a new edition of the same editors' *Research in progress in English and historical studies in the universities of the British Isles* (1971). Now includes listings of work of scholars being carried on privately or under other than university auspices, and also work in progress in the other Commonwealth nations mentioned in the title. Z6201.B59

Writings on British history, 1946/48–1960/61. London, Inst. of Historical Research, 1973–78. (In progress) **DC51**

For earlier volumes and annotation *see Guide* DC185–DC186.

Contents: 1946/48, ed. by D. J. Munro; 1949/51, ed. by D. J. Munro; 1952/54, ed. by J. M. Sims; 1955/57, ed. by J. M. Sims and P. M. Jacobs; 1958/59, ed. by H. J. Creaton; 1960/61, ed. by C. H. E. Philpin and H. J. Creaton. Z2016.W74

Dissertations

See also Suppl. DA7.

Bell, S. Peter. Dissertations on British history, 1815–1914; an index to British and American theses. Metuchen, N.J., Scarecrow Pr., 1974. 232p. $7.50. **DC52**

In five main sections: (1) political history; (2) economic history; (3) social history; (4) ecclesiastical history; (5) history of education. Sections are subdivided as necessary. Indexes of authors, persons, places and subjects. About 2,300 entries. British master's essays are included, but not American; also, theses submitted prior to 1914 are omitted. Z2016.B43

Guides to records

Cook, Chris. Sources in British political history, 1900–1951. Comp. for the British Library of Political and Economic Science. London, Macmillan; N.Y., St. Martin's Pr., 1975–77. 4v. **DC53**

Contents: v.1, A guide to the archives of selected organisations and societies (£10; $16.95); v.2, A guide to the private papers of selected public servants (£15; $16.95); v.3–4, A guide to the private papers of Members of Parliament (£15; $17.95 per v.).

A report on "the results of a survey of twentieth-century British political archives."—*Foreword*. The project was "intended to locate the papers of all persons and organisations influential in British politics between 1900 and 1951, encourage their preservation, and publish a guide," but certain priorities have necessarily been established: "Whilst a comprehensive search is being made for the papers of all members of the House of Commons, the papers of individual members of other categories are being sought more selectively, on the basis either of their rank or of their known political activity."

In v.1, entry is alphabetical by name of organization, society, or political movement. A historical note is followed by notes on the papers, indication of their location, and availability. v.2 "is concerned with the private papers of some 1,500 senior public servants who were active and influential in British public life between 1900 and 1951" (*Introd.*), including diplomats, civil servants, colonial administrators, and the armed forces.

v.3–4 "are concerned with the surviving private papers of all Members of Parliament from the General Election of September 1900 to the fall of the Atlee Government in the election of October 1951 . . . [and] attempt to include every M.P. elected during this period, together with every holder of a ministerial appointment."—*Introd.* CD1042.A2C66

Gt. Brit. Public Record Office. Catalogue of microfilm. 1976. [London, P.R.O., 1977] unpaged. **DC54**

Previous ed. (1970) entitled *Public Record Office film catalogue*.

"... lists most of those records of which the Public Record Office holds master negatives on microfilm" (*Introd.*), but omits films "for which commercial publishers have been granted overseas sales rights." Arranged by group (e.g., Foreign Office), with reference to more extensive descriptions when available.

Dictionaries and handbooks

Cook, Chris and **Keith, Brendan.** British historical facts, 1830–1900. [London, Macmillan, 1975] 279p. £15. **DC55**

Serves as a chronological predecessor to Butler's *British political facts* (*Guide* CJ176).

A compilation of lists, tables, etc., bringing together a great deal of political information from many sources. Emphasis is on people, listing "almost all those who held high political, judicial, military or administrative office in Britain between 1830 and 1900."—*Pref.* JN216.C65

Powell, Ken and **Cook, Chris.** English historical facts, 1485–1603. [London, Macmillan]; Totowa, N.J., Rowman & Littlefield, [1977]. 288p. $21.50. **DC56**

Offers a variety of lists, chronologies, and background information on historical events and developments of the Tudor period, presented in chapters on: The crown and central government; Parliament; The judicature and the courts; Local government; The church; Education; War, rebellion and diplomacy; Scotland and Ireland; Tudor economic legislation; Population and growth of towns. "Selected Tudor biographies," pp. 206–20; brief bibliography, pp. 221–28. Lacks an index which would have greatly enhanced the ready reference value. DA315.P68

Sainty, John Christopher. Office-holders in modern Britain. London, Athlone Pr. [for] Univ. of London, Inst. of Historical Research, 1975–76. v.4–6. **DC57**

For v.1–3 and annotation *see Guide* DC197.

Contents: v.4, Admiralty officials, 1660–1870. 161p. £6.50; v.5, Home office, 1782–1870. 62p. £4 ; v.6, Colonial office: Secretaries of State for War, 1794–1801; Secretaries of State for War and Colonies, 1801–1854; Secretaries of State for Colonies, 1854–70. 52p. £4.

Source books

English historical documents. London, Eyre Methuen, 1975–77. v.3, 12². (In progress) **DC58**

For previously published volumes and annotation *see Guide* DC202.

Contents: v.3, 1189–1327, by Henry Rothwell; v.12, pt.2, 1874–1914, by W. D. Handcock.

Regional

Stephens, W. B. Sources for English local history. [Manchester], Manchester Univ. Pr. [distr. in U.S. by Rowman & Littlefield], [1975]. 260p. £3.60. **DC59**

First published 1973; reprinted with minor amendments 1975.

A fairly detailed guide (to both published and unpublished source materials) intended to be of use "to undergraduates reading history, to college of education students, to postgraduate students training for teaching or archive work, to those beginning research for higher degrees, to members of adult education classes, and to teachers at various levels, as well as to the many interested amateurs who wish to pursue seriously the study of their neighbourhood."—*Pref.* An introductory section is followed by chapters on population and social structure; local government and politics; poor relief, charities, prices and wages; industry, trade and communications; agriculture; education; religion. Indexed. Z2023.S8

Victoria history of the counties of England. London & N.Y., Oxford Univ. Pr. for the Inst. of Historical Research, 1974–78. (In progress) **DC60**

For previously published volumes and annotation *see Guide* DC226.

Contents: *Cambridge and the Isle of Ely*: v.6, ed. by A. P. M. Wright. 1978; *Gloucester*: v.11, ed. by N. M. Herbert. 1976; *Middlesex*: v.5, ed. by T. F. T. Baker. 1976; *Somerset*: v.3, ed. by R. W. Dunning. 1974; *Stafford*: v.17, ed. by M. W. Greenslade. 1976; *Wiltshire*: v.10, ed. by Elizabeth Crittall. 1975; *York, East Riding*: v.3, ed. by K. J. Allison. 1976.

Atlases

Historic towns; maps and plans of towns and cities in the British Isles, with historical commentaries from earliest times to 1800. Gen. ed., M. D. Lobel. Oxford & London, Lovell Johns, 1969–75. v.1–2. 41cm. (In progress) **DC61**

Contents: v.1, Banbury, Caernarvon, Glasgow, Gloucester, Hereford, Nottingham, Reading, Salisbury. 151p.; v.2, Bristol, Cambridge, Coventry, Norwich. various pagings. (Each town also published separately.)

Publisher varies.

"Not facsimiles of early maps, but modern scientific plans which should incorporate data derived from early maps, documents, and material remains."—*Introd.* The base map is "a large-scale plan (1:5000 scale) of each selected town as it was in the first quarter of the 19th century before it had been much affected by the Industrial Revolution and the accompanying rise in population." On this map are imposed features of the medieval town, including medieval street names; it is preceded by maps showing the site within the region, with principal roads. The historical introduction for each town presents "the relevant factors in the story of the town's origin, physical growth or contraction." No indexes. G1814.A1H5

British Commonwealth

Royal Commonwealth Society, London. Library. Subject catalogue of the Royal Commonwealth Society. Boston, G. K. Hall, 1971. 7v. (4477p.) $615. **DC62**

Contents: v.1, British Commonwealth and Europe, Asia in general, Mideast, India; v.2, Other Asian areas, Africa in general, North Africa; v.3, West Africa, East Africa; v.4, Noncommonwealth Africa including former foreign colonies, Republic of South Africa, other southern African countries; v.5, The Americas; v.6, Australia, New Zealand, Pacific; v.7, Biography, voyages and travels, World War I and II.

Supplements the 1930–37 edition of the *Subject catalogue* (*Guide* DC219) and the *Biography catalogue* (*Guide* AJ182) "by reproducing all the cards between their publication and March 1971."—*Pref.* Z7164.C7R83

———First supplement. Boston, G. K. Hall, 1977. 2v. $240.

Covers additions to the Library for Mar. 1971–Dec. 1976 and adds a list of periodical holdings, as well as indexing of certain albums and collections of photographs and volumes of engravings.

Scotland

An historical atlas of Scotland, c.400–c.1600; ed. Peter McNeill and Ranald Nicolson; cartographer W. J. Davie. St. Andrews, Atlas Committee of Scottish Medievalists, 1975. 213p. 29cm. £2.60 pa. **DC63**

Offers very clear, black-and-white maps with accompanying text (signed by contributors) and selected bibliography. No index. G1826.S1H5

GREECE

American School of Classical Studies at Athens. Gennadius Library. Catalogue. First supplement. Boston, G. K. Hall, 1973. 872p. $120. **DC64**

For the main set *see Guide* DA83.

The supplement reproduces cards added Dec. 1968–Feb. 1973.

Cincinnati. University. Libraries. Catalog of the Modern Greek collection. Boston, G. K. Hall, 1978. 5v. $375. **DC65**

Reproduction of the catalog cards (in dictionary arrangement) for this outstanding collection. Lists both monographic and serial holdings. The collection was originally devoted to "works of Greek scholars on Ancient Greek authors, history and archaeology" (*Introd.*), but collecting policy was soon extended to encompass works "on Byzantium, Modern Greek literature, linguistics, history, folklore, religion, philosophy, economics and sociology." Z2281.C55

HUNGARY

Harvard University. Library. Hungarian history and literature: classification schedule, classified listing by call number, chronological listing, author and title listing. Cambridge, publ. by Harvard Univ. Lib., distr. by Harvard Univ. Pr., 1974. 186p. (Widener Library shelflist, 44) $25. **DC66**

For a note on the series *see Guide* AA111.

"This volume ... lists 6,550 titles concerning the history and literature of Hungary. The present boundaries of the country define the scope of local history coverage."—*Pref.* Z2146.H37

U.S. National Archives and Records Service. Guide to the collection of Hungarian political and military records, 1909–1945. Wash., 1972. 20p. **DC67**

A guide to 21 rolls of microfilm deposited in the National Archives (Archives designation T973) and consisting of Hungarian records seized at the end of World War II. Most of the papers concern the war years. CD3028.H9U54

Vardy, Steven Bela. Modern Hungarian historiography. Boulder, Colo., East European Quarterly (distr. by Columbia Univ. Pr.), 1976. 333p. (East European monographs, 17) $16.50. **DC68**

A survey "of the development of Hungarian historical sciences from the eleventh to the middle of the twentieth century" (*Pref.*), with special emphasis on the 20th century. Appendix, pp.299–309: "Significant source publication series since 1857." Detailed name and subject index. DB923.V372

IRELAND

New history of Ireland. T. W. Moody, F. X. Martin, F. J. Byrne, eds. Oxford, Clarendon Pr., 1976. v.3. maps. il. (In progress; to be in 9v.) **DC69**

Contents: v.3, Early modern Ireland, 1534–1691. 1976. 736p. £17.

Comp. under the auspices of the Royal Irish Academy.

Planned to be the authoritative history of Ireland, with "history" broadly interpreted to include sections on literature, the arts, the church, etc. Each section contributed by a specialist. In writing the articles for v.3 (the first volume published) contemporary scholarship published through 1974 was taken into account.

Other volumes are to cover: v.1, Prehistoric and early medieval Ireland; v.2, Medieval Ireland (1169–1534); v.4, 18th century Ireland (1691–1800); v.5, Ireland under the union, I (1801–1870); v.6, Ireland under the union, II (1870–1921); v.7, Ireland since 1921; v.8, Chronology, maps, and other reference matters; v.9, General bibliography, illustrations, and other reference matter.

An extensive review appears in the *English historical review* 93:117–21 (Jan. 1978).

ITALY

Bibliography

Harvard University. Library. Italian history and literature: classification schedule, classified listing by call number, chronological listing, author and title listing. Cambridge, publ. by Harvard Univ. Lib., distr. by Harvard Univ. Pr., 1974. 2v. (Widener Library shelflist, 51–52) $90. **DC70**

For a note on the series *see Guide* AA111.

These volumes "cover Italian history and literature, a collection comprising more than 72,000 titles. Historical topics include the government and administration, religious affairs, civilization, social life and customs, and geography and description of peninsular Italy, Sicily, and Sardinia, as well as Malta, Monaco, and San Marino. Literary histories, anthologies, and works by and about authors writing in Italian from the Duecento to the present are included in the sections for literature."—*Pref.* Z2341.H37

Pine-Coffin, R. S. Bibliography of British and American travel in Italy to 1860. Firenze, Olschki, 1974. 371p. (Biblioteca di bibliografia italiana, 76) L14,000. **DC71**

British and American works are listed in separate chronological sections. Brief annotations. Indexes of (1) persons; (2) anonymous titles; (3) places; (4) publishers, printers and booksellers. Z2356.P55

Periodicals

Istituto Nazionale per la Storia del Movimento di Liberazione in Italia. Catalogo della stampa periodica della Biblioteche dell' Istituto Nazionale per la Storia del Movimento di Liberazione in Italia e degli Istituti associati, 1900/1975, a cura di Francesca Ferratini Tosi [et al.]. Milano, 1977. 374p. **DC72**

A catalog of periodicals relating to antifascism and the Italian resistance. Locates files in some 23 Italian libraries.

Encyclopedias

Enciclopedia dell' antifascismo e della Resistenza. [Milano], La Pietra, [1976]. v.3. (In progress) **DC73**

For earlier volumes and annotation *see Guide* DC274.

Contents: v.3, H–M.

LITHUANIA

Encyclopedia Lituanica. Boston, [Juozas Kapočius, 1975–76]. v.4–5. (In progress) **DC74**

For earlier volumes and annotation *see Guide* DC282.

Contents: v.4–5, N–U.

Kantautas, Adam and **Kantautas, Filomena.** A Lithuanian bibliography: a check-list of books and articles held by the major libraries of Canada and the United States. [Edmonton], Univ. of Alberta Pr., 1975. 725p. $10. **DC75**

A classed bibliography with author and title indexes. More than 10,000 items. Locates copies. Includes sections for Lithuanians abroad. Z2537.K33

POLAND

Bibliography

Bibliografia historii Polski XIX wieku. Wrocław, Zakład Narodowy im. Ossolińskich, 1972–76. v.2$^{2-3}$. (In progress) **DC76**

For earlier parts and annotation *see Guide* DC296.
Contents: v.2^{2-3}, 1832–1864. (Część 3 in 2 pts.)

Davies, Norman. Poland, past and present; a select bibliography of works in English. Newtonville, Mass., Oriental Research Partners, 1977. 187p. $13. **DC77**

English-language books and articles (plus a few items in French, German or Italian) relating to any period of Polish history are listed in topical arrangement with an author index. Addenda of materials published Dec. 1975–Autumn 1976. Appendixes include a glossary of Polish terms most likely to be encountered, a gazetteer, and an international list of periodicals most relevant to the study of Polish history. For the beginning researcher or general reader. Z2526.A1

Polska Akademia Nauk. Instytut Historii. Bibliografia historii Polski. . . . Warszawa, Państwowe Wydawnictwo Naukowe, 1974. v. 3, pt. 1. (In progress) **DC78**

For earlier volumes and annotation *see Guide* DC299.
Contents: v. 3, pt. 1, 1918–1945.

Schrifttum über Polen (ohne Posener Land). Bearb. von Johanna Stiller. Marburg/Lahn, J. G. Herder-Instituts, 1971– . (Wissenschaftliche Beiträge zur Geschichte und Landeskunde Ost-Mitteleuropas, 90, 95–) **DC79**

"Im Auftrage der Historisch-Landeskundlichen Kommission für Posen und das Deutschtum in Polen."—*t.p.*

Contents: 1961–1962 und Nachträge (Auswahl) (publ. 1971. 431p.); 1963–1965 und Nachträge (Auswahl) (publ. 1974. 395p.).

Represents a continuation of Rister's *Schrifttum über Polen* (*Guide* DC300). Because the literature for the Poznań region has become so extensive, a separate bibliography is being published for that area: *Schrifttum über das Posener Land 1961–1970,* ed. by Herbert Rister (Marburg/Lahn, 1976–).

Encyclopedias and handbooks

Poland, a handbook. Warsaw, Interpress Publ., 1974. 573p. il. maps. zł.175. **DC80**

A collection of English-language articles by Polish writers on all aspects of life in Poland: history; social, economic, political policy; sports; tourism; art (including cinema); foreign relations, etc. No bibliography, but many statistical tables and other illustrative material. DK404.P625613

Polska. Zarys encyklopedyczny. Wyd. 1. Warszawa, Państwowe Wydawnictwo Naukowe, 1974. 820p. il. maps. zł.280. **DC81**

A topical encyclopedia treating Polish history, economy, industry, art, culture, etc. Detailed table of contents, but no general index. DK403.P65

PORTUGAL

Verbo; enciclopédia luso-brasileira de cultura. Lisboa, Ed. Verbo, 1970–76. v.10–18. **DC82**

For earlier volumes and annotation *see Guide* DC311.
Contents: v.10–18, Hermenêutica–Zyl. Completes the set.

SCANDINAVIA

See also under names of individual countries.

Kulturhistorisk Leksikon for nordisk Middelalder fra Vikingetid til Reformationstid. . . . København, Rosenkilde og Bagger, 1974–78. v.18–22. **DC83**

For earlier volumes and annotation *see Guide* DC318.
Contents: v.18–21, Sätesgårdsnamn – Øyreting; v.22, Register. (Completes the set.)
v.21 contains a supplement to the full set, including additions and corrections, a list of collaborators, and a list of abbreviations used.

SPAIN

Bardi, Ubaldo. La guerra civile di Spagna; saggio per una bibliografia italiana. Urbino, Argalìa Editore, [1974]. 134p. L.2800 pa. **DC84**

A classed list of Italian writings on the Spanish Civil War of 1936–39. Lacks an index. Z2700.B37

Cortada, James W. A bibliographic guide to Spanish diplomatic history, 1460–1977. Westport, Conn., Greenwood Pr., [1977]. 390p. $25. **DC85**

Organized by reign, then by country (with occasional topical subdivisions). Author index, but none of subjects. Only published books, pamphlets, government documents, and periodical articles are included. Z2696.C67

González Ollé, Fernando. Manual bibliográfico de estudios españoles. Pamplona, Ediciones Universidad de Navarra, 1976. 1375p. **DC86**

A classed bibliography covering the whole range of Spanish studies. Arranged in 22 main categories, each closely subdivided, with chronological and geographical sub-sections where appropriate. Author and subject indexes in addition to a very detailed table of contents. Z2681.G58

Russell, Peter Edward, ed. Spain, a companion to Spanish studies. [New ed.] London, Methuen, 1973. 592p. £6.60. **DC87**

"An entirely new version of the work of the same title, edited by the late Prof. E. Allison Peers, which was first published in 1929." —*Pref.* Each area of Spanish studies (literature, music, history, Spanish-American literature, etc.) was contributed by a specialist and is designed to be a complete survey of the field. Bibliography (emphasizing English-language works when possible) at the end of each chapter. DP48.R87

TURKEY

Kornrumpf, Hans-Jürgen and **Kornrumpf, Jutta.** Osmanische Bibliographie mit Besonderer Berücksichtigung der Turkei in Europa. Leiden, Brill, 1973. 1378p. (Handbuch der Orientalistik. 1 Abt. Der Nahe und der Mittlere Osten. Ergänzungsband, 8) 290 fl. **DC88**

Pp.1–726 comprise an alphabetical author listing of books (including book reviews), essays, and articles in all languages. A second section, pp. 729–1378, provides a listing in classed arrangement of the items in the first section. A useful feature is the indication at the end of each entry in the author part of the classification used for that item in the subject section. Z2831.K67

Shaw, Stanford J. History of the Ottoman Empire and modern Turkey. Cambridge, Cambridge Univ. Pr., 1976–77. 2v. **DC89**

Contents: v.1, Empire of the Gazis: the rise of the Ottoman Empire, 1280–1808 ($23.50; $12.95 pa.); v.2, Reform, revolution, and republic: the rise of modern Turkey, 1808–1975 ($29.95; $13.95 pa.).

Based on both Ottoman and European sources, the work attempts to present a balanced history from the foundations of the Ottoman Empire through the beginning of the Republic of Turkey. Bibliography at the end of each volume.

For contrasting scholarly opinions of the work *see* reviews in the *English historical review* 93:393–95 (Apr. 1978), in the *Bulletin* of the School of Oriental and African Studies 41:160–62 (1978), and in the *Slavic review* 37:162–63 (Mar. 1978). DR440.S5

Suzuki, Peter T. French, German, and Swiss university dissertations on twentieth century Turkey; a bibliography of 593 titles, with English translations. Wiesbaden, WDS-Schnelldruck, 1970. 138p. (Newsletter for European researchers on modern Turkey. Suppl. no.1, rev.) **DC90**

An author listing with broad subject index. Covers French dissertations accepted 1900–67; German dissertations, 1900–65; Swiss dissertations, 1900–68. Includes some works completed at the universities of Graz and Vienna.

UKRAINE

Weres, Roman. Ukraine, selected references in the English language. 2d ed. enl. & up-to-date. Chicago, Ukrainian Research and Information Inst., 1974. 312p. (Ukrainian Bibliographical Reference Center, Chicago. Ukrainian reference ser., no.1) **DC91**

1st ed. 1961.

A topical bibliography of books, chapters of books, pamphlets, and periodical articles on all aspects of Ukrainian studies. All entries are in English except for a few bibliographies, reference works, sources on the history of the Ukraine, and works of exceptional importance. Z2514.U5W4

UNION OF SOVIET SOCIALIST REPUBLICS

See also Eastern and Southeastern Europe.

Guides

An introduction to Russian history, ed. by Robert Auty and Dimitri Obolensky. Cambridge, London & N.Y., Cambridge Univ. Pr., [1976]. 403p. (Companion to Russian studies, 1) $32.50. **DC92**

Offered as a "first orientation" for students beginning work in Russian studies. Each of the ten sections was contributed by a specialist; a "Guide to further reading" concludes each section. Index. DK40.I57

Bibliography

Istoriia dorevoliutsionnoi rossii v dnevnikakh i vospominaniiakh; annotirovann'ia ukazatel' knig i publikatsiia v zhurnalakh. Sost. G. A. Glavatskikh [et al.]. Moskva, Izd. "Kniga," 1976– . v.1– . (In progress) **DC93**

At head of title: Nauchnaia Biblioteka imeni A. M. Gor'kogo, Moskovskogo Gosudarstvennogo Universiteta imeni M. V. Lomonosova, Gosudarstvennaia Biblioteka SSR imeni V. I. Lenina.

Contents: t.1, XV–XVIII veka (1.46r.); t.2, ch.1, 1801–1856.

An annotated bibliography of pre-Revolutionary Russian diaries, memoirs, travel accounts, etc., published in books, journals and collections. Foreign-language accounts are cited if published in Russia. Topically arranged within historical period. To be in 4v. Indexes in v.1; Names and titles cited; Geographic and ethnic names; Collections used for v.1; Periodicals and other serials used for v.1–4. Z2506.I87

Jones, David Lewis. Books in English on the Soviet Union, 1917–73: a bibliography. N.Y., Garland, 1975. 331p. $20. (Garland reference library of social science, v.3) **DC94**

Limited to "books written in the English language . . . which are wholly concerned with the Soviet Union."—*Foreword.* Pamphlets are excluded, as are books which deal with both the Tsarist and Soviet periods. Classed arrangement, with name index. Nearly 4,600 items. Z2491.J65

Sovetskaia strana v period vosstanovleniia narodnogo khoziaistva (1921–1925gg.): bibliograficheskii ukazatel' dokumental'nykh publikatsii. Sost. L. A. Kotel'nikova [et al.]. Moskva, Kniga, 1975. 629p. 2.42r. **DC95**

At head of title: Gosudarstvennaia Publichnaia Istoricheskaia Biblioteka RSFSR.

Offers citations to 9,611 documents published 1921–25, arranged topically and with a geographical index. Published in series with *Velikaia oktiabr'skaia sotsialisticheskaia revoliutsiia* (*see Guide* BD979) and *Sovetskaia strana v period grazhdanskoi voiny (1918–1922gg.)* (Moscow, 1961). Z2510.S67

Dissertations

Bruhn, Peter. Russika und Sowjetika unter den deutschsprachigen Hochschulschriften, 1961–1973: bibliographisches Verzeichnis. Wiesbaden, Harrassowitz; Berlin, Osteuropa-Inst. an d. Freien Univ., 1975. 166p. (Bibliographische Mitteilungen des Osteuropas-Instituts an der Freien Universität Berlin, 11) **DC96**

Serves as a continuation of Gerhard Hanusch's list of "Osteuropa-Dissertationen" covering the period 1945–60, which appeared as supplements in the *Jahrbücher für Geschichte Osteuropas,* 1953–60. Z2491.B88

Dossick, Jesse John. Doctoral research on Russia and the Soviet Union, 1960–1975; a classified list of 3,150 American, Canadian, and British dissertations, with some critical and statistical analysis. N.Y., Garland, 1976. 345p. (Garland reference library of social science, 7) $32. **DC97**

Continues the listings in the compiler's 1960 publication of similar title (*Guide* DC372), supersedes the annual supplements appearing in the *Slavic review* 1964–1974, and adds some items missed in the earlier volume.

Arranged by subject (agriculture to sports), with American and Canadian works in one scheme and the British in a second, similar scheme. Indexes of Russian/Soviet names, American and Canadian authors, and British authors. Annual supplementary lists continue to appear in the *Slavic review,* Dec. 1976– . A list of corrections and some suggestions for improving the next edition appear in *Slavonic and East European review* 40:134–35 (Jan. 1977). Z2491.D62

Manuscripts

Moscow. Publichnaia Biblioteka. Otdel Rukopisei. Vospominaniia i dnevniki XVIII-XX vv.: ukazatel' rukopisei. Red. S. V. Zhitomirskaia. Moskva, "Kniga," 1976. 619p. 2.50r. **DC98**

A catalog of manuscripts of personal memoirs and diaries in the Lenin State Library. Many of the manuscripts are described at some length, and the contents notes are fully indexed. Z6611.B6M76

Guides to records and archives

Grant, Steven A. Scholars' guide to Washington, D.C. for Russian/Soviet studies. Wash., Smithsonian Inst. Pr. for Kennan Inst. for Advanced Russian Studies of the Woodrow Wilson Internatl. Center for Scholars, 1977. 403p. $19.95; $5.95 pa. **DC99**

Intended as the first of a series of scholars' guides to the Washington, D.C. area. In two main sections: (1) Collections (i.e., libraries, archives, museums, data banks, etc.); (2) Organizations (i.e., associations, government agencies, research centers, etc.). Indexed. Z2491.G67

Grimsted, Patricia Kennedy. Archives and manuscript repositories in the USSR: Moscow and Leningrad. Supplement 1: Bibliographical addenda. Zug, Switzerland, Inter-Documentation Co., [1976]. 203p. (Bibliotheca Slavica, 9) 37.50Sw.Fr. **DC100**

For full information *see Suppl.* AB29.

Union of Soviet Socialist Republics. Glavnoe Arkhivnoe Upravlenie. Katalog arkhivovedcheskoi literatury i sbornikov dokumentov, 1964–1967gg. Pod red. G. P. Lebedeva. Moskva, 1970. 181p. **DC101**

For volumes covering earlier periods *see Guide* DC377–DC378.

Extends the coverage of this bibliography of archival publications and articles and books relating to archives.

Historiography

Mazour, Anatole Gregory. Modern Russian historiography. Rev. ed. Westport, Conn., Greenwood Pr., 1975. 224p. $13.95. **DC102**

First published 1939 as *An outline of modern Russian historiography.*

Surveys the "historiographic development in Russia prior to 1917."—*Pref.* The same author has treated developments after 1917 in *The writing of history in the Soviet Union* (Stanford, Hoover Inst. Pr., 1971). DK38.M3

Encyclopedias and handbooks

Handbook of major Soviet nationalities. Zev Katz, ed. N.Y., Free Pr.; London, Collier Macmillan, [1975]. 481p. $25. **DC103**

In five main parts: (1) The Slavs; (2) The Baltics; (3) The Transcaucasus; (4) Central Asia; (5) Other nationalities (i.e., Jews, Tatars, Moldavians). Within these main sections are chapters on 17 Soviet nationalities, 15 of which have their own Union republics. Chapters, in turn, are in three main sections: "*General Information* deals with territory, economy, history, demography, culture, and external relations. *Media* treats questions of language and media, as well as educational, cultural, and scientific institutions. *National Attitudes* analyzes national attitude formation, views of scholars, and current evidences of nationalism"—*Notes.* Appendix of "Comparative tables for the major Soviet nationalities." Each chapter by a specialist. Bibliographies; index. DK33.H35

McLane, Charles B. Soviet-Third world relations. London, Central Asian Research Centre; distr. by Columbia Univ. Pr., 1973-74. 3v. **DC104**

For volume on the Middle East *see Suppl.* DE23; on Asia, *see Suppl.* DE3; on Africa, *see Suppl.* DD21.

The modern encyclopedia of Russian and Soviet history. Ed. by Joseph L. Wieczynski. [Gulf Breeze, Fla.], Academic Internatl. Pr., 1976–79. v.1–11. (In progress) $27.50 per v. **DC105**

Contents: v.1–11, Aachen–Franco-Russian.

To be in 40 to 50v. Aims "to become the most comprehensive aid to the study of the Russian past ever created in the English language" (v.1,*p.vi*), with information encompassing "all major facts, events, personalities and institutions important to the history of the Russian Empire and the Soviet Union." While the editor's note states that the work "will reproduce in English information contained in the many standard Russian reference series," the sources of specific articles are not given (nor is there an indication whether the information is a direct translation from a single source). Additional information is derived from monographs and research studies, and new articles have been contributed by an international roster of contemporary scholars. Longer articles are signed, and include bibliographies of both Russian- and English-language materials. Intended to be useful "to undergraduate students, government and private researchers and even high school students as well as to professional historians and scholars," but highly specialized information of narrow interest is omitted on the assumption that the specialist can obtain it from Russian-language sources. Supplements are anticipated to cover material inadvertently omitted from volumes already published. DK14.M6

YUGOSLAVIA

Horton, John J. Yugoslavia. Oxford, Clio Pr., [1977]. 195p. (World bibliographical ser., 1) $25.25. **DC106**

Primarily a listing of English-language materials, with a few titles in French, German, and Serbo-Croatian. The books and articles cited are those considered most useful for the general reader, for specialists in related areas, the beginning researcher, and the librarian building a collection. Critical annotations. Topical arrangement with author, title, subject index. Z2951.H67

Terry, Garth M. Yugoslav studies: an annotated list of basic bibliographies and reference works. [Twickenham, Eng.], Anthony C. Hall, 1977. 89p. £4.25. **DC107**

In three sections: (1) General reference works (including handbooks, statistical compilations, encyclopedias, dictionaries, library catalogs, atlases, etc.); (2) General bibliographies (subdivided by geographical area); (3) Subject bibliographies and reference works. About 550 items; indexes of authors and of titles as main entries.

A review by Richard Kindersley in *TLS,* Mar. 24, 1978, p.340, suggests additional language and biographical dictionaries for inclusion, as well as sources for maps.

D D

Africa

GENERAL WORKS

Guides

Hartwig, Gerald W. and **O'Barr, William M.** The student Africanist's handbook; a guide to resources. [Cambridge, Mass.], Schenkman, [1974]. 152p. $5.95. **DD1**

Includes chapters on the nature of African studies; a brief overview of the societies, cultures and modern nations of Africa; general references and disciplinary sources; bibliography of African regions and countries; aids for intensive research; and special topics. Lacks an index. Z3501.H27

Bibliography

Asamani, J. O. Index Africanus. Stanford, Calif., Hoover Inst. Pr., [1975]. 659p. $25. (Hoover Inst. bibliographies, 53) **DD2**

". . . a catalogue of articles in Western languages dealing with Africa and published from 1885 to 1965 in periodicals, Festschriften or memorial volumes, symposia, and proceedings of congresses and conferences."—*Pref.*

A general section is followed by sections for North Africa, West Africa, Central Africa, East Africa, and Southern Africa, each subdivided by country, then by subject. More than 24,600 entries; author index. A more detailed table of contents or a subject index would have greatly facilitated use of the volume. Z3501.A73

Chicago. Center for Research Libraries. Cooperative Africana Microform Project. CAMP catalog, 1977 cumulative edition. Chicago, publ. by the Cooperative Africana Microform Project and the Center for Research Libraries, 1977. 203p. **DD3**

——— ——— 1978 supplement. Chicago, 1978. 27p.

"The Cooperative Africana Microform Project (CAMP) was created in 1963 to bring together in microform a collection of research materials [books, pamphlets, government documents, journals] related to Africa for the cooperative use of the members."—*Introd.* These materials are acquired, housed, and cataloged by the Center for Research Libraries. In the basic volume all materials cataloged as of Sept. 1976 are listed alphabetically by main entry, with a name and topic index. The supplement adds items cataloged between Sept. 1976 and Nov. 1977, and is not indexed.

Panofsky, Hans E. A bibliography of Africana. Westport, Conn., Greenwood Pr., [1975]. 350p. $15. (Contributions in librarianship and information science, no.11) **DD4**

"The author has attempted to compile a handbook for students of Africa (particularly those with bibliographic needs beyond their own discipline or geographic area of specialization), librarians other than those fully specialized in African bibliography, and, not least, laymen who want to gain more depth on some aspects of Africa."—*Introd.* Sections for: (1) The study of Africa; (2) Bibliographies and serials; (3) Guide to resources by subject and discipline; (4) Guide to resources in non-African areas; (5) Guide to resources in African nations; and (6) On collecting and disseminating Africana. Subject index (with a few titles included), but no author/title index to the great bulk of citations in the text. Z3501.P15

U.S. Dept. of the Army. Army Library. Africa: a bibliographic survey of literature. [Wash., Headquarters, Dept. of the Army, 1973] 545p. maps, part folded. (DA pamphlet 550-17) $17.50. **DD5**

Earlier editions appeared 1962 and 1967.

Attempts "to assess the problems and prospects in the vast continent. . . . The work includes data on the strategic importance of Africa as a continent, and also provides facts and figures on the political, sociological, economic, and military aspects that contribute to the viability of individual African states."—*Analysts' note.* In four main sections: (1) The African continent: an overview; (2) The regions of the continent: problems and prospects; (3) The countries of the African continent: national profiles; (4) Source materials for further research and reference. Index of maps, but no general index. Z3501.U47

Witherill, Julian W. The United States and Africa: guide to U.S. official documents and government-sponsored publications on Africa, 1785–1975. Wash., Lib. of Congress, 1978. 949p. $14.75. **DD6**

A partially annotated bibliography of selected publications issued by or for the United States government relating to any part of Africa, including the southeast Atlantic and the Western Indian Ocean islands; Egypt is excluded. Sections covering the periods 1820 through 1951 are "limited primarily to congressional and presidential documents, commercial reports, diplomatic papers and treaties" (*Pref.*), whereas the 1952–75 period also includes "translations issued by JPRS and printed and mimeographed studies concerning American assistance programs prepared by or for federal government agencies." Arranged by geographic area, subdivided by topic in the 1952–75 section. Index by topic, issuing body, main entry. Z3501.W57

Current

African Studies Association. Research Liaison Committee. Research in progress, 1970/71– . Waltham, Mass., African Studies Assoc., [1971?–]. Annual. **DD6a**

Issues for 1970/71–1972/74 had subtitle: A selected listing of current Africanist research.

Based on questionnaires sent to members of the Association and other Africanists. Each issue cites current projects at the doctorate and post-doctorate level. Topical arrangement with author index.

Dissertations

Sims, Michael and **Kagan, Alfred.** American & Canadian doctoral dissertations & master's theses on Africa, 1886–1974. Waltham, Mass., African Studies Assoc., Brandeis Univ., [1976]. 365p. **DD7**

Based on *American doctoral dissertations on Africa 1886–1972* by Anne Schneller and Michael Bratton (*Guide* DD17).

Arranged by country or geographic area, then by broad subject field. Subject and author indexes. More than 6,000 items. Z3501.S5

Manuscripts and archives

Guide to federal archives relating to Africa. Comp. by Aloha South. [Waltham, Mass., African Studies Assoc., 1977] 556p. $65. **DD8**

Comp. and ed. by the National Archives and Records Service for the African Studies Association.

Describes the "known Africa-related records in the National Archives of the United States. The records, which include textual material, maps, sound recordings, motion and still pictures, are located in the National Archives Building, the General Archives Division in the Washington National Records Center, Presidential libraries, and the regional archives branches that are part of the Federal Archives and Records Centers."—*Introd.* Arranged alphabetically by name of agency, with subordinate agencies thereunder. Indexes of subjects, of places, of proper names, of ships, and of ethnic groups.

A second volume is to cover Africa-related material in non-governmental archives and libraries.

Although published separately, this is part of the series "Guides to the sources of the history of nations: Africa" (*Guide* DD58; *Suppl.* DD19).

Chronology

Freeman-Grenville, Greville Stewart Parker. Chronology of African history. [London & N.Y.], Oxford Univ. Pr., 1973. 312p. £5. **DD9**

"These historical tables display, in a calendrical fashion, the whole course, so far as it is known, of the principal events and dates in the whole continent of Africa from c.1000 BC until the end of 1971."—*Introd.* Indexed. DT17.F73

General history

Cambridge history of Africa. J. D. Fage and Roland Oliver, gen. eds. Cambridge, University Pr., 1975–77. v.3–5. (In progress; to be in 8v.) **DD10**

Contents: v.3, From ca.1050 to ca.1600, ed. Roland Oliver. 1977. 803p. $48.50; v.4, The sixteenth and seventeenth centuries, ed. Richard Gray. 1975. 738p. $42.50; v.5, From ca.1790 to ca. 1870, ed. John E. Flint. 1977. 617p. $42.50.

Chapters written by specialists include full bibliographies; there is also a bibliographical essay at the end of each volume. Detailed index; maps. Of the same high caliber as other Cambridge histories. DT20.C28

Atlases

Fage, John D. An atlas of African history. Maps drawn by Maureen Verity. 2d ed. [London], Edward Arnold, [1978]. unpaged. 69 cm. £10. **DD11**

1st ed. 1958 (*Guide* DD41).

A complete revision reflecting advances in archaeological and historical knowledge of the pre-Colonial period in particular. 21 new maps.

Freeman-Grenville, Greville Stewart Parker. A modern atlas of African history. Cartography by E. Hausman. London, Rex Collings, 1976. 63p. 25cm. £3; £1.50 pa. **DD12**

Based on an earlier edition designed for school use. Like the earlier volume, this one "covers the whole period from the earliest relics of prehistoric man in Africa up to 1975. . . . The seventy maps of this atlas are designed solely to illustrate the more important themes, facts, episodes or sequences of events" (*Pref.*) in African history. G2446.S1F7

AFRICA, SOUTHERN

Bibliography

American-Southern African relations: bibliographic essays. Ed. by Mohamed A. El-Khawas and Francis A. Kornegay, Jr. Westport, Conn., Greenwood Pr., [1975]. 188p. $11.95. (African Bibliographic Center. Special bibliographic ser., n.s., no.1) **DD13**

Contents: American involvement in Angola and Mozambique by M. A. El-Khawas; A short bibliographic essay on U.S. policy toward Southern Rhodesia (Zimbabwe), by S. Nyang; Namibia, by B. Rogers; United States investments in Southern Africa, by T. Hultman and R. Kramer; Black America and U.S.-Southern African relations, by F. A. Kornegay, Jr.

Each essay is followed by full citations to works cited in the text. Not indexed.

Scheven, Yvette. Bibliographies for African studies, 1970–1975. Waltham, Mass., African Studies Assoc., 1977. 135p. $12. **DD14**

Cites about 1,000 bibliographies issued as books, articles, parts of edited volumes, etc., relating to sub-Saharan Africa. Topical/geographical arrangement, with continuing bibliographies cited at the end of each section. Index of names, titles, and subjects.

Zoghby, Samir M. Arab-African relations, 1973–1975; a guide. Wash., General Reference and Bibliography Div., Reader Services Dept., Lib. of Congress, 1976. 26p. (Maktaba-African relations, no.1) **DD15**

"Books and periodical articles on contemporary relations between Arab states and Sub-Saharan Africa" (*Pref.*) published during the 1973–75 period are arranged by author, with a subject index. Brief annotations. Z3013.Z63

——— Islam in sub-Saharan Africa, a partially annotated guide. Wash., Lib. of Congress, 1978. 318p. $8.50. **DD16**

A partially annotated bibliography of selected books and periodical articles pertaining to the social, religious, and political structure of the Muslim populations, the Islamization of sub-Saharan Africa, "the resistance of Muslim leaders and reformers to European imperial designs, and the role of Islam as a major variable in political relations between Muslim states in the twentieth century."—*Pref.* Chronological arrangement subdivided by geographical area, then by topic. Indexed. Z7835.M6Z63

Dissertations

Pollak, Oliver B. and **Pollak, Karen.** Theses and dissertations on Southern Africa: an international bibliography. Boston, G. K. Hall, [1976]. 236p. $18. **DD18**

Arranged by broad subject headings, each subdivided by country or other geographical area. Author index, but no detailed subject approach. Lists some 2,400 academic theses (including B.Litt. and B.Ed., as well as M.A. and Ph.D. papers) accepted for advanced degrees between 1884 and 1974. Represents work at more than 200 institutions in 30 countries. Z3518.P55

Manuscripts and archives

Guide to the sources of the history of the nations. B. Africa . . . Zug, Inter Documentation, 1974–76. v.4, 6, Index v.3–4. (In progress) **DD19**

For previously published volumes *see Guide* DD58.

Contents: v.4, Sources de l'histoire de l'Afrique au Sud du Sahara dans les archives et bibliothèques françaises, pt.II, Bibliothèques (1976; 195 Sw.Fr.); Index, v.3–4 (1976; 48 Sw.Fr.); v.6, Guida delle fonti per la storia dell' Africa a Sud del Sahara esistenti in Italia, pt.2 (1974; 95 Sw.Fr.).

The volumes for Belgian, British, and American archives have been or are to be published outside this series (*see Guide* DD59 and *Suppl.* DD8).

Dictionaries and handbooks

African historical dictionaries. no.1– . Metuchen, N.J., Scarecrow Pr., 1974– . no.1– . (In progress) **DD20**

Contents: no.1, Historical dictionary of Cameroon, by Victor T. LeVine (1974. 198p.); no.2, People's Republic of the Congo, by V. McL. Thompson and R. Adloff (1974. 139p.); no.3, Swaziland, by John J. Grotpeter (1975. 251p.); no.4, Gambia, by Harry A. Gailey (1975. 172p.); no.6, Somalia, by Margaret Castagno (1975. 213p.); no.7, Dahomey (People's Republic of Benin), by Samuel Decalo (1976. 201p.); no.8, Burundi, by Warren Weinstein (1976. 368p.); no.9, Togo, by Samuel Decalo (1976. 243p.); no.10, Lesotho, by Gordon Haliburton (1977. 223p.); no.11, Mali, by Pascal J. Imperato (1977. 204p.); no.12, Sierra Leone, by C. P. Foray (1977. 279p.); no.13, Chad, by Samuel Decalo (1977. 413p.); no.14, Upper Volta, by D. M. McFarland (1978. 239p.); no.15, Tanzania, by L. S. Kurtz (1978. 363p.); no.16, Guinea, by T. E. O'Toole (1978. 183p.); no.17, Sudan, by J. O. Voll (1978. 193p.).

Following a brief survey of the history and economics of the country, each dictionary is an alphabetical arrangement of entries for people and topics. Most volumes end with a selective bibliography.

For a description of one of the better volumes in the series *see* the Subscription Books Committee review of the Togo dictionary in the *Booklist* 74: 1758–59 (July 15, 1978).

McLane, Charles B. Soviet-African relations. London, Central Asian Research Centre; distr. by Columbia Univ. Pr., 1974. 190p. (Soviet–Third world relations, v.3) £5; $15. **DD21**

Surveys "Soviet relations with 36 sovereign African nations south of the Sahara" (*Pref.*), excluding those countries which were still colonies or dependencies in 1972 as well as South Africa and Rhodesia. Soviet relationship with each country is presented in tabular form—political, economic, cultural—chronologically arranged. List of references for each country section. A "Regional perspective" section offers a "discussion of the broad tendencies of Soviet interest in Africa from the late 1950s to the end of 1972, as measured by the substance of Soviet press commentaries, the volume of aid and trade and the diplomatic response to competition from other non-African powers, notably China. . . ."—*Pref.*

For companion volumes on Asian and Middle East relations *see Suppl.* DE3, DE23. DT38.9.R8M27

Rosenthal, Eric. Encyclopaedia of Southern Africa. 6th ed. London & N.Y., F. Warne & Co., [1973]. 662p. il. $15. **DD22**

5th ed. 1970 (*Guide* DD62).

Special attention was given to updating articles involving population statistics, technology, finance and industry, legislation, and education; new material was added on "Bantu homelands."

ALGERIA

Lawless, Richard I. Algerian bibliography: English language publications, 1830–1973. London & N.Y., Bowker, in assoc. with the Centre for Middle Eastern and Islamic Studies of the Univ. of Durham, [1976]. 114p. (Centre for Middle East and Islamic Studies publs., 4) £9.50; $22.50. **DD23**

Some 1,490 books and periodical articles are listed under 12 topics, subdivided as appropriate. The first section, "Bibliography," includes titles in all languages; the other sections cite only English-language materials. Author index. Z3683.A4L38

CAMEROON

DeLancey, Mark W. and **DeLancey, Virginia H.** A bibliography of Cameroon. N.Y., Africana Publ. Co., [1975]. 673p. (African bibliography ser., 4) $27.50. **DD24**

Covers "from the onset of German colonization (1884) through the beginning of 1972," with some later publications. Books, articles, some documents and recordings are listed; book reviews and abstract references are noted. Z3761.D44

EGYPT

Helck, Hans Wolfgang and **Otto, Eberhard.** Lexikon der Ägyptologie. Wiesbaden, O. Harrassowitz, 1972–78. v.1–3². maps. il. (In progress) **DD25**

Contents: v.1–3², A–Kanopus. Separate indexes have been published for v.1 and v.2. Price per volume varies: e.g., v.1, DM368; v.2, DM396.

An authoritative encyclopedia of Egyptian civilization intended for both the specialist and the student. Signed articles with lengthy bibliographies; a few articles are in English or French. Focus is on Egypt of the Pharoahs to the Hellenistic period, with sketchy treatment given to later periods, prehistory, and countries of conquest (the user being referred to more comprehensive encyclopedias such as the *Reallexikon für Assyriologie*). Excellent indexes for each completed volume. PJ1031.H4

ETHIOPIA

Brown, Clifton F. Ethiopian perspectives, a bibliographical guide to the history of Ethiopa. Westport, Conn., Greenwood Pr., [1978]. 264p. (African Bibliographic Center. Special bibliographic ser., n.s., no.5) $19.50. **DD26**

"Ethiopian history" is interpreted in the broadest sense, so that ethnology, health, religion, etc., are included. Books and periodical articles in all languages are listed in topical sections alphabetically arranged; index of authors and anonymous titles.

Hidaru, Alula and **Rahmato, Dessalegn.** A short guide to the study of Ethiopia; a general bibliography. Westport, Conn., Greenwood Pr., [1976]. 176p. (African Bibliographic Center. Special bibliographic ser., n.s., no.2) $12.75. **DD27**

Covers most of the same topics as the Brown compilation (*Suppl.* DD26), but stresses government publications and archival sources. Many entries are annotated. Author index.

Marcus, Harold G. The modern history of Ethiopia and the horn of Africa, a select and annotated bibliography. Stanford, Hoover Inst. Pr., [1972]. 641p. (Hoover Inst. bibliographical ser., 56) $30. **DD28**

2,042 annotated entries for articles appearing in 19th-century geographical journals; includes materials on history, economics, political science, anthropology, geology, climatology. Entries are grouped mainly by language; author, geographical, and subject indexes. Z3521.M35

GHANA

Afre, S. A. Ashanti region of Ghana: an annotated bibliography, from earliest times to 1973. Boston, G. K. Hall, [1975]. 494p. $33. **DD29**

A revised and updated edition of the author's 1967 thesis for Fellowship of the British Library Association.

Attempts "to list all books, pamphlets and periodical articles; academic theses, dissertations, and project reports; maps and atlases; and unpublished seminar and conference papers relating or containing important references to Ashanti published or produced up to and including the year 1973."—*Introd.* Broad subject listing with author and subject indexes. 2,781 items. Z3785.A64

GUINEA-BISSAU

McCarthy, Joseph M. Guinea-Bissau and Cape Verde Islands, a comprehensive bibliography. N.Y., Garland, 1977. 196p. $17.50. **DD30**

A topically arranged bibliography of books, periodical articles, and government publications in English and Portuguese. Author index. Z3873.G8M3

NIGERIA

Červenka, Zdenek. The Nigerian War, 1967–1970: history of the war, selected bibliography and documents. Frankfurt am Main, Bernard u. Graefe Verlag für Wehrwesen, 1971. 459p. (Schriften der Bibliothek für Zeitgeschichte, n.F., Heft 10) **DD31**

Offers "a selection of what was written about the Nigerian crisis and the war in Great Britain, the United States, France, the Soviet Union, the Federal Republic of Germany, and other European countries."—*Introd.* "History of the war," pp.1-213; "Selected documents [reprinted]," pp.217-380; bibliography, pp.382-451. Author index. DT515.9.E3C4

RHODESIA

Encyclopaedia Rhodesia. Gen. ed., Mary Akers. [Salisbury, Rhodesia, College Pr., 1973] 445p. il. $12.50 (Rhod.). **DD32**

Offers brief articles "on Rhodesian history, geography, flora and fauna, the way of life of its peoples, law, central Government and various other aspects of Rhodesia." A short bibliography precedes the main text, but bibliographical references are not provided with the articles themselves. DT962.2.E53

Pollak, Oliver B. and **Pollak, Karen.** Rhodesia/Zimbabwe: an international bibliography. Boston, G. K. Hall, [1977]. 621p. $50. **DD33**

A comprehensive bibliography "based on searches in over 230 bibliographies which produced over 11,300 citations including monographs, academic theses, essays within books as well as periodical literature in over 1,100 journals."—*Introd.* Classed arrangement with author index. Covers anthropology, ethnology, religion, sociology, communications, economics, education, fine arts, geography, history, natural science, political science and international relations. Z3578.P64

SOMALIA

Salad, Mohamed Khalief. Somalia, a bibliographical survey. Westport, Conn., Greenwood Pr., 1977. 468p. (African Bibliographic Center. Special bibliographic ser., n.s., no.4) $22.50. **DD34**

A bibliography of books, journal and newspaper articles, and maps. Concentrates on the present-day Somali Democratic Republic but includes some material relating to "other Somali territories and their constituent populations still under foreign administrations."—*Introd.* Covers all disciplines. No index.

SOUTH AFRICA

Bibliography

Bibliografie van buitelandse publikasies oor Suid-Afrika, insluitende publikasies van Suid-Afrikaners en vertalings van Suid-Afrikaanse werke in die buiteland uitgegee, 1969/71– . Pretoria, Die Staatsbiblioteek, 1973– . Irregular. (1972/73 publ. 1974: R3) **DD35**

Added title page in English: Bibliography of overseas publications about South Africa, including publications by South Africans and translations of South African works published abroad.

Arranged by Dewey Decimal Classification, with index of authors, titles, editors, etc.

Muller, C. F. J., Van Jaarsveld, F. A. and **Van Wijk, Theo.** Supplement to A select bibliography of South African history; a guide for historical research. Pretoria, Univ. of South Africa, 1974. 166p. **DD36**

For the basic volume *see Guide* DD102.

Intends to add "items covering the period to 1965 omitted for various reasons from the earlier compilation and to include recent publications to about the end of May 1973."—*Introd.*

Encyclopedias

Standard encyclopaedia of Southern Africa. [Cape Town], NASOU Ltd., [1976]. v.12. **DD37**

For earlier volumes and annotation *see Guide* DD105.

Contents: v.12, Suppl. and index. The index covers both the main set and the supplement.

SWAZILAND

Wallace, Charles Stewart. Swaziland; a bibliography. Johannesburg, Univ. of the Witwatersrand, Dept. of Bibliography, Librarianship and Typography, 1967. 87p. **DD38**

The author's thesis for the Diploma in Librarianship.

A continuation of the bibliography by Johanna Arnheim (*Swaziland, a bibliography*. Cape Town, Univ. of Cape Town Libs., 1969. 23p.; completed 1950 for Higher Certificate in Librarianship). Mainly materials from the 1950–65 period, with some earlier publications. Classed arrangement; author and geographical indexes.

Z3607.S9W34

ZAÏRE

Vellut, Jean Luc. Guide de l'étudiant en histoire du Zaïre. Kinshasa, Éditions du Mont Noir, [1974]. 207p. ([Collection "Objectif 80"], Série "Essais," no.8; Collection cours universitaires, no.1) **DD39**

Chapters surveying archival and printed sources and discussing research methods, etc., are followed by a classed bibliography. Index to the bibliography.

Z3631.V4

D E

Asia

GENERAL WORKS

Bibliography

Dissertations

Doctoral dissertations on Asia; an annotated bibliographical journal of current international research. v.1, no.1– , Wint. 1975– . [Ann Arbor, Mich.], publ. for the Assoc. for Asian Studies by Xerox University Microfilms, [1975]– . Semiannual (v.2, 1976/77 issued in 1v.). **DE1**

Comp. and ed. by Frank J. Shulman.

". . . continues the bibliographical listings that appeared in the *Association for Asian Studies Newsletter* between 1969 and 1971 and in the *Asian Studies Professional Review* from its beginning in the fall of 1971 through the spring 1974 issue."—*Introd.* Lists both recently completed dissertations and dissertations in progress. Includes references to *Dissertation abstracts international;* permanent address of the author is given when available.

Manuscripts and archives

Matthews, Noel and **Wainwright, M. Doreen.** A guide to manuscripts and documents in the British Isles relating to the Far East. [London], Oxford Univ. Pr. for the School of Oriental and African Studies, 1977. 182p. £17.50. **DE2**

A survey of English, Welsh, Scots, and Irish (both Northern Ireland and the Republic) depositories, including some papers in private custody.

Handbooks

McLane, Charles B. Soviet-Asian relations. London, Central Asian Research Centre; distr. by Columbia Univ. Pr., 1973. 150p. (Soviet–Third world relations, v.2) £5; $16. **DE3**

"The present volume deals with Soviet relations with 14 developing nations in Asia stretching from Afghanistan to the Philippines." —*Pref.* The data, presented in three columns—political, economic, cultural—are drawn primarily from Soviet sources and are arranged chronologically. List of references for each country section.

For companion volumes on African and Middle East relations *see Suppl.* DD21, DE23.

DK68.M15

Dictionaries and encyclopedias

Frédéric, Louis. Encyclopedia of Asian civilizations. [Villecresnes, France], Louis Frédéric, [1977–]. v.1–3. (In progress; distr. in U.S. by Cheng & Tsui Co., Cambridge, Mass.) **DE4**

Contents: v.1–3, A–I.

Introductory matter in English and French.

To be in 10v. Intended as "a practical and multidisciplinary reference work" (*Introd.*) on the various civilizations of Asia. Oriental names, terms, etc., have been romanized and are entered in a single alphabet. Includes entries for personal and place names; terms in literature, art and religion; titles of written works; historical events, etc. Each entry is identified according to the culture from which it derives. Numerous cross references. A general bibliography is promised for the final volume.

DS4.L68

Historical and cultural dictionaries of Asia. Metuchen, N.J., Scarecrow Pr., 1972–76. no.1–9. (In progress) **DE5**

Contents: no.1, Saudi Arabia, by Carroll L. Riley (1972. 139p. $6); no.2, Nepal, by Basil C. Hedrick and Anne K. Hedrick (1972. 205p. $7); no.3, Philippines, by Ester G. Maring and Joel M. Maring (1973. 240p. $8.50); no.4, Burma, by Joel M. Maring and Ester G. Maring (1973. 296p. $8.50); no.5, Afghanistan, by M. Jamil Hanifi (1976. 149p. $6); no.6, Thailand, by Harold E. Smith (1976. 219p. $8); no.7, Vietnam, by Danny J. Whitfield (1976. 377p. $13.50); no.8, India, by George T. Kurian (1976. 329p. $12); no.9, Sultanate of Oman and the Emirates of Eastern Arabia, by J. D. Anthony [et al.] (1976. 144p. $6).

Following a brief survey of the history and economics of the country, each dictionary is an alphabetical arrangement of entries for personal names and topical subjects. Most volumes end with a selective bibliography.

NEAR AND MIDDLE EAST

Guides

Simon, Reeva S. The modern Middle East; a guide to research tools in the social sciences. Boulder, Colo., Westview Pr., [1978]. 283p. $17.50; $7.75 pa. **DE6**

Intended as a working, selective handbook for students, scholars, librarians, specialists and non-specialists doing research on the Middle East of the 19th and 20th centuries. Arrangement is by type of reference material (e.g., bibliography of bibliography, printed library catalogs, current bibliography) within five main divisions: (1) Bibliography, (2) Periodicals, (3) Primary source material, (4) Reference sources, (5) Report literature. Annotated. Author, title, subject index. Z3013.S55

Bibliography

Arab Islamic bibliography; the Middle East Library Committee guide. Ed. by Diana Grimwood-Jones, Derek Hopwood, J. D. Pearson. [Hassocks, Eng.], Harvester Pr.; [Atlantic Highlands, N.J.], Humanities Pr., [1977]. 292p. **DE7**

"Based on Giuseppe Gabrieli's *Manuale di bibliografia musulmana* [1916]."—*t.p.*

Offered as a "new guide to reference materials for Islamic studies along the same lines as Gabrieli's work, retaining or referring to all that remains useful in the original publication and supplementing this with information on what has been contributed by scholars, librarians, bibliographers and others since the publication of the *Manuale.*" —*Foreword.* Sections contributed by scholars and librarians on bibliographies, encyclopedias and reference works, Arabic grammars, genealogy and biographical dictionaries, press and periodicals, maps and atlases, geographical names, *Festschriften,* scientific expeditions, institutions, manuscripts, archives, epigraphy, numismatics, printing and book production, libraries. Index of authors and anonymous titles. Z3013.A66

Atiyeh, George Nicholas. The contemporary Middle East, 1948–1973; a selective and annotated bibliography. Boston, G. K. Hall, [1975]. 664p. $49. **DE8**

A classed bibliography with author and subject indexes. Emphasis is on the social sciences. Materials are mainly in English, French, German, Italian and Spanish, with some works in Arabic, Turkish and Persian included "either because they represent new trends in their fields or because they complete the coverage of topics that otherwise would not be well represented."—*Introd.* Nearly 6,500 items. Intended for the student and beginning researcher. Z3013.A85

Beirut. Université Saint-Joseph. Centre d'Études pour le Monde Arabe Moderne. Arab culture and society in change, a partially annotated bibliography of books and articles in English, French, German and Italian, comp. by the staff of CEMAM ("Centre d'Études pour le Monde Arabe Moderne"). . . . Beirut, Dar el-Mashreq Publ., [1973]. 318p. $15. **DE9**

Lists books and articles dealing with the Arab countries of the Middle East and North Africa in their contacts with "Western" culture from the period of the first World War to the present. Topical arrangement with indexes by authors, persons, regions, and broad subjects. Z3013.B43

Bevis, Richard W. Bibliotheca cisorientalia; an annotated checklist of early English travel books on the Near and Middle East. Boston, G. K. Hall, 1973. 317p. **DE10**

Provides " a reasonably complete checklist of books reporting at first hand on the Mideast after the Moslem conquest, published in English before 1915."—*Introd.* Author listing within five sections: English language travel books; Translations into English; Collections; Biography, criticism and scholarship; Bibliography. Most entries are briefly annotated; library locations are indicated. Z3013.B47

Chicago. University. Library. Catalog of the Middle Eastern Collection [formerly the Oriental Institute Library]. Boston, G. K. Hall, 1970–77. 16v. and Suppl. 1. ($1350; Suppl. 1, 962p., $90) **DE11**

The library aims "to collect all useful printed material on every aspect of the Near East" (*Pref.*) and is especially strong in materials on the ancient Near East and medieval Islam. Dictionary arrangement. Includes books, periodical articles, periodicals and series, pamphlets, and book reviews. The supplement is a main entry catalog of recently added materials relating to all aspects of the Middle East, plus works written in the Arabic, Persian, and Turkish languages regardless of subject. (The library has been integrated into the Regenstein Library, although the catalog remains separate.) Z3013.C43

Clements, Frank, comp. The emergence of Arab nationalism from the nineteenth century to 1921. [London], Diploma Pr., [1976]; Wilmington, Del., Scholarly Resources Inc., 1977. 289p. $14.95. **DE12**

An annotated bibliography of books, periodical articles, and pamphlets. In three main sections: (1) The struggle between the Arabs and Turks; (2) The peace settlement and its consequences; (3) The fertile crescent under the mandate system. Extensive annotations; index.

Littlefield, David W. The Islamic Near East and North Africa; an annotated guide to books in English for non-specialists. Littleton, Colo., Libraries Unlimited, 1977. 375p. $19.50. **DE13**

A guide for the general reader and the librarian. Some 1,166 numbered items are fully annotated as a basic collection for the field. Additional, supplementary items are noted in the annotations. Separate author, title, and subject indexes. Z3013.L653

The study of the Middle East: research and scholarship in the humanities and the social sciences. Ed. by Leonard Binder. N.Y., Wiley, [1976]. 648p. $26.50. **DE14**

"A project of the Research and Training Committee of the Middle East Studies Association."—*t.p.*

Each chapter is a bibliographic survey and assessment of research and scholarship on an aspect of Middle Eastern studies. Each essay by a different scholar or team of scholars. Chapters on: Area studies; Islamic religious tradition; History; Anthropology; Islamic art and archaeology; Political science; Philosophy; Linguistics; Literature; Sociology; and Economics. Separate author and subject indexes. DS61.8.S78

Zoghby, Samir M. Arab-African relations, 1973–1975; a guide. Wash., 1976. 26p. **DE15**

For full citation and annotation *see Suppl.* DD15.

Current

The Middle East: abstracts and index. v.1, no.1– , Mar. 1978– . Pittsburgh, Library Information and Research Service, 1978– . Quarterly. $60 per yr. **DE16**

Amy C. Lowenstein, ed.

Offers citations, with abstracts, of English-language materials in the humanities and social sciences relating to countries of the Middle East. A section of general materials applicable to the entire area is followed by one on the Arab-Israeli conflict and another on the "Arab World"; then follow sections on individual countries. Within sections the materials are grouped by type: journal articles (drawn from a wide range of periodicals), editorials, government documents, interviews, NTIS documents, speeches and statements, doctoral dissertations, reprints, statistics, books and reviews. Each issue has author and subject indexes which cumulate annually in the December issue.

Dissertations

Selim, George Dimitri. American doctoral dissertations on the Arab world, 1883–1974. 2d ed. Wash., Lib. of Congress, 1976. 173p. **DE17**

1st ed. 1970 (*Guide* DE35).

Lists 1,825 dissertations, coverage being extended through 1974 in this edition. Z3013.S43

Arab-Israeli conflict

Bibliography

DeVore, Ronald M. The Arab-Israeli conflict; a historical, political, social, and military bibliography. Santa Barbara, Calif., Clio Books, [1976]. 273p. $17.50. **DE18**

Directed toward the undergraduate student, the bibliography concentrates almost exclusively on important English-language books and articles published before 1974. "An attempt was made to include works which present a diversity of views on a given subject in order to give the user a broad perspective on the evolution of the conflict." —*Note.* Detailed subject arrangement with name index. Z3479.R4D48

Khalidi, Walid and **Khadduri, Jill.** Palestine and the Arab-Israeli conflict, an annotated bibliography. Beirut, Inst. for Palestine Studies; Kuwait, Univ. of Kuwait, 1974. 736p. **DE19**

"The focus of the bibliography is on Palestine as a political problem during, roughly, the past century (1880–1971)."—*Pref.* Books, articles, easily accessible academic theses, government documents, and private papers are included in a classified arrangement based on time periods. Materials are mainly in English, Arabic and Hebrew; most entries are annotated. Index of authors, titles, and persons. 5-year supplements are planned. Z3479.R4K45

Source books

The Arab-Israeli conflict, ed. by John Norton Moore, sponsored by the American Society of International Law. Princeton, Princeton Univ. Pr., 1974. 3v. $95. **DE20**

Contents: v.1–2, Readings; v.3, Documents.

In v.1–2 is assembled a selection of scholarly readings from the international legal literature on the principal issues and alternatives for their settlement; v.3 reprints the principal documents regarding the international legal aspects of the conflict. "Selected bibliography on the Arab-Israeli conflict and international law," v.3, pp.1200–23. DS119.7.A6718

Atlases

Gilbert, Martin. The Arab-Israeli conflict: its history in maps. 2d ed. London, Weidenfeld & Nicolson, 1976. 109p. 26cm. £4.25; £2.50 pa. **DE21**

1st ed. 1974.

Some 109 maps in black-and-white trace "the history of the Arab-Jewish conflict from the turn of the century to the present day [i.e., Nov. 1975]."—*Pref.* G2206.S1G5

Source books

Hurewitz, Jacob Coleman. The Middle East and North Africa in world politics, a documentary record. 2d ed., rev. & enl. New Haven, Yale Univ. Pr., 1975– . v.1– . (In progress) **DE22**

1st ed. (1956) had title: *Diplomacy in the Near and Middle East.*

Contents: v.1, European expansion, 1535–1914 (616p. $30).

A collection of English translations of important documents relating to Western European and American contacts with countries of the Middle East—Afghanistan to non-Soviet southwest Asia—and North Africa. Each document is preceded by a short essay indicating its importance. Lengthy bibliography at the end of v.1.

v.2 is to deal with "British-French supremacy, 1914–1945"; v.3 with "British-French withdrawal and Soviet-American rivalry, 1945–1975." DS42.H78

Encyclopedias and handbooks

McLane, Charles B. Soviet-Middle East relations. London, Central Asian Research Centre; distr. by Columbia Univ. Pr., 1973. 126p. (Soviet–Third world relations, v.1) £5; $15. **DE23**

Provides an overview of Soviet relations with 16 countries in the Middle East and North Africa (including Cyprus, but not Afghanistan and Sudan) by giving for each country an introductory account followed by a chronology. Each chronology lists in parallel columns political, economic, and cultural events (e.g., diplomatic agreements and exchanges, major credit and technical assistance agreements, exchange of economic and cultural delegations and, to a lesser extent, trade union and professional exchanges) through 1970. Bibliography, pp.123–26. No index.

For companion volumes on Asian and African relations *see Suppl.* DE3, DD21. DS63.2.R9M3

Shimoni, Yaacov and **Levine, Evyatar.** Political dictionary of the Middle East in the twentieth century. Rev. & updated ed. N.Y., Quadrangle, 1974. 510p. il. $6.95. **DE24**

1st ed. 1972 (*Guide* DE41).

Includes a supplement for the years 1971–74, edited by Itamar Rabinovich and Haim Shaked, pp.[435]–510. An asterisk before the entry in the main section of the work indicates that there is updated information in the supplement. DS61.S52

ASIA, SOUTH

Bibliography

Chicago. Center for Research Libraries. South Asia Microform Project. SAMP catalog. Chicago, 1974. 35p. **DE25**

—— —— Supplement 1–2. Chicago, 1976–78. 2v.

"The South Asia Microform Project (SAMP) exists to make available in microform [to member libraries] research materials related to the study of South Asia. This catalog represents all SAMP material cataloged through February 1974."—*Introd.* The supplements add materials cataloged through Dec. 1977. Items are listed alphabetically by main entry; there is no index.

Dissertations

Krishan Gopal. Theses on Indian Sub-continent, 1877–1971: an annotated bibliography of dissertations in social sciences and humanities accepted with the universities of Australia, Canada, Great Britain and Ireland, and United States of America. Ed. by Dhanpat Rai. Delhi, Hindustan Publ. Corp., [1977]. 462p. (Bibliographical research ser., 1) Rs.140. **DE26**

Intended as "a comprehensive and interdisciplinary guide to all dissertations, published during 1877–1971, that deal in whole or in parts with Bangladesh, India, Nepal-Sikkim-Bhutan, Pakistan and Sri Lanka."—*Pref.* Topical arrangement within geographical divisions; author and subject indexes. Z3185.K74

ASIA, SOUTHEAST

Cornell University. Libraries. Southeast Asia catalog. Boston, G. K. Hall, 1976. 7v. $595. **DE27**

Contents: v.1–3, Western language monographs; v.4–5, Vernacular monographs; v.6, Vernacular monographs (cont'd); Other language monographs; Serials; v.7, Serials (cont'd.); Newspapers; Maps.

Photographic reproduction of catalog cards for all monographs, serials, newspapers, maps, and microfilms relating to Burma, Cambodia, Indonesia, Laos, Malaysia, Singapore, Brunei, the Philippines, Portuguese Timor, Thailand, and Vietnam. Includes many subjects of wider interest, e.g., Buddhism, Islam, ethnic minorities, and languages of bordering regions. Z3221.C86

ASIA, EAST

Bibliography

California. University. Library. East Asiatic Library. Author-title catalog; Subject catalog. 1st supplement. Boston, G. K. Hall, 1973. 4v. (Author-title cat., 2v. $230; Subj. cat., 2v. $230) **DE28**

For main set and annotation *see Guide* DE73.

Covers materials added 1968–72. Cross references and added entries are not included in the supplement.

Chicago. University. Library. Far Eastern Library. Catalogs of the Far Eastern Library. Boston, G. K. Hall, 1973. 18v. $1980. **DE29**

Contents: Author-title Chinese catalog, 8v. ($940); Author-title Japanese catalog, 4v. ($510); Classified catalog and subject index, 6v. ($740).

The Chinese collection was established in 1936 with emphasis on selecting research materials on "Chinese literature, history and institutions, especially of the ancient period."—*Pref., v.1.* Added to this strength are the collections in archaeology and the fine arts, the pre-modern period, and local gazetteers. Arranged in romanized order with romanization based on the Wade-Giles system and subjects divided according to the Harvard-Yenching classification.

The Japanese collection was established in 1958 and is especially strong in the humanities and history; there is also a notable collection of Japanese works in Chinese studies. Entries are arranged in romanized order according to the modified Hepburn system and use of the Harvard-Yenching classification. Z881.C5365

Michigan. University. Library. Asia Library. Catalogs of the Asia Library. . . . Boston, G. K. Hall, 1978. 25v. $2350. **DE30**

Contents: v1–13, Chinese catalog; v.14–25, Japanese catalog.

Photographic reproduction of the dictionary card catalog of this extensive collection of materials from China, Japan and Korea (the Japanese section includes Korean materials). Comprehensive coverage in the humanities and social sciences, with special strengths for modern and contemporary China, local histories, the theater, and legislation and statistical publications of Japan.

U.S. Library of Congress. Orientalia Division. Far Eastern languages catalog. Boston, G. K. Hall, 1972. 22v. $2175. **DE31**

Photographic reproduction of the catalog cards for Chinese, Japanese, and Korean works processed at the Library of Congress since 1958. Special strengths are in the humanities, social sciences, and law; relatively strong in science and technology, although the collection does not try to duplicate holdings of the National Library of Medicine and the National Agricultural Library. Dictionary arrangement. Z3009.U56

Library resources

Yang, Teresa S., Kuo, Thomas C. and **Shulman, Frank Joseph.** East Asian resources in American libraries. N.Y., Paragon Book Gallery, 1977. 143p. $8.95 pa. **DE32**

An outgrowth of Yang and Yang's *Asian resources in American libraries* (1968; *Guide* DE14), but concentrating on East Asia rather than sources relating to the whole of Asia.

Contains two essays, "American library resources on East Asia," by T. S. Yang, and "East Asian collections in American libraries," by T. C. Kuo; a bibliographical guide to East Asian resources by F. J. Shulman; and a directory of East Asian collections in American libraries by T. S. Yang. The bibliographic guide concentrates on publications of the 1968–76 period—i.e., works appearing since publication of the earlier guide mentioned above. Index of authors and other main entries. Z3001.Y35

BANGLADESH

Satyaprakash. Bangla Desh: a select bibliography. Gurgaon, Indian Documentation Service, 1976. 218p. (International bibliography ser., 3) Rs.50. **DE33**

Lists some 2,500 titles (3,699 entries) of books, book reviews, journal articles and articles from the *Times of India* dealing with Bangladesh and published 1962–76. Arranged by author and topic. Z3186.S27

CHINA

Guides

Wilkinson, Endymion. The history of imperial China, a research guide. Cambridge, East Asian Research Center, Harvard Univ.; distr. by Harvard Univ. Pr., 1973. 213p. (Harvard East Asian monographs, 49) $9. **DE34**

A survey of "primary sources and the reference aids to them in Chinese, Japanese, and Western languages."—*Pref.* Concentrates on the period from the third century B.C. to the 18th century. An introductory section, "Research hints" discusses the main problems (i.e., converting dates, locating places, finding biographical information, etc.) encountered in using primary materials. Subject and author/title indexes. DS734.7.W5

Bibliography

Kamachi, Noriko, Fairbank, John K. and **Ichiko, Chūzō.** Japanese studies of modern China since 1953; a bibliographical guide to historical and social science research on the nineteenth and twentieth centuries. Supplementary volume for 1953–1969. Cambridge, Mass., East Asian Research Center, Harvard Univ.; distr. by Harvard Univ. Pr., 1975. 603p. (Harvard East Asian monographs, 60) **DE35**

A supplement to the volume by Fairbank, Banno and Yamamoto (*Guide* DE87). Z3106.K28

Lieberthal, Kenneth. A research guide to Central Party and government meetings in China, 1949–1975, with a foreword by Michael Oksenberg. White Plains, N.Y., Internat. Arts and Sciences Pr., [1976]. 322p. (Michigan studies on China, special no.) $7.95 pa. **DE36**

A chronological listing of the meetings, giving topic, dates, place, major agenda items, attendance, summaries of speeches and reports, indication of documents passed, reference to published accounts of the meeting and to any important secondary works. Index to meeting summaries.

Wang, James C. F. The cultural revolution in China: an annotated bibliography. N.Y., Garland, 1976. 246p. (Garland reference library of social science, v.16) $23. **DE37**

A topical listing of 364 English-language books and periodical articles widely available in American libraries. Annotations; author and subject index. Z3108.A5W35

Dissertations

Shulman, Frank Joseph. Doctoral dissertations on China, 1971–1975; a bibliography of studies in Western languages. Seattle, Univ. of Wash. Pr., [1978]. 329p. **DE38**

Forms a supplement to Gordon and Shulman's earlier bibliography covering 1945–70 (*Guide* DE99). 1,573 entries for the 1971–75 period, with an appendix of 228 pre-1971 theses not listed in the earlier compilation. Z3106.G65 Suppl.

Periodicals

London. University. Contemporary China Institute. A bibliography of Chinese newspapers and periodicals in European libraries. Cambridge, Cambridge Univ. Pr., 1975. 1025p. $65. **DE39**

Listing is by name of periodical or newspaper, with indication of holdings in libraries of both Eastern and Western Europe (although more libraries in the latter section were surveyed). No index, nor cross references in the body of the work, but there is a lengthy list of Western-language titles with corresponding Chinese titles, pp. 15–68. Z6955.Z9L66

Historiography

Hsieh, Winston. Chinese historiography on the Revolution of 1911, a critical survey and a select bibliography. Stanford, Calif., Hoover Inst. Pr., 1975. 165p. (Hoover Institution studies, 34) $9. **DE40**

A bibliographical essay (pp.3–103) is followed by "A selected bibliography on the 1911 Revolution, with addenda," pp.104–42, giving citations to Chinese works with English translation of titles, and notes on any English translation or summary of the complete work. Subject index. DS773.H7

Handbooks and general histories

Cambridge history of China. Gen. eds., John K. Fairbank and Denis Twitchett. London, Cambridge Univ. Pr., [1978–]. v.10. (In progress) **DE41**

Contents: v.10, Late Ch'ing, 1800–1870, ed. by John K. Fairbank. 713p. £18.50.

The first published volume of a projected 14v. work. Similar to the other "Cambridge histories," and with sections written by specialists, the series will offer a survey of the "current state of knowledge" of the history of China, excluding the pre-dynastic period. DS735.C3I45

Franke, Wolfgang. China Handbuch, hrsg. . . . unter Mitarbeit von Brunhild Staiger. Eine Veröffentlichung der Deutschen Gesellschaft für Ostasienkunde in Verbindung mit dem Institut für Asienkunde. [Düsseldorf], Bertelsmann Universitätsverlag, [1974]. 1768 col. il. DM164. **DE42**

A compact, one-volume encyclopedia of China, primarily of the 19th and 20th centuries. Signed articles with bibliographical references. Personal name and detailed subject indexes. DS706.F73

HONG KONG

Rydings, H. Anthony. A Hong Kong union catalogue: works relating to Hong Kong in Hong Kong libraries. [Hong Kong], Centre of Asian Studies, Univ. of Hong Kong, 1976. 2v. (967p.) (Centre of Asian Studies bibliographies and guides, no.10) HK$250. **DE43**

Attempts to list by subject all books, essays and parts of books, periodical articles, periodicals published in Hong Kong, maps, theses, and mimeographed materials dealing mainly with Hong Kong which are located in Hong Kong libraries. Author/title index. Supplements are planned. Z3107.H7R93

INDIA

Early writings on India: a union catalogue of books on India in English language published upto [*sic*] 1900 and available in Delhi libraries. Ed. by H. K. Kaul. New Delhi, Arnold-Heinemann, [1975]. 324p. Rs.65. **DE44**

A classified catalog of 3,277 items with author/title index. Z3209.E22

Scholberg, Henry. Bibliographie des français dans l'Inde. [Pondicherry, Historical Soc. of Pondicherry, 1973] 216p. Rs.55. **DE45**

Brief survey chapters of "Historical writing on the French in India" and "Bibliographic resources for a study of the French in India" are followed by a bibliography of books, government publications, and a few theses in topical arrangement. Lists of maps and atlases and of titles of periodicals (including government serials) most relevant to the French presence in India are also included. Index of authors, subjects and anonymous titles. Z3208.A39S36

Sharma, Jagdish Saran. Sources of Indian civilization; a bibliography of works by world orientalists other than Indian. Delhi, Vikas, [1974]. 360p. Rs.55. **DE46**

A bibliography of more than 3,500 books in classed arrangement according to broad Dewey classes. Brief subject index; some annotations. A high percentage of the works listed is in English, but Indologists from 15 countries are represented. Z3206.S49

IRAN

Bibliography

Pearson, James Douglas. A bibliography of pre-Islamic Persia. [London], Mansell, 1975. 288p. (Persian studies ser., 2) £15. **DE48**

About 7,300 items in classed arrangement, with author index. The principal sections are: (A) Languages and literatures; (B) History; (C) Religion; and (D) Art and archaeology; each is appropriately subdivided. Full table of contents but no detailed subject index. International in coverage (but omitting Russian materials); generally speaking, the cutoff date is 1970. Z3366.P36

General histories

Cambridge history of Iran. Cambridge, University Pr., 1975. v.4. (In progress) **DE49**

For previously published volumes and annotation *see Guide* DE140.

Contents: v.4, The period from the Arab invasion to the Saljugs, ed. by R. N. Frye.

JAPAN

Bibliography

Introductory bibliography for Japanese studies. Tokyo, Univ. of Tokyo Pr.; distr. by Internatl. Scholarly Book Services, Portland, Ore., 1974– . v.1– . (v.1, pts.1–2, $28.50) (In progress) **DE50**

Prep. for the Japanese Foundation.

A continuation of *K.B.S. bibliography of standard reference books* (*Guide* DE151), with emphasis on materials published since 1970.

v.1,pt.1 covers law, political science, economics, sociology, geography, cultural anthropology; pt.2, history, archaeology, religion, language, literature, art. Each part has an index of authors and editors cited in that volume. Supplementary volumes updating the two parts are promised in alternate years. Z3306.I57

Dissertations

Shulman, Frank Joseph. Doctoral dissertations on Japan and Korea, 1969–1974: a classified bibliographical listing of international research. Ann Arbor, Mich., University Microfilms Internatl., 1976. 78p. **DE51**

Serves as a supplement to Shulman's *Japan and Korea: an annotated bibliography of doctoral dissertations . . . 1877–1969* (*Guide* DE157).

Separate sections for Japan and Korea, each in topical subject arrangement, listing 914 theses on Japan, 314 on Korea, and 88 on both Japan and Korea. Two appendixes, one listing 108 theses defended before 1969; the other listing "39 recently completed Soviet dissertations."—*Introd.* Author, institutional, and "modified subject" indexes. Includes order information for dissertations available from University Microfilms International.

Source books

Lu, David John. Sources of Japanese history. N.Y., McGraw-Hill, 1974. 2v. $8.95. **DE52**

A selection of English translations of Japanese documents which picture the development of social, economic, and political institutions. Covers all periods, the most recent document being dated 1968. Chronological arrangement; headnotes for each document; index. DS803.L8

KOREA

Bibliography

Ginsburgs, George. Soviet works on Korea 1945–1970. Los Angeles, Univ. of Southern Calif. Pr., 1973. 179p. (Univ. of Southern Calif. School of Internatl. Relations. Far Eastern and Russian research ser., 4) $9.50; $6.50 pa. **DE53**

Prep. for the Joint Committee on Korean Studies of the American Council of Learned Societies and the Social Science Research Council.

An extensive listing of books and pamphlets, articles, and dissertations written in the Soviet Union concerning Korea. Titles are given in Russian, followed by an English translation in parentheses. Topical arrangement with author index. Essays on the history of Soviet research on Korea and the state-of-the-art, pp.17–62. Z3316.G55

Dissertations

Shulman, Frank Joseph. Doctoral dissertations on Japan and Korea, 1969–1974: a classified bibliographical listing of international research. Ann Arbor, Mich., University Microfilms Internat., 1976. 78p. **DE54**

For full information *see Suppl.* DE51.

NEPAL

Bibliographie du Népal. Paris, Éditions C.N.R.S., 1973–75. v.3[1] and suppl. **DE55**

For previously published parts and annotation *see Guide* DE184.

Contents: v.3,t.1, Cartes du Népal dans les bibliothèques de Paris et de Londres, par L. Boulnois; Supplément, 1967–1973, par L. Boulnois.

Bibliography of Nepal. Comp. and ed. by Khadga Man Malla. Kathmandu, Royal Nepal Academy, 1975. 529p. Rs.74. **DE56**

Title and introductory matter in English and Nepali.

A classified bibliography of some 8,300 books and periodical articles on various aspects of Nepalese history, life and culture published up to 1972. Annotations in Nepali. Indexed. Z3207.N4B52

PAKISTAN

Bibliography

Pakistan and Bangladesh; bibliographical essays in social science. Ed. by W. Eric Gustafson. [Islamabad], Univ. of Islamabad Pr., 1976. 364p. **DE57**

"This collection of bibliographical essays is a product of the National Seminar on Pakistan and Bangladesh which has met at the Southern Asian Institute, Columbia University, since Nov. 1970."—*Pref.* Seven essays survey scholarship in the areas of foreign policy, economics, social science, anthropology, political science, and Muslim separatism. Z3196.P34

Satyaprakash. Pakistan: a bibliography 1962–1974. Gurgaon, Indian Documentation Service, [1975]. 338p. Rs.65 ($13). **DE58**

An author and subject listing of some 6,500 items—significant signed periodical articles, research papers, book reviews, and editorials from 109 Indian journals and the daily *Times of India*. Z3196.S28

Dissertations

Anwar, Muhammad. Doctoral dissertations on Pakistan. Islamabad, Pakistan, Nat. Commission on Historical and Cultural Research, 1976. 124p. **DE59**

Attempts to list "all the theses accepted for doctoral degrees by universities abroad up to the academic year 1975, which in some way or other deal with Pakistan."—*Pref.* Cites 877 dissertations in classed arrangement, with author index.

Anwar, Mumtaz A. Doctoral research on Pakistan; a bibliography of dissertations accepted by foreign universities up to 1971. Lahore, Pak Book Corp., 1976. 72p. **DE60**

A classed bibliography with author index. More than 600 entries. "Research done prior to 1947 and relating to areas constituting Pakistan or to subjects directly relating to Pakistan have also been included."—*Pref.*

SRI LANKA

Goonetileke, H. A. I. A bibliography of Ceylon. Zug, Inter Documentation Co. AG, 1976. v.3. **DE61**

For v.1–2 and annotation *see Guide* DE191.

Contents: v.3, Supplementing v.I & II, and containing additional materials up to June 1973.

VIETNAM

Cotter, Michael. Vietnam: a guide to reference sources. Boston, G. K. Hall, [1977]. 272p. $50. **DE62**

Presented as the "first known compilation of reference works about Vietnam. It lists about 1400 books, periodical articles, serials, government publications, and other materials in the human and natural sciences, primarily in romanized Vietnamese (quôc-ngữ), French, and English from 1651 (the date of the first dictionary using romanized Vietnamese . . .) until 1976."—*Introd.* Classified arrangement; annotations; name/title index. Z3228.V5C68

Legler, Anton and **Bauer, Frieda.** Der Krieg in Vietnam; Bericht und Bibliographie. Frankfurt am Main, Bernard und Graefe, 1969–76. 4v. (Schriften der Bibliothek für Zeitgeschichte, n.F., Heft 8, 11, 13, 16) **DE63**

Contents: [v.1] Bis 30.9.1962; [v.2] Oktober 1968–September 1969; v.3, Oktober 1969–September 1971; v.4, Oktober 1971–Januar 1973.

An extensive bibliography of periodical articles, government publications, and books in Western languages. Topical arrangement with author index. Each volume has an introductory survey of Vietnam, Laos, and conduct of the war during the period covered. DS557.A6L32

Leitenberg, Milton and **Burns, Richard Dean.** The Vietnam conflict; its geographical dimensions, political traumas, and military developments. Santa Barbara, Calif., Clio Books, 1973. 163p. **DE64**

Presents a "working" bibliography of books, articles, and government publications dealing with background and ongoing aspects of the war. Primarily English-language materials, with some French titles. Index. Z3228.V5L44

D F

Australia and New Zealand

NEW ZEALAND

Bagnall, Austin Graham. New Zealand national bibliography to the year 1960. Wellington, A. R. Shearer, Govt. Printer, 1975. v.4. (In progress) **DF1**

For full information *see Suppl.* AA138.

D G

Oceania

GENERAL WORKS

Bibliography

Bibliography of periodical articles relating to the South Pacific. v.1– , 1974– . Suva, Fiji, Univ. of the South Pacific Lib., 1976– . Annual. Fiji $4 per yr. **DG1**

Esther Dam, comp. and ed.

A classed listing within geographical sections for Oceania, Melanesia, Micronesia, Polynesia. Author index. References are drawn from about 200 periodicals received in the University of the South Pacific Library.

FIJI ISLANDS

Coppell, William G. Catalogue of theses and dissertations relating to Fiji & Rotuma. [Suva, Fiji], Univ. of the South Pacific Lib., 1976. 29p. (Selected bibliography, no.3) **DG2**

An author listing, with subject index. Includes undergraduate honors theses as well as master's theses and doctoral dissertations. Aims to be more inclusive, as well as more up-to-date, than the relevant sections of Dickson and Dossor's *World catalogue of theses on the Pacific Islands* (*Guide* DG11).

PAPUA NEW GUINEA

Jones, Gregory. Papua New Guinean history & politics; an annotated bibliography, 1950–1974. [Canberra], Canberra College of Advanced Education Lib., 1975. 133*l*. (Library bibliography ser., no.2) $5 (Austral.) **DG3**

A classified arrangement of books and government publications, with author, subject and series indexes. Z4811.J64

D H

Arctic and Antarctic

BIBLIOGRAPHY

Arctic Institute of North America, Montreal. Library. Catalogue of the Library. . . . 1st–2d supplement. Boston, G. K. Hall, 1971–74. 3v. (Suppl. 1, 902p., $115; Suppl. 2, 2v., $230) **DH1**

For main set and annotation *see Guide* DH3.

The supplements cover additions to the library from 1968 through mid-1974. A third supplement was listed as "in press" in 1978.

E

Pure and Applied Sciences

E A

General Works

GUIDES

Grogan, Denis Joseph. Science and technology; an introduction to the literature. 3d ed. [Hamden, Conn.], Linnet Books; London, Clive Bingley, 1976. 343p. $12.50. **EA1**

2d ed. 1973 (*Guide* EA3).

Revised and expanded—"most visibly in the areas of computerized data bases and of microforms which now have chapters to themselves."—*Introd.*

Malinowsky, Harold Robert, Gray, Richard A. and **Gray, Dorothy.** Science and engineering literature; a guide to current reference sources. 2d ed. Littleton, Colo., Libraries Unlimited, 1976. 368p. $14. **EA2**

1st ed., 1967, had title: *Science and engineering reference sources* (*Guide* EA8).

The change of title for this edition "reflects its substantial restructuring and its expanded coverage of reference books (the 1967 edition covered 435 reference books, while this second edition covers 1,096)."—*Pref.*

BIBLIOGRAPHY

Current

Kyed, James M. and **Matarazzo, James M.** Scientific, engineering, and medical societies publications in print, 1976–1977. N.Y., Bowker, 1976. 509p. $19.95. **EA3**

1974 ed. publ. under title: *Scientific, technical and engineering societies publications in print, 1974–75* (*Guide* EA35).

Contains in-print lists of 369 societies. Arrangement of lists is alphabetical by society. Information includes: society address, order or sales office address, and publications with prices. Z7911.K92

General and juvenile

Wolff, Kathryn and **Storey, Jill.** AAAS book list supplement. Wash., Amer. Assoc. for the Advancement of Science, 1978. 457p. $16.50. **EA4**

"A selected and annotated list of science and mathematics books which supplements the *AAAS science book list* (3d ed; 1970 [*Guide* EA41]) for secondary school students, undergraduates, teachers and nonspecialist readers."—*t.p.* Arranged by Dewey Decimal Classification. Author index; title and subject index. Z7401.W64

Periodicals

BioSciences Information Service of Biological Abstracts. Bibliographic guide for editors and authors. [By] Biosciences Information Service of Biological Abstracts, Chemical Abstracts Service, Division of the American Chemical Society [and] Engineering Index, Inc. Wash., Amer. Chemical Soc., 1974. 362p. **EA5**

Prepared through the combined efforts of BIOSIS, CAS, and EI, Inc. to aid in improving the reliability and usefulness of bibliographic information found in scientific and technical publications. Contents divided into three sections: (1) *Guideline for use of the coded bibliographic strip;* (2) *Bibliographic standards,* an annotated list of international standards especially relevant for editors and authors; (3) *Serial titles, abbreviations and codes,* giving the complete titles with the standardized abbreviations and ASTM CODEN for some 27,700 serial publications.

Superseded in part by: Z6945.A2B55

International Council of Scientific Unions. Abstracting Board. International serials catalogue. [Paris], Internatl. Council of Scientific Unions, Abstracting Board; distr. by Biosciences Information Service, Philadelphia [1978]. 2v. $50. **EA5a**

Contents: Pt. I, Catalogue; Pt. II, Index/Concordance.

The *Catalogue* lists in alphabetical order the serial publications abstracted and indexed by the member services of the ICSUAB, and includes journal abbreviation, CODEN, ISSN, and the initials of the services indexing the journal. The *Index/Concordance* includes an ISSN to CODEN list in numerical order and a CODEN to ISSN list in alphabetical order; each is associated with corresponding page numbers in the *Catalogue.*

Directory of Japanese scientific periodicals. Tokyo, Natl. Diet Lib., 1974. 1000p. **EA6**

Published irregularly. Previous ed. 1967 (*Guide* EA66). Z6958.J3D5

Abbreviations

International CODEN directory. Columbus, Ohio, Chemical Abstracts Service. Annual, with annual suppl. microfiche (24x). $300 per year. **EA7**

A directory of all CODEN assigned since 1954 (approximately 145,000). In three parts: an alphabetical listing by title, an alphabetical listing by CODEN, and a KWOC index of titles. Subscriptions must be accompanied by a "License to copy" agreement with CAS. The directory is reissued at the beginning of each year, and the outdated directory and supplement must be returned to CAS.

Audio-visual materials

AAAS science film catalog. Wash., Amer. Assoc. for the Advancement of Science; N.Y., Bowker, 1975. 398p. $18.50. **EA8**

Ann Seltz-Petrash, project ed. and comp.; Kathryn Wolff, managing ed.

Provides selection and ordering information for about 5,600 science films (pure sciences, technology, and social sciences) for elementary grades through adult level that can be bought, borrowed, or rented from United States producers and/or distributors. Arranged by subject; indexed by title. Q192.A17

INDEXES AND ABSTRACT JOURNALS

Bibliography

International Federation for Documentation. Abstracting services. 2d ed. The Hague, Internatl. Federation for Documentation (available from Internatl. Publications Service, N.Y.), 1969. 2v. (FID publ. 455) v.1, $30; v.2, $15. **EA9**

1st ed. 1965.

Contents: v.1, Science, technology, medicine, agriculture; v.2, Social sciences, humanities.

Approximately 1,500 abstracting services arranged by title—1,300 in v.1; 200 in v.2. The descriptions of the services include editorial body, publisher, publishing history and availability, number of journals covered, language and subject. A second section gives titles arranged by UDC number and alphabetical lists of subject headings in English, French, Russian, and Spanish. Z695.I62

Owen, Dolores B. and **Hanchey, Marguerite.** Abstracts and indexes in science and technology; a descriptive guide. Metuchen, N.J., Scarecrow Pr., 1974. 154p. $6. **EA10**

Gives descriptions of 125 abstracts and indexes arranged in 11 subject categories, with information on arrangement, coverage, scope, a description of the abstract, and indexing provided in each of the reference tools. "We do [not] intend it to be a definitive bibliography. . . . Rather, we hope to facilitate the use of these materials by means of a simple straight-forward outline. . . ."—*Pref.* Indexed. Z7403.O95

Indexes

General science index. v.1– , July 1978– . N.Y., Wilson, 1978– . Monthly (except June and December), with annual bound cumulation. Service basis. **EA11**

A cumulative subject index to 90 English-language general science periodicals not completely covered by other abstracts and indexes. In addition, an author listing of citations to book reviews follows the main body of the index. No author entries.

Science citation index. 1962–63. Philadelphia, Inst. for Scientific Information, 1973. $1800 per yr. **EA12**

These volumes represent a retrospective filling-in of the "Citation index" and "Source index" (*see Guide* EA87) for the years indicated.

Five-year cumulations of the *Science citation index* are now available for later periods, as follows: 1965–69, $12,000 (or $7,000 for Source and Citation index; $5,000 for Permuterm); 1970–74, $13,000 (or $8,000 for Source and Citation index; $5,000 for Permuterm). Previously published annual volumes are returnable for credit towards cumulations.

ENCYCLOPEDIAS AND HANDBOOKS

McGraw-Hill encyclopedia of science and technology. 4th ed. N.Y., McGraw-Hill, 1977. 15v. $490. **EA13**

An updating, with appropriate additions and revisions, of 3d ed., 1971; for annotation *see Guide* EA107. Between editions updating is continued by *McGraw-Hill yearbook of science and technology,* 1977–. Q121.M3

Van Nostrand's Scientific encyclopedia. 5th ed. N.Y., Van Nostrand Reinhold, 1976. 2370p. $67.50. **EA14**

Douglas M. Considine, ed.
4th ed., 1968 (*Guide* EA110).
Revised and updated. "Selected reference material is added to the end of most major entries for the first time in this edition."—*Pref.*

The way things work; an illustrated encyclopedia of modern technology. N.Y., Simon & Schuster, [1967]–1971. 2v. il. $27.90. **EA15**

Translated and adapted from *Wie funktioniert das?* by "an English-American team," using English terminology with footnotes giving American equivalents. "... not a reference book in the ordinary sense. It has been designed to give the layman an understanding of *how things work,* from the simplest mechanical functions of modern life to the most basic scientific principles and complex industrial processes that affect our well-being."—*Foreword.* T47.W3913

Style manuals and report writing

O'Connor, Maeve and **Woodford, F. Peter.** Writing scientific papers in English; an ELSE-Ciba Foundation guide for authors. N.Y. & Amsterdam, Elsevier, 1976. 108p. $12.75. **EA16**

"Sponsored by the International Union of Biological Sciences, the International Union of Geological Sciences, and EDITERRA [European Association of Earth-Science Editors]."—*t.p.*
"This guide is for scientists of any nationality who want to submit papers to journals published in English.... Our guidelines are in general agreement with the recommendations to authors contained in the (American) *CBE Style Manual,* but they take both British and American English usage into account as well as certain European printing practices that differ from those in the USA."—*Introd.*
T11.O25

DICTIONARIES

Daintith, John. A dictionary of physical sciences. N.Y., Pica; distr. by Universe Books, 1977 [c.1976]. 333p. il. $16.50. **EA17**

A companion to *A dictionary of earth sciences* (*Suppl.* EE1) and *A dictionary of life sciences* (*Suppl.* EC4). A handy, easy-to-use, concise dictionary for the physical sciences. Q123.D22

Dictionary of science and technology. Eds.: T. C. Collocott and A. B. Dobson. Rev. ed. [London], Chambers, 1975. 2v. £2.80. **EA18**

1st ed. 1971 (*Guide* EA124). Q123.D53

McGraw-Hill dictionary of scientific and technical terms. Daniel N. Lapedes, ed.-in-chief. 2d ed. N.Y., McGraw-Hill, [1978]. 1771p. il. $39.50. **EA19**

1st ed. 1974.
Offers almost 108,000 definitions of terms from science and technology. Definitions are clear and concise; each is identified according to field of science or technology. Pronunciation is not indicated. Uses SI (Système International d'Unités) units and includes an appendix giving conversion factors. Q123.M15

Abbreviations

Wennrich, Peter. Anglo-American and German abbreviations in science and technology. 1st ed. N.Y. & London, Bowker; München, Verlag Dokumentation, 1976–77. v.1–2. (In progress) $29.95 per v. **EA20**

Subtitle: *Anglo-amerikanische und deutsche Abkürzungen in Wissenschaft und Technik.*
Contents: v.1, A–E; v.2, F–O. To be complete in 3v.
A compilation of more than 150,000 German and Anglo-American abbreviations taken from some 800 international journals. "More than 60% [of the abbreviations] are found in the Anglo-American sphere...."—*Foreword.* German and English words are interfiled in a single alphabetical sequence. Q179.W44

Foreign terms

French

DeVries, Louis. French-English science and technology dictionary. 4th ed. N.Y., McGraw-Hill, 1976. 683p. $13.50. **EA21**

1st–3d ed. (1940–62) publ. under title: *French-English science dictionary for students in agricultural, biological, and physical sciences* (*Guide* EA133). This ed. rev. and enl. by Stanley Hochman.
"This new edition has been revised to include some 4,500 terms.... The new entries have been incorporated into the Supplement which follows the main body of the dictionary."—*Introd.*
Q123.D37

German

DeVries, Louis. German-English science dictionary. 4th ed. N.Y., McGraw-Hill, [1978]. 628p. $14.50. **EA22**

"Updated and expanded by Leon Jacolev with the assistance of Phyllis L. Bolton."—*t.p.*
3d ed. 1959 (*Guide* EA134).
"The Fourth Edition introduces the newly specialized terminologies of nuclear science and engineering, computer science and data processing, solid state physics, molecular biology, genetics, automation, soil and environmental sciences, electronics, etc.... For the sake of expediency ... the new terms have again been ... incorporated into the Addendum."—*Pref.* Q123.D42

Dorian, Angelo Francis. Dictionary of science and technology. English-German. 2d rev. ed. N.Y. & Amsterdam, Elsevier, 1978, 1401p. $81.75. **EA23**

Added title page: *Handwörterbuch der Naturwissenschaft und Technik. Englisch-Deutsch.*
1st ed. 1967 (*Guide* EA137).
"A large number of terms which could rightly be regarded as ballast has been eliminated and about 16,000 new lemmata inserted, mainly relating to those branches of science and technology which are being constantly developed in our times."—*Pref.* Q123.D67

Russian

Chernukhin, Adol'f Efimovich. English-Russian polytechnical dictionary. 3d ed. N.Y., Pergamon, [1976]. 647p. $50. **EA24**

Added title page: *Russko-angliiski tekhnicheskii slovar'.*
About 80,000 terms. T10.C45

TABLES

Landolt, Hans Heinrich. Landolt-Börnstein Zahlenwerte und Funktionen aus Naturwissenschaften und Technik. Neue Serie. Gesamtherausgabe: K. H. Hellwege. N.Y. & Berlin, Springer, 1974–78. Gruppe 4 (in various pts.). (In progress) v.1, pt.a, $215.60, pt.b, $120; v.2, $255.20; v.3, $140.80. **EA25**

Previous *Gruppe,* 1961–74; *see Guide* EA169.
Contents: Gruppe IV, Makroskopische und technische Eigenschaften der Materie. Macroscopic and technical properties of matter. QC61.L332

DIRECTORIES

Scientific research in British universities and colleges. 1951/52–1974/75. London, Stat. Off., 1952–75. Annual. **EA26**

For annotation *see Guide* EA182.

Ceased publication with the volumes covering 1974/75. To be superseded by *Research in British universities, polytechnics and colleges,* a publication of the Lending Division, British Library, Boston Spa, England. Announced for late 1978 publication, the new series will also be in three sections: v.1, Physical sciences (due Dec. 1978; £15); v.2, Biological sciences (due mid-1979; £10); v.3, Social sciences (due late 1979; £10).

Swannack-Nunn, Susan. Directory of scientific research institutes in the People's Republic of China. Wash., Nat. Council for U.S.-China Trade, 1977–78. 3v. $150. **EA27**

Contents: v.1, Agriculture, fisheries, forestry; v.2, Chemicals, construction; v.3 (in 2 pts.), Electrical and electronics; energy; light industry; machinery, including metals and mining; transportation.

Contains introductory material on the organization and state of scientific research in the People's Republic of China, followed by listings of research organizations by subject area. Includes institutional names both in English and in Chinese characters, address, organizational structure, journals in which the institution has recently published, areas of research activity, staff when known; sometimes includes abstracts of recent publications. "The institutions in the directory do not represent a definitive listing. . . . We are limited to institutions mentioned in PRC publications and those visited by foreign delegations. . . . Universities and social science institutions are not included."—[*Note*] Q180.C5S92

Who is publishing in science. 1971– . Philadelphia, Inst. for Scientific Information, 1971– . Annual. (1979: $200) **EA28**

Supersedes *International directory of research & development scientists* (1967–69).

Provides affiliation and addresses for first authors of publications included in *Current contents, Science citation index,* and *Social sciences citation index.* In three sections: Author, Organization, Geographic. Q145.W46

SOCIETIES AND CONGRESSES

Directories

World guide to scientific associations and learned societies. 2d ed. N.Y., Bowker; München, Verlag Dokumentation, 1978. 510p. $49.50. **EA29**

For full information *see Suppl.* CA36.

Publications

Bibliographic guide to conference publications, 1975– . Boston, G. K. Hall, 1976– . Annual. **EA30**

For full information *see Suppl.* CK88.

British Library. Lending Division. BLL conference index, 1964–1973. Boston Spa, [Eng.], British Library, Lending Division, 1974. 1220p. £10. **EA31**

"Cumulated publication containing details of all conferences . . . listed, up to the end of 1973 in the *Index of conference proceedings received by NLL* [National Lending Library], Numbers 1–75 inclusive."—*Pref.* Coverage from inception tried to be comprehensive for subject fields of science and technology, then extended to the social sciences in 1966. Contains 46,500 conferences cross-indexed under 27,500 keyword headings. Entries are arranged in four columns: (1) date of conference; (2) title in language of document and sponsoring organization, truncated to fit one line; (3) place of conference; (4) location within BLLD. In 1973 coverage was extended to all subject fields; for annual cumulation (no.69–) *see Suppl.* EA32. Z7403.B8

——— Index of conference proceedings received. Boston Spa, [Eng.], British Library, Lending Division, 1973– . no.69– . Annual. **EA32**

Continues a publication started in 1965 with same title and issued by the National Lending Library. Coverage from 1973 forward "includes all subject fields."—*Pref.* Each entry consists of the title (in the language of the document, with English preferred when multilingual), sponsoring organization, date and place of conference, and location within BLLD. Entries are arranged under subject keywords. For cumulation of previous years see *BLL conference index, 1964–1973* (*Suppl.* EA31). Z7403.B768

Cambridge. University. Library. Union catalogue of scientific libraries in the University of Cambridge; scientific conference proceedings 1644–1974. London, Mansell, 1975. 2v. 1221p. £27.50. **EA33**

"Compiled at the Scientific Periodicals Library, University of Cambridge."—*t.p.*

A computer-produced catalog of "about 25,000 entries for approximately 6,000 conferences and symposia" (*Pref.*) of the period 1644–1972. A name and keyword catalog with entries for each conference under several headings—official name of conference, title of published proceedings, corporate bodies involved, and venues. Z7409.C35

Conference papers index. Louisville, Ky., Data Courier, 1978– . v.6– . Monthly, with cumulated annual index available separately. $245 per yr.; annual index $140. **EA34**

Continues *Current programs,* v.1–5, 1973–77, and assumes its numbering. Frequency of indexing varies.

Monthly issues have programs of scientific and technological conferences grouped by subject. Information includes the full title of the meeting, inclusive dates, location, names of sponsoring organizations, ordering information for publications, and a list of papers presented. This list includes the name and mailing address for the first author, complete title of paper, and any order number assigned to the paper in the printed program. Since *Conference papers index* is derived from the final program of the meeting rather than from subsequently published conference proceedings, it is timelier than other conference indexes; on the other hand, order information for the published proceedings may not be available. Beginning with v.7 (1979) each monthly issue includes both author and keyword indexes which cumulate into the separate annual index volume.

Index to scientific and technical proceedings. Philadelphia, Inst. for Scientific Information, Jan., 1978– , v.1– . Monthly with semiannual cumulations. $500 per yr. **EA35**

Indexes published conference proceedings at the individual paper level with Permuterm indexing of keywords from titles of papers, an author/editor index, and an index of authors' corporate affiliation. Also indexes conferences by category (i.e., subject), sponsor, and meeting location, but does not index by date of conference. Publishes full information about published proceedings including title, date, and place held, sponsor, editors, how published, price, and order information. Includes tables of contents of papers presented, giving title of paper, authors' names and corporate affiliation, and page number. Does not attempt to give comprehensive coverage of published proceedings; it attempts to select the more important proceedings. The publisher estimates that the 3,000 proceedings covered in 1978 are about half of the proceedings published that year and make up about 75%–90% of the significant conference literature.

LABORATORIES

Industrial research laboratories of the United States. 15th ed. Ed. by Jaques Cattell Pr. N.Y., Bowker, 1977. 828p. $65. **EA36**

14th ed. 1972; for previous editions and annotation *see Guide* EA204.

"This edition contains information on 10,028 R&D facilities belonging to 6947 organizations engaged in fundamental and applied research, including development of products and processes."—*Pref.* T176.N37

HISTORY OF SCIENCE

Isis cumulative bibliography; a bibliography of the history of science formed from Isis critical bibliographies 1–90, 1913–65. Ed. by Magda Whitrow. v.3, Subjects. [London], Mansell, 1976. 678p. $56. **EA37**

For v.1–2 *see Guide* EA214.

Includes "all those entries [from the *Isis critical bibliographies* no.1–90] that deal with the history of science or of individual sciences without reference to a particular period or civilization, those that refer to more than two centuries during the modern period, and those that deal with two or more civilizations but are not restricted to a particular period in history."—*Introd.* Classed arrangement with an alphabetical index to the subject classmarks. Z7405.H6I2

BIOGRAPHY

American men and women of science. 13th ed. Ed. by Jaques Cattell Pr. N.Y., Bowker, 1976. 7v. $300. **EA38**

12th ed. 1971–73 (*Guide* EA222).

Although the subtitle is no longer *Physical and biological sciences,* the coverage and criteria for inclusion are the same as for preceding editions. The seven volumes, containing almost 110,000 biographies, were completed in ten months and released simultaneously "a radical, and beneficial departure from the production of the 12th edition. . . ."—*Pref.*

"A former biographee whose current status could not be verified is given a reference to the 12th edition if the probability exists of a continued activity in science. References are also given to scientists who have died since publication of the last edition. Omitted are the names of those previously listed as retired and those who have entered fields or activities not covered by the scope of the directory." v.7 is entitled "Discipline and geographic indexes."

For the "Social and behavioral sciences" volume *see Suppl.* CA42. Q141.A47

Dictionary of scientific biography. Charles Coulston Gillispie, ed. in chief. N.Y., Scribner's, [1976]. v.14. $40. **EA39**

Contents: v.14, Verrill–Zwelfer. Main set complete in 14v.; for v.1–13 and annotation *see Guide* EA225. Q141.D5

——— Supplement I. N.Y., Scribner's, [1978]. 818p. il. $55. **EA40**

Numbered as v.15 of *Dictionary of scientific biography.*

In two parts: the first part consists of biographical articles on scientists not included in the main work, either because they only recently died, or because the article was planned for the *Dictionary* but not included in the main work (in which case there is a reference to the Supplement under the scientist's name in the main work) or simply because the scientist was previously overlooked. The second part offers topical essays "on the scientific outlook and accomplishments of certain ancient civilizations."—*Pref.* Q141.D5

Poggendorff, Johann Christian. Biographisch-literarisches Handwörterbuch der exakten Naturwissenschaften, unter Mitwirkung der Akademien der Wissenschaften zu Berlin, Göttingen, Heidelberg, München und Wien, hrsg. von der Sächischen Akademie der Wissenschaften zu Leipzig. Red. von Rudolph Zaunick und Hans Salié. Berlin, Akademie-Verlag, 1974–78. v.7b, T.5–6$^{1-2}$. (In progress) **EA41**

For previously published parts and annotation *see Guide* EA231. Contents: v.7b, 1932 bis 1962, T.5–6, Lfg.1–2, L–Othmer.

Who was who in American history—science and technology. Chicago, Marquis, [1976]. 688p. $47.50. **EA42**

"A component of *Who's who in American history.*"—*t.p.*

A compilation of biographical information for "some 90,000 deceased American notables within the covers of the [*Who was who in America*] volumes . . . from the early days of the colonies to mid-1973."—*Pref.* Q141.W43

Who's who in engineering. 3d ed. N.Y., Engineers Joint Council, [1977]. 605p. **EA43**

Ed. by Jean Gregory.

2d ed. 1973 had title: *Engineers of distinction* (*Guide* EA225a).

Gives biographical data on engineers in the United States who have met stated criteria for distinction. Also has a section on American and Canadian engineering societies. Includes a geographic index and an index to specialization. TA139.E53

Who's who in science in Europe. 3d ed. Guernsey, C.I., Hodgson, 1978. 4v. $350. **EA44**

For 2d ed. (1972) and annotation *see Guide* EA239. Q141.W5

Who's who of British engineers, 1974/75. [4th ed.] London, Eurobooks; Athens, Ohio, Ohio Univ. Pr., 1974. 526p. $10. **EA45**

2d ed. 1968 (*Guide* EA241).

An addenda section (pp.467–71) provides information from questionnaires received too late for inclusion in the main alphabet. The sections on professional institutions and publications have been updated and expanded.

PATENTS

Maynard, John T. Understanding chemical patents: a guide for the inventor. Wash., Amer. Chemical Soc., 1978. 146p. $12.50. **EA46**

"This is in no sense a book about patent law or about patent licensing and management. . . . This book tries to answer immediate practical questions of chemists and engineers about how to read and to understand patents, how to use patents as a source of information, how to recognize that an invention has been made, how to work with attorneys or agents in seeking patent protection for inventions, how to keep adequate notebook records, how to watch for infringement of patents, and so on."—*Pref.* QD39.2.M38

STANDARDS

Chumas, Sophie J., ed. Directory of United States standardization activities. Wash., Nat. Bureau of Standards, 1975. 223p. (Nat. Bureau of Standards. Special publ. 417) $6.75. **EA47**

Supersedes *Miscellaneous publication* 288 (dated 1967), which superseded *Miscellaneous publication* 230, *Standardization activities in the United States* (*Guide* EA256).

——— Index of international standards. Wash., Nat. Bureau of Standards, 1974. 206p. (Nat. Bureau of Standards. Special publ. 390) $5.60. **EA48**

A KWIC index to over 2,700 titles of the International Organization for Standardization, the International Electrotechnical Commission, the International Commission on Rules for the Approval of Electrical Equipment, the International Special Committee on Radio Interference, and the International Organization of Legal Metrology.

U.S. National Bureau of Standards. Publications of the National Bureau of Standards, catalog; a compilation of abstracts and key word and author indexes. 1966–67; 1968–69; 1970– . Wash., Govt. Prt. Off., 1969– . Annual. (National Bureau of Standards. Special publ. 305, and suppls.) **EA49**

Betty L. Hurdle, ed.

Supplements NBS Circular 460, *Publications of the Bureau of Standards complete from the establishment of the Bureau (1901) to June 30, 1947*, and its supplements: 1947–57; 1957–60; 1960–66 (*Guide* EA259).

FORMULAS AND RECIPES

Chemical formulary. Cumulative index for v.1–15. N.Y., Chemical Publ. Co., 1972. 396p. $26.50. **EA50**

Supersedes *Cumulative index for v.1–10*, 1958, *see Guide* EA260.

E B

Astronomy

GENERAL WORKS

Guides

Seal, Robert A. A guide to the literature of astronomy. Littleton, Colo., Libraries Unlimited, 1977. 306p. $25. **EB1**

An annotated list of current books and periodicals on astronomy and closely related fields. Indexed. Z5151.S4

Bibliography

Collins, Mike. Astronomical catalogues 1951–75. [Old Working, Eng.], Inst. of Electrical Engineers, [1977]. 325p. (INSPEC bibliography series no.2) £55. **EB2**

"Presents a collection of nearly 2500 catalogues . . . covering . . . 1951 to 1975 inclusive. Some catalogues published in 1976 and 1977 are also included. The bibliography contains lists of celestial objects, phenomena and equipment as well as books and slides. Each entry contains full bibliographic details and most have an abstract and a summary. . . ."—*Abstract.* Author, corporate author, and designation indexes. Z5154.S8C64

Zinner, Ernst. Geschichte und Bibliographie der astronomischen Literatur in Deutschland zur Zeit der Renaissance. Stuttgart, Anton Hiersemann, 1964. 480p. **EB3**

1st ed. 1941 (*Guide* EB9).

An unaltered reprint of the 1941 ed., together with a new supplement.

Dictionaries and encyclopedias

The Cambridge encyclopedia of astronomy. Ed.-in-chief, Simon Mitton. N.Y., Crown, 1977. 481p. il. $35. **EB4**

Prepared by astronomers, the encyclopedia presents a broad-based survey of astronomy with emphasis on firmly established new results. The 23 major topics, which have "been gathered into cohesive themes in order to present a more accurate and understandable guide to the new Universe" (*Introd.*), are intended for amateur and professional. The index is specific and extensive with references to the main text, photographs, and diagrams. A 14-page "Star atlas" of stars visible to the naked eye in the Northern and Southern hemispheres, and "An outline of physics" are provided in the appendixes. QB43.2.C35

Hopkins, Jeanne. Glossary of astronomy and astrophysics. Chicago, Univ. of Chicago Pr., [1976]. 169p. $10.95. **EB5**

"This volume is published under the auspices of *Astrophysical journal.*"—*verso of t.p.*

Offers brief definitions of the most commonly used terms in astronomy and astrophysics. QB14.H69

Weigert, Alfred and **Zimmermann, Helmut.** Concise encyclopedia of astronomy. 2d English ed. London, Adam Hilger; dist. by Crane, Russak, N.Y., [1976]. 532p. il. maps. $19.75. **EB6**

Translation of *ABC der Astronomie*, 3d ed. 1971, rev. by H. Zimmermann. Tr. by J. Home Dickson.

1st English ed. (1967) had title: *ABC of astronomy*.

A publication in dictionary format combining concise definitions with more extended articles, intended for a general audience. Up-to-date and comprehensive. QB14.W4513

Handbooks

Allen, Clabon Walter. Astrophysical quantities. 3d ed. London, Athlone Pr.; Atlantic Highlands, N.J., Humanities Pr., 1973. 310p. $20.25. **EB7**

1st ed. 1955; 2d ed. 1963.

"The intention of this book is to present the essential information of astrophysics in a form that can be readily used. . . . The information is as up to date as possible."—*Pref.* "The book should contain all experimental and theoretical values, constants, and conversion factors that are fundamental to astrophysical arguments."—*Introd.* QB461.A55

Robinson, J. Hedley. Astronomy data book. N.Y., Wiley, [1972]. 271p. $10.95. **EB8**

"This book is intended as a reference tool for the student and amateur astronomer and for those interested in the earth sciences. . . . It is intended that the observer shall use this book in conjunction with a Star Atlas."—*Introd.* Brings together basic data and information, and includes a 15-page glossary of astronomical terms. QB64.R58

Roth, Günther Dietmar, ed. Astronomy; a handbook. Tr. and rev. by Arthur Beer. N.Y. & Berlin, Springer, 1975. 567p. il. $24.80. **EB9**

Based on 2d ed. of *Handbuch für Sternfreunde*, 1967.

Consists of 21 signed chapters on astronomical topics, including chapters on astronomical literature and nomenclature, and on astronomical instruments. Indexed; contains bibliographies. QB64.R59

Directories

Kirby-Smith, H. T. U.S. observatories: directory and travel guide. N.Y., Van Nostrand Reinhold, [1976]. 173p. il. $11.95. **EB10**

A compilation of information about United States observatories and some important museums and planetariums. Gives descriptions of facilities, equipment, and the kind of work done, as well as histories and information on the availability of public tours. Indexed. QB81.K57

E C

Biological Sciences

GENERAL WORKS

Bibliography

Smit, Pieter. History of the life sciences; an annotated bibliography. N.Y., Hafner Pr., [1974]. 1074p. $55. **EC1**

Contents: Chap. I, General references and tools; Chap. II, Historiography of the life and medical sciences; Selected list of biographies, bibliographies, etc., of famous biologists, medical men, etc., including some modern reissues of their publications; Index of personal names.

" . . . originated as a plan to produce an extension of the parts of Sarton's 'Guide to the History of Science' [*Guide* EA216] that deal with the life sciences."—*Introd.* More than 4,000 entries with full bibliographical information and short summary review (about 90 words). Z5320.S55

Dictionaries

Abercrombie, Michael, Hickman, C. J. and **Johnson, M. L.** Penguin dictionary of biology. [New ed.] London, Allen Lane; N.Y., Viking Pr., [1977]. 311p. $12.50. **EC2**

1966 ed. entitled: *Dictionary of biology* (*Guide* EC14).

"This hardback edition, based on sixth paperback edition, 1977" —*verso of t.p.* QH203.A2

Cowan, Samuel Tertius. A dictionary of microbial taxonomy. N.Y., Cambridge Univ. Pr., [1978]. 285p. $28.50. **EC3**

Ed. by L. R. Hill.

Revision and expansion, with widened scope, of *A dictionary of microbial taxonomic usage*, 1968 (*Guide* EC15).

"It is not intended only, or even mainly, for taxonomists . . . but it is written for those whose work brings them to taxonomy, often reluctantly."—*Pref.* QR9.C66

A dictionary of life sciences. Ed. by Elizabeth A. Martin. N.Y., Pica; distr. by Universe Books, 1977 [c.1976]. 374p. $16.50. **EC4**

A companion to *A dictionary of earth sciences* (*Suppl.* EE1) and *A dictionary of physical sciences* (*Suppl.* EA17). A handy, easy-to-use, concise dictionary for the life sciences. QH302.5.D52

Herbert, W. J. and **Wilkinson, P. C.,** eds. A dictionary of immunology. 2d ed. Oxford, Blackwell Scientific; distr. by J. B. Lippincott, Philadelphia, 1977. 197p. il. $9.75 pa. **EC5**

"Compiled by members of [*sic*] staff of the Department of Bacteriology and Immunology, Department of Pathology, and Institute of Virology, University of Glasgow."—*t.p.*

1st ed. 1971.

The purpose is to provide a glossary for use in undergraduate teaching and "to include a range of terms wide enough to satisfy the needs of any biologist, clinician or biochemist who requires easy reference to current immunological usage . . . the definitions given are not intended to reflect our personal views as to how the terms *should* be used but, rather, to tell the reader how they *have been* used in the literature."—*Pref.* QR180.4.H47

Jeffrey, Charles. Biological nomenclature. 2d ed. N.Y., Crane, Russak, [1977]. 72p. $11.50. **EC6**

1st ed. 1973.

"The purpose of this handbook is to provide a practical guide to the use of the nomenclatural parts of taxonomic literature, to promote understanding of the problems, principles and practice of biological nomenclature and to act as an introduction to the Codes of Nomenclature themselves."—*Pref.* QH83.J43

Steen, Edwin B. Dictionary of biology. N.Y., Barnes & Noble, [1971]. 630p. $12.50. **EC7**

Provides brief definitions of about 12,000 terms. "Taxonomic names, except for some of the major groups, are not included as entries with definitions; however, under their common names, representatives of the principal groups are listed and the groups are characterized."—*Pref.* QH13.S74

Handbooks

Altman, Philip L. and **Katz, Dorothy Dittmer,** eds. Cell biology. Bethesda, Md., Federation of Amer. Societies for Experimental Biology, [1976]. 454p. (Biological handbooks, n.s., v.1) $45. **EC8**

A detailed tabulation of data on the cell, with emphasis on vertebrate cells. 102 tables are arranged in seven sections: (1) General cell characteristics; (2) Cell environment; (3) Cell periphery; (4) Mitochondria: (5) Endoplasmic reticulum, microsomes, ribosomes, and Golgi; (6) Lysosomes, peroxisomes, granules, and microbodies; (7) Nuclei. Includes appendixes of animal and plant names. QH581.2.C34

——— and **Dittmer, Dorothy S.,** eds. Respiration and circulation. Bethesda, Md., Federation of Amer. Societies for Experimental Biology, [1971]. 930p. (Biological handbooks) $30. **EC9**

Constitutes a complete revision and combination of *Handbook of respiration* (1958) and *Handbook of circulation* (1959).

A collection of authoritative data, quantitative and descriptive, on respiration and circulation. For the most part concerned with man and other vertebrates but includes sections on invertebrates and on plants. QP101.R47

CRC handbook of microbiology. 2d ed. Cleveland, CRC Pr., 1977– . v.1– . (In progress) (v.1: $69.95) **EC10**

1st ed. 1973.

Contents: v.1, Bacteria, ed. by Allen I. Laskin and Hubert A. Lechevalier.

Provides up-to-date data on the properties of microorganisms, their composition, products, and activities. v.1 (covering general information, paleomicrobiology, cytology, the bacteria) features information on organismic microbiology and presents data of taxonomic value. Taxonomic and topical indexes.

v.2, announced for late 1978 publication, will cover fungi, algae, and protozoa; v.3, projected for 1979, will deal with amino acids and protein; v.4, also planned for 1979, will be devoted to carbohydrates, lipids and minerals. QR6.C2

Handbook of the biology of aging. Eds., Caleb E. Finch and Leonard Hayflick; with the assistance of associate eds. Harold Brody [and others]. N.Y., Van Nostrand Reinhold, 1977–. v.1– . il. (In progress) (v.1: $32.50) **EC11**

First of a 3-volume set. Contains 27 detailed chapters on the biological aspects of aging written by recognized experts in the field.

Directories

American Institute of Biological Sciences. AIBS directory of bioscience departments and faculties in the United States and Canada. 2d ed., comp. by Peter Gray. Stroudsburg, Pa., Dowden, Hutchinson & Ross; distr. by Halsted Pr., N.Y., [1975]. 660p. $29. **EC12**

1st ed. (1967) had title: *Directory of bioscience departments in the United States and Canada* (*Guide* EC30).

Revised and expanded to include more than 2,400 individuals and some 2,500 institutions. QH319.A1A44

Style manuals

Council of Biology Editors. Style Manual Committee. Council of Biology Editors style manual; a guide for authors, editors, and publishers in the biological sciences. 4th ed. Arlington, Va., Council of Biology Editors, Inc. (available from Amer. Inst. of Biological Sciences), [1978]. 265p. il. $12. **EC13**

3d ed. (1972) entitled *CBE style manual (Guide* EC32).

"The sequence of chapters has been changed; most chapters have been thoroughly rewritten."—*Pref.* Z250.6.B5C65

ECOLOGY

Burke, John Gordon and **Reddig, Jill Swanson.** Guide to ecology information and organizations. N.Y., Wilson, 1976. 292p. $12.50. **EC14**

Intended primarily for public libraries and their patrons. Includes "both print and nonprint materials, as well as names of persons who are willing to share their expertise."—*Introd.*

In various sections: Citizen action guides, Indexes, Reference books, Histories, Monographs, Government publications, Nonprint media, Periodicals, Organizations, Government officials. Includes a directory of publishers and distributors, and a detailed index. Z5861.B87

Grzimek's Encyclopedia of ecology. Ed.-in-chief, Bernhard Grzimek. English ed. N.Y., Van Nostrand Reinhold, [1976]. 705p. il. $39.50. **EC15**

Ed. by Bernhard Grzimek, Joachim Illies, Wolfgang Klausewitz.

Translation of the 1973 German ed.

". . . a supplement to the thirteen-volume Grzimek's Animal Life Encyclopedia [*Guide* EC148]."—*Foreword.*

Over 40 experts have made contributions to the 33 essays in this one-volume encyclopedia. In pt. 1, "The environment of animals," the 22 essays are arranged under four headings: (1) Adaptations to the abiotic environment; (2) Adaptations to the biotic environment; (3) Habitats and their fauna; (4) Man as a factor in the environment of animals. Pt. 2 entitled "The environment of man." Index. QL45.G7913 Suppl.

NATURAL HISTORY

Bibliography

American Museum of Natural History, New York. Library. Research catalog of the Library of the American Museum of Natural History; authors. Boston, G. K. Hall, 1977. 13v. $1095. **EC16**

"Provides access by personal, corporate, and joint authors, compilers, editors, and illustrators of note, as well as biographical and critical materials. . . . Of particular value are author entries for journal articles and chapters in books."—*Pref.* Z7409.A43

Indexes

Thompson, John W., comp. Index to illustrations of the natural world. Nedra Slauson, ed. Syracuse, N.Y., Gaylord Professional Publ., 1977. 265p. $29.95. **EC17**

Subtitle: Where to find pictures of the living things of North America.

Approximately 6,200 entries for plants, birds, and animals. For each item is listed the common name, scientific name, and citations to three to ten illustrations. The pictures cited are found in a total of 178 books which "have been published since 1960, but some classic works published earlier have been included. . . . The availability of the books in most medium-size and large libraries was an important criterion in selection."—*Introd.* Includes a 77-page index from the scientific name to the common name. Z7998.N67T45

Encyclopedias

Grzimek's Encyclopedia of evolution. Ed.-in-chief, Bernhard Grzimek. English ed. N.Y., Van Nostrand Reinhold,[1976]. 560p. il. $39.50. **EC18**

Ed. by Gerhard Heberer and Herbert Wendt.

Translation of the 1972 German ed.

Over 200 contributors from all over the world have prepared the 23 essays in this one-volume encyclopedia. The many general aspects of evolutionary theory, phylogeny, genetics effect, paleontology, paleobotany, paleogeology, and the evolution of man are covered, as well as such subjects as the origin of life, early history of the earth, the path to warm-bloodedness, origin of mammals, the conquest of the air, etc. Includes supplementary readings and index. QE711.2.G79

Handbooks

Peterson, Roger Tory. The Peterson field guide series. Boston, Houghton Mifflin, 1947– . **EC19**

Designed as basic guides for the nature student, beginner, or expert, each volume by a specialist in the subject.

The series includes *A field guide to*: birds; Western birds; shells of the Atlantic and Gulf coasts and the West Indies; butterflies; mammals; Pacific coast shells (including shells of Hawaii and the Gulf of California); rocks and minerals; birds of Britain and Europe; animal tracks; ferns and their related families of Northeastern and Central North America; trees and shrubs; reptiles and amphibians of Eastern and Central North America; birds of Texas and adjacent states; Rocky Mountain wildflowers; stars and planets; Western reptiles and amphibians; wildflowers of Northeastern and North-central North America; mammals of Britain and Europe; insects of America north of Mexico; Mexican birds; birds' nests (found east of Mississippi River); Pacific states wildflowers; edible wild plants of Eastern and Central North America.

Directories

The naturalists' directory international. 42d ed. South Orange, N.J., PCL Publications, 1975. 259p. **EC20**

41st ed. 1972; *see Guide* EC43.

A name index and a discipline/specialty index have been added.

BOTANY

General works

Bibliography

Beale, Helen Purdy. Bibliography of plant viruses and index to research. N.Y., Columbia Univ. Pr., 1976. 1495p. $75. **EC21**

This international bibliography of plant virus articles covers a span of 78 years, from 1892 to 1970. Over 29,000 entries arranged alphabetically by author. The virus diseases included are chiefly those of higher plants. Extensive subject indexes. Z5185.V5B42

Nissen, Claus. Die botanische Buchillustration, ihre Geschichte und Bibliographie. 2. Aufl. Stuttgart, A. Hiersemann, 1966. 3v. in 1. DM440. **EC22**

1st ed. in 2v., 1951–52 (*Guide* EC58).

Consists of a reproduction of the two volumes of the 1st ed. together with a 94p. supplement as v.3. Z5351.N49

Stafleu, Frans Anthonie and **Cowan, Richard S.** Taxonomic literature. 2d ed. Utrecht, Bohn, Scheltema & Holkema, 1976– . v.1– . (In progress) (Regnum vegetabile, v.94) (v.1: $100) **EC23**

Subtitle: A selective guide to botanical publications and collections with dates, commentaries and types.

Previous ed. 1967 (*Guide* EC61).

Contents: v.1, A–G. QK96.R4

Indexes

Torrey Botanical Club. Index to American botanical literature; first supplement. 1967–76. Boston, G. K. Hall, 1977. 740p. $100. **EC24**

A supplement to the *Index* publ. in 4v., 1969 (*Guide* EC68). Z5358.A4T6

Dictionaries

International Botanical Congress, 11th, Seattle, 1969. International code of botanical nomenclature, adopted by the eleventh International Botanical Congress, Seattle, August 1969. Prep. and ed. by F. A. Stafleu, chairman [and others]. Utrecht, Oosthoek's Uitgeversmaatschappij N.V. (available from Bohn, Scheltema & Holkema), 1972; 426p. (Regnum vegetabile, v. 82) $31. **EC25**

Added title pages in French and German; text published in the three languages.

This code supersedes the 1961 ed. (*Guide* EC77). QK96.R4

Directories

Henderson, D. M. and **Prentice, H.T.** International directory of botanical gardens. 3d ed. Utrecht, Bohn, Scheltema & Holkema, 1977. 270p. (Regnum vegetabile, v.95) $17. **EC26**

2d ed. 1969 (*Guide* EC89).

Index herbariorum: a guide to the location and contents of the world's herbaria. Utrecht, Bohn, Scheltema & Holkema, 1976. pt.2 (4). (Regnum vegetabile, v.93) $16. **EC27**

For previously published parts *see Guide* EC92.

Contents: pt.2(4), Collectors, M, by I. H. Vegter. QK96.R4

Handbooks

Hortus third; a concise dictionary of plants cultivated in the United States and Canada. N.Y., Macmillan, [1976]. 1290p. il. $99.50. **EC28**

"Initially compiled by Liberty Hyde Bailey and Ethel Zoe Bailey. Revised and expanded by the Staff of the Liberty Hyde Bailey Hortorium."—*t.p.*

1941 ed. had title: *Hortus second* (*Guide* EL39).

"Provides a contemporary assessment of the kinds and the names of plants cultivated in the continental United States and Canada, Puerto Rico, and Hawaii. Initially planned as a simple revision of *Hortus second, Hortus third* evolved ... into an essentially new work.... Innovations included are: author or authors for each botanical name, illustrations of representative members of most families, a separate glossary of botanical terms, an index to common names, and a list of authors cited."—*Pref.* SB45.H67

Biography

Desmond, Ray. Dictionary of British and Irish botanists and horticulturists: including plant collectors and botanical artists. London, Taylor & Francis, 1977. 747p. $87.50. **EC29**

2d ed. (1931) had title: *A biographical index of deceased British and Irish botanists* (*Guide* EC96).

Extensive revision and expansion. Although limited to deceased botanists, the dictionary's coverage has quadrupled. Z5358.G7B7

Flora

Graf, Alfred Byrd. Tropica: color cyclopedia of exotic plants and trees from the tropics and subtropics for warm-region horticulture—in cool climate the sheltered indoors. East Rutherford, N.J., Roehrs Co., [1978]. 1120p. $115. **EC30**

Contents: The tropics and subtropics; Warm area horticulture; Plants indoors; Colorama of plants and trees [main section]; Plant descriptions.

Includes 7,000 photographs representing 1,630 genera. "Most species in this book, except such as Fruit trees, Conifers, Ferns, and Carnivorous plants, are classified within their natural systemic families."—*Prelude.* Includes bibliography and literature references. Common names index of exotic plants; generic botanical index. SB407.G73

Newcomb, Lawrence. Newcomb's Wildflower guide. Boston & Toronto, Little, Brown, [1977]. 490p. il. $6.95. **EC31**

Il. by Gordon Morrison.

"An ingenious new key system for quick, positive field identification of the wildflowers, flowering shrubs and vines of Northeastern and North-central North America."—*t.p.* "This guide provides a new and eminently workable key system, which is based on the most easily seen features that make each species unique."—*Introd.* Identification is based on examining a specimen for flower type, plant type, and leaf type and referring to the locator key with the information derived. The locator key refers the user to the page on which the wildflower is identified. QK118.N38

Rickett, Harold William. Wild flowers of the United States. Complete index for the six volumes. N.Y., McGraw-Hill, [1975]. 152p. $29.50. **EC32**

For v.1–6 and annotation *see Guide* EC107.

Index comp. by Lee Pennington from the separate indexes in the six individual volumes.

Lists artists, photographers, common and botanical names. The latter gives families, genera, and species. QK115.R5

Tutin, Thomas Gaskell [and others], eds. Flora Europaea. Cambridge, University Pr., 1976. v.4. (In progress) $65. **EC33**

For v.1–3 (1964–72) *see Guide* EC108.

Contents: v.4, Plantaginaceae to compositae (and rubiaceae); v.5, Alismataceae to orchidaceae, in press 1978. QK281.T8

Fungi

Ainsworth, Geoffrey Clough, ed. The fungi; an advanced treatise. N.Y., Academic Pr., 1965–73. 4v. il. $210. **EC34**

Supersedes Wolf and Wolf *The fungi,* 1947 (*Guide* EC116).

Contents: v.1, The fungal cell; v.2, The fungal organism; v.3, The fungal population; v.4 (in 2 pts.), A taxonomic review with keys.

"The object of this work is . . . to summarize what is known about fungi as fungi. . . . The work, as the subtitle implies, is also intended as a reference book."—*Pref.* QK603.A33

Smith, Alexander Hanchett. A field guide to western mushrooms. Ann Arbor, Univ. of Michigan Pr., [1975]. 280p. il. $16.50. **EC35**

Seeks to provide information on 201 species of western mushrooms. "Seventy of the species included here were known only from the western area or were described from it originally but have since been found elsewhere. Over twenty-five poisonous or very undesirable species for the table from the areas are illustrated and described. Many species are in the 'edible' column meaning that as far as it is known they are not poisonous. About fifteen of these are considered to be of 'gourmet' calibre. Finally there is the residuum of species of which the edibility is still apparently unrecorded. These have for the most part been listed as 'not recommended'."—*Introd.* Glossary; bibliography; index. QK617.S55

ZOOLOGY

General works

Bibliography

Harvard University. Museum of Comparative Zoology. Library. Catalogue. First supplement. Boston, G. K. Hall, 1976. 770p. $120. **EC36**

Main work in 8v., publ. 1968 (*Guide* EC130).

"The First supplement . . . includes new titles added to the Library since 1966 as well as cataloging information for many older titles revised according to the Anglo-American cataloging rules."—*Pref.* Z7999.H32

Nissen, Claus. Die zoologische Buchillustration, ihre Bibliographie und Geschichte. Stuttgart, A. Hiersemann, 1966– . v.1– . (In progress) **EC37**

Contents: v.1, Bibliographie; v.2, Geschichte der zoologischen Buchillustration.

Issued serially: 15 pts. issued through 1978, to be complete in 16. v.1 is a bibliography of illustrated works listed alphabetically by first author and by illustrator, with indexes to subject, geographic area, animal, and author (including coauthors and editors). v.2 is a history of zoological illustration and is indexed by author, illustrator, geographic area, subject and animal; it also includes a supplement to v.1 which has a closing date of Sept. 1975. Z7991.N5

Handbooks

International zoo yearbook. 1959– . Ed. by P. J. S. Olney. London, Zoological Soc., 1959– . v.1– . Annual. (v.18, 1978: £15) **EC38**

Consists of two sections: (1) signed articles (some with references) pertaining to the management of zoos and zoo animals; and (2) reference section, which includes: Zoos and aquaria of the world; New buildings and exhibits; Species . . . bred in captivity during 1976 and multiple generation births; Census of rare animals in captivity 1977; Studbooks and world registers for rare species of wild animals in captivity. Author and subject indexes. QL76.A1I5

Melby, Edward C. and **Altman, Norman H.** CRC handbook of laboratory animal sciences. Cleveland, CRC Pr., 1974–76. 3v. (v.1, $47.95; v.2, $52.95; v.3, $69.95) **EC39**

v.1 deals with legislative regulations pertaining to laboratory animals for the United States and for Canada, and includes general and specific information for the management and control of various types of animals, e.g., fish, dogs. v.2 discusses neoplasias, zoonoses, and diseases of laboratory animals. v.3 covers new and additional information about laboratory animals, such as: nutrition, physiological data, effect of drugs on nervous system, spontaneous viral infections, hematology, immunology, virology. Cumulated index in v.3. QL55.M45

Generic indexes

Nomenclator zoologicus. . . . London, Zoological Soc. of London, 1966–75. v.6–7. **EC40**

For v.1–5 and annotation *see Guide* EC147.

Contents: v.6, 1946–55, ed. by Marcia A. Edwards and A. Tindell Hopwood (£10); v.7, 1956–65, ed. by Marcia A. Edwards and H. Gwynne Vevers (£20).

Encyclopedias

Grzimek, Bernhard, ed. Grzimek's Animal life encyclopedia. N.Y., Van Nostrand Reinhold, [1972–75]. 13v. **EC41**

Publication was completed 1975; for contents note and annotation *see Guide* EC148.

Birds

Cramp, Stanley, ed. Handbook of the birds of Europe, the Middle East, and North Africa: the birds of the western palearctic. N.Y. & Oxford, Oxford Univ. Pr., 1978– . v.1– . il., maps. (v.1, $55) (In progress, to be complete in 7v.) **EC42**

Contents: v.1, Ostrich to ducks.

Based on H. F. Witherby's *Handbook of British birds*, 1938–41, expanded and updated. Authoritative, encyclopedic in scope. Concise entries arranged taxonomically. QL679.H35

Gruson, Edward S. Checklist of the world's birds; a complete list of the species, with names, authorities and areas of distribution. N.Y., Times Books, [1976]. 212p. $10.95. **EC43**

"It is the purpose of this book to provide as complete a listing of the species of birds of the world as possible, to give the scientific name and an English common name for each of the species, to provide a source to which the reader is referred if more information about the species is wanted and to give a gross idea of its range."—*Introd.* QL677.G76

Palmer, Ralph S., ed. Handbook of North American birds. New Haven, Conn., Yale Univ. Pr., [1962]–76. 3v. il., maps. $32.50 per v. **EC44**

"Sponsored by American Ornithologists' Union and New York State Museum and Science Service."—*p.[i].*

Contents: v.1, Loons through flamingos; v.2, Waterfowl (first part); v.3, Waterfowl (concluded).

An encyclopedic treatment. Entries are arranged taxonomically, mainly according to the Wetmore classification; indexed. QL681.P3

Fishes

Wheeler, Alwyne C. Fishes of the world; an illustrated dictionary. N.Y., Macmillan, [1975]. 366p. il. $27.50. **EC45**

"The dictionary entries are arranged in alphabetical order, separate entries being made for families (cross-referenced to genera included), and under the scientific name of the species of fish. . . . Widely used vernacular names mostly in the English language are also given and cross-indexed. The [500 color] plates are arranged in systematic order of families, thus bringing the closest related groups together."—*Introd.* Over 2,000 entries, which include some 700 line drawings. "Common names are fully cross-referred in the dictionary section."—*Contents.* QL614.7.W47

Shells

Abbott, Robert Tucker. American seashells: the marine mollusca of the Atlantic and Pacific coasts of North America. 2d ed. N.Y., Van Nostrand Reinhold, [1974]. 663p. il. $49.50. **EC46**

1st ed. 1954.

For the advanced amateur and professional. Describes in detail about 2,000 species and lists another 4,500. Basically a taxonomic survey of marine species found along the shores and continental shelf of North America. QL411.A19

BIOCHEMISTRY

Barman, Thomas E. Enzyme handbook. Supplement 1. N.Y., Springer, 1974. 517p. $25. **EC47**

For basic volume (1969) *see Guide* EC183.

"In the five years since the appearance of the *Enzyme Handbook* several hundred new enzymes have been described. The *Supplement* includes molecular and kinetic data on about half of these and also on several enzymes omitted from the *Handbook*."—*Pref.* QP601.B26

Commission on Biochemical Nomenclature. Enzyme nomenclature; recommendations (1972) of the Commission on Biochemical Nomenclature on the nomenclature and classification of enzymes together with their units and the symbols of enzyme kinetics. N.Y. & Amsterdam, Elsevier, 1973. 443p. $5.95 pa. **EC48**

Also published as *Comprehensive biochemistry*, v.13, 3d ed.

"This edition is a revision of the Recommendations (1964) of the International Union of Biochemistry. It was prepared by the Commission on Biochemical Nomenclature with the assistance of an Expert Committee and approved by the International Union of Pure and Applied Chemistry and the International Union of Biochemistry."—*t.p.* Gives Enzyme Code (E.C.) number, recommended name, systematic name, other names, reaction catalyzed, and references for 1,770 enzymes. Indexed. QP601.C645

Handbook of biochemistry and molecular biology. Gerald D. Fasman, ed. 3d ed. Cleveland, CRC Pr., [1976–77]. 9v. $529.60. **EC49**

Herbert A. Sober, consulting ed.

2d ed., 1970, had title: *Handbook of biochemistry* (*Guide* EC186).

Contents: Proteins—amino acids, peptides, polypeptides, proteins (3v.); Nucleic acids—purines, pyrimidines, nucleotides, oligonucleotides, tRNA, DNA, RNA (2v.); Lipids, carbohydrates, steroids (1v.); Physical and chemical data, miscellaneous—ion exchange, chromatography, buffers, miscellaneous [e.g. vitamins] (2v.); Cumulative series index. QP514.H34

National Research Council. Committee on Specifications and Criteria for Biochemical Compounds. Specifications and criteria for biochemical compounds. 3d ed. Wash., Nat. Academy of Sciences, 1972. 216p. $21.25. **EC50**

2d ed. 1967 (*Guide* EC188).

"This edition contains criteria and specifications for 521 compounds. The first edition ... [covered] 225 compounds, and the second ... 392 compounds."—*Pref.* QD415.7.N37

—— —— Supplement: biogenic amines and related compounds. Wash., Nat. Academy of Sciences, 1977. 20p. $5.

Stenesh, J. Dictionary of biochemistry. N.Y., Wiley, [1975]. 344p. $22.50. **EC51**

"... contains approximately 12,000 entries drawn from ... textbooks and reference books ... and from the research literature ... ; all the source material consulted has been published since 1962. The recommendations of the Commission on Biological Nomenclature of the International Union of Pure and Applied Chemistry and the International Union of Biochemistry were among the sources used." —*Pref.* QP512.S73

ENTOMOLOGY

Gilbert, Pamela. A compendium of biographical literature on deceased entomologists. London, British Museum (Natural History), 1977. 455p. £25. **EC52**

Contains references to biographical information and bibliographical listings published before the end of 1975 for some 7,500 deceased entomologists. Z5856.G55

Howe, William H. The butterflies of North America. Garden City, N.Y., Doubleday, 1975. 633p. il. $39.95. **EC53**

"*The Butterflies of North America* is a comprehensive volume on the butterflies and skippers of Canada and the United States, including Alaska and Hawaii."—*Pref.* QL548.H68

Johnson, Warren T. and **Lyon, Howard H.** Insects that feed on trees and shrubs: an illustrated practical guide. Ithaca, N.Y., Cornell Univ. Pr., [1976]. 464p. il. $35. **EC54**

"With the collaboration of C. S. Loehler, N. E. Johnson, and J. A. Weidhaas."—*t.p.*

Contents: Insects that feed on conifers; Insects that feed on broad-leaved evergreens, and deciduous plants; Sources of information on pest control; Selected references; Glossary; Index of insects, mites and animals; Index to insects by host plants.

"This book is a reference manual. It covers essential information about many of the important insects, mites, and other animals associated with woody ornamental plants. Its audience is intended to be agricultural advisor, teacher, student, nurseryman, arborist, forester, gardener, scientist, as well as any person having direct or peripheral responsibility for the maintenance of trees and shrubs. It deals in a pragmatic way with the science of entomology, and provides assistance in the identification of insects and related animals often considered pests."—*Introd.* More than 700 insects and mites are discussed, listed, or illustrated. Over 1,000 photographs of the pests and their damage to the host tree or shrub, including some 200 color plates. SB931.J64

E D

Chemistry

GENERAL WORKS

Guides

Woodburn, Henry M. Using the chemical literature; a practical guide. N.Y., Marcel Dekker, [1974]. 302p. $9.75. **ED1**

Intended for instruction in the use of the chemical literature, "the book is a practical guide and not a bibliography of sources."—*Pref.* QD8.5.W66

Indexes and abstract journals

Chemical abstracts, publ. by the American Chemical Society. 9th collective index, 1972/76. Columbus, Ohio, Chemical Abstracts Service, 1977–78. 57v. $6000. **ED2**

For annotation to abstracts and previous collective indexes *see Guide* ED19. QD1.A51

Parent compound handbook. A publication of the Chemical Abstracts Service. Columbus, Ohio, Amer. Chemical Soc., 1976– . 4v. $300, including 1979 ed. and suppls. for 1979–80. **ED3**

Supersedes *The ring index* (1st ed. 1940; 2d ed. 1960 with suppls. 1–3, 1963–65).

In two parts: (1) Parent compound file, in 2v., one of which is a looseleaf binder with supplementary and replacement pages issued periodically; and (2) Index of parent compounds, in 2v. A cumulative supplement is issued bimonthly and is biennially merged into v.2 of the "Index."

"The *Parent Compound Handbook* is intended as a major reference work for chemists and for those who use *Chemical Abstracts (CA)*.... The *Parent Compound File* (PCF) contains structural diagrams and related data about [more than 44,000] unique, representative *CA* index parents, collectively called parent compounds.... The PCF also includes data on cyclic and acyclic stereoparents as well as cage parents.... Information accompanying each parent compound includes the CAS Registry Number, a structural diagram illustrating the numbering system, a unique alphabetic Parent Compound Identifier, the current *CA* index name, the molecular formula, and, in most cases, the Wiswesser Line Notation. For cyclic parents (other than cage parents) a ring analysis is also provided. The second part of the *Handbook* is the *Index of Parent Compounds.* It is ... designed to afford ... access ... (a) by ring analysis, (b) by ring substructure, (c) by parent name, (d) by Wiswesser Line Notation, (e) by molecular formula, and (f) by CAS Registry Number."—*Introd.* QD291.P37

Encyclopedias

Encyclopédie des gaz. Gas encyclopaedia. [Comp. by Société] L'Air Liquide, Division Scientifique. N.Y. & Amsterdam, Elsevier, [1976]. 1150p. $183.75. **ED4**

Text in French and English.

Offers articles on 138 gases from air to xenon, with an "enormous scope of the subjects covered: chemical and physical properties, operating conditions, flammability limits, toxicity, biological properties, materials of construction, uses, etc. . . . [with] short but effective bibliography."—*Pref.* TP247.E52

Dictionaries

Bennett, Harry. Concise chemical and technical dictionary. 3d ed. enl. N.Y., Chemical Publ. Co., 1974. 1175p. $35. **ED5**

2d ed. 1962.

Over 50,000 definitions of scientific terms, chemicals, trademark products (with manufacturer for American products) and drugs. "Brevity rather than extended definition has been the rule."—*Pref.* QD5.B45

The condensed chemical dictionary. 9th ed. Rev. by Gessner G. Hawley. N.Y., Van Nostrand Reinhold, [1977]. 957p. $34.50. **ED6**

8th ed. 1971 (*Guide* ED33).

"It is not a dictionary in the usual sense of an assemblage of brief definitions, but rather a compendium of technical data and descriptive information covering many thousand chemicals and chemical phenomena, organized in such a way as to meet the needs of those who have only minutes to devote to any given substance or topic." —*Introd.* Entries for trademark names include a number corresponding to a list of manufacturers, given in an appendix; manufacturers' addresses are also given. QD5.C5

Foreign terms

Callaham, Ludmilla Ignatiev. Russian-English chemical and polytechnical dictionary. 3d ed. N.Y., Wiley, [1975]. 852p. $34.95. **ED7**

2d ed. 1962 (*Guide* ED46).

A revised and updated edition. Rather than aiming for "completeness," the compiler has given "preference to the most frequently used terms and to the rare, hard-to-find definitions."—*Pref.* QD5.C33

Handbooks

American Public Health Association. Standard methods for the examination of water and wastewater. 14th ed. Wash., Amer. Public Health Assoc., 1975. 1193p. il. $35. **ED8**

1st ed. 1905; 13th ed. 1971.

"Prepared and published jointly by: American Public Health Association, American Water Works Association, Water Pollution Control Federation."—*t.p.*

The major divisions of the text are: General introduction, Physical examination, Determination of metals, Determination of organic constituents, Automated laboratory analyses, Examination of water and wastewater for radioactivity, Bioassay methods for aquatic organisms, Microbiological examination of water, and Biological examination of water. Each section has a bibliography and/or references. The separation of test methods for water from those for wastewater has been discontinued. Indexed. QD142.A5

Association of Official Analytical Chemists. Official methods of analysis of the Association of Official Analytical Chemists. 12th ed. Wash., Assoc. of Official Analytical Chemists, 1975. 1094p. $40. **ED9**

William Horowitz, ed.

Eds. 1–10, 1920–65, publ. by Association of Official Agricultural Chemists; ed. 11– , 1970– , by Association of Official Analytical Chemists.

Gives qualitative and quantitative methods for analysis of foods, fertilizers, pesticides, hazardous substances, drugs, cosmetics, color additives, poisons, and other materials. Has a section on preparation of standard solutions. Indexed. S587.A8

Dow Chemical Company. Thermal Research Laboratory. JANAF thermochemical tables. D. R. Stull and H. Prophet, project directors. 2d ed. Wash., Nat. Bureau of Standards, 1971. 1v., various paging. (National standard reference data series. NSRDS-NBS-37) $9.75. **ED10**

1st ed. 1964.

Provides, for elements, inorganic compounds, and simple organic compounds, "thermodynamic reference data of the highest quality and timeliness."—*Pref.* Filing order of tables is according to the modified Hill indexing system. An index to the filing order is given before the tables. QC100.U573

Gardner, William. Chemical synonyms and trade names; a dictionary and commercial handbook containing over 35,000 definitions. 8th ed., rev. and enl. by Edward I. Cooke and Richard W. I. Cooke. West Palm Beach, Fla., CRC Pr.; Oxford, Technical Pr., 1978. 769p. $54.95. **ED11**

7th ed. 1972 (*Guide* ED50).

This revision includes 3,300 new entries, with 400 new names added to the index of manufacturers. TP9.G28

Merck index; an encyclopedia of chemicals and drugs. 9th ed. Rahway, N.J., Merck, 1976. 1v., various paging. $18. **ED12**

Martha Windholz, ed.

8th ed. 1968 (*Guide* ED60).

"The exceptional growth in the volume of scientific information published in the last few years has made it necessary to abandon the traditional and time-consuming editing and printing methods used in previous editions and to develop new computer-assisted methods that allow for rapid publication of new information. As of this edition, all the information contained in the monograph section has been stored in a computer data base; editing and correcting were done on-line; and the cross-reference and formula-indices were generated and alphabetized by computer."—*Pref.* RS356.M4

Table of molecular weights; a companion volume to the Merck index, 9th edition. Rahway, N.J., Merck, 1978. 257p. $12. **ED13**

Martha Windholz, Susan Budavari, Margaret Noether Fertig and Georg Albers-Schönberg, eds.

"The book contains high-resolution molecular weights, arranged in ascending order associated with empirical formulae, compound names, and monograph numbers under which the specific compounds are listed in *The Merck Index.* We hope that this volume used with the *The Merck Index* will serve as an important tool in making the identification of chemical compounds easier."—*Pref.* RS57.T2

Style manuals

American Chemical Society. Handbook for authors of papers in American Chemical Society publications. 3d ed. Wash., Amer. Chemical Soc., 1978. 122p. il. $7.50. **ED14**

1st ed. (1965) entitled: *Handbook for authors of papers in the research journals of the American Chemical Society;* 2d ed. (1967) entitled: *Handbook for authors of papers in the journals of the American Chemical Society.*

A manual on manuscript preparation, giving information on preferred use of terms, illustrations, presentation of data, and typing of final copy. Includes a section on the editorial process. T11.A4

INORGANIC

International Union of Pure and Applied Chemistry. Commission on the Nomenclature of Inorganic Chemistry. Nomenclature of inorganic chemistry. 2d ed. N.Y., Pergamon, [1971]. 110p. $12.25. **ED15**

1st ed. 1959 (*Guide* ED73).

Also published as v.28, no.1 of *Pure and applied chemistry.*

"Definitive rules 1970."—*t.p.*

"A major revision and extension of Section 7 has been undertaken.... The former Section 4 which dealt with crystalline phases of variable composition has been ... revised and extended, and now becomes Section 9. Its place as Section 4 is taken by a fuller treatment of polyanions, formerly briefly dealt with in a sub-section of Section 7. The rules for the nomenclature of inorganic boron compounds are outlined in Section 11."—*Introd.* QD7.I58

ORGANIC

Dictionary of organic compounds. 4th ed. Formula index for the dictionary and fifth cumulative supplement. N.Y., Oxford Univ. Pr.; London, Eyre & Spottiswoode, 1971. 558p. $36. **ED16**

For 4th ed. (1965) and fifth (cumulative) supplement *see Guide* ED79.

An index, with elements listed in alphabetical order after carbon and hydrogen, to formulae of compounds given in the main work and its fifth (cumulative) supplement.

——— 4th ed. Tenth and cumulative supplement. N.Y., Oxford Univ. Pr.; London, Eyre & Spottiswoode, 1974. 1156p. $98.

Collates material published in the annual volumes since the fifth and cumulative supplement (*see Guide* ED79). QD251.D53

Fieser, Louis Frederick and **Fieser, Mary.** Reagents for organic synthesis. N.Y., Wiley, [1975–77]. v.5-6. (v.5, $32.75; v.6, $29.50). **ED17**

For v. 1-4 *see Guide* ED82.

v.5 treats about 350 reagents for the first time and about 400 reviewed in earlier volumes; v.6 treats about 400 reagents for the first time and about the same number previously reviewed.

Molecular structures and dimensions. Utrecht, Bohn, Scheltema & Holkema; distr. by Polycrystal Book Service, Pittsburgh, 1970– . v.1– . Annual. **ED18**

"Published for the Crystallographic Data Centre Cambridge and the International Union of Crystallography."—*t.p.*

Ed. by Olga Kennard, David G. Watson, Frank H. Allen and Stella M. Weeds.

A classified bibliography of organic and organometallic crystal structures, with author, formula, and transition metal indexes. Indexing both by standard formula and permuted formula; beginning with v.8 includes a KWIC index of compound names. v.1 and v.2 cover the literature from 1935–69; v.3, 1969–71; v.4, 1971–72; v.5, 1972–73; v.6, 1973–74; v.7, 1974–75; v.8, 1975–76. Z5524.C8M6

Pouchert, Charles J. The Aldrich library of infrared spectra. 2d ed. [Milwaukee], Aldrich Chemical Co., [1976]. 1576p. $67.50. **ED19**

1st ed. 1970.

"... it is ... the intention of this book to present a large number of spectra on each of the important organic functional groups along with a short written description and graphic representation of their spectral features for the purpose of review by the average chemist who is not a specialist in infrared spectroscopy."—*Pref.* QD96.I5P67

BIOGRAPHY

American chemists and chemical engineers. Ed. by Wyndham D. Miles. Wash., Amer. Chemical Soc., 1976. 544p. $28.50. **ED20**

Contains biographical sketches, ranging from a few paragraphs to several pages, of over 500 deceased American chemists and chemical engineers. Biographies cover the period from colonial times to the present; bibliographies of biographical information are included. Index of names mentioned in the biographies. QD21.A43

E E

Earth Sciences

GENERAL WORKS

Dictionaries and encyclopedias

A dictionary of earth sciences. Ed. by Stella E. Stiegeler. N.Y., Pica; distr. by Universe Books, 1977 [c.1976]. 301p. $16.50. **EE1**

A companion to *A dictionary of life sciences* (*Suppl.* EC4) and *A dictionary of physical sciences* (*Suppl.* EA17). A handy, easy-to-use, concise dictionary for the earth sciences. QE5.D54

The planet we live on; illustrated encyclopedia of the earth sciences, ed. by Cornelius S. Hurlbut, Jr. N.Y., Abrams, [1976]. 527p. il. $37.50. **EE2**

A reference book for the general reader, having short articles in nontechnical language, arranged alphabetically and with cross references. No bibliographies are given. QE5.P55

Handbooks

Reeves, Robert G., ed. Manual of remote sensing. Falls Church, Va., Amer. Soc. of Photogrammetry, [1975]. 2v. $45. **EE3**

Contents: v.1, Theory, principles and techniques; v.2, Photographic interpretation and applications.

A substantial revision and expansion of the American Society of Photogrammetry's *Mannual of photographic interpretation* (1960), also using material from its *Manual of photogrammetry* (3d. ed., 1966), *Manual of color aerial photography* (1968), and the periodical *Photogrammetric engineering.* "The two volumes of this manual contain comprehensive treatments of remote-sensing theory, instruments, and techniques and their applications to agricultural, earth, and environmental sciences, natural resources, and engineering."—*Pref.* G70.4.M36

GEOLOGY

Encyclopedias and handbooks

Fairbridge, Rhodes Whitmore and **Bourgeois, Joanne,** eds. The encyclopedia of sedimentology. Stroudsburg, Pa., Dowden, Hutchinson & Ross; distr. by Academic Pr., N.Y., [1978]. 901p. il., maps. (Encyclopedia of earth sciences, v.6) $65. **EE4**

"The *Encyclopedia of sedimentology* is a comprehensive, alphabetical treatment of the discipline of sedimentology. It is intended to be a reference book for sedimentologists, geologists, and others who come in contact with sediments.... Some attempt has been made to define terms and to adhere to definitions in this volume, but an encyclopedia is *not* a dictionary."—*Pref.* Signed articles have bibliographies and cross references. Index. QE471.E49

——— The encyclopedia of world regional geology. Stroudsburg, Pa., Dowden, Hutchinson & Ross; distr. by Academic Pr., N.Y., 1975– . pt.1– . il., maps. (Encyclopedia of earth sciences, v.8) pt.1, $40. **EE5**

Contents: pt.1, Western hemisphere (including Antarctica and Australia); pt.2, Eastern hemisphere, to be published.

Provides geologic and geomorphic data by continent, region, country, and island group. Signed articles, with cross references and bibliographies, are arranged alphabetically. Indexed. QE5.F33

International Union of Geological Sciences. International Subcommission on Stratigraphic Classification. International stratigraphic guide: a guide to stratigraphic classification, terminology, and procedure. N.Y., Wiley, [1976]. 200p. il. $9.50. **EE6**

Hollis D. Hedberg, ed.

An international standard to replace national and regional codes and unify stratigraphic usage; an essential reference. Has an extensive bibliography. Indexed. QE651.I57

Dictionaries

American Geological Institute. Dictionary of geological terms, prepared under the direction of the American Geological Institute. Garden City, N.Y., Anchor/Doubleday, 1976. 472p. $3.50 pa. **EE7**

Ed. by William H. Matthews III and Robert E. Boyer.

1st ed. 1957.

An abridgment of the *Glossary of geology,* 1972 (*Guide* EE63).

"Intended for use by students of geology; elementary and secondary school science teachers; hobbyists . . . and others who have occasion to use but are unfamiliar with geological terminology."—*Pref.* QE5.A48

Challinor, John. A dictionary of geology. 5th ed. N.Y. & Oxford, Oxford Univ. Pr., 1978. 368p. $14.95. **EE8**

4th ed. 1973 (*Guide* EE62).

"This edition is again thoroughly revised and considerably enlarged."—*Pref.* QE5.C45

Atlases

Shell Oil Company. Exploration Department. Stratigraphic atlas of North and Central America. Prepared by the Exploration Department of Shell Oil Company, Houston, Texas. Princeton, N.J., Princeton Univ. Pr., [1975]. 272p. il. maps. 43cm. $50; $15 spiral bound. **EE9**

Ed. by T. D. Cook and A. W. Balley.

A collection of black-and-white maps, on a scale of 1:25,000,000, and stratigraphic sections, together with extensive bibliographies. G1106.C57S54

METEOROLOGY

Handbooks

World Meteorological Organization. Guide to hydrological practices. 3d ed. Geneva, World Meteorological Organization (available from Unipub, N.Y.), 1974. 1v., looseleaf, various paging. (*Its* WMO [publ.] no. 168) $29.50. **EE10**

1st ed. (1965) entitled: *Guide to hydrometeorological practices* (*Guide* EE120).

A revised and improved edition, the new title indicating the broader scope of its contents. QC925.W667

——— Guide to meteorological instrument and observing practices. 4th ed. Geneva, World Meteorological Organization (available from Unipub, N.Y.), 1971. 1v., looseleaf, various paging. (*Its* WMO [publ.] no.8-TP-3) $30. **EE11**

2d ed. 1961 (*Guide* EE121).

Climatology

Grayson, Donald K. A bibliography of the literature on North American climates of the past 13,000 years. N.Y., Garland, 1975. 206p. (Garland reference library of natural science, v.2) $18. **EE12**

Not an exhaustive bibliography of its subject area, nor a critical compilation of the literature, although it includes "much, perhaps even most, of the pertinent literature."—*Introd.* Publications are listed by author and numbered; an index gives access to the literature by seven broad geographic subdivisions of North America. Z6683.C5G66

Ruffner, James A. and **Bair, Frank E.** The weather almanac. 2d ed. Detroit, Gale, [1977]. 728p. il., maps. $20. **EE13**

1st ed. 1974.

"A reference guide to weather, climate, and air quality in the United States and its key cities, comprising statistics, principles, and terminology. Provides weather/health information and safety rules for environmental hazards associated with storms, weather extremes, and earthquakes. Also includes world climatological highlights and a special feature on Alaskan Pipeline climatology."—*t.p.* QC983.R83

U.S. Environmental Data Service. Selective guide to climatic data sources. Prep. by Staff, National Weather Records Center, Asheville, N.C. Wash., Govt. Prt. Off., 1969. 90p. (*Its* Key to meteorological records documentation, no.4.11) **EE13a**

Previous ed. (1963) had title: *Selective guide to published climatic data sources* (*Guide* EE127).

Arranged alphabetically by title within four groups: (1) Current publications; (2) Publications carrying additional time-sequential tables; (3) Special climatological publications; (4) Collateral climatological publications.

U.S. National Oceanic and Atmospheric Administration. Climates of the states. Port Washington, N.Y., Water Information Center, [1974]. 2v. $45. **EE14**

A compilation of the "fifty-one individual state climatological reports issued during the last decade. . . . [Covers] the climate of each of the fifty states plus Puerto Rico and the U.S. Virgin Islands. Each state section contains a general summary of climatic conditions followed by detailed tables of freeze data; normals of temperature and precipitation by climatic divisions and stations; normals, means, and extremes of selected individual stations; and maps showing temperature, precipitation and locations of stations. Also included are miscellaneous data on snowfall, sunshine and occurrence of tropical storms."—*Foreword.* QC983.U58

World survey of climatology. H. E. Landsberg, ed.-in-chief. N.Y. & Amsterdam, Elsevier, 1976–77. v.6–7, 12. (In progress) v.6, $67.50; v.7, $81.75; v.12, $93.95. **EE15**

For previously published volumes *see Guide* EE128.

Contents: v.6, Climate of Central and Southern Europe, ed. by C. C. Wallen; v.7, Climates of the Soviet Union, ed. by P. E. Lydolph; v.12, Climates of Central and South America, ed. by W. Schwerdtfeger. QC981.W67

MINERALOGY

Bibliography

Ridge, John Drew. Annotated bibliographies of mineral deposits in the Western hemisphere. Boulder, Colo., Geological Soc. of America, 1972. 681p. maps. (Geological Soc. of America, Memoir 131) $28. **EE16**

Together with *Annotated bibliographies of mineral deposits in Africa, Asia (exclusive of the USSR) and Australasia* (below) and a projected third volume, this will form a revised and expanded version of *Selected bibliographies of hydrothermal and magmatic mineral deposits,* 1958.

"I have included in these bibliographies all deposits that have, in my opinion, been formed in whole or in part by magmatic or hydrothermal processes, including those produced by volcanic exhalations reaching the sea floor, for which I believe a worthwhile literature exists."—*Introd.* Thoroughly annotated. Arranged geographically; indexed by author, by deposit, by age of mineralization, by metals or minerals produced, and by Lindgren Classification Index. Z6738.O75R53

——— Annotated bibliographies of mineral deposits in Africa, Asia (exclusive of the USSR) and Australasia. Oxford & N.Y., Pergamon, [1976]. 545p. maps. $35. **EE17**

For annotation *see* previous entry. Z6739.A3R53

Dictionaries

Webster, Robert. Gems: their sources, descriptions and identification. 3d ed. [Hamden, Conn.], Archon, [1975; repr. 1977]. 938p. il. $50. **EE18**

2d ed. 1970 (*Guide* EE141).

A revised and updated edition, with a completely rewritten chapter on synthetic gems.

Handbooks

Pough, Frederick H. A field guide to rocks and minerals. 4th ed. Boston, Houghton Mifflin, 1976. 317p. il. $10.95; $5.95 pa. **EE19**

3d ed. 1960 (*Guide* EE153).

In this edition "the text has been completely reset; several new minerals have been added and the localities of occurrence have been updated and expanded."—*Pref.* QE367.P6

Roberts, Willard Lincoln, Rapp, George Robert and **Weber, Julius.** Encyclopedia of minerals. N.Y., Van Nostrand Reinhold, [1974]. 693p. il. $69.50. **EE20**

Alphabetically arranged descriptions of 2,200 minerals, giving chemical composition, crystallographic data, physical properties and description, mode of occurrence, best reference in English, and a color photograph. Includes a brief glossary. QE355.R63

OCEANOGRAPHY

Atlases

Rand McNally atlas of the oceans. N.Y., Rand McNally, [1977]. 208p. il., maps. 38cm. $29.95. **EE21**

A clearly written, profusely illustrated, and well-indexed encyclopedic guide for the non-specialist. Includes information on physical and biological oceanography and on man's interactions with the ocean. The final chapter is a brief encyclopedia of marine life, arranged taxonomically. GC11.2.R35

World ocean atlas. Sergei Georgievich Gorshkov, editor-in-chief. Oxford & Elmsford, N.Y., Pergamon, 1976–78. 2v. maps. 46cm. v.1, $330; v.2, $300. **EE22**

Contents: v.1, Pacific ocean; v.2, Atlantic ocean.

Includes charts on ocean bed, climate, hydrology, hydrochemistry, biogeography, navigation, and many other topics, presented with great care on beautifully colored plates. Text, keys, and captions to figures are in Russian. A translation (poorly done) is provided only for the brief introductory text and index.

Handbooks

Handbook of marine science. West Palm Beach, Fla., CRC Pr., 1974– . [Sec. I] v.1– . (In progress) [Sec.I] v.1, $54.95; v.2, $48.95; [Sec.II] v.1, $36.50. **EE23**

Contents: [Sec.I] Oceanography—v.1, Physical (F. G. Walton Smith, ed.); v.2, Biological (Frederick A. Kalber and F. G. Walton Smith, eds.); [Sec.II] Marine products—v.1, Compounds from marine organisms (Joseph T. Baker and Vreni Murphy, eds.). Projected are [Sec.III] Mariculture; [Sec.IV] Fisheries.

Sec.I consists of tables assembled from many sources to provide a convenient source of information for oceanographers; each volume is separately indexed. Sec.II is a compilation of information about organic compounds derived from marine organisms. GC11.C17

E F

Mathematics

GENERAL WORKS

Guides

Dorling, Alison Rosemary, ed. Use of mathematical literature. Woburn, Mass., Butterworths, 1977. 260p. (Information sources for research and development) $24.95. **EF1**

Chapters on mathematical literature, organizations, reference materials, mathematics education, and the history of mathematics are followed by nine chapters on topical areas in mathematics, with bibliographies. Includes author and subject indexes.

Bibliography

Mathematical Association of America. Committee on the Undergraduate Program in Mathematics. A basic library list for four-year colleges. 2d ed. Wash., Mathematical Assoc. of America, 1976. 106p. $4.50. **EF2**

1st ed. 1966.

Lists approximately 700 books and journals arranged by broad subject areas. Author index.

Abstract journals

Mathematical reviews. Indexes: author index, v.29–44 (1965–72). Providence, R.I., Amer. Mathematical Soc., 1974. 4v. $200. **EF3**

For main series and annotation *see Guide* EF14. QA1.M76

Dictionaries and encyclopedias

James, Glenn and **James, Robert C.** Mathematics dictionary. 4th ed. N.Y., Van Nostrand, 1976. 509p. $17.95. **EF4**

An expansion and revision of 3d ed., 1968 (*Guide* EF20). QA5.J32

Mathematical Society of Japan (Nihon Sūgakkai). Encyclopedic dictionary of mathematics. Cambridge, Mass., M.I.T. Pr., [1977]. 2v. il. $125. **EF5**

Ed. by Shôkichi Iyanaga and Yukiyosi Kawada. Tr. by the Mathematical Society of Japan with the cooperation of the American Mathematical Society. Translation reviewed by Kenneth O. May.

A translation of *Iwanami sūgaku jiten* (Tokyo, 1954; 2d ed. 1968).

A scholarly, comprehensive, and up-to-date encyclopedia consisting of 436 medium-length articles arranged alphabetically, and thoroughly indexed. Technical terms are set in boldface and defined where they initially appear; subsequent appearances are marked with a dagger, indicating that they appear in the subject index. Articles contain references to the technical literature. Cross references. QA5.N513

Sneddon, Ian Naismith, ed. Encyclopaedic dictionary of mathematics for engineers and applied scientists. N.Y., Pergamon Pr., [1976]. 800p. $100. **EF6**

"The aim has been to select those mathematical concepts and techniques which are most widely and frequently used in engineering, and by an extensive cross-reference system to bind together a vast amount of information giving easy access to the fundamental definitions and main results of each of the major branches of mathematics. While the mathematics is always sound, it is the applications rather than the theory which is emphasized."—*Foreword.* Indexed. TA330.S66

Handbooks

Bartsch, Hans-Jochen. Handbook of mathematical formulas. N.Y., Academic Pr., [1974]. 528p. $9.50. **EF7**

"Translation of the 9th ed. of *Mathematische Formeln* by Herbert Liebscher, Leipzig."—*verso of t.p.*

"The scope of this collection of formulas covers the whole field from the fundamental rules of arithmetic, via analytic geometry and infinitesimal calculus through to Fourier's series and fundamentals of probability calculus."—*Pref.* QA41.B313

Pearson, Carl E., ed. Handbook of applied mathematics: selected results and methods. N.Y., Van Nostrand Reinhold, [1974]. 1265p. $39.50. **EF8**

"Most of the topics in applied mathematics dealt with in this handbook can be grouped rather loosely under the term *analysis.* They involve results and techniques which experience has shown to be of utility in a very broad variety of applications."—*Pref.* The emphasis is on technique. The 21 chapters, contributed by 20 mathematicians, include bibliographic references and have been extensively indexed. QA40.P38

Tables

Bibliography

Schütte, Karl. Index mathematischer Tafelwerke und Tabellen aus allen Gebieten der Naturwissenschaften. 2., verb. u. erhebl. erw. Aufl. München, Oldenbourg, 1966. 239p. **EF9**

Added title page (*Index of mathematical tables from all branches of sciences*) and preface in English; section headings in German and English.

1st ed. 1955 (*Guide* EF47.)

Coverage expanded from the 1,200 tables indexed in 1st ed. to over 2,800 tables. Z6654.T3S34

Compendiums

Hansen, Eldon R. A table of series and products. Englewood Cliffs, N.J., Prentice-Hall, [1975]. 523p. $74. **EF10**

A systematic table of series and products, including about 1,200 new entries. Provides systematic access not only to series involving elementary and special functions, but also to numerical power series, which are written "in a canonical form so that a given numerical power series can be found . . . about as easily as one finds a given numbered page in a book. . . . The 'average' reader finding a series in the literature will almost certainly also find his series in this table." —*Pref.* QA295.H25

Pearson, Egon Sharpe and **Hartley, H. O.,** eds. Biometrika tables for statisticians. [Reprinted with corrections] London, Biometrika Trust (available from Charles Griffin & Co., Buckinghamshire, Eng.), 1976. 2v. (v.1, £8.50; v.2, £10) **EF11**

v.1 is a corrected reprint of the 3d ed., 1976 (originally publ. 1954; 2d ed. 1958); v.2 is a corrected reprint of the 1st ed. of that volume published 1972. The work represents a revision and expansion of *Tables for statisticians and biometricians,* ed. by Karl Pearson (1st ed. 1924; 3d ed. 1948).

Taken together, these two volumes of tables cover the vast majority of situations encountered by statisticians. v.1 contains all of the more commonly used tables; more specialized tables are in v.2. Each volume has an extensive introduction defining the functions covered and describing their use; illustrative examples are given. QA276.P431

E G

Physics

GENERAL WORKS

Abstract journals and indexes

Science abstracts: Sec.A, Physics abstracts. Cumulative indexes, 1969–72, 1973–76. London, [1973, 1978]. (1969–72, $890; 1973–76, $1800). **EG1**

For annotation and previous cumulative indexes *see Guide* EG10.

Contents: Cumulative author index, 1969–72, 3v.; 1973–76, 4v. Cumulative subject index, 1969–72, 4v.; 1973–76, 8v.

Dictionaries and encyclopedias

Encyclopaedic dictionary of physics; general, nuclear, solid state, molecular, chemical, metal and vacuum physics, astronomy, geophysics, biophysics and related subjects. Ed. in chief, J. Thewlis. Supplementary v.5. N.Y. & Oxford, Pergamon, [1975]. 379p. il. $44. **EG2**

Main series in 9v. publ. 1961–64; supplements 1–4 publ. 1966–71 (*Guide* EG14).

Gray, Harold James and **Isaacs, Alan,** eds. A new dictionary of physics. N.Y., Longman, 1975. 619p. $35. **EG3**

1958 ed. had title: *Dictionary of physics* (*Guide* EG16).

Major revision, updating, and expansion; many old entries rewritten and shortened; rather lengthy entries on the elements omitted since information is provided elsewhere. QC5.G7

Handbuch der Physik, hrsg. von S. Flügge. Berlin, Springer, 1974–76. v.6a[4]; v.49, pt.5. (In progress) v.6a[4], $81.40; v.49, pt.5, $87.20. **EG4**

For previously published volumes and annotation *see Guide* EG18.

Contents: v.6a[4], Mechanics of solids (1974); v.49, pt.5, Geophysics (1976).

Lexikon der Physik, hrsg. von Hermann Franke. 3d ed. Stuttgart, Franckh, [1969]. 3v. il. **EG5**

2d ed. 1959 (*Guide* EG22).

A completely revised edition.

Directories

American Institute of Physics. Graduate programs in physics, astronomy, and related fields, 1976/77– . N.Y., Amer. Inst. of Physics, 1976– . Annual. $10. **EG6**

Supersedes *Graduate programs in physics and astronomy,* 1968.

"... designed to provide easily accessible, comparative information on graduate programs and research in physics and in fields based upon the principles of physics.... Each entry in the book describes the graduate programs offered by an academic department at an institution of higher learning in North America ... with separate parts for ... the United States and Canada. Within these parts, entries are organized ... by state or province."—*Introd.*

Information for each department includes address and telephone number, admissions information, information on degree programs, size and budget of department, and lists of faculty (including fields of specialization); recent publications are included for some departments. QC30.A48

Directory of physics and astronomy staff members: North American colleges and universities, federally funded research & development centers, [and] government laboratories, 1975/76– . N.Y., Amer. Inst. of Physics, [1975–]. Annual. $20. **EG7**

Continues *Directory of physics and astronomy faculties: United States/Canada/Mexico,* 1959/60–1974/75.

Lists physics staffs by institution, giving address and telephone number of institution, name and telephone extension of staff members, and for academic institutions gives academic rank. Indexed by personal name. QC30.D57

Handbooks

Handbook of optics, ed. by Walter G. Driscoll and William Vaughan. N.Y., McGraw-Hill, [1978]. 1v., various paging. il. $55. **EG8**

"Sponsored by the Optical Society of America."—*t.p.*

Intended to fill "a need for a convenient compilation of optical information [as expressed by members of the Society, including] not only those engaged in optical physics, lens design, vision, color and other specializations traditionally associated with optics but also chemists, engineering scientists, and medical scientists.... "—*Pref.* QC369.H35

Tables

Lang, Kenneth R. Astrophysical formulae; a compendium for the physicist and astrophysicist. N.Y. & Berlin, Springer, 1974. 735p. il. $78.80; $29.50 pa. **EG9**

"This book is meant to be a reference source for the fundamental formulae of astrophysics. Wherever possible, the original source ... is referenced, together with references to more recent modifications and applications."—*Pref.* Uses centimeter-gram-second units. Indexed by subject and author; includes extensive bibliographies. QB461.L35

Lederer, Charles Michael and **Shirley, Virginia S.,** eds. Table of isotopes. 7th ed. N.Y., Wiley, 1978. 1523p. il. $32.50. **EG10**

Edgardo Browne, Janis M. Dairiki, and Raymond E. Doebler, principal authors.

6th ed. 1967 (*Guide* EG42).

"An Isotope Index, ordered by atomic number (Z) and subordered by mass number (A), precedes the main table. It contains all stable nuclei, radioisotopes, and isomers that appear in the *Table of isotopes.* ... The main table is ordered by mass number and subordered by atomic number. For each mass number there is an abbreviated mass-chain decay scheme.... Following the mass-chain decay scheme, tabulated data and detailed nuclear level schemes are given for individual isotopes.... As in the 6th edition, each tabulated entry consists of a critical selection of reported data."—*Introd.* QD466.L37

Bibliography

Datensammlungen in der Physik; data compilations in physics. Karlsruhe, Zentralstelle für Atomkernenergie-Dokumentation; available from Atomic Energy Documentation Service, Larchmont, N.Y., 1976–78. v.1–3 (In progress) (Physik Daten. Physics data. nos. 3-1, 3-2, 3-3) v. 3-1, $6; v. 3-2, $3.80; v. 3-3, $5.90. **EG11**

A main volume and two supplements which together index about 2,400 data compilations published through February 1978. "The aim of this bibliography is to inform about existing data compilations in the field of physics and to facilitate the search for data.... We have endeavored to make this survey as complete as possible for physics." —*Introd.* Compilations are arranged under topical headings in German and English; subject index in English. QC52.P49

COLORS

Smithe, Frank B. Naturalist's color guide. N.Y., Amer. Museum of Natural History, [1975]. 2pts. pt.I, looseleaf, 24p., $9; pt.II, 229p., $5. **EG12**

Pt.I, *Naturalist's color guide,* consists of 86 swatches, named and numbered. Pt.II, *Naturalist's color guide supplement,* retains much of the terminology from Robert Ridgway's *Color standards and color nomenclature* (Wash., 1912), analyzes each color, correlates each color with many similar colors, and mentions numerous others. QL767.S63

E H

Psychology and Psychiatry

GENERAL WORKS

Bibliography

Mental Health Materials Center, Inc., New York. A selective guide to materials for mental health and family life education. 1976 ed. N.Y., Mental Health Materials Center; distr. by Gale, 1976. 947p. $65. **EH1**

This 3d rev. ed. includes 200 more titles than the 1973 ed. (*Guide* EH17). RA790.M3855

Watson, Robert Irving, ed. Eminent contributors to psychology. N.Y., Springer, 1974–76. 2v. (v.1, $24; v.2, $80) **EH2**

Contents: v.1, A bibliography of primary references; v.2, A bibliography of secondary references.

v.1 deals with references to the works of deceased eminent contributors to psychology. v.2 is a collection of references to sources in which the contributors and their contributions are discussed by others. Coverage is from the Renaissance to the present day. The major contributors to the study of mind and behavior are drawn from philosophy, biology, anthropology, medicine, psychology, etc. Z7201.W37

Periodicals

Markle, Allen and **Rinn, Roger C.**, eds. Author's guide to journals in psychology, psychiatry and social work. N.Y., Haworth Pr., [1977]. 256p. $14.95. **EH3**

A guide to help authors locate the professional journals in which acceptance of their articles is most probable. *Psychological abstracts* and the 1976 edition of *Ulrich's International guide to periodicals* were used as the guides for choosing the English-language journals for inclusion. The types of information given for the journals include: address, major content areas, type of articles usually accepted and inappropriate manuscripts, topics preferred, publication lag time, acceptance rate, style requirement, location of indexing and abstracting, and circulation. BF76.8.M37

Tompkins, Margaret and **Shirley, Norma.** Serials in psychology and allied fields. 2d ed. Troy, N.Y., Whitston, 1976. 472p. $22.50. **EH4**

1st ed. (1969) had title: *A checklist of serials in psychology and allied fields* (*Guide* EH30).

More than 800 serials listed. A title and subject index and a listing of serials by subject are added to this edition. Z7203.T65

Dictionaries and encyclopedias

American Psychiatric Association. Committee on Public Information. A psychiatric glossary: the meaning of terms frequently used in psychiatry. 4th ed. N.Y., Basic Books, 1975. 157p. $7.95. **EH5**

Ed. by the subcommittee of the Committee on Public Information, Shervert H. Frazier, chairman.

3d ed. 1969 (*Guide* EH40).

About 400 new terms have been added since the 3d ed. RC437.A5

Chaplin, James Patrick. Dictionary of psychology. New rev. ed. [N.Y., Dell, 1975] 576p. $1.95. **EH6**

1st ed. 1968.

Aims to provide accurate, concise meanings of technical terms in the field of psychology. "Terms from the related disciplines of psychoanalysis, psychiatry, and biology have been freely included where these have found wide usage in the literature of psychology."—*Introd.* BF31.C45

International encyclopedia of psychiatry, psychology, psychoanalysis, and neurology. N.Y., Van Nostrand Reinhold (publ. for Aesculapius Pubs.), [1977]. 12v. il. $675. **EH7**

Ed. by Benjamin B. Wolman.

Authoritative survey articles include brief bibliographies. Cross references; indexed. RC334.I57

Die Psychologie des 20. Jahrhunderts. Zürich, Kindler, 1976– . Bd. 1– .(In progress; 5v. issued through 1978.) (v.1–3, $98.88 each; v.4, $95; v.5, $102) **EH8**

Contents: Bd.1, Die Europäische Tradition, hrsg. Heinrich Balmer (1976); Bd.2–3, Freud und die Folgen, hrsg. Dieter Eicke (1976); Bd.4, Pawlaw und die Folgen, hrsg. Hans Zeier (1977); Bd.5, Binet und die Folgen, hrsg. Gerhard Strube (1978); Bd.6, Lorenz und die Folgen, hrsg. Roger A. Stamm; Bd.7, Piaget und die Folgen, hrsg. Gerhard Steiner; Bd.8, Lewin und die Folgen, hrsg. Annelise Heigl-Evers; Bd.9, Ergebnisse für die Medizin: Psychosomatik, hrsg. Peter Hahn; Bd.10, Ergebnisse für die Medizin: Psychiatrie, hrsg. Uwe H. Peters; Bd.11–12, Konsequenzen für die Pädagogik, hrsg. Walter Spiel; Bd.13, Anwendungen im Berufsleben, Arbeits-, Wirtschafts- und Verkehrpsychologie, hrsg. François Stoll; Bd.14, Auswirkungen auf die Kriminologie, hrsg. Ulrich Ehebald; Bd.15, Imagination, Kreativität und Transzendenz . . . , hrsg. Gion Condrau. (Bd.6–15 not yet publ.)

A massive and important encyclopedia to be published in 15v. of approximately 1200 pages per volume. Represents the work of more than 600 contributors, predominantly from Western Europe. Each volume deals with a specific dimension, subdiscipline, or allied field. Each volume has a separate subject and author index and a glossary. BF105.P78

Handbooks

American handbook of psychiatry. Silvano Arieti, ed.-in-chief. 2d ed. N.Y., Basic Books, 1974–75. 6v. $169.50. **EH9**

Previous ed. 1959–60 in 3v. (*Guide* EH59).

Contents: v.1, The foundation of psychiatry; v.2, Child and adolescent psychiatry, sociocultural and community psychiatry; v.3, Adult clinical psychiatry; v.4, Organic disorders and psychosomatic medicine; v.5, Treatment; v.6, New psychiatric frontiers.

The *Handbook* has been completely revised, updated, and expanded. RC435.A562

Handbook of industrial and organizational psychology. Marvin D. Dunnette, ed. Chicago, Rand McNally, [1976]. 1740p. $49.95. **EH10**

Contents: pt.1, Theoretical and methodological foundations of industrial and organizational psychology; pt.2, Individual and job measurement and the management of individual behavior in organizations; pt.3, Description and measurement of organizations and of behavioral processes in organizations.

". . . the plan is to produce a *Handbook* that is broad in scope, giving strong emphases to both conceptual and methodological issues relevant to the study of industrial and organizational behavior."—*Pref.* Contains 37 signed chapters; most include references. Subject index. HF5548.8.H355

Handbook of parapsychology. Ed. by Benjamin B. Wolman. N.Y., Van Nostrand Reinhold, [1977]. 967p. $35. **EH11**

Contains 34 signed chapters on various aspects of parapsychology, all with extensive lists of references, followed by a list of suggested readings and a glossary. The chapters range from balanced treatments of research methods to some highly credulous chapters on alleged phenomena. Useful for references to the enormous recent literature. Indexed. BF1031.H254

Directories

U.S. National Institute of Mental Health. Mental health directory. Wash., Govt. Prt. Off., 1977. (DHEW publ. no. (ADM) 77-266) $7. **EH12**

First publ. 1964.

"NIMH has provided listings of treatment resources in every State and Territory . . . gathered from the Division's 1976 inventory of mental health facilities. . . . The Institute's National Clearinghouse for Mental Health Information has supplemented this material with information about Regional, State, and voluntary mental health agencies as well as mental health-related resources in other Federal agencies and in professional and private organizations."—*Pref.* Entries are arranged by state, then city, town, or county. Data include name, address, phone number, and services provided.

Style manuals

American Psychological Association. Publication manual. 2d ed. [Wash., Amer. Psychological Assoc., 1974] 136p. $5 pa. **EH13**

1st ed. publ. as v.49, no.4, pt.2 (July 1952) of *Psychological bulletin.*

"This *Publication Manual* draws its rules from a large body of psychological literature, from editors and authors experienced in psychological writing, and from recognized authorities on publication practices. Writers who employ this Manual conscientiously will express their ideas in a form and style both accepted by and familiar to a broad readership in psychology."—*Introd.* BF76.7.A46

History and biography

American Psychiatric Association. Biographical directory of the Fellows and Members of the American Psychiatric Association as of October, 1977. 7th ed. N.Y., Bowker, 1977. 1573p. $45. **EH14**

Comp. for the APA by the Jaques Cattell Press.
6th ed. 1973 (*Guide* EH69). RC326.A54A2

Nordby, Vernon. A guide to psychologists and their concepts. San Francisco, Freeman, 1974. 187p. $8. **EH15**

"The aims of this book are twofold: first, to present brief biographies of [42] persons whose thinking has been influential and sometimes decisive in establishing the conceptual horizons of contemporary psychology; second, to set forth as clearly and as succinctly as we can their principal concepts. This guide is written for the general reader. . . . "—*Introd.* BF109.A1N67

Zusne, Leonard. Names in the history of psychology: a biographical sourcebook. Wash., Hemisphere Publ.; distr. by Wiley, [1975]. 489p. il. $17.95. **EH16**

A list of 526 biographies chosen by a panel of 9 judges. "The statements describing these individuals are not standard or even short, dictionary versions of standard biographies. They have one main function, namely, to explain the specific contribution or contributions the subject made to psychology."—*Pref.* Entries are arranged chronologically according to birth dates, covering a period from 540 B.C. to 1961. BF109.A1Z85

Tests and measurements

Goldman, Bert A. and **Saunders, John L.** Directory of unpublished experimental mental measures, 1974– . N.Y., Behavioral Publ., 1974– . Irregular. (v.1, 1974: $13.95; v.2, 1978: $14.95) **EH17**

"The *Directory of Unpublished Experimental Mental Measures: Volume I* proposes to supplement the *Mental Measurements Yearbooks* by publishing periodic surveys of tests not available commercially, using as sources those journals that carry studies and reports employing experimental instruments. The present volume is offered as the first in a series, this one is based on the 1970 issues of 29 journals. Its orientation is predominantly educational, but it includes material related to psychology, sociology, and personnel work as well."—*Foreword v.1.* Each entry gives test name, purpose, author, article, and journal. Subject index. BF431.G625

Taulbee, Earl S., Wright, H. Wilkes and **Stenmark, David E.** The Minnesota multiphasic personality inventory (MMPI): a comprehensive annotated bibliography (1940–1965). Troy, N.Y., Whitston, 1977. 603p. $35. **EH18**

A comprehensive, annotated bibliography of 2,144 references on the MMPI from 1940 to 1965. The overall coverage includes: abstracts of MMPI articles; non-abstracted MMPI articles; manifest anxiety references; foreign references; doctoral dissertations; master's theses, books, manuals, and test reviews. Author and subject indexes.

OCCULTISM

See also Suppl. EH11.

Encyclopedia of occultism and parapsychology. Ed. by Leslie Shepard. Detroit, Gale, 1978. 2v. $48. **EH19**

Subtitle: A compendium of information on the occult sciences, magic, demonology, superstitions, spiritism, mysticism, metaphysics, physical science, and parapsychology, with biographical and bibliographical notes and comprehensive indexes.

Includes "more than 3000 entries from Lewis Spence's *Encyclopedia of the Occult* (1920) and Nandor Fodor's *Encyclopedia of Psychic Science* (1934) . . . [which have been augmented] with over 1000 new entries dealing with modern development in occultism and parapsychology. Special attention has been given to biographies of parapsychologists and the fields of their investigations."—*Introd.*
BF1407.E52

E J

Engineering

GENERAL WORKS

Guides

Mount, Ellis. Guide to basic information sources in engineering. N.Y., Wiley, [1976]. 196p. $11.95. **EJ1**

Not a comprehensive list of sources, but rather a book designed to orient an engineering student unfamiliar with library research.
T10.7.M68

Bibliography

New York. Public Library. Research Libraries. Bibliographic guide to technology, 1975– . Boston, G. K. Hall, 1976– . Annual. **EJ2**

Issue covering 1977 publ. 1978 in 2v., $110.

Serves as a supplement to the Engineering Societies Library's *Classed subject catalog* (*Guide* EJ3) and its supplements 1–9; the same publisher's *Technology book guide,* 1974, may be considered the 10th suppl.

Includes relevant publications cataloged during the year by the New York Public Library, with additional entries from Library of Congress MARC tapes and conference publications cataloged by the Engineering Societies Library. Z5854.N48a

Handbooks

Souders, Mott. Handbook of engineering fundamentals. 3d ed. N.Y., Wiley, [1975]. 1562p. il. (Wiley engineering handbook ser.) $33.50. **EJ3**

2d ed. (1952) ed. by O. W. Eshbach (*Guide* EJ5).

A thorough revision, including the complete rewriting of the sections on aeronautics and chemistry, and the inclusion of new sections on astronautics, heat transfer, electronics, automatic control, and engineering economy. The section on engineering law has been omitted. TA151.E8

Materials

Lynch, Charles T., ed. CRC handbook of materials science. Cleveland, CRC Pr., [1974–75]. 3v. (v.1, $64.95; v.2, $44.95; v.3, $59.95) **EJ4**

Contents: v.1, General properties; v.2, Metals, composites, and refractory materials; v.3, Nonmetallic materials and applications.

"It has been the goal of the CRC *Handbook of Materials Science* to provide a current and readily accessible guide to the physical properties of solid state and structural materials. . . . Most of the information is in tabular format. . . . This reference is particularly aimed at the nonexperts, or those who are experts in one field but seek information on materials in another."—*Pref.* Each volume indexed separately. TA403.4.L94

AERONAUTICAL AND SPACE ENGINEERING

Handbooks

Wilding-White, T. M., ed. Jane's Pocket book of space exploration. N.Y., Collier Macmillan, 1977. 238p. il. $5.95. **EJ5**

Contains illustrations of over 200 manned and unmanned space craft and launch vehicles, along with concise technical and historical data. TL796.W48

CHEMICAL ENGINEERING

Encyclopedias

Chemical technology: an encyclopedic treatment. N.Y., Barnes & Noble, 1975. v.7–8 with general index. $40 each. **EJ6**

For v.1–6, publ. 1968–73, and annotation *see Guide* EJ81.

Contents: v.7, Vegetable food products and luxuries; v.8, Edible oils and fats, Animal products, Material resources, General index, Appendix—Recent developments in materials and technology. Set complete with v.8. TP200.M35

Kirk-Othmer encyclopedia of chemical technology. 3d ed. N.Y., Wiley, [1978–]. v.1–3. il. (In progress) (25v. planned, to be issued at the rate of 4 per yr.) $120 per v. **EJ7**

Editorial board: Herman F. Mark, Donald F. Othmer, Charles G. Overberger, and Glen T. Seaborg.

2d ed. 1963–72 in 24v. (*Guide* EJ82).

All of the articles in this new edition have been rewritten and updated; many new subjects have been added. Articles are written by specialists, are signed, and include bibliographies. This edition uses SI (Système international d'unités) as well as English units, and includes Chemical Abstracts Service Registry Numbers. TP9.E55

Plastics

Brandrup, Johannes and **Immergut, E. H.,** eds. Polymer handbook. 2d ed. N.Y., Wiley, [1975]. 1v., various paging. $38.75. **EJ8**

1st ed. 1966 (*Guide* EJ90).

Because of space limitations in this greatly expanded edition, it is "limited to synthetic polymers plus poly(saccharides) and their derivatives."—*Pref.* QD388.B72

Encyclopedia of polymer science and technology: plastics, resins, rubbers, fibers. Supplement. N.Y., Wiley, [1976–77]. v.1–2. il. (In progress) $65 per v. **EJ9**

Supplements the 16v. set publ. 1964–72 (*Guide* EJ92).

Handbook of plastics and elastomers, ed. by Charles A. Harper. N.Y., McGraw-Hill, [1975]. 1008p. in various pagings. il. $39.50. **EJ10**

"The *Handbook of Plastics and Elastomers* was prepared as a thorough sourcebook of practical data for all ranges of interest. It contains an extensive array of property and performance data."—*Pref.* Cross references. Indexed. TP1130.H36

Society of the Plastics Industry. Plastics engineering handbook of the Society of the Plastics Industry, Inc., ed. by Joel Frados. 4th ed. N.Y., Van Nostrand Reinhold, [1976]. 909p. il. $39.95. **EJ11**

3d ed. 1960 had title: *SPI plastics engineering handbook* (*Guide* EJ98).

"Virtually every chapter from the Third Edition has either been completely rewritten or revised extensively and a number of new chapters have been added."—*Pref.* TP1130.S58

CIVIL ENGINEERING

Handbooks

Civil engineer's reference book, ed. by Leslie Spencer Blake. 3d ed. London, Butterworths; Levittown, N.Y., Transatlantic Arts, 1975. 1v., various paging. il. $60. **EJ12**

2d ed. (1969) had title: *Civil engineering reference book* (*Guide* EJ102).

Completely revised, with additional material, especially in contract management and control, site setting up, and equipment procurement and management. Includes extensive bibliographies. TA151.C58

Godel, Jules B. Sources of construction information; an annotated guide to reports, books, periodicals, standards and colors. Metuchen, N.J., Scarecrow Pr., 1977– . v.1– . (In progress) **EJ13**

Contents: v.1, Books. 673p. $25.

Three additional volumes are expected. TA145.G62

Standard handbook for civil engineers. Frederick S. Merritt, ed. 2d ed. N.Y., McGraw-Hill, 1976. 1v., various paging. il. $39.95. **EJ14**

1st ed. 1968 (*Guide* EJ103).

Revised and updated. "The sections . . . dealing with design and construction with concrete, structural steel, cold-formed steel, and wood have been rewritten . . . because of major changes in standard design specifications."—*Pref.* Other changes reflect advances in computer applications, emphasis on environmental control and prevention of pollution, etc. TA151.S8

Environment and environmental problems

General works

Bibliography

EPA cumulative bibliography, 1970–1976. Springfield, Va., NTIS, 1976. 2v. (PB-265920) **EJ15**

Provides a cumulative listing of all reports entered into the NTIS collection through 1976 by the U.S. Environmental Protection Agency (EPA) and its predecessor agencies. v.1 contains bibliographic citations and abstracts, and title index; v.2 contains the subject, corporate source, author, contract number, and access/report number indexes. Updated quarterly by *EPA publication bibliography: quarterly abstract bulletin* (*Suppl.* EJ18). Z5861.E15

Man and the environment information guide series. Seymour M. Gold, series ed. Detroit, Gale, 1975– . v.1– . $18 per v. (In progress) **EJ16**

Contents: v.1, Environmental education, by William B. Stapp and Mary Dawn Liston (1975. 225p.); v.2, Wastewater management, by George Tchobanoglous (1976. 202p.); v.3, Environmental planning, by Michael J. Meshenberg (1976. 492p.); v.4, Environmental values, 1860–1972, by Loren C. Owings (1976. 324p.); v.5 not yet published; v.6, Environmental law, by Mortimer D. Schwartz (1977. 191p.); v.7, Environmental toxicology, by Robert L. Rudd (1977. 266p.).

A monographic series of guides to information sources.

Oi Committee International. International development and the human environment; an annotated bibliography. N.Y., Macmillan Information, [1974]. 334p. $14.95. **EJ17**

"Compiled to acquaint the reader with the various aspects of ecology and international development in greater depth than an ordinary annotated bibliography, it still functions as an instrument of quick and efficient references. Each annotation and citation is indexed by author, subject, and publisher. Each of these refers to the entry by number."—*Introd.* Most material listed was published between 1968 and 1972. Z5861.O4

Indexes and abstract journals

EPA publications bibliography: quarterly abstract bulletin. Springfield, Va., NTIS, 1977– . Quarterly, with annual cumulative index. $50. **EJ18**

Includes abstracts and bibliography, title index, subject index, sponsoring EPA Office index, corporate author index, personal author index, accession/report number index, order form, and list of EPA libraries. For previous EPA publications *see EPA cumulative bibliography, 1970–1976* (*Suppl.* EJ15).

Dictionaries

Allaby, Michael. A dictionary of the environment. N.Y., Van Nostrand Reinhold, [1977]. 532p. $17.95. **EJ19**

Compiled by an interdisciplinary panel of specialists. Defines and explains 6,000 words and phrases used in all sciences that relate to the environment. QH540.4.A44

Directories

See also Suppl. CL25.

Institute of Ecology. Directory of environmental life scientists. Wash., Govt. Prt. Off., 1974. 9v. $50.55. (EP1105-2-3) **EJ20**

Prepared for the U.S. Army Corps of Engineers to provide a directory of environmental life scientists for engineers in environmental studies and activities. Each of the 9v. is for a major region of the continental United States. The arrangement of data in each volume is under the organization's or individual's name. There are 4 indexes to assist in the location of experts when a specialty or specific information is important for: (1) a specific ecosystem or pollutant; (2) environmental impact experiences; (3) geographical familiarity; and (4) species, projects, research topics, etc. QH35.I48

World environmental directory. 3d ed. [Silver Spring, Md., Business Publishers], 1977–78. 2v. $57. **EJ21**

2d ed. 1975.

Contents: v.1, United States and Canada; v.2, Africa, Asia, Australia-New Zealand, Europe, Middle America, South America.

"Pollution Control Product Manufacturers—Air, Water, Solid Waste, Noise; Professional Services, including Consulting Design, Research, Laboratory, and Engineering Services; Government Agencies; Independent Agencies and Commissions; Professional/Scientific, Trade, Labor, and Public Interest Organizations; Universities and Other Educational Institutions; Law Firms with Environmental Interests; Environmental Libraries; Corporate Environmental Officials; Washington Representatives for Industry; State Offices for Air Implementation Plans; State Analytical Laboratories; Periodical Publications; International Environmental Organizations—throughout the World."—*t.p., v.1.*

Factual data include name, address, phone number, cable address, etc., of the organization and names of persons to contact or in positions of responsibility. Personnel index. TD12.W67

Handbooks

Burchell, Robert W. and **Listokin, David.** The environmental impact handbook. [New Brunswick, N.J.], Center for Urban Policy Research, 1975. 234p. il. $8.95 pa. **EJ22**

A guide for land-use planners when preparing environmental impact studies in accordance with the National Environment Policy Act of 1969. Gives detailed, comprehensive explanations of the content, format, responsibilities, recommended procedures, and review processes used in preparing environmental impact studies. HC110.E5B87

CRC handbook of environmental control. Cleveland, CRC Pr., 1973–78. 5v. and series index. **EJ23**

Coordinating ed., Richard Prober.

Contents: v.1, Air pollution. 1973. 576p. $44.95. Ed. by Richard G. Bond and Conrad P. Straub. Section headings: The atmosphere and air pollutants; Effect of air pollution; Emission sources; Air pollution control measures. Index. v.2, Solid waste. 1973. 580p. $44.95. Ed. by Richard G. Bond and Conrad P. Straub. Section headings: Solid wastes—sources and composition; Effects of solid wastes; Solid waste controls and management. Index. v.3, Water supply and treatment. 1973. 835p. $51.95. Ed. by Richard G. Bond and Conrad P. Straub. Section headings: Sources and quality; Needs; Quality criteria; Water treatment; Water distribution; Biological control in water supply systems; Recreational waters; Analytical methods; Monitoring. Index. v.4, Waste water: treatment and disposal. 1974. 928p. $53.95. Ed. by Richard G. Bond and Conrad P. Straub. Section headings: Domestic sewage; Industrial wastes; River waters: oxygen balance; Nutrients, lakes, eutrophication. Index. v.5, Hospital and health care facilities. 1975. 440p. $42.95. Ed. by Conrad P. Straub. Section headings: Kinds and numbers of institutions; Microbial considerations; Environmental hygiene and environmental health; Safety; General sanitation; Nursing homes. Index. Series index. 1978. 128p. $34.95.

"The aim of this series is to bring together pertinent information in tabular form that will be useful in evaluating the environment, not only from the standpoint of effects on the ecosystem, aquatic and terrestrial, but also on man's relationship to the environment and the environment's relationship to man."—*Pref.* TD176.4.H35

Stern, Arthur Cecil, ed. Air pollution. 3d ed. N.Y., Academic Pr., 1976–77. 5v. $200. **EJ24**

2d ed. 1968 (*Guide* EJ122).

Contents: v.1, Air pollutants, their transformation and transport; v.2, The effects of air pollution; v.3, Measuring, monitoring and surveillance of air pollution; v.4, Engineering control of air pollution; v.5, Air quality management.

Revised and greatly expanded, with many new contributors represented. Each volume has its own subject index. TD883.S83

Verschueren, Karel. Handbook of environmental data on organic chemicals. N.Y., Van Nostrand, 1977. 659p. $37.50. **EJ25**

Presents information on physical and chemical data, air pollution factors, water pollution factors, and biological effects. More than 1,000 organic compounds are listed, but not all of the above categories of information are given for each compound. TD196.O73V47

Water resources and water pollution

Bibliography

Giefer, Gerald J. and **Todd, David K.,** eds. Water publications of state agencies. Port Washington, N.Y., Water Information Center, [1972]. 319p. **EJ26**

With the assistance of Mary Louise Quinn.

Subtitle: *A bibliography of publications on water resources and their management published by the states of the United States.*

"A listing of water resources publications issued by 335 state agencies in 50 states of the United States. Information is listed by state with publications grouped under the issuing agencies of each state." —*Pref.* Information on how to obtain publications is included.

——— ——— First supplement, 1971–1974, with the assistance of Beverly Fish. 1976. 189p. $23.

Ralston, Valerie Hunter. Water resources; a bibliographic guide to reference sources. Storrs, Univ. of Connecticut, 1975. 123p. (The Library. Bibliography series no. 2) (Institute of Water Resources. Report no.23) **EJ27**

More than 400 entries arranged by type, e.g., guides, dictionaries, encyclopedias, handbooks, statistical sources, with author and keyword indexes. Many items are annotated. TD224.C8A3

Summers, W. Kelly and **Spiegel, Zane.** Ground water pollution: a bibliography. Ann Arbor, Mich., Ann Arbor Science, 1974. 83p. $12.50. **EJ28**

A partially annotated bibliography "of ground water contamination of nitrates, heavy metals, pesticides and herbicides. The impact of urbanization and the effects of solid waste disposal, animal wastes and petroleum products on ground water quality are covered in the more than 400 entries."—*Pref.* Z5862.2.W3S9

Unger, Samuel G., Jordening, David L., and **Tihansky, Dennis.** Bibliography of water pollution control benefits and costs. Wash., Govt. Prt. Off., 1974. 181p. (EPA-600/5-74-028) **EJ29**

Prep. for the Office of Research and Development, U.S. Environmental Protection Agency.

The computerized "bibliography includes approximately 3000 relevant references, alphabetized by author.... The references listed have been screened and are considered relevant to the problems inherent in estimating water pollution control benefits and costs."—*Pref.* Z5862.2.W3U53

Directories

Giefer, Gerald J. Sources of information in water resources; an annotated guide to printed materials. Port Washington, N.Y., Water Information Center, [1976]. 290p. $23.50. **EJ30**

"This guide, compiled for the use of the student and researcher, cites and annotates over 1100 titles found useful for reference purposes in the water resources field.... The emphasis here has been upon the literature of the United States."—*Pref.* Z7935.G53

Handbooks

Van der Leeden, Frits. Water resources of the world: selected statistics. Port Washington, N.Y., Water Information Center, [1975]. 568p. il. $32.50. **EJ31**

A compilation and summary tabulation of world-wide water resources statistics. Presents data on the characteristics of major lakes, rivers, and reservoirs; desalination; hydrologic cycle, including glaciers and the oceans; water supplies in developing nations; and international water development and financing programs. The 578 tables and numerous maps and diagrams are arranged by continents. Detailed references. GB661.V34

Hydraulic engineering and hydrodynamics

Brater, Ernest Frederick and **King, Horace Williams.** Handbook of hydraulics for the solution of hydraulic engineering problems. 6th ed. N.Y., McGraw-Hill, [1976]. 1v., various paging. il. $26.50. **EJ32**

5th ed. 1963 (*Guide* EJ141).

Revised and updated. This edition "includes new material on the metric system and on the design of pipe networks, and a completely new section describing the applications of numerical methods and digital computers to hydraulic engineering."—*Pref.* TC160.K5

Structural engineering

Merritt, Frederick S., ed. Building construction handbook. 3d ed. N.Y., McGraw-Hill, 1975. 1v., various paging. il. $43.50. **EJ33**

2d ed. 1965 (*Guide* EJ146).

This edition "is virtually a new book. It contains several new sections and almost complete revisions of previous sections to include important new developments. Many of the revisions were necessary because of drastic changes in the specifications for design and construction with commonly used construction materials."—*Pref.* TH151.M4

Transportation engineering

Transportation and traffic engineering handbook. Institute of Traffic Engineers. John Edward Baerwald, ed; Matthew J. Huber and Louis E. Keefer, assoc. eds. Englewood Cliffs, N.J., Prentice-Hall, 1976. 1080p. il. $24.95. **EJ34**

A revision and enlargement of *The traffic engineering handbook,* 1965.

Chapters written by different authorities, with emphasis on practical application. Little material on mass transportation. Well indexed. HE333.T68

ELECTRICAL AND ELECTRONIC ENGINEERING

Bibliography

Electronics: a bibliographical guide. [v.3], by Lindsay Corbett. London, Macdonald, [1973]. 799p. £20. **EJ35**

v.1–2 (1961–65) by C. K. Moore and K. J. Spencer (*Guide* EJ160).

Abstract journals

Science abstracts: Sec.B, Electrical & electronics abstracts. Cumulative indexes, 1969–72, 1973–76. London, [1973, 1978]. 1969–72, $340; 1973–76, $800. **EJ36**

For annotation and previous cumulative indexes *see Guide* EJ163.

Contents: Cumulative author index, 1969–72, 1v.; 1973–76, 2v. Cumulative subject index, 1969–72, 2v.; 1973–76, 3v.

——— Sec.C, Computer & control abstracts. Cumulative indexes, 1969–72, 1973–76. London, [1973, 1978]. 1969–72, $210; 1973–76, $450. **EJ37**

For annotation and previous cumulative indexes *see Guide* EJ164.

Contents: Cumulative author index, 1969–72, 1v.; 1973–76, 1v. Cumulative subject index, 1969–72, 1v.; 1973–76, 2v.

Dictionaries

Institute of Electrical and Electronics Engineers. IEEE standard dictionary of electrical and electronics terms. 2d ed. Piscataway, N.J., IEEE Service Center; distr. N.Y., Wiley, 1977. 882p. $37.50. **EJ38**

1st ed. 1972 (*Guide* EJ168).

"The current edition derives the bulk of its new definitions from standards published between 1968 and 1977. Most of the definitions that have been continued from the 1972 edition have been reaffirmed because of their inherent usefulness. The committees that generated the definitions originally still consider them to be equally appropriate at the present time."—*Introd.* Alphabetic arrangement of words and phrases with a reference number leading to the source of the standardization. Includes an 85p. listing of abbreviations, symbols, acronyms, functional designations, sigla, and letter combinations. TK9.I478

Markus, John. Electronics dictionary. 4th ed. N.Y., McGraw-Hill, [1978]. 745p. il. $24.50. **EJ39**

3d ed.(1966) had title: *Electronics and nucleonics dictionary* (*Guide* EJ165).

"Accurate, easy-to-understand, and up-to-date definitions for 17,090 terms used in solid-state electronics, computers, television, radio, medical electronics, industrial electronics, satellite communication, and military electronics."—*t.p.* TK7804.M35

Handbooks

Fink, Donald G. and **McKenzie, Alexander A.,** eds. Electronics engineers' handbook. N.Y., McGraw-Hill, [1975]. 1v., various paging. il. $42.50. **EJ40**

A companion volume to the *Standard handbook for electrical engineers* (*Suppl.* EJ44), this is the first handbook addressed to the field of electronics engineering as a whole. Attempts to contain all pertinent data within its scope; oriented toward application rather than theory. TK7825.F56

Giacoletto, L. J., ed. Electronics designers' handbook. 2d ed. N.Y., McGraw-Hill, [1977]. 1v., various paging. il. $47.50. **EJ41**

1st ed. (1957) by Robert W. Landee, Donovan C. Davis, and Albert P. Albrecht.

"This Handbook has been organized with the basic developments first, followed by numerical tabulation of material properties. Next, components, circuit analysis, and circuit design are introduced, and one progresses from smaller to larger systems."—*Pref.* TK7825.L3

Instrument engineers' handbook. Bēla G. Liptāk, ed. Supplement one. Philadelphia, Chilton, 1972. 633p. $24.95. **EJ42**

For v.1–2 (1969–70) *see Guide* EJ190.

"This first supplement adds the following new topics to subjects covered in Volumes I and II: pollution instrumentation, human engineering, physical properties analyzers, ion selective electrodes, and instrument installation materials. Furthermore, it reports on the new developments in the already discussed areas of process measurement, computers, displays and control systems."—*Pref.*

National Fire Protection Association. NFPA handbook of the National electrical code, ed. by John H. Watt and W. I. Summers. 4th ed. N.Y., McGraw-Hill, 1975. 832p. $17.50. **EJ43**

3d ed. 1972 (*Guide* EJ193).

"Based on the current 1975 code."—*t.p.*

Includes a "Resume of code changes" indicating deletions, revisions and new sections reflected in the 1975 code through changes to the 1971 edition.

Standard handbook for electrical engineers. Donald G. Fink and H. Wayne Beaty, eds. 11th ed. N.Y., McGraw-Hill, [1978]. 1v., various paging. il. $46.50. **EJ44**

10th ed. 1968 (*Guide* EJ196).

An extensively revised and reorganized edition. TK151.S83

Turner, L. W., ed. Electronics engineer's reference book. 4th ed. London & Woburn, Mass., Butterworths, [1976]. 1v., various paging. il. $54.95. **EJ45**

3d ed. 1967 (*Guide* EJ188).

Entirely rewritten, with revised arrangement. TK151.E43

Electronic data processing

Dictionaries and encyclopedias

Burton, Philip E. A dictionary of microcomputing. N.Y., Garland, 1976. 171p. il. (Reference library of science & technology, v.5) $14.50. **EJ46**

Very concise definitions may be difficult for readers with no previous knowledge of computers. QA76.15.B89

Encyclopedia of computer science. 1st ed. N.Y., Petrocelli/Charter, 1976. 1523p. il. $60. **EJ47**

Ed. by Anthony Ralston and Chester L. Meek.

A reference work for the non-specialist, consisting of 500 signed survey articles, some of which have brief bibliographies. Excellent index. QA76.15.E48

Directories

Kruzas, Anthony Thomas, ed. Encyclopedia of information systems and services. 3d ed. Detroit, Gale, 1978. 1030p. $95. **EJ48**

1st ed. 1971 (*Guide* AB184); 2d ed. 1974, 1271p.

Subtitle: A guide to information storage and retrieval services, data base producers and publishers, online vendors, computer service companies, computerized retrieval systems, micrographic firms, libraries, government agencies, networks and consortia, information centers, data banks, clearinghouses, research centers, associations, and consultants.

Revised and expanded, following the plan of the earlier editions. Z674.3.K78

Williams, Martha E. and **Rouse, Sandra H.** Computer-readable bibliographic data bases: a directory and sourcebook. Wash., Amer. Soc. for Information Science, 1976. 1v., looseleaf. $68. **EJ49**

Updated replacement pages furnished at 6-month intervals.

An updated version of *Survey of commercially available computer-readable bibliographic data bases,* ed. by J. H. Schneider, M. Gechman and S. E. Furth (1973).

Covers about 300 data bases as opposed to 81 in the 1973 publication. Information was acquired in various ways, including questionnaire, with telephone follow-up and verification. For each data base the directory aims, as far as possible, to provide the following: (1) Basic information (name, frequency of update, time span covered, etc.); (2) Producer/distributor/generator information; (3) Availability and charges for data base tapes; (4) Subject matter and scope of data on tape; (5) Subject analysis/indexing data; (6) Bibliographic data base elements present on tape; (7) Tape specifications; (8) Search programs; (9) Data base services offered; (10) User aids.

A new edition is promised for 1979. Z699.22.C635

Radio and television

Reference data for radio engineers. 6th ed. Indianapolis, H. W. Sams, [1975]. 1v., various paging. il. $30. **EJ50**

5th ed. 1968 (*Guide* EJ220).

Originally a production of the International Telephone and Telegraph Corporation, this reference work has in recent editions obtained material from outside the ITT system. TK6552.R44

ENERGY

The energy directory update service. N.Y. Environment Information Center, 1975– . (1978: $125; 1978 and backfile: $250) **EJ51**

Started with one volume, *The energy directory*, 1974, then expanded into a set of individually bound chapters which are updated periodically. Some of the chapters are: "Energy information locator" (1975, 1977); "Federal government-executive branch" (1976– . Annual); "Federal energy agencies in transition" (1977); "Industry" (1976); "Regional and state government" (1976, 1977); "Solar energy update" (1977); "Trade, professional and non-government organizations" (1976); "Energy Congress '78" (1978). A comprehensive guide to national energy organizations, decision-makers, and sources of information. Factual data include names, titles, addresses, phone numbers, mission statements, programs, projects, publications, advisory board members, maps, and organizational charts. Indexes in each chapter; master cumulative indexes, 1976 and 1978. HD9502.U5E54

Energy technology handbook, prepared by 142 specialists. Douglas M. Considine, ed.-in-chief. N.Y., McGraw-Hill, [1977]. 1v., various paging. il. $49.50. **EJ52**

"This Handbook concentrates on those fundamental technologies which relate to energy sources, energy reserves, energy conversion, energy transportation and transmission, and to an extent limited both by time and space in the preparation of this volume, energy distribution, utilization, and the energy/environmental interface."—*Pref.* TJ163.9.E54

McGraw-Hill encyclopedia of energy. Daniel N. Lapedes, ed.-in-chief. N.Y., McGraw-Hill, [1976]. 785p. il. $24.50. **EJ53**

More than 300 signed articles (some drawn from the *McGraw-Hill encyclopedia of science and technology*; *Suppl.* EA13), including brief bibliographies, on technological and economic aspects of energy. Cross-references; indexed. TJ163.2.M3

U.S. Department of Energy. Energy research abstracts, 1976– . Oak Ridge, Tenn., Technical Information Center, v.1– , 1976– . Semimonthly, with semiannual and annual indexes. $184 per yr. **EJ54**

Partially supersedes U.S. Atomic Energy Commission's *Nuclear science abstracts* (*Guide* EJ324). Supersedes U.S. Energy Research and Development, *ERDA research abstracts* (1975), nos.1–4 of which were titled *ERDA reports abstracts*. v.1–v.2, no.21 (1977) issued by the U.S. Energy Research and Development Administration as *ERDA energy research abstracts*.

"... provides abstracting and indexing coverage of all scientific and technical reports, journal articles, conference papers and proceedings, books, patents, theses, and monographs originated by the U.S. Department of Energy, its laboratories, energy centers, and contractors. ... ERA also covers other U.S. Government sponsored energy information and the international literature on reactor technology, waste processing and storage, and fusion technology. In addition, nonnuclear information obtained from foreign governments under agreements for cooperation is covered."—*[Note], 1978*. Z5853.P83U533

MECHANICAL ENGINEERING

Handbooks

Davidson, A., ed. Handbook of precision engineering. London, Macmillan; N.Y., McGraw-Hill, 1972–74. v.3–4, 7–10. (In progress) il. $29.50 per v. **EJ55**

For previously published volumes *see Guide* EJ259.

Contents: v.3, Fabrication of non-metals; v.4, Physical and chemical fabrication techniques; v.7, Electrical design applications; v.8, Surface treatment; v.9, Production engineering; v.10, Forming processes. TJ145.D33213

Harris, Cyril M. and **Crede, Charles E.**, eds. Shock and vibration handbook. 2d ed. N.Y., McGraw-Hill, [1976]. 1v., various paging. il. $32.50. **EJ56**

1st ed. 1961 (*Guide* EJ262).

This edition has major changes, including the deletion of archival material and chapters whose importance has diminished because of technical developments; the treatment of current engineering problems of major interest has been expanded. TA355.H35

Machinery's Handbook; a reference book for the mechanical engineer, draftsman, toolmaker and machinist, by Erik Oberg, Franklin D. Jones, and Holbrook L. Horton. 20th ed. N.Y., Industrial Pr., 1975. 2482p. il. $25. **EJ57**

19th ed. 1972 (*Guide* EJ265).

In this edition "the new material covers a large variety of subjects that are important to designers and builders of everything mechanical. Recent or revised engineering standards, both American and British, are included, together with a large amount of general information and mechanical data representing the latest designing and manufacturing practice."—*Pref*.

Society of Manufacturing Engineers. Tool and manufacturing engineers handbook, a reference work for manufacturing engineers. 3d ed. N.Y., McGraw-Hill, [1976]. 1v., various paging. il. $49.50. **EJ58**

2d ed. (1959) had title: *Tool engineers handbook* (*Guide* EJ256). Extensively revised.

MILITARY AND NAVAL ENGINEERING

Albion, Robert Greenhalgh. Naval & maritime history: an annotated bibliography. 4th rev. and exp. ed. Newton Abbot, [Eng.], David and Charles, [1973]. 370p. £6.95. **EJ59**

3d ed. 1968 (*Guide* EJ271).

This edition combines the listings from the 3d ed. and its supplements with new listings published through mid-1971. Now includes more than 5,000 entries. Z6834.H5A4

MINING AND METALLURGICAL ENGINEERING

Bibliography

U.S. Bureau of Mines. List of Bureau of Mines publications and articles, with subject and author index, by Rita D. Sylvester. 1960–64; 1965–69; 1970–74. Wash., Govt. Prt. Off., [1966, 1970, 1975]. (*Its* Special publ.), 1965–69, $3.75; 1970–74, $7. **EJ60**

Supplements the U.S. Bureau of Mines, *List of journal articles ... July 1, 1910, to Jan. 1, 1960* ... (*Guide* EJ276) and the U.S. Bureau of Mines, *List of publications ... July 1, 1910 to Jan. 1, 1960* ... (*Guide* EJ277). Z6736.U759

Handbooks

Metals handbook. 8th ed. Metals Park, Ohio, Amer. Soc. for Metals, 1975–76. v.10–11. $52 per v. **EJ61**

For previously published volumes *see Guide* EJ307.

Contents: v.10, Failure analysis and prevention; v.11, Nondestructive testing and quality.

A new edition is now in progress:

——— 9th ed. Metals Park, Ohio, Amer. Soc. for Metals, 1978– . v.1– . (In progress) (v.1, $56) **EJ62**

Contents: v.1, Properties and selection: irons and steels.

A complete revision of this comprehensive, multi-author handbook. This edition uses both metric and U.S. units.

Smithells, Colin J., ed. Metals reference book. 5th ed. London & Boston, Butterworths, [1976]. 1566p. il. $105. **EJ63**

Eric A. Brandes, asst. ed.

4th ed. (1967) in 3v. (*Guide* EJ311).

"The object of this reference book is to provide a convenient summary of data relating to metallurgy. So far as possible, the data are presented in the form of tables or diagrams with a minimum of descriptive matter, although short monographs have been included where information could not otherwise have been adequately presented. This edition has been the subject of very thorough revision .... Values are given in both [SI (Système international d'unités) and traditional] units ... and, in addition, complete conversion tables ... are provided. The values given are those which contributors have selected as the most reliable, after a critical review of the published data."—*Pref*. TN671.S55

NUCLEAR ENGINEERING

Abstract journals

INIS atomindex: an international abstracting service. Vienna, Internatl. Atomic Energy Agency; distr. by Unipub., N.Y., 1970– . v.1– . Semimonthly with semiannual indexes. $150 per yr. **EJ64**

Partially supersedes U.S. Atomic Energy Commission, *Nuclear science abstracts* (*Guide* EJ324). Supersedes International Atomic Energy Agency, *List of references on nuclear energy*, 1959–68 (*Guide* EJ321).

"INIS is a cooperative, decentralized information system set up by the International Atomic Energy Agency and its Member States. Its purpose is to construct a data base identifying publications relating to nuclear science and its peaceful applications."—*Introd*. Availability of the report literature is indicated; many of the reports are available on microfiche from INIS. Z7144.N8I15

U.S. Atomic Energy Commission. Nuclear science abstracts. Oak Ridge, Tenn., Technical Information Branch, 1948–June, 1976. v.1–33. **EJ65**

In governmental reorganization the U.S. Atomic Energy Commission was eliminated and its publication, *Nuclear science abstracts* (*Guide* EJ324), ceased. Some of the functions of the AEC were taken over by the new agency, U.S. Energy Research and Development Administration and, subsequently, by the U.S. Department of Energy. Much of the coverage of *NSA* was taken over by *Energy research abstracts* (*Suppl.* EJ53). *NSA* is also partially superseded by *INIS Atomindex* (above). QC770.U64

E K

Medical Sciences

MEDICINE

Guides

Blake, John Ballard and **Roos, Charles,** eds. Medical reference works . . . ; a selected bibliography. Supplement 3, 1973–1974, comp. by Joy S. Richmond. Chicago, Medical Lib. Assoc., 1975. 89p. **EK1.**

For main volume and earlier supplements *see Guide* EK1.

Offers "244 annotated citations to reference works that appeared in the *National Library of Medicine Current Catalog* during 1973 and 1974."—*Pref.* Computer-produced from the NLM *Current catalog* data base.

Bibliography

Andrews, Theodora. A bibliography of the socioeconomic aspects of medicine. Littleton, Colo., Libraries Unlimited, 1975. 209p. $10. **EK2**

Guide to the literature concerning the socio-economic aspects of health care. "It is hoped that the librarians who wish to build collections in fields of health care and related areas will find this bibliography valuable."—*Introd.* Author and title index. A6675.E2A53

Manning, Diana Helen. Disaster technology: an annotated bibliography. N.Y., Pergamon, 1976. 282p. $15. **EK3**

An earlier ed. appeared 1973.

Contents: (1) Annotated references—Relief organizations; Medical aspects: planning; Medical aspects: general; Medical aspects: nutrition; Sociological aspects; Physical aspects: general; Physical aspects: earthquakes; (2) Reviews; (3) Subject classification.

"The purpose of this bibliography is to supply relief agencies with information on published and unpublished literature available concerning technical aspects of disaster relief and prevention with special emphasis on developing countries. It is also intended to provide those involved in relevant research with information on disaster topics from other disciplines."—*Introd.*

Each review is a brief discussion of general points with indications of controversial issues. The subject classification includes broad subject headings with reference numbers that refer to the annotated references or reviews. Author index. Z5776.M35

Current

Medical books and serials in print, an index to literature in the health sciences, 1978– . N.Y., Bowker, 1978– . [Ed.7–] Annual. (7th ed., 1978: $39.95) **EK4**

[Ed.1–6] entitled *Bowker's Medical books in print* (*Guide* EK26).

Subject and title listings of serials have been added beginning with the 7th ed.

Films

Health sciences video directory, 1977– . [N.Y.], Shelter Books, 1977– . Annual. **EK5**

Lawrence Eidelberg, ed.

An annotated directory of programs or series for all areas of professional health education available on videocassette or videotape. The programs are listed alphabetically by title and include order information, format, intended audience, authority, and a synopsis of the contents. The index uses the Medical Subject Headings System (MESH), with as many as three index entries for each title. R835.H4

Indexes

Medical socioeconomic research sources. Chicago, Amer. Medical Assoc. Division of Library and Archival Services; distr. by Aspen System Corp., Germantown, Md., 1971– . v.1– , 1971– . Quarterly with annual cumulation. **EK6**

Frequency varies: v.1–5, 1971–75, monthly with annual cumulations.

Supersedes *Index to medical socioeconomic literature* (v.1–9, 1962–70).

"A guide to current publications in the sociology and economics of medicine. Source documents include pamphlets, journal articles, theses, books, reports, legislation and unpublished speeches, as well as selected newspapers."—*Introd.* The items indexed are broadly defined to include the literature of the social sciences as related to health care and are taken from the general areas of economics, education, ethics, international relations, legislation, medical practice, political science, psychology, public health, and sociology. The annual cumulation also includes lists of books for the year and regularly reviewed serials. Subject and author indexes. Z6660.M47

Dictionaries

Black's Medical dictionary, by William A. R. Thompson. 31st ed. London, Adam & Charles Black; N.Y., Barnes & Noble, 1976. 950p. il. $15. **EK7**

30th ed. 1974 (*Guide* EK68).

"New sections have been added on cot deaths, drop attacks, Lassa fever, shin splints, sterilization, tattooing, and vasectomy, as well as many other subjects. There has also been the ongoing revision that characterizes each new edition, some of the more radically revised sections in this edition being those on autism, death, frostbite, prostaglandins, sleep, and transplantation."—*Pref.* R121.B598

Butterworths Medical dictionary. Macdonald Critchley, ed.-in-chief. 2d ed. London & Boston, Butterworths, [1978]. 1942p. $79.95. **EK8**

First published in 1961 as *The British medical dictionary*, ed. by Sir Arthur Salusbury MacNalty.

Includes an appendix on anatomical nomenclature, relating Nomina Anatomica nomenclature to English equivalent. R121.B75

Dorland's Illustrated medical dictionary. 25th ed. Philadelphia, Saunders, 1974. 1748p. il. $23.50. **EK9**

24th ed. 1965 (*Guide* EK70).

A group of 84 consultants reviewed all entries, resulting in "the most extensively revised edition of this Dictionary yet to be published."—*Pref.*

Stedman, Thomas Lathrop. Stedman's Medical dictionary. 23d ed. Baltimore, Williams & Wilkins, [1976]. 1678p. il. $21.95. **EK10**

22d ed. 1972 (*Guide* EK74).
This edition offers 10,322 new definitions. R121.S8

Specialized dictionaries

Regal, Waldo A. The inverted medical dictionary: a method of finding medical terms quickly. Westport, Conn., Technomic Publ. Co., 1976. 261p. $20; $14.50 pa. **EK11**

"When the correct term is known, it is a simple matter of looking for its meaning in a standard medical dictionary. Conversely, when the meaning or situation is apparent but the proper medical term must be identified, the same dictionary is of little help. This book is a medical dictionary in reverse. Each 'meaning' has been reduced to a brief key phrase. Alphabetically arranged, each phrase is followed by the appropriate medical term. In many cases synonymous terms are included to enable the reader to select the most applicable one." —*Pref.* R121.R54

Abbreviations

Hughes, Harold Kenneth. Dictionary of abbreviations in medicine and the health sciences. Lexington, Mass., Lexington Books, 1977. 313p. $23. **EK12**

Covers usage in the United States, Canada, Great Britain, Ireland, other parts of English-using Europe, Australasia, southern Africa, and the United Nations. Contains more than 12,000 entries with some 20,000 meanings. The abbreviations included are used in all areas of medicine and the health sciences, e.g., clinical, research, and production activities in all phases of professional care; food and energy resources; remedial education; veterinary science; and safety. The appendix provides conversion tables for weights, measures, and temperatures. R121.H89

Roody, Peter, Forman, Robert E. and **Schweitzer, Howard B.** Medical abbreviations and acronyms. N.Y., McGraw-Hill, 1976. 255p. $5.95 pa. **EK13**

Attempts to "set forth, in an orderly and easily accessible fashion, the most common medical and health-related abbreviations and their preferred forms . . . efforts were directed at standardization."—*Pref.* Over 14,000 entries with cross references. R121.R77

Handbooks

Altman, Philip L. and **Katz, Dorothy Dittmer,** eds. Human health and disease. Bethesda, Md., Federation of Amer. Societies for Experimental Biology, [1977]. 435p. (Biological handbooks, new series, v.2) $45. **EK14**

Contains "186 tables of quantitative and descriptive data. With few exceptions, which are clearly indicated, coverage throughout the book is for man."—*Introd.* RB37.2.A48

Child health encyclopedia: the complete guide for parents. The Boston Children's Medical Center and Richard I. Feinbloom. N.Y., Delacorte Pr., [1975]. 561p. $15. **EK15**

An encyclopedia with detailed information contributed by specialists about children's diseases and conditions from infancy to adolescence. RJ26.C45

Clark, Randolph Lee and **Cumley, Russell W.** The book of health: a medical encyclopedia for everyone. 3d ed. N.Y., Van Nostrand Reinhold, 1973. 925p. il. $29.95. **EK16**

1st ed. 1953; 2d ed. 1962.
"There are many things about the body and about the various diseases that the doctor does not have time to explain—things the patient should know in order to hold up his end of the medical partnership between physician and patient. It is hoped that these necessary explanations, which the physician often has to omit, may be found here. . . . many of today's physicians and scientists destined for future renown have edited the accounts of their contributions to medicine. Further, the care in its preparation and the expertness of knowledge of those who assisted make *The Book of Health* an acceptable source of information for the student of physiology and hygiene and for those preparing themselves for the study of medicine, nursing, dentistry, and technology."—*Foreword.*
Includes comprehensive index and glossary. RC81.C59

Medical risks: patterns of mortality and survival. Lexington, Mass., D. C. Heath, Lexington Books, [1976]. 1v., various paging. $27.50. **EK17**

A reference volume sponsored by The Association of Life Insurance Medical Directors of America and The Society of Actuaries.—*t.p.*
Richard B. Singer and Louis Levinson, eds.
"This book is a compilation of mortality and survival statistics in relation to risk factors identified in groups of people under follow-up observation."—*Chap. 1.* The data were "known to exist in many published articles scattered throughout the medical literature. If articles could be retrieved, critically evaluated, and useful data presented on a comparative basis within a uniform format, it was thought that the resulting tables would be of value not only to medical directors, underwriters, and actuaries in the life insurance industry but also to many workers in the health sciences."—*Pref.*
The broad topical arrangement in pt.I, The text, and in pt. II, The tables, is the same: Physical, toxic and other risks; Cancer; Neuropsychiatric disorders; Cardiovascular disorders; Respiratory disorders; Digestive system diseases; Genitourinary diseases; Systemic disorders; Endocrine and metabolic diseases. Includes author and subject indexes. RA407.M4

Merck manual of diagnosis and therapy. 13th ed. Rahway, N.J., Merck, 1977. 2165p. $10. **EK18**

Robert Berkow, ed.
12th ed. 1972 (*Guide* EK95).
"This edition . . . follows the basic format of its immediate predecessor, but it has been almost completely rewritten and the content has been increased by more than 60%. While emphasis remains on diagnosis and treatment, the discussions of basic physiologic, pathologic, and other factors essential to rational diagnostic reasoning and effective therapy have been enriched. More discussions of symptons and signs have been added . . . . Almost every section is larger . . . . A new section has been added to reflect advances in Clinical Pharmacology, and some sections, such as Immunology and Allergic Disorders, have been totally redone and greatly expanded."—*Foreword.* RC71.A1M47

Directories

Foreign medical school catalogue, 1971– . Bay Shore, N.Y., Foreign Medical School Information Center, 1971– . Annual. $19.95. **EK19**

Charles R. Modica, ed.
Includes medical schools from 65 foreign countries. Introductory section discusses the Education Commission for Foreign Medical Graduates (ECFMG) and the Coordinated Transfer Application System. The college listings are accompanied by statistics of their admissions, graduates, and performances on the ECFMG exams. The individual school programs and admission requirements do not have in-depth coverage. R711.F65

United States

Health care directory, 77–78, ed. by Craig T. Norback and Peter G. Norback. Oradell, N.J., Medical Economics Co., Book Div., [1977]. 1v., various paging. **EK20**

The table of contents reflects the alphabetical arrangement of the text's sixty broad subject headings which start with Adoption information, Aged, Ambulance manufacturers, Ambulance service, through Sex counselling & education, Shows & conventions, Social welfare organizations, and end with Volunteer work opportunities. Arrangement under the headings is by state then alphabetically by names of agencies, businesses, institutions, organizations, societies, etc. RA7.5.H42

Medical and health information directory. Detroit, Gale, 1977. 664p. $48. **EK21**

Subtitle: A guide to state, national and international organizations, government agencies, education institutions, hospitals, grant-award sources, health care delivery agencies, journals, newsletters, review serials, abstracting services, publishers, research centers, computerized data banks, audiovisual services, and libraries and information centers.

Anthony T. Kruzas and Robert Fitch Allen, eds.

R118.4.U6M4

National health directory. 2d ed. Wash., Science and Health Publ., 1978. 500p. $22.50. **EK22**

1st ed. 1977.

Contents arranged in 9 sections: (1) Table of contents/Agency index; (2) Congressional name index; (3) Name index (other than U.S. senators and representatives); (4) Key congressional health subcommittees; (5) Congressional delegations; (6) Congressional full committees and their subcommittees dealing with health matters; (7) Federal agencies; (8) Federal regional officers; (9) State officials.

"A complete directory including the name, title, address and telephone number of more than 7,500 key information sources on health programs and legislation. Includes congressmen, their health legislative aides and appointment secretaries in Washington and district offices . . . ."—*t.p.* RA7.5.N37

Who's who in health care: first edition 1977. N.Y., Hanover Publ., 1977. 746p. $60. **EK23**

Contains over 8,000 biographical sketches, detailing professional background and achievements. "Every effort was made to insure the inclusion of the Nation's leadership in every possible aspect of the health care field, including: schools, pharmaceutical and insurance industries, voluntary associations, researchers, consultants, hospital executives, etc."—*Pref.* R712.A1W35

History

Bibliography of the history of medicine, 1970–74. Bethesda, Md., Nat. Lib. of Medicine, [1975]. 1069p. $16. **EK24**

The second cumulative index, cumulating nos.6–10 of the *Bibliography* (*Guide* EK117). Z6660.B5822

DENTISTRY

Guides

American Dental Association. Bureau of Library Services. Basic dental reference works. Chicago, Amer. Dental Assoc., 1975. 26p. **EK25**

Prepared by Aletha Kowitz.

"This annotated listing of 104 titles is yet another attempt to provide a guide to the most pertinent works that the dental reference librarian and others who use the dental literature cannot work without."—*t.p.* The lists of basic dental reference works, with short annotations, are arranged under the headings: dictionaries, indexes, surveys, syndromes, directories, bibliographies, current practice, histories, sources, and miscellaneous. RK51.A54

Directories

Admission requirements of U.S. and Canadian dental schools, 1974/75– . Wash., Amer. Assoc. of Dental Schools, 1974– . Annual. (1978/79: $7.50) **EK26**

Continues *Admission requirements of American dental schools*, 1963–74.

Provides an extensive range of information for each school: general information, description of programs, admission requirements, applications processes, costs, etc. RK91.A54

NURSING

Miller, Benjamin Frank and **Keane, Claire B.** Encyclopedia and dictionary of medicine, nursing and allied health. 2d ed. Philadelphia, Saunders, 1978. 1148p. il. $16.95. **EK27**

1st ed (1972) had title: *Encyclopedia and dictionary of medicine and nursing* (*Guide* EK168).

The greater emphasis on patient care and patient education is reflected in the title change. Updated list of "Agencies and organizations concerned with the promotion of health and management of disease." R121.M65

NUTRITION

Bibliography

Food and Agriculture Organization of the United Nations. Food composition tables: updated annotated bibliography. Rome, FAO; distr. by Unipub, N.Y., 1975. 181p. $12 pa. **EK28**

1965 ed. had title: *Review of food composition tables*; 1970 ed. had title: *Food composition tables: annotated bibliography.*

Arranged (1) by continent, (2) by country. Includes information on techniques of gathering data.

Dictionaries and handbooks

Adams, Catherine F. Nutritive value of American foods in common units. Wash., Agricultural Research Service, U.S. Dept. of Agriculture, 1975. 291p. (Agriculture handbook, no.456) $5.15. **EK29**

Based on Agriculture handbook no. 8 *Composition of foods: raw, processed, prepared* (*Guide* EK179).

"This publication has been prepared to serve as a basic reference for data on nutrients in frequently used household measures and market units of food."—*Introd.* Two basic sections: Táble 1, Nutritive values for household measures and market units of foods; Table 2, Fatty acid values for household measures and market units of foods. Uses generic names of foods. TX551.A35

Consumer and Food Economics Institute. Composition of foods. Wash., Agricultural Research Service, U.S. Dept. of Agriculture, 1976–77. looseleaf. (In progress) (Agriculture handbook, no.8–1–) no.8–1, $3; no.8–2, $1.30. **EK30**

Contents: no.8–1, Dairy and egg products: raw, processed, prepared; no.8–2, Spices and herbs: raw, processed, prepared.

"This publication is a major revision of the 1963 edition of USDA Agriculture Handbook No.8, 'Composition of Foods . . . Raw, Processed, Prepared,' currently a basic source of food composition data in this country."—*Foreword.* "This revision . . . is being issued in sections so as to expedite release of data to the public. Each section contains a table of nutrient data for a major food group. The entire series will cover a wide range of food products."—*Pref.*

TX556.M5C68

Fenaroli, Giovanni. Fenaroli's Handbook of flavor ingredients: adapted from [his] Italian language works. 2d ed. Cleveland, CRC Pr., [1975]. 2v. (928p.) il. v.1, $49.95; v.2, $59.95. **EK31**

At head of title: CRC.

Ed., trans., and rev. by Thomas E. Furia and Nicolo Bellanca.

1st ed. 1971.

Contents: v.1, pt.1, General considerations; pt.2, Natural flavor; v.2, pt.3, Synthetic flavor; pt.4, Use of flavor ingredients.

The scope of these volumes is the same as for the 1st ed., "to present a current, authoritative, first-source description of natural and synthetic flavor ingredients, their detailed characteristics, and their application in food. It is primarily intended for those using flavors rather than for the accomplished *flavorist.*"—*Editorial foreword, 1st ed.* "New material presented includes the following: (1)

Data on new synthetic flavor ingredients; (2) Updating of natural occurrence of flavor ingredients; (3) Addition of references, augmenting many of the topics . . . ; (4) Through the cooperation of CRC Press utilization of new, comprehensive reviews on significant flavor topics."—*Pref.* Indexed. TP418.F4613

McGraw-Hill encyclopedia of food, agriculture & nutrition. Daniel N. Lapedes, ed. in chief. N.Y., McGraw-Hill, 1977. 732p. il. $24.50. **EK32**

Most of the material is drawn from the *McGraw-Hill encyclopedia of science and technology* (*Suppl.* EA13). Cross references; indexed.

National Research Council. Food and Nutrition Board. Recommended dietary allowances. 8th rev. ed. Wash., 1974. 128p. $4.25 pa. **EK33**

For previous editions *see Guide* EK177.

In this revision the latest research cited seems to be mainly 1972, with a few references to early 1973 noted. Bibliography of references, pp.103–28.

PHARMACOLOGY

Guides

Sewell, Winifred. Guide to drug information. Hamilton, Ill., Drug Intelligence Publ., [1976]. 218p. il. $12. **EK34**

Prepared by librarian-bibliographers; primarily oriented toward problem-solving. Arranged in four parts: (1) handbooks, drug compendia, and related works with tables of comparative information and data; (2) use of primary sources—periodicals, monographs, etc.; (3) searching patterns and secondary sources—abstracts, indexes, etc.; (4) methods and use of current awareness searching and technology—computers, etc.

Dictionaries

Marler, E. E. J., comp. Pharmacological and chemical synonyms; a collection of names of drugs, pesticides and other compounds drawn from the medical literature of the world. 6th ed. with suppl. New York & Amsterdam, Elsevier, 1978. 510p. $49.75. **EK35**

5th ed. 1973 (*Guide* EK192).

A reprint in paperback of the 6th ed. (1976) together with a supplement of new drugs which have appeared since, new synonyms, and updated entries.

Handbooks

AMA drug evaluations. 3d ed. Acton, Mass., Publishing Sciences Group, 1977. 1326p. **EK36**

2d ed. 1973 (*Guide* EK194).

This edition "marks the initiation of a joint cooperative effort between the AMA Department of Drugs and the American Society for Clinical Pharmacology and Therapeutics. . . . The successful format of previous editions has been retained, but most of the text has been completely rewritten or rigorously revised. Evaluations of over 50 new drugs marketed since the last edition have been included, as well as information on some investigational agents. The use of tables has been expanded . . . , and an extensive listing for normal values of clinical laboratory tests have been added in an appendix."—*Pref.* RM300.A57

Handbook of non-prescription drugs. 5th ed. Wash., Amer. Pharmaceutical Assoc., 1977. 388p. $12.50. **EK37**

1st ed. 1969.

"The American Pharmaceutical Association offers this Fifth Edition of the *Handbook of Non-prescription Drugs*, the only definitive compilation of facts on home remedies . . . we feel confident that the *Handbook* will make the reader a little safer, and nonprescription drugs a little more useful."—*Pref.* There are 32 chapters with broad headings such as: Antacid products, Laxative products, Asthma products. Each chapter discusses the etiology of the condition; the anatomy, physiology, and pathophysiology of the affected systems; the signs and symptoms; the treatment and adjunctive measures; an evaluation of ingredients in over-the-counter products; and important patient and product considerations. RM671.A1H35

Long, James W. The essential guide to prescription drugs; what you need to know for safe drug use. N.Y., Harper & Row, 1977. 751p. $25; $8.95 pa. **EK38**

"This book is meant to be a source of basic information about the most commonly used drugs—the equivalent of a 'patient package insert'—presented in an accessible form for you and your family. It is *not* a do-it-yourself manual that can substitute for professional judgment and the direction of the physician."—*Pref.* The data are arranged under the generic drug names, for which are given dosage, side effects, adverse reactions, etc. There is a cross-index from over 1,500 brand names to the generic names. RM300.L64

Modern drug encyclopedia and therapeutic index. 14th ed. N.Y., Yorke Medical, 1977. 1009p. $37. **EK39**

Arthur J. Lewis, ed.

12th ed. 1973 (*Guide* EK198).

Updated, with some new entries added. Now includes sections on the Drug Enforcement Administration and on drug and chemical blood level data. RS153.M57

TOXICOLOGY

Handbooks

Dreisbach, Robert Hastings. Handbook of poisoning: diagnosis & treatment. 9th ed. Los Altos, Calif., Lange Medical Publ., 1977. 559p. $8. **EK40**

1st–8th eds. publ. 1955–74; 1st ed. had title: *Handbook of poisons.*

Contents: I, General considerations; II, Agricultural poisons; III, Industrial hazards; IV, Household hazards—cosmetics, food poisoning, miscellaneous chemicals; V, Medicinal poisons; VI, Animal and plant hazards—reptiles, arachnids & insects, marine animals, plants.

"The purpose of this Handbook is to provide a concise summary of the diagnosis and treatment of clinically important poisons. Many other potentially poisonous agents which have not been important clinically are included in tabular form."—*Pref.* RA1211.D7

Gosselin, Robert E. [and others]. Clinical toxicology of commercial products: acute poisoning. 4th ed. Baltimore, Williams & Wilkins, [1976]. 1v., various paging. $54. **EK41**

3d ed. 1969 (*Guide* EK223).

"The increasing number of poisonings by drugs, both proprietary and prescription drugs, impelled us to increase the number of such items included in this edition . . . . Contributing manufacturers were given the opportunity to edit descriptions of their products as they appeared in the 1963 and 1969 editions. Many manufacturers were given this opportunity again in 1973 and 1974."—*Pref.*

A monthly supplement, "Clinical toxicology of commercial products," is distributed to state public health offices and poison control centers throughout the United States. RA1211.G5

Plunkett, Edmond Robert. Handbook of industrial toxicology. 2d ed. N.Y., Chemical Publ. Co., 1976. 552p. **EK42**

1st ed. 1966 (*Guide* EK99).

"The previous data has been reviewed and revised, and new material has been introduced. . . . Bibliographic footnotes have been added where they represent good general review articles or where they contain excellent bibliographies to which the reader may refer." —*Pref.* RA1216.P55

Registry of toxic effects of chemical substances. Rockville, Md., U.S. Dept. of Health, Education, and Welfare, 1976– . Annual. (U.S. Dept. of Health, Education, and Welfare, NIOSH series) $17.50. **EK43**

Edward J. Fairchild, ed.

Continues National Institute for Occupational Safety and Health, *Toxic substances list*, 1971–75.

The 1977 ed. is in 2v.: v.1 is an index volume, containing an alphabetical index to all substances covered as well as separate indexes to subfiles of compounds that are (a) carcinogenic and neoplastic, (b) teratogenic, (c) mutagenic, and (d) toxic to humans; v.2 contains, when available, Chemical Abstracts Service compound name, CAS registry number, synonyms, common or trade names, molecular weight, molecular formula, toxic levels with literature references, standards and regulations, and references to review articles. RA1215.N37

VETERINARY MEDICINE

Merck veterinary manual; a handbook of diagnosis and therapy for the veterinarian. 4th ed. Rahway, N.J., Merck, 1973. 1600p. $13.25. **EK44**

O. H. Siegmund, ed.

2d ed. 1967 (*Guide* EK231).

A considerably revised edition. Now in eight parts, with more attention to diseases, especially those occurring outside North America, and those found in poultry and laboratory animals. SF745.M4

Universities Federation for Animal Welfare. The UFAW handbook on the care and management of laboratory animals. 5th ed. Edinburgh, Churchill Livingstone, 1976. 635p. £15. **EK45**

1st ed. 1949; 4th ed. 1972.

A detailed and practical approach to the care and management of laboratory animals. Chapters 1–15 give general information on such topics as: genetic aspects of breeding methods, the animal house and its equipment, transportation of laboratory animals, anaesthesia, euthanasia, and post-mortem techniques for laboratory animals. Chapters 16–51 give information for specific animals or groups of animals. Includes the more common animals such as: anura, cats, dogs, guinea pigs, hamsters, mice, rabbits, rats, primates; and the less common such as: gerbils, ferrets, fowl, reptiles, freshwater fish, land freshwater molluscs, blowflies, beetles, wild rats, etc. Information given for specific animals or animal groups includes: standard biological data, husbandry, feeding, diseases, disease control and treatment, uses, and a list of references for additional and/or more specific information. Indexed. SF406.U54

E L

Agricultural Sciences

AGRICULTURE

Encyclopedias

Wyman, Donald. Wyman's Gardening encyclopedia. Revised and expanded. N.Y., Macmillan, [1977]. 1221p. $19.95. **EL1**

1st ed. 1971.

"This Revised Edition contains many plant name changes that have been recorded in the recently published *Hortus III.*"—*Foreword.* A table of contents has been added. Authoritative; geared to United States conditions. SB45.W97

Handbooks

Pesticide handbook—Entoma, 1975–76. College Park, Md., Entomological Soc. of America, 1975– . Ed.26– . Biennial. (27th ed., 1977/78: $7.50) **EL2**

Pesticide handbook (1st ed. 1949) merged with *Entoma* and continues the volume numbering of the *Handbook.*

Contents of the 27th ed.: Consolidated list of approved common names of insecticides and certain other pesticides; Up-to-date listings of commercial products and equipment; General reference information, regulations, pesticide companies, poison control centers, etc. SB951.P415

Pesticide index. 5th ed. College Park, Md., Entomological Soc. of America, 1976. 328p. $12. **EL3**

Comp. and ed. by William J. Wiswesser.

1st ed. 1961.

Contents: Pesticide index—Alphabetic listings, numeric listings; CAS nomenclature index; Molecular formulas; Wiswesser line notations; Appendix I, A selected list of some basic chemical manufacturers owning registered trademarks; Appendix II, A selected list of some recent publications dealing with pesticide names.

The alphabetic listings contain all the available information for the pesticide, *i.e.*, CAS nomenclature, CAS registry number, molecular formula, use, physical appearance. SB951.P42

U.S. Forest Service. Seeds of woody plants in the United States. Wash., Forest Service, 1974. 883p. il. (Agricultural handbook no.450) $20.50. **EL4**

Completely rewritten and greatly expanded edition of *Woody-plant seed manual*, 1948 (U.S. Dept. of Agriculture. Misc. publ. no.654).

"Part 1 includes chapters on the principles and general methods of producing and handling seeds. Part 2 is a compilation of seed data on 188 genera of woody plants including flowering and fruiting dates, seed processing methods, storage conditions, seed yields and weights, methods of breaking seed dormancy, germination tests, and a large collection of fruit and seed photographs."—*verso of t.p.* S501.U53

The world's worst weeds: distribution and biology. LeRoy G. Holm [and others]. Honolulu, publ. for the East-West Center by Univ. Pr. of Hawaii, [1977]. 609p. il. maps. $35. **EL5**

"This is an inventory of the [about 300] principal weeds of the world's [16] major crops, with particular emphasis on their distribution, seriousness, and their known biology."—*Pref.*

The arrangement is by weeds (pt.I) and by crops (pt.II). Appendix A lists useful publications on weed distribution, identification, biology and control. Appendix B lists books and special publications on poisonous plants. The index is comprehensive and is international in the choice of common names. SB611.W67

History

Schapsmeier, Edward L. and **Schapsmeier, Frederick H.** Encyclopedia of American agricultural history. Westport, Conn., Greenwood Pr., [1975]. 467p. $25. **EL6**

Aims "to provide information on all areas bearing on agricultural history" (*Pref.*) for the beginning student as well as the scholar. Includes entries for terms, persons, events, organizations, publications, legislative acts, etc. Some bibliographic references. Includes a general index and a number of special indexes, which group references topically. S441.S36

FORESTRY

Bibliography

Davis, Richard C. North American forest history: a guide to archives and manuscripts in the United States and Canada. Santa Barbara, Calif., ABC-Clio, 1977. 376p. $63.75. **EL7**

Sponsored by Forest History Society, Inc. Companion to the Fahl volume (below).

A guide to the 108 repositories in forest archives which were identified in 1956. Each of the 3,830 groups or collections of documents is numbered and arranged by state. Subject index is to entry number. Z5991.D33

Fahl, Ronald J. North American forest and conservation history: a bibliography. Santa Barbara, Calif., ABC-Clio, 1977. 408p. $39.75. **EL8**

Sponsored by Forest History Society, Inc. Companion to the Davis volume (above).

A historical bibliography listing primary and secondary sources covering the exploitation, utilization, and appreciation of the forest and its resources. Over 8,000 annotated references, listed alphabetically, and indexed by subject. Z5991.F33

Handbooks

The international book of wood. Martyn Bramwell and Janette Place, eds. N.Y., Simon and Schuster, 1976. 276p. il. $29.95. **EL9**

Major sections of text: anatomy of wood, renewable resources, architecture in wood, sacred buildings, living with wood, ships and shipwrights, artistry in wood, lore and legend and belief, and survey of world timbers. In the last section 144 hard and soft woods are described in detail, giving their use, treatment, and properties that make them commercially important. Index. TS820.I56

HOME ECONOMICS

Food and cookery

Bibliography

Axford, Lavonne B. English language cookbooks, 1600–1973. Detroit, Gale, 1976. 675p. $45. **EL10**

Title-ordered list of over 11,000 cookbooks. No annotations. Author index; subject index.

Patten, Marguerite. Books for cooks: a bibliography of cookery. N.Y., Bowker, 1975. 526p. $19.50. **EL11**

An annotated bibliography of more than 1,700 cookery books of relatively recent publication date, mainly in print at time of compilation. Aims "to cover every available type of cuisine and cookery."—*Introd.* Author listing with subject and title indexes.

Cookbooks

Rombauer, Irma S. and **Becker, Marion.** Joy of cooking. Newly rev. and expanded ed. N.Y., Bobbs-Merrill, 1975. 915p. $10. **EL12**

For 1964 ed. *see Guide* EL93.

A greatly revised and expanded edition of this standard cookbook, now including more than 4,500 recipes.

Wines

Johnson, Hugh. The world atlas of wine; a complete guide to the wines & spirits of the world. [enl. and completely rev.] N.Y., Simon and Schuster, [1978]. 288p. il., maps. $29.95. **EL13**

1st ed. 1971.

Contents: Introduction, Choosing and serving wine, France, Germany, Southern and eastern Europe and the Mediterranean, The new world, Spirits.

Describes the wines of specific parts of the world. Each area is accompanied by a map, generally detailed. Index; gazetteer.

F

Data Bases

❖The use of computer-readable data bases, and particularly their use through on-line systems, has developed rapidly in the past few years and is now considered to be a normal part of library reference work. More than 500 computer-readable data bases are publicly available. They contain more than seventy million references to journal articles, monographs, and newspaper articles; approximately fifty million of the references are searchable through on-line systems in the United States, Canada, and Europe. Since on-line searching requires a relatively small initial investment in equipment (a terminal and an acoustic coupler are all that is required for a searcher to query a multiplicity of systems and data bases), the tremendous resource of data bases is available to large and small libraries and information centers. It must be kept in mind, however, that charges for on-line search time are often significant and must either be borne by the library or passed along to the patron requesting the search.

Organizations that offer on-line data base searches (libraries, information centers, and information brokers) must have trained searchers who are familiar with features and characteristics of the systems used as well as the content, coverage, and indexing practices of the data bases searched. Data bases may be used for retrospective searches (limited by the time span of the data base searched), quick answers to questions, current-awareness services, data base analysis, and bibliometric studies. To make proper use of each data base the searcher must have access to appropriate user aids—manuals, thesauri, dictionaries, etc.—for the system and data base employed.

The major on-line service organizations for bibliographic

data base searching are: Lockheed Information Systems, Bibliographic Retrieval Services, the National Library of Medicine, System Development Corporation, and the New York Times in the United States; the Canada Institute for Science and Technology and QL Systems in Canada; and Information Retrieval Services of the European Space Agency, the British Library, DIMDINET, and SCANNET in Europe.

In addition to systems for searching bibliographic and natural-language data bases, there are numerous systems for searching numeric and factographic data bases. Numeric data bases are used by "end users" and specialist technicians more than by librarians or other intermediaries. However, some of these systems are being used in special libraries. Among the major systems providing on-line access to numeric data bases are: Data Resources, Chase Econometric Associates, Cyphernet, IDC, Telstat Systems, General Electric, On-Line Systems, ADP Network Services, The Computer Company, IMS, IDC, Bowne Time Sharing, and Time Share Corporation.

The survey which follows is limited to a selection of representative and major data bases. A brief bibliography of directories, periodicals, yearbooks, and current sources of information on new developments in the field of data bases and on-line searching is appended.

DATA BASE DESCRIPTIONS

The data bases described below are grouped into five broad categories according to subject content: (1) general, (2) humanities, (3) social sciences, (4) history and area studies, and (5) pure and applied sciences. Descriptions generally include the following elements:

Data base full name (with acronym); former name or acronym if appropriate

Producer name and address

Correspondence with printed source

Description of contents

Coverage in terms of years for literature or items included; cumulative number of citations or items from initiation through 1978; anticipated number added annually; number of journals used for source material; type of indexing used for access points in searching and availability of abstracts; on-line access sites or batch searching sites when data base is not on-line.

Not every data base description includes every one of these elements. Some were not known, others were not appropriate. In some cases, if an element description included data for another element, the data were not requested. The cumulative number of citations is a total for the data base as a whole; if a data base is comprised of several files, records are totaled in the one number. The number of citations or items in the data base does not necessarily indicate the number of references that are on-line through a specific vendor or available for batch searching through centers. If a data base corresponds to several printed sources, there is no implication that the first year of coverage includes material for all printed sources; the first year as here cited refers to the first year for any one of the component files. The indication of number of journals for source material ignores other types of sources unless an individual source type contributes a large percentage of citations or items to the data base. When it is indicated that the data base "corresponds with printed source of same name," the printed source may actually be multiple sources (e.g., specific years of named source, indexes to the named source, and cumulative or other special combinations of the named source). The indication of types of access points used for searching is not all inclusive. The intent here is to show whether controlled vocabulary is used. In most cases several other types of subject access are available, and in almost all cases free language terms in titles can be searched. Where abstracts are included, they are generally searchable. The indication of on-line and batch access is not exhaustive; it includes the names of those vendors or centers named by the data base producer as licensed users. Additional data base vendors or processors may be added at any time, or a given vendor may drop a data base. Names of major vendors have been abbreviated as follows:

BRS	Bibliographic Retrieval Service
CISTI	Canada Institute for Scientific and Technical Information
DIMDI	Deutsches Institut für Medizinische Dokumentation und Information
ESA	European Space Agency
LIS	Lockheed Information Systems
NERAC	New England Research and Applications Center
OCLC	OCLC, Inc.
SDC	System Development Corporation.

Fuller information on all of the data bases in this listing may be found in the Williams and O'Donnell directory cited in the appended bibliography and *Suppl.* EJ49.

FA

General

Comprehensive dissertation index (CDI). University Microfilms Internatl., Ann Arbor, Mich. **FA1**

Corresponds to printed source of same name (*Guide* AH10). Covers citations to U.S. and Canadian doctoral dissertations from 1861 to the present and master's theses published by U.M.I. (Does not search the abstracts found in *Dissertation abstracts international.*) Approximately 660,000 citations through 1978; adds 39,000 per year; controlled terms and numeric subject codes; on-line through BRS, LIS, and SDC.

The information bank. The New York Times Information Services, Parsippany, N.J. **FA2**

Covers all news and editorial matter from the *New York Times* plus material from more than 60 additional general circulation, business, and financial newspapers and magazines. Data base covers 1969 to present; approximately 1,600,000 citations through 1978; adds 200,000 per year; controlled terms and abstracts; on-line through the Information Bank.

Library and information science abstracts (LISA). Library Assoc., London. **FA3**

Corresponds to printed source of same name (*Guide* AB12). Worldwide coverage of the field of library and information science, including generation, processing, storage, retrieval, and reproduction of information in hard copy, microform, and computer-readable form. Data base covers 1969 to present; approximately 27,000 citations through 1978; adds 4,000 per year; from 300 journals; controlled and uncontrolled terms and abstracts; on-line through LIS and SDC, batch searched through NERAC.

Machine-readable cataloging (Books) (MARC (Books)). Lib. of Congress, Wash., D.C. **FA4**

Corresponds to the *National union catalog* (*Guide* AA95). Includes books on all subjects collected by Library of Congress in English from 1968 to present, in French from 1973 to present, and in German from 1975 to present; approximately 909,100 records through 1978; adds 20,000 per year; Library of Congress call numbers and Dewey Decimal Classification numbers; on-line through OCLC and batch searched through CISTI and the Mechanized Information Center at Ohio State University.

MARC (Films). Lib. of Congress, Wash., D.C. **FA5**

Corresponds to *Library of Congress catalogs: films and other materials for projection* (*Guide* BG117). Includes records for all films cataloged by Library of Congress since 1972, plus some materials released in the United States and Canada which have an educational or institutional value. Data base covers 1972 to present; approximately 50,000 items through 1978; adds 7,400 per year; Library of Congress and Dewey classification numbers; on-line through OCLC and batch searched by producer.

——— **(Maps).** Lib. of Congress, Wash., D.C. **FA6**

Includes all single and multi-sheet thematic maps, map sets, and maps treated as serials in all languages currently received, cataloged, or re-cataloged by Library of Congress. Data base covers 1973 to present; approximately 36,000 citations through 1978; adds 6,000 per year; Library of Congress call numbers and map classification codes; batch searched by producer.

——— **(Serials).** Lib. of Congress, Wash., D.C. **FA7**

Includes all serials in all Roman and non-Roman alphabet languages that are currently cataloged or re-cataloged by Library of Congress. Data base covers 1973 to present; approximately 93,000 citations through 1978; adds 39,000 per year; Library of Congress and Dewey classification numbers; on-line through OCLC and batch searched by the producer.

MARC distribution service—GPO monthly catalog. Govt. Prt. Off., Alexandria, Va. **FA8**

Corresponds to the *Monthly catalog of United States government publications* (*Guide* AG25). Includes unclassified documents produced at the government's expense. Data base covers 1976 to present; approximately 50,000 citations through 1978; adds 20,000 per year; subject headings and subject codes; on-line through BRS and LIS.

Magazine index (MI). Information Access Corp., Los Altos, Calif. **FA9**

Corresponds to microfilm source of same name. Covers articles, news reports, editorials on major issues, product evaluations, biographies, short stories, poetry, recipes, and reviews from popular American magazines. Data base covers 1976 to present; approximately 180,000 citations through 1978; adds 75,000 per year; from 374 journals; subject headings and free language terms; on-line through LIS.

F B

The Humanities

See also Suppl. FC9.

Artbibliographies modern (ABM). Clio Pr., Ltd., Oxford, England. **FB1**

Corresponds to printed source of same name (*Suppl.* BE21). Covers publications on modern art and design for the period 1800 to the present; data base covers 1973 to present; approximately 28,000 citations through 1978; adds 8,000 per year; from 500 journals plus monographs; controlled and free language index terms and abstracts; on-line through LIS.

Philosopher's index data base. Philosophy Documentation Center, Bowling Green State Univ., Ohio. **FB2**

Corresponds to printed source, the *Philosopher's index* (*Guide* BA24). Covers American philosophy journals and books published from 1940 to the present and international philosophy journals from 1967. Data base covers 1940 to present; approximately 60,000 citations; adds 13,000 per year; controlled index terms and abstracts included; batch searching available through the producer.

Religion index one: periodicals and Religion index two: multi-author works (RIO-RIT). American Theological Library Association Indexes, Chicago. (Formerly *Index to religious periodical literature*) **FB3**

Corresponds to printed source of same name (*Suppl.* BB9). Citations to articles and monographs on religion, theology, church history, ethics, and other fields as they relate to religion. Data base covers 1974 to present; approximately 28,000 citations through 1978; adds 12,000 per year from 200 journals; controlled index terms and abstracts included; batch searching available through the producer.

F C

Social Sciences

See also Suppl. FE11, FE15.

ABI/INFORM. Data Courier, Louisville, Ky. **FC1**

United States and international coverage of all phases of management and administration. Data base covers 1971 to present; approximately 82,000 citations through 1978; adds 14,500 per year; from 400 journals; controlled index terms and abstracting; on-line through BRS, LIS, and SDC.

American statistics index (ASI). Congressional Information Service, Wash., D.C. **FC2**

Corresponds to printed source of same name (*Guide* CG76). Covers the spectrum of social, economic, and demographic data collected and analyzed by all branches and agencies of the United States government, including publications generated by the major federal statistical agencies (Bureau of the Census, Bureau of Labor Statistics, National Center for Social Statistics, National Center for Education Statistics, and the Statistical Reporting Center for the Department of Agriculture) as well as other branches and agencies. Data base covers 1973 to present; approximately 60,000 records through 1978; adds 10,000 per year; controlled index terms, free language terms, and abstracts; on-line through SDC.

Congressional Information Service/Index to congressional publications and public laws (CIS index). Congressional Information Service, Wash., D.C. **FC3**

Corresponds to printed source of same name (*Guide* CJ83). Covers significant publications issued by nearly 300 House, Senate, and joint committees and subcommittees of the U.S. Congress. Data base covers 1970 to present; approximately 100,000 citations through 1978; adds 14,000 per year; controlled index terms, free language terms and abstracts; on-line through SDC.

Congressional record abstracts (CRECORD). Capital Services, Wash., D.C. **FC4**

Corresponds to printed source of same name. Covers the *Congressional record*, bills and resolutions, amendments to bills and resolutions, committee and subcommittee reports, legislation recently signed into law, floor actions, schedules of committees and their floor activities, executive communications, speeches, and debates. Data base covers 1976 to present; approximately 150,000 citations through 1978; adds 80,000 per year; subject codes and free language terms; on-line through SDC.

Current index to journals in education (CIJE). Educational Resources Information Center (ERIC), Nat. Inst. of Education, Wash., D.C. **FC5**

Corresponds to printed source of same name (*Guide* CB81). References to journal articles dealing with education and curriculum materials. Data base covers 1969 to present; approximately 186,000 citations through 1978; adds 20,000 per year; from 730 journals; controlled index terms, free language terms and abstracts; on-line through BRS, LIS, and SDC.

Data base on European doctoral theses in management (DISSERT 1). European Inst. for Advanced Studies in Management, Brussels. **FC6**

Corresponds to *Bibliography on European doctoral theses in management*. Approximately 2,300 citations through 1978; adds 400 per year; controlled terms and abstracts; on-line through the producer.

Defense market measures system (DM2). Frost and Sullivan, N.Y. **FC7**

Corresponds to the *Commerce business daily*. Covers contracts awarded, requests for proposals, and R&D sources sought by the federal government related to defense and the space industry as issued by DOD, ERDA, FAA, NASA, all civil agencies, plus key sub-contracts. Data base covers 1960 to present; 1,750,000 citations through 1978; adds 75,000 per year; "system product categories" and "capability product categories"; on-line through LIS and available for batch searching through the producer.

F&S index of corporations and industries (F&S index). Predicasts, Cleveland. **FC8**

Corresponds to printed source of same name (*Guide* CH111). Includes domestic and international coverage of significant business information on a country, company, and industry basis. Data base covers 1970 to present; approximately 1,100,000 records through 1978; adds 301,000 per year; from 950 journals and government reports; controlled index terms; on-line through LIS and SDC.

Language and language behavior abstracts (LLBA). Sociological Abstracts, San Diego, Calif. **FC9**

Corresponds to printed source of same name (*Guide* BC18). Citations to the world's literature on speech and language pathology. Data base covers 1973 to present; approximately 32,000 citations through 1978; adds 6,000 per year; from 1,000 domestic and foreign journals; controlled index terms, free language terms, and abstracts; on-line through LIS.

LEXIS (formerly called OBAR). Mead Data Central, N.Y. **FC10**

Covers federal and state court reported cases; federal and state constitutions, codes, rules and regulations; decisions from certain government agencies; and material related to specific subject matters. Comprises 25 component files: 5 federal files, 19 state files, and an "All states" file covering decisions of all state courts in the LEXIS service. Data base years of coverage vary with files, the earliest going back to 1890; approximately eleven billion characters through 1978; adds 500 million characters per year; full text searching; on-line through producer.

Management contents data base. Management Contents, Skokie, Ill. **FC11**

Corresponds to printed source entitled *Management contents* (*Suppl.* CH49). Includes business and management literature from 220 journals. Data base covers 1974 to present; approximately 55,000 citations through 1978; adds 15,000 per year; controlled index terms, subject headings, and abstracts; on-line through BRS, LIS, and SDC; batch searching through NERAC.

Predicasts overview of markets and technologies (PROMPT). Predicasts, Cleveland. **FC12**

Corresponds to *Chemical market abstracts* and *Electronics and equipment market abstracts*, thus representing a merger of the data bases formerly designated as CMA and EMA. Worldwide coverage of all significant literature pertaining to chemical process industries and literature significant to the electronics market, including computers, communications systems and equipment, consumer electronics, and aerospace. Data base covers 1972 to present; approximately 250,000 citations through 1978; adds 79,500 per year; controlled index terms and abstracts; on-line through LIS.

Resources in education (RIE). Educational Resources Information Center (ERIC), Nat. Inst. of Education, Wash., D.C. **FC13**

Corresponds to printed source of same name (*Suppl.* CB30). Includes references to reports filed by contractors and grantees on the results of funded educational research, curriculum materials, information science, library science, and other education-related materials. Data base covers 1966 to present; approximately 151,000 citations through 1978; adds 15,500 per year; controlled index terms, free language terms, and abstracts; on-line through BRS, LIS, SDC, ERIC Processing and Reference Facility, ERIC Clearinghouse on Information Resources, Tokyo Shibaura Electric Co., and University of Wisconsin Academic Computing Center.

Social sciences citation index (SSCI). Inst. for Scientific Information, Philadelphia. **FC14**

Corresponds to printed source of same name (*Guide* CA37). Provides worldwide coverage of the principal journals of the social sciences and also to related journals in the natural, physical, and biomedical sciences. Data base covers 1969 to present; approximately 856,000 references through 1978; adds 30,000 per year; citation indexing; on-line through BRS, LIS, and SDC.

United States political science documents (USPSD). Univ. Center for Internatl. Studies, Univ. of Pittsburgh, Pittsburgh, Pa. **FC15**

Corresponds to printed source of same name (*Suppl.* CJ23). Covers the broad field of political science, including government, international relations, public policy, area studies, social sciences, public administration, law and legislation, and urban and regional planning. Data base covers 1975 to present; approximately 10,000 citations through 1978; adds 3,600 per year; indexed with controlled and free language terms; abstracts included; available on-line through LIS and SDC.

F D

History and Area Studies

America: history and life (AHL). Amer. Bibliographical Center (ABC-Clio, Inc.), Santa Barbara, Calif. **FD1**

Corresponds to printed source of same name (*Guide* DB29). Citations to journal articles, book reviews, and dissertations on United States and Canadian history and culture from prehistoric times to the present. Data base covers 1954 to present; approximately 98,000 citations through 1978; adds 11,500 per year; from 1,900 journals and other sources; indexed with controlled and free language terms; abstracts included; on-line through LIS.

Historical abstracts (HA). Amer. Bibliographical Center (ABC-Clio, Inc.), Santa Barbara, Calif. **FD2**

Corresponds to printed source of same name (*Guide* DA24). Includes: Pt.A, Modern history abstracts, 1450–1914; Pt.B, Twentieth century abstracts, 1914 to present. Offers abstracts of articles on world history excluding the United States and Canada. Data base covers 1954 to present; approximately 64,000 citations through 1978; adds 15,000 per year; from 1,900 journal sources; indexed with controlled and free language terms, abstracts included; on-line through LIS.

F E

Pure and Applied Sciences

See also Suppl. FC7, FC12.

AGRICultural on line access (AGRICOLA: formerly CAIN). U.S. Dept. of Agriculture, Beltsville, Md. **FE1**

Corresponds to the *National Agricultural Library catalog* (*Guide* EL12), *Bibliography of agriculture* (*Guide* EL15), and *Catalog* of the Food and Nutrition Information and Educational Materials Center. Worldwide coverage of the literature related to agriculture, including agricultural economics, rural sociology, agricultural products, animal industry, agricultural engineering, entomology, food and human nutrition, forestry, pesticides, plant science, soils and fertilizers and related fields. Data base covers 1970 to present; approximately 1,250,000 references through 1978; adds 145,000 per year; from 6,500 journals; National Agricultural Library classification codes and abstracts; on-line through BRS, LIS, and SDC; batch searched by many organizations.

Air Pollution Technical Information Center (APTIC). Environmental Protection Agency, Research Triangle Park, N.C. **FE2**

Corresponds to *Air pollution abstracts* (*Guide* EJ117). Worldwide coverage of the literature on air quality and air pollution prevention and control. Data base covers 1966 to present; approximately 100,000 references through 1978; no increment; from 7,000 journals, controlled index terms, free language terms, and abstracts; on-line through LIS.

BIOSIS previews. (Formerly *BA previews*) BioSciences Information Service, Philadelphia. **FE3**

Corresponds to *Biological abstracts* (*Guide* EC11) and *BioResearch index*. International coverage of life sciences research, including agriculture, toxicology, food technology, chemotherapy, and microbiology among the many areas covered. Data base covers 1969 to present; approximately 2,400,000 citations through 1978; adds 275,000 per year; concept codes, "Biosystematic" (taxonomic) codes, and free language terms; on-line through BRS, LIS, SDC, CISTI, ESA, and DIMDI; batch searched through numerous organizations.

CA search. (Formerly *CA condensates and CA subject index alert*) Chemical Abstracts Service, Columbus, Ohio. **FE4**

Corresponds to *Chemical abstracts* (*Guide* ED19) citations without abstracts. Worldwide coverage of chemical and chemical engineering literature. Data base covers 1968 to present; approximately 3,560,000 citations through 1978; adds 387,000 per year; from 14,000 journals plus patents; controlled index terms; on-line through BRS, LIS, SDC, ESA, NLM, and the Japan Information Center of Science and Technology; batch searched by many organizations.

Computerized engineering index (COMPENDEX). Engineering Index, New York. **FE5**

Corresponds to printed source of same name (*Guide* EJ4). Worldwide coverage of significant engineering literature as found in journals, proceedings of conferences, symposia, and technical reports of associations, government agencies, universities and laboratories. Data base covers 1969 to present; approximately 875,000 citations through 1978; adds 100,000 per year; from 1,700 journals plus monographs; controlled index terms, free language terms, "Ei" codes and abstracts; on-line through CISTI, LIS, ESA, SDC, Tokyo Shibaura Electric Co., and Council for Scientific and Industrial Research of South Africa; batch searched through numerous organizations.

Excerpta medica (EM). Excerpta Medica Foundation, Amsterdam. **FE6**

Corresponds to many Excerpta Medica publications (*Guide* EK61). International coverage of the biomedical area, i.e., human medicine and related disciplines, and those aspects of the basic biological sciences with some relevance to human medicine. Data base covers 1968 to present; approximately 1,440,000 citations through 1978; adds 280,000 per year; from 3,500 journals; on-line through LIS; batch searched by producer.

Geological reference file (Geo Ref). Amer. Geological Inst. (AGI), Falls Church, Va. **FE7**

Corresponds to *Bibliography and index of geology* (*Guide* EE23), *Bibliography and index of micropaleontology* (*Guide* EE174), *Bibliography and index of North American geology* (*Guide* EE23), *Geophysical abstracts* (*Guide* EE56), *Bibliography and index of geology exclusive of North America* (*Guide* EE22), and *Bibliography of theses in geology* (*Guide* EE48–EE51). Worldwide coverage of the geosciences literature. Data base covers 1961 to present; approximately 530,000 citations through 1978; adds 50,000 per year; from 4,200 journals plus monographs; controlled index terms, free language terms, and AGI codes; on-line through SDC and batch searched by NERAC and CISTI.

Index to scientific reviews (ISR). Inst. for Scientific Information, Philadelphia. **FE8**

Corresponds to printed source of same name. Includes significant review articles published throughout the world on any subject in science. Data base covers 1974 to present; approximately 120,000 references through 1978; adds 25,000 per year; from 2,700 journals; citation indexing; batch searched through producer.

International information services for the physics and engineering communities (INSPEC). Inst. of Electrical Engineers, London. **FE9**

The INSPEC system includes three major data bases, INSPEC A, INSPEC B, and INSPEC C, which correspond respectively to *Physics abstracts* (*Guide* EG10), *Electrical and electronics abstracts* (*Guide* EJ163), and *Computer and control abstracts* (*Guide* EJ164). Worldwide coverage of the literature of physics, electronics and electrical engineering, computers and control engineering, and mechanical engineering. Data base covers 1969 to present; approximately 1,826,000 citations through 1978; adds 1,000 per year; from 2,000 journals; controlled index terms, free language terms and abstracts; on-line through BRS, LIS, SDC, ESA, CISTI, Info-Line Ltd., and Council for Scientific and Industrial Research of South Africa.

MEDLARS On-line (MEDLINE). Nat. Lib. of Medicine, Bethesda, Md. **FE10**

Corresponds to *Index medicus* (*Guide* EK45). Worldwide coverage of the medical and biomedical literature. Data base covers 1971 to present; approximately 2,800,000 citations through 1978; adds 240,000 per year; from 3,000 journals; controlled (MeSH) terms, MeSH classes; on-line through NLM, BRS, CISTI, DIMDI, Medical Information Center, Tokyo Shibaura Electric Co., and SCANNET.

NTIS bibliographic data file. Natl. Technical Information Service, Springfield, Va. **FE11**

Corresponds to the printed source, *Government reports announcement* (*Guide* EA92). Covers the unclassified multi-disciplinary technical reports generated for NASA, DDC, ERDA and many departments and independent agencies (e.g., Departments of Commerce; Health, Education and Welfare; Housing and Urban Development; Interior; Labor; State; Transportation; Treasury; the Environmental Protection Agency; and the National Science Foundation). Data base covers 1964 to present; approximately 650,000 citations as of Dec. 1978; adds 60,000 per year; controlled terms, free language terms and abstracts; on-line through BRS, ESA, LIS, and SDC.

Pharmaceutical literature documentation (RINGDOC). Derwent Publications, London. **FE12**

Covers the pharmaceutical literature. Data base covers 1964 to present; approximately 584,000 references through 1978; adds 40,000 per year; from 370 journals; on-line through SDC.

Psychological abstracts tape editions lease license (PATELL). Amer. Psychological Assoc., Wash., D.C. **FE13**

Corresponds to *Psychological abstracts* (*Guide* EH33). Covers nonevaluative summaries of the world's literature in psychology and other behavioral sciences. Data base covers 1967 to present; approximately 260,000 citations through 1978; adds 25,000 per year; from 850 journals; controlled index terms, APA subject codes and abstracts; on-line through BRS, ERIC/IR, LIS, SDC, and Informationszentrum Sozialwissenschaften.

Science citation index (SCI). Inst. for Scientific Information, Philadelphia. **FE14**

Corresponds to printed source of same name (*Guide* EA87). International coverage of the principal journals of science—basic and applied, engineering, technology, life sciences, and medicine. Data base covers 1961 to present; approximately 5,752,900 references through 1978; adds 500,000 per year; from more than 2,500 journals; citation indexing; on-line through LIS.

Smithsonian Science Information Exchange (SSIE). Smithsonian Science Information Exchange, Wash., D.C. **FE15**

Corresponds to *Notices of research projects*. Includes descriptions of research projects sponsored by the federal government, by major foundations and fund-raising organizations, and by some universities, state and local governments, industrial and foreign organizations. Data base exists in two files: 1965–74 and 1975 to present. The historical file includes administrative data and 800,000 references but no abstracts. The current file includes 500,000 references through 1978 and adds 108,000 per year; controlled index terms, SSIE codes and abstracts; on-line through LIS and SDC.

World patents index (WPI). Derwent Publications, London. **FE16**

Corresponds to *Central patents index* and *World patents index*. Worldwide coverage of the patent literature of 24 leading countries using IPC codes for the following areas: human necessities, performing operations, transportation, chemistry, textiles, building, construction, mechanics, lighting, heating, instruments, nuclear science, and electricity. Data base periods of coverage vary with disciplines and have starting dates as follows: pharmaceuticals, 1963; agriculture, 1965; plastics, 1966; chemistry, 1970; mechanical, electrical and general, 1974. Approximately 1,472,470 references through 1978; adds 624,000 per year; on-line through SDC.

Bibliography

SOURCEBOOKS

Hall, James Logan. On-line information retrieval sourcebook. London, Aslib, 1977. 267p. £14.50.

Includes an extensive bibliography (pp. 209–42) in addition to the text. Z699.3.H34

DIRECTORIES

Data bases in Europe: a directory to machine-readable data bases and data banks in Europe. Alex Tomberg, ed. 3d ed. London, publ. for EUSIDIC by Aslib, 1977. 73p. £7.60.

A new edition is announced for 1979 publication. Z699.22.D37

Hall, James Logan. On-line bibliographic data bases: 1979 directory. London, Aslib, 1979. 94p. $28.50 ($24 to Aslib members).

A directory of 116 data bases, with an additional 40 entries in the appendix.

Williams, Martha E. and **Rouse, Sandra H.** Computer-readable bibliographic data bases: a directory and data sourcebook. Wash., Amer. Soc. for Information Science, 1976– . looseleaf. $68.

An updated version of *Survey of commercially available computer-readable bibliographic data bases*, ed. by J. H. Schneider [and others] (Wash., 1973).

Offers detailed information on more than 300 data bases; kept up-to-date by supplements (*see Suppl.* EJ49). A new edition is in press:

——— and **O'Donnell, R.** Computer-readable data bases: a directory and data sourcebook. Wash., Amer. Soc. for Information Science, [to be publ. 1979].

This edition will cover more than 500 data bases and will be fully indexed.

PERIODICALS

❖Most of the journals that cover various aspects of information science and/or librarianship occasionally contain articles dealing with data bases.

Advanced technology/libraries. v.1, no.1– , Jan. 1972– . White Plains, N.Y., Knowledge Industry Publs., 1971– . Monthly. $36.

Running title: AT/L.

A newsletter which frequently contains reports on data bases.

American Society for Information Science. Bulletin . . . . v.1, no.1– , June/July, 1974– . Wash., The Society, 1974– . Bimonthly. $27.50.

Regularly includes a column on data bases.

Database. v.1, no.1– , Sept. 1978– . Weston, Conn., Online, Inc., 1978– . Quarterly. $52.

Subtitle: The magazine of data base reference and review.

Devoted to reviews and reference articles concerning on-line data bases.

Information hotline. v.8, no.1– , Jan. 1976– . N.Y., Science Associates Internatl., 1976– . 11 issues per yr. $35.

Continues *Information news and sources* (Sept. 1974–Dec. 1975), which in turn continued *Information, part 1: News, sources, profiles* (Mar./Apr. 1972–July/Aug. 1974), which was a continuation of *Information—news/sources/profiles* (Jan./Feb. 1969–Jan./Feb. 1972); numbering is continuous throughout the changes of title.

Contains information on sources, profiles of organizations, and news of data bases. A companion publication appears as:

Information reports and bibliographies. v.1, no.1– , Jan./Feb. 1972– . N.Y., Science Associates Internatl., 1972– . 6 issues per yr. $35.

Title varies: 1972–74 issues had title: *Information, part 2: Reports, bibliographies*.

On-line review. v.1, no.1– . Mar. 1977– . Oxford & N.Y., Learned Information, 1977– . Quarterly. $45.

Subtitle: The international journal of on-line information systems.

Offers articles and news related to the on-line use of data bases. An ongoing feature is an annual bibliography of on-line data base publications; the first in the series, "Online information retrieval bibliography" by D. Hawkins (v.1, no.1, Mar. 1977) covers publications of the period 1965–76.

Online. v.1, no.1– , Jan. 1977– . Weston, Conn., Online, Inc., 1977– . Quarterly. $48.

Provides practical information for on-line use of data bases.

ANNUALS

See also annotation for *On-line review* (above).

American Library Association. The ALA yearbook, 1976– . Chicago, Amer. Lib. Assoc., 1976– . Annual.

Subtitle: A review of library events.
Contains a section on computer-readable data bases.

Annual review of information science and technology. v.1– , 1966– . Wash., Amer. Soc. for Information Science, 1966– . Annual. $35 to non-members.

Frequently includes chapters on bibliographic data bases, numeric data bases, and on-line systems.

Index

❖*This is an index of authors, editors, compilers, and sponsoring bodies which appear as main entries, of titles, and of subjects. Many personal and corporate names appearing in bibliographic notes and annotations are also included. In cases where a subject entry for a single item corresponds directly to a title and would merely repeat the same information, no subject entry is made.*

Designed by Vladimir Reichl
Composed by Datagraphics
in Times Roman; produced on III's Videocomp
Printed on 60# white offset stock
and bound by Webcrafters, Inc.